# How to Know When to Go
## The Art and Science of Predicting
## The Best Times to Fish and Hunt

### Rick Taylor

Copyright © 2008 by Rick Taylor

Published and distributed in the United States by: Jer-Ben Publications, Inc:
www.primetimes2.com

All rights reserved. No part of this book may be reproduced by any mechanical, photographic, or electronic process, or in the form of a phonographic recording; nor may it be stored in a retrieval system, transmitted, or otherwise be copied for public or private use—other than for "fair use" as brief quotations embodied in articles and reviews—without prior written permission of the publisher.

ISBN-13: 978-0-9789238-1-5 (trade pbk.)
ISBN-10: 0-9789238-1-2 (trade pbk.)
First Printing 1995
Second Printing 1997
Revised Printing 1998
Fourth Printing 2000
Fifth Printing 2002
Sixth Printing 2004
Seventh Printing 2006
Eight Printing 2008

Printed in the United States

# Contents

**Introduction** 1

**1. Overview: Best Times of the Day** 5

    Sunlight: The Primary Factor 7
    Fish and Water Temperature 8
    The Electromagnetic Element 10
    The Seven Potential Periods 12
    Assigning Priorities to the Seven Major Periods 16
    Summary 20

**2. Overview: Best Months and Days** 21

    Fish and Water Temperature...Again 21
    The Fish's Food Supply 24
    Fish and the Sun's Seasonal Cycle 25
    A Seasonal Activity Chart for Fishing 26
    The Best Days to Fish and Hunt 28
    The Lunar Phase Cycle 30
    The Moon's High-Low Cycle 31
    The Moon's Apogee-Perigee Cycle 32
    The Complete Solar/Lunar Element 32
    Summary 33

**3. The Energy Behind the Solar/Lunar Effect** 35

    Electromagnetic (EM) Energy 35
    The Angle and Proximity Factors in a Day's Best Times 37
    The Angle Factor in a Month's Best Days 41
    The Rhythm Theory 42
    Summary 44

**4. Polishing Your When-to-Go Game Plan** 45

    Fishing:
        *Regional Adjustments 46; The Weather 47; Water Clarity 51;*
        *Fishing Pressure 54; Rivers and Streams 54; Salt Water 55*
    Hunting 57
    Summary 58

**5. Fine-Tuning to the Individual Species** 61

    Fishing:
        *Bass 61; Panfish 62; Catfish 63; Northerns/Muskies 63;*
        *Stream Trout 64; Walleyes 64*
    Hunting:
        *Deer 65; Turkey 72; Upland Birds 74; Water Fowl 75; Squirrels 75;*
        *Crows, Fox, Coyote, Opossum, Raccoon, Rabbits 76*

**6. Inside PrimeTimes** 79

    The Solar Activity Base 79
    The Solar Peaks 80
    The Lunar Peaks 84
    Q & A: Activity Periods 87; Seasons, Time Zones 90;
        Times vs Days 92; Other Uses for PrimeTimes 95
    A Final Word 95

# *Introduction*

Each spring Harold Hinshaw's farm pond was graced with a dozen newly-hatched ducklings from his prized pair of mallards. But this year two of the youngsters had mysteriously disappeared before reaching their two-month birthday. The old farmer was perplexed, until one May morning he witnessed first-hand a large northern pike boiling the surface to inhale one of the hapless quackers.

Seeing his chance to finally beat Ernie Three-Bears in the local bait shop's big fish contest, Harold fetched his trusty rod-n-reel from the garage, selected the best pike lure in his tackle box, and set out to eradicate the demon fish from his waters. But after three days of periodically pounding the one-acre impoundment, Harold had nothing to show for the effort, except one less duckling.

Desperate to save the remaining brood, he swallowed his pride and called Ernie. Through gritted teeth, Harold offered to pay the old Cherokee for his trouble, if would come out and catch the fish for him.

Two days and another duckling passed before Ernie appeared at his back door, asking for Harold's rod, reel, lure, and directions to the pond. Mumbling under his breath that he could have come sooner and brought his own outfit, Harold handed over the gear and pointed the way. Ernie was back 45 minutes later, hoisting the 15-pound pike up for inspection with one hand, handing Harold a bill for $104 with the other.

Outraged, partly by being outfished once again and partly by the exorbitant fee, Harold demanded that Mr. Three-Bears itemize the bill, explaining every facet of his charge.

Calmly retrieving the invoice from Harold's hand and a pen from his pocket, Ernie scratched a few more lines on the paper, then handed it back.

It read:
Coming out from town to catch pike......$2.00
Catching pike..........................................$2.00
Knowing when to catch pike..............$100.00

The old adage of doing the right thing in the right place at the right time is still as true as it ever was for success in the outdoors. None of those three factors is more important than the other two, yet the *right-time* aspect is often last in our thinking. You need only thumb through your favorite fishing or hunting magazine to see the bulk of the pages are devoted to *how-to*, followed by *where-to-go*. Finishing a distant third is the *when-to-go* element, usually in the form of some type of "moon table."

In some respects, the *how-to* factor has a right to be number-one. New products are always coming and techniques are always improving. No one wants to be the only angler in the boat not catching fish or the lone hunter returning to camp without a deer. But this can cause a loss of perspective. It becomes easy to think that *when-to-go* is always the last consideration, when in fact it's the one thing that can turn a dead pool into a honey hole, a bad day into a great one, or make a novice look like an expert. Think back to the most productive fishing or hunting trip you ever had. The odds are it was mostly the result of being there at the right time.

If you took a poll of your outdoor acquaintances, you'd find that roughly 70 percent *say* they do not use a moon table. Right away you can suspect something is fishy, because most of America's sportsmen do consult one quite regularly. They either don't want anyone catching on to their little secret, or fear a good ribbing by their fishing buddies--who, if the truth be known, probably checked a table just that morning in the privacy of their pick-up!

The reason most would give you for not using a table is, "The best time to go is when I can." Actually, that's a self-defeating statement, because who needs to go at the right time more than sometime who has so little of it? Besides, most of us have more flexibility in our schedules than we'll admit. Sure, the boss may dictate our vacation time to within a certain time frame. But couldn't we pick the week of June 4 over June 11, if we knew the fishing would be better? Yes, we have household chores on the weekend. But if the prime time to fish is Saturday morning, can't the lawn's mowing or Tabby's neutering be scheduled for Saturday afternoon? More than one person with a good, fish and game activity calendar has rescheduled his work hours or even his daughter's wedding to be in field or stream at zero hour.

Unfortunately, some folks have tried consulting such tables, only to dump that idea the first time results did not meet expectations. The fault here can lie with both the forecaster and the follower. By its very nature, most tables imply (whether expressed or not) that all fish and game activity is contingent on lunar cycles. In truth, the moon is only one factor in a line of many, and needs to be kept in perspective. The reader expects too much from the table, and is equally let down when it produces results less than anticipated. He comes home feeling foolish for the attempt, never to give the moon a second chance. That's a mistake.

Conversely, there's the sportsman who won't make a move unless the moon is right. There's a good chance that the first time he tried a lunar table it worked, and that's all it took. From then on, no lake sees his lure nor field his form, if it's not a "good" day or a "primary period." That's a mistake, as well.

This book will take an honest look at our ability, as

well as lack of ability, in predicting the activity periods of many fish and game species. We'll begin by seeing how all creatures in general are influenced by everything from the conditions of their immediate environment to the contents of their stomachs. You'll see why and how the moon influences life on earth, plus the way its role can vary from one day to the next. We'll discuss how the sun's light and heat energy have been ignored by moon tables and their followers alike, when these energies are the most important daily activity coordinators there are.

We'll also take a closer look at your *PrimeTimes* calendar, a highly comprehensive concept in fish and game activity forecasting. You'll see how its incorporation of all the predictable elements—the sun and moon's electromagnetic rhythms, plus the sun's hourly light and heat cycles, elevates *PrimeTimes* above the rank of "moon table" to become the world's first and only true *activity* table. We'll offer you insights to using it effectively when going after your favorite quarry—everything from bass and bucks to water fowl and walleye, and see how to adjust it for changes in the weather and other unpredictable variables. Finally, we'll take a real nuts and bolts inspection of how the *PrimeTimes Wall Calendar*—the crux of our system, arrives at its predicted times and values, then wrap up with some pertinent Q & A.

Hopefully, you'll close this book knowing not only how to devise a strong, when-to-go game plan before each outing, but the fact that the *PrimeTimes* calendar—with its foundation of astrophysical fact, supported scientific theories, and the general consensus of expert outdoorsmen, has already done most of the legwork for you.

# 1
## *Overview: Best Times of the Day*

There are too many unknowns to make the when-to-go element an exact science. And thank goodness for that. If every activity period of every finned, feathered and furred creature were predictable, at the prescribed hour lakes and fields would be deluged by the salivating hoards, then just as quickly left to desolate silence in a cloud of dust. A few weeks later, with nothing left to stalk, our outdoor adventures would be reduced to precious old magazines and reruns of Sunday afternoon fishing and hunting shows.

Take a typical largemouth bass, for example. As Bufford hangs out under the roots of an old stump on a nice, early spring afternoon, imagine all the variables working on his willingness to hit a lure. One is his present state of hunger, something quite difficult for us to know. It depends largely on when he last ate, how much he ate, his digestion rate, his amount of body fat, and his general feeding posture.

Then there's the question of his "personality," meaning any individual traits of this particular bass. Has he been caught before, and now shies away from things that shake, rattle or roll? Is he aggressively defending a territory or just passing through? Are there other bass in the area, perhaps setting his switch to the competitive mode? Are both eyes in good shape? Is he worn out from nesting or a recent fight with an alligator gar? How old is Bufford; is he anxious to feed and grow some more, or is this stump his retirement condo?

All are difficult questions to answer, yet any one of which can have a direct bearing on his likelihood to enter what we affectionately call an "activity period."

Luckily, there are a number of important influences we can know something about in this scenario. We have learned that in the spring his species is basically in a feeding mood to restore the body fat lost during winter. Many are aggressively defending feeding or nesting territories. The water temperature is on an upward trend, causing the metabolisms of all fish to increase proportionately. While the food supply is relatively low right now, it's on the upswing, as new life is born and old life slithers out of hibernation. And we know that, thanks to the sun beating down, the upper layer of this lake is getting warmer by the minute, which could have a more immediate effect on the activity of any fish within it.

Of these known variables, almost all are positive for some kind of feeding sometime during this spring day. The question, of course, is when will this feeding most likely occur. And for that we need to look no farther than to the most predictable element this day has to offer: the warming rays of the sun. We know that the longer the shallows receive this radiation, the warmer they will get. And history, if not a good thermometer, tells us that this peak normally is achieved midway between high noon and sunset. On that evidence alone, we can conclude the following with a reasonable degree of certainty: *The best time of day to catch shallow bass under these conditions is in the middle of the afternoon,* or what has become to be known as the "heat-of-the-day."

Now, that's not to say some bass couldn't be caught during another time of day. They certainly could. Nor is it a guarantee that mid-afternoon will see activity. It may not. But in the long run—day after sunny day, year after normal year—that mid-afternoon period in the early spring will surrender the most shallow bass.

What we can't say with as much confidence is whether *Bufford* will be among them. If the first step to successfully predicting fish and game activity is to study the species as a whole, the second step is to understand that each creature is an individual, with it's own blueprint and experiences, and may not comply with the rest.

So, let's begin with the first step and see how the behavior of fish and game as a whole is governed by a variety of predictable elements, from changes in light and heat levels to an erratic rhythm of electromagnetic energy.

**Sunlight: The Primary Factor**

With the exception of entities living underground or inside some object of perpetual darkness, the daily and seasonal schedule of all life on earth is regulated mostly by the *sun's light cycle*. The changing lengths of daylight throughout a year are known to influence everything from mating and migrations to feeding and hibernation. On a daily level, the dawning of the sun spurs all to some degree of activity or inactivity, while dusk basically reverses it. It's difficult to live on the earth without having the sun as a major dictator of your schedule.

If we were to devise a general, when-to-go calendar based on nothing other than the sun's light cycle, each day may look like Figure 1-1. It's basically wake up at dawn's early light, move out to the feeding area, hunt or graze until dusk, then head home for the night. Of course, there will be minor variations during the day for the different species under different conditions. The grazers, knowing the grass or berries aren't going to run away, may take intermittent "naps"

*FIGURE 1-1*
**DAILY FISH AND GAME ACTIVITY
BASED ON THE SUN'S LIGHT CYCLE**

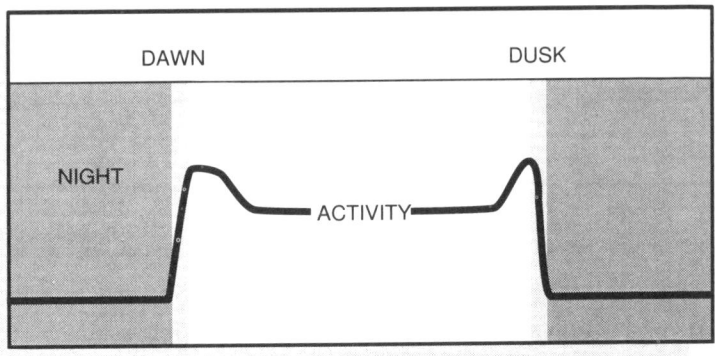

throughout the day. No self-respecting pheasant is flying to the corn in a driving rain. And nocturnal creatures will be active at night and rest during the day. But this is the general pattern most animals follow day after normal day. If our when-to-go calendar followed nothing more than the solar light cycle, we would do quite well, particularly when hunting. Fish are also affected by this light cycle, yet another element comes into play that can be even more crucial.

**Fish and Water Temperature**

Being cold-blooded means a fish's body temperature will be the same as its surroundings. When the temperature rises or falls, the metabolism goes right along with it, making the fish more active or less active, respectively. This allows changes in water temperature to be one of the best weapons we have in predicting piscatorial activity periods.

Fortunately, we know a great deal about how this warming and cooling occurs, and can generally predict it well in advance. Dawn, for example, is usually the coolest time of any 24-hour stretch, because the sun's warming mechanism has been absent for at least ten hours, and the water has had all night to transfer some of its heat back into the air. As the sun breaks the horizon, its rays once again strike the body of water, and a gradual rise in temperature begins. By high noon (equidistant between sunrise and sunset) the sun's heat energy is at its most direct angle of the day, making its deepest and hottest penetration. By mid-afternoon, the accumulated heat has reached it's peak for that day, and we have the period

*FIGURE 1-2*
**DAILY FISH ACTIVITY BASED ON SEASONAL WATER TEMPERATURE**

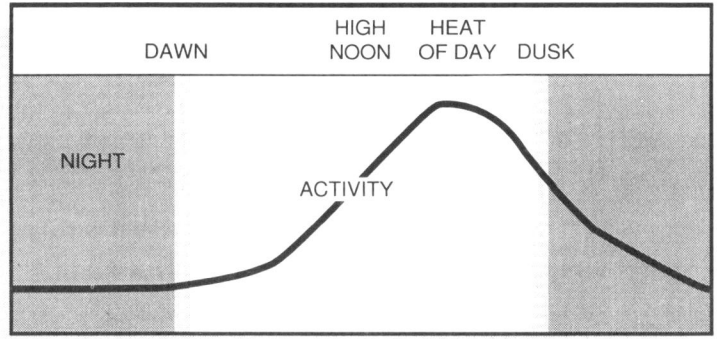

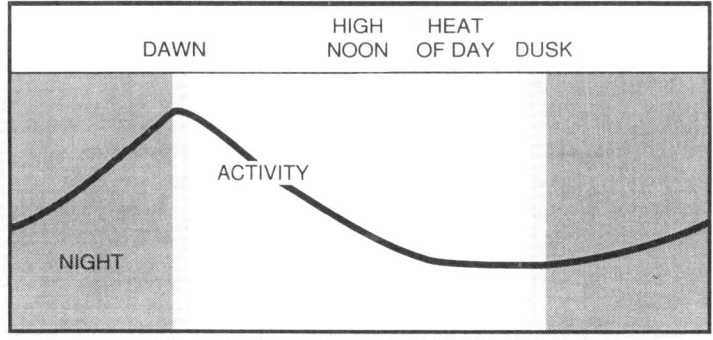

Overview: Best Times of the Day

known appropriately as the heat-of-the-day. A gradual cooling occurs after that, picking up speed as the sun sets and nighttime unfolds. The thermal decline continues throughout the night, completing the cycle at dawn.

The first chart (see "a.") in Figure 1-2 shows our daily game plan—if based strictly on water temperature, during the spring and fall, when the water is cooler than the fish's ideal. While activity could occur at any time, the better period would be during the Heat-of-the-Day, when the shallows are at their warmest.

The second chart (see "b.") shows the same daily game plan anytime the water is above the fish's ideal. Now our quarry would prefer the coolest stretch of any 24-hour span, which would be around Dawn.

Those are good additions to our activity calendar. Of course, there are still more things to consider, but devising a when-to-go gameplan on seasonal water temperature alone would bring far better results than just "going when we can go."

**The Electromagnetic Element**

Combining the sun's light and heat energy just discussed, we find three potentially active periods each day: Dawn, Dusk, and in the cooler months, Heat-of-the-Day. All three are fairly obvious to the observant eye, and it's not difficult to believe the effect each can have on fish and game behavior. However, such may not be the case with a different type of influence coming from both the sun and moon: Electromagnetism (EM, for short).

We'll explore this more thoroughly in Chapter 3, so for now let's just say that every object in the universe is surrounded by its own, invisible, yet very real, electromagnetic field. You have one, your beer has one, the dead bug in

*FIGURE 1-3*
**DAILY FISH AND GAME ACTIVITY BASED ON ELECTROMAGNETIC ENERGY OF THE MOON**

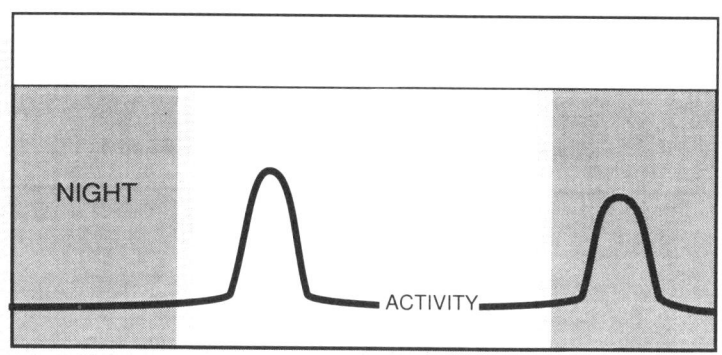

your beer has one, as does the glass holding your beer, the table holding your glass, etc. etc. The closer two objects are to each other, the greater the interaction between their two electromagnetic fields. Other important factors include their angle to each other, their size, and composition.

To all life on earth, the three objects exerting the greatest amount of EM energy every second of every day are the sun, the moon, and the earth itself. And because the moon is circling the earth, while the earth is circling the sun, these three bodies are constantly changing their angle and distance from the others. This means an equally constant altering of the amount of electromagnetic influence a bass or deer experiences from hour to hour, day to day.

What we outdoor folks have learned is that when the moon is passing over our heads each day, fish and game may be more active. This also seems to happen—although to a lesser degree, some 12 1/2 hours later when the moon is "underfoot," meaning on the opposite side of the planet (see Figure 1-3). Consequently, two more potential periods need to be added to our when-to-go calendar/game plan. But unlike the solar influences, which occur at virtually the same times from one day to the next, the moon passes overhead anywhere from 45-60 minutes later each day. So it's rather difficult to keep track of it without some type of lunar schedule.

While many folks consult the moon's daily position before heading out, for some reason they totally ignore the sun's, which by all reasons of logic and scientific evidence

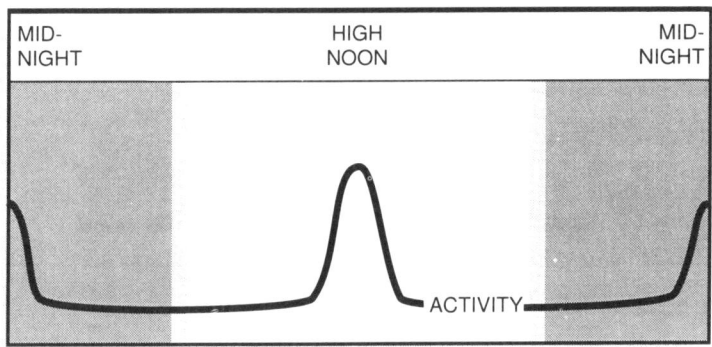

*FIGURE 1-4*
**DAILY FISH AND GAME ACTIVITY
BASED ON ELECTROMAGNETIC ENERGY OF THE SUN**

generates at least as much electromagnetic influence. Again, dealing with size, distance, and angle (like the moon), the sun's better EM periods are when it's Overhead and Underfoot (see Figure 1-4). But as we said, unlike the moon's, this cycle changes relatively little from day to day.

**The Seven Potential Periods**

That brings us to a total of seven periods having some degree of positive or negative influence over fish and game each day. In chronological order they are Dawn, Sun Overhead (high noon), Heat-of-the-Day, Dusk, and Sun Underfoot (mid-night). The list concludes with the Overhead Moon and

Underfoot Moon, both of which are never locked into one certain time each day. If we put them all together and gave each a relatively equal value, our daily calendar/game plan would look something like Figure 1-5.

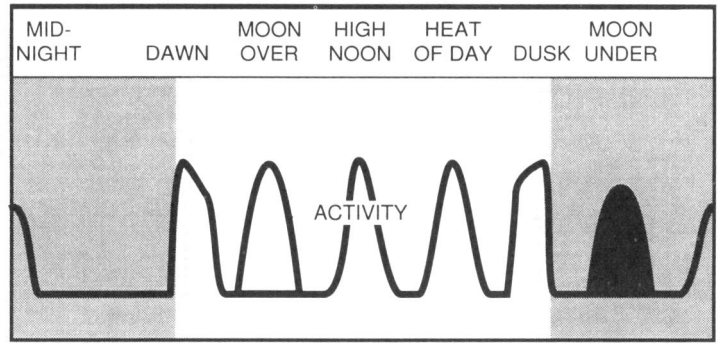

*FIGURE 1-5*
**THE SEVEN PREDICTABLE PERIODS
OF POTENTIAL INFLUENCE**

Let's take a look at the seven individually to see the special significance each carries.

*Dawn*

1. Begins at first light, peaks at sunrise, then tapers off at different times, depending on the season and species.
2. In the long run, the most influential stimulus of any 24 hours, as darkness turns to light, urging most diurnal (active during daylight) fish and game into activity.
3. Is generally the first beat in the activity rhythm for the rest of the 24 hour period.
4. Will usually be the most important period for diurnal game. For fish, will often be the most important in waters close to and warmer than their ideal, because it offers

the coolest water of most 24-hour periods.

    4. Increasing, yet still-low light, gives some predators the visual edge over their optically-inferior prey.

*High Noon*

    1. Can be one to three hours in duration, depending on the season; but it's peak is always half way between sunrise and sunset.
    2. Can be a "lunch period" for some species of game year-round and for fish during the warmer months.
    3. Is the sun's highest electromagnetic influence of the day, with the sun being directly overhead. Is also when both the sun's light and heat penetrate the deepest into water, often sparking plankton blooms.
    4. During cooler months, its ending can blend into the beginning of the Heat-of-the-Day period.

*Heat-of-the-Day*

    1. Runs for two to four hours, depending on the season and weather.
    2. Peaks roughly between "high noon" and sunset, when the land and water reach their highest daily temperature.
    3. Is a positive time for fish only during the colder months. Some game may use it as a resting time year-round.

*Dusk*

    1. Begins as the sun gets low to the western horizon and usually ends at twilight.
    2. Is a key movement time for game year-round, as the diurnal species head back to bedding areas, and the nocturnal species move out to hunt for food.

3. Is a semi-active period for fish in colder water, as the shallows still hold some of the warmth accumulated throughout the day. For the same reason in summer temperatures, may be an inactive period, especially for lunkers.

4. Fading light gives some predators the visual edge over their prey.

*Mid-Night*

1. Falls directly between sunset and sunrise, and peaks exactly 12 hours before and after "high noon."

2. Is a strong period year-round only for nocturnal animals.

3. Some predator fish may become active now in warmer waters, due to the need to feed more, plus daytime shallows being too warm or experiencing too much traffic.

4. Is the sun's underfoot period in terms of electromagnetism.

*Overhead Moon*

1. Reaches the same point in our sky 45-60 minutes later each day, making it the most variable element of all.

2. Is subject to a number of cycles affecting its angle, distance and therefore strength of EM energy.

3. Is often most effective during periods of stable weather, or when the more conventional solar periods are not producing.

*Underfoot Moon*

1. Basically the same as the overhead moon, except is effective some 12 1/2 hours later and to a lesser degree.

## Assigning Priorities to the Seven Major Periods

Of course, an even distribution of the seven periods each day is highly unlikely in the real outdoor world. The time of year, the species we're interested in, and how the moon interacts with the daily solar periods will all play a role in each period's time of occurrence, duration, and importance from week to week, if not day to day or even hour to hour.

*FIGURE 1-6*

**A TYPICAL, SUNNY, MARCH DAY FOR BASS IN OHIO**

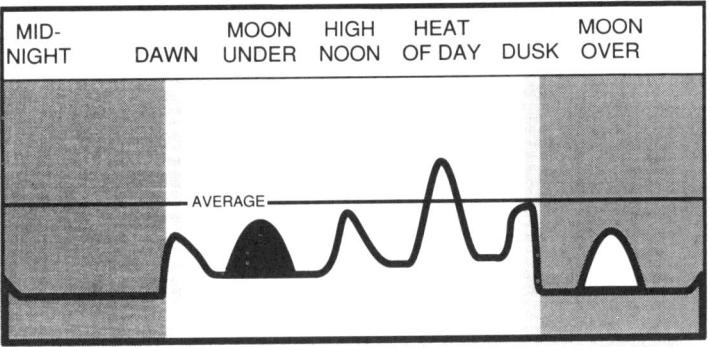

In Figure 1-6 we've adjusted the seven periods to show their relative importance on a typical, sunny day in Ohio, while we're fishing for bass. Since the water probably will be well below the bass's ideal temperature of 70 degrees, the Heat-of-the-Day period offers the best chance for shallow water activity. Dusk comes next, both for its still-warm shallows and dimming light, the latter of which not only signals one last chance to grab a bite, it's also a time when bass have the visual edge over their optically inferior prey. Close behind dusk is the High Noon period, offering the combination of electromagnetic energy, some warming from the strong heat penetration, and a possible plankton bloom that stirs prey to feed, followed by the predators. Also right up there and in a toss-up for fourth place is Dawn for its beginning of the day, the Underfoot Moon, for it's electromagnetic energy streaming down during mid-morning, and the Overhead Moon, which is generally stronger than its underfoot counterpart, yet today is occurring well into the night, when the overall activity is low anyway. For this same reason, the electromagnetism of the Sun Underfoot (mid-night) period is less influential.

*FIGURE 1-7*
**A TYPICAL, EARLY-JULY DAY FOR BASS IN OHIO**

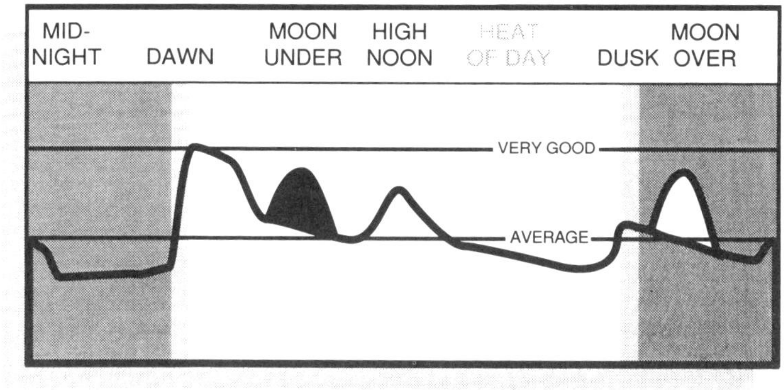

[Chart showing activity levels across time periods: MID-NIGHT, DAWN, MOON UNDER, HIGH NOON, HEAT OF DAY, DUSK, MOON OVER — with reference lines for VERY GOOD and AVERAGE]

Figure 1-7 takes us four months into the future on the same Ohio lake. Now our calendar has an entirely different look. Again water temperature is a major factor, now being, say, 84 degrees down to five feet. Not only is the Heat-of-the-Day period no longer primary, it has become a negative influence. With little opposition, Dawn claims the number-one slot for both its darkness-breaking-into-light stimulus and for offering the coolest water of this 24-hour stretch. Both lunar periods are strong, as well, because they coincide with good solar periods: the Moon Overhead occurs right after dark when many bass, especially the lunkers, begin thinking about food (the last six or so hours were too hot to roam the shallows); and the Moon Underfoot may be riding on Dawn's coattails. The Sun Overhead (high noon) period hangs in there as always, mainly for it's electromagnetic energy and plankton bloom, but now also because some six hours have passed since the dawn feeding, and most fish will look for food more than one or two times each 24 hours during summer. Dusk loses some of its positive influence due to its over-heated shallows, while the Sun Underfoot (mid-night) period comes into it own, with night activity at its best of the year in clear waters, especially if there is a high degree of human activity.

*FIGURE 1-8*
**GAME MOVEMENT ON A TYPICAL DAY**

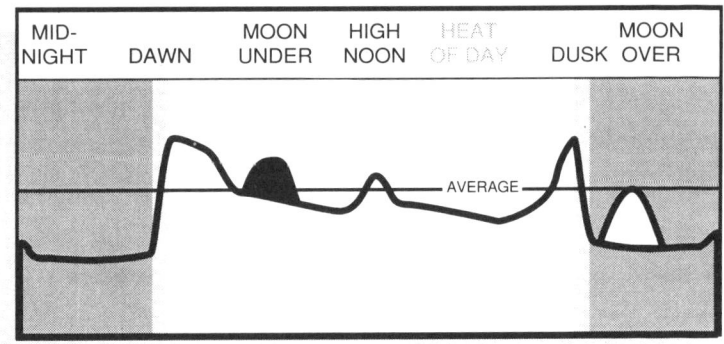

Figure 1-8 shows what the activity curve would look like for most diurnal animals. The only real change is Dusk rising to be as important as Dawn, with everything that moved out to feed during daybreak now returning to bed down. And since the nighttime hours are a virtual zero for activity among the daytime creatures, the Moon Overhead period we see occurring after dark loses much of its stature, being applicable only to the "night owls." The other minor adjustment is a slight drop in the Sun Overhead period, because its direct light and heat mean little to warm-blooded animals.

*Now* our when-to-go calendar has taken on a more viable, useful shape. It offers us a comprehensive overview of those seven daily periods capable of being predicted well in advance, and places each one into a theoretical, if not downright accurate, order of importance. All that's left is to apply it in a logical manner.

That means using the calendar as a guide, not a gospel. In the long term, the order of this magnificent seven will hold up. But on any given day it may not, because you can't know everything that's going on with your quarry. Besides the individuality of each creature, you may be dealing with an out-of-whack oxygen content or pH balance. The bass could have been subjected to a large tournament yesterday, or the deer to a roving pack of wild dogs. Maybe this is a down year for the population. Maybe a grocery truck overturned up yonder two days ago and every woodland critter in the area is so full they've been snoring since noon yesterday.

In a more practical vein, any discrepancies you do experience with the calendar's forecasts will probably be in the *order* of the periods' priorities. For some reason the Heat-of-the-Day period doesn't produce one early spring day, while the Sun Overhead does. Or that maverick Underfoot Moon, while only in the fifth slot today, takes center stage and brings in your year's largest largemouth. These things can and will happen. You should stay flexible enough to adjust the calendar temporarily when necessary, while not losing confidence in its long term accuracy. You should also be objective in your evaluations. Were the bass really hitting better at high noon, or did you change locations, lures or tactics? Did that trophy come because it was the Underfoot Moon period, or because its stomach was very empty and your lure was the first potential meal it had seen all day?

Finally, by all means keep complete records of your outings and continually look for patterns relevant to your particular situation. Even if some low period on the calendar consistently presents activity, you have exactly what you are looking for: a highly accurate, when-to-go guide.

**Summary**

While we can never know all the variables that may be affecting our fish and game at any given time, there are seven periods of influence each day we can predict quite accurately and well in advance. These periods and the type of influence—positive or negative—they are capable of providing are (in no particular order):

1. Dawn (darkness to light; day's coolest)
2. Dusk (light to darkness; relatively warm)
3. Heat-of-the-Day (day's warmest)
4. Moon Overhead (EM energy)
5. Moon Underfoot (EM energy)
6. Sun Overhead (EM energy; day's most direct light and heat)
7. Sun Underfoot (EM energy)

How important each of these will be during an outing depends largely on the nature of your quarry, the time of year (mainly for fish), and how the moon interacts with the daily solar periods that day. While *PrimeTimes* has already done most of the calculations for you, it's important to understand that other factors, like the weather or fishing/hunting pressure, may need to be tossed into the mix at the last minute. We'll be discussing these a little later in Chapter 4, "Polishing Your When-to-go Game Plan."

# 2

## *Overview: Best Months and Days*

In Chapter 1 we studied the general ins and outs—or should we say, ons and offs, of when to go during any day. Here we'll deal with the other part of forecasting, determining the best months and days of a month. This subject is dear to all who plan their outings anywhere from a couple days to a couple years in advance.

We may have only four bullets in this battle, but each can pack a considerable punch. They are t*emperature, the food supply, the sun*, and *the moon*. While the first three are important to game, they have little impact on the best *months* to hunt each year. Most mammals generally eat all year-round, and move as circumstances dictate. Their activity curve is basically a straight line across the months, interrupted only by spikes during the mating season. Besides, there's little point in trying to figure out the best times of year to hunt, when state-regulated hunting seasons have already solved that problem for us. Consequently, the first part of this chapter will deal mostly with fish.

**Fish and Water Temperature...Again**

Just as the changing temperature of a lake, pond or

river provides excellent clues to fish activity on an hour to hour basis, so it does over the course of a year. And while we can't predict what exactly will happen temperature-wise on any particular day, we do know the general trends.

Figure 2-1 is a documented, daily thermal history of a typical Midwest lake for an eight-week period during sum-

*FIGURE 2-1*
**WEEKLY VARIATIONS IN WATER TEMPERATURE**

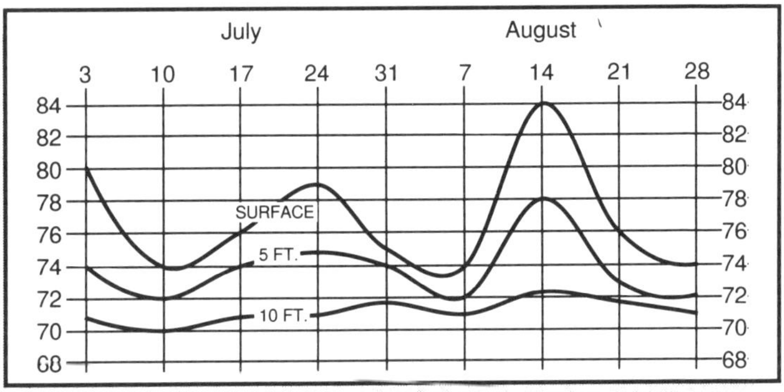

mer. We show this to demonstrate how much the surface temperature changes from week to week when compared to the ten-foot depth. The weather's immediate influence on the shallows becomes obvious, able to vary the temperature by five to ten degrees over the course of one 24-hour stretch under optimal conditions (ie: sunny, low winds, warm air).

While the ten-foot depth changes at a slower, more methodical rate, especially during summer, it can get as radical as the surface in the spring and fall when a lake is less stratified thermally. Figure 2-2 shows the daily temperature at ten feet on the same lake in the same year, from late-March to mid-November. The spikes and plummets pertain to warming trends and cold fronts, respectively, while the general trend is upward in the spring, stabilizing during summer,

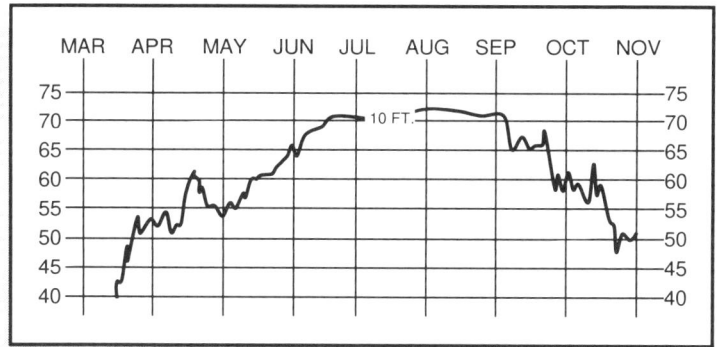

*FIGURE 2-2*
**MONTHLY VARIATIONS IN WATER TEMPERATURE**

then downward in the fall.

Consequently, even though much of the better fishing comes in the shallows, it's that medium layer of 10 or so feet (depending on your water clarity and climate) that is a better indicator of the general fishing quality throughout a year. For example, in water colder than 40 degrees, which is often under ice, there's little going on in a fish's life. We may catch a few, but patience is a virtue. When the ice goes out, even a slight breeze can cause the pond or lake to "turn over," mixing all the thermal layers together and raising the temperature of the upper layers a degree or two almost immediately. The sun's angle continues to increase throughout the spring and penetrate more deeply, the water warms, the fish's metabolism improves, and we keep witnessing more and more activity. By mid-summer the upper layers may get too warm in most parts of the country, and many fish shift downward to cooler layers. The onset of fall cools the shallows back to a more ideal range, and activity picks up here once again. Eventually, the entire body of water cools past the fish's ideal, and we have a gradual downgrading of activity right into winter.

## The Fish's Food Supply

The availability of food is always a primary factor, as well. The better the fish's food supply, the better our chances of getting them to strike. It may seem that lures stand little chance competing against the real thing for our quarry's attention, but the fact is when those shad or crayfish are few and far between, those who eat them often shut down operations to conserve energy. As Jonah, the great whaler, is rumored to have said, "Tis far better to cast thy offering among the baitfish and maketh it appear vulnerable than tis to swim it through foodless waters past lock-jawed fish."

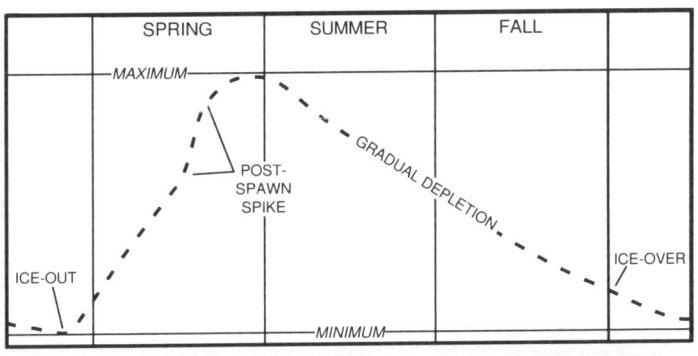

FIGURE 2-3
SEASONAL CHANGES IN THE FISH'S FOOD SUPPLY

Not too coincidentally, the seasonal food supply follows the same, general curve as water temperature (see Figure 2-3). In the spring, when the water begins warming for the first time, the signal is given for the reactivation of life. First, crayfish, salamanders, and other species hibernating in the mud and rocks come out, especially around the 50-degree mark. Baitfish move off the bottom to take advantage of minor plankton blooms occurring in the warming shallows, and eventually insects enter the menu. When temperatures in the upper layers transcend the low 70's and the spawning season comes to an end, a relatively sharp spike occurs in the food supply, as the waters flood with billions of young edibles. However, after reaching its peak in mid-summer, the food curve begins to drop faster than and independent of the water temperature. This is because more and more of those free-swimmers disappear from the picture, while the water temperature continues to rise or stay the same.

**Fish and the Sun's Seasonal Cycle**

Somewhere in elementary school we learned that the four seasons are the result of how directly overhead the sun is to our northern hemisphere each time of the year. When at it's most direct angle (June 21, give or take a day) we have the first day of summer. The sun's heat energy is never stronger, as evidenced by the fact that if you don't leave one of your car windows open a crack, you may be sweeping tempered glass off the asphalt. When at its lowest angle (December 21 or so), it's the first day of winter, and we feel only a fraction of the

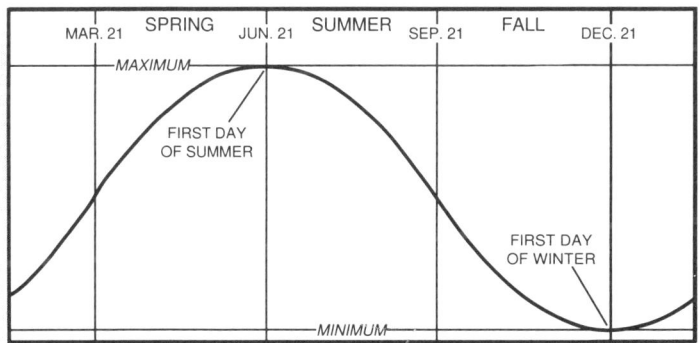

FIGURE 2-4
**SEASONAL CHANGES IN THE SUN'S ANGLE**
(HEAT, LIGHT, AND ELECTROMAGNETIC ENERGY)

sun's potential heat energy (see Figure 2-4).

Meanwhile, the sun's *electromagnetic energy* follows the same curve exactly, being stronger in summer, weaker in winter, peaking on June 21 and bottoming out on December 21. The stronger this EM flow, the more positive the influence on fish and game. (For more detail on electromagnetism, see Chapter 3.)

It's no coincidence that the sun's seasonal curve corresponds closely to the water temperature curve, which in turn parallels the food supply curve. The three go hand-in-hand. The higher the sun, the stronger the EM and heat energy. The stronger the heat energy, the warmer the water. The warmer the water, the better the food supply (up to its saturation point in summer). The better the food supply, the more a fish is in the feeding mode. And the more he's willing to open his mouth, the better our chances of catching him.

### A Seasonal Activity Chart for Fishing

Figure 2-5 shows the similarity among these three when put together on the same graph. Figure 2-6 takes it a step

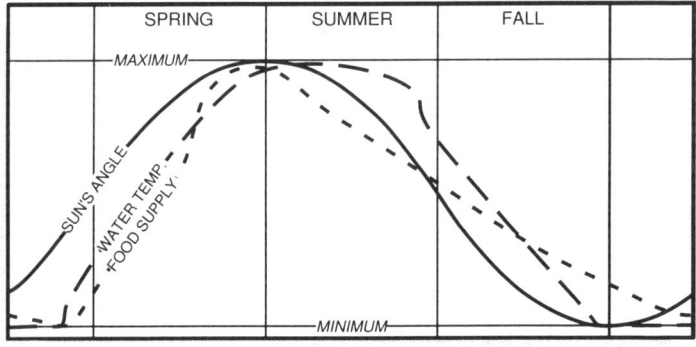

FIGURE 2-5
**COMPARING SEASONAL CHANGES IN WATER TEMP., AVAILABLE FOOD, AND THE SUN'S ANGLE**

*FIGURE 2-6*
**SEASONAL ACTIVITY CHART FOR FISH**
(BY AVERAGING THE MAIN ELEMENTS OF WATER TEMP., FOOD, AND THE SUN'S ANGLE)

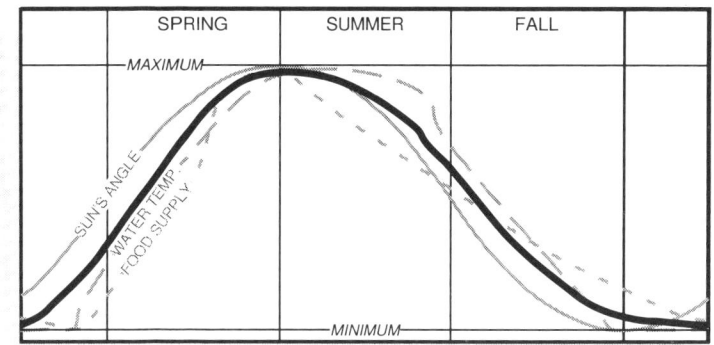

farther by averaging them into one, heavy, black line, depicting the general feeding patterns for fish from season to season. Of course, any given month in any given year will have fluctuations which no one can predict in advance.

Certain adjustments may also have to be made if you are fishing in waters colder or warmer than this average. Figure 2-7 compares the extremes found from north to south in the U. S., using northern Minnesota and southern Texas as examples. In the former, the ice may not go out until mid-to-late spring, then seal the lake back up by mid-fall. The fish have a relatively short feeding and growing season, so they don't waste time when the lid is off. With all the action packed into a few months, the angler here has some of the best fishing anywhere in the U. S.

Meanwhile, his Texas cousin, who thinks ice is only something to keep drinks cold, finds open water and willing fish even in the dead of winter, while his summers can last six months or more. There's never a prolonged, semi-hibernation season like in the north, and the prime feeding periods are spread out over many months, making this southern curve far less extreme in both directions.

*FIGURE 2-7*
**HOW SEASONAL FISH ACTIVITY CAN VARY FROM NORTH TO SOUTH IN THE U.S.**

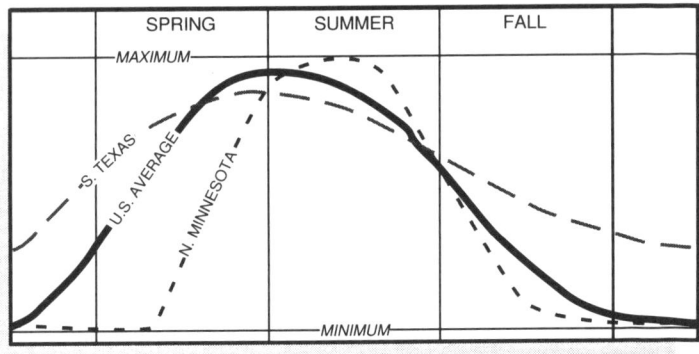

So, there it is. We've taken the three seasonal variables of water temperature, available food, and the sun's angle, and found them to parallel each other so closely that we can average them into one, seasonal activity curve. Then by adjusting this curve to each particular region, and understanding there will be fluctuations all along it, especially in the spring and fall, we end up with a reasonably reliable, month-to-month fishing forecaster that should apply year after year.

### The Best Days to Fish and Hunt

We started this book learning to zero in on the best *hours* to go fishing or hunting. And in this chapter so far we have seen how to determine the best *months*. But that still leaves a big hole in our over all, when-to-go-fishing-and-hunting calendar. We have yet to know how to predict perhaps the most important matter of all: the best *days* of any month.

Enter the solar/lunar element, or what is commonly labeled, "the moon." Unlikely, controversial and mysterious as it may be, the moon is the only thing we know influencing the earth that is both predictable well in advance and has a cycle that starts over every month (29.530588 days, to be exact), with noticeable distinctions every week. Even our most powerful fish and game regulator, the sun, has only its hourly, dawn-to-dusk-to-dawn cycle, and its seasonal, winter-to-summer-to-winter cycle. There is nothing about old Sol that circles back to the beginning once a month like the moon.

Weekly and monthly cycles occur around us continuously. On a large scale, coastal tides, which rise and fall daily in tune with the moon's gravitational pull, also come up higher every two weeks (called "spring tides") . The female menstrual cycle occurs once a month, and a fetus' gestation period is nine lunar months. Some rose bushes bloom every two weeks to the day. Corn planted one week grows better than corn planted a week earlier or later. And more to our point, how many times has it seemed that the fishing is good for a week or two, then poor for the next week or two? Over 90 percent of the entires in a recent *Texas Fish & Game Magazine* lunker contest were caught during a major moon phase, which, as we know, occurs at two-week intervals.

When patterns like this catch our eye, patterns that can't be explained by the obvious solar cycles, we start looking for something that does operate on a weekly or monthly basis. Our search usually goes no farther than the moon. In some cases the connection is a scientific fact, such as those spring tides, which happen when the moon and sun come into alignment with the earth (ie: new and full moon phase). In other cases, like the roses and corn, we can only suspect there is a correlation with the moon. But as to whether or not the moon affects fish and game behavior, one needs only note how many sportsmen across the world consult the moon before heading out. We can't pinpoint that figure, but it's easier to find a fishing or hunting magazine that carries lunar information than one that doesn't. The majority of outdoor enthusiasts can't all be barking up the wrong tree.

**The Lunar Phase Cycle**

Perhaps gently refined over the years, the general consensus today is that fish and game become more active during the full and new phases, with each month's two half moons also being a productive time, although to a lesser degree and shorter in duration. So, when we add the moon's phase cycle to our seasonal gameplan, the activity curve takes on a whole new look. The general trend is still the same, but now we have a series of ups and downs occurring at roughly one week intervals (see Figure 2-8). On the average, it takes the moon one week to go from full to half, then another seven days to go from half to new, and so on. Figure 2-8 shows this trend for a whole year, while Figure 2-9 zooms into for a close-up of any one month.

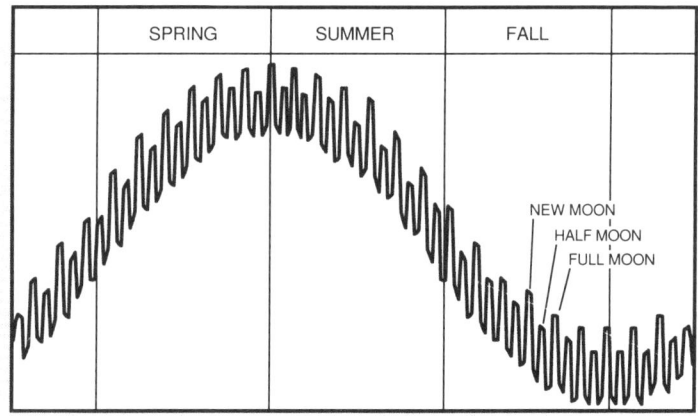

*FIGURE 2-8*
**FISH ACTIVITY BASED ON MONTHLY MOON PHASES ALONG SEASONAL TRENDS**

*FIGURE 2-9*
**WEEKLY FISH ACTIVITY BASED ON MOON PHASE**

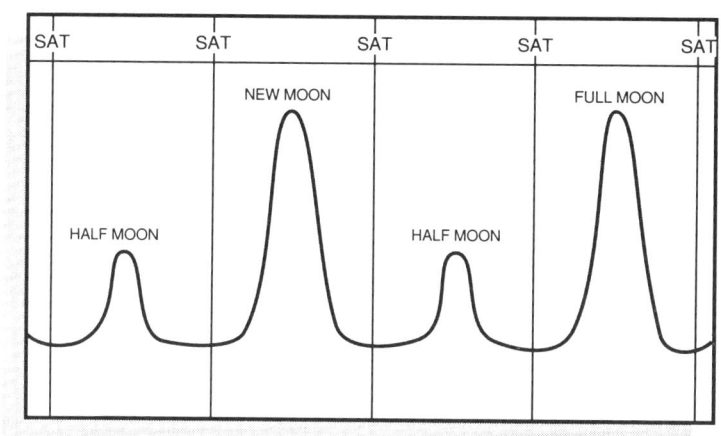

Most respectable moon tables today gauge their predictions in this manner. What they don't consider, however, is that all full and new moons are not created equal astrophysically. Nor do two full moons, two new moons, or two half moons have exactly the same amount of influence from one month to the next. Other lunar cycles need to be factored into the equation for a truly accurate picture.

**The Moon's High-Low Cycle**

One of the more important secondary cycles is the moon's "high-low" cycle, which is very much like the sun's winter-to-summer-to-winter seasonal cycle. The difference is that while the sun's takes exactly one year to complete, the moon's is accomplished in only 27 days on the average. Just as the sun comes higher and higher overhead each day as we head towards summer, the moon does basically the same thing each day as it moves toward its "high" of the month. The higher it is, the stronger its electromagnetic energy strikes the earth and its inhabitants.

Therefore, during a month when the lunar "high" would land on the same day as say, the full moon, that particular full moon would have extra influence on the entire six-seven-day period, as well as during its "hourly" overhead prime time each day (see Chapter 1). Two weeks later, when the new moon corresponded closely to the "low" moon, that new moon would have less influence in both respects. As you may have suspected from the high-low cycle taking 27 days versus the phase's 29.5 days, they are like two wheels spinning at slightly different rpm's, coming into sync only about once a year.

### The Moon's Apogee-Perigee Cycle

To a lesser degree, but worth consideration, is the distance the moon is from the earth at various times each month. This apogee-perigee cycle (with apogee being when the moon is the farthest and perigee when it is the closest) can account for about a ten percent deviation in the moon's potential power. It also takes slightly less than one month to complete, and is slightly out of sync with the phase and high-low cycles.

### The Complete Solar/Lunar Element

By factoring in these important high-low and apogee-perigee cycles of the moon, our activity calendar gives a more scientific accounting of the energy emanating from any given new, full, or half moon. In Figure 2-10 the new moon period is clearly the strongest for this hypothetical month, followed by the full moon, the first half moon, then the second half moon. We can accurately assume the new moon period is occurring relatively closely to at least the high moon, and possibly perigee, as well.

*FIGURE 2-10*
**WEEKLY FISH ACTIVITY BASED ON MOON PHASE, THE HIGH-LOW AND APOGEE-PERIGEE CYCLES, PLUS SEASONAL TRENDS**

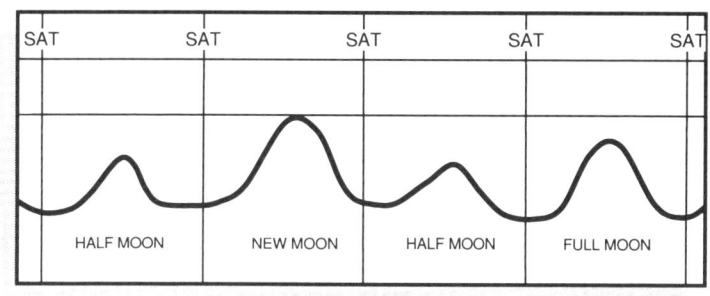

If all three phenomena were to land on the same day and in conjunction with the high sun (first day of summer), that peak would peg out at 100, the highest it can ever get. The strongest day we've had in recent history was June 22, 1990, the day of a new moon, high moon, and just one day after both perigee and the high sun. The day rated a 99 on our scale, which is rare indeed. We had numerous calls from our calendar users, saying they had experienced terrific fishing. "We," unfortunately, were busy making the 1991 calendars and never got out that day.

**Summary**

While the best months to hunt are regulated mostly by your state legislature, fishermen can look to seasonal patterns in water temperature, the food supply, and the sun. All three go hand-in-hand, making their seasonal curves quite similar.

On a best-day basis, the main regulator is the moon. By formulating its high-low, apogee-perigee, and phase cycles, in conjunction with the sun's high-low cycle, we can put the results on a sliding scale of 0-100 to accurately describe the amount of solar/lunar energy each day is receiving.

# 3

# *The Energy Behind the Solar/Lunar Effect*

In the previous two chapters we discussed how activity periods can be affected by the sun's light and heat—tangible elements that are relatively easy to understand. Here we'll go into the electromagnetic aspects of the sun and moon, a subject somewhat more nebulous, but just as important.

If you have a copy of our other book, "Under the Solar/Lunar Influence," you'll find this chapter to be a synopsis of Part One, which deals with the scientific facts and theories behind the electromagnetic theory. If you don't own that book, you might consider getting a copy, as it covers the subject in much more detail than we have the space to do here.

**Electromagnetic (EM) Energy**

As we touched on briefly in Chapter 2, every object in the universe, from the smallest subatomic particle to the largest star, emits its own electromagnetic energy field. We can't see, feel nor hear these fields, but the results of one interacting with another are evident in all corners of everyday life, such as the circular patterns formed by iron filings around a magnet, high and low tides on our coasts, pictures and sounds coming from a tv set.

Science also knows that the closer two objects are to each other, the stronger their EM fields interact. Furthermore, the larger an object's mass, the farther and stronger its energy is felt.

With these factors in mind, let's see how fish and game may be affected by the ever-changing interaction of the three largest objects in their lives—the earth, the sun and the moon.

The earth, of course, has the strongest influence, since it literally holds all creatures directly to its surface. This intimacy apparently creates an ongoing electromagnetic interchange between the two factions. Scientists suspect, for example, that migratory birds may follow "paths" in the earth's EM field, as may bees, caribou, fish, and any other transient animal that seems capable of finding its way to and from key locations. Some people seem to sleep or work better when pointed in a certain direction. It's documented that water absorption by the simple bean seed can be altered by turning it a few degrees. Modern science now suspects that such phenomena are made possible by the traces of lodestone (ie: magnets) recently discovered in the brains of the subjects.

Meanwhile, the sun and moon traverse our sky each day, tossing their electromagnetic influence into the mix. When the alignment is right, things seem to happen, like the grunion always spawning on the first four nights after a full or new moon, or oysters opening their shells each time the moon is overhead or underfoot, whether they are in the ocean or not. Mostly, it seems to depend on the angle and the proximity of the sun and the moon in relation to the earth at any given time.

In determining the *best days of the month* to go fishing or hunting, it's a matter of how these two celestial bodies line up with the earth in general, while on a *best times of the day* basis, it's more how they relate to that immediate area of earth presently holding the quarry in question.

**The Angle and Proximity Factors in a Day's Best Times**

When considering the celestial configuration of an Overhead or Underfoot Moon, the first thing we may notice is the straight line formed by the moon, that immediate area of the earth (plus any creature in that area), and the earth's center. One theory suggests the moon's EM energy waves are coming in parallel to the earth's at this location (see section "a." of Figure 3-1), generating some kind of positive interaction between the two.

This becomes more evident when we move ahead three hours to when the moon is about half-way down toward the horizon at a 45-degree angle, a lunar position usually associated with poorer fishing and hunting (see section "b."). Now the moon's incoming energy waves are striking the earth's at an odd angle, apparently causing some decrease in the lunar influence.

Moving ahead another three hours, the moon is on the horizon, striking the earth's energy waves at a 90-degree angle (see section "c."). Some moon tables show this as a minor activity period, and PrimeTimes may also, were it not for too many other factors (ie: Dawn, Dusk, Sun Overhead, etc.) being deemed more important.

Jumping ahead another 6 1/2 hours to the moon's Underfoot position (see section "d."), we find a configuration also known as a good time to be in the outdoors, although not quite as influential as the Overhead Moon. Here the moon's energy waves are coming from the opposite direction, yet they are back in a parallel alignment with the earth's.

That's one possible cause for the sun and moons effect on our quarry. Let's call it the "EM Wave Alignment" theory.

*FIGURE 3-1*
**ALIGNMENT OF EARTH AND MOON'S ENERGY WAVES**

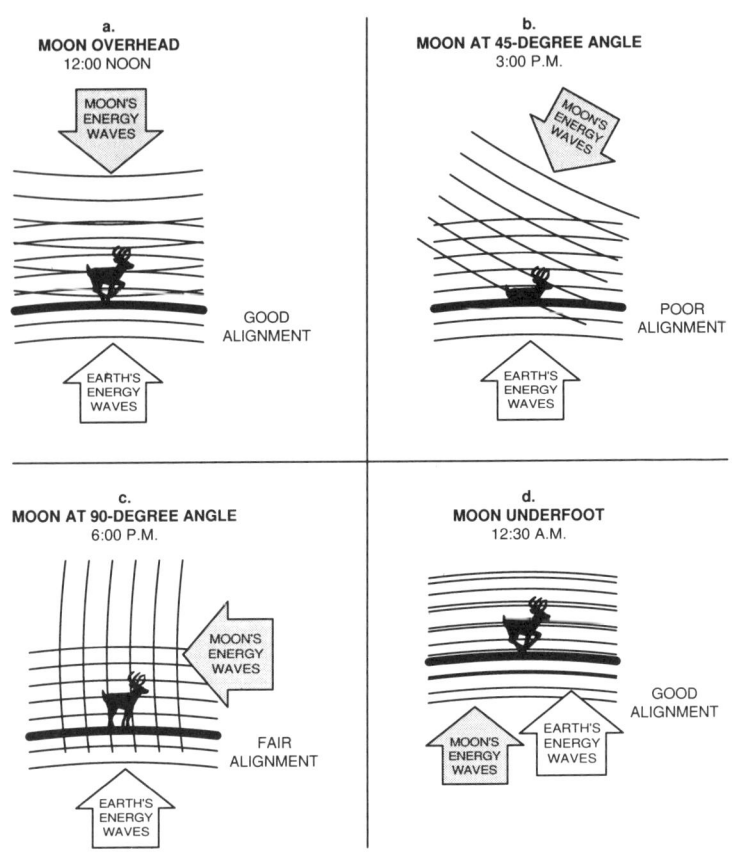

And although we used the moon as an example here, remember that all this applies equally to the sun's energy.

Another theory says the greater the angle of the sun or moon to our location, the more of the earth's atmosphere that energy must pass through to reach us. Since our atmosphere, which is approximately 1,000 miles thick, filters out all forms of incoming cosmic energy and debris, the angle at which the energy approaches has a great deal to do with how much ultimately arrives.

*FIGURE 3-2.*
**MILES OF ATMOSPHERE THE MOON'S ENERGY MUST PASS THROUGH AT VARIOUS ANGLES**

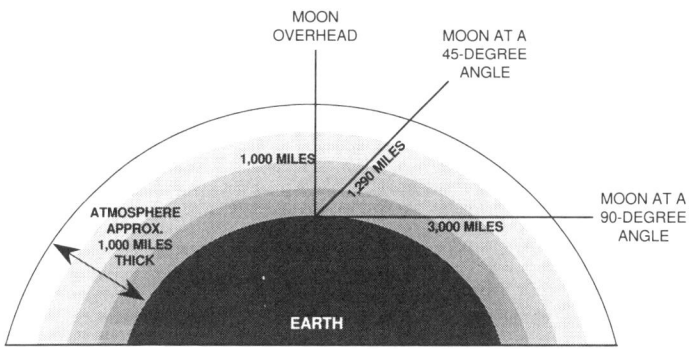

For the purpose of illustration, say there are three, identically-sized meteors coming straight at your property at the same speed from three different angles in outer space. The first enters earth's 1,000 miles of atmosphere directly overhead, disintegrates considerably along the way, and smacks into your garden weighing only 100 pounds. The second comes in at a 45-degree angle, and arrives weighing only 77 pounds, because it had to travel through an extra 290 miles of rock-eating atmosphere to reach the same spot. Meanwhile, since the final projectile comes in at a 90 degree angle (ie: from the horizon), it has to endure a total of 3,000 miles of atmosphere, three times more than the first meteorite. Consequently, it arrives tipping the scales at a mere 33 pounds.

We'll label this one as the "Atmospheric Filter" theory. And while the figures and percentages used in this example are arbitrary, it's not unreasonable to surmise that EM energy from the sun and moon, coming in a various angles, would go through similar degrees of filtration (see Figure 3-2).

The sun and moon's ever-varying positions in the sky also mean their distances from any given location of earth are constantly changing. When directly overhead, either is as

*FIGURE 3-3.*
**THE MOON'S VARYING DISTANCE FROM YOUR QUARRY EACH DAY**

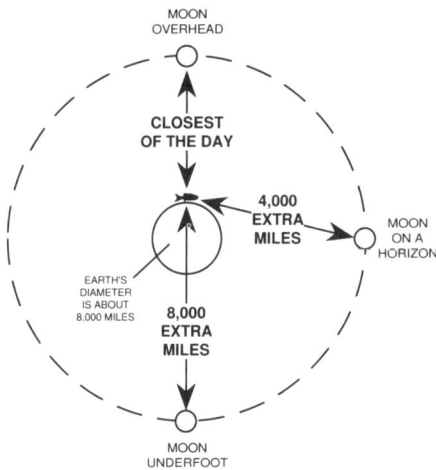

close as it can get to us that day. When on the horizon, however, both are some 4,000 miles farther away from that same spot. And when on the other side of the earth, they are some 8,000 miles farther (see Figure 3-3). Since the sun is 93 million miles from us, these few extra miles will not account for much change in solar energy. But the moon is less than one-quarter of a million miles from earth, so 4,000 extra miles means a two percent increase in distance, and 8,000 miles about four percent. Although not the biggest hitter in our EM ballgame, this "Distance" theory could find a spot in right field.

Viable as any of these three theories are in causing each day's best times, only one holds up when we look at the sun-moon-earth relationship in terms of the best days of each month.

## The Angle Factor in a Month's Best Days

Again starting at the result and working backwards to find a cause, we know that the full and new moons—and to a lesser degree the half moon phases, generally produce the best days for fish and game activity. Checking the sun and the moon's positions in relation to the earth during these conditions reveals all three being in a relatively straight line during a new and full moon, while at a right angle to one another during a half moon (see Figure 3-4).

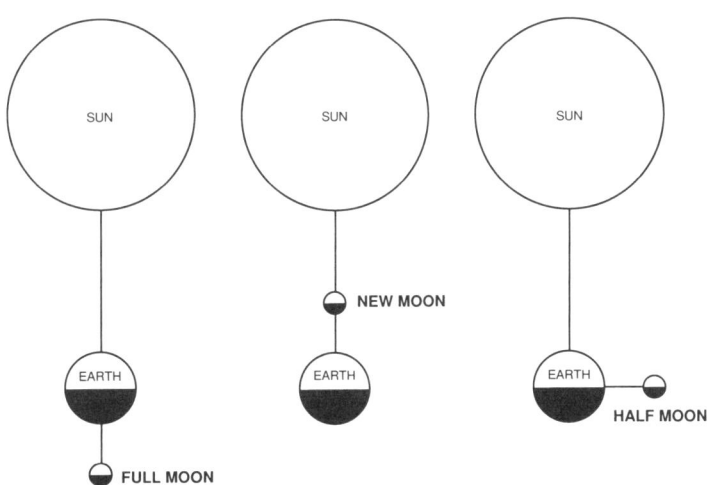

FIGURE 3-4.
**THE SUN-MOON-EARTH ALIGNMENT DURING A FULL, NEW, AND HALF MOON PHASE**

The alignment of these three heavenly bodies during the new and full moons is very similar to the straight line we saw during the period of the Overhead or Underfoot Moon (see "a." and "d." in Figure 3-1). And their alignment during a half moon mimics the minor periods of the moon being on either horizon (see section "c." in Figure 3-1). While there really isn't way to apply the "Atmospheric Filter" and "Distance" theories here, we could conclude that the "EM Wave Alignment" of Figure 3-1 theory works quite nicely in this best-days context.

**The Rhythm Theory**

One other possible explanation for the virility of new, full, and half moon phases is the cadence in which the moon and sun come directly over our heads and under our feet during each 24-hour stretch (see Figure 3-5). Take the full moon for example: At noon, while the sun is passing overhead, sending down strong energy, the moon is underfoot,

*FIGURE 3-5.*
**THE RHYTHM THEORY**

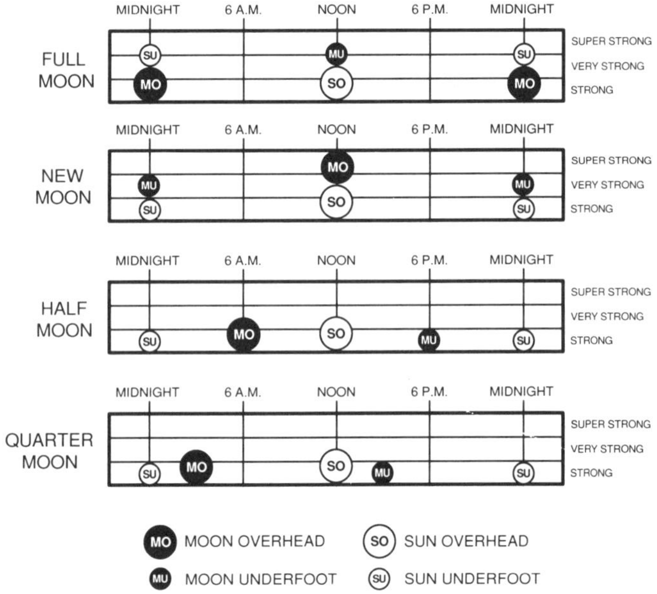

| | MIDNIGHT | 6 A.M. | NOON | 6 P.M. | MIDNIGHT | |
|---|---|---|---|---|---|---|
| FULL MOON | (SU) / MO | | (MU) / (SO) | | (SU) / MO | SUPER STRONG / VERY STRONG / STRONG |
| NEW MOON | MU / (SU) | | MO / (SO) | | MU / (SU) | SUPER STRONG / VERY STRONG / STRONG |
| HALF MOON | | (SU) | MO | (SO) | (MU) | (SU) | SUPER STRONG / VERY STRONG / STRONG |
| QUARTER MOON | (SU) / MO | | (SO) / (MU) | | (SU) | SUPER STRONG / VERY STRONG / STRONG |

MO MOON OVERHEAD   (SO) SUN OVERHEAD
(MU) MOON UNDERFOOT   (SU) SUN UNDERFOOT

sending up energy, giving us a double dose. Some 12 hours later, the two have reversed their positions and we get another double dose. This creates a relatively steady, two beat rhythm of very strong energy at 12-hour intervals.

Basically, the same cadence occurs under a new moon, except the sun and moon are traveling the sky together, instead of directly opposed. So, its two beats are of different strengths, being super strong when overhead, and very strong when underfoot.

During a half moon period the sun and moon are at right angles to each other, meaning when one is overhead, the other is not underfoot, rather, on one horizon or the other. So there's no teaming up of solar and lunar energy, just a nice, steady rhythm at 6-hour intervals.

Most of the month, however, is out-of-sync, as illustrated by the bottom box of Figure 3-5. Labeled "Quarter Moon," to signify any day that is not within the full, new, or half moon phase, the intervals between energy spurts is probably too irregular for our quarry to maintain an organized activity rhythm based on the solar/lunar influence. If this rhythm theory is to hold water, it must presuppose that 1) fish and game fare better when active at regular intervals, just as we humans do, and 2) solar/lunar energy plays a role in the timing of these periods. Consequently, the days when this energy comes at irregular intervals theoretically could be the days when conflicts emerge among the properties normally responsible for our quarry's activity level and schedule.

Those are the basic theories. Since each is just that—a theory, you're free to pick and choose which one(s) you like the best. Eventually, scientists will probably pinpoint the exact cause of the sun and moon's influence. If it turns out to be the "EM Wave Alignment" theory—which at this point seems a good possibility, you can yawn and say, "Oh, I knew that back in the 20th Century."

**Summary**

Every object in the universe is surrounded by its own electromagnetic (EM) field, which can interact with other fields, the degree of which will depend on angle, distance, and mass of the two.

To fish and game, the strongest EM influence comes from the earth, followed by the sun and moon. How much of this energy is received from the sun and moon at any particular moment depends on their distance, angle, and their alignment with the earth.

There are a few theories on why angle is important in deciding each day's best times, the best probably being the "EM Wave Alignment" (see Figure 3-1). The other is the "Atmospheric Filter" theory (Figure 3-2). The "EM Wave Alignment" also could help account for each month's best days, along with the "Distance" theory (Figure 3-3) and the "Rhythm" theory (Figure 3-5).

# 4

## *Polishing Your When-to-Go Game Plan*

The goal of *PrimeTimes* is to provide outdoors enthusiasts with a quick, accurate, and easy-to-follow overview of the potential activity days and times for the more popular fish and game species. From the beginner, who may not yet know when the best periods are, to the veteran, who may be too short on time this week to study all the variables, you need do nothing more than glance at *PrimeTimes* to have a relatively accurate activity forecast for just about anything that swims, saunters, or soars.

Still, you may be the type who won't always settle for being 90 percent of the way there. You want your best-times-of-the-day game plan honed to a razor's edge, and that's what we'll try to do in this chapter and the next. Here we'll see how some anglers can make a simple adjustment in *PrimeTimes* to better suit their region, and hunters to better suit most game in general. We'll deal with those variables, like the weather, environmental conditions, and fishing/hunting pressure, that no person or activity calendar can predict in advance, yet need to be worked into the formula, perhaps at the last minute.

Remember that *PrimeTimes* is geared more toward fishing, so there's relatively little an angler needs to do in the way of adjusting it to better suit his purposes. Also, virtually all suggested alterations deal only with the priority (strength) of certain periods, not their time of occurrence. The only minor exception to this comes in customizing the calendar to your exact, geographic location within any given time zone, which is a topic for Chapter 6.

## FISHING

While lures and techniques can vary appreciably from one fish to the next, we can pretty much lump the various aquatic species together when discussing the effects of geography, weather, water clarity, and fishing pressure on their activity periods. And only small divisions occur when comparing lakes to streams and salt water to fresh.

**Regional Adjustments**

If you use *PrimeTimes* to fish anywhere in the middle latitudes of the northern hemisphere for bass, crappie, northern, muskie, bluegills, catfish, or any other specie that prefers the shallow-to-medium depths, your when-to-go game plan is basically set. *PrimeTimes* is designed mostly with these subjects in mind, because they provide the centerpiece for the vast majority of our recreational hours. Even if you go for those fish that prefer deeper, colder water—like walleyes or lake trout, or the offshore gamefish like billfish or marlin, there is little extra to do.

However, if you fish in the far north or far south, one period of *PrimeTimes* could be increased or decreased to some degree during certain months of the year. This is the Heat-of-the-Day peak, which comes into play only when the water temperature is colder than your favorite species' ideal. (The term "ideal" is used by biologists to describe the temperature in which the metabolism of a particular specie operates at peak efficiency, and which that fish may actually seek out when available.)

To be as accurate as possible for the most people, *PrimeTimes* is geared for these middle latitudes where 70-degree water (the average preferred temperature for the more popular species of fish) usually arrives in April or May and exits in September or October. So, if you live in, say, Dallas, Texas, where 70-plus water is often found in March and can hang on until November, you'll want to downgrade that Heat-of-the-Day period *PrimeTimes* may still be showing in March and April, then again in late-September and October.

Here's a simple rule of thumb for those of you in the south: *Anytime the upper layers of your water are 70 degrees or above, ignore the Heat-of-the-Day period, even if* PrimeTimes *is showing it.*

And for those of you in the north: *Anytime the upper layers of your water are below 70 degrees, include the Heat-of-the-Day period, even if* PrimeTimes *is not showing it.*

**The Weather**

Since no one can accurately predict the weather more than a day or two in advance (we know some meteorologists who are lucky to get this afternoon's forecast right), *PrimeTimes* operates on the premise that the day in question is fairly typical. This means relatively stable weather with mostly sunny skies, seasonal temperatures, and winds that haven't recently changed directions nor velocity to any large extent. Because the water temperature is staying constant, or possibly rising slightly, whatever pattern your fish are presently on should hold up, and your *PrimeTimes* calendar can be followed with relative confidence.

Weather change will inevitably come, however, with the most common deviation being cloud cover. If it's just a little haze or high, cirrus clouds, the effects may be minimal. Under a heavy overcast, on the other hand, some upgrading and downgrading to *PrimeTimes'* daily peaks and valleys may be necessary.

Figure 4-1 shows an example of this during a typical cold-season situation (the date used here is March 22, randomly chosen from the *1995 PrimeTimes Wall Calendar*). When you compare the top section ("Sunny") with the lower

FIGURE 4-1
**PRIMETIMES FOR FISH:
SUNNY VERSUS OVERCAST IN THE COOLER MONTHS**

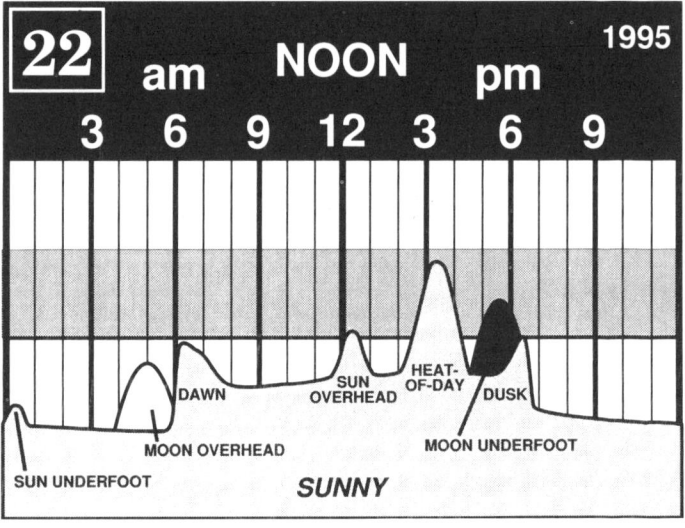

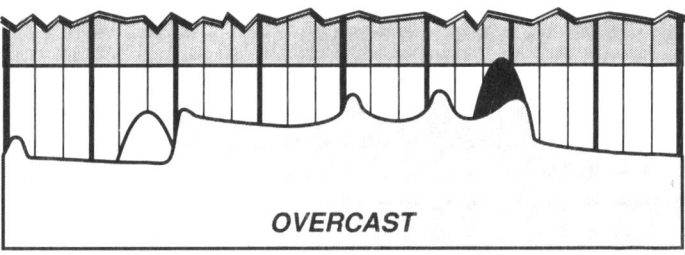

48  How to Know When to Go

one ("Overcast"), you'll notice how the Heat-of-the-Day peak in particular loses most of its punch under heavy cloud cover. Without the sun's heat, there will be little temperature change in either the air or water throughout the entire day, so one time is basically the same as another in this respect.

In terms of solar light, Dawn on an overcast day still begins with a sharp increase in activity, because things do get noticeably brighter at sunrise, even through thick clouds. But by mid-morning, with no high, brightening skies to curtail feeding activity, this Dawn period may continue on unimpeded, tapering only slightly as more and more predators feed successfully.

Meanwhile, electromagnetic energy from the sun or moon is probably less affected by cloud cover, so any downgrading of the four periods dealing with this force (the Overhead and Underfoot Moon and Sun) is less severe.

You may have noticed that the total number of active hours on this day dropped when we went from sunny to overcast. This will often be the case under these conditions, because heavy cloud cover can be associated with an air temperature that's cooler than the water. Especially if there is a wind, this would then translate into a drop in water temperature, one of the main turn-offs in fishing during the colder months. If it's a warm, overcast day, such may not be the case. It's important, therefore, to know both your present air and water temperatures.

Overcast days during the warmer months, however, often signal a general increase in the total activity curve (see Figure 4-2), because the shallows are already at or above the fish's ideal temperature. Heavy cloud cover prevents any additional warming, and may even cool the shallows down, making them a more comfortable place to be. And with the sun's light greatly subdued, predator fish—feeling more secure, tend to wander out from their cover and roam the

FIGURE 4-2
**PRIMETIMES FOR FISH:
SUNNY VERSUS OVERCAST IN THE WARMER MONTHS**

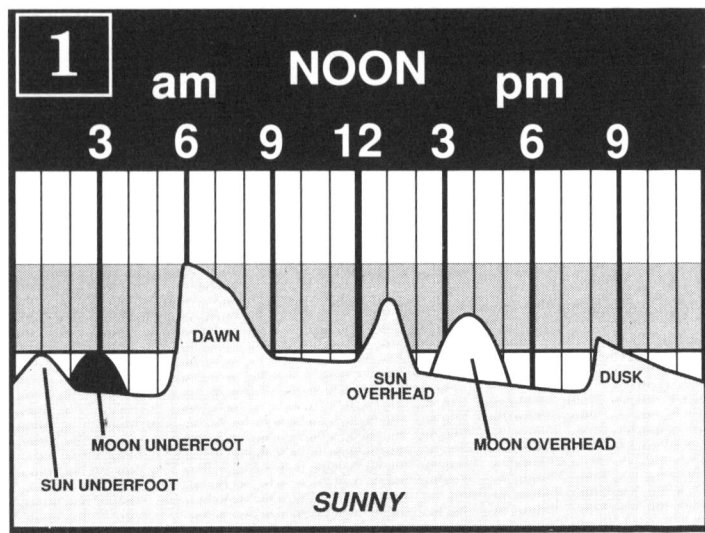

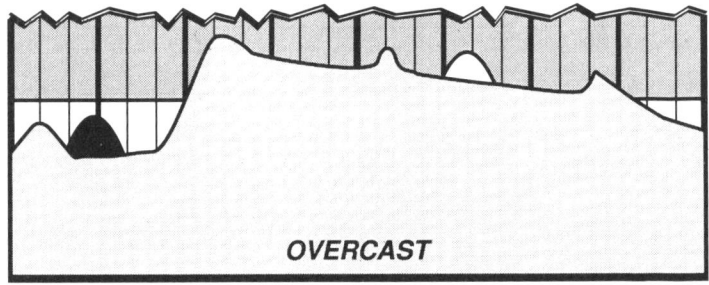

shallows for longer periods in search of food. So, while a major peak, like Dawn, may not have the exclusivity it does on a sunny day and, consequently, require a little downgrading, the subsequent upgrading of the valleys more than makes up for it.

Again, the electromagnetic lunar and solar periods are less affected by cloud cover, so little downgrading is necessary. They do, however, lose potential by virtue of the normally poor times (valleys) experiencing an upgrade now. In other words, with the whole day being a good time, these EM times do not stand out as much.

What often follows an overcast period is the infamous cold front, long deemed the angler's curse from fall through spring. A warm, southerly breeze suddenly gives way to a cold blast from the north, changing currents and cooling the shallow layers a few degrees. Concurrently, the sun explodes onto the environment, unimpeded by its previous screen of clouds, haze and humidity, and even the larger gamefish begin feeling a little insecure.

While cold fronts do usher in less than ideal variables, they do not necessarily alter a fish's best feeding periods (and therefore *PrimeTimes*' predicted daily times). Imagine you are a five-pound largemouth roaming the shallows in search of threadfin shad under an overcast, spring sky, when a cold front comes through and starts generating all the typical changes. For the first few hours the temperature in your immediate surroundings will change little if at all, because it takes time for water to transfer heat to the air, and vice versa. And even after the water has cooled a couple degrees, the change has been so gradual that it may not be enough to throw you completely off your feed. The suddenly bright sky offers a much more immediate change, but with a couple kicks of your tail you can be in the shade of weeds or a fallen tree and feeling just as secure. Your feeding activity does not have to end for this reason; it simply can change from search-and-destroy to less-mobile ambushing.

The real culprit in a cold front is usually the shift in wind direction. And not because it turns off the gamefish, but because it simply repositions their food supply. When the wind has been out of the same direction for a few days, concentrations of plankton become established in certain areas. This draws in the baitfish, which in turn draws in our quarry. A wind shift alters the currents and blows the plankton into new areas of the lake, and the baitfish go right along with it, possibly followed by the predators. The angler who suddenly finds his hot spot unproductive may be inclined to believe the fish have developed lockjaw, when the fact is they may have only moved into nearby cover or to another area of the lake. He would be wise to change his location and maybe tactics, but not the predictions of his *PrimeTimes* calendar.

**Water Clarity**

If your water is anywhere from muddy to slightly colored, it fits *PrimeTimes*' criteria. If it's super clear, and you want to fish only in the shallows, you could downgrade the Heat-of-the-Day period a little during the cooler months. The problem is that clear water does not absorb the sun's light and heat very well, at least not in any concentrated, noticeable form in the shallows.

Say there are two ponds side-by-side: one has clear water, one has murky water, and both begin this sunny day with a base temperature of 52 degrees (see Figure 4-3). As the Heat-of-the-Day period rolls around at mid-afternoon, each pond will exhibit considerably different thermal layering. The murky water, being darker in color, will naturally absorb more heat (just as your shoulders feel the sun more when wearing a black shirt). Also, because the sun penetrates only the first few feet of murky water, all the warming gets concentrated there, thus raising the shallows to the high 50's in this example.

Meanwhile, over at the clear pond, some of the sun's heat/light gets reflected back into the atmosphere, due to the water's lighter color. That which could penetrate did so much deeper, spreading its allotment of heat over a larger volume of water. As a result, the pond's surface here reached only 54

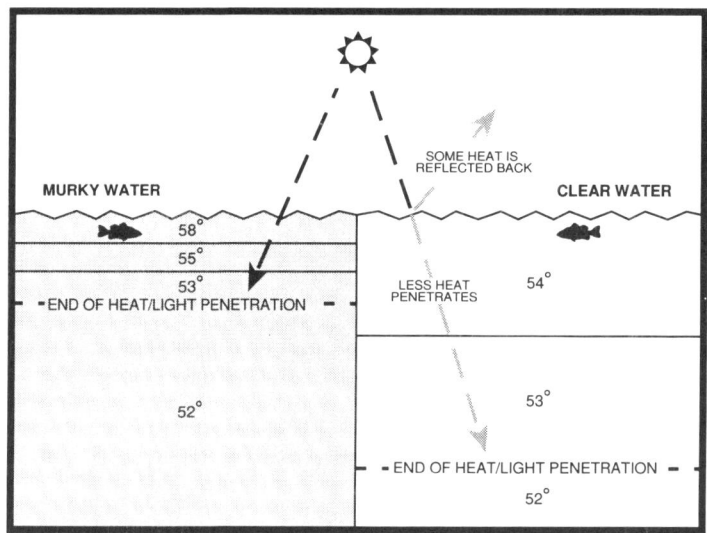

FIGURE 4-3
**WHY CLEAR WATER CAN DIMINISH THE "HEAT-OF-THE-DAY'S" STRENGTH IN SHALLOWS**

degrees, four degrees cooler than its murky counterpart. Any gamefish in the clear pond would find less advantage coming to the shallows during the Heat-of-the-Day, so the shallow-water angler here could downgrade this period to some degree, while upgrading the low-light periods.

In most clear water situations, however, the fish basically live and feed in proportionately deeper water, especially during daylight hours. You'll notice in Figure 4-3 that any fish in the medium depths will actually experience a one-degree rise in temperature today, while over at the murky pond the same depth did not warm at all. Although this does score a point for the Heat-of-the-Day in clear water, the low-light periods of Dawn and Dusk usually still win the match.

For daytime fishing in clear water you should also pay more attention to the Overhead/Underfoot Moon and Sun. Since the shallows of any body of water act as a buffer against weather changes, those fish which inhabit deep water experience a filtered version of any changes in light, temperature, and the wind. And without these variables working on them as much, there's little else during the day except the electromagnetic elements of the moon and sun, on which water depth seems to have no effect. So, if you fish clear water where your quarry is relatively deep most of the time during daylight, you could place less emphasis on the weather and more on the EM periods of the sun and moon.

Clear water anglers also notice that the daytime fishing can often be poor during a full moon. This is probably due to the extra illumination cast upon the after-hours waters (when the skies are clear), allowing many game species to see better than their optically-inferior prey. To whatever degree night feeding does occur, it's logical that the daytime bites may be that much reduced. Under any other lunar phase, which will have little or no extra night light, things remain status quo. So, in clear water and especially during the spring and fall months when the below-ideal water temperature has fish feeding only once or twice each 24 hours, the week of the full moon may require some serious night fishing. During the summer, with feeding spells popping up around the clock, that week may still be a good time for launching at sundown, but not to the exclusion of all others.

So far we've been discussing water clarity in terms of its average color over the long run. There's also the issue of those short term changes in clarity brought on by rains, winds, or massive plankton blooms. For example, when your lake suddenly turns cloudier than normal, you will want to diminish *PrimeTimes*' light-related periods (ie: Dawn and Dusk) proportionately until conditions improve. If the murkiness is not severe enough to inhibit feeding, the Heat-of-the-Day peak could actually intensify for shallow fishing, as that heat energy gets concentrated in the upper layer and raises the water temperature higher and quicker than normal. If your quarry resides in the deeper regions, you should downgrade Heat-of-the-Day to zilch.

## Fishing Pressure

*PrimeTimes* said it was going to be good fishing from 3:00 to 4:30 on Thursday afternoon, so you sneaked out of the office and waylaid some nice, summertime fish. Now it's Sunday, you're on the same spot during another predicted prime time, but nothing is hitting. What happened?

If this is an average lake during the warmer months, you're probably contending with a myriad of other anglers, boaters, skiers, and even rock-throwing kids that weren't here last Thursday. This kind of topside commotion can move fish out of productive areas and even shut down their feeding urge. Working deeper during any of the four electromagnetic periods (Sun/Moon Overhead/Underfoot) is one possible solution. The other is to see what *PrimeTimes* periods occur after the sun goes down, and come out then. Keep in mind that as a rule, the clearer your water, the better the night fishing.

## Rivers and Streams

For the most part, rivers and streams can be treated the same as the shallows of a lake or pond. So, what we just discussed under "Weather" and "Water Clarity" will apply here, as well. The major difference, of course, is that rivers and streams have a steady, uni-directional current, while ponds and lakes do not. And therein lies two things to consider.

The first is that wind shifts, such as those associated with a cold front, will have less effect on the fish. It's not likely that a river's current will change direction or velocity due to anything less than a tornado. So, if you have the fish located, don't move just because the wind has.

Secondly, a cold front in the spring or fall may be more immediate and severe, due to the shallowness of the stream, and the fact that flowing water exchanges heat more readily with the air.

**Salt Water**

As rivers vary from lakes basically in terms of currents, oceans vary from lakes basically in terms of size. Consequently, while the changing light values of Dawn and Dusk hold up well in salt water, as do the Sun Overhead and Underfoot periods, oceans are often too vast and too turbulent to be affected much by the Heat-of-the-Day. So scratch that one, unless you are fishing in a shallow backwater, estuary, or just beneath a calm surface.

The ocean's size also means it will have tides, those twice-a-day events that are a direct result of gravitational pull from the sun—on a global scale, and the moon—on a local scale. (The same pull is exerted on inland lakes, but here the surface volume is so relatively small the tides go unnoticed.) Since the rise and fall of shoreline depths move the foodfish around, tides can be a factor in when certain gamefish become active. On the one hand, a falling tide washes the food away from their shallow sanctuaries, making them vulnerable to predation. On the other hand, a rising tide freshly inundates shoreline cover and any morsels within. Which is the better time to fish depends on a variety of factors, particularly the species.

Of course, *PrimeTimes*' two lunar periods (Overhead and Underfoot Moon) correspond closely to the day's two high tides. Halfway in between come the two low tides, when the moon is on either horizon. So, you could use *PrimeTimes* as a tidal chart, although it won't be as precise as one devised strictly for your location, because other factors, like topography, are involved. But what really gets interesting here is that while the moon's gravitational pull is causing the tides, its peak electromagnetic force is simultaneously working on the fish itself. This means if your salt water quarry traditionally feeds at high tide, the double stimulation of the higher water level and the EM element will be acting upon it. If your fish feeds on a low tide, a conflict develops and you may want to downgrade the Overhead and Underfoot Moon periods in *PrimeTimes*. In most offshore cases, however, the gamefish's activity schedule is not totally tide-contingent, so *PrimeTimes*' EM periods remain as factors to consider.

Moonlight can illuminate salt water just as it does freshwater, and those species with advanced optical systems are just as likely to take advantage of the full moon phase on clear nights. Billfish, for example, are known to provide better daytime fishing during the dark of the moon (new moon), because they apparently feed too much at night when the moon is full. Meanwhile, stripers may prefer the first days following each half moon, for reasons of their own. So again, it is vital that you know the feeding habits of your particular quarry, and adapt them accordingly to *PrimeTimes*.

## HUNTING

With virtually all game animals and birds, you'll want to emphasize *PrimeTimes*' Dawn and Dusk periods, which contain the primary movements between feeding and bedding areas (see Figure 4-4).

Also, if *PrimeTimes* has a Heat-of-the-Day period on the day in question, ignore it. Daily high temperatures generally do little to activate warm-blooded creatures, and may, in fact, find them snoozing. Of course, if that works into

*FIGURE 4-4*
**ADJUSTING PRIMETIMES FOR MOST DIURNAL GAME**

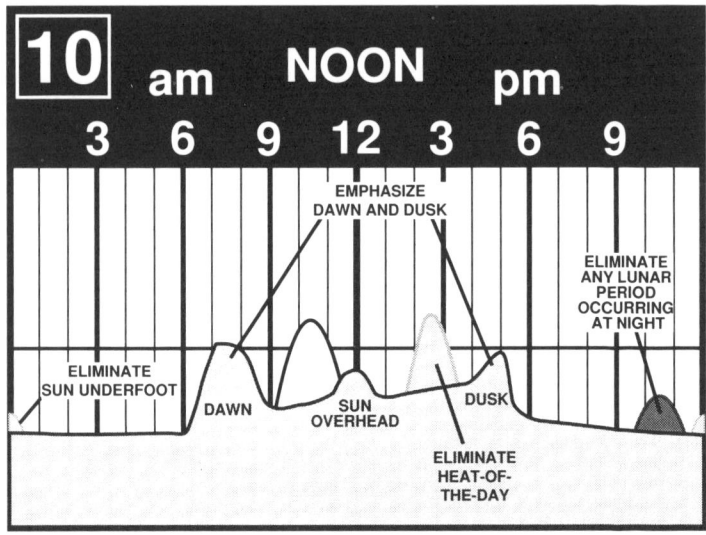

your attack plan, by all means consider this period.

Finally, if your species cannot be legally hunted at night or simply is not active then, you'll obviously want to ignore any solar or lunar period occurring during these hours.

That's really all there is to it for the animal kingdom in general. Individually, however, the various species can require their own adjustments to *PrimeTimes*, especially those known to prowl the nighttime hours as well as daylight. And that's the subject for our next chapter.

**Summary**

*PrimeTimes* is formulated for fishing, so most of you will have little else to consider in your when-to-go game plan under most conditions. When alteration is required, it will rarely be to the time of day that period occurs, but to its importance (height of its peak). Most of these are minor changes that you will probably make automatically anyway, if and when the situation rises. To summarize, they are:

1. When your water is 70 degrees or above, downgrade or even completely eliminate the Heat-of-the-Day period.

2. When the sky is overcast...
    a. if the water temperature is below your quarry's ideal (ie: fall through early-spring), downgrade the Heat-of-the-Day period considerably, and the Sun Overhead period (high noon) a little. If the day is also cool and dropping the water temperature, downgrade the entire day proportionately;
    b. if the water temperature is above the fish's ideal (ie: mid-spring through early-fall), upgrade the entire day, especially *PrimeTimes*' valleys.

3. In very clear water, or anytime you are fishing deep during the day...
    a. downgrade the Heat-of-the-Day's influence, and upgrade the Sun Overhead (high noon) period;
    b. upgrade whichever lunar period is occurring during daylight;
    c. your better times are often Dawn, Dusk, and—during the warmer months, don't forget the night, especially under a bright moon.

4. When your lake suddenly turns cloudier than normal...
    a. diminish *PrimeTimes*' light-related periods (ie: Dawn and Dusk) proportionately;
    b. if you are fishing in the shallows, upgrade the Heat-of-the-Day period;
    c. if you are fishing deep, ignore the Heat-of-the-Day period altogether.

5. In high-traffic waters...
    a. if your water is clear, upgrade the after-hours prime times and go at night;
    b. if your water is murky or you can't go at night, upgrade the daytime EM periods and move out to deeper water.

6. In shallow rivers and streams...
    a. wind shifts have little effect;
    b. cold fronts can be more detrimental because moving water loses (and gains) heat faster.

7. In oceans...
    a. down-grade the Heat-of-the-Day period, unless in a calm, shallow area;
    b. the Moon Overhead and Underfoot periods can be especially strong for species that feed when the tide is high, and weakened for species that feed when the tide is low;
    c. the extra light at night associated with a full moon phase can have some species feeding more at night and less during the day.

8. For hunting in general...
    a. emphasize Dawn and Dusk;
    b. forget the Heat-of-the-Day period;
    c. ignore any solar or lunar period occurring after hours.

# 5

# *Fine-Tuning to the Individual Species*

The final step in making a when-to-go game plan as accurate as possible is to understand the nature of your particular quarry. While all creatures in the area receive an equal dose of solar/lunar energies at any given moment, their individual needs, instincts, and behavior patterns may cause different reactions to these influences. Here we'll look at the more popular fish and game species to see if and how you may adjust the "Best Times of the Day" section of *PrimeTimes* in your approach to each of them.

## Fishing

As you undoubtedly know by now, *PrimeTimes* is geared mostly for the angler. That, and the fact that in terms of solar/lunar influence a fish is basically a fish, means very little fine-tuning is required between the individual species. Still, each can have its little quirks.

### *Bass*

If there is one creature *PrimeTimes* pertains to more than any other it's the largemouth bass. About the only thing you may want to keep in mind is that most big bass are individuals, and some have been known to go their own way on occasion with no rhyme nor reason. There are also those variables to which we can never be privy, such as knowing that the lake's biggest, juiciest crayfish just departed this earth via ol' Bufford's digestive system, and now our target is in anything but a feeding mood.

Still, in the long run most bass activity patterns are reasonably predictable. So go ahead and follow *PrimeTimes* as is, while always staying flexible.

*Panfish (ie: Bluegill and Crappie)*

Hanging around in schools, panfish often have a mob mentality. When one gets an idea, they all have the same little light bulb going off over their heads. That can work to our advantage, because introducing a jig-n-minnow to a group of crappie or bluegill can sometimes get the action going without any help from the sun or moon. On the negative side, when one gets spooked they all may. A common cause of this is having one depart your hook—either from fighting free or being intentionally released, and it rejoins the school with blood or some other bodily fluid oozing from its mouth. The action can come to a screeching halt.

And since panfish are a little lower on the food chain, they react more quickly to changes in the weather and sky conditions. This happens because one of the items on their menu is small minnows, which feed on plankton, which in turn can react almost instantaneously to changes in their environment. Say, for example, the wind shifts directions and starts blowing a plankton bloom out of a heretofore productive area. The minnows may go right along with it, followed closely behind by the crappie, bluegills, white bass or other schoolfish. Meanwhile, for reasons previously given, the larger gamefish may not be this reactionary, and thus take longer to show the effects of that wind shift.

So, you don't need to adjust *PrimeTimes* much to suit schooling panfish. Just keep in mind that their collective and competitive nature opens them up more to outside influences, including any that you may personally import.

## *Catfish*

Being mostly nocturnal, bottom-feeding scavengers, cats are less dependent on the patterns of their prey. A rotting pile of post-bluegill probably isn't following any solar or lunar influence, and is likely to be there whenever the catfish feels like scooping it up. Still, those same factors which influence most fish and game work on catfish in much the same fashion.

While the bigger ones are individuals, they all share the common trait of caring less whether it's day or night. Cats have poor eyesight and very sensitive "noses," so how much light is permeating their environment means little to them. Consequently, you could downgrade the Dawn and Dusk periods, while consistently upgraded all four of the electro-magnetic periods (Moon/Sun Overhead/Underfoot), especially those that occur after dark. You should also consider the Heat-of-the-Day period only when fishing in shallow water that is colder than 70 degrees, and then to less degree than for most other gamefish.

## *Northerns and Muskies*

These two predators rely heavily on their vision when feeding, preferring to lie back in the weeds or other heavy cover, waiting to ambush passing foodfish. Consequently, you could emphasize the low-light periods of Dawn and Dusk a little more, since these are times when the northern and muskie hold a strong visual edge over their prey.

*Stream Trout*

When trout or any shallow-river gamefish have their sights on insects, you may want to concentrate more on Dusk, Heat-of-the-Day (in cool water) and Dawn, in that order. Dawn is often good for the usual reasons, but by mid-afternoon the water and air are their warmest of the day, inducing insect hatches and activity. Then, a few hours later at Dusk, the number of bugs reaches its apex just as the fading daylight may be making our predator fish more aggressive.

*Walleyes*

You need only look at a walleye's enlarged pupils to see how sensitive they are to light. While they will and do come to the shallows occasionally for food, by and large this specie prefers the medium to lower depths for residing during the day. And as we just discussed in the "Water Clarity" section, being down here removes them somewhat from the immediate effects of light and temperature changes. So, your hours on the water may be more productive if they are in line with the moon, plus the Sun Overhead period of high-noon.

In the shallows, look for them at the early part of Dawn and the latter part of Dusk. When night fishing in either the shallows or depths, upgrade any corresponding lunar time, plus the Sun Underfoot period of midnight. Also, since the walleye's preferred temperature is closer to 60 degrees, the Heat-of-the-Day period will cease being a positive influence earlier in the spring and start up later in the fall.

**Hunting**

The game segment presents more diversity among its members. Some have fur and walk to feeding areas, other have feathers and fly. Some are crafty loners, others need the collective intelligence of a group to be slightly smarter than a hedge apple.

We'll begin by going into considerable detail on deer, using the whitetail as kind of a template for the other popular species. This way we won't have to keep repeating the universal points for each, rather just key on the differences.

So, even if you don't hunt deer, you should read this section, since it will cover aspects that may apply to your favorite species, yet may not be discussed at any length in that particular section.

*Deer*

With their acute senses, especially the ability to see in low-light conditions, whitetails generally prefer the Dawn and Dusk hours for their major movements. But more and more experts are discovering that the moon can also play a key role in a deer's daily routine. They've noticed movements occurring quite regularly during the Moon Overhead and Moon Underfoot periods, sometimes almost exclusively.

Meanwhile, other experts say some whitetails will also move and feed on clear nights during the full moon period. The lunar illumination offers the deer ample light to see, while not exposing them as much to their few enemies. During this phase, the normal activity of Dawn and Dusk can be reduced, while mid-day (Sun Overhead) may see an increase, since it is half-way between the mid-night feeding spells.

According to Jeff Murray, an outdoor writer and co-originator of the *"Deer Hunter's Moon Guide"* (see acknowledgments in front of this book), the optimum days are during the half moon periods, when the Overhead or Underfoot Moon coincides with Dawn and/or Dusk. Here we have the triple-whammy effect of high electromagnetic energy and extra lunar illumination from the moon, occurring at the already-proven activity periods of first and last light. This causes deer to start earlier and/or linger longer in their feeding grounds.

When you factor in other vital variables, such as wind direction, deer populations, hunting pressure, food availability, rutting, and the fact that whitetails—especially bucks, are notorious for being individuals, predicting prime times for deer can become a veritable science. The best plan is to start with a general outline for deer as a species, then be flexible enough to adjust it as your specific situation and quarry dictate.

Figure 5-1 is an actual day from the *1995 PrimeTimes Wall Calendar*, showing the solar and lunar positions during November's full moon. Since deer are warm-blooded mammals, we can ignore that Heat-of-the-Day period, because it pertains mostly to fish, whose metabolisms are directly connected to the temperature of their environment. Deer, of course, do not have this characteristic.

With that done, we have a reasonably reliable activity curve for the average deer. If, however, you suspect the specific whitetails being stalked are also under some lunar influence, you may want to factor in the times of the Overhead and Underfoot Moons. As Figure 5-1 shows, during this full moon period the Moon Underfoot is coinciding with the Sun Overhead period of mid-day, while the Moon Overhead occurs at midnight in conjunction with the Sun Underfoot period. Of course, you are not allowed to hunt during the night, so that leaves the Sun Overhead period as a strong

*FIGURE 5-1*
**PRIMETIMES FOR DEER
DURING A FULL MOON (ie: NOV. 7, 1995)**

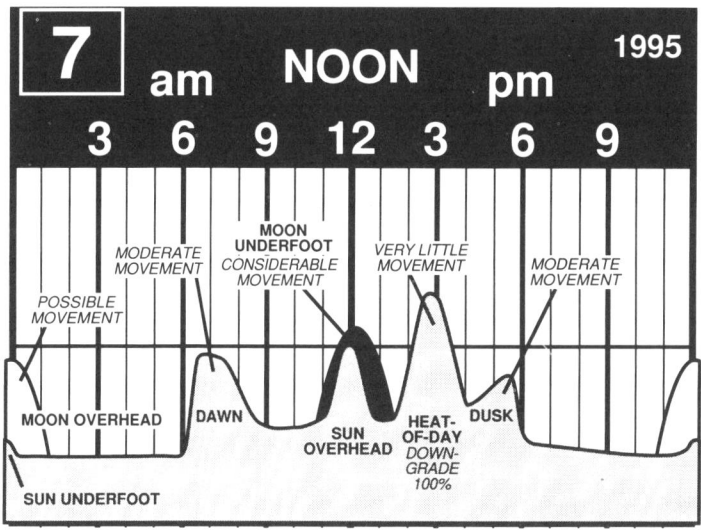

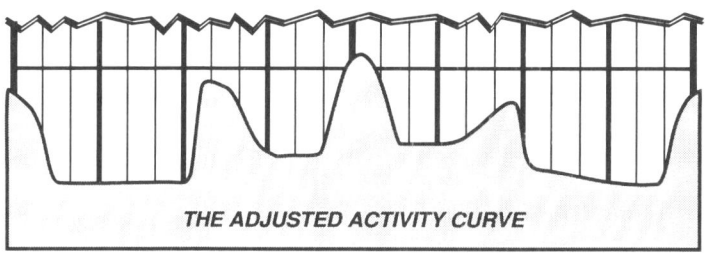

possibility, with Dawn and Dusk the other considerations. The bottom section of Figure 5-1 shows the activity curve once adjusted for the lunar influence, plus the elimination of the Heat-of-the-Day period.

Figure 5-2 moves us up to November 16 in the 1995 calendar to demonstrate one of the month's two half moon phases (actually, it's the day after the half moon, to better suit our purposes). Here the Moon Overhead period lands right on

FIGURE 5-2
**PRIMETIMES FOR DEER
DURING A HALF MOON (ie: NOV. 16, 1995)**

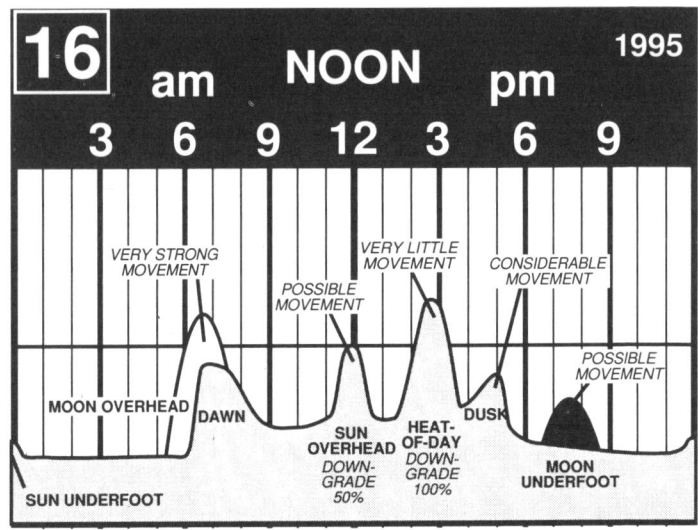

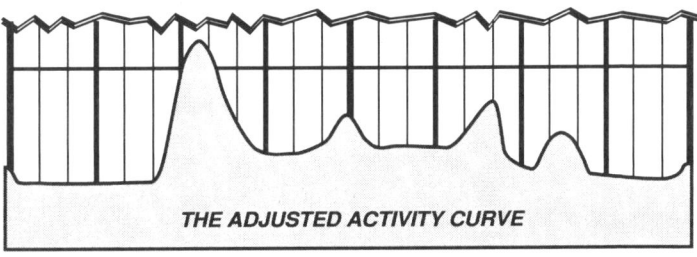

top of Dawn, offering that triple-whammy effect which should get a good share of the deer up and moving. If there is some strong feeding during the morning, we may expect mid-day to become a resting time; consequently, that Sun Overhead period at noon could be downgraded by about 50 percent. Of course, the Heat-of-the-Day spell is not much of a factor now, so it can be downgraded to virtual zero. As the sun drops in the west, we can expect many deer to feed again before heading back to the bedding areas, so Dusk remains a period to keep an eye on. Any lunar influence from the Moon Underfoot may be reduced somewhat in this situation, since it occurs just a couple of hours after the last feed.

Again, the bottom section of Figure 5-2 shows how this day's activity curve for deer may look once adjusted for all the major factors. Notice how the Dawn period has extended to account for the extra lunar influence. The Sun Overhead's peak is downgraded, because it's more likely a resting time now, plus it basically was high in the first place for fish, not deer. The Heat-of-the-Day peak is gone for the same reason. Dusk remains steady, and the Underfoot Moon drops a bit.

(NOTE: 15 days later on November 30, one day after the next half moon phase, the two lunar periods shown in Figure 5-2 are reversed [ie: the Moon Overhead will be occurring a couple hours after dusk and the Moon Underfoot at Dawn]. While our activity curve won't change all that much, there will be the addition of some lunar illumination in the early night hours. So, theoretically, that peak could be extended a little.)

Figure 5-3 takes us to November 22, the day of the new moon. This may be a time of balance, with the three main periods of Dawn, Sun Overhead, and Dusk fairly even in potential for the general population of whitetails. With the Overhead Moon transpiring at high-noon right along with the Overhead Sun, a lot of electromagnetic energy is reigning down about now, giving this time of day one of its strongest boosts of the month. The same is happening at mid-night, where the Moon Underfoot overlaps the Sun Underfoot. There is, however, no extra illumination associated here, so mid-night during a new moon may have less potential than it does under a full moon.

It's important to keep in mind the unlikelihood of having only one active period per day for deer under any normal circumstance. As we discussed earlier in this book, perhaps the most controlling factor of any creature's daily feeding pattern is hunger. And being warm-blooded, deer digest their food at the same rate day after day, month after month, just as we humans do. That means that even after a full meal, six hours later they may not mind eating again. Twelve hours later they would be very hungry, and 24 hours between meals could find them downright cranky. Also, since deer are herbivores, they are fairly assured their food will be waiting for them anytime of the day or night. They need not submit to the patterns of their prey, nor weigh the energy cost of hunting and chasing it down, as the carnivorous wolf or fox must do.

So, using the new moon scenario in Figure 5-3 as an example, let's design a logical pattern of activity for deer over a 24-hour stretch:

    1) Some get up at first light and move to a feeding area as usual, while those more tuned to the moon sleep in (there is no electromagnetic solar or lunar influence working on them at Dawn, only the solar light element of night turning into day);

    2) By late morning both the sun and moon are beginning to pour down EM energy, spurring those still in bed to get moving and perhaps those already feeding to continue a little longer (on most other days, this is a time for resting);

    3) The late-risers remain active until about 1:00 or 2:00 p.m., then head to their daytime resting areas;

    4) As dusk approaches, many head back to the feeding areas for a bite, then by last light move to the bedding area;

    5) Some, probably those that slept in initially, may find their stomachs growling during the night and select to do some after-hours feeding (even though there is no moonlight,

*FIGURE 5-3*
**PRIMETIMES FOR DEER
DURING A NEW MOON (ie: NOV. 22, 1995)**

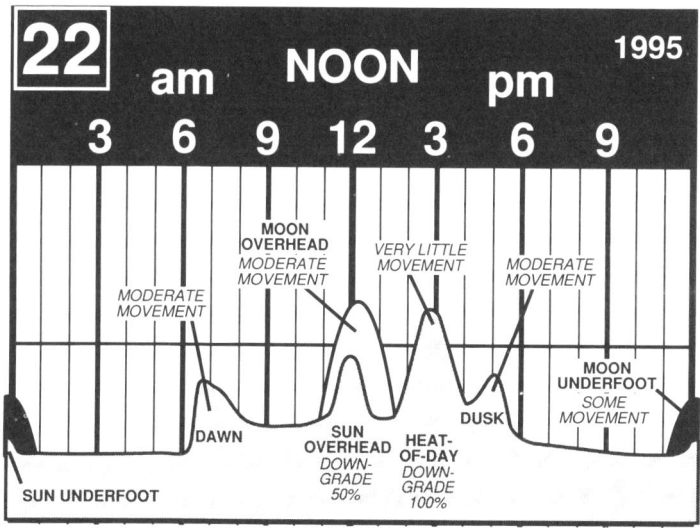

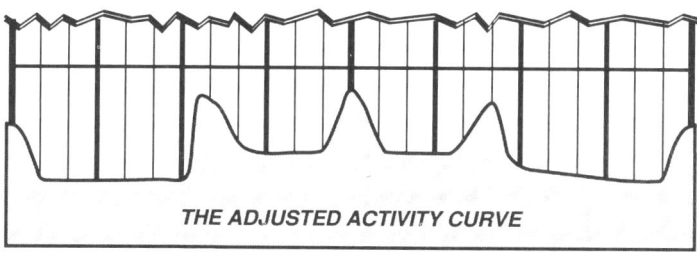

the deer can see well enough);

6) By dawn the cycle starts over, with the night feeders sleeping in again and the daytime feeders feeling some need for sustenance.

That is just a sampling. It does not take into account a number of the variables listed earlier, such as weather, which could have most game holding in their bedding areas for

Fine-Tuning to the Individual Species

extended periods during heavy rain, or nibbling corn from sunrise to sunset on a bluebird day. If there's a lot of hunting pressure, you'll probably find more nighttime feeding, as deer learn to associate daylight with snapping twigs, odd odors, and an occasional column of walking camouflage. And you must always consider the idiosyncrasies of the individual animal. Big bucks with huge racks don't get that way following the herd. Because deer are one of the few creatures that can move anytime of the day or night, the smarter ones probably do.

Also keep in mind that the moon's interaction with the solar peaks is an ever-changing array of peaks and valleys. Be careful in thinking that all full, new, half or in-between moons are the same, because they never are. Study your *PrimeTimes Wall Calendar* carefully before each outing.

Perhaps the recommended hunting strategy in most cases is to spend the first day on your stand from pre-dawn to at least 1:00 or 2:00 p.m. That is a long time, but it should go a long way in telling you what pattern those deer are following. Whether it proves to be a lunar format, with Dawn and Dusk as quiet periods, or a solar one, with Dawn and Dusk as the primaries, you will know where to concentrate your efforts from here on.

*Turkey*

One of the most difficult game birds to bag, the male turkey is a wary daytime creature that pretty much follows *PrimeTimes*' activity curve, leaving the roost at first light and returning at dusk. However, as in the case of deer, more and more turkey hunters are discovering frequent activity in tune with the Overhead or Underfoot Moon, whichever is occurring during daylight hours. For example, Jan Chase, a touring lecturer on the sport, reported killing all four of her Grand

Slam turkeys in 1994 during lunar times predicted by our calendar. And it wasn't that she went out only at these prescribed times; most came after having no success during the normal activity hours of early morning.

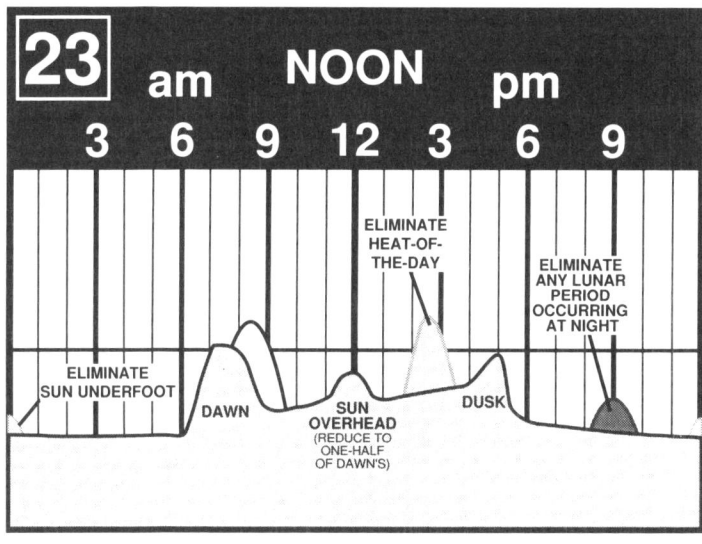

FIGURE 5-4
**SAMPLE PRIMETIMES FOR TURKEY**

Of course, the mating season disrupts most normal patterns. Dr. James Earl Kinamer, a wildlife biologist with the National Wild Turkey Federation, says that in the spring, as the days get longer, toms get more horny and begin feeding less, living off their breast sponges instead. When they do go for grain, it's often during the mid-morning to mid-afternoon (Sun Overhead) period. But mostly they are preoccupied with attracting and servicing the hens, which is usually announced with considerable gobbling while on the roost in the early morning. Later in the spring, as the hens leave to nest, the gobbling occurs later in the morning. According to Dr. Kinamer, these are the times hunters should try to call in the toms. During the non-mating season, he recommends setting up along the turkey's migration route to and from the feeding areas.

So, all in all, *PrimeTimes* is well set up for turkeys. You still need to incorporate the weather and mating variables when necessary, plus do the usual downgrade of the Heat-of-the-Day period, if you want your quarry on the move. And because turkeys are neither active nor legally hunted at night, you can completely ignore any *PrimeTimes* solar or lunar periods occurring between dusk and dawn (see Figure 5-4).

*Upland Birds*

Pheasants, quail, grouse, and partridge are all diurnal birds that generally begin each day at Dawn by moving to areas of grain, and end it by heading back again to the roost at Dusk. At noon (Sun Overhead), there is often another move to feed, as may be the case under any lunar period occurring during the day.

In the typical hunting scenario, we prefer finding the birds in some type of heavy cover, like the roost, where they are less likely to run ahead of our approach, giving the dogs a chance to get on point. But with the exception of stalking uneducated birds on opening day, it can be quite difficult to locate many in their roost from sunrise to one-half-hour later, when the day's shooting hours begin. The early-season dummies are already statistics, while the smarter ones quickly learned to get out by first light before the bipeds arrive, and not return until after the sun is well below the horizon.

For this reason, the Heat-of-the-Day period in *PrimeTimes* can be a good time to hunt upland birds on sunny days. When the morning and mid-day feeds were successful, some birds like to catnap in sun-baked areas—like thick, short grass, during these mid-afternoon hours.

So, of all the game animals, upland birds probably follow the *PrimeTimes* activity curve the most closely. There is little we need to adjust.

*Water Fowl*

For all practical purposes, ducks and geese are quite similar to upland birds, except they roost on water instead of land. So, what we just covered in the previous section applies here, as well, with a couple exceptions.

First, since we do not normally hunt water fowl with pointers, the Heat-of-the-Day period should be ignored. As we said, this is a time when the birds may be resting. And for ducks and geese that means in open fields or on open water. So, unless you are puddle-jumping or belly-crawling, mid-afternoon can be a poor time to hunt.

Also, since geese, especially, will fly at night, particularly during major migrations, the normal daytime routine can be upset for that flock. While their departure time could be influenced by a solar or lunar EM period, arrival time is probably based more on wing fatigue and/or reaching appropriate landing areas.

*Squirrels*

Besides the obvious anatomical structuring, the difference between squirrels and the only other mammal we covered so far (deer) is that the former has no nocturnal activity inclinations whatsoever. And while we can wait for them in ambush, it's usually more productive to walk along through the woods, watching ahead for signs of movement. Squirrel activity is regularly associated with Dawn, Dusk, Sun Overhead, and maybe daytime's lunar period. (For more details, see the "*Deer*" section.)

*Crows*

Also strictly diurnal, the crow leaves the roost—which he may share with a few thousand of his relatives, between first light and Dawn, then returns during the same twilight hour of Dusk. If you are hunting along their flyways, these may be the only times you'll find them in large numbers.

The most used method, however, is to lure a few into your blind with decoys and a call. Since this is often best achieved when they are feeling cantankerous, set up during the Sun Overhead period, plus whichever lunar time is transpiring during daylight hours.

*Fox, Coyote, Opossum, Raccoon, and Rabbits*

As diverse as these furbearers may seem, they all share the common trait of spending much of their active hours in the nocturnal setting. According to Dave DeBolt, a professional hunting guide and game farm owner from Granger, Iowa, the raccoon, opossum, and rabbit are especially prone to the nighttime, probably because their low stature on the food web has them high on the menu of many predators. And while some of their enemies will also hunt by night, it's more difficult to spot prey after the sun sets. The coyote and fox, with their excellent night vision, prowl mostly after hours, but are often active during the low-light hours of Dawn and Dusk, as well.

As is the case with any nighttime activity, the roles of Dawn and Dusk simply reverse: Dusk signals the beginning of activity, while Dawn marks its conclusion. Concurrently, the night hours in *PrimeTimes* would be raised considerably across the board, and the daytime hours lowered proportionately. And with the sun's light and heat energy pretty much out of the picture, it's only logical to turn more of our attention to the electromagnetic elements of the moon and sun (see Figure 5-5).

Dave says he's been following these solar/lunar periods for many years, finding them to be an excellent when-to-go tool for virtually all furbearers. Yet he cautions that you must still apply the data with some degree of logic. On nights of a bright moon, for example, you may have the urge to head out because you'll be able to see better. But your quarry, especially the raccoon, opossum, and rabbit, will often be staying home for the same reason. Also, when winter sets in, these species do not like trudging through snow to dig for food, so may spend two or three days at a time in a semi-hibernating state. The best times to hunt them are in the fall before the snows come.

*FIGURE 5-5*
**SAMPLE PRIMETIMES FOR NOCTURNAL FURBEARERS**

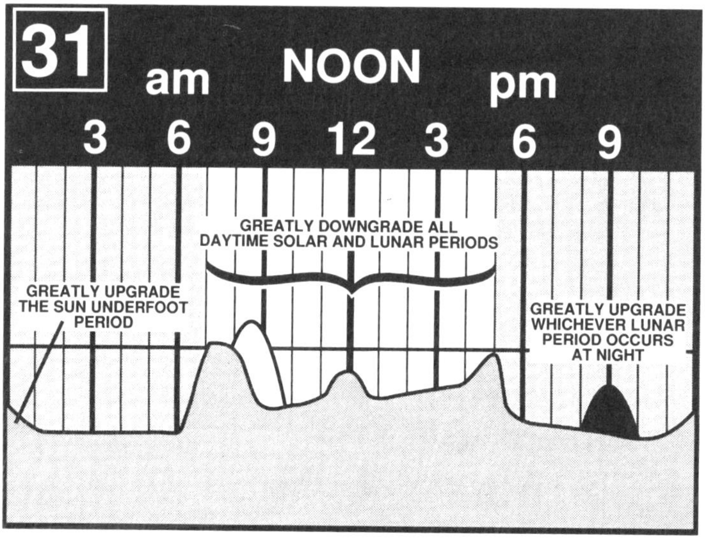

[Figure showing a 24-hour timeline with markings at 3, 6, 9 am, 12 NOON, 3, 6, 9 pm, labeled "31". Annotations read: "GREATLY UPGRADE THE SUN UNDERFOOT PERIOD", "GREATLY DOWNGRADE ALL DAYTIME SOLAR AND LUNAR PERIODS", "GREATLY UPGRADE WHICHEVER LUNAR PERIOD OCCURS AT NIGHT".]

Fine-Tuning to the Individual Species

# *6*

## *Inside PrimeTimes*

In this final chapter we are going to dissect the "Best Times of the Day" section of the *Wall Calendar* for an in-depth look at how it arrives at its predicted times and values, plus answer any left-over questions you may have.

As we've said, the concept, formulas, calculations, and layout are well founded in astrophysical and biological fact, so some of this matter may get a little technical in places. Don't worry if you don't remember it all; the system will still work just fine. We thought that by sharing its blueprint, some of you "techies" would come to better understand the true comprehensiveness and accuracy of *PrimeTimes*, and thereby use each year's calendar more confidently.

**The Solar Activity Base**

Each day in the "Best Times of the Day" section of the *Wall Calendar* starts from a foundation of solar energy, designated by the white area at its base. This area actually starts as a rectangle with no humps or valleys. How thick (high) this base is on any given day depends on the time of year, being at its thinnest (lowest) on the first day of winter (see lightly-shaded base in Figure 6-1), and thickest on the first day of summer (the white base in Figure 6-1). The thickness changes weekly, the degree of which is determined by a number of factors, the most important being the sun's high-low cycle (see Figure 2-4 in Chapter 2). By comparing these two samples in Figure 6-1, you can see how much this base will change over the course of half a year. These weekly changes pertain almost entirely to fishing, as water is cool in the winter (slower fishing) and warm in the summer (more active fish). The basic activity curve of game changes very little from one week to the next.

FIGURE 6-1
**SEASONAL CHANGES IN THE SOLAR ACTIVTY BASE**

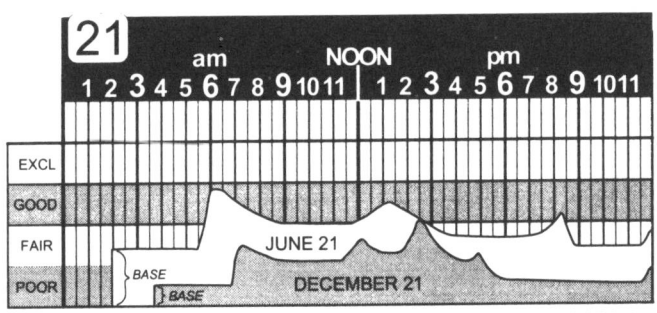

THE BASE REACHES ITS MAXIMUM THICKNESS ON THE FIRST DAY
OF SUMMER, AND ITS MINIMUM ON THE FIRST DAY OF WINTER

**The Solar Peaks**

Springing up from each day's base are the solar peaks of Dawn, Sun Overhead, Heat-of-the-Day (when in season), Dusk, and the Sun Underfoot. Again comparing the two samples is Figure 6-1, you can see how each solar period's basic height, duration, time of occurrence, and relativity to the others change from summer to winter, or vise versa.

Let's look at how the beginning time, ending time, and

strength (height) of each solar period is achieved.

*Dawn*

The Dawn period in *PrimeTimes* (see Figure 6-2) always begins 30 minutes prior to sunrise, at a time commonly called "first light." You don't need professional guide status to know that most creatures don't wait for the sun to break the horizon before entering an active state. In that half hour before sunrise things can go from dead to alive faster and further than any other time of day. That's why the activity line on this particular part of Dawn always rises so sharply and to the height that it does.

For the 30-60 minutes following sunrise, the activity of many fish and game remains high, as they continue en route to feeding areas or simply entering a feeding posture. Then as the morning progresses, this mode may gradually wane, a result of the creature's own rhythm, a successful feed, the brightening sky, all three, or something else. *PrimeTimes* shows this by the slow taper of Dawn's activity curve, which levels off at various times of the morning, depending on the time of year. Designating an exact ending time for the "time boxes" (above each corresponding hump), is one of the least precise calculations *PrimeTimes* makes, since this period seldom ends sharply (see Figure 6-3).

And although Dawn does taper off, it does not descend to the level of activity we saw just prior to first light. Mid-morning may find many fish and game winding down a little, but they are still more active than before the sun's wake-up call.

*Sun Overhead (High Noon)*

The next period's beginning, zenith, ending, and strength are rooted in astrophysical data, so its dimensions can

FIGURE 6-2
**ANATOMY OF THE SOLAR PERIODS**

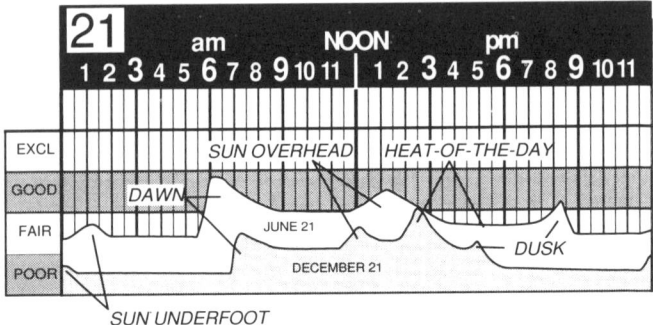

be quite precise. The higher the sun's daily path is across the northern hemisphere, the stronger and wider the Sun Overhead period is shown in *PrimeTimes*. It depicts the seasonal changes in the sun's heat, light, and electromagnetic energy, as determined by its angle (see Figure 2-4 in Chapter 2).

In Figure 6-2 compare this period's dimensions from one extreme to the other, being narrow in winter and wide in the summer. You'll also note that after reaching its peak in summer, the activity curve drops off more when compared to winter. This is because the Sun Overhead period basically coincides with the beginning of each day's Heat-of-the-Day period. In the summer, the building heat of mid-afternoon is often a negative, so the Sun Overhead period finds itself concluding when the water is getting too warm. In winter, the Heat-of-the-Day is a positive, so the Sun Overhead period ends just as another good period is beginning. In fact, its ending time actually levels off at a point higher than it began.

*Heat-of-the-Day*

The day's warmest period historically hits mid-way

between high noon and sunset, which also can be calculated accurately. Applying only to fish in water colder than their ideal, the strength (height) of this period is based on it's ability to supply activity stimuli—namely heat, to the fish's environment in relation to the other periods. Being cold-blooded, the warmer the water (to a point), the more active the fish.

Again, in the summer the Heat-of-the-Day time frame offers a negative influence, and thereby is more of a valley than a peak. The temperature in the shallows simply can get too warm for many species. Meanwhile, in the winter, just as the Sun Overhead period tapers right into the Heat-of-the-Day, the Heat-of-the-Day tapers right into Dusk. This signifies how the earth and water may still be holding some of that mid-afternoon heat as Dusk approaches.

*Dusk*

The beginning of this period can be as hard to pinpoint as the end of Dawn's. But it's peak usually hits right on sunset. A sharp decline then occurs in the 30 minute span from sunset to last light, designating the end to virtually all the primary stimuli associated with the daylight hours.

In terms of strength and width, Dusk is one solar period that changes relatively little from summer to winter. This happens because there is a balancing out of the positive/negative influences. For example, in the winter Dusk is bolstered by being on the coattails of the Heat-of-the-Day, and degraded by the seasonally cold water. In the summer, just the opposite occurs: it loses strength, because the shallows may be too warm from the Heat-of-the-Day, yet the warm, seasonal water has fish generally quite active.

The exception is in clear waters where fish often feed after the sun goes down, especially during the summer months. Now the Dusk period may not taper at all after sunset, as the end of light is actually a cue for some fish to come shallow.

*Sun Underfoot*

From the standpoint of electromagnetic energy, this period would pretty much mimic the Sun Overhead period, except its daytime counterpart has a couple elements this one doesn't: namely, heat energy and light energy. So, the Sun Underfoot does not deserve as much height and width, especially during the colder months when fish are less active after hours. Still, you can use its peak on the *PrimeTimes Wall Calendar* to see the exact time the sun is on the other side of our planet.

**The Lunar Peaks**

The two *PrimeTimes* periods not connected to the solar base are, of course, the Overhead and Underfoot Moons. Both begin and end independently of any solar activity, yet their strength is determined in part by their current placement along that solar curve. Let's take a closer look.

*Moon Overhead*

To determine the beginning and ending times of this lunar period, we begin with the moon's "zenith," which is that exact hour and minute it reaches its highest point in the sky for that day. From there, calculations are made to determine how many minutes beyond the zenith this period will extend, and how many minutes before. The result is the total length that period lasts on that day. The factors involved in this calculation include the moon's present position within its high-low and apogee-perigee cycle.

In Figure 6-3, the arrow labeled "1" points out the

beginning time for the Overhead Moon, both on the hump and its corresponding bar directly above it. (Please be advised that this is not the time of moonrise; it is the beginning of this day's activity window.) Arrow "2" shows the moon's zenith, which is the exact center of the hump, and its highest point. Arrow "3" designates the end of the activity window.

*FIGURE 6-3*
**ANATOMY OF THE LUNAR PERIODS**

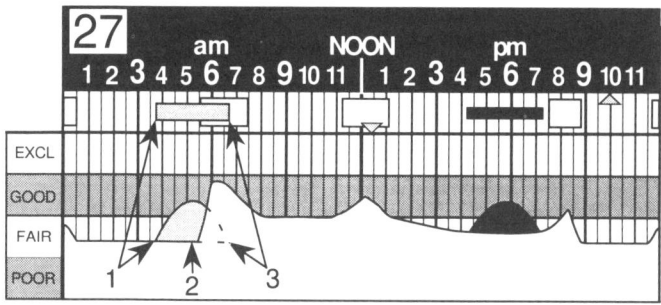

ONE DAY LATER

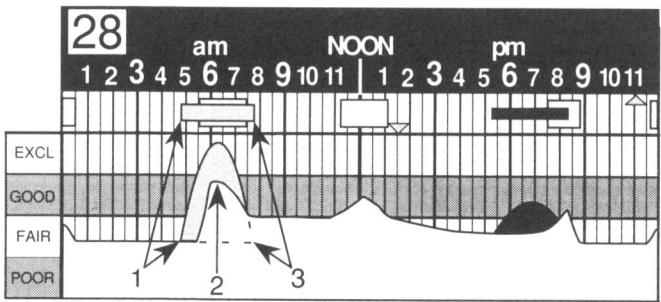

The moon's strength, on the other hand, while also derived from its high-low and apogee-perigee cycles, depends as well on its location along the solar activity base. *PrimeTimes* always finds the zenith point along a lunar hump's base (the "2" arrow), then places this point flush against the solar activity curve. For example, on the day of the 27th in Figure

6-3 the moon's zenith occurs at 5:10 a.m. (see arrow "2"). This is about 50 minutes before sunrise and 20 minutes before first light, so it gains no additional strength from any solar peak. On the next day, however (see the 28th in Figure 6-3), the zenith time hits about one hour later, which does overlap the Dawn period. Consequently, *PrimeTimes* slides that lunar hump straight up until the zenith point along its base meets Dawn's activity line at that same time of day. The result is a lunar hump extended to demonstrate the "double whammy" influence of the Moon Overhead period overlapping Dawn on this day. And while extending the hump may appear to narrow it—and therefore make it shorter in time, it does not. The beginning and ending times are not altered.

By the way, the only reason the *PrimeTimes Wall Calendar* always has the moon sliding behind the solar base is because otherwise the lunar humps would occasionally block out any solar period with which it was sharing space and time. Granted, the way it is in the *Wall Calendar*, parts of the lunar hump do get obscured by the solar base, and that poses a problem with seeing exactly when a few lunar periods begin or end. But that's what the time line is for: with its corresponding time boxes above the humps, you have a clear look at the start and finish of all periods.

We just discussed how the length and strength of a lunar period is based on its high-low and apogee-perigee cycles. Figure 6-4 shows how these humps can vary from one extreme to the other, such as from a high moon to a low one. There's not enough room to show the entire range, which can last from 12-15 days, but you get the idea. Generally, periods last anywhere from a little less than 1 hour to 3 1/2 hours. But even this range changes from one year to the next, because so do the variables responsible. These varying widths and heights also help represent the moon's ever-changing strength from one day to the next.

FIGURE 6-4
**DURATIONS AND STRENGTHS
OF THE DAILY LUNAR PERIODS**

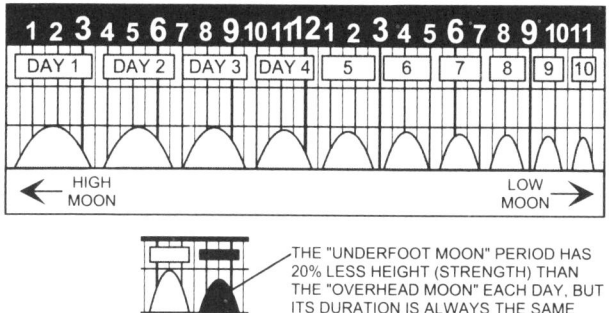

*The Underfoot Moon*

Everything we just explained about the Overhead Moon applies to the Underfoot one, as well, with the exception that the height (strength) of the Underfoot Moon's humps is about 20% less across the board (see Figure 6-4). For reasons explained in earlier chapters, this is more than just a token decrease. From both astrophysical theory and the general consensus of outdoor experts, the Underfoot Moon's influence on fish and game seems to be slightly less.

## Q & A

*Can I Expect Activity During All of* PrimeTimes' *Periods Each Day?*

Although the *Wall Calendar* will always show six or seven activity periods, this does not necessarily mean that our quarry will be active during all those times. A lot will depend on the species, whether we're hunting or fishing, and, in the case of the latter, your water temperature.

Say you're bass fishing on November 19, 1995, and the water temperature is 48 degrees (see Figure 6-5, which is the actual *PrimeTimes* listing for that day). There are three things you can safely assume: 1) there will probably be no more than one activity period per bass today; 2) not all bass will be active during the same period; and 3) some won't turn on at all.

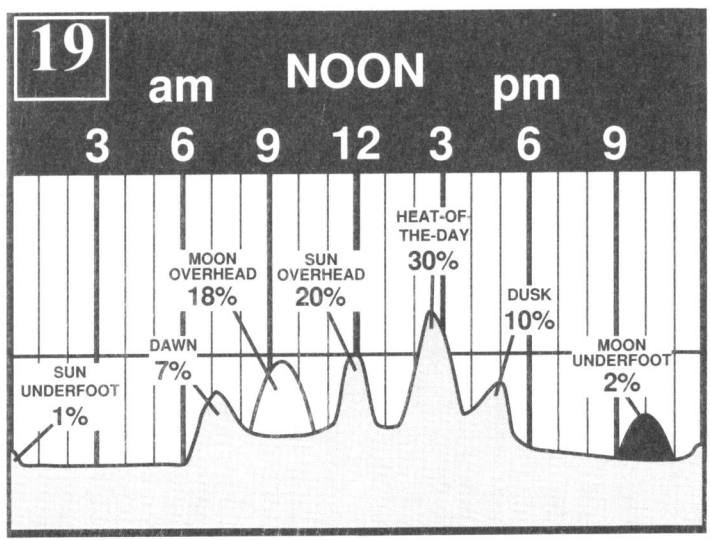

FIGURE 6-5
**SEEING THE HEIGHT OF EACH PERIOD AS A PERCENTAGE OF THE DAY'S TOTAL POTENTIAL**

Consequently, you could read *PrimeTimes*' suggested peaks to mean something like: 30% of the bass population will be relatively active during the Heat-of-the-Day period (which is listed as the best today), 20% may be so during the Overhead Sun period (the second best), 18% when the Moon is Overhead (a close third), 10% at Dusk (fourth best), 7% at Dawn (fifth), 2% when the Moon is Underfoot (which hits at a bad solar time: around 10:00 p.m. that night), and 1% when the Sun is Underfoot. The remaining 12% either activate at some other time or not at all on this particular day.

Or you could use these same percentages to describe each period's potential for being the one any given bass uses for feeding today (ie: there's a 30% chance he'll turn on during the Heat-of-the-Day, a 20% chance during the Noon period, 18% during the Overhead Moon, etc.) And during the warmer months, when our fish's metabolism is operating in high gear, you could use them to describe how he may distribute his activity over the course of a day (ie: he may do 30% of his feeding at Dawn, 20% at Noon, etc.). This latter method would also apply to most warm-blooded animals, which can have five or six to-and-from-feeding movements each day year-round.

However, what the *PrimeTimes* peaks are truly saying is this: *Of all the known, predictable energy from heat, light, and electromagnetism during this 24-hour period, 30% is coming from when the build-up of solar heat energy is at its highest (Heat-of-the-Day), 20% is from when the solar electromagnetic, light and heat energy is at its highest (Sun Overhead), 18% from the peak in lunar electromagnetic energy (the Overhead Moon), 10% from the combination of daylight fading into darkness and a relatively warm time of day (Dusk), 7% from darkness turning into daylight (Dawn), 10% from secondary lunar electromagnetic energy (Moon Underfoot) that occurs at a cold, dark time, so is reduced to only 2%, and 1% from the secondary solar electromagnetic energy (Sun Underfoot); the remaining 12% is simply a buffer that recognizes some fish may feed at other times due to other influences, or may not turn on at all today.*

So, again, *PrimeTimes*' various-sized peaks each day are an accurate description of the predictable, influential energy coming from the sun and moon in the form of light, heat, and EM energy. How these elements affect your fish and game may be open to interpretation, but *PrimeTimes* bases its conclusions on radio-tracking studies, fish/game surveys, and the general consensus of expert outdoors people.

*Is the Solar/Lunar EM Element More Effective During Certain Seasons?*

The weather, which can be an overriding factor in fish and game behavior, tends to stabilize during summer and winter, thereby becoming less of a factor. Any moon table's batting average often improves during these two seasons.

*Why Does* PrimeTimes *Work Regardless of Geography?*

*PrimeTimes* is effective anywhere in the northern hemisphere, and doesn't do too badly in the southern one, either. It's all due to the world being divided into 24 time zones back in 1883, each one spanning 15 degrees of longitude, which is a little more than 1,000 miles across at the equator, and more like 750 miles across the center of the U. S. They divided it up this way, because it takes the earth 24 hours to complete each rotation, or what we call one day. From our perspective on the ground, then, the sun takes about one hour to travel from one time zone to the next, always moving east to west. The moon takes just a couple minutes longer.

With this in mind, let's say you live in New York, your brother lives in Los Angeles, and you're both using the *PrimeTimes* calendar, which says the moon will be directly overhead at noon today. As predicted, around noontime it is over your head in New York. Wondering if the same is happening on the west coast, you immediately call your bro in L.A., who reports that for him the moon is only about half way up from the eastern horizon. You wonder how that can be, then he points out that it's only 9:00 a.m. there in L. A. Three hours from now the moon will be passing overhead there, and the time will be noon, just as it happened for you in New York.

What no such calendar can do, however, is be pinpoint accurate for everyone within any one time zone. This time let's say you both live in the central time zone, you in Montgomery, Alabama, on the eastern side, your brother in Pecos, Texas, on the western side, making the distance between you to be about 1,000 miles (actually, this is one of the few places in the U. S. where a time zone is this wide; all are anything but symmetric, and average more like 700-800 miles across). There are a couple factors we need to consider here. 1) *PrimeTimes* is geared for the center of any time zone, which in this case would be the 93rd Parallel dissecting the Central Time Zone (see Figure 6-6). That means you both are about 500 miles "off center." 2) From our perspective in the northern hemisphere, the moon seems to traverse the sky at

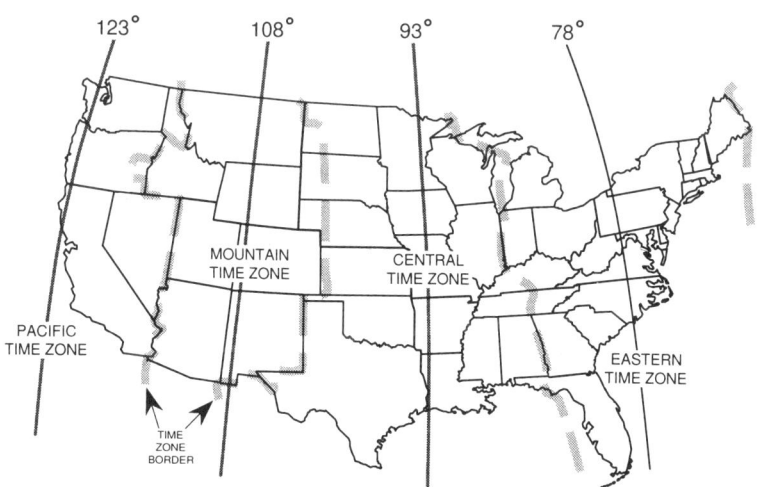

FIGURE 6-6
**EACH TIME ZONE'S LONGITUDE FOR WHICH PRIMETIMES' "BEST TIMES OF THE DAY" ARE ZEROED**

Inside PrimeTimes

approximately 750 mph from east to west, meaning it will take about one hour and 20 minutes to travel from your town to his. Consequently, it will be over your head in Montgomery approximately 40 minutes before the time listed in *PrimeTimes*, and over his head in Pacos 40 minutes after the same listing. The two of you could adjust *PrimeTimes* accordingly for both now and all future outings.

The "center" of each time zone, as we mentioned, is actually a particular longitude. As you can see in Figure 6-6, for the Pacific time zone this is 123 degrees N. longitude, for Mountain Time it's 108 degrees, Central is 93 degrees, and Eastern is 78 degrees. If you live along one of these longitudes, *PrimeTimes* will be dead-on accurate for you. But don't feel badly if you're a few hundred miles on either side of the line; 100 miles off means only an eight-minute difference, and 200 miles is only 16 minutes. As we just saw, the worst case scenario is 500 or so miles, and that translates to only about 40 minutes.

So, for most of us in the U. S., *PrimeTimes'* listings are accurate to within 15 minutes or less, which really isn't worth worrying about. Still, if you wish to adjust the calendars to your exact location within any time zone, simply *find the number of miles you are from its center, then divide that by 12.* If you are to the *west* of that center line, *add* the result to the times listed. If you are to *east, subtract* it.

Also keep in mind that this adjustment applies only to the "Best Times of the Day" sections. The "Best Days of the Month" are not affected by the time zones or where you live within one.

*When a Good Period--denoted by a Fish or Game Symbol, Occurs on a Day with a Poor Rating, Which Should I Believe?*

As you undoubtedly know by now, there are always

two key elements to consider when picking a time to fish or hunt: 1) The best days of that week, month, and even year; and 2) The best period(s) within any given day. For the most part, these two are unrelated. The "Best Days of the Month" chart of *PrimeTimes* is based largely on various solar/lunar electromagnetic influences and shows each day's overall potential in relation to the others that month. The fish/game symbols simply alert you to those lunar periods that are overlapping key solar periods. However, that's not to say you shouldn't use these two features together. A period with a solar/lunar overlap should be all that much better on a highly-rated day, just as it could poorer on a day with a relatively low rating.

*Do People Use PrimeTimes for Purposes Other Than Fishing and Hunting?*

While the great outdoors has always been the main arena for employing the solar/lunar effect, it may surprise you to learn how many other ways followers have said they use it. A number of retail store owners, for example, say they watch the Moon Overhead and Underfoot periods for sudden surges in the number of customers through the door. Other readers have claimed using our calendars to determine the best times to buy and sell stocks, bet the horses, and call on clients. Three different police departments have ordered from us, knowing the crime rate increases around full moons. He didn't explain why, but a defense attorney bought one to use in court, as did a prosecutor, also without explanation (no, it wasn't the same case).

More than one has claimed it's easier to meet people at dances or bars on a full moon, and we've heard of increased sexual peaks during the same phase. A lot of customers say their own daily peaks and valleys correspond to those in *PrimeTimes*, and some claim to often experiencing some

*FIGURE 6-7*
## THE *PRIMETIMES WALL CALENDAR* FORMAT

A. HOW A TYPICAL DAY LOOKS IN THE WALL CALENDAR*

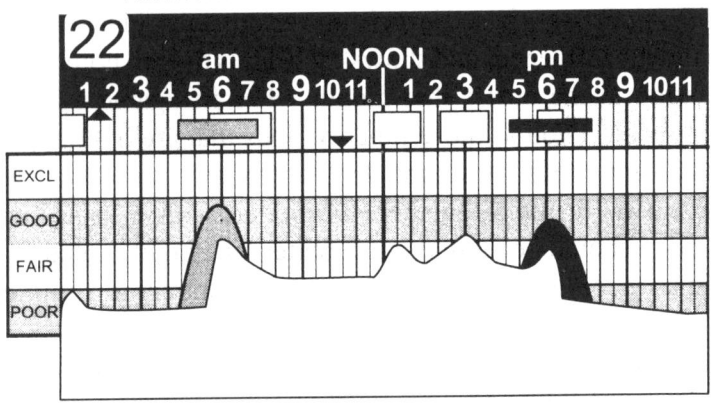

B. THE SAME DAY WITH DESCRIPTIONS*

THIS TIME LINE HAS BOXES TO BETTER SHOW THE BEGIN AND END TIMES OF THE PERIODS. RISE AND SET TIMES ARE ALSO SHOWN FOR THE MOON (BLACK TRIANGLES) AND THE SUN (BEGIN/END OF GRAY SHADED AREAS).

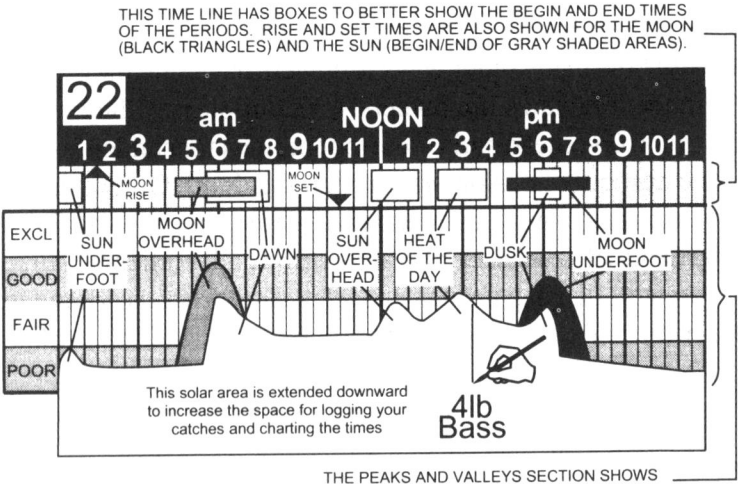

THE PEAKS AND VALLEYS SECTION SHOWS EACH PERIOD'S RELATIVE STRENGTH

*When the Wall Calendar was published in black & white (1996-1998), the shading of the two lunar periods was reversed: black signified the Overhead Moon, gray signified the Underfoot Moon. Here, and throughout this book, the drawings represent the calendar being in color, where the Overhead Moon is bright yellow (shown here as gray) and the Underfoot Moon is dull yellow (shown here as black).

degree of insomnia on nights the moon is overhead at bedtime. And then there's the lady who used to do horoscopes for people, but has switched over to the sun and moon, because she found them to be more reliable than the stars.

*Since the sun and moon cause our oceanic tides, they obviously do generate some kind of "pull" on the earth. But how can a relatively tiny fish or animal be affected?*

A long-standing theory states that since an animal's body is composed mostly of water, minor "tides" may occur within and cause some kind of response. After all, when life was forming in the sea billions of years ago, the moon was five times closer to the earth and generated tides a mile high. That could have left a genetic imprint that all creatures still carry today. A more recent theory suggests that since blood contains iron--a magnetically-susceptible element, it can be directly affected by the ever-changing angles and strengths in the electromagnetic energies of the sun and moon, along the same principles of a magnet pulling and rearranging iron filings. The whole dilemma is not unlike electricity, light, radio waves, or any other such phenomenon: We don't understand *how* it works...only that it does.

## A Final Word

Throughout this book we've tried to view all the factors that go into constructing an effective, when-to-go fishing/hunting game plan, both for the immediate and distant futures. We've recognized, categorized, and scrutinized the predictable as well as unpredictable to see if, how, and when each becomes an influence. When it's all put together, the end result is perhaps better than we thought possible. But getting there was certainly no small chore, and the thought of having to do it all prior to each outing can leave us wallowing in piles of data and self pity.

The only practical option is to get someone else to do it for you. We at Jer-Ben Publications have gladly accepted this role, and plan to continue for many years to come. What we tentatively tossed out to the public as an alternative to the present moon tables in 1986 has somehow blossomed into the most widely-followed, when-to-go system in the world, being circulated to some 4 million readers monthly via magazines, newspapers, TV, specialty calendars, and even computer disks. In fact, after studying all such tables America has to offer, a large Japanese company selected ours to import overseas. We are either onto something here, or the parakeet owners of the world have discovered a special use for the *PrimeTimes* pages.

Maybe it's that we don't claim to be an omnipotent oracle that will get you out there at the right time everytime...implying you used an improper technique or piece of equipment when it fails. Maybe it's that we have never hidden what our calendar is founded on, preferring to openly explain its facts and theories, what it can and cannot do. (We must be the only prognosticator to write two books about its system.) Maybe it's simply our layout—how we provide the *Pocket Calendar* format for you "numbers people," the *Wall Calendar* for you "graphics," and keep trying to improve them both year after year.

Or maybe it's because our calendars work to a higher degree than the others. If that is so, we take only a small part of the credit. It's those magnificent, celestial bodies that really do all the work. All we do is predict their next move.

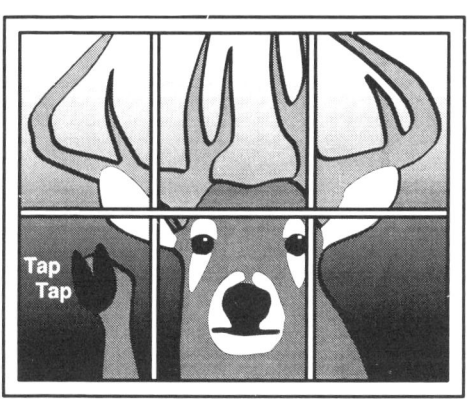

# The Pathophysiology and Pharmacotherapy of Myocardial Infarction

# Physiologic and Pharmacologic Bases of Drug Therapy

Series Editor

Stanley Greenberg

Berlex Laboratories, Inc.
Cedar Knolls, New Jersey

*Gene C. Palmer* (Editor) Neuropharmacology of Central Nervous System and Behavioral Disorders, 1981

*R. Douglas Wilkerson* (Editor) Cardiac Pharmacology, 1982

*Nicholas A. Mortillaro* (Editor) The Physiology and Pharmacology of the Microcirculation, Volume 1, 1983; Volume 2, 1984

*Gesina L. Longenecker* (Editor) The Platelets: Physiology and Pharmacology, 1985

*Nabil El-Sherif and C. V. Ramana Reddy* (Editors) The Pathophysiology and Pharmacotherapy of Myocardial Infarction, 1986

# The Pathophysiology and Pharmacotherapy of Myocardial Infarction

EDITED BY

## Nabil El-Sherif

Division of Cardiology
State University of New York
Downstate Medical Center
and Veterans Administration Medical Center
Brooklyn, New York

## C. V. Ramana Reddy

Division of Cardiology
State University of New York
Downstate Medical Center
Brooklyn, New York

1986

ACADEMIC PRESS, INC.

**Harcourt Brace Jovanovich, Publishers**
Orlando   San Diego   New York   Austin
Boston   London   Sydney   Tokyo   Toronto

COPYRIGHT © 1986 BY ACADEMIC PRESS, INC.
ALL RIGHTS RESERVED.
NO PART OF THIS PUBLICATION MAY BE REPRODUCED OR
TRANSMITTED IN ANY FORM OR BY ANY MEANS, ELECTRONIC
OR MECHANICAL, INCLUDING PHOTOCOPY, RECORDING, OR
ANY INFORMATION STORAGE AND RETRIEVAL SYSTEM, WITHOUT
PERMISSION IN WRITING FROM THE PUBLISHER.

ACADEMIC PRESS, INC.
Orlando, Florida 32887

*United Kingdom Edition published by*
ACADEMIC PRESS INC. (LONDON) LTD.
24–28 Oval Road, London NW1 7DX

**Library of Congress Cataloging in Publication Data**
Main entry under title:

The Pathophysiology and pharmacotherapy of myocardial
　 infarction.

(Physiologic and pharmacologic bases of drug
therapy)
　 Includes index.
　 1. Heart—Infarction.　 2. Heart—Infarction—
Chemotherapy.　 I. El-Sherif, Nabil, Date
II. Reddy, C. V. Ramana (Chatla V. Ramana), Date
III. Series.　 [DNLM: 1. Myocardial Infarction—drug
therapy. 2. Myocardial Infarction—physiopathology.
WG 300 P2972]
RC685.I6P38　 1986　　 616.1'237　　 85-30671
ISBN 0–12–238045–2 (alk. paper)

PRINTED IN THE UNITED STATES OF AMERICA

86 87 88 89　　 9 8 7 6 5 4 3 2 1

To the memory of my parents and to my wife, Laila,
and her wonderful gifts, Tarek, Yasir, Khalid, and Mona.

*Nabil El-Sherif*


To my loving wife, Nydia, and children, Chandra and Padma,
and to the memory of my beloved parents.

*C. V. Ramana Reddy*

# Contents

Contributors     xi
Preface     xiii

1. Pathogenesis of Coronary Atherosclerosis: Prevention of Atherogenesis
   Assaad S. Daoud, Katherine E. Fritz, and John Jarmolych

   I. The Atherosclerotic Lesion     1
   II. Pathogenesis of Atherosclerosis     7
   III. Risk Factors in Atherogenesis     15
   IV. Clinical Trials     19
   V. Regression of Atheroma in Humans     26
   VI. Regression of Atheroma in Experimental Animals     27
   References     31

2. Hemodynamic Consequences of Myocardial Infarction and the Role of Vasodilators in Acute and Chronic Management
   Dennis W. Wahr and Kanu Chatterjee

   I. Introduction     39
   II. Hemodynamic Consequences of Heart Failure     40
   III. Potential Benefits of Vasodilators in Congestive Heart Failure     47
   IV. Classification and Mechanisms of Vasodilation     52
   V. Site of Action of the Vasodilators     53
   VI. Vasodilator Agents: Pharmacology, Hemodynamics, and Side Effects     55
   VII. Clinical Applications     70

VIII. Summary 77
References 78

3. Pump Failure: Role of Vasopressor Agents
   C. V. Ramana Reddy and Nabil El-Sherif

   I. Introduction 85
   II. Pathophysiology 86
   III. Role of Vasopressor Agents in the Treatment of Pump Failure 96
   IV. Future Directions 108
   References 110

4. Coronary Artery Spasm and Pharmacology of Coronary Vasodilators
   Charles R. Lambert and Carl J. Pepine

   I. Introduction 117
   II. Coronary Artery Spasm: Evolution of Current Concepts 117
   III. Coronary Artery Spasm and Myocardial Infarction 122
   IV. Pathophysiological Mechanisms 133
   V. Pharmacology of Coronary Vasodilators 139
   VI. Summary 147
   References 148

5. Physiologic Basis and Results of Thrombolytic Therapy in Acute Myocardial Infarction
   Barry S. Denenberg and James F. Spann

   I. Introduction 155
   II. Physiology of Thrombus Formation and Fibrinolytic Enzyme System 156
   III. Early Trials of Long-Duration, Late Intravenous Thrombolytic Therapy in Acute Myocardial Infarction 158
   IV. Intracoronary Streptokinase 159
   V. Intravenous Streptokinase 173
   VI. Management of Patients after Thrombolytic Therapy 179
   VII. Future Directions 181
   References 182

6. Electrophysiology of Ventricular Arrhythmias in Myocardial Infarction
   Nabil El-Sherif

   I. Introduction 187
   II. Electrophysiological Mechanisms of Ventricular Arrhythmias 187
   III. Electrophysiological Mechanisms of Ventricular Arrhythmias in Myocardial Infarction 203
   IV. Conclusion 235
   References 236

7. The Pharmacology of Antiarrhythmic Drugs
   Pasquale F. Nestico and Joel Morganroth

   I. Introduction    241
   II. Pharmacokinetics    241
   III. Antiarrhythmic Drugs    248
   IV. Summary    265
   References    265

8. Mechanisms and Management of Myocardial Infarction Arrhythmias
   Karen J. Friday and Ralph Lazzara

   I. Introduction    269
   II. Mechanisms of Cardiac Arrhythmias    271
   III. Mechanisms of Arrhythmias during Infarction    274
   IV. Clinical Studies    279
   V. Pharmacology of Antiarrhythmic Drugs    285
   VI. Effects of Antiarrhythmic Drugs in Ischemic Tissue    290
   VII. Drug Therapy of Arrhythmias during Acute Myocardial Infarction    294
   VIII. Prophylaxis for Postinfarction Sudden Death    304
   IX. Conclusions    307
   References    308

9. Pharmacologic and Surgical Therapy of Postinfarction Ventricular Arrhythmias
   E. Wayne Grogan, Jr. and Mark E. Josephson

   I. Introduction    317
   II. Ventricular Ectopy and Nonsustained Ventricular Tachycardia    317
   III. Ventricular Fibrillation    319
   IV. Ventricular Tachycardia    322
   V. Summary    341
   References    342

10. The Role of Beta Blockers in the Prevention of Sudden Cardiac Death in the Postinfarction Patient
    Peter L. Frommer and Curt D. Furberg

    I. Introduction    347
    II. Methods    349
    III. Results    351
    IV. Discussion    358
    V. Summary    368
    References    368

Index    371

# Contributors

Numbers in parentheses indicate the pages on which the authors' contributions begin.

*Kanu Chatterjee* (39), Cardiovascular Division, Coronary Care Unit, Moffitt Hospital, University of California, San Francisco, California 94143

*Assaad S. Daoud* (1), Department of Pathology, Albany Medical College and Laboratory Service, Veterans Administration Medical Center, Albany, New York 12208

*Barry S. Denenberg* (155), Cardiology Section, Department of Medicine, Temple University Hospital, Philadelphia, Pennsylvania 19140

*Nabil El-Sherif* (85, 187), Division of Cardiology, State University of New York, Downstate Medical Center, and Veterans Administration Medical Center, Brooklyn, New York 11203

*Karen J. Friday* (269), University of Oklahoma Health Sciences Center, and Department of Medicine and Coronary Care Unit, Oklahoma Memorial Hospital, Veterans Administration Medical Center, Oklahoma City, Oklahoma 73104

*Katherine E. Fritz* (1), Department of Pathology, Albany Medical College, and Atherosclerosis Research Laboratory, Veterans Administration Medical Center, Albany, New York 12208

*Peter L. Frommer* (347), National Heart, Lung and Blood Institute, Bethesda, Maryland 20892

Contributors

*Curt D. Furberg* (347), Clinical Application and Prevention Program, National Health, Lung and Blood Institute, Bethesda, Maryland 20205

*E. Wayne Grogan, Jr.* (317), Cardiac Electrophysiology Laboratory, Hospital of the University of Pennsylvania, Philadelphia, Pennsylvania 19104

*John Jarmolych* (1), Department of Pathology, Albany Medical College, and Anatomic Pathology, Veterans Administration Medical Center, Albany, New York 12208

*Mark E. Josephson* (317), Department of Medicine, University of Pennsylvania School of Medicine, and Cardiovascular Section, Hospital of the University of Pennsylvania, Philadelphia, Pennsylvania 19104

*Charles R. Lambert* (117), Veterans Administration Medical Center, Gainesville, Florida 32610

*Ralph Lazzara* (269), University of Oklahoma Health Sciences Center, and Department of Medicine and Cardiovascular Disease Section, Oklahoma Memorial Hospital, Veterans Administration Medical Center, Oklahoma City, Oklahoma 73104

*Joel Morganroth* (241), Department of Pharmacology, Hahnemann University, and Sudden Death Prevention Program, Likoff Cardiovascular Institute, Philadelphia, Pennsylvania 19102

*Pasquale F. Nestico* (241), Likoff Cardiovascular Institute, and Hahnemann University, Philadelphia, Pennsylvania 19102

*Carl J. Pepine* (117), Division of Cardiovascular Medicine, University of Florida, and Veterans Administration Medical Center, Gainesville, Florida 32610

*C. V. Ramana Reddy* (85), Division of Cardiology, State University of New York, Downstate Medical Center, Brooklyn, New York 11203

*James F. Spann* (155), Cardiology Section, Department of Medicine, Temple University Hospital, Philadelphia, Pennsylvania 19140

*Dennis W. Wahr* (39), Cardiovascular Division, Department of Medicine, University of California, San Francisco, California 94143

# Preface

The heart may be represented in a straightforward manner as a muscular pump with an intricate and specialized electrical conduction system that is responsible for the rhythmic and organized driving of the pump. The coronary arteries supply the cardiac muscle and the conduction system, and both can suffer from diminished or interrupted blood supply. Atherosclerosis is the major pathologic process that affects the coronary arteries, and its consequence, myocardial ischemia or infarction, is the number one killer of people in the United States. Myocardial ischemia or infarction can be fatal either by leading to failure of the cardiac muscle (pump failure) or by disrupting the organized electrical activity of the cardiac muscle. The latter process leads to inefficient or disorganized contraction of the cardiac muscle secondary to ventricular tachycardia or to ventricular fibrillation and is the most common underlying cause of sudden cardiac (electrical) death. Not uncommonly sudden cardiac electrical death occurs in people whose hearts otherwise have adequate cardiac muscle function.

The past decade has witnessed an explosion in new knowledge that has contributed to better understanding of the mechanisms and clinical management of myocardial infarction. The advances have come so rapidly in recent years that it is important to review and examine critically the new perspectives and clinical strategies in the management of acute myocardial infarction. In this volume we have reviewed the advances in the pathophysiology and pharmacotherapy of acute myocardial infarction and related complications. The topics were selected to cover its two major consequences: cardiac muscle dysfunction and cardiac electrical dysfunction.

The first chapter reviews the controversy surrounding the pathogenetic mechanisms of atheroma formation and its potential reversibility and reappraises the current status of coronary risk factors and the benefits of primary prevention. The pathophysiologic mechanisms of pump failure and the current approach to its management are then reviewed with one chapter discussing the rational use of vasodilators in postinfarction heart failure and another chapter focusing on the pharmacotherapy of cardiogenic shock. Both chapters outline future directions in the development of new drugs in dealing with these disorders. The rationale for the renewed interest in the role of coronary vasospasm and the current knowledge of the use of calcium channel blockers are considered separately. Also reviewed is the status of "the newest kid on the block," the thrombolytic therapy for acute myocardial infarction.

The contribution of this volume to the understanding and management of ischemia-related sudden cardiac electrical death includes a detailed presentation of the electrophysiologic mechanisms of ventricular arrhythmias in myocardial infarction. The three current approaches for the management of postinfarction ventricular tachyarrhythmias are pharmacologic therapy, surgical therapy, and the use of electrical devices. Of the three approaches, pharmacologic therapy remains the mainstay of management. Two chapters consider the pharmacology and pharmacokinetics of conventional and new antiarrhythmic agents as well as the clinical use of those agents for postinfarction ventricular arrhythmias. Another chapter discusses the use of antiarrhythmic therapy based on programmed electrical stimulation and compares the role of pharmacologic therapy with that of antiarrhythmic surgery and the use of antitachycardia pacemakers and implantable defibrillators. Finally, the concept of secondary prevention of sudden cardiac death is amplified by a comprehensive review of the various trials using beta-blocking agents that were conducted in the last few years.

The chapters in this volume were written by cardiologists who have a particular interest in the subject as well as considerable personal experience with most of the conditions described. Many of the statements are therefore influenced by the authors' own observations, and the editors have made no effort to eliminate personal views nor have we tried to unify them. In this regard, we have also allowed a certain degree of overlap between chapters.

Our goal is to provide easily accessible information on the most relevant topics related to acute myocardial infarction for medical students, primary care physicians, and cardiovascular specialists. Although the reader may feel that certain aspects of this broad field are overlooked, we hope that what is included here will be of interest and will broaden the knowledge and horizons of all readers.

Nabil El-Sherif
C. V. Ramana Reddy

# The Pathophysiology and Pharmacotherapy of Myocardial Infarction

# 1
# Pathogenesis of Coronary Atherosclerosis: Prevention of Atherogenesis

Assaad S. Daoud, Katherine E. Fritz, and John Jarmolych

## I. The Atherosclerotic Lesion

There is general agreement that the atheroma, the elevated, whitish-yellow lesion with a necrotic, lipid-rich core, is the hallmark of atherosclerosis. However, there is no agreement as to the characterization of the earlier intimal changes which lead to the development of the atheroma. It is still debatable if the flat, yellow lesion, designated "fatty streak," which is characterized by an abnormal accumulation of intra- and extracellular lipid, is a precursor of the atheroma or whether the latter arises independently. More controversial is the role of the focal fibromuscular intimal thickening (cushion or intimal cell mass), which shows no abnormal lipid deposition, in the genesis of the atherosclerotic lesion. In this communication the above three "lesions" will be described separately and their possible relationship to each other will be discussed.

### A. Atheroma or Fibrous Plaque

In non-pressure-perfused specimens the lesion is elevated and protrudes into the lumen of the artery (Fig. 1A). The lumen cross section is roughly crescent-shaped. It is white to whitish-yellow in color. On sectioning, the large atheroma shows a necrotic, yellow, grumous center ("gruel"), and a white, firm intimal part. When arteries are fixed under normal intraluminal pressure, the lumen is circular or slightly oval, more or less symmetrical, regardless of the size of the intimal lesion (Fig. 1B) (Glagov and Zarins, 1983). Histologically, the atheroma is characterized by cell proliferation and accumulation of connective tissue and lipids. The deeper and central parts of the lesion consist of a mass of lipid material with cholesterol clefts, cell debris, fibrin and other plasma proteins, and

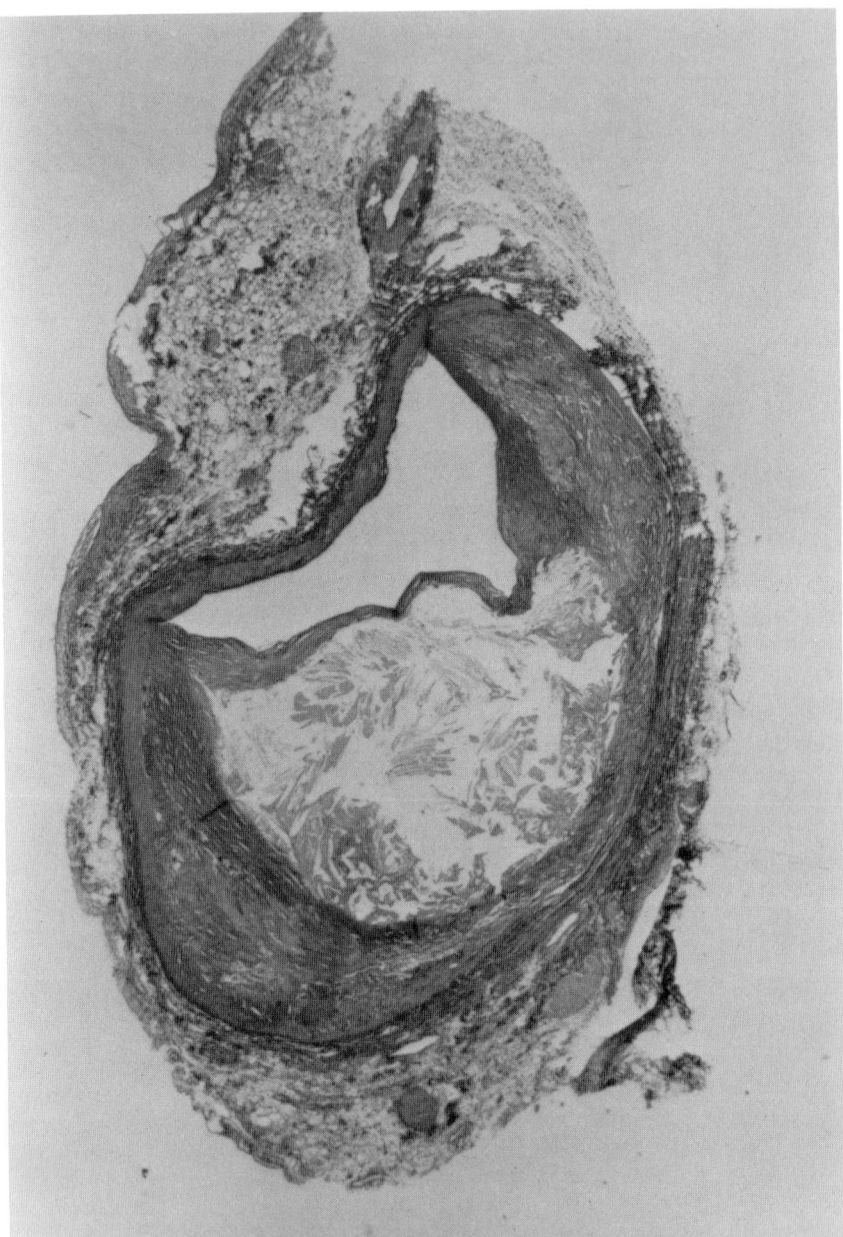

**Fig. 1A.** Cross section of immersion-fixed coronary artery with partially intact wall. The lumen is collapsed and irregular. The lesion tends to bulge into the lumen and shows central necrosis and a fibrous cap. There is focal involvement of the subjacent media (Lawson's elastic tissue stain after decalcification).

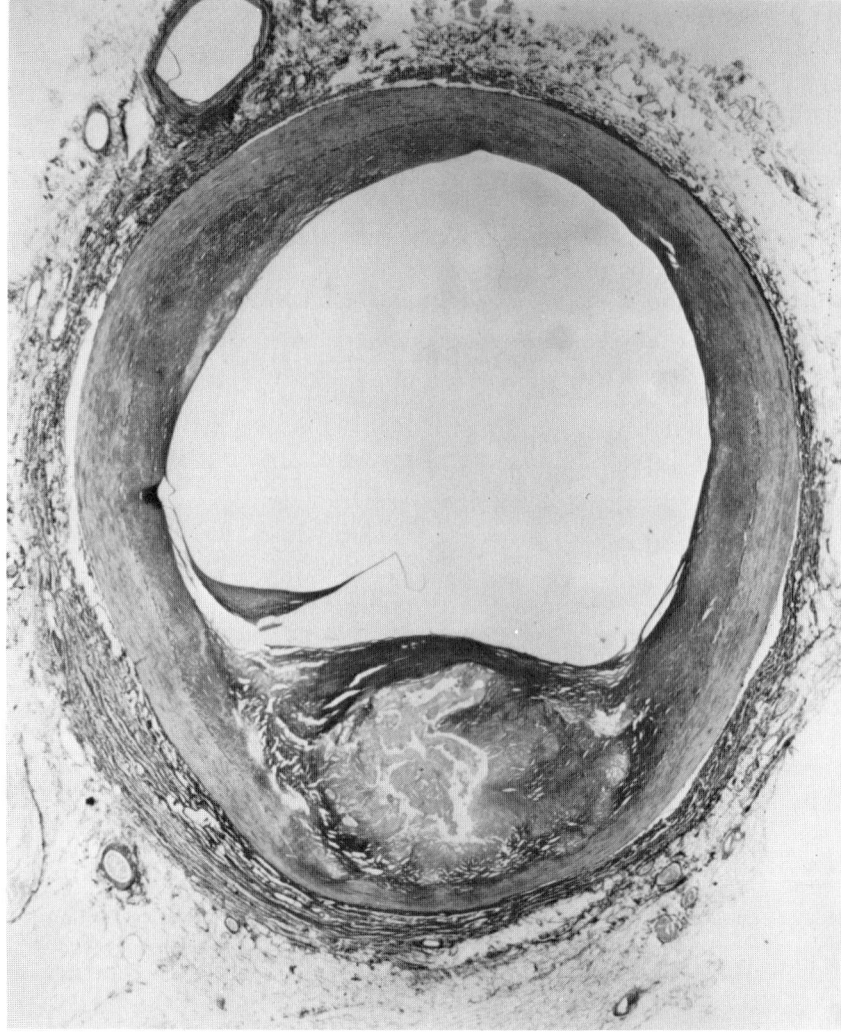

**Fig. 1B.** Cross section of a perfusion-fixed coronary artery with an eccentric lesion. The lumen is regular and almost round. There is a fibrous cap at the luminal surface and thinning of the media subjacent to the lesion (Lawson's elastic tissue stain after decalcification).

varying numbers of spindle and foam cells. The superficial or luminar portion of the plaque is composed mostly of spindle cells and fibrous stroma. Electron microscopic study reveals that the spindle cells are smooth muscle cells (SMC) and the foam cells are SMC or macrophages. The origin of many of the foam cells cannot be determined with certainty;

however, they are believed by many to be fat-laden macrophages. The fibrous stroma consists of collagen, elastic tissue, and glycosaminoglycans. These cellular and extracellular elements of the atheroma occur in varying proportions, giving the lesion a heterogenous appearance which varies from one lesion to another, not only in different arteries but within the same artery. Some are mostly necrotic with large amounts of lipid, while others are mostly fibrotic and resemble a scar.

In the advanced phase of the disease, the atheroma undergoes progression changes known as complications. These are (1) calcification, which is usually present in most advanced disease and varies in form from patchy granular deposits to massive amounts converting the artery to a pipestem-like structure; (2) hemorrhage into the plaque, which may rupture into the lumen and lead to the formation of thrombus; and (3) ulceration, which may either predispose to thrombosis, or, by discharging the necrotic material ("gruel") into the blood stream, lead to atheromatous emboli.

### B. Fatty Streaks

Fatty streak is a descriptive term applied to the flat or slightly elevated yellow lesions which, when stained with Sudan IV, take on a bright orange-red color (Constantinides, 1965; Haust, 1971). The fatty streak in man is made up of SMC that contain varying numbers of lipid droplets and large lipid-filled cells resembling macrophages (Haust, 1971; Geer and Haust, 1972). The extracellular substance is scarce and consists of extracellular lipid, collagen, elastic tissue, glycosaminoglycans, and microfibrils. In the aorta, these lesions may occur at birth and are present in almost all children after the age of 3 years (Holman et al., 1959; McGill, 1968; Strong and McGill, 1969). They increase in extent with age until about the fourth decade. In the coronary arteries, fatty streaks begin to appear in the second decade and increase in extent in the third decade (Strong and McGill, 1962, 1969; McGill, 1968; Eggen and Solberg, 1968). In the fourth and subsequent decades the fatty streaks became mixed with or replaced by fibrous plaques.

The relationship of fatty streaks to fibrous plaques is still controversial. In the late 1950s Holman et al. (1959) proposed that fatty streaks are the precursors of fibrous plaques. This theory is still the prevailing concept on the natural history of atherosclerosis because

1. There is histologic resemblance between the two lesions. Both fatty streaks and fibrous plaques involve the intima and are characterized by lipid deposition, smooth muscle proliferation, and the presence of large foam cells, probably macrophagic in origin.

2. Fibrous plaques and fatty streaks are often mixed or superimposed on each other. This is especially obvious in the coronary arteries, where fatty streaks in young individuals among white populations parallel the extent of severe atherosclerosis in older persons from the same group (McGill, 1968).

3. In young adult males there are transitional lesions having the gross and microscopic appearance of both fatty streaks and fibrous plaques. Such lesions are relatively common in the coronary arteries of North American males between the ages of 20 and 40 years (McGill, 1974).

4. Finally, experimental data suggest that lesions similar to human fatty streaks may progress to become fibrolipid plaques (Moore, 1975). Indeed, in monkeys and in swine, species which develop atherosclerotic lesions similar to those of man, the early changes observed after feeding an atherogenic diet are very similar to the human fatty streaks while the advanced lesions are comparable to the fibrous plaque in man (Daoud *et al.*, 1975).

Several investigators have challenged this conventional concept because

1. The extent and localization of fatty streaks in the aortas of young persons do not correlate well with the extent and localization of fibrous plaques in older persons. Aortic fatty streaks appear first in the proximal portion of the arch, later in the thoracic and last in the abdominal aorta (Holman *et al.*, 1959; Mitchell and Schwartz, 1965).

2. Black children have more extensive fatty streaks than do white children, while black adults have less extensive fibrous plaques than do white adults (McGill, 1968).

3. Young females, of all ethnic groups in many geographic areas, have more extensive aortic fatty streaks than young males of the corresponding populations, while the reverse is true as to incidence of fibrous plaques in these populations between females and males (Tejada *et al.*, 1968; McGill, 1968).

## C. Fibromuscular Intimal Thickening

Fibromuscular intimal thickening, also referred to as intimal cushion, intimal pad, or intimal cell mass (Thomas *et al.*, 1978b), is a term used to describe focal or diffuse thickening of the intima without abnormal lipid deposition. The thickened intima is made up mostly of smooth muscle cells, collagen, elastic tissue, and glycosaminoglycans (Fig. 2). These lesions in older age groups become mixed with focal lipid deposition and associated chronic inflammatory and proliferative reactions typical of ath-

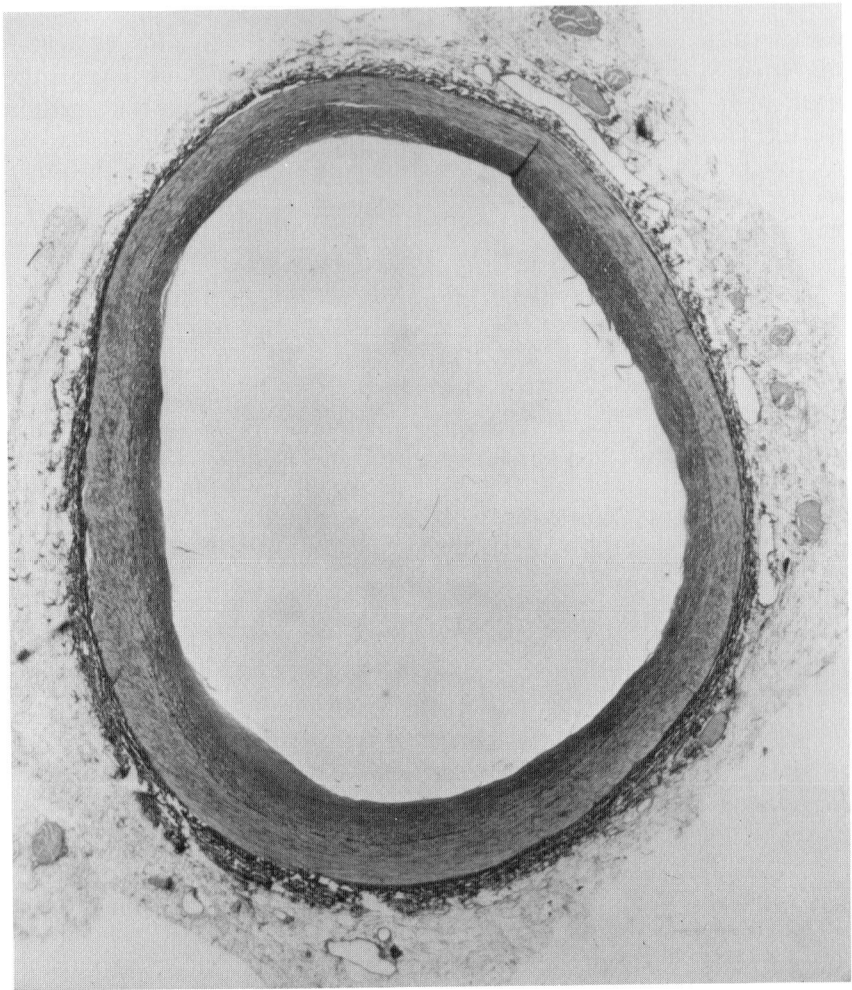

**Fig. 2.** Diffuse fibromuscular thickening of the intima of the proximal segment of the coronary artery. The thickened intima is devoid of necrosis and contains few intra- or extracellular fat deposits. The internal elastic membrane is, in general, intact with only focal small defects (Lawson's elastic tissue stain).

erosclerosis (McGill, 1974). Fibromuscular intimal thickening has been the subject of many studies (Gross *et al.*, 1934; Dock, 1946; Moon, 1957; Neufeld *et al.*, 1962; Geer and Haust, 1972; Thomas *et al.*, 1978b) but its relationship to atherosclerosis is still controversial. There are some who believe that the intimal thickening is a normal response to the hemodynamic stress at branching points, while others consider it a stage of the evolution of atherosclerosis (Fry, 1974; Texon, 1974). Data on fibromuscular intimal thickening among children of different populations are also conflicting. Vlodaver *et al.* (1969) found differences that correspond with the severity of adult atherosclerosis. Other studies showed no such differences in young persons (Robertson, 1960; Robertson *et al.*, 1963; Scott *et al.*, 1966; Geer *et al.*, 1968). Fibromuscular intimal thickening is a common finding in the arteries of experimental animals, even when not subjected to experimental manipulation, and was interpreted by some as response to hemodynamic stress, especially when it occurs at the points of branching. The most comprehensive work on the fibromuscular intimal thickening in animals has been done by Thomas and his co-workers in the aortas of swine. These authors found that fibromuscular intimal thickening, designated by them as intimal cell masses (ICM), is present in the swine abdominal aorta at birth. These ICM are concentrated in fairly specific anatomical locations, not necessarily at points of branching. In normal swine fed a low-fat, low-cholesterol commercial mash diet, the number of cells in these ICM does not increase significantly up to 1 year (Thomas and Kim, 1983; Thomas *et al.*, 1978b; Scott *et al.*, 1979a,b). From their studies, the Albany group believes that cell proliferation, which usually occurs in the ICM after exposure to atherogenic stimulus, is the initiating event in the formation of the atherosclerotic lesion. They consider the fatty streaks as representing one form of an atherosclerotic lesion developing after the proliferative process is already well established. They state that whether or not the lesion will appear grossly as a fatty streak depends upon the amount of lipid it accumulates. In theory, a lesion should be able to progress to the advanced stage without ever going through a fatty streak stage.

## II. Pathogenesis of Atherosclerosis

The lack of definitive characterization of the early lesion led to multiple hypotheses as to its pathogenesis. Among the leading theories offered to explain the pathogenesis of the disease are the senescence theory (Moschowitz, 1950), the hypoxic theory (Hueper, 1944), the lipid infiltration theory (Virchow, 1958), the thrombus–incrustation theory (Rokitansky, 1841; Duguid, 1949), etc. In the 1950s and 1960s the lipid infiltration and the thrombus–incrustation theories became the two dominant theories. Ross and Glomset (1976) melded these two theories together under the "injury and repair" hypothesis. Finally, Benditt and Benditt (1973) put forth the "monoclonal" theory which was, perhaps, the only new theory of the recent past. Since none of these theories, singly or in combination, can explain all the phenomena observed in atherogenesis we will briefly discuss the injury and repair theory, because most investigators subscribe to it at the present time, and the monoclonal theory, because of its novelty.

## A. The Injury and Repair Hypothesis

This hypothesis postulates that the initial event in atherogenesis is damage to the endothelial cells which leads to their desquamation. This endothelial injury may result from several factors, including hemodynamic stress, as is the case in hypertension, hyperlipidemia, cigarette smoking, various chemical agents, infections, and immunologic injury. Desquamation of the endothelium exposes the underlying collagen, which in turn predisposes to platelet adherence and microthrombus formation. Organization of surface mural thrombi would contribute to the progression and development of the atheroma. The endothelial injury would also potentiate the infiltration of plasma constituents, including lipoproteins, into the intima. This injury concept considers the role of cholesterol infiltration during atherogenesis as a secondary additive factor and emphasizes the interaction between damaged endothelium and platelets. This emphasis on the role of endothelial injury–platelet interaction is supported by the work of Mustard and co-workers (1968a,b) and Ross and Vogel (1978), who found that the platelet component presumably released at the site of endothelial injury, platelet-derived growth factor (PDGF), is a mitogen for smooth muscle cells. In addition, endothelial cells themselves are able to secrete a factor which causes smooth muscle proliferation (Gajdusek *et al.*, 1980).

While this injury hypothesis is the most popular one at present, there has not been convincing evidence that areas of spontaneous denudation occur. However, as stated by Schwartz *et al.* (1981), lack of convincing evidence for spontaneous denudation makes it worthwhile to consider the possible role of nondenuding injury in atherogenesis. This nondenuding injury may be effective independently of the platelet factors. Indeed, for some, lipoprotein, especially low density lipoprotein (LDL), is the initiating factor of the atheroma. In favor of this assumption are (1) the fact that lipids are major constituents of the atheroma, especially in its necrotic center; and (2) the development of premature atherosclerosis in patients having marked hypercholesterolemia. In addition, LDL, which is the major class of lipoproteins associated with atherosclerosis, appears to cause several manifestations of the disease. LDL may cause injury to the endothelium (Ross and Harker, 1976), which will disturb the endothelial barrier and lead to abnormal accumulation of lipoprotein in the intima. A special category of LDL obtained from hyperlipemic monkeys is reported to be a mitogen for smooth muscle cells (Fischer-Dzoga *et al.*, 1976). Finally, both smooth muscle cells and macrophages possess surface membrane receptors for binding LDL (Goldstein and Brown, 1977), which is important in the development of foam cells.

## B. Monoclonal Theory

This hypothesis, which was proposed by Benditt and Benditt (1973), suggests that the initiation of atherosclerotic lesions resides in smooth muscle cells that undergo somatic mutation. Benditt found that many foci of smooth muscle cells from atheromas of black women who were heterozygous for the enzymes glucose-6-phosphate dehydrogenase (G-6-PD), usually showed only one form of this enzyme, which suggested that this collection of cells was monoclonal in origin. Similar findings are reported in benign tumors of smooth muscle cells (Linder and Gartler, 1965). The findings of Benditt have been confirmed by others (Thomas *et al.*, 1978a; Pearson *et al.*, 1975). While Pearson subscribes to the monoclonal theory of Benditt, Thomas and his group tend to support a "natural selection" mechanism to explain the origin of these "monotypic" cells rather than a somatic mutation.

## C. Function and Interaction of Lesion Components

From the multiplicity of hypotheses, it is obvious that the pathogenesis of atherosclerosis is still obscure. However, in recent years a large amount of work has elucidated many of the functions of the arterial cells and their interaction with each other and with elements of the circulating blood. In this chapter we will summarize some of the functions and interactions which may be pertinent in atherogenesis. The primary function of the SMC, which is the most abundant cell in the lesion, is contraction (Ives *et al.*, 1978), but the capacity for contraction apparently is modulated by the secretory and/or replicative state of the cell, judging by the results of *in vitro* experiments which showed that SMC are less contractile when actively secreting or replacing (Ross, 1981; Chamley-Campbell *et al.*, 1981). Perhaps nearly as important as contraction is their ability to migrate, because a substantial number of lesion SMC are presumed to have migrated into the lesion from the media. Experimental confirmation of this function derives from *in vitro* studies of both aortic explants and from aortic cell cultures. Free-floating explants of swine aortas cultured longer than 4 days produce a variably luxuriant growth at the periphery (Daoud et al., 1973). While the proliferation of cells demonstrably contributes to this accumulation of cells, it is obvious that migration of cells from the explant proper must also be an important factor. Similarly, in the "classical" method of establishing SMC cell cultures, explants, instead of being allowed to remain free-floating, are caused to adhere to a glass or plastic substrate. Cells will then migrate from the explant proper onto the substrate and eventually, in combination with proliferation of the migrating cells, form a sheet of SMC more or less covering the entire substrate (Ross, 1981). In a specialized application of this general procedure, the distance that SMC will migrate onto the substrate from an attached explant has been used as a measure of the effects of different additives to culture media on the growth patterns (Fischer-Dzoga and Wissler, 1976). Further support for the migration potential even of cells in a confluent monolayer is provided by the speed with which adjacent cells fill in the denuded area of a "wound" produced in an SMC culture (Gottlieb and Spector, 1981; Thorgeirsson et al., 1979).

Wherever arterial SMC are found, as, for instance, either in normal media or in an atherosclerotic lesion, they are major contributors to their extracellular milieu. In the media, they are the producers of the collagen, the elastic tissue, and the glycosaminoglycans, which are the major extracellular components (Daoud et al., 1977; Wight and Ross, 1975; Wight, 1980a; Larjava et al., 1980; McCullagh and Balian, 1975). They also secrete hydrolytic enzymes, among them $\beta$-glucuronidase, cholesteryl ester hydrolase (Fritz et al., 1981b), and collagenase (Fritz et al., 1982), although these enzymes are demonstrable at only a low level in normal aortic media. In cell culture, SMC also secrete cathepsin D (Hayes et al., 1979), and they demonstrate a capacity for partial control of the level of at least one enzymatic activity by secreting an inhibitor of collagenase (Kerwar et al., 1980). Thus, through the capacity for production and/or degradation of the predominant constituents of their environment they are major determinants of their total environment.

SMC exercise a degree of homeostasis of their internal composition through a variety of mechanisms. For instance, under normal circumstances, uptake of LDL via specific receptors controls the synthesis of cholesterol and the intracellular accumulation of cholesteryl ester, except in the presence of large excesses of LDL (Goldstein and Brown, 1977). This cholesterol control mechanism is modulated by the rate of synthesis of LDL receptors (Bierman and Albers, 1977). Other substances whose binding are specific receptor-mediated are heparin (Karnovsky, 1981) and PDGF (Ross, 1981). Pinocytosis, another function of SMC, is important in the internalization of relatively low molecular weight substances (sucrose and horseradish peroxidase have been studied), and its rate is sensitive to the concentration of PDGF (Davies and Ross, 1978). Although it is less important in determining internal composition in SMC than in other cells, such as macrophages, SMC have been shown to have a phagocytic capability (Simpson, 1977; Garfield et al., 1975).

The capacity to divide, which SMC share with most cells, is of major importance in the development of atherosclerotic lesions. Under normal circumstances, arterial SMC have a very low proliferative rate, whether measured autoradiographically (Thomas et al., 1968) or biochemically (Fritz et al., 1981a) but the SMC in lesions contribute to the characteristically marked accumulation of cells by a greatly enhanced rate of proliferation (Fritz et al., 1981a), probably in response to exposure to a number of mitogenic substances.

Even when aging, SMC are important contributors to the atherosclerotic process, being the source of matrix vesicles on which hydroxyapatite crystals are deposited (Anderson, 1983; Kim, 1976; Tanimura et al., 1983).

The other major cell of the normal artery is the endothelial cell (EC), which exhibits a wide range of functions. Perhaps the most obvious is as a barrier between the circulating blood and the underlying arterial wall. This barrier is more effective against albumin than against glucose and water in rabbits (Chobanian et al., 1983). Simultaneously with their exclusion, under most circumstances, of formed blood elements such as erythrocytes, leukocytes, and platelets, from the subendothelial space, they must provide selective transport of essential plasma constituents. Details of the mode of transport of a large number of substances are still unknown, although apparently size of the molecule or particle is an important determinant (Huttner et al., 1973). A large protein molecule, such as ferritin, is apparently transported via vesicles, while small hemepeptides also require vesicles or vesicles arranged in chains to form transendothelial channels (Simionescu et al., 1975).

Another function which EC share with the underlying SMC is migration. This is especially important in the repair of small areas of denudation, which can be demonstrated even in normal arteries (Gottlieb and Spector, 1981). Migration does not require a growth factor (Schwartz et al., 1981), and its control is clearly separable from that of multiplication (Thorgeirsson et al., 1979; Sholley et al., 1977). In vitro studies have documented the ability of EC to spread, which is also important in wound healing, as distinct from migrating (Gold and Pearlstein, 1980).

The array of substances which EC can synthesize and secrete is impressive. Like SMC they contribute to, and modify, their external environment by production of collagen [Types I (Cotta-Pereira et al., 1980), III

(Sage et al., 1979, 1981), and V (Sage et al., 1981; Jaffe et al., 1976)], elastic fibers (Jaffe et al., 1976), and fibronectin (Saba and Jaffe, 1980), as well as hydrolytic enzymes (Hayes et al., 1979). They also exercise a degree of control over SMC by producing factors, one of which stimulates (Gajdusek et al., 1980; Ross et al., 1982), and another (heparinlike), which inhibits SMC growth (Castellot, 1981). They play an important role in the coagulation process by being a source of Factor VIII (Jaffe et al., 1973) and prostaglandin $I_2$ ($PGI_2$) (Jaffe and Weksler, 1979). They produce endothelial cell-relaxing factor, which is essential for acetylcholine-mediated relaxation of arteries (Furchgott, 1983). They modulate their internal environment, and processes controlled by it, by production of specific receptors for a variety of substances, such as LDL (Goldstein and Brown, 1977; Vlodavsky et al., 1978; Fielding et al., 1979), chylomicrons (Fielding et al., 1979), fibroblast growth factor (Gospodarowicz et al., 1978), platelet factor IV (Busch et al., 1979), $\beta$-thromboglobulin (Hope et al., 1979), chemotactic agents (Hoover et al., 1980), and even, under certain injurious conditions, Fc and C3b (Ryan et al., 1981).

In addition to SMC and EC of normal artery, the macrophage becomes a varyingly important cell type in lesions (Daoud et al., 1981; Stary, 1979; Gerrity, 1981a; Schaffner et al., 1980). We will consider only the many functions of this cell which are quite separate from its role in the immune response. However, the possibility that there is an immune component in the initiation or development of the lesion should not be dismissed, although the mechanisms involved remain to be elucidated (Hollander et al., 1974a; Lamberson and Fritz, 1974; Hardin et al., 1973). Primary among macrophage attributes is their ability to migrate, as is obvious by their very presence in the lesion, since they are derived from the circulating blood monocyte (Gerrity et al., 1981; Gerrity, 1981b; Issekutz et al., 1981). Perhaps of equal consequence is their phagocytic function, which is so important in the resolution of inflammation and bacterial infection (Steinman and Cohn, 1974). They have also been shown to phagocytize mineral calcium as well as collagenous matrix (Rifkin et al., 1980). Support for the concept that macrophages in lesions are actively phagocytic has been provided by the successful recovery from atherosclerotic lesions of a suspension of cells with many characteristics of macrophages which demonstrably phagocytized opsonized particles (Schaffner et al., 1980). This phagocytic capacity, as well as pinocytosis, is increased when macrophages are "activated" (Cohn, 1978).

Macrophages affect their environment in a number of ways. For instance, to some degree, they control the synthesis of collagen and glycosaminoglycans (GAG) (Kulonen and Potila, 1980), and they produce proteinases which degrade elastin (Werb et al., 1980; Werb and Gordon,

1975a), glycoproteins, and collagen (Werb et al., 1980; Werb and Gordon, 1975b); acid hydrolases (Unanue, 1976; Cohn and Wiener, 1963); enzyme inhibitors (Ross, 1981); peroxidase, superoxide dismutase (Ross, 1981), reactive $O_2$ metabolites (Cohn, 1978); and chemotactic factors (Ross, 1981), as well as complement components (Unanue, 1976), lysozyme (Cohn and Weiner, 1963), and plasminogen activator (Unkeless et al., 1974). They especially influence the other two cell types in lesions, SMC and EC, by producing a growth factor which stimulates proliferation of both cell types (Martin et al., 1981; Glenn and Ross, 1981; Ross et al., 1982). They also modulate their own function by the secretion of fibronectin, which is important both in cell adhesion and in nonimmune opsonization of phagocytizable particles (Villiger et al., 1981; Alitalo et al., 1980; Johansson et al., 1979), and by the production of specific LDL and $\beta$-VLDL (very low density lipoproteins) receptors, which affords a measure of control of cholesterol metabolism (Schechter et al., 1981; Mahley, 1983).

In the normal arterial wall, in addition to various ions, notably calcium, the major extracellular components are collagen, elastic tissue, GAG, and glycoproteins. Two types of collagen, III and I, are to be found in the approximate proportions 70:30 (McCullogh and Balian, 1975). As for GAG, chondroitin sulfates A and C, dermatan sulfate, and hyaluronic acid are secreted by SMC (Merrilees and Scott, 1981), while heparan sulfate or the less sufated GAG, heparin, is secreted by EC (Buonassisi, 1973). A low level of cholesterol, predominantly free, is also present in normal artery, as are phospholipids and triglycerides (Fritz et al., 1981a). Changes in the concentrations or compositions of any of these various substances can have a profound effect on not only other extracellular components, but also on various functions of constituent cells. Examples of interactions among extracellular components include the binding and precipitation of $\beta$- and pre-$\beta$-lipoprotein by GAG as insoluble complexes. Here, the type of GAG is important, with heparin having the greatest affinity (Berenson et al., 1971; Stevens et al., 1976; Avila et al., 1978; Biheri-Varga, 1978; Iverius, 1977). Chondroitin sulfate and dermatan sulfate tend to bind to collagen, while heparan sulfate has a greater affinity for elastin (Radhakrishnamurthy et al., 1977). A reaction of GAG with circulating components has been demonstrated. For instance, both hyaluronic acid and heparin, but not chondroitin sulfate (Yamada et al., 1980), bind to fibronectin. Heparin also retards the rate of thrombin formation, potentiates the action of antithrombin III, and reversibly binds and neutralizes complement (Wight, 1980b; Perlin, 1977; Stivala, 1977; Engelberg, 1977).

Since GAG content has been shown to change with varying stages of atherosclerotic lesions, the possibility that the GAG composition is responsible for characteristic differences in both permeability and fibrinolytic activity among lesion types has been raised (Klynstra et al., 1967). The amino acid composition of elastin is apparently an important determinant in the binding of lipid (Kramsch et al., 1971) and of $Ca^{2+}$ (Keeley and Partridge, 1974), while cholesterol accumulation in lesions favors a simultaneous accumulation of $Ca^{2+}$.

Although the lesion cells have wide-ranging potential functions, as cited above, all functions are not active simultaneously or under all circumstances. Obviously, the control mechanisms which determine the expression of various functions are of prime importance in the development or control of the lesion, but these controls are largely undefined, and at best poorly understood. However, there is abundant evidence that extracellular components do affect some cell functions. For instance GAG, through their binding of LDL and thus increasing the LDL concentration, influence the synthesis of LDL receptors and ultimately the synthesis of cholesterol and the accumulation of cholesteryl esters in SMC (Goldstein and Brown, 1977) and macrophages (Traber and Kayden, 1980). Heparin has been associated with a spectrum of effects from decreasing SMC proliferation (Clowes and Karnovsky, 1977), binding lipoprotein lipase to EC (Olivecrona et al., 1977), facilitating the release of LDL from its receptor (Goldstein and Brown, 1977), and activation of lipoprotein lipase (true also of heparan sulfate) (Wight, 1980a), to facilitating macrophage phagocytosis via its binding to fibronectin (Van de Water et al., 1981). Hyaluronic acid acts to aggregate macrophages (Love et al., 1979). There is also evidence that glycoproteins depress the elastolytic activity of macrophages (Jones and Werb, 1980).

Lipid accumulation affects the cells in a variety of ways. For instance, LDL has been shown to enhance the proliferation of SMC (Fischer-Dzoga, 1979) but to depress the phagocytic activity of macrophages (Feo et al., 1976; Klurfeld et al., 1979). On the other hand, $\beta$-VLDL increases synthesis of cholesteryl esters by macrophages (Mahley et al., 1980). Increased cholesterol accumulation has even been related to an increased level of collagen synthesis (Modrak and Langner, 1980).

The role of $Ca^{2+}$ is very complex. It is involved in a variety of processes, among them, the binding of LDL to its receptors, or the activity of metalloproteinases, such as collagenase.

The possibility that such extracellular components as collagen, GAG, or cholesteryl esters may exert a measure of control over the production of hydrolytic enzymes by SMC and/or macrophages must be considered. Evidence that cholesteryl ester hydrolase, $\beta$-glucuronidase, and a cathepsin B-1-like enzyme, which hydrolyzes collagen, are more active in lesion tissue than in adjacent normal tissue has been presented (Fritz et al., 1981b; 1982), and this, together with the demonstration of differences in concentrations of these substances in various arterial tissues (Fritz et al., 1981b) suggests that substrate induction of enzymes may be one important mechanism of control of these activities.

Finally, there is evidence that the functions of a given lesion cell type may be influenced by other cells of the lesion. Outstanding among these is the stimulation of SMC proliferation by both EC and macrophages by virtue of mitogens produced by each cell type. Conversely, SMC have been shown to enhance production of GAG, especially hyaluronic acid and chondroitin sulfate by EC (Merrilees and Scott, 1981).

## III. Risk Factors in Atherogenesis

While the pathogenesis of atherosclerosis is still unknown, epidemiological and clinical studies have identified several factors which appear to predispose to the disease. These factors are called "risk factors."

### A. Hyperlipidemia

Probably the most significant of these risk factors is hypercholesterolemia or hyperlipoproteinemia, because in its absence, other risk factors alone do not result in premature clinical events of atherosclerosis. However, these other risk factors, especially cigarette smoking, hypertension, and diabetes mellitus, greatly influence the effect of hyperlipoproteinemia on atherogenesis. The evidence of the association of hypercholesterolemia and atherosclerosis is overwhelming:

1. Cholesterol and cholesteryl esters are major components of the atheroma.
2. Defects in lipid metabolisms such as congenital hyperlipidemias lead to premature atherosclerosis and ischemic heart disease (IHD)[1].
3. Hypercholesterolemia is often encountered in patients vulnerable to IHD, such as those suffering from diabetes mellitus, hypothyroidism, and nephrotic syndrome.
4. Epidemiologic studies show that populations with high serum cho-

---

[1] In this text the interchangeable terms coronary heart disease (CHD), coronary artery disease (CAD), and ischemic heart disease (IHD) are used as they are referred to in references quoted.

lesterol concentration have a higher incidence of IHD events than populations with low serum cholesterol concentrations.

5. Dietary regimens which increase serum cholesterol levels in the blood in various animal species invariably result in the development of atherosclerotic lesions in the aorta and major arterial beds.

6. Animals which do not develop atherosclerosis spontaneously or when fed an atherogenic diet, such as the rat and dog, do not usually respond with high serum cholesterol concentrations when challenged by an atherogenic stimulus.

Elevation of serum cholesterol is controlled by several endogenous and exogenous factors. Among the endogenous factors are defects in lipid metabolism, as in familial hyperlipidemias, or they may be associated with diseases such as diabetes and hypothyroidism. The most important exogenous cause of hyperlipidemia is dietary overload with lipids. Epidemiological studies of large population groups in different parts of the world have shown a correlation between fat ingestion, especially cholesterol and saturated fats, and the concentration of cholesterol in the serum (Keys, 1970). Well-controlled studies of people confined to institutions or to metabolic wards also showed a good correlation between cholesterol consumption and serum cholesterol (Hegsted et al., 1965). This was particularly true when the amount of cholesterol consumed was between 0 and 600 mg/day. The amount of fat ingested is not the only important factor in influencing the concentration of cholesterol in the serum. Saturation of fatty acids is also important. A diet rich in saturated fatty acids significantly increases the total plasma cholesterol while a diet rich in polyunsaturated fatty acids decreases the concentration. Monosaturated fatty acids have little effect (United States Department of Health, Education and Welfare Report, 1980).

Cholesterol and other plasma lipids, such as triglycerides, do not circulate in the blood as free lipids; they exist in the form of lipoprotein complexes. These can be divided on the basis of their density and electrophoretic mobility into lipoprotein families, chylomicrons, VLDL, LDL, and high density lipoproteins (HDL). These are also known as pre-$\beta$, $\beta$, and $\alpha$ lipoproteins in the above order, based on the apoproteins predominant in each class. Most of the cholesterol in the plasma (60–75%) is transported in the form of LDL. Hence, total plasma cholesterol reflects largely LDL cholesterol.

Many investigations have shown that the cholesterol carried within the various lipoprotein particles has different effects on atherogenesis. It appears that VLDL and LDL cholesterols are atherogenic if elevated, while HDL cholesterol has a protective effect against the disease (Castelli, 1983). Patients with familial hypercholesterolemia (Type II disease) provide a striking example of the role of high levels of LDL in the development of atherosclerosis. These patients, who lack LDL receptors in their tissue (Goldstein and Brown, 1975), have very high concentrations of LDL in their plasma. They usually die from coronary heart disease very early in life.

Feeding a high-fat, high-cholesterol diet to various species of animals promotes an increase in the concentration of LDL in the plasma (Mahley, 1983). In man, hypercholesterolemia resulting from feeding a high-cholesterol diet is largely the result of an increase in LDL cholesterol (LDL-C) (Rudel *et al.,* 1979).

Several epidemiologic studies have suggested that HDL may play a role in preventing atherogenesis (Eder and Gidez, 1982) by facilitating the uptake of cholesterol from the arterial wall, and thus, people with low plasma HDL might be subject to the development of accelerated atherosclerosis (Miller, 1978). Several authorities have suggested that the ratio of total cholesterol (TC) to HDL cholesterol (HDL-C) or LDL-C to HDL-C may be more important determinants of the risk of developing atherosclerotic heart disease than TC, LDL-C, or HDL-C levels alone (Adner and Castelli, 1980; Castelli, 1982, 1983; Durant *et al.,* 1982; Enger *et al.,* 1977).

## B. Hypertension

Epidemiologic evidence indicates that hypertension is one of the major risk factors of coronary heart disease (Kannel *et al.,* 1964, 1979; Castelli, 1982), and it is the strongest risk factor for stroke and congestive heart failure (Kannel *et al.,* 1970, Kannel *et al.,* 1979). The risk is related to both systolic and diastolic blood pressure, although diastolic seems to be more predictive (Leren *et al.,* 1983). In the Framingham Study a borderline hypertension of 140/90–94 mm Hg was accompanied by a 50% increase of coronary heart disease and three times the risk of stroke. A person with hypertension of 160/95 mm Hg or greater runs two to three times the risk of coronary heart disease and seven times the risk of stroke (Castelli, 1982). In the United States National Cooperative Pooling Project, the risk of ischemic heart disease in individuals with diastolic pressure greater than 105 mm Hg was four times that of individuals with pressure 84 mm Hg or less (Pooling Project Research Group, 1978).

## C. Cigarette Smoking

The reports of the Surgeon General on smoking and health have established cigarette smoking as a major contributor to atherosclerotic heart disease (U.S. Department of Health, Education and Welfare Reports,

1979, 1980). The Framingham Study shows that smoking, at least in persons under 60 years of age, continues to be one of the three most significant risk factors of coronary heart disease (CHD). The risk is reversible within a short period of time. In persons who stop smoking cigarettes, CHD risk declines to the level of a nonsmoker within 1 year, while the risk of lung cancer returns to normal only in 10 to 15 years. The striking aspect of cigarette smoking is its special relationship to sudden death. Persons who smoke more than a pack a day are at five times greater risk of sudden death at a young age than nonsmokers (Castelli, 1983). At autopsy, coronary and aortic atherosclerosis is greater in smokers than nonsmokers (Strong and McGill, 1969).

### D. Diabetes Mellitus

It is generally assumed that diabetes mellitus predisposes to coronary atherosclerosis. This is based on epidemiologic and pathologic findings (Keen and Jarrett, 1975; Brownlee and Cahill, 1979; West, 1978; Castelli, 1983; Goodale *et al.*, 1962; Thomas *et al.*, 1956). Some of the longitudinal epidemiological studies indicated that impaired glucose tolerance and hyperglycemia without frank clinical diabetes were also associated with increased frequency of cardiovascular disease. The association appears to be limited to the Western industrialized countries. There appears to be no increase in coronary heart disease and coronary atherosclerosis among people with maturity-onset diabetes in nonindustrialized countries (Keen and Jarrett, 1975).

### E. Other Factors

A host of other factors have been identified which are associated with an increase in the incidence of coronary heart disease. Among these are obesity, physical activity, stress, and genetic predisposition; but the data supporting these factors are less convincing than in the major risk factors cited above. Obesity has long been recognized as having as association with coronary heart disease. This association may be indirect. Obese individuals tend to have more severe hyperlipidemia, hypertension and diabetes mellitus. However, the recent Framingham Report (Castelli, 1982) shows that obese persons free of the other major risk factors still have higher incidence of coronary heart disease episodes.

Several recent studies indicate that physical activity protects against coronary atherosclerosis. In the Framingham Study, the higher one scored on a physical activity scale, the lower were the subsequent rates of death and heart attack (Castelli, 1982). In a Harvard Alumni Study, death and heart attack rates were related to the continuing level of physical activity of the graduate (Castelli, 1982; Paffenbarger, 1978). The London Transport Worker Study showed that subjects who reported vigorous exercise did much better than the exercising group as a whole.

The role of stress in atherogenesis is still a matter of controversy. It is a common belief that a stressful life predisposes to coronary heart disease. Some investigators have proposed that people with characteristic patterns of behavior, which they termed Type A, were more likely to develop coronary heart disease than those with a contrasting pattern of behavior, which they termed Type B. These same investigators have reported data indicating that the Type A personality is associated with an increased risk for coronary heart disease even when other risk factors were taken into account (Rosenman *et al.*, 1975, 1976). In the Framingham Study, individuals with Type A personality were found to have about twice the risk of developing coronary heart disease than individuals with Type B traits. This relationship exists only among white-collar working men and does not hold for the blue-collar working men. Among women, Type A personalities are at high risk whether they work as employees or housewives (Haynes *et al.*, 1978; Castelli, 1983).

## IV. Clinical Trials

When one considers the prevalence of coronary artery disease in the Western world, and the complexity of the disease, with at least epidemiological evidence of such a variety of risk factors, it is not surprising that there have been many clinical trials of a wide variety of regimens in the search for a logical and effective approach to the prevention and/or treatment of this disease. The trials range in scope from those involving a few patients, perhaps sharing only one common characteristic and involving a single precise mode of intervention, for a relatively short time (weeks or months) to massive studies, wherein several thousand subjects followed fairly complex protocols involving multiple facets such as dietary changes and one or more drugs, continuing over several years. The most numerous clinical trials have been based on intervention with drugs and/or diet; less numerous are other regimens directed toward a variety of risk factors. A major component of many clinical trials is the demonstration of the coincidence of one or more risk factors with atherosclerotic disease. One complicating factor in the summary of results from these many trials lies in the variation of choice or end point. Parameters as diverse as angiographic evidence of disease, changes in blood lipid levels, EKG changes, and amount of disease histologically detected at autopsy have been used as measures of disease status during or after a trial.

Each trial has contributed to some degree to our evaluation of treatment modalities and/or the mechanisms by which external factors influence the development or arrest of the disease. Because of this we will review and summarize briefly a number of such trials and their results.

First, let us consider some surveys which did not involve intervention, but, instead, hoped to define differences among groups, to provide a basis for assessment of future changes, or to delineate an association with one or more risk factors. Among these, two very large studies of essentially normal, largely male populations, directly involving approximately 20,000 individuals, defined the relationship of cardiac-associated death over 10 to 18 years to a variety of characteristics, social as well as biochemical (Leren et al., 1983; Castelli, 1983). In spite of differences in design and endpoint, both studies showed a positive association of mortality with elevated total cholesterol, high blood pressure, smoking, and a Type A, "overachiever" personality. In addition. elevated blood glucose and obesity were identified in one study as being associated with coronary heart disease (Castelli, 1983), while in the second, increased HDL and HDL/TC ratios, as well as level of education, were inversely related to heart-related death (Leren et al., 1983). In another study (Schwertner et al., 1984), 618 young men, each of whom had some medical problem which could preclude their flying, were studied by the United States Air Force to define a possible relationship between elevated serum cholesterol and cortisol levels, angiographically detectable coronary artery narrowing, and behavior patterns. Among those with no coronary artery disease (CAD) there was no relation between levels of cholesterol and cortisol, but a significant association between cholesterol and cortisol was found in those individuals with CAD of any degree and also in those with Type A behavior patterns, suggesting a hormonal component to CAD. A Finnish study of 264 8-year old boys was designed to provide background information on serum lipid levels and dietary habits of boys from rural and urban areas for an ongoing study of blood pressure, anthropometric, biochemical, and socioeconomic variables. Differences in diet between urban (more vegetable margarine) and rural, and between eastern (less fruit, vegetables, and low-fat milk) and western areas were brought out (Viikari et al., 1982).

At least three studies involving no intervention have addressed the relationship between diabetes and atherosclerosis. Plasma lipid levels were endpoints in two of the three. In the first of these, plasma insulin levels of 323 nondiabetic, first-degree relatives of insulin-dependent diabetics were found to be significantly correlated with total and LDL cholesterol (LDL-C) and triglycerides (TG), whereas there was an inverse correlation with HDL cholesterol (HDL-C) (Orchard *et al.,* 1983). The second compared HDL-C levels of insulin-dependent diabetic men and women with those of age and sex-matched controls, and found, unexpectedly, that HDL-C levels of diabetic men were significantly higher than those of controls. This was not true of the diabetic women, however, in whom a nonsignificant elevation in HDL-C levels was associated with poor metabolic control of diabetes (Mattock *et al.,* 1982). Since insulin-dependent diabetics have an increased risk of CAD, while there is considerable evidence that elevated HDL-C levels are protective against CAD, the findings of this study are somewhat paradoxical. The third study, extended over 2 years, with assessment of lower extremity atherosclerotic occlusive (ASO) disease as endpoint, documented that while 98 of the 274 participants had demonstrable ASO on entry into the study, an additional 92 were positive at the end of 2 years. Further, an association of progression of the existing disease was associated with older age groups, longer duration of diabetes, and elevated serum cholesterol levels (Bendick *et al.,* 1983).

An example of a large study involving no intervention was one designed to test the hypothesis, suggested by some work with experimental animals, that vasectomized men were more at risk for CAD. All of the 7420 men involved in the 9-year study underwent coronary angiography, and angiographically detectable CAD was the endpoint. The results showed no evidence of a relationship of a previous vasectomy to extent of CAD (Rimm *et al.,* 1983). In Russia, in a 2-year prospective study of 278 patients with stable angina, wherein extent of CAD was determined angiographically at the outset and fatal or nonfatal myocardial infarct (MI) was the endpoint, a direct relation between MI and number of vessels with disease was found. It also documented an association between frequency of MI and disease of the left anterior descending artery (Gasilin *et al.,* 1983).

The effect of exercise was studied over 3 years in a study of 750 postinfarct patients, with morbidity and mortality as endpoints. There was no change in morbidity as a result of the training program of vigorous exercise three times per week, but there was a 37% (but not significant) decrease in total mortality in this group, and a significant (87%) decrease in fatal MI occurrence (Oberman and Pitt, 1982). Exercise in conjunction with a moderately restricted diet was studied in a small group of prepubertal boys over 31 weeks, with weight loss and plasma lipid composition as endpoints. The regimen was successful in lowering weight and TC, LDL-C, and TG levels (Kahle *et al.,* 1982).

The effect of a regimen of prudent diet and decreased smoking, as opposed to no intervention, was monitored in 1232 men who were healthy but a high risk for CHD. After 6 to $7\frac{1}{2}$ years, there was a 47% decrease in fatal or nonfatal MI in the diet, less-smoking group (Leren et al., 1983).

Because of the complexity of interpreting the significance of relatively small changes in plasma lipid levels likely to be achieved in a random population sample and the huge numbers of subjects needed to achieve meaningful results of intervention trials with such subjects, numerous investigators have attempted to simplify the problem by using as subjects patients with hereditary hyperlipidemia, since these patients have exaggerated risk as well as potential for change in plasma lipids. These trials have in common the fact that the intervention has been directed toward lowering plasma lipid levels. In addition to dietary recommendations which stressed decreased total fat intake, with emphasis on cholesterol and saturated fats, a number of lipid-lowering drugs have been used. Among them, clofibrate and its analogs gemfibrozil, ciprofibrate, and fenofibrate, as well as mevinolin, apparently act by decreasing cholesteryl ester synthesis (Hudson and Day, 1982), while colestipol and colestyramine are nonabsorbed bile acid sequestrants. Probucol, a lipid-soluble bisphenyl, and nicotinic acid, which lowers cholesterol levels by an as yet poorly understood mechanism, were also tested. For instance, in one study 24 men and women, all typed hyperlipidemics, who had 6 months of stable intermittent claudication due to femoral–popliteal disease, were randomized to diet only or diet plus an appropriate drug (cholestyramine for Type II, clofibrate for Type III, and nicotinic acid for Type IV hyperlipidemias). The regimens were maintained for 15 to 24 months and the endpoints were plasma lipids and angiographically determined amount of disease, defined as edge irregularity. Each type of combined drug–diet regimen resulted in a significant decrease in TC, LDL-C, and TG and increase in HDL-C as compared to diet only subjects, and this change was associated with a 60% decrease in progression of the disease (Duffield et al., 1982, 1983).

The recently released results of the Lipid Research Clinics Primary Prevention Trial are most impressive. This optimally designed and executed double-blind study involved 3806 men age 35–59, all of whom on entry were Type II hyperlipidemics with TC levels over 250 mg/dl, yet with no CAD, diabetes, or hypertension. The duration of the study was 10 years. All patients were instructed to follow a moderate cholesterol-lowering diet, and each received either cholestyramine or a placebo. Endpoints were (1) a definite CHD death or nonfatal MI and (2) change in plasma TC or LDL-C. Those taking cholestyramine showed a significant decrease in CHD death or nonfatal MI which appears to have been mediated by the concommitant decrease in TC and LDL-C (Lipid Research Clinics Program, 1984a, b).

A smaller group (Heideman and Hoff, 1982) of hyperlipoproteinemics, Types IIA, IIB, and IV were assigned to a "prudent"diet for 6 months, with added fenofibrate the first and last 2 months. The endpoint in this case was a change in TC, TG, and ApoA/ApoB ratio. TG level was significantly decreased in patients in all three types of hyperlipoproteinemia, TC in types IIA and IIB, and the ApoA/ApoB ratio increased in all types, all very encouraging results. However, intestinal side effects were a problem with several patients (Avogaro et al., 1983). Ciprofibrate at either 50 or 100 mg/day was shown in a group of 20 type II patients to decrease LDL-C and TC while simultaneously increasing HDL-C over a period of 12 weeks. In another trial comparing gemfibrozil and clofibrate, the endpoint was change in plasma lipid levels. Forty hyperlipidemic patients received one or the other of these drugs for 18 weeks. Results showed that, while both were effective, gemfibrozil caused a greater decrease in TG, VLDL, and LDL/HDL ratios and a greater increase in HDL than clofibrate (Nash, 1982a). In one case of clofibrate and niceritrol intervention, with concentrations of mono- or polyunsaturated fat as the endpoint, clofibrate was found to cause a shift of polyunsaturated to monounsaturated fats, a change which presumably could be counteracted with diet (Vessby et al., 1980). Mevinolin, in a small trial with patients refractory to other drugs, proved effective at lowering LDL-C levels without affecting HDL-C; addition of colestipol enhanced these results, and no adverse results of either regimen were noted (Illingworth, 1983). Probucol has been shown to lower TC and LDL-C (McCaughan, 1981; Glueck, 1982; Nash, 1982b), but has the added undesired effect of lowering HDL-C and ApoA levels (Glueck, 1982). In a study of 65 primary hypercholesterolemic patients treated over 9 months with clofibrate or colestipol with clofibrate added the last 2 months, both regimens were found to decrease TC and LDL-C without change in HDL-C, but there were more responders to colestipol than to clofibrate (Seplowitz et al., 1981). A trial involving 42 patients, each of whom had greater than 50% narrowing of a least one nongrafted coronary artery and plasma cholesterol over 250 mg/dl at entry into the study, surveyed the results of 2 years' treatment with colestipol or placebo. A significant reduction in TC and angiographically determined progression of lesions in fewer of the colestipol-treated patients was found as compared to controls (Nash et al., 1982b).

Definitely warranting consideration is the World Health Organization Cooperative Trial on Primary Prevention of Ischemic Heart Disease. From about 10,500 men free of overt IHD, 4700 were actually studied for

9 years. Their experimental regimen was either clofibrate or an olive oil placebo; grouping was based on plasma cholesterol levels at entry into the study, where the top and bottom third were used, and half of the top third wererandomized to clofibrate treatment. The endpoint in this study was death, and, surprisingly, the overall death rate of the clofibrate-treated men was significantly higher than for the placebo group; this increase could not be ascribed to any one disease, and no explanation for this finding is apparent. (W.H.O. Cooperative Trial, 1980).

Three other lipid-lowering drugs have each been tested in at least one trial. Three months' treatment with thyroxin lowered TC, LDL-C, and ApoB in the plasma of Type IIA hypercholesterolemic patients (Schwandt and Weisweiler, 1980). Short-term treatment (4–9 weeks) with acipimox (an analog of nicotinic acid) was effective in raising HDL-C and lowering LDL-C in Type IIA patients and lowering TG in Type IV patients (Sirtori *et al.*, 1981), and lecithin (35 g/day), given for 5 months to Alzheimer's disease patients who had no heart disease, resulted in lowered plasma TC and LDL/HDL ratio and elevated HDL (Vroulis *et al.*, 1982).

In summary, most studies involving lipid-lowering drugs were effective, to varying degrees, in changing plasma lipid profiles, and some improved the course of disease as measured by angiography or incidence of MI or death.

Several other approaches, either to treatment of risk factors, as, for instance, hypertension, or interfering with some mechanism, such as platelet aggregation, have been subjected to clinical trial. Aspirin has been extensively studied with conflicting results, probably due in part to differences in dose as well as to widely differing populations and/or endpoints (Marcus, 1983; Mustard *et al.*, 1983; Fuster and Chesebro, 1981). For instance, in most studies the role of thrombin, a potent mediator of thrombosis which is unaffected by antiplatelet drugs, has not been assessed, and may, indeed, have masked a beneficial aspirin effect (Mustard *et al.*, 1983). Aspirin in low doses inhibits platelet cyclo-oxygenase and subsequent production of thromboxane $A_2$ (Burch *et al.*, 1978), and in a double-blind VA Cooperative study of 1266 men with unstable angina, who took 324 mg aspirin per day for 12 weeks, there were highly significant (51%) decreases in death and in nonfatal myocardial infarction in the aspirin-treated group as compared to the placebo group (Lewis *et al.*, 1983). At higher doses, aspirin has been shown to decrease the production of prostacyclin, which is derived from blood vessel walls and serves as a vasodilator as well as preventing platelet aggregation (Moncada and Vane, 1979). Thus, the ideal dosage would decrease thromboxane $A_2$ concentration without decreasing prostacyclin. The addition of dipyridimole to a low-dose aspirin regimen has shown promising results (Fuster and Chesebto, 1981), based presumably on the phosphodiesterase-inhibiting capacity of dipyridamole, the quality by which it produces its anthithrombotic effect (Moncada and Vane, 1979). The relative efficacy of aspirin in men and women is currently clouded and needs to be studied. Ticlopidine, another inhibitor of platelet aggregation, was shown to be effective, as compared to placebo, in relieving chronic arterial occlusion in a double-blind Japanese study involving 193 patients (Katsumura et al., 1982).

Because of the relationship between hypertension and coronary atherosclerosis, clinical trials involving various drugs used in the treatment of hypertension have been made using as endpoints CHD events or changes in blood lipids. One survey, involving over 16,000 patients treated from 1 to 5 years, compared two antidiuretics, chlorohalidone and hydrochlorothiazide, and the antihypertensive spironolactone and found no difference in CHD events among those treated as compared to untreated controls. It also brought out the fact that both of the diuretics tested caused an increase in TC to the same extent, while chlorohalidone was more effective in reducing blood pressure. In contrast, spironolactone did not result in elevation of TC but also caused less reduction of blood pressure (Ames, 1983). The effect of treatment of mild hypertension over 5 years with alpha- and beta- adrenergic blocking drugs, alone and in combination, was studied in 785 patients, with changes in blood lipids as endpoint. Propranolol, atenolol, and pindolol, all beta-adrenergic blockers, were found to decrease the concentration of HDL, a presumably negative effect. The most effective regimen was found to be pindolol plus the alpha-adrenergic blocker, prazosin, which resulted in decreased levels of LDL and VLDL without changes in HDL (Leren et al., 1983).

Approaches to the treatment of angina and/or coronary artery spasm have been tested clinically. Calcium channel entry blockers verapamil and nifedipine were tested in 37 patients with coronary spasm but only minor or no CAD for a mean of 21 months, with angina as endpoint. Both effectively reduced the angina, and some patients remained free of angina as much as 10 months after cessation of the treatment (Freedman et al., 1982). Diltiazem was shown to prolong the duration of exercise and delay the onset of angina almost as well as nitroglycerine (Koiwaya et al., 1981), and, in a small group of patients with stable angina and over 70% occulsion, diltiazem, and another beta blocker, propranolol, both increased work capacity significantly over placebo, as measured by exercise ECG (Bounhoure et al., 1983).

Taken as a whole, the clinical trials are continually adding to our understanding of the mechanisms underlying, and roles of risk factors in, atherosclerotic disease, as well as helping to provide rational therapeutic approaches to its control.

## V. Regression of Atheroma in Humans

Although in the long run the control of the mortality and morbidity associated with atherosclerosis by prevention is the ideal approach, its implementation, were it to be realized tomorrow, would not help the millions who already have coronary atherosclerosis to a substantial degree. For them, the imperative is the prevention of progression, and, hopefully, the regression, of established lesions.

While there is ample evidence that diet-induced atherosclerosis in experimental animals, at least in its early and moderate forms, regresses, the evidence of regression of human atherosclerosis is still circumstantial. The data suggesting that human atherosclerosis can regress are epidemiological, morphological, biochemical, and angiographic.

The epidemiologic studies derived mostly from the experience during World War II in Russia, Sweden, and Norway (Brozek et al., 1946; Malmros, 1950; Strom and Jensen, 1951). These studies indicated a decrease in the rate of myocardial infarct and stroke among populations which were subjected to marked food deprivation, especially animal fats. The morphologic studies are also derived from the experience of World Wars I and II, and from individuals dying from wasting diseases. Aschoff (1924) reported a diminution in the amount of aortic atherosclerosis observed at autopsy during the period of semistarvation in Germany at the end of World War I. Similar findings were also reported by Beitzke (1928) and Variainen and Kanerva (1947). Unfortunately, all these studies were poorly controlled and largely impressionistic, and, thus, cannot be accepted as clearly established facts (Thomas et al., 1978a).

Wilens (1947) showed that aortas and coronary arteries from individuals dying from a wasting disease, with extensive terminal weight loss, had less atherosclerosis than those from autopsied individuals without extensive weight loss. The findings of Wilens were confirmed by Wanscher et al. in 1951 in autopsied cancer and noncancer patients. The effects of wasting diseases on human atherosclerosis was biochemically evaluated by Eilersen and Faber (1960) in aortas from autopsied tuberculous individuals. The control material consisted of aortas of individuals who died accidentally or of disease of short duration, with the exclusion of individuals with heart disease, diabetes, and hyypertension. For comparison, they used two ages for the tubercular group: age at death and age at which weight loss began. Measurement of calcium and cholesterol content of intima and media of aortas indicated that there was a cessation of cholesterol deposition during the period of final emaciation. However, calcium deposition was unchanged during this period.

Probably, the most significant data indicating that human atherosclerosis can regress are derived from arteriography. A group of investigators (Knight *et al.*, 1972; Buchwald *et al.*, 1980) showed by sequential coronary arteriograms that some individuals whose serum cholesterol was reduced by partial ileal bypass exhibited a decrease in plaque size. Similar results were reported in the femoral artery from patients with Type IV and Type II hyperlipoproteinemia. Elevated blood lipids and blood pressure were treated with medication and diet. After an interval of 13 months on the regimen, repeated angiograms showed regression of atherosclerosis in nine out of 25 patients. A recent report from the Helsinki Prospective Angiographic Study (Nikkila *et al.*, 1983) showed that after lowering of serum lipids by diet and clofibrate, repeated angiographic study, after 2 and 7 years, revealed that the lesion remained unchanged in 40%. In the NHLBI Type II Coronary Intervention Study, sequential coronary angiography indicated that prevention of the progression of angiographically demonstrable coronary disease can be accomplished by lowering serum cholesterol by diet and cholestyramine. Their results support the hypothesis that increase in HDL and decrease in total cholesterol or LDL, or preferably both together, can prevent or delay coronary artery disease progression (Levy, 1983).

## VI. Regression of Atheroma in Experimental Animals

In the last few decades, several studies have shown that diet-induced atherosclerotic lesions regress after withdrawal of the dietary stimulus. In this communication, we will discuss regression in rabbits, dogs, fowl, nonhuman primates, and swine.

The first documented study of the regression of atherosclerotic lesions was reported in the rabbit by Anitschkow (1933) in the 1930s. He found that atherosclerotic plaques produced in the aorta by high cholesterol feeding showed a gradual loss of their lipid. Microscopically, there was a disintegration and disappearance of the foam-cell masses and their replacement by newly developing collagenous and elastic tissue. He also noticed that cholesterol crystals persisted after the other lipids had been removed. Subsequent work on regression in the rabbit model produced contradictory results. Friedman and Byers (1963) reported that, after cessation of the high-cholesterol diet, rabbits showed an increase in the amount of atherosclerosis and in their cholesterol content. When the animal attained its normal serum cholesterol, however, there was no further increase in the size of the lesion or in its cholesterol content. Constantinides (1965) and Constantinides *et al.* (1960) found that the aortas of rabbits fed a high-cholesterol diet for 2 months followed by 2 years on a normal diet had more extensive atherosclerosis than the aortas of the animals sacrificed immediately after the period of cholesterol feeding. Moreover, the former aortas had thicker plaques and approximately seven times greater cholesterol content. Prior and Ziegler (1965) reported minor shrinkage of the plaque in rabbits fed an atherogenic diet for a period of 6 months, then returned to a normal diet for a period up to 16 months, as compared with those in animals killed immediately after 6 months of cholesterol feeding. Minor shrinkage of the plaque was also reported by McMillan *et al.* (1955) and by Duff and McMillan (1951). Positive results in regression in these animals were reported by Bortz (1968) on early atherosclerosis and Vesselinovitch *et al.* (1974) of moderate to severe atherosclerosis. The latter investigators attempted to effect regression of rabbit atherosclerosis by means of a low-fat diet and hyperoxia either alone or in combination with cholestyramine or estrogen. They found that the most effective regression regimen in rabbit is a combination of hyperoxia and low-fat diet with cholestyramine or estrogen.

In 1949, Horlick and Katz reported that, in chickens, after withdrawal of an atherogenic diet, early lesions might completely be resorbed while more severe lesions might undergo regression and reparative changes. Pick *et al.* (1952) have shown that in chickens, regression is enhanced by estrogen.

Regression of diet-induced atherosclerosis in pigeons has also been reported. St. Clair *et al.* (1972) demonstrated that in white Carneau pigeons diet-induced atherosclerosis regressed. The features of regression were a reduction of the atherogenic index and a reduction in free and esterified cholesterol. Wagner and Clarkson (1977) reported that atherosclerosis produced in white Carneau pigeons, either by intermittent or continuous cholesterol feeding, regressed as evidenced by a decrease in the thickness of lesions. However, the pattern of regression was different in the two groups. Among the differences was a higher concentration of calcium in the intermittent group at 8 months regression. These authors also found that this increase in mineralization during regression could be prevented by EHDP (ethane-1-hydroxy-1,1-diphosphonate) treatment (Wagner *et al.*, 1977).

Bevans, in 1951, reported regression of atherosclerosis produced in aortas of dogs by a cholesterol–thioracil regimen when the animals were shifted to a stock diet (Bevams *et al.*, 1951). De Palma *et al.* (1970), using sequential observations of canine atherosclerosis produced by cholesterol feeding and oblation of the thyroid by $^{131}$I, reported regression of established plaque over a period of 12 to 14 months.

In the monkey, Armstrong and his associates (1970) reported convincing evidence that coronary atherosclerotic lesions, produced in rhesus monkeys by an atherogenic diet, decreased significantly in size when the animals were shifted to a cholesterol-free diet for long periods of time (9 months). They also showed that there was a decrease in both free and esterified cholesterol (Armstrong and Megan, 1972). Eggen *et al.* (1974) reported regression of fatty streaks produced in the rhesus monkeys by an atherogenic diet after withdrawal of the diet. The features of regression were a decrease in surface involvement by fatty streaks in the aorta and its major branches and in a decrease in cholesterol plus cholesteryl ester concentration in the intima media preparations. The cholesterol concentration returned to control levels after 64 weeks on a basal diet (Eggen *et al.*, 1974; Kokatnur *et al.*, 1975). Vesselinovitch *et al.* (1976) studied the regression of moderate to severe diet-induced atherosclerosis in the rhesus monkey. After 18 months on regression regimens the aortas from the regression animals showed about two-thirds as many lesions, which were, on the average, about half as severe as those of the baseline.

Some investigators studied the effect of a moderate reduction of serum cholesterol on regression in the rhesus monkey. Following the production of atherosclerotic lesions by a high-cholesterol diet a group of animals was sacrificed as a baseline; the remaining animals were divided in two groups. By manipulation of the diet, the serum cholesterol was maintained at a concentration of 280 to 320 mg/dl in one group and at 180 to 220 mg/dl in the other. Animals were sacrificed at 24 and 48 months. At 24 months of regression, there was striking regression of fatty streaks in the animals changed to 200 mg/dl levels when compared with those from the baseline or from the 300 mg/dl level. Regression of fibrous plaques did not occur in either of the regression groups (Bond *et al.*, 1977). Chemical analysis of the abdominal aortas showed at 24 months a decrease in the concentration of the various lipids including cholesterol and cholesteryl ester in both regression groups, especially so in those with serum cholesterol levels of 200 mg/dl (Wagner *et al.*, 1980). Several studies on monkeys have used a drug and/or a dietary additive to induce an accelerated regression. Positive results were reported following the use of cholestyramine (Wissler and Vesselinovitch, 1976), the calcium antagonist EHDP (Hollander *et al.*, 1974a; Kramsch and Chan, 1975), and antihypertensive drugs (Hollander *et al.*, 1974b).

Daoud *et al.* (1976) have reported that advanced atherosclerosis produced in the abdominal aortas of miniature swine by a combination of injury in the form of abrasion with a balloon catheter and an atherogenic diet, regressed after 14 months of withdrawal of the dietary stimulus. The features of regression were a decrease in the size of the lesion with remodeling of the intima toward a smooth surface; a significant decrease in intimal surface stained with Sudan IV; and the virtual disappearance of necrosis, hemorrhage in plaque, and thrombosis. There was no decrease in the number of sections showing calcification. Biochemical studies showed that the regressed lesions had a decreased level of DNA, total and esterified cholesterol and phospholipid concentration, and DNA synthesis (Fritz et al., 1976). Since the regression diet used was so severe as to be unacceptable to Western man, the Albany group carried out another experiment in which they studied the effect of a dietary regimen that resulted in a serum cholesterol level of approximately 200 mg/dl on the fate of swine atherosclerosis produced by feeding the animals a high-cholesterol diet for 17 months without injury (Augustyn et al., 1978; Jarmolych et al., 1978). Further, these effects were compared with those obtained from the addition of clofibrate to the same dietary regimen. The serum cholesterol levels of the latter regimen were around 100 mg/dl. Morphologically, there was no regression observed in the animals on the regimen without clofibrate. The addition of clofibrate caused regression that involved a significant decrease in size, gross sudanophilia, and disappearance of foam cell lesions. Biochemically, the clofibrate regimen resulted in a significant decrease in DNA and esterified cholesterol concentration and in the rate of DNA synthesis. This experiment emphasized the importance of serum cholesterol rather than the amount of dietary cholesterol in causing regression. In a sequential study aimed to explore the natural history of regression, the same group of investigators found that in the early phase of regression (6 weeks) there was little change from the baseline in both morphological and biochemical features except for an increase in the number of macrophages. By 5 months, there was a significant decrease in the amount of necrosis, DNA and cholesterol concentration, and in cholesterol synthesis. There was also a decrease in the number of macrophages and an increase in collagen synthesis. At 14 months, the lesions in the aortas and coronary arteries were almost completely devoid of necrosis and composed mostly of collagen. There was no change in the size between the baseline and the fourteenth-month regression lesion in the aorta. However, in the coronary the latter was significantly smaller. Biochemically, at 14 months, in the aorta lesions synthesis of DNA and total protein had reached control levels. The concentrations of cholesterol and cholesteryl esters, while significantly below the baseline level, remained substantially higher than in the controls (Daoud et al., 1981; Fritz et al., 1981a).

Overall, evidence from experiments in a variety of species, if extrapolated to man, provides the basis for hope that at least some features of atherosclerotic lesions in most stages of development will regress in response to lowering of serum cholesterol levels. We must await the development of more precise noninvasive methods of assessing the progression or regression of established coronary artery lesions in man before we can state unequivocally that a regression regimen can be effective in man. However, in the interim, based on the mass of data available, it would seem reasonable to prescribe prudent diets and/or serum lipid-lowering regimens for those individuals with elevated serum cholesterol levels.

## References

Adner, M. M., and Castelli, W. P. (1980). *J.A.M.A.* **342**, 534.
Alitalo, K., Hovi, T., and Vaheri, A. (1980). *J. Exp. Med.* **151**, 602–613.
Ames, R. P. (1983). *Am. Heart J.* **106**, 1207–1213.
Anderson, H. C. (1983). *Arch. Pathol. Lab. Med.* **107**, 341–348.
Anitschkow, N. (1933). *In* "Experimental Atherosclerosis in Animals" (E. V. Cowdry, ed.), pp. 271–322. MacMillan.
Armstrong, M. L., and Megan, M. B. (1972). *Circ. Res.* **30**, 675–680.
Armstrong, M. L., Warner, E. D., and Connor, W. E. (1970). *Circ. Res.* **27**, 59–67.
Aschoff, L. (1924). *In* "Lectures in Pathology," pp. 247–259. Hoeber, New York.
Augustyn, J. M., Fritz, K. E., Daoud, A. S., Jarmolych, J., and Lee, K. T. (1978). *Arch. Pathol. Lab. Med.* **102**, 294–297.
Avila, E. M., Lopex, F., and Camejo, G. (1978). *Artery* **4**, 36–60.
Avogaro, P., Bittolo-Bon, G., Belussi, F., Pontoglio, E., and Cazzolato, G. (1983). *Atherosclerosis* **95**, 100.
Beitzke, H. (1928). *Virchows Arch. Pathol. Anat.* **267**, 625.
Bendick, P. J., Glover, J. L., Kuebler, T. W., and Dilley, R. S. (1983). *Surgery* **93**(6), 834–838.
Benditt, E. P., and Benditt, J. M. (1973). *Proc. Natl. Acad. Sci.* **70**, 1753–1756.
Berenson, G. S., Radhakrishnamurthy, B., Dalferes, E. R., Jr., and Srinivasan, S. R. (1971). *Hum. Pathol.* **2**, 57–79.
Bevans, M., Davidson, J. D., and Kendalls, F. F. (1951). *Arch. Pathol.* **51**, 288–292.
Bierman, E. L., and Albers, J. (1977). *Biochim. Biophys. Acta* **488**, 152–160.
Biheri-Varga, M. (1978). *Artery* **4**, 504–511.
Bond, M. G., Bullock, B. C., Lehner, N. D. M., and Clarkson, T. B. (1977). *In* "Atherosclerosis IV" (G. Schettler, Y. Goto, Y. Hata, and G. Klose, eds.), pp. 278–280. Springer-Verlag, New York.
Bortz, W. M. (1968). *Circ. Res.* **22**, 135–139.
Bounhoure, J. P., Fauvel, J. M., Puel, J., Sabot, G., and Miguel, J. P. (1983). *Arch. Mal. Couer.* **76**, 97–102.
Brownlee, M., and Cahill, G. F., Jr. (1979). *Atheroscler. Rev.* **4**, 29–70.
Brozek, J., Wells, S., and Keyes, A. (1946). *Am. Rev. Sov. Med.* **4**, 70.
Buchwald, H., Rucker, R. D., Moore, R. B., and Varco, R. L. (1980). *In* "Atherosclerosis V" (A. M. Gotto, L. C. Smith, and B. Allen, eds.), pp. 735–738. Springer-Verlag, New York.
Buonassisi, V. (1973). *Exp. Cell Res.* **76**, 363–368.
Burch, J. W., Stanford, N., and Majeries, P. W. (1978). *J. Clin. Invest.* **61**, 314–319.

Busch, C., Dawes, D. S., Wasteson, P., and Wasteson, A. (1979). *Thromb. Haemost.* **42,** 43.
Castelli, W. P. (1982). *Am. J. Forensic Med. Pathol.* **3**(4), 323–327.
Castelli, W. P. (1983). *Am. Heart J.* **106,** 1191–1200.
Castellot, J. J., Jr. (1981). *J. Cell Biol.* **90,** 372–379.
Chamley-Campbell, J. H., Campbell, G. R., and Ross, R. (1981). *J. Cell Biol.* **89,** 379–383.
Chobanian, A. V., Menzoian, J. O., Shipman, J., Heath, K., and Haudenschild, C. C. (1983). *Circ. Res.* **53,** 805–814.
Clowes, A. W., and Karnovsky, M. J. (1977). *Nature* **265,** 625–626.
Cohn, Z. A. (1978). *J. Immunol.* **121,** 813–816.
Cohn, Z. A., and Wiener, E. (1963). *J. Exp. Med.* **118,** 991–1008.
Constantinides, P. (1965). In "Experimental Atherosclerosis," p. 42. Elsevier Publishers, Amsterdam.
Constantinides, P., Booth, J., and Carlson, G. (1960). *Arch. Pathol.* **70,** 712–724.
Cotta-Pereira, G., Sage, H., Bornstein, P., Ross, R., and Schwartz, S. M. (1980). *J. Cell Physiol.* **102,** 183–191.
Daoud, A. S., Fritz, K. E., Jarmolych, J., and Augustyn, J. M. (1973). *Exp. Mol. Pathol.* **18,** 177–189.
Daoud, A. S., Jarmolych, J., Augustyn, J. M., Fritz, K. E., Singh, J. K., and Lee, K. T. (1976). *Arch. Pathol. Lab. Med.* **100,** 372–379.
Daoud, A. S. Fritz, K. E., Jarmolych, J., Augustyn, J. M., and Mawhinney, T. M. (1977). In "Atherosclerosis. Metabolic and Clinical Aspects" (G. W. Manning and M. D. Haust, eds.), pp. 928–933. Plenum Publishing Corp., New York.
Daoud, A. S., Jarmolych, J., Augustyn, J. M., and Fritz, K. E. (1981). *Arch. Pathol. Lab. Med.* **105,** 233–239.
Davies, P. F., and Ross, R. (1978). *J. Cell Biol.* **79,** 663–671.
De Palma, R. G., Hubay, C. A., and Insull, W., Jr. (1970). *Surg. Gynecol. Obstet.* **131,** 633–647.
Dock, W. (1946). *J.A.M.A.* **131,** 875–878.
Duff, G. L., and McMillan, G. C. (1951). *Am. J. Med.* **11,** 92.
Duffield, R. G., Miller, N. E., Jamieson, C. W., and Lewis, B. (1982). *Br. J. Surg.* **69,** 3–5.
Duffield, R. G., Lewis, B., Miller, N. E., Jamieson, C. W., Brunt, J. N., and Colchester, A. C. (1983). *Lancet* **2,** 639–642.
Duguid, J. B. (1949). *Lancet* **2,** 925–927.
Durant, R. H., Linder, C. W., and Jay, S. (1982). *J. Adolesc. Health Care* **3,** 75–78.
Eder, H. A., and Gidez, L. E. (1982). *Med. Clin. North Am.* **66,** 431–440.
Eggen, D. A., and Solberg, L. A. (1968). *Lab. Invest.* **18,** 571–579.
Eggen, D. A., Strong, J. P., and Newman, W. P., III. (1974). *Lab. Invest.* **31,** 294–301.
Eilersen, P., and Faber, M. (1960). *Arch. Pathol.* **70,** 103–107.
Engelberg, H. (1977). *Fed. Proc.* **36,** 70–72.
Enger, S. C., Herbjornsen, K., and Erikson, J. (1977). *Scan. J. Clin. Lab. Invest.* **37,** 251.
Feo, F., Canuto, R. A., Torrielli, M. V., Garcea, R., and Dianzani, M. U. (1976). *Agents and Actions* **6,** 135–142.
Fielding, C. J., Vlodavsky, I., Fielding, P. E., and Gospadarowicz, D. (1979). *J. Biol. Chem.* **254,** 8861–8868.
Fischer-Dzoga, K. (1979). *Artery* **5,** 222–236.
Fischer-Dzoga, K., and Wissler, R. W. (1976). *Atherosclerosis* **24,** 515–525.
Fischer-Dzoga, K., Fraser, R., and Wissler, R. W. (1976). *Exp. Mol. Pathol.* **24,** 346–359.
Freedman, S. B., Richmond, D. R., and Kelly, D. T. (1982). *Am. J. Cardiol.* **50,** 711–715.
Friedman, M., and Byers, S. O. (1963). *Am. J. Pathol.* **43,** 349–354.

Fritz, K. E., Augustyn, J. M., Jarmolych, J., Daoud, A. S., and Lee, K. T. (1976). *Arch. Pathol. Lab. Med.* **100**, 380–385.
Fritz, K. E., Augustyn, J. M., Jarmolych, J., and Daoud, A. S. (1981a). *Arch. Pathol. Lab. Med.* **105**, 240–246.
Fritz, K. E., Daoud, A. S., and Jarmolych, J. (1981b). *Fed. Proc.* **40**, 351.
Fritz, K. E., Daoud, A. S., and Jarmolych, J. (1982). *Fed. Proc.* **41**, 452.
Fry, D. L. (1974). *Ciba Found. Symp.* **12**, 93.
Furchgott, R. F. (1983). *Circ. Res.* **53**, 557.
Fuster, V., and Chesebro, J. H. (1981). *Mayo Clin. Proc.* **56**, 265–273.
Gadjusek, C. M., Dicorleto. P., Ross, R., and Schwartz, S. M. (1980). *J. Cell Biol.* **85**, 467–472.
Garfield, R. E., Chacka, S., and Blose, S. (1975). *Lab. Invest.* **33**, 418–427.
Gasilin, V. S., Sidorenko, B. A., Sidelnikova, T. I. A., Lupanov, V. P. and Sergeeva, L. N. (1983). *Kardiologiia* **23**, 74–79.
Geer, J. C., and Haust, M. D. (1972). *Mongr. on Atheroscler.* **2**, 361.
Geer, J. C., McGill. H. C., and Strong, J. P. (1968). *Am. J. Pathol.* **38**, 263–287.
Gerrity, R. G. (1981a). *Am. J. Pathol.* **103**, 181–190.
Gerrity, R. G. (1981b). *Am. J. Pathol.* **103**, 191–200.
Glagov, S., and Zarins, C. K. (1983). *In* "Clinical Diagnosis of Atherosclerosis" (M. G. Bond, W. Insull, Jr., S. Glagov, A. B. Chandler, and J. F. Cornhill, eds.), pp. 11–35 Springer-Verlag, New York.
Glenn, K. C., and Ross, R. (1981). *Cell* **25**, 603–615.
Glueck, C. J. (1982). *Ann. Intern. Med.* **96**, 475–482.
Gold, L. I., and Pearlstein, E. (1980). *Biochem. J.* **186**, 551–559.
Goldstein, J. L., and Brown, M. S. (1975). *Arch. Pathol. Lab. Med.* **99**, 181–184.
Goldstein, J. L., and Brown, M. S. (1977). *Annu. Rev. Biochem.* **46**, 897–930.
Goodale, F., Daoud, A. S., Florentin, R., Lee, K. T., and Gittelsohn, A. (1962). *Exp. & Mol. Pathol.* **1**, 353–363.
Gospodarowicz, D., Brown, K. D., Birdwell, C. R., and Zetter, B. R. (1978). *J. Cell Biol.* **77**, 774–788.
Gottlieb, A. I., and Spector, W. (1981). *Am. J. Pathol.* **103**, 271–282.
Gross, L., Epstein, E. Z., and Kugel, M. A. (1934). *Am. J. Pathol.* **10**, 253–274.
Hardin, N. J., Minick, R., and Murphy, G. E. (1973). *Am. J. Pathol.* **73**, 301–325.
Haust, M. D. (1971). *Human Pathol.* **1**, 1–29.
Hayes, L. W., Goguen, C. A., Stevens, A. L., Magaral, W. W., and Slakey, L. L. (1979). *Proc. Natl. Acad. Sci. U.S.A.* **76**, 2532–2535.
Haynes, S. G., Feinlieb, M., and Kannel, W. B. (1978). *Am. J. Epidemiol.* **107**, 384–402.
Hegsted, D. M., McGandy, R. B., Myers, M. L., and Stare, F. J. (1965). *Am. J. Clin. Nutr.* **17**, 281–295.
Heideman, C. L., and Hoff, H. F.(1982). *J. Biochim. Biophys. Acta* **711**(3) 431–444.
Hollander, W., Columbo, M. A., Kramsch, D. M., and Kirkpatrick, B. (1974a). *Adv. Cardiol.* **13**, 192–207.
Hollander, W., McCombs, H. L., Franzblau, C., Kirkpatrick, B., and Schmid, K. (1974b). *Circulation* **50**(Suppl. III), 93.
Holman, R. L., McGill, H. C., Strong, J. P., and Geer, J. C. (1959). *Am. J. Pathol.* **34**, 209–235.
Hoover, R. L., Folger, R., Haering, W. A., Ware, B. R., and Karnovsky, M. J. (1980). *J. Cell Sci.* **45**, 73–86.
Hope, W., Martin, T. J., Chesterman, C. N., and Morgan, F. J. (1979). *Nature* **282**, 210–212.

Horlick, L., and Katz, L. N. (1949). *J. Lab. Med.* **34,** 1427–1442.
Hudson, K., and Day, A. L. (1982). *Atherosclerosis* **45,** 109–113.
Hueper, W. C. (1944). *Arch. Pathol. Lab. Med.* **38,** 162, 245, 350.
Huttner, I., Boutet, M., and More, R. H. (1973). *Lab. Invest.* **28,** 672–677.
Illingworth, D. R. (1983). *Circulation* **68**(Suppl. III), 188.
Issekutz, T. B., Issekutz, A. C., and Movat, H. C. (1981). *Am. J. Pathol.* **103,** 47–55.
Iverius, P. H. (1977). *In* "Atherogenesis Initiating Factors," Ciba Symposium 12, pp. 185–196. Elsevier, Amsterdam.
Ives, H. E., Schultz, G. S., Galardy, R. E., and Jamieson, J. D. (1978). *J. Exp. Med.* **148,** 1400–1413.
Jaffe, E. A., and Weksler, B. R. (1979). *J. Clin. Invest.* **63,** 532–535.
Jaffe, E. A., Hoyer, L. W., and Nachman, R. L. (1973). *J. Clin. Invest.* **52,** 2757–2764.
Jaffe, E. A., Minick, C. R., Adelman, B., Becker, C. G., and Nachman, R. (1976). *J. Exp. Med.* **144,** 209–225.
Jarmolych, J., Daoud, A. S., Fritz, K. E., Augustyn, J. M., Singh, J. K., and Kim, D. N. (1978). *Arch. Pathol. Lab. Med.* **102,** 289–293.
Johansson, S., Rubin, K., Ahlgren, T., and Seljelid, R. (1979). *F.E.B.S. Letters* **105,** 213–216.
Jones, P. A., and Werb, Z. (1980). *J. Exp. Med.* **152,** 1527–1536.
Kahle, E. B., Walker, R. B., Eisenman, P. A., Behall, K. M., Hallfrisch, J., and Reiser, S. (1982). *Am. J. Clin. Nutr.* **35**(5), 950–957.
Kannel, W. B., Dawber, T. R., Friedman, G. D., Glennon, W. E., and McNamara, P. M. (1964). *Ann. Intern. Med.* **61,** 188–899.
Kannel, W. B., Wolf, P. A., Verter, J., and McNamara, P. M. (1970). *J.A.M.A.* **214,** 301–310.
Kannel. W. B., Castelli, W. P., and Gordon, T. (1979). *Ann. Intern. Med.* **90,** 85–91.
Karnovsky, M. J. (1981). *Am. J. Pathol.* **105,** 200–206.
Katsumura, T., Mishima, Y., Kamiya, K., Sakaguchi, S., Tanabe, T., and Sakuma, A. (1982). *Angiology* **33**(6), 357–367.
Keeley, F. W., and Partridge, S. M. (1974). *Atherosclerosis* **19,** 287–296.
Keen, H., and Jarrett, J. (1975). "Complications of Diabetes" Yearbook Medical Publishers, Inc., Chicago, Illinois.
Kerwar, S. S., Nolan, J. C., Ridge, S. C., Oronsky, A. L., and Slakey, L. L. (1980). *Biochim. Biophys. Acta* **632,** 183–191.
Keys, A. (1970). *Circulation* **41**(Suppl. I), 1–211.
Kim, K. M. (1976). *Fed. Proc.* **35,** 156–162.
Klurfeld, D. M., Allison, M. J., Gerszten, E., and Dalton, H. P. (1979). *J. Med.* **10,** 49–64.
Klynstra, F. B., Bottcher, C. J. F., Van Melsen, J. A., and Van der Laan, E. J. (1967). *J. Atheroscler. Res.* **7,** 301–309.
Knight, L., Scheibel, R., Amplatz, K., Vacro, R. L., and Buchwald, L. (1972). *Surg. Forum* **23,** 141.
Koiwaya, Y., Makamura, M., Mitsutake, A., Tanaka, S., Takeshita, A. (1981). *Am. Heart J.* **101**(2), 143–149.
Kokatnur, M. G., Malcom, G. T., Eggen, D. A., and Strong, J. P. (1975). *Atherosclerosis* **21,** 195–203.
Kramsch, D. M., and Chan, C. T. (1975). *Fed. Proc.* **34,** 235.
Kramsch, D. M., Franzblau, C., and Hollander, W. (1971). *J. Clin. Invest.* **50,** 1666–1677.
Kulonen, E., and Potila, M. (1980). *Acta Pathol. Microbiol. Scand.* (C) **88,** 7–13.
Lamberson, H. V., Jr., and Fritz, K. E. (1974). *Arch. Pathol.* **98,** 9–16.
Larjava, H., Saarni, H., Tammi, M., Penttinen, R., and Ronnemaa, T. (1980). *Atherosclerosis* **35,** 135–143.

# 1. Atherosclerosis: Genesis and Prevention 35

Leren, P., Helgeland, A., Hjermann, I., and Holme, I. (1983). *Am. Heart J.* **106**, 1200–1206.
Levy, R. I. (1983). *Circulation*(Part II) **68**, 188.
Lewis, H. D., Davis, J. W., Archibald, D. G., Steinke, W. E., Smitherman, T. C., Doherty, J. M., III, Schnaper, H. W., Lewinter, M. M., Linares, E., Pouget, J. M., Sabharwal, S. C., Chesler, E., and De Mots, H. (1983). *N. Engl. J. Med.* **309**, 396–403.
Linder, D., and Gartler, S. M. (1965). *Am. J. Hum. Genetics* **17**, 212–220.
Lipid Research Clinics Program (1984a). *J.A.M.A.* **251**, 351–364.
Lipid Research Clinics Program (1984b). *J.A.M.A.* **251**, 365–374.
Love, S. H., Shannon, B. T., Myrvik, Q. N., and Lynn, W. S. (1979). *J. Reticuloendothel. Soc.* **25**, 269–282.
McCaughan, D. (1981). *Arch. Intern. Med.* **141**, 1428–1432.
NcCullagh, K. A., and Balian, G. (1975). *Nature* **258**, 73–75.
McGill, H. C., Jr. (1968). *Lab. Invest.* **18**, 560–564.
McGill, H. C., Jr. (1975). *In* "Atherosclerosis III" (G. Schlettler and A. Weizel, eds.), pp. 27–38. Springer-Verlag, New York.
McMillan, G. C., Horlick, L., and Duff, G. L. (1955). *Arch. Pathol. Lab. Med.* **59**, 63.
Mahley, R. W. (1983). *Arch. Pathol. Lab. Med.* **107**, 393–399.
Mahley, R. W., Innerarity, T. L., Brown, M. S., Ho, Y. K., and Goldstein, J. L. (1980). *J. Lipid Res.* **21**, 970–980.
Malmros, H. (1950). *Acta Med. Scand.* **246**, 137–153.
Marcus, A. J. (1983). *N. Engl. J. Med.* **309**, 1515–1516.
Martin, B. M., Gimbrone, M. A., Jr., Unanue, E. R., and Cotran, R. S. (1981). *J. Immunol.* **126**, 1510–1515.
Mattock, M. B., Slater, A. M., Fuller, J. H., Omer, T., El-Gohart, R., Redmond, S. D., and Keen, H. (1982). *Atherosclerosis* **45**(1), 67–79.
Merriless, M. J., and Scott, L. (1981). *Atherosclerosis* **39**, 147–161.
Miller, N. (1978). *Lipids* **13**, 914.
Mitchell, J. R. A., and Schwartz, C. J. (1965). Blackwell Scientific Publications, London.
Modrak, J. B., and Langner, R. O. (1980). *Atherosclerosis* **37**, 211–218.
Moncada, S., and Vane, J. R. (1979). *N. Engl. J. Med.* **300**, 1142–1147.
Moon, H. D. (1957). *Circulation* **16**, 263–267.
Moore, S. (1975). *Fed. Proc.* **34**, 875.
Moschowitz, E. (1950). *J.A.M.A.* **143**, 861–865.
Mustard, J. F., Glynn, M. F., Jorgensen, L., Nishizawa, E. E., Packham, M. A., and Roswell, H. C. (1968a). *In* "Progress in Biochemical Pharmacology" (L. J. Miras, A. N. Howard, and R. Paoletti, eds.), pp. 508–532. S. Karger, New York.
Mustard, J. F., Packham, M. A., Rowsell, H. C., and Jorgensen, L. (1968b). *Ann. NY Acad. Sci.* **149**, 848–859.
Mustard, J. F., Kinlough-Rathborne, R. L., and Packham, M. A. (1983). *Am. J. Med.* **74**(6A), 43–49.
Nash, D. T. (1982a). *Angiology* **33**(9), 594–602.
Nash, D. T. (1982b). *Postgrad. Med.* **72**(2), 207–211.
Nash, D. T., Gensini, G., and Esente, P. (1982). *Int. J. Cardiol.* **2**(1), 43–55.
Neufeld, H. N., Wagenvoort, C. A., and Edwards, J. E. (1962). *Lab. Invest.* **11**, 937–944.
Nikkila, E. A., Viikinkoski, P., and Valle, M. (1983). *Circulation* (Part II) **68**, 188.
Oberman, A., and Pitt, B. (1982). *Hosp. Pract.* **17**(10), 94A, 941J.
Olivecrona, T., Bengtsson, G., Marklund, S. E., Lindahl, U., and Hook, M. (1977). *Fed. Proc.* **36**, 60–65.
Oliver, M. F., Heady, J. A., Morris, J. N., and Cooper, J. (1980). *Lancet* **2**, 379–385.
Orchard, T. J., Becker, D. J., Bates, M., Kuller, L. H., and Drash, A. L. (1983). *Am. J. Epidemiol.* **118**(3), 326–327.

Paffenbarger, R. S. (1978). *Am. J. Epidemiol.* **108**, 161.
Pearson, T. A., Wary, A., Solez, K., and Heptinstall, R. H. (1975). *Am. J. Pathol.* **81**, 379–387.
Perlin, A. S. (1977). *Fed. Proc.* **36**, 106–109.
Pick, R., Stamler, J., and Rodbard, S. (1952). *Circulation* **6**, 858–861.
Pooling Project Research Group. (1978). *J. Chron. Dis.* **31**, 201–306.
Prior, J. T., and Ziegler, D. D. (1965). *Arch. Pathol.* **80**, 50–57.
Radhakrishnamurthy, B., Ruiz, H. A., Jr., and Berenson, G. S. (1977). *J. Biol. Chem.* **252**, 4831–4841.
Rifkin, B. R., Baker, R. L., Somerman, M. J., Pointon, S. E., Coleman, S. J., and Au, W. Y. W. (1980). *Cell Tissue Res.* **210**, 493–500.
Rimm, A. A., Hoffman, R. G., Anderson, A. J., Gruchow, H. W., and Barboriak, J. J. (1983). *Prev. Med.* **12**(2), 262–273.
Robertson, J. H. (1960). *Arch. Dis. Child.* **35**, 588–590.
Roberston, W. B., Geer, J. C., Strong, J. P., and McGill, H. C., Jr. (1963). *Exp. Mol. Pathol.* **1**(Suppl. I), 28–39.
Rokitansky, C. (1841). *In* "Handbuch der Pathologischen Anatomie"
Rosenman, R. H., Brand, R. J., Jenkins, C. D., Friedman, M., Straus, R., and Wurm, M. (1975). *J.A.M.A.* **233**, 872–877.
Rosenman, R. H., Brand, R. J., Sholtz, R. I., and Friedman, M. (1976). *Am. J. Card.* **37**, 903–910.
Ross, R. (1981). *Arteriosclerosis* **1**, 293–311.
Ross, R., and Glomset, J. A. (1976). *N. Engl. J. Med.* **295**, 420–425.
Ross, R., and Harker, L. (1976). *Science* **193**, 1094–1100.
Ross, R., and Vogel, A. (1978). *Cell* **14**, 203–210.
Ross, R., Raines, E., and Bowen-Pope, D. (1982). *Ann. NY Acad. Sci.* **397**, 18–24.
Rudel, L. L., Shah, R., and Greene, D. G. (1979). *J. Lipid Res.* **20**, 55–65.
Ryan, U. S., Schultz, D. R., and Ryan, J. W. (1981). *Science* **214**, 557–558.
Saba, T. M., and Jaffe, E. A. (1980). *Am. J. Med.* **68**, 577–594.
Sage, H., Crouch, E., and Bornstein, P. (1979). *Biochemistry* **18**, 5433–5442.
Sage, H., Pritzl, P., and Bornstein, P. (1981). *Biochemistry* **20**, 436–442.
Schaffner, T., Taylor, K., Bartucci, E. J., Fischer-Dzoga, K., Beeson, J. H., Glagov, S., and Wissler, R. W. (1980). *Am. J. Pathol.* **100**, 57–80.
Schechter, I., Fogelman, A. M., Haberland, M. E., Seager, J., Hokom, M., and Edwards, P. A. (1981). *J. Lipid Res.* **22**, 863–871.
Schwandt, P., and Weisweiler, P. (1980). *Atherosclerosis* **35**(3), 301–306.
Schwartz, S. M., Gajdusek, C. M., and Selden, S. C., III. (1981). *Arteriosclerosis* **1**, 107–126.
Schwertner, H. A., Troxler, R. G., Whl, G. S., and Jackson, W. G. (1984). *Arteriosclerosis* **4**, 59–64.
Scott, R. F., Florentin, R. A., Daoud, A. S., Morrison, E. S., Jones, R. M., and Hutt, M. S. R. (1966). *Exp. Mol. Pathol.* **5**, 12–42.
Scott, R. F., Thomas, W. A., Lee, W. M., Reiner, J. M., and Florentin, R. A. (1970a). *Atherosclerosis* **34**, 291–301.
Scott, R. F., Thomas, W. A., Reiner, J. M., and Florentin, R. A. (1979b). *Exp. Mol. Pathol.* **31**, 145–153.
Seplowitz, A. H., Smith, F. R., Berns, L., Eder, H. H., and Goodman, D. S. (1981). *Atherosclerosis* **39**(1), 35–43.
Sholley, M. M., Gimbrone, M. A., and Cotran, R. S. (1977). *Lab. Invest.* **36**, 18–25.
Simionescu, N., Simionescu, M., and Palade, G. E. (1975). *J. Cell Biol.* **64**, 586–607.
Simpson, C. F. (1977). *Artery* **3**, 210–217.

# 1. Atherosclerosis: Genesis and Prevention

Sirtori, C. R., Gianfranceschi, G., Sirtori, M., Bernini, F., Descovich, G., Montaguti, U., Fuccella, L. M., and Musatti, L. (1981). *Atherosclerosis* **38**(3–4), 267–271.
Stary, H. C. (1979). *Virchows Arch. Pathol. Anat.* **383**, 117–134.
St. Clair, R. W., Clarkson, T. B., and Loland, H. B. (1972). *Circ. Res.* **31**, 664–671.
Steinman, R. M., and Cohn, Z. A. (1974). *In* "The Inflammatory Process" (B. W. Zweifach, L. Grant, and R. T. McClusky, eds.), pp. 449–510. Academic Press, New York.
Stevens, R. L., Colombo, M., Gonzales, J. J., Hollander, W., and Schmid, K. (1976). *J. Clin. Invest.* **58**, 470–481.
Stivala, S. S. (1977). *Fed. Proc.* **36**, 83–88.
Strom, A., and Jensen, R. A. (1951). *Lancet* **1**, 126.
Strong, J. P. (1969). *J. Atheroscler. Res.* **10**, 303–317.
Strong, J. P., and McGill, H. C., Jr. (1962). *Am. J. Pathol.* **40**, 37–49.
Strong, J. P., and McGill, H. C., Jr., (1969). *J. Atheroscler. Res.* **9**, 215–265.
Tanimura, A., McGregor, D. H., and Anderson, H. C. (1983). *Proc. Soc. Exp. Biol. Med.* **172**, 173–177.
Tejada, C., Strong, J. P., Montenegro, M. R., Restrepo, C., and Solberg, L. A. (1968). *Lab. Invest.* **18**, 509–526.
Texon, M. (1974). *Med. Clin, N. Am.* **58**, 257–268.
Thomas, W. A., and Kim, D. N. (1983). *Lab. Invest.* **48**(3), 245–255.
Thomas, W. A., Florentin, R. A., Nam, S. C., Jones, R. M., and Lee, K, T. (1968). *Arch. Pathol. Lab. Med.* **86**, 621–643.
Thomas, W. A., Lee, K. T., and Rabin, E. R. (1956). *Arch. Intern. Med.* **98**, 489–494.
Thomas, W. A., Janakidevi, K., Florentin, R. A., and Reiner, J. M. (1978a). *In* "State of Prevention and Therapy in Human Arteriosclerosis and in Animal Models" (W. H. Hauss, R. W. Wissler, and R. Lehman, eds.), pp. 73–80. Westdeutscher-Verlag, Germany.
Thomas, W. A., Scott, R. F., Lee, W. M., Florentin, R. A., and Reiner, J. M. (1978b). *Exp. Mol. Pathol.* **29**, 371.
Thorgeirsson, G., Robertson, A. L., Jr., and Cowan, D. H. (1979). *Lab. Invest.* **41**, 51–62.
Traber, M. G., and Kayden, H. J. (1980). *Proc. Natl. Acad. Sci.* **77**, 5466–5470.
Unanue, E. R. (1976). *Am. J. Pathol.* **83**, 396–417.
Unkeless, J. C., Gordon, S., and Reich, E. (1974). *J. Exp. Med.* **139**, 834–850.
United States Department of Health, Education and Welfare, Public Health Service, Office of the Assistant Secretary for Health, Office of Smoking and Health. (1979). [DHEW Publication No. (PHS) 79-50066].
United States Department of Health, Education and Welfare, Public Health Service, Office of the Assistant Secretary for Health, Office of Smoking and Health. (1980). [DHEW Publication No. (PHS) 80-50057].
Van de Water, L., III, Schroeder, S., Crenshaw, E. B., III, and Hynes, R. O. (1981). *J. Cell Biol.* **90**, 32–39.
Variainen. E., and Kanerva, K. (1947). *Ann. Med. Biol. Fenn.* **36**, 748.
Vessby, B., Lithell, H., Gustafsson, I. B., and Boberg, J. (1980). *Atherosclerosis* **35**(1), 51–65.
Vesselinovitch, D., Wissler, R. W., Fisher-Dzoga, K., Hughes, R., and Dubien, L. (1974). *Atherosclerosis* **19**, 259–275.
Vesselinovitch, D., Wissler, R. W., Hughes, R., and Borensztajn, J. (1976). *Atherosclerosis* **23**, 155–176.
Viikari, J., Akerblom, H. K., Nikkari, T., Rasanen, L., Vudri, I., Pyorala, K., Dahl, M., Lahde, P. L., Pesonen, E., Sudninen, P., and Uhari, M. (1982). *Ann. Clin. Res.* **14**(2), 103–110.

Villiger, B., Kelley, D. G., Engleman, W., Kuhn, C., III, and McDonald, J. A. (1981). *J. Cell Biol.* **90**, 711–720.
Virchow, R. (1858). *In* "Die Cellularpathologie in Ihrer Bergrundung and Physiologische und Pathologische Gewebelehre."
Vlodaver, Z., Kahn, H. A., and Neufeld, H. N. (1969). *Circulation* **39**, 541–550.
Vlodavsky, I., Fielding, P. E., Fielding, C. J., and Gospodarowicz, D. (1978). *Proc. Natl. Acad. Sci.* **75**, 356–360.
Vroulis, G., Smith, R. C., Schoolar, J. C., Dahlen, G., Katz, E., and Misra, C. H. (1982). *Am. J. Psychiatry* **139**(12), 1633–1634.
Wagner, W. D., and Clarkson, T. B. (1977). *Atherosclerosis* **27**, 369–381.
Wagner, W. D., Clarkson, T. B., and Foster, J. (1977). *Atherosclerosis* **27**, 419–435.
Wagner, W. D., Clarkson, T. B., and Foster, J. (1980). *Exp. Mol. Pathol.* **32**, 162–174.
Wanscher, O., Clemmesen, J., Nielson, A. (1951). *Brit. J. Cancer* **5**, 172–174.
Werb, Z., and Gordon, S. (1975a). *J. Exp. Med.* **142**, 346–360.
Werb, Z., and Grodon, S. (1975b). *J. Exp. Med.* **142**, 361–377.
Werb, Z., Banda, M. J., and Jones, P. A. (1980). *J. Exp. Med.* **152**, 1340–1357.
West, K. M. (1978). *In* "Epidemiology of Diabetes and its Vascular Lesions." Elsevier, New York.
W. H. O. European Collaborative Group (1980). *Eur. Heart J.* **1** 73–80.
Wight, T. N. (1980a). *Am. J. Pathol.* **101**, 127–142.
Wight, T. N. (1980b). *In* "Progress in Hemostasis and Thrombosis" (H. Spaet, ed.), 5th edition, pp. 1–39. Grune and Stratton, New York.
Wight, T. N., and Ross, R. (1975). *J. Cell Biol.* **67**, 675–686.
Wilens, S. L. (1974). *Am. J. Pathol.* **23**, 293–804.
Wissler, R. W., and Vesselinovitch, D. (1976). *Ann. NY Acad. Sci.* **275**, 363–378.
Yamada, K. M., Kennedy, D. W., Kimata, K., and Pratt, R. M. (1980). *J. Biol. Chem.* **255**, 6055–6063.

# 2 Hemodynamic Consequences of Myocardial Infarction and the Role of Vasodilators in Acute and Chronic Management

Dennis W. Wahr and Kanu Chatterjee

## I. Introduction

The most common clinically significant hemodynamic consequence of acute myocardial infarction is the development of a low output state. In the absence of rhythm abnormalities, left ventricular failure is the most common cause of the low output state. However, right ventricular infarction, acute papillary muscle rupture or dysfunction, ventricular septal rupture, or hypovolemia are less common, but important, potential causes. There are a number of compensatory mechanisms that attempt to restore normal circulatory hemostasis. Adverse hemodynamic results of these compensatory mechanisms include inappropriate elevation of systemic vascular resistance (afterload) and/or elevated pulmonary venous pressure (preload). While the potential benefits of vasodilation in the treatment of heart failure were recognized more than 40 years ago (Sarnoff and Farr, 1944; Burch, 1956; Judson *et al.*, 1956), major clinical interest did not develop until the late 1970s, when accurate invasive bedside hemodynamic monitoring was available (Swan *et al.*, 1970; Forrester *et al.*, 1972). Marked improvement in cardiac performance was demonstrated by several researchers in patients with acute and chronic heart failure during vasodilator therapy (Taylor *et al.*, 1965; Gould *et al.*, 1970b; Franciosa *et al.*, 1972; Chatterjee *et al.*, 1973a). Since then, vasodilator therapy of acute myocardial infarction has remained an area of intense clinical investigation. Today there is a large and expanding number of potent vasodilator agents. These agents have highly variable mechanisms of vasodilation and sites of action. The purpose of this chapter is to review the currently available vasodilator agents and their clinical application in the acute and chronic treatment of heart failure. The rational use of these agents necessitates a basic understanding of the pathophysiology of the low output state that may complicate myocardial infarction.

## II. Hemodynamic Consequences of Heart Failure

Heart failure is associated with low cardiac output, inadequate to meet metabolic demand. Clinically, the low cardiac output may be manifested by hypotension, reflex tachycardia, or manifestations of diminished organ perfusion, such as oliguria, mental obtundation, and cold, clammy skin. Low cardiac output is frequently accompanied by both elevated systemic vascular resistance (afterload) and by elevated pulmonary venous pressure (preload). Low cardiac output, without a compensatory increase in systemic vascular resistance, results in systemic hypotension, because blood pressure = cardiac output × systemic vascular resistance. However, blood pressure can be maintained in the presence of low output when the systemic vascular resistance is increased by a proportional amount. Patients with low cardiac output without increased preload may complain of fatigue, lack of energy, decreased exercise tolerance, but may not have "congestive" symptoms, (e.g, dyspnea, paroxysmal nocturnal dyspnea, or orthopnea). The frequently used term, "congestive heart failure," is associated with increased preload, which is the cause of the typical "congestive" symptoms. Increased preload is an important compensatory mechanism, because increased preload is associated with increased end-diastolic volume, which results in increased stroke volume, according to the Frank–Starling mechanism. However, increased end-diastolic volume is associated with elevated pulmonary and systemic venous pressures, accounting for congestive symptoms. An understanding of the hemodynamic mechanisms of the various symptoms of heart failure is necessary for employing rational therapy with vasodilating agents. Several mechanisms contribute to increased afterload and preload in heart failure.

### A. Mechanism of Increased Systemic Vascular Resistance

#### 1. Catecholamine Release

It is clear that circulating norepinephrine levels are markedly elevated in heart failure (Chatterjee and Parmley, 1983; Cohn, 1981; Thomas and Marks, 1978; Kubo et al., 1980). It has been postulated that this results primarily from spillover into the circulation of catecholamines released at the neuromuscular junction during neurogenic stimulation. It appears that the vasoconstriction that contributes to elevated systemic vascular resistance results from increased stimulation of vascular alpha receptors; extensive reviews of this mechanism have been published (Zelis and Flaim, 1982; Francis, 1985). There is currently considerable interest in determining how pharmacologic therapy of heart failure may affect the neurohumoral response, both at rest and during exercise (Francis et al., 1982; Minami et al., 1983). Presently, the potential clinical application of determination of catecholamines is unknown.

## 2. Angiotensin II

Angiotensin II contributes to elevated systemic vascular resistance in heart failure by means of a direct potent vasoconstrictor effect (Merril et al., 1946; Genest et al., 1968; Brown et al., 1970; Johnston et al., 1968; Gavras et al., 1977; Curtiss et al., 1979; Turini et al., 1979; Watkins et al., 1976; Dario, 1962). The precise mechanism for activation of the renin–angiotensin–aldosterone system in heart failure is not known. Increased renal sympathetic activity with beta-receptor stimulation, renal vasoconstriction with redistribution of cortical blood flow to the medullary glomeruli, and a reduction in perfusion pressure in the afferent arterioles—all can promote renin release from the juxtaglomerular apparatus. Irrespective of the mechanism, increased renin release is accompanied by increased levels of angiotensin II, which is a potent direct vasoconstrictor. Angiotensin also facilitates norepinephrine release at neuromuscular junctions and thus further contributes to the increase in systemic vascular resistance. Increased aldosterone levels promote salt and water retention with consequent elevation of preload (Ichikawa et al., 1985). In some patients with severe heart failure, angiotensin II contributes significantly to elevating systemic vascular resistance. When these patients are treated with angiotensin converting enzyme inhibitors, systemic vascular resistance decreases and renal function and cardiac function improve.

## 3. Vasopressin (antidiuretic hormone)

In many patients with chronic heart failure, a higher level of the hormone vasopressin has been observed (Zucker et al., 1977, 1979). The increase in vasopressin occurs despite cardiac dilatation and left atrial stretching, which usually inhibits the secretion of antidiuretic hormone. The significance of this increase is not apparent. However, it may contribute to plasma volume expansion and to the increase in systemic vascular resistance.

### 4. Increased Vascular Stiffness

Increased vascular stiffness in congestive heart failure has been considered an important contributing factor in elevating systemic vascular resistance (Zelis and Flaim, 1982; Fouad et al., 1982). Increased sodium content of blood vessels has been suggested as the possible mechanism for this stiffness, based on the observation that the vascular sodium content of large and small arteries of animals with heart failure is higher. Furthermore, increased tissue pressure, associated with apparent or subclinical edema, may also be contributory. Thus, there are several interacting mechanisms that may contribute to the elevation of systemic vascular resistance.

## B. Mechanism of Increase in Preload in Heart Failure

There are several mechanisms for the increase in preload in heart failure. The decrease in left ventricular function directly induces an increase in left ventricular end-diastolic volume, consequent upon decreased stroke volume and increased residual volume. This increase in diastolic volume may be accentuated by the increase in afterload, which may decrease left ventricular function further, leading to a vicious cycle. Intravascular volume is also increased by activation of the neuroadrenergic system, which can increase venous tone and increase venous return to the heart. Volume expansion is further increased by the activation of the renin–angiotensin–aldosterone system. The elevation in intraventricular and intracardiac volume, however, leads to elevation in systemic and pulmonary venous hypertension.

## C. "Low Output" in Acute Myocardial Infarction

### 1. Left Ventricular Infarction

Depression of left ventricular function is not uniform in patients with acute myocardial infarction. A wide range of changes in ejection fraction occurs, despite acute myocardial necrosis. When one determines global ejection fraction, it may remain normal in many patients, but a markedly depressed ejection fraction can be observed in others. Regional myocardial ejection fraction at the site of infarction, however, as expected, is virtually zero. Noninvolved myocardial segments are usually hypercontractile at the onset of myocardial infarction, which compensates for the loss of function of the infarcted myocardial segments and maintains a normal or near-normal global ejection fraction. With larger infarction, global ejection fraction declines, despite hypercontractility of the normal myocardium, because of inadequate compensation. A new but relatively small myocardial infarction in a patient with previous infarction may cause marked reduction in global ejection fraction and precipitate pump failure. The severity of pump failure is related to the total extent of nonfunctioning or hypofunctioning myocardium.

As the change in ejection fraction after acute myocardial infarction is variable, the hemodynamic consequences are also variable and nonuniform. In many patients, no hemodynamic abnormalities are detected; in others profound hypotension, low cardiac output, and markedly elevated ventricular filling pressures accompany acute myocardial infarction.

The initial hemodynamics soon after the onset of myocardial infarction (within 72 hr), in a group of patients with acute myocardial infarction, are summarized in Table I. Based on initial cardiac output and pulmonary capillary wedge pressure, the patients were divided into three groups. In Group I patients, cardiac output and pulmonary capillary wedge pressure were within the normal range. Clinical evidence of pump failure was absent in these patients. In patients in Group II, pulmonary capillary wedge pressure was elevated, along with tachycardia. The average cardiac index was at the lower limit of normal. Clinically, these patients had symptoms and signs of pulmonary venous hypertension with or without features of diminished organ perfusion. The patients in Group III had clinical features of diminished organ perfusion, and about half of these patients had clinical cardiogenic shock, as well as pulmonary congestion. The hemodynamic abnormalities were also most severe in this group: pulmonary capillary wedge pressure was markedly elevated and cardiac

**TABLE I**

Hemodynamic Profile in Left Ventricular Infarction

|  | Group I[a] | Group II[a] | Group III[a] |
|---|---|---|---|
| Number of patients | 9 | 14 | 15 |
| Heart rate (beats/min) | 88 ± 6.7 | 93 ± 3.2 | 100 ± 3.3 |
| Mean arterial pressure (mm Hg) | 92 ± 1.6 | 101 ± 3.6 | 83 ± 2.2 |
| Mean pulmonary capillary wedge pressure (mm Hg) | 11 ± 0.7 | 22 ± 0.9 | 27 ± 3.1 |
| Cardiac index (Liters/min/m$^2$) | 2.7 ± 0.18 | 2.5 ± 0.17 | 1.7 ± 0.12 |
| Systemic vascular resistance (dynes/sec/cm$^{-5}$) | 1517 ± 124 | 1744 ± 163 | 1768 ± 1290 |

[a] Group I, no clinical heart failure; Group II, patients with pulmonary congestion; Group III, patients with severe pump failure.

index was very low. Low cardiac index was associated with tachycardia and elevated systemic vascular resistance. In many patients mean arterial pressure was maintained, despite low cardiac output, presumably due to elevated systemic vascular resistance. It is apparent that the severity of hemodynamic abnormalities and depression of cardiac function is not uniform in all patients with acute myocardial infarction.

Determination of hemodynamic abnormalities is helpful for rational therapy. In patients with normal cardiac output and pulmonary venous pressure (Group I), no specific therapy is required until a complication such as angina or low output state occurs. In patients with high pulmonary venous pressure, but with normal cardiac output (Group II), diuretics and venodilators (nitroglycerin and nitrates) are appropriate therapy. If cardiac output is also low, vasodilators with combined arteriolar and venodilating effects (nitroprusside) are preferable, provided hypotension is not present and systemic vascular resistance is elevated. In patients with hypotension, vasopressors, inotropic agents, and/or intra-aortic balloon, counterpulsation should be instituted before vasodilator therapy is begun.

## 2. Right Ventricular Infarction

Right ventricular infarction occurs almost exclusively in patients with inferior or inferoposterior myocardial infarction secondary to proximal occlusion of the right coronary artery (Haupt et al., 1983). Pathologic data suggest that up to one-third of all patients who have inferior myocardial infarction also have involvement of the right ventricle, but only 5% develop clinically significant hemodynamic deterioration (Lorell et al., 1979; Wartman and Hellerstein, 1948). In patients with pre-existent structural heart disease, such as pulmonary artery hypertension or atrial septal defect, the hemodynamic complications are more common (Ratliff and Hackel, 1980; Rietveld et al., 1983). Noninvasive tests, such as electrocardiography, employing the $V_3R$ and $V_4R$ lead (Candell-Riera et al., 1981; Klein et al., 1983), $Tc_{99m}$ myocardial scintigraphy (Wackers et al., 1978), two-dimensional echocardiography (Sharpe et al., 1978), or nuclear wall motion studies (Rigo et al., 1975) can be employed to diagnose right ventricular infarction with good sensitivity in the majority of patients suffering inferior wall infarction (Baigrie et al., 1975). However, clinically significant right ventricular infarction, associated with low cardiac output, requires invasive hemodynamic monitoring for appropriate management.

The hemodynamic findings of right ventricular infarction are well described (Lorell et al., 1979). The most frequent hemodynamic abnormality is disproportionate elevation of right atrial pressure compared to pulmonary capillary wedge pressure. In severe right ventricular infarction, an acute increase in right ventricular end-diastolic volume occurs (Goldstein et al., 1982). Because the pericardium is a stiff membrane characterized by a relatively steep pressure–volume relationship, an acute increase in intrapericardial pressure may occur. This increased intrapericardial pressure may result in equalization of diastolic pressures and decreased left ventricular volume, similar to patients with constrictive pericarditis or cardiac tamponade. Right atrial pressure tracing may demonstrate a sharp Y descent and an increase with inspiration (Kussmaul's sign). Right ventricular pressure tracing demonstrates a "square root sign." Right ventricular systolic pressure may decrease and right ventricular stroke volume and stroke work index are typically decreased. These hemodynamic alterations ultimately lead to decreased cardiac output. The primary mechanism for decreased output is the reduction in left ventricular preload and reduced left ventricular diastolic size. The absolute left ventricular diastolic pressure may be elevated; however, left ventricular transmural pressure (diastolic pressure − intrapericardial pressure), the true filling pressure, is decreased.

It is apparent that the hemodynamics of right ventricular infarction may closely resemble that of cardiac tamponade, acute pulmonary embolism, or constrictive pericarditis. The differential diagnosis is dependent on the derived setting and appropriate use of diagnostic studies. Therapy will be discussed in a later section.

## 3. Ventricular Septal Rupture

Acute intraventricular septal rupture may complicate either transmural infarction of the inferior myocardial wall or transmural anterior-septal myocardial infarction (Vlodarer and Edwards, 1977). Ruptures of the septum with inferior myocardial infarction tend to be located in the basal portion of the septum, while ruptures associated with anterior infarction tend to be apical in location. In either case, the perforation tends to be single and can range in size from a millimeter to several centimeters. The size of the defect and the relative difference between systemic vascular and pulmonary vascular resistance are the major determinants of the magnitude of left-to-right shunt, and thus, the extent of hemodynamic deterioration (Synhorst et al., 1976). If the size of the defect is small, systemic vascular resistance is less important. If the ventricular septal defect is large, the magnitude of left-to-right shunt is primarily determined by the ratio of the pulmonary and systemic vascular resistance, as the ventricular septal defect itself offers minimal resistance to left-to-right shunt.

As with right ventricular infarction, hemodynamic monitoring of these patients is essential. The sudden, severe volume overload of the right and left ventricles, the greatly increased pulmonary artery flow, elevated pulmonary capillary wedge pressure, and rapidly declining systemic output are a catastrophic combination of events. Furthermore, it may be difficult on clinical grounds to distinguish between acute mitral regurgitation and rupture of the ventricular septum in patients who suddenly develop a loud systolic murmur (Meister and Helfant, 1972). A right heart catherization can readily distinguish between these two complications. Patients with ventricular septal defect will demonstrate a "stepup" in oxygen saturation in the right ventricle and pulmonary artery, compared to the right atrium. Patients with acute mitral regurgitation lack this stepup, but have a large V wave in the pulmonary capillary wedge pressure. Without appropriate, urgent therapy, mortality close to 100% can be expected. However, as opposed to patients with rupture of the free wall of the left ventricle, who die suddenly, these patients can often be stabilized with vasodilator therapy and/or intra-aortic balloon pumping to lower afterload, allowing enough time for definitive surgical correction. Hemodynamic pressure monitoring allows serial determination of intracardiac pressure, pulmonary vascular resistance, systemic vascular resistance, and left-to-right shunt ratio to guide therapy. Details of therapy will be discussed later.

### 4. Acute Papillary Muscle Rupture or Dysfunction

Papillary muscle infarction, with or without partial or complete rupture of a papillary muscle, is a rare but catastrophic complication of myocardial infarction. The posteromedial papillary muscle of the left ventricle is most commonly affected. This papillary muscle derives its blood supply from the right coronary artery and, thus, inferior infarction is the most common clinical setting for papillary muscle rupture. The anterolateral papillary muscle is supplied by the left coronary artery and, therefore, papillary muscle rupture is relatively less common. Rupture of a right ventricular papillary muscle is rare. The hemodynamic sequela of papillary muscle rupture is dependent on the extent of necrosis and rupture. If the entire trunk of the papillary muscle ruptures, mitral regurgitation will be massive and incompatible with life (Roberts and Cohen, 1972). Rupture of only a portion of the papillary muscle, or even infarction without rupture, may result in a severe, though not catastrophic, degree of regurgitation potential, which may be amenable to therapy (Roberts and Perloff, 1972; Wei et al., 1979).

Invasive hemodynamic monitoring is essential in this situation. Patients typically have severe elevation of the pulmonary capillary wedge pressure, with a prominent V wave and decreased cardiac output. Therapy includes vasodilator therapy and/or intra-aortic balloon therapy to lower afterload and improve forward output. As with ventricular septal defect, medical therapy is only supportive and surgical correction should be considered at the earliest possible time. Details of therapy will be discussed later.

### 5. *Hypovolemia*

Frank shock, as a result of hypovolemia, is an uncommon complication of acute myocardial infarction. When encountered, it is often seen in those patients with severe diaphoresis and vomiting at the onset of infarction, or in those who have received repeated doses of diuretics or nitrates. The hemodynamic abnormalities of hypovolemia are decreased right atrial and pulmonary capillary wedge pressures, as well as low cardiac output. Therapy is simple administration of fluid.

## III. Potential Benefits of Vasodilators in Congestive Heart Failure

### A. Afterload Reduction

Vasodilator therapy for low cardiac output is based on the principle of afterload reduction in the failing heart. As has been discussed previously, there are many mechanisms that may cause inappropriate elevation of afterload in heart failure. Studies of the mechanics of contraction of isolated heart muscle have shown that increasing the load against which a muscle shortens (afterload) will decrease the magnitude of shortening and the velocity of shortening (Sonnenblick, 1962). Conversely, if one reduces the afterload, the muscle shortens further and with greater velocity.

In the isolated heart muscle preparation, the concepts of preload and afterload are simple. Preload represents the initial load on the muscle that stretches it to its initial length before contraction. Afterload represents the additional load the muscle must lift as it shortens. In the intact heart, the accurate measurement of afterload requires calculation of wall stress throughout systole from measurement of intraventricular pressure, radius, and wall thickness (Ross, 1976; Peterson *et al.*, 1974). In clinical practice, such calculations are difficult to make. Therefore, the clinician is forced to use other approximations of afterload, all of which have limitations. These include aortic pressure, aortic impedance, and systemic vascular resistance.

### 1. *Arterial Pressure*

Arterial pressure is the most easily measured index of afterload in the intact heart, but it is also the most imprecise. Assuming no aortic outflow tract obstruction is present, the absolute arterial blood pressure is equal to left ventricular cavity pressure during systole. However, as mentioned above, intracavity pressure is only one of the variables that determines wall stress. Depending on the dynamic changes that occur in chamber radius and wall thickness with therapy, it is actually possible to have significant falls in afterload without any change in absolute arterial pressure. This has been observed clinically when initiation of vasodilator therapy causes significant increases in cardiac output without any fall in blood pressure. Nevertheless, arterial pressure is useful as a rough estimate of afterload and, within limits, increases in intraventricular systolic pressure are associated with decreased shortening of the left ventricular diameter during systole and with decreased mean velocity of circumferential shortening ($V_{cf}$) (Mahler *et al.*, 1975; Chatterjee *et al.*, 1971).

## 2. Aortic Input Impedance

Some investigators believe that the external force to ventricular ejection (afterload) is better represented by the aortic input impedance, which can be described by the relation of aortic pulsatile pressure and flow wave forms throughout the cardiac cycle (Patel *et al.*, 1963; Noble *et al.*, 1967; Nichols *et al.*, 1977; Murgo *et al.*, 1980). In general, "impedance" implies a mesure of the opposition to flow presented by a system and is a *frequency-dependent function*. "Resistance" conveys a meaning similar to impedance but is confined to *average or steady-state conditions*. In the arterial system, blood pressure and flow exist as pulsatile wave forms superimposed on a mean (or nonpulsatile) component. Thus, total opposition to arterial flow encompasses both frequency-dependent pulsatile components and a frequency-independent nonpulsative steady state component. "Aortic input impedance" is a measure of both components (Milnar, 1975; O'Rourke and Taylor, 1967; Pepine and Nichols, 1982; Nichols and Pepine, 1982).

The influence of each individual component of vascular load on ventricular ejection has been evaluated in experimental animals and human beings. Decreased arterial compliance (i.e., increased impedance) with constant resistance is associated with reduced stoke volume and mean aortic pressure (Elzinga and Westerhof, 1973). Increased resistance alone causes a decrease in stroke volume but increases mean aortic pressure. Careful consideration of these findings has important implications during vasodilator therapy of heart failure. Mean blood pressure may actually fall, despite an actual increase in afterload in some patients. Unless the changes in the arterial wave form (impedance) are analyzed, invalid conclusions concerning the hemodynamic effects of a drug can be made.

Aortic input impedance spectra were determined in patients with clinical and hemodynamic evidence of chronic heart failure and compared with those in subjects without heart failure, matched for age and arterial pressure. In patients with heart failure, both input resistance and characteristic impedance were significantly increased compared to normals (Pepine et al., 1978). It was also demonstrated that vasodilators like sodium nitroprusside can decrease characteristic impedance and increase ventricular ejection without changing arterial pressure (Pepine et al., 1979). These studies indicate that a vasodilator-induced increase in arterial compliance is a potentially important mechanism for improving left ventricular function. At the present time, the calculation of "aortic input impedance" is difficult and is not available for application to routine clinical practice.

### 3. Systemic Vascular Resistance (SVR)

Systemic vascular resistance is currently the preferred method for estimating afterload in clinical practice. It is less precise than aortic input impedance, because it ignores the dynamics of pulsatile flow and pressure but instead is only the average of this relation throughout the cardiac cycle. It is much easier to calculate systemic vascular resistance from measurement of the pressure drop across the arterial system and cardiac output. For the systemic arterial system, systemic vascular resistance (SVR) is calculated as follows: SVR = (mean arterial pressure − right atrial pressure)/cardiac output. Systemic vascular resistance is preferred as an estimate of afterload to simple blood pressure. The use of systemic vascular resistance calculation is important for evaluating response to vasodilator agents in patients with congestive heart failure (Chatterjee and Parmley, 1977). Reduction of systemic vascular resistance or aortic impedance appears to be the principal mechanism for the improvement of left ventricular function with vasodilators (Chatterjee and Parmley, 1977; Parmley and Chatterjee, 1978).

## B. Preload Reduction

As stated previously, increased preload is an important compensatory mechanism for increasing left ventricular function based on the Frank–Starling relationship. It is only when preload becomes inappropriately elevated that congestive symptomatology is initiated. It is, therefore, important that preload-reducing agents be avoided in heart failure in those patients with normal or only slightly elevated wedge pressures. Reduction of preload in these patients will tend to lower stroke volume as the ventricle moves down the ascending limb of the Frank–Starling curve. It is only in those patients with a very high preload and congestive symptomatology that preload reduction is important. At high filling pressures, the Frank–Starling curve is relatively flat and lowering the filling pressure serves to decrease congestion without decreasing forward output significantly.

Preload reduction can be achieved in several ways. Vasodilators with predominant effect on the venous system will acutely increase venous capacitance, leading to peripheral pooling of blood and decreased venous return to the heart, thus lowering preload. Vasodilators with a predominant effect on the arterial system can also decrease preload, if there is a marked increase in forward stroke volume and decrease in residual volume. Chronically, preload may be best controlled with liberal use of diuretic agents which, by decreasing intravascular volume, decrease venous return to the heart (Nelson et al., 1983).

## C. Relief of Myocardial Ischemia

It has been demonstrated that segmental reversible myocardial ischemia can contribute to decreased left ventricular function and that relief of ischemia is beneficial (McAnulty et al., 1975; Helfant et al., 1974; Klausner et al., 1976). The major determinants of myocardial oxygen consumption include contractility (inotropic state), intraventricular volume (preload), intraventricular pressure (afterload), and heart rate. Most vasodilators have been shown to have no inotropic effects. Heart rate tends not to change and, with the use of captopril and nitroprusside, may actually decline; preload and afterload are usually significantly decreased. Thus, the overall effect of vasodilator therapy is to lower the determinants of myocardial oxygen consumption. Some vasodilators may also increase regional myocardial perfusion by enhancing collateral blood flow to ischemic myocardial segments (daLuz et al., 1975; Becker et al., 1971). One can argue that while decreased afterload is advantageous in decreasing oxygen consumption, it may be disadvantageous because decreased arterial pressure may decrease coronary artery perfusion pressure and hence reduce oxygen supply to the myocardium. The interactions between these two antagonistic factors are important in determining the overall effect on the ischemic myocardium. The transmyocardial pressure gradient (arterial diastolic pressure − left ventricular diastolic pressure) is also an important determinant of myocardial perfusion. It has been demonstrated that reduction of elevated left ventricular end-diastolic pressure tends to enhance relative perfusion to the subendocardial layers of the myocardium by increasing the "transmyocardial pressure gradient" or by increasing collateral flow (Chiariello et al., 1976; Kirk et al., 1978).

In summary, vasodilators, if administered to patients with initially elevated preload and afterload, have the potential to decrease segmental myocardial ischemia by decreasing myocardial oxygen requirements or increasing myocardial perfusion, or both. This decreased myocardial ischemia may improve overall cardiac performance (Dunn et al., 1982; Parmley et al., 1976). Because of these potentially favorable effects on myocardial ischemia, vasodilator therapy is particularly attractive in the treatment of heart failure due to ischemic heart disease.

## D. Improvement in Diastolic Compliance

Another possible mechanism by which vasodilators can produce beneficial effects in patients with heart failure is by improving left ventricular diastolic compliance. The pressure–volume relationship of the left ventricle is curvilinear (Fig. 1), so that at small end-diastolic volumes, with increased compliance, a given volume increment will produce only a minor rise in ventricular diastolic pressure. At high end-diastolic volumes,

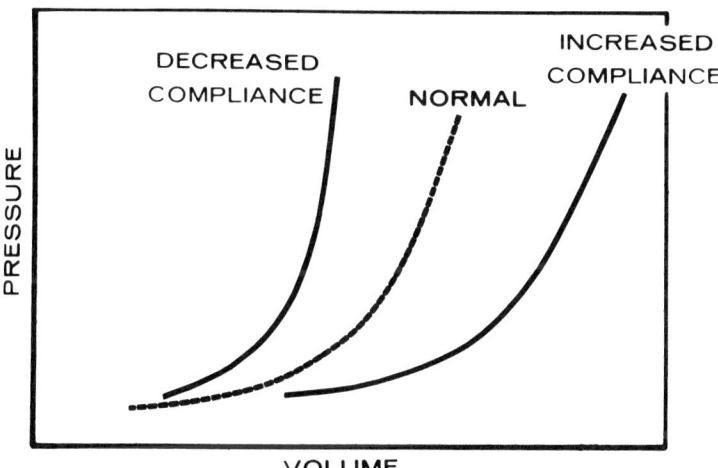

**Fig. 1.** Schematic diagrams of left ventricular diastolic pressure–volume relations. With a rightward shift of the diastolic pressure–volume curve, a larger volume at the same end-diastolic pressure results. As the end-diastolic volume, not the end-diastolic pressure, determines the changes in stroke volume, a rightward shift of the pressure–volume curve will cause a leftward shift of the left ventricular function curve. Vasodilators, nitroprusside or nitroglycerin, can cause an acute increase in left ventricular diastolic compliance.

typical of patients with heart failure, there is a greater increase in diastolic pressure with each volume increment. Because left ventricular end-diastolic volume is the most important determinant of stroke volume, it is apparent that a shift in compliance could markedly alter the relationship between filling pressure and cardiac performane. Thus, if the pressure–volume relation was shifted to the right, a larger volume at the same end-diastolic pressure would result. This would result in a leftward shift of the ventricular function curve.

The mechanism of improved diastolic compliance is controversial. Some investigators believe improved compliance is due to a reduction of ischemia by the vasodilator agents. Others feel that a more important factor is the interaction of right and left ventricular volumes within a confined pericardial space (Alderman and Glantz, 1976; Brodie *et al.*, 1977). Because the pericardium is a stiff structure, it tends to maintain a constant overall heart volume at high filling pressures. A vasodilator that lowers right heart pressure will also reduce the end-diastolic volume of the right ventricle and allow a larger left ventricular volume at the same left ventricular diastolic pressure. Thus, agents that lower right-sided pressures will tend to produce an apparent increase in the compliance of the left ventricle. In chronic, severe left ventricular failure, elevated right heart pressure is a frequent hemodynamic abnormality. This fact emphasizes the importance of treating these patients with drugs that have the potential to decrease right heart volume and pressure.

## IV. Classification and Mechanisms of Vasodilation

We have previously described various mechanisms that can lead to elevated vascular tone. It follows, therefore, that there are several pharmacological mechanisms by which vasodilation and subsequent reduction of systemic vascular resistance can be achieved. Vasodilator agents such as hydralazine, nitrates, and nitroprusside cause direct smooth muscle relaxation of the peripheral vascular bed. Other agents cause vasodilation by decreasing or inhibiting the vasoconstricting effects mediated by the sympathetic adrenergic nervous system. Clonidine decreases peripheral sympathetic outflow by stimulating the alpha-adrenergic receptors located in the central nervous system (Hermiller *et al.*, 1983). Drugs like phentolamine or prazosin cause vasodilation by peripheral alpha-adrenergic receptor blockade. Ganglionic blocking agents, trimethaphan or hexamethonium, also cause vasodilation and have been used for the treatment of heart failure. Stimulation of beta$_2$ receptors with salbutamol and pirbuterol is associated with peripheral vasodilation and decreased systemic vascular resistance. Drugs like nifedipine and verapamil decrease systemic vascular resistance and arterial pressure by inhibiting the inward calcium current to the smooth muscles of the peripheral vascular beds. Cyclic AMP (cAMP) is a potent mediator of smooth muscle relaxation in the vascular bed and its intracellular concentration can be increased by the administration of prostacylins, prostaglandins E, or dibutyryl cAMP (Matsui *et al.*, 1983). Saralasin is a competitive antagonist of angiotensin II. Teprotide, captopril, and enalapril decrease production of angiotensin II from angiotensin I by inhibiting angiotensin-converting enzyme. Attenuation or inhibition of the effects of angiotensin II are associated with arteriolar dilation, reduction of systemic vascular resistance, and a fall in arterial pressure.

While these agents can be grouped according to their primary mechanism of action, it should be emphasized that they have additional secondary effects that may contribute either to additional vasodilation or to adverse compensatory mechanisms that may seem to counteract the initial benefits of vasodilation. For this reason, each agent will be discussed individually in a subsequent section, and its relative role in the treatment of congestive heart failure will be critically assessed.

## V. Site of Action of the Vasodilators

In addition to the heterogeneous mechanisms of action of the various vasodilators, there is a clinically more relevant difference in their site of action on the peripheral vascular bed. Vasodilators such as nitroglycerin have a predominant action on the peripheral venous system, with little effect on systemic arteries. The expected hemodynamic changes with a venodilator include a decrease in pulmonary venous pressure (wedge pressure) and a fall in right atrial pressure. These changes are a direct result of an increase in the volume capacitance of the venous system and an effect of redistribution of the intravascular volume from the arterial system to the venous beds. This leads to improvement in "congestive symptomatology." The effects of these changes on cardiac output are variable. In the setting of high filling pressure, a reduction in filling pressure will occur along the flat portion of the ventricular function curve. Therefore, no reduction in stroke volume will occur. In contrast, with a normal initial filling pressure, a reduction in filling pressure will tend to lower stroke volume as the ventricle moves down the ascending limb of its curve. In such circumstances, hypotension and reflex tachycardia might occur.

Predominantly arterial vasodilators, such as hydralazine, decrease systemic vascular resistance and thereby increase stroke volume and cardiac output with little or no change in pulmonary venous pressure or right atrial pressure. Drugs such as captopril or prazosin seem to have a balanced effect and produce both arterial and venous vasodilation. With these agents, the net increase in stroke volume is necessarily less than that expected from their arteriolar dilating effects, because of the concomitant reduction of filling pressure related to venodilation. The important hemodynamic effects of commonly used vasodilators are summarized in Table II.

**TABLE II**

Important Hemodynamic Effects of Commonly Used Parenteral and Nonparenteral Vasodilators Used for Treatment of Heart Failure

| Vasodilator | Heart rate | Blood pressure | Cardiac output | Systemic and pulmonary venous pressures |
|---|---|---|---|---|
| Nitroprusside | No change or increase | Decrease or no change | Increase | Decrease |
| Phentolamine | Increase | Decrease or no change | Increase | Decrease |
| Nitroglycerin and nitrates | No change or increase | Decrease or no change | No change or slight increase | Decrease |
| Hydralazine and endralazine | No change or increase | Decrease or no change | Increase | No change or slight decrease |
| Minoxidil | No change or increase | Decrease or no change | Increase | No change or slight decrease |
| Prazosin and trimazosin | No change or increase | Decrease | Increase | Decrease |
| Captopril and enalapril | No change or decrease | Decrease | Increase | Decrease |
| Nifedipine | Increase or no change | Decrease | Increase | No change or decrease |
| Diltiazem | No change | Decrease or no change | Increase | Decrease or no change |

## VI. Vasodilator Agents: Pharmacology, Hemodynamics, and Side Effects

### A. Sodium Nitroprusside

Sodium nitroprusside is a potent vasodilator that causes relaxation of both the arteriolar resistance and the venous capacitance bed by a direct action of the free nitroprusside radical (nitroso moiety) on vascular smooth muscle. Nitroprusside solution must be administered only by slow intravenous infusion using a microdrip regulator to ensure pressure flow rate. Effective dosage varies between 0.5 µg/kg/min (35 µg/min) to 10.0 µg/kg/min (700 µg/min). In the treatment of heart failure, hemodynamic monitoring is mandatory during nitroprusside therapy. Changes in arterial and pulmonary capillary wedge pressures, cardiac output, and systemic vascular resistance should be determined. The hemodynamic effects of nitroprusside decline rapidly when the intravenous infusion is stopped because of its rapid metabolism to cyanide and subsequently to thiocyanate through the mediation of a hepatic enzyme, rhodanase. The rate of conversion from cyanide to thiocyanate is dependent on the availability of thiosulfate. Cyanide toxicity only occurs when thiosulfate supplies of the body are depleted and is thus very rare. The blood thiocyanate levels, however, do not reflect cyanide levels. The best screening test for cyanide toxicity is acid–base balance, as metabolic acidosis is the earliest and most reliable sign. Thiocyanate is generally a nontoxic compound that is excreted in the urine. However, if prolonged therapy is anticipated in patients with renal failure, serum thiocyanate levels should be monitored daily.

The hemodynamic effects of nitroprusside result from its balanced effect on the arteriolar resistance and systemic venous capacitance beds and are characterized by a significant reduction of systemic vascular resistance, an increase in cardiac output and stroke volume, and a concomitant decrease in systemic and pulmonary venous pressure. Systemic and pulmonary arterial pressures tend to decrease, while heart rate tends to remain unchanged (Chatterjee *et al.*, 1979; Franciosa *et al.*, 1972). Furthermore, it has been demonstrated (Chatterjee *et al.*, 1973a; Chatterjee and Parmley, 1977; Armstrong *et al.*, 1975) that the improvement in cardiac output is related to the initial elevation of the systemic vascular resistance and the pulmonary venous pressure (Fig. 2). Patients with initially normal pulmonary venous pressure may experience a further decrease in filling pressure and no change, or even a fall, in cardiac output. The lack of increase in cardiac output may also be observed in some patients with initially elevated pulmonary venous pressure, if it is

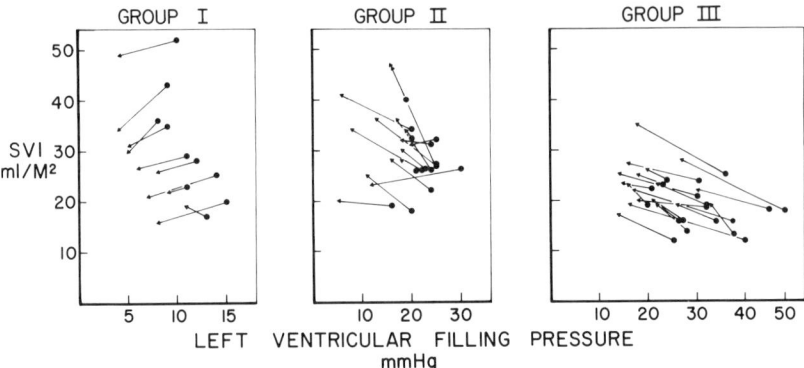

**Fig. 2.** Changes in stroke volume index (SVI) and left ventricular filling pressure with sodium nitroprusside in patients with acute myocardial infarction. In patients in Group I, with normal initial left ventricular pressure and no clinical evidence of heart failure, SVI decreased, along with decreased left ventricular filling pressure, indicating no improvement in left ventricular function. In patients in Group II and III, with initially elevated left ventricular filling pressure, and with clinical evidence of moderate (Group II) or severe (Group III) pump failure, SVI increased along with decreased left ventricular filling pressure, indicating improved left ventricular function. (From Chatterjee *et al.*, 1973.)

lowered to a very low level. It is essential, therefore, to determine the initial hemodynamics in order to identify the subset of patients likely to benefit from sodium nitroprusside therapy. The effects of sodium nitroprusside on coronary hemodynamics are varied. An increase in coronary blood flow due to a primary decrease in coronary vascular resistance has been reported (Cohn *et al.*, 1974a; Powers *et al.*, 1982). In contrast, a decrease in coronary blood flow, along with decreased myocardial oxygen demand, has also been observed (Chatterjee *et al.*, 1973a). These findings suggest that changes in coronary blood flow are likely to be determined not only by changes in coronary vascular resistance, but also by changes in the determinants of myocardial oxygen demand.

Changes in regional myocardial function, and the extent of myocardial injury during sodium nitroprusside therapy, in patients with acute myocardial infarction have been the subject of a number of investigations, resulting in conflicting reports. In some studies, an increase in infarct size was seen, and in other studies, a reduction of infarct size was observed (Awan *et al.*, 1976; Chiariello *et al.*, 1976; Gold *et al.*, 1976). The influence of this therapy on the mortality of patients with acute myocardial infarction has been evaluated in both prospective randomized studies and in uncontrolled studies (Chatterjee *et al.*, 1976c; Cohn *et al.*, 1982; Durrer *et al.*, 1982). Again, conflicting results have emerged. In some studies, decreased infarct size, along with improved prognosis, has been reported (Durrer *et al.*, 1982). In other studies, higher mortality with nitroprusside therapy has been reported (Cohn *et al.*, 1982). In patients with severe pump failure, the hospital mortality with sodium nitroprusside therapy appears to be lower than expected with conventional therapy (Chatterjee *et al.*, 1976c). However, the *long-term prognosis still remains unfavorable. At present, routine use of sodium nitroprusside therapy in patients with an acute myocardial infarction is not recommended.* It should be reserved for the treatment of severe pump failure complicating myocardial infarction.

Renal hemodynamics and function may be variably affected by nitroprosside, depending on whether or not heart failure and low cardiac output coexist. In the absence of heart failure, renal blood flow increases due to decreased renal vascular resistance, provided a marked fall in arterial pressure does not occur (Bastrow and Kalayanides, 1972). In patients with congestive heart failure, sodium nitroprusside increases renal blood flow and sodium and potassium excretion without any change in the glomerular filtration rate (Cogan *et al.*, 1979). However, marked reduction in arterial pressure may decrease glomerular filtration rate and sodium excretion and elevate plasma renin activity (Kaneho *et al.*, 1967). The side effects of sodium nitroprusside are primarily related to a marked fall in systemic blood pressure. Symptoms include those of end-organ hypoperfusion and include nausea, vomiting, sweating, restlessness, substernal distress, or myocardial ischemia. Therapy includes immediate discontinuation of the infusion and administration of vasopressors, if necessary. Cyanide toxicity, while extremely rare, can occur in patients with depleted thiosulfate stores or liver failure. Cyanide toxicity is manifested by dizziness, ataxia, coma, dilated pupils, and shallow breathing. As mentioned previously, metabolic acidosis is an early screening test. In patients with renal failure, thiocyanate levels can reach high levels and induce hypothyroidism if nitroprusside therapy is continued for several days.

## B. Nitroglycerin and Nitrates

Nitroglycerin and other organic nitrates are also direct-acting vasodilators with a predominant affect on the venous capacitance beds and a lesser effect on the arteriolar resistance bed. Vasodilation may be mediated, in part, by a nitroglycerin-induced prostacyclin release from endothelial cells (Mehta *et al.*, 1983), and by the activation of guanylate cyclase (Horowitz *et al.*, 1983). Currently, there are a large number of nitroglycerin preparations available with highly variable pharmacokinetics and routes of administration, but all produce similar hemodynamic changes. The effect of sublingual nitroglycerin occurs within 2 min and lasts for 20 to 30 min. Obviously, this short duration of action is not practical for treatment of heart failure, which is typically treated with longer-acting agents. Nitroglycerin agents can generally be administered sublingually, orally, or topically. An important distinction must be made between dosage in sublingual versus oral administration. While oral nitrates are absorbed well from the gastrointestinal tract, first-pass hepatic biotransformation by glutathione reductase reduces the amount of active drug available, thus requiring much larger doses (Opie, 1980). Also, the more gradual absorption from the gastrointestinal tract may result in a longer duration of action, compared to sublingual administration. For example, the effective dosage of sublingual isosorbide dinitrate is 2.5–10 mg and lasts 2–3 hr. Effective oral dosage is 20–80 mg and lasts 4–6 hr. Pentaerythitol tetranitrate is another long-acting nitrate with a duration of action of 6 hr and can be administered orally (Klein *et al.*, 1978). The duration of action of topical nitroglycerin (nitroglycerin paste) is 4–6 hr and can last as long as 8 hr. The newer transdermal patch (30–90 cm$^2$) can provide sustained effects for 24 hr (Olivari *et al.*, 1983a,b). Nitroglycerin can also be administered intravenously in acute clinical situations. Intravenous dosage should be titrated by continuous invasive hemodynamic monitoring. Effective dosage varies between 0.5 $\mu$g/kg/min (35 $\mu$g/min) and 15 $\mu$g/kg/min (1050 $\mu$g/min). This route of administration provides a constant effective blood level of nitroglycerin, which might be advantageous in the management of acute heart failure.

Nitroglycerin and isosorbide dinitrate produce qualitatively similar hemodynamic effects in patients with acute or chronic heart failure, whether administered intravenously, sublingually, orally, or topically (Taylor *et al.*, 1976). Reduction in pulmonary capillary wedge pressure and right atrial pressure are the most consistent effects. A modest decrease in arterial pressure usually occurs, and pulmonary artery pressure and pulmonary vascular resistance tend to decrease in the majority of patients. Variable changes in systemic vascular resistance, cardiac output, and stroke volume are observed. In patients with normal left ventricular filling pressure, or in those in whom it falls to a very low level, cardiac output and stroke volume tend to decrease and systemic vascular resistance may not change. In the presence of elevated left ventricular filling pressure, cardiac output and stroke volume either remain unchanged or increase slightly (Chatterjee *et al.*, 1978; Gray *et al.*, 1975; Leier *et al.*, 1983).

Nitroglycerin can be used for the treatment of heart failure complicating myocardial infarction. Because of its predominant effect on the venous capacitance vessels, it is most effective in patients with mild or moderate heart failure with elevated pulmonary capillary wedge pressure and near-normal cardiac output without elevated systemic vascular resistance. Patients with decreased cardiac output and elevated systemic vascular resistance would be better treated with sodium nitroprusside because of its combined arterial and venodilator action. There are some data, however, that suggest that at high doses, nitroglycerin or nitrates may also cause potent systemic arterial vasodilation. Very large doses of isosorbide dinitrate may have the same effect.

Despite its relatively weak effect on systemic arteries, nitroglycerin is a potent vasodilator of the coronary arteries. This effect is most pronounced on the epicardial vessels, with little or no effect on the small intramyocardial arteries and arterioles (Feldman and Conti, 1981). This observation, as well as the potent antianginal effects of nitroglycerin, have led to a number of investigations evaluating the myocardial metabolic effects of nitroglycerin in chronic coronary artery disease (McGregor, 1982; Feldman and Conti, 1981). It is clear that no single explanation of "how nitrates work" to relieve myocardial ischemia is applicable to all circumstances. There are several potential mechanisms: (1) nitrate-induced reduction of venous tone resulting in venous pooling, resulting in decreased ventricular end-diastolic pressure and volume, and thus decreased wall stress, which reduces myocardial oxygen requirements; (2) with decreased systolic pressure, there may be significant oxygen sparing, especially if reflex tachycardia is prevented; (3) nitrates may enhance collateral flow to the ischemic myocardium; and (4) reduction of epicardial coronary artery vasospasm with improvement in myocardial perfusion.

Because of these potential beneficial effects on myocardial ischemia, nitroglycerin and isosorbide dinitrate have also been used to decrease the extent of myocardial ischemia and infarct size in patients with acute myocardial infarction. Nitroglycerin has been shown to decrease the extent of myocardial injury (Chiariello *et al.*, 1976). An increase in transmyocardial blood flow and subendocardial flow to the ischemic myocardial segments has been reported in experimental myocardial infarction. In a limited number of patients with acute myocardial infarction, intravenous nitroglycerin has been shown to decrease infarct size calculated from creatine phosphokinase (CPK) and CPK-MB activity curves (Bussman *et al.*, 1979), although this has not been confirmed by others (Brown *et al.*, 1976; Jugdutt, 1983). Several prospective, randomized studies on the use of intraveous nitroglycerin in acute myocardial infarction have reported conflicting and inconclusive results regarding reduction of infarct size or mortality (Bussman *et al.*, 1979; Chiche *et al.*, 1979; Flaherty *et al.*, 1983; Hockings *et al.*, 1981). In a randomized study (Flaherty *et al.*, 1983), no benefit was observed from intravenous nitroglycerin therapy. Thus, the routine use of nitroglycerin cannot be recommended, and it should be used only for treatment of heart failure or control of angina.

The most common side effect of nitrate therapy is headache, which is most prominent initially and usually decreases during chronic treatment. In patients with right ventricular infarction, nitroglycerin should not be used without concomitant fluid administration, otherwise, severe hypotension and a shocklike syndrome may be precipitated. In some patients with acute myocardial infarction, extreme bradycardia and hypotension may occur, which can be reversed by intravenous atropine. Postural dizziness and weakness occur less frequently in patients with heart failure. Methemoglobinemia, although extremely rare, has been reported during long term treatment with larger doses of nitrates.

### C. Hydralazine and Endralazine

Hydralazine is a direct acting vasodilator that causes smooth muscle relaxation, primarily of the arterial, precapillary resistance vessels with minimal effect on veins (Koch-Weser, 1976). It can be administered orally, intravenously, or intramuscularly. The usual oral dose of hydralazine which is effective in the treatment of chronic heart failure is variable, ranging between 200 and 400 mg daily. Typically, the drug is divided into two to four equal daily doses. The effective dose is at least partly related to the acetylator phenotype of the patient. Slow acetylators have significantly decreased hepatic biotransformation of hydralazine and, thus, greater and prolonged bioavailability of the active compound. The metabolic products of hydralazine are excreted in the urine.

The important hemodynamic effects of hydralazine have been well described by several investigators and are typical of agents with a predominant arteriolar vasodilatory effect (Chatterjee *et al.*, 1976b; Fitchett *et al.*, 1979; Franciosa *et al.*, 1977). They are characterized by a marked increase in cardiac index and stroke volume index and a marked fall in systemic vascular resistance. Arterial pressure remains unchanged or decreases slightly. There is a slight or no change in systemic or pulmonary venous pressures. Unlike the experience with hypertensive patients, reflex tachycardia usually does not occur in patients with congestive heart failure. Pulmonary vascular resistance also decreases.

Hydralazine has a variable effect on myocardial metabolism. In the absence of obstructive coronary artery disease, coronary vascular resistance decreases and coronary blood flow increases (Magorien et al., 1982). In patients with ischemic heart failure, however, changes in coronary blood flow and myocardial oxygen consumption appear to be dependent on changes in the determinants of myocardial oxygen demand. A variable effect on rate–pressure product occurs following hydralazine, increasing in some and decreasing in others (Rouleau et al., 1981).

Hydralazine, particularly in combination with nitrates, has been found useful for the treatment of patients with chronic heart failure. Beneficial hemodynamic and clinical effects have been reported in patients with both ischemic and primary cardiomyopathy. These effects are present at both rest and exercise (Franciosa and Cohn, 1979). The patients most likely to have the greatest response to hydralazine are those with the higher initial systemic vascular resistance (Goldberg et al., 1983; Wilson et al., 1983). End-diastolic volume or initial ejection fraction are not predictive. Although several investigators have reported sustained effects of hydralazine, some papers have described the development of tolerance (Packer et al., 1982). It may be possible to attenuate the development of tolerance by increasing the dose of diuretics. Plasma renin levels increase after the administration of hydralazine, activating alodesterone-mediated sodium retention.

The most serious side effect of hydralazine is a drug-induced lupus syndrome, which is seen in 15 to 20% of patients receiving daily doses of 400 mg or more. A genetic deficiency of the hepatic enzyme $N$-acetyl transferase, which inactivates hydralazine, is a risk factor for the development of this side effect (Perry, 1973; Talseth, 1976). Some patients with severe coronary artery disease develop angina during hydralazine therapy (Massie et al., 1981). Increased diuretic dosage is often required to avoid fluid retention. Gastrointestinal symptoms include nausea and diarrhea, which are frequent. Polyneuropathy due to pyridoxin deficiency has been reported (Raskin and Rishman, 1965). Other infrequent side effects include acute febrile illness and a syndrome of flushing, sweating, and urticaria, which may be secondary to hydralazine-induced inhibition of histamine.

Endralazine, a new structural analog of hydralazine, has undergone initial testing (Quyyami et al., 1983). These studies have demonstrated hemodynamic effects essentially identical to those of hydralazine. However, a major advantage of endralazine is that its metabolism is independent of the patient's acetylator status and, thus, has a more narrow effective dose range. Largely due to this advantage, there have not been any cases of lupus erythematosus reported with the use of endralazine, indicating that it may be potentially safer than hydralazine.

## D. Minoxidil

Minoxidil is a potent, direct-acting, smooth muscle-relaxing agent, predominantly affecting arteriolar resistance vessels with a slight effect on the venous capacitance vessels (Chatterjee et al., 1976a). In hypertensive patients, reflex stimulation of renin and norepinephrine is observed in response to a fall in blood pressure (Pettinger, 1980). The pharmacokinetics of this drug in humans have not been entirely elucidated, and information has been obtained mostly from animal studies. Minoxidil is almost completely absorbed (95%) after oral dose, appearing in plasma within 30 min and reaching a peak concentration in 1 hr. The elimination half-life is about 4 hr. Approximately 10% of a dose of minoxidil is excreted unchanged in the urine. The normal dose of minoxidil in the management of chronic heart failure ranges from 10 to 20 mg twice daily.

The hemodynamic effects of minoxidil are similar to those of hydralazine (McKay et al., 1982). Cardiac, index, stroke volume index, and stroke work index increase, accompanied by a decrease in systemic vascular resistance. No significant changes in systemic and pulmonary venous pressure occurs. In general, heart rate and mean arterial pressure remain unchanged. In some patients with chronic congestive heart failure, marked hypotension and tachycardia are occasionally seen.

The clinical uses of minoxidil are similar to those of hydralazine. The most common side effect is hypertrichosis. The major clinical problem for chronic minoxidil therapy, however, is fluid retention and weight gain, occurring in almost 100% of patients with heart failure. Fluid retention is a greater problem with minoxidil than any of the other pure vasodilators, such as hydralazine (Markham et al., 1983). In some patients fluid retention can be prevented by increasing the dose of diuretics.

## E. Phentolamine

Phentolamine is a alpha-adrenergic blocking agent possessing direct smooth muscle-relaxing effect. An immediate and significant reversal of the insulin suppression that occurs in heart failure is observed after phentolamine. Although this can potentially improve myocardial metabolism, the significance of this pharmacologic effect in the management of heart failure is unclear (Gould and Reddy, 1979).

Phentolamine can be administered by the intravenous and oral routes. When administered intravenously, the onset of hemodynamic effect is observed within 5 min. The effects are quickly reversed within minutes of discontinuation of therapy. Intravenous phentolamine therapy is indicated for the treatment of acute heart failure or before the initiation of nonparenteral vasodilator therapy in patients with severe chronic congestive heart failure.

The hemodynamic effects of phentolamine are similar to those of sodium nitroprusside. Arterial pressure, systemic vascular resistance, pulmonary capillary wedge pressure, and right atrial and pulmonary artery pressures decline, while cardiac output and stroke volume increase. In contrast to sodium nitroprusside, phentolamine tends to increase heart rate, even in patients with heart failure. The changes in left ventricular function are influenced by the initial level of left ventricular filling pressure. In patients with high initial left ventricular filling pressure, stroke volume and cardiac output increase, along with a decrease in filling pressure, indicating improved left ventricular function. In the presence of normal filling pressure, stroke volume increases infrequently, even though left ventricular filling pressure decreases.

Gould *et al.* (1975) reported that phentolamine may decrease coronary vascular resistance and increase coronary blood flow. In patients with acute myocardial infarction, the effects of phentolamine on coronary blood flow and myocardial oxygen consumption appear to be related to the changes in myocardial oxygen demand. In most patients, arterial pressure decreases significantly and heart rate increases. However, the product of the systolic blood pressure × heart rate (an index of myocardial oxygen demand) and the coronary blood flow and myocardial oxygen consumption usually remain unchanged (Chatterjee, 1982). Thus, improved cardiac function occurs after phentolamine, with little or no increase in metabolic cost.

The major complication associated with phentolamine therapy is hypotension, requiring cautious dosage titration. Thus, in normotensive patients with heart failure, the initial dose of intravenous phentolamine should be low (0.1 mg/min). Changes in arterial pressure, systemic vascular resistance, cardiac output, and left ventricular filling pressure should be monitored as the dose is increased by 0.1 mg/min every 10 min. In most patients, the beneficial hemodynamic effects are observed with a 1–2 mg/min infusion of phentolamine. Palpitations and gastrointestinal symptoms are occasionally seen and angina can be precipitated.

### F. Trimethaphan

Trimethaphan is a ganglion-blocking agent which has been used in a limited number of patients with acute myocardial infarction (Shell and Sobel, 1974). Following intravenous administration, pulmonary capillary wedge pressure usually decreases without any significant change in cardiac output. Arterial pressure and heart rate also decrease. The hemodynamics of trimethaphan in these patients are similar to those seen with nitroglycerin. Because of the potential for the development of tachyphylaxis, trimethaphan is rarely used for the treatment of heart failure.

### G. Trimazosin

Trimazosin is a quinazoline derivative which has a mechanism of action and hemodynamic response similar to prazosin (Awan et al., 1979; Weber et al., 1980). Experience with this drug in treating patients with congestive heart failure is limited. Following administration of trimazosin to patients with heart failure, cardiac output and stroke volume increased, while systemic and pulmonary venous pressures and pulmonary arterial pressure decreased. Systemic and pulmonary vascular resistance are also reduced. Heart rate and mean arterial pressure remain unchanged. These hemodynamic effects seem to be sustained during chronic therapy (Ports et al., 1983). During maintenance trimazosin therapy, exercise tolerance and maximum oxygen consumption increase (Weber et al., 1980). Trimazosin has produced beneficial effects in patients with heart failure after doses ranging from 25 to 100 mg three times daily (Chatterjee et al., 1981). The advantage of using this drug over other vasodilators and its potential adverse reactions after chronic treatment will require further study.

### H. Prazosin

Prazosin is a quinazoline derivative which selectively blocks postsynaptic (alpha$_1$) receptors in the blood vessels, leading to vasodilation. Prazosin also inhibits phosphodiesterase, which causes smooth muscle relaxation and interferes with norepinephrine synthesis. The usual dose for treating congestive heart failure ranges from 3 to 5 mg, three to four times daily. The drug is rapidly absorbed from the gastrointestinal tract. Most of the drug (79%) is excreted in the feces. Approximately 6% of the drug is excreted in the urine unchanged. Patients with renal failure have increased plasma levels and longer elimination half-life.

Prazosin exerts a balanced vasodilator effect on precapillary resistance and postcapillary venous capacitance vessels. Hemodynamic effects include a fall in systemic vascular resistance and arterial pressure, with concomitant increases in cardiac output and stroke volume. Pulmonary and systemic venous pressures and pulmonary artery pressure decrease (Chatterjee et al., 1981). In patients with heart failure, prazosin improves left ventricular function during exercise (Goldman *et al.*, 1980). However, prospective, controlled studies do not suggest that prazosin improves exercise tolerance of patients with chronic heart failure.

The effects of prazosin on coronary hemodynamics are variable. In some patients with ischemic heart failure, coronary blood flow and myocardial oxygen consumption decrease, along with reduction in the determinants of myocardial oxygen demand. In others, coronary blood flow and myocardial oxygen consumption tend to increase, despite a decrease in myocardial oxygen demand (Rouleau *et al.*, 1982). The mechanism for this divergent response is not clear. A primary decrease of the coronary vascular resistance due to alpha-adrenergic receptor blockade and, therefore, an increase in coronary blood flow, despite a decreased oxygen demand, cannot be excluded.

Although a number of studies have demonstrated sustained hemodynamic effects in patients with chronic heart failure (Goldman *et al.*, 1980; Rouleau *et al.*, 1981), attenuation of beneficial hemodynamic effects with chronic therapy has been reported by others (Arnold *et al.*, 1979; Packer *et al.*, 1979a,b) (Fig. 3). The mechanism of this attenuation is not clear. Plasma norepinephrine has been shown to be increased following chronic therapy, which may result in peripheral vasoconstriction. Sodium retention due to aldosterone stimulation has also been postulated to account for attenuation of effects. The addition of antialdosterone agents can potentially prevent attenuation of clinical response (Rouleau *et al.*, 1981).

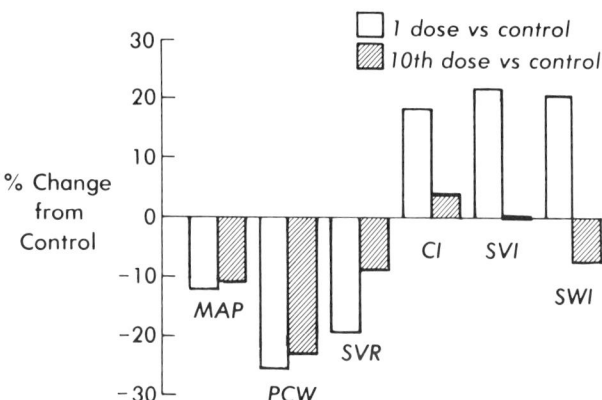

**Fig. 3.** Comparative hemodynamic effects between the first and tenth dose of 5 mg of prazosin in congestive heart failure. After the first dose, cardiac index (CI), stroke volume index (SVI), and stroke work index (SWI) increased, and mean arterial pressure (MAP), pulmonary capillary wedge pressure (PCW), and systemic vascular resistance (SVR) decreased. After the tenth dose, however, CI, SVI, and SWI returned to the control levels. (From Arnold *et al.*, 1979, by permission of the American Heart Association, Inc.)

Side effects of prazosin are uncommon. Occasionally hypotension occurs after the first dose, which can be minimized by starting with a small initial dose. This effect is typically seen only in patients with hypertension, and is not observed in chronic heart failure patients. Gastrointestinal symptoms are seen in a few patients. Palpitations, drowsiness, depression, and nervousness are infrequent. Sexual dysfunction is rare.

## I. Converting Enzyme Inhibitors

### 1. Captopril

Captopril is the first angiotensin-converting enzyme inhibitor to be approved for the treatment of chronic severe heart failure. Captopril has both venous and arterial vasodilating properties. While vasodilation secondary to the decreased synthesis of angiotensin II is a principal mechanism of action of this drug, it is clear that vasodilation by captopril is not solely related to this mechanism. Captopril also prevents the degradation of the vasodilator bradykinin, which also causes an increased synthesis and release of vasodilator prostaglandins (Dzau et al., 1984; Swartz and Williams, 1982; Moore et al., 1981; Goldstone et al., 1981; Heel et al., 1980). That prostaglandins contribute in vasodilation is also suggested, as well as that the concomitant use of indomethacin attenuates the effects of captopril, particularly in the subset of patients with initially low renin levels (Witzgall et al., 1982). Serum catecholamine levels fall after administration of captopril, suggesting a decrease in sympathetic activity, which usually tends to increase following administration of other vasodilator agents (Nicholls et al., 1981). Captopril appears to reduce degradation of bradykinin (Heel et al., 1980). Finally, because captopril also inhibits the synthesis of aldosterone, a reduction in body weight associated with diuresis and natriuresis typically occurs with its use (Dzau et al., 1980).

Captopril is administered orally in dosages from 6.25 mg twice daily to 100 mg orally twice daily. The most commonly used dose, however, is 25 mg three times daily. The peak effect is achieved approximately $1\frac{1}{2}$–2 hr after administrations and persists for 6 to 8 hr. Approximately 50% of the drug is metabolized to inactive compounds in the liver. Both metabolites and active drug are excreted in the urine. In patients with renal impairment, adjustment of the dose may be indicated (Onoyama et al., 1981). Hemodialysis is effective in removing captopril from the system. The important therapeutic hemodynamic effects of captopril in patients with chronic heart failure are well documented by several studies, all of which have noted the same results (Ader et al., 1980; Awan et al., 1981; Davis et al., 1979; Turini et al., 1978). In general, the hemodynamic changes reflect those of a vasodilator with combined arterial and venous vasodila-

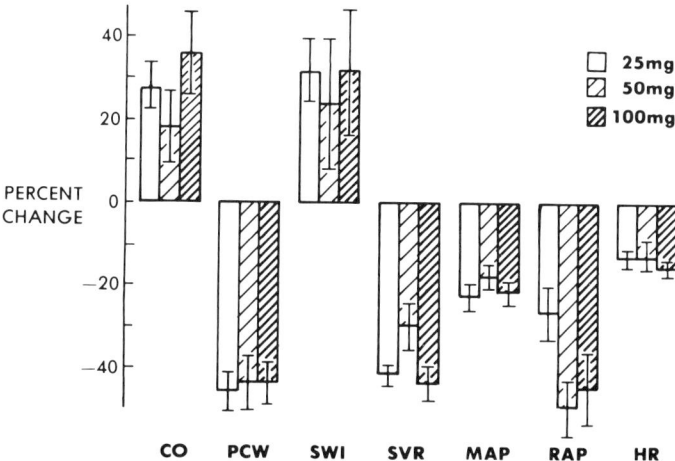

**Fig. 4.** Changes in cardiac output (CO), pulmonary capillary wedge pressure (PCW), stroke work index (SWI), systemic vascular resistance (SVR), mean arterial pressure (MAP), right atrial pressure (RAP), and heart rate (HR) after 25, 50, and 100 mg of oral captopril in patients with chronic congestive heart failure. The hemodynamic effects of captopril were characterized by a significant increase in CO and SWI and a decrease in PCW, MAP, RAP, and SVR. The magnitude of hemodynamic change following 25, 50, and 100 mg of captopril was similar. (From Ader et al., 1980.)

tion. Following captopril administration, a decrease in systemic vascular resistance and systemic blood pressure, associated with a significant increase in cardiac output, occurs. This reflects the arterial vasodilation properties of captopril. There is also a striking fall in pulmonary capillary wedge pressure, pulmonary artery pressure, and right atrial pressure, probably secondary to venodilation (Fig. 4). Because angiotensin II does not cause direct venoconstriction, the fall in right heart pressures is felt to be related to decreased sympathetic tone. As with most arterial vasodilator agents, those patients with the highest initial systemic vascular resistance have the greatest increase in cardiac output.

Captopril appears to have beneficial effects on myocardial metabolism in patients with ischemic heart disease (Chatterjee et al., 1982; Halperin et al., 1982). Captopril consistently decreases the rate–pressure product, an index of myocardial oxygen demand which is associated with decreased coronary blood flow and myocardial oxygen consumption. Thus, the beneficial hemodynamic changes seem to occur at a lower myocardial oxygen cost.

Captopril seems to decrease renal vascular resistance and increase renal blood flow (Creager et al., 1981). Accompanying these changes is an increase in sodium excretion and potassium retention. Changes in renal function, however, also depend on the changes in mean arterial pressure (Pierpont *et al.*, 1981). Correlation between the change in blood pressure and creatinine clearance has been demonstrated, suggesting that it is critical to avoid profound hypotension and prevent deterioration of renal function following captopril. During maintenance therapy in patients with chronic heart failure, captopril has produced a sustained improvement in renal function (Dzau *et al.*, 1980).

Captopril appears to produce sustained beneficial hemodynamic and clinical effects (Ader *et al.*, 1980; Awan *et al.*, 1982; Dzau *et al.*, 1980; Fouad *et al.*, 1982; Levine *et al.*, 1980; Kramer *et al.*, 1983). This includes both resting and exercise hemodynamics, and a general improved state of well-being. These sustained effects seem to be a major advantage of captopril over other orally administered vasodilator agents for the treatment of heart failure. Tolerance to both hydralazine and prazosin has been reported by several investigators (Colucci *et al.*, 1980; Packer *et al.*, 1982). The sustained effect of captopril is probably related to sustained decrease in aldosterone and angiotensin II, which promotes diuresis and sodium excretion, in addition to peripheral vasodilation. Prazosin and hydralazine, while potent vasodilators, promote activation of the renin system, leading to sodium and fluid retention. It has been shown that the tolerance to hydralazine and prazosin can be overcome with increasing doses of diuretics or the addition of spironolactone (Rouleau *et al.*, 1981).

Captopril has been well tolerated by most patients treated for heart failure (Packer *et al.*, 1984). The most common important side effect is hypotension, which seems to be most likely to occur following the first dose. Blood pressure seems to return to higher, well-tolerated levels with continued use (Chatterjee *et al.*, 1982; Sharpe *et al.*, 1980). For this reason in patients with severe heart failure, dosage should be begun at low levels (6.25 mg three times daily). Other rarely noted side effects include dizziness, renal insufficiency, rash, nausea, anorexia, diarrhea, neutropenia, and proteinuria (Romankiewicz *et al.*, 1983).

### 2. *Enalapril (MK-421)*

Very recently, a new oral angiotensin-converting enzyme inhibitor, enalapril (MK-421), has been under investigation. Preliminary results suggest that its hemodynamic effects are similar to those of captopril, and it may also be useful in the long-term management of heart failure. The major difference between captopril and enalapril is the prolonged duration of action, which may allow twice daily administration (DiCarlo *et al.*, 1983; Cody *et al.*, 1983; Levine *et al.*, 1983b; Cody, 1985; Franciosa *et al.*, 1985).

## J. *Calcium Entry Blockers* (Calcium Channel Antagonists)

### 1. Nifedipine

All calcium entry blocking agents cause smooth muscle relaxation by interfering with muscular excitation–contraction coupling and are potent vasodilators with predominant effect on arteriolar beds. Arteriolar relaxation appears to be related to inhibition of transmembrane calcium influx. Recent studies have also demonstrated that vasoconstriction, induced by stimulation of vascular postsynaptic alpha$_1$ adrenoceptors, is reduced by calcium entry blockers through a noncompetitive antagonism (van Zwieten *et al.*, 1983). This mechanism may further contribute to the vasodilator effect of calcium entry blockers.

Pharmacokinetic data about nifedipine is not complete. However, it is well absorbed from the gastrointestinal tract. Bioavailability is approximately 60 to 70%. After a 10-mg dose, maximum effect is achieved in 30 to 60 min and appears to be sustained for 6 to 8 hr. Duration of action seems to be longer with larger initial doses. Recommended dosage is 10–40 mg three times daily. Nifedipine is eliminated from the body by hepatic metabolism. For acute therapy, sublingual nifedipine, 10 mg, is very rapidly absorbed, achieving significant serum levels in only 6 min (Raemsch and Sommer, 1983).

Although all calcium entry blocking agents, including nifedipine, exert negative inotropic effects because of their potential to decrease systemic vascular resistance, it has been used in the treatment of chronic congestive heart failure (Elkayam *et al.*, 1983; Polese *et al.*, 1979; Anderson and Vik-Mo, 1983). The hemodynamic changes were characterized by a reduction in systemic vascular resistance and an increase in cardiac index. Blood pressure declined modestly and was associated with no significant change in heart rate. Pulmonary capillary wedge pressure, right atrial pressure, and pulmonary vascular resistance showed no significant change. Heart rate remained the same or decreased.

The effect of nifedipine on coronary hemodynamics and myocardial metabolism in congestive heart failure has not been evaluated, although in patients with coronary artery disease, without heart failure, it tends to increase coronary artery blood flow. Nifedipine does not activate the renin–aldosterone system, despite its potent hypotensive effects (Bianchetti *et al.*, 1983; Fifer *et al.*, 1985), and also has a potent natriuretic effect on the kidney (Garthoff *et al.*, 1983; Pederson, 1983).

Adverse reactions to calcium antagonists have been extensively reviewed (Krebs, 1983), and, in general, are better tolerated than nitrates or beta blockers. In general, the most common side effects related to the potent vasodilators include hypotension, flushing, headache, palpitations, and edema of the ankles. Gastrointestinal effects include rare episodes of nausea, constipation, or diarrhea. Conduction disturbances with nifedipine do not occur.

All of these factors suggest that nifedipine may be of value in the treatment of severe congestive heart failure. More extensive clinical testing is indicated.

### 2. *Verapamil*

Because it has more potent negative inotropic effects than nifedipine, verapamil has not been as extensively tested in severe heart failure. Nevertheless, some papers (Ferlinz and Citron, 1983; Hanrath et al., 1983) have suggested that it may also be effective. The potent arteriolar vasodilation seems to more than compensate for the negative inotropic effect. Further clinical studies with verapamil in congestive heart failure are indicated.

### 3. *Diltiazem*

Hemodynamic effects of both intravenous and oral diltiazem have been evaluated in a small number of patients with severe chronic congestive heart failure, and beneficial effects have been reported (Walsh et al., 1984). An increase in cardiac output, stroke volume, and stroke work index, together with a decrease in mean arterial and pulmonary capillary wedge pressure have been observed. There was no change in maximal first derivation of left ventricular pressure ($dP/dT_{max}$). Transient junctional rhythm occurred in occasional patients.

It needs to be emphasized that all calcium entry blocking agents can exert negative inotropic effects and have the potential to produce deleterious effects on left ventricular function. In some patients, cardiac output may decrease, along with hypotension, despite decreased left ventricular outflow resistance. These adverse effects are more likely to occur in patients with severe heart failure, and more often with verapamil.

## VII. Clinical Applications

### A. Acute Myocardial Infarction Complicated by Heart Failure

When it is clinically suspected that a patient with acute myocardial infarction is in significant heart failure, hemodynamic monitoring is required to establish the diagnosis and choose the mode of therapy. Based

**TABLE III**

Therapy in Relation to the Hemodynamic Subsets of Acute Myocardial Infarction

| Subset | Clinical presentation | Left ventricular stroke work index (gm/m/m²) | Pulmonary capillary wedge pressure (mm Hg) | Therapy |
|---|---|---|---|---|
| 1 | Stable | ≥40 | ≤15 | None required |
| 2 | Pulmonary congestion | >20 | >15 | Diuretics; venodilators |
| 3A | Pulmonary congestion ↓ Perfusion | 10–20 | >15 | Combined arteriolar and venodilators |
| 3B | Shock | ≤10 | >15 | Inotropes; mechanical assist devices; vasopressors |

upon measurements of stroke work index and left ventricular filling pressures, patients with left ventricular failure can be divided into hemodynamic subsets (Table III). In patients in Subset 1, no specific therapy is necessary. For patients in Subset 2, the degree of depression of left ventricular function may be very mild and the only abnormal hemodynamic finding will be mild elevation of pulmonary capillary wedge pressure. These patients can usually be treated with diuretics alone. If, despite diuretic therapy, pulmonary venous pressure remains high, venodilators (nitroglycerin) can be effective. Patients with more moderate degrees of heart failure, in Subset 3A, have higher pulmonary capillary wedge pressure with decreased cardiac output. These patients should be considered for vasodilator therapy. Patients in Subset 3B have severely decreased left ventricular function, along with hypotension. Thus, this subset requires the initial institution of inotropic and vasopressor therapy, or mechanical assist devices to maintain arterial pressure.

In the management of pump failure complicating recent myocardial infarction, intravenous vasodilators with a rapid onset of action and short half-life are preferable to orally administered agents, to allow rapid adjustment of dosage. Sodium nitroprusside, nitroglycerin, and phentolamine are the most frequently used vasodilator agents. In general, the hemodynamic effect of phentolamine is similar to nitroprusside, except that there is more of a tendency to develop reflex tachycardia (Kotter et al., 1977; Gould et al., 1974). There has been a great deal of controversy over the clinical application of nitroglycerin versus nitroprusside in this setting.

Armstrong et al. (1975) compared the hemodynamic effects of both intravenous nitroprusside and intravenous nitroglycerin in the same group of patients with acute myocardial infarction. A greater increment in the ratio of systemic vascular resistance to pulmonary capillary wedge pressure was noted with nitroglycerin than with nitroprusside at a comparable decrease in arterial pressure. Stinson et al. (1975) compared the hemodynamic effect of intravenous nitroglycerin and nitroprusside in early postsurgical patients. Although both drugs decreased left atrial pressure, nitroprusside increased stroke volume and cardiac output, while nitroglycerin decreased cardiac output and stroke volume. These findings confirm the impression of multiple previous studies with these agents (i.e., nitroprusside has a balanced effect on arterial and venous beds, while nitroglycerin is predominantly a venodilator). These studies provide clear guidelines to the rational clinical application of these agents. In patients with heart failure characterized by low forward output and elevated pulmonary capillary wedge pressure, nitroprusside is the agent of choice. However, during nitroprusside therapy, if there is marked reduction in pulmonary capillary wedge pressure, cardiac output may be increased. Marked decrease in preload may override the potential benefits of afterload reduction and the net effect may be a decrease in forward output (Walinsky et al., 1974).

In patients with severe congestive symptoms characterized by very high pulmonary capillary wedge pressure and only mildly decreased forward output, intravenous nitroglycerin is the preferred agent, because of its predominant effect on the venous system.

*Despite an immense volume of clinical data on the variable effects of nitroglycerin versus nitroprusside in preserving myocardial tissue and decreasing ischemia during myocardial infarction, there is no conclusive evidence that either agent can significantly decrease the extent of myocardial injury.* Therefore, these studies cannot be used to justify the preferential use of either agent to decrease the extent of myocardial injury. It is apparent, however, that both nitroprusside and nitroglycerin can decrease myocardial ischemia by decreasing the determinants of myocardial oxygen demand. However, in most patients with an acute myocardial infarction, there is a thrombotic occlusion of the stenosed coronary artery supplying the infarcted area. Increased perfusion to the peri-infarction zones, therefore, can occur only if there is an increase in collateral blood flow. Controversy exists regarding the effects of vasodilator agents on collateral flow to the infarcted myocardial segments. Investigators have attempted to evaluate these effects indirectly by evaluating changes in regional wall motion effects (Brown et al., 1976), regional metabolic effects (Gold et al., 1976; Mueller et al., 1974), changes in ST segment elevation on the electrocardiogram (Mulkherje *et al.*, 1975), and serum CPK activity (Magnusson *et al.*, 1976). In general, both positive and negative results have been reported with each of these techniques. Furthermore, even if enhanced collateral flow occurred, it is not clear whether it would be sufficient to cause a *clinically meaningful decrease* in the extent of myocardial injury.

*There is also no conclusive evidence to suggest that the routine use of either nitroglycerin or nitroprusside will improve the prognosis of patients with acute myocardial infarction.* Both agents have undergone large-scale, prospective, randomized trials to evaluate potential improvement in prognosis. Two such studies with nitroprusside demonstrated that no benefit in either early or late prognosis (Cohn *et al.*, 1982; Hacking *et al.*, 1981), while another reported decreased mortality (Durrer *et al.*, 1982). In the prospective studies using nitroglycerin (Bowen *et al.*, 1979; Chiche *et al.*, 1979), no conclusive benefits were demonstrated. It should be noted that all of these studies excluded patients with severe cardiogenic shock.

In uncontrolled studies, vasodilators have been reported to improve immediate prognosis in patients with severe left ventricular failure (Chatterjee *et al.*, 1976b). This study reported a mortality rate of 44% in this severely ill subgroup compared to a previous reported expected mortality of at least 75% (Scheidt *et al.*, 1973; Chatterjee and Swan, 1973): Unfortunately, despite an improved early survival, the late prognosis of these patients is very poor. The projected 2-year survival rate is only 28%.

## B. Acute Myocardial Infarction Complicated by Mechanical Defects

The pathologic and hemodynamic consequences of acute papillary muscle rupture and ventricular septal defect have been previously described. Hemodynamic monitoring is essential in both groups of patients for accurate diagnosis and to guide therapy. In the case of acute papillary muscle rupture, arteriolar vasodilator agents like nitroprusside have beneficial hemodynamic effects (Chatterjee *et al.*, 1973b; Greenberg *et al.*, 1978). With decreased afterload, forward stroke volume increases and the regurgitant volume decreases without any significant change in left ventricular stroke volume. Thus, during vasodilator therapy, a redistribution of the left ventricular total stroke volume occurs; more blood is pumped forward into the aorta and less backward to the left atrium. This results in a decrease in the magnitude of the regurgitant wave (V wave on the wedge pressure tracing), a fall in mean wedge pressure, and increased cardiac output.

In the case of ventricular septal rupture, the size of the left-to-right shunt is dependent on the ratio of systemic vascular resistance to pulmonary vascular resistance. Thus, if systemic vascular resistance can be reduced with nitroprusside, decreased shunting will occur. This has been demonstrated clinically (Tecklenberg et al., 1976). Unfortunately, agents like nitroprusside also reduce pulmonary vascular resistance and the potential exists to actually increase the size of the shunt. Thus, monitoring is required to detect the actual effect of vasodilator therapy in all of these patients.

Although vasodilator agents like sodium nitroprusside, nitrates, and phentolamine produce hemodynamic benefits in these patients, vasodilator therapy must be regarded as supportive rather than definitive. Surgical correction should be considered as soon as the patient's condition is stabilized. It appears that early surgical intervention provides a better prognosis in these critically ill patients.

## C. Therapy of Right Ventricular Infarction

The clinical presentation, pathologic findings, and hemodynamic consequences of right ventricular infarction were described previously. In general, the primary mechanism of the hypotensive-low output state in this condition is due to a functional, severe reduction in left ventricular preload and reduced left ventricular size, similar to that seen in cardiac tamponade. Vasodilators alone should be used with great caution in patients with clinically significant right ventricular infarction, because of the potential for further decrease in left ventricular preload.

First-line therapy for right ventricular infarction is well described (Cohn et al., 1974b; Lorell et al., 1979; Goldstein et al., 1982). In general, therapy involves aggressive fluid administration, despite initially elevated right atrial pressure, to increase left ventricular preload. Diuretics, or any preload-reducing agent, should be avoided. Vasodilators which have the potential to decrease pulmonary vascular resistance (nitroglycerin, nitroprusside) can increase right ventricular stroke volume and, hence, venous return to the left ventricle. However, concomitant administration of intravenous fluids is necessary to maintain adequate right ventricular filling pressure. Occasionally, combined use of inotropic agents such as dobutamine, vasodilators, and intravenous fluids is required to maintain adequate systemic output. Hemodynamic monitoring is essential to determine response to therapy. A–V sequential pacing can be lifesaving in patients with bradyarrhythmia and A–V conduction disturbances. Pulmonary artery balloon counterpulsation has been used in occasional patients.

## D. Chronic Congestive Heart Failure

### 1. Rationale for Selection of a Specific Agent

From this discussion, it is apparent that there are many orally administered vasodilator agents with an ability to produce substantial clinical benefits in patients with severe heart failure characterized by elevated pulmonary capillary wedge pressure and decreased cardiac output. Unfortunately, the clinical application of these agents has frequently failed to achieve the desired clinical results, and many clinicians are frustrated by the relatively large number of side effects they may produce. It is clear that there is no uniformly effective or safe vasodilator agent for patients with heart failure.

*Of the currently available vasodilator agents, long-term therapy with converting enzyme inhibitors appears to produce the most consistent hemodynamic and clinical benefits.* Approximately 60% of all heart failure patients improve with long term captopril therapy (Packer, 1983; Captopril Multicenter Research Group, 1983). Captopril therapy is less frequently complicated by the development of tolerance than other agents. This is probably due to its inhibition of the aldosterone pathway, preventing sodium retention and fluid retention, which commonly occur with other pure vasodilating agents. Concomitant diuretic dosage with captopril is commonly less than with other vasodilator agents. Reflex tachycardia does not occur, probably due to captopril's inhibition of the sympathetic nervous system. Dosage requirements with captopril are relatively simple. Because only 10–20 mg of captopril completely inhibits the angiotensin-converting enzyme (Ferguson *et al.,* 1977), doses of 25, 50, 100, and 150 mg tend to produce the same clinical result (Fig. 4). Captopril has relatively few adverse effects. The most noticeable is hypotension. However, hypotensive events tend to occur in the first 24 hr of therapy, predominantly in those patients with severe hyponatremia or with previous intravenous diuretic therapy. The reason for this is relatively hyponatremic patients tend to have higher plasma renin activity. Nevertheless, 20–30% of patients will require the substitution or addition of a second vasodilator.

Hydralazine may cause a mildly greater increase in cardiac output than captopril (Rouleau *et al.,* 1982); however, there are several relative disadvantages compared to captopril. The dose requirements of hydralazine are highly variable, as previously described. There is a greater tendency to develop tolerance. Sodium and fluid retention can occur, requiring increased doses of diuretics. The important side effects are more common and include headaches, flushing, exacerbation of ischemia, and systemic lupus erythematosus. It is estimated that only 30–40% of all heart failure patients benefit from hydralazine (Packer, 1983).

Prazosin also has limitations compared to captopril. The most important is a relatively greater tendency for the development of tolerance, which may occur within 48 hr of initiation of therapy, and fluid retention.

Calcium channel agonists, such as nifedipine, are relatively less well studied in patients with heart failure. More studies are needed before these agents can be recommended for the treatment of heart failure.

Nitroglycerin is of value in the treatment of chronic heart failure. However, because it is a predominant venodilator, it does not increase forward cardiac output. For this reason it is not an alternative therapy to captopril or hydralazine but may be clinically useful as *adjunct* therapy with arteriolar vasodilating agents in patients with congestive symptoms.

### 2. Combination Therapy

The relative different hemodynamic effects of the vasodilator agents suggest that rational combination therapy can be employed clinically. The hemodynamic effects of nitrates and hydralazine alone and in combination have been studied in the same patients (Massie *et al.*, 1977). As expected, nitrates reduced right atrial and pulmonary capillary wedge pressure. Hydralazine alone produced a marked increase in cardiac output, along with a decrease in systemic vascular resistance, but right atrial and pulmonary capillary wedge pressure remained unchanged. The combination of hydralazine and nitrates caused a substantial increase in cardiac output and a reduction of systemic and pulmonary venous pressures.

Comparative crossover hemodynamic studies of captopril, prazosin, and hydralazine in the same patients have been performed (Rouleau *et al.*, 1982). As expected, the pure arteriolar vasodilator hydralazine produced relatively greater increase in cardiac output than either captopril or prazosin. However, prazosin and captopril produced a greater decrease in the pulmonary capillary wedge pressure. Heart rate decreased with captopril but increased with hydralazine and prazosin. A combination of hydralazine and captopril also appeared to produce better hemodynamic effects. Indeed, combination therapy produced a greater increase in cardiac output and a decrease in pulmonary capillary wedge pressure, mean arterial pressure, and heart rate (Massie *et al.*, 1983). However, long-term studies are required to evaluate the clinical effectiveness and potential hazards of combination therapy.

### 3. Influence of Vasodilator Therapy on the Prognosis of Patients with Chronic Refractory Heart Failure

Currently, there are no adequately controlled studies to evaluate the influence of vasodilator therapy on the long-term prognosis of patients with chronic heart failure. It is well known that the natural history of untreated severe heart failure is extremely poor, with a reported mortality of 39 to 80% within 1 to 2 years of follow-up (Massie *et al.*, 1981). Unfortunately, follow-up studies of patients treated with vasodilator agents suggest that the overall prognosis remains unfavorable. Certain subsets of patients, however, can be predicted to do better than others. The severity of depression of cardiac function, based on the calculated stroke work index, correlates with a progressively worsening prognosis. The lack of progressive heart failure, as judged clinically, was associated with a better prognosis. Finally, the magnitude of hemodynamic improvement during the initiation of vasodilator therapy seems to identify patients with a relatively better prognosis. This does not imply that the vasodilator agent was responsible for the better prognosis but can be merely used to identify patients with better myocardial function. Currently, vasodilator agents are employed clinically to achieve symptomatic improvement. Recently, a large scale multicenter cooperative study has reported improved survival of patients with mild to moderate congestive heart failure treated with hydralazine 300 mg/day combined with isosorbide dinitrate 160 mg/day (Preliminary report of V-Heft, 1986, unpublished).

## VIII. Summary

Myocardial failure, irrespective of the etiology, and whether acute or chronic, may result in low output state. Compensatory mechanisms include increased catecholamine release, increased production of angiotensin II, increased vasopressin secretion by the pituitary, and a general increase in vascular stiffness. However, in an attempt to maintain arterial pressure, an increased afterload decreases forward stroke volume and increases residual and end-diastolic volumes. Increased preload also occurs due to an increase in the intravascular volume, secondary to activation of the renin–angiotensin–aldosterone system. Decreased forward cardiac output and increased preload are the hemodynamic determinants of the majority of symptoms that patients with heart failure experience. Vasodilator agents have the potential to alter both abnormally elevated afterload and preload favorably and cause symptomatic improvement. There is a large number of currently available vasodilating agents with highly variable mechanisms of vasodilation and variable sites of action. Applied rationally, vasodilator agents can be of significant value in the therapy of pump failure complicating acute myocardial infarction, and for the treatment of chronic congestive heart failure.

## Acknowledgments

The authors wish to thank Mrs. Kathleen Hecker and Mr. Kenneth Payne for their editorial assistance in preparing this manuscript.

## References

Ader, R., Chatterjee, K., Ports, T. A., Brundage, B. H., Hiramatsu, B., and Parmley, W. W. (1980). *Circulation* **61**, 931–937.
Alderman, E., and Glantz, S. A. (1976). *Circulation* **54**, 622–667.
Anderson, K., and Vik-Mo, H. (1983). *Circulation* **69**, 490–496.
Armstrong, P. W., Walker, D. C., Burton, J. R., and Parker, J. O. (1975). *Circulation* **52**, 1118–1127.
Arnold, S., Williams, R., Ports, T. A., Baughman, R. A., Benet, L. Z., Parmley, W. W., and Chatterjee, K. (1979). *Ann. Intern. Med.* **91**, 345–349.
Awan, N. A., Miller, R. R., Vera, Z., DeMaria, A. N., Amsterdam, E. A., and Mason, D. T. (1976). *Am. J. Cardiol.* **38**, 435–447.
Awan, N. A., Hermanovich, J., Whitcomb, C., Skinner, P., and Mason, D. T. (1979). *Am. J. Cardiol.* **44**, 126–131.
Awan, N. A., Evenson, M. K., Needham, K. E., Win, A., and Mason, D. T. (1981). *Am. Heart J.* **101**, 22–31.
Awan, N. A., Amsterdam, E. A., Hermanovich, J., Bommer, W. J., Needham, K. E., and Mason, D. T. (1982). *Am. Heart J.* **103**, 474–479.
Baigrie, R., Has, A., Morgan, C., Rakowski, H., Droback, M., and MacLaughlin, P. (1975). *J. Am. Coll. Cardiol.* **1**, 1396–1404.
Bastrow, R. D., and Kalayanides, G. J. (1972). *J. Pharmacol. & Exp. Ther.* **181**, 244–249.
Becker, L., Fortuin, N., and Pitt, B. (1971). *Circ. Res.* **28**, 263–269.
Bianchetti, M. G., Beretta-Piccoli, C., Weidman, P., Link, L., Boehringer, K., Ferrier, C., and Morton, J. J. (1983). *Hypertension* **5** (Suppl. II), II-57–II-65.
Bowen, W. G., Branconi, J. M., Goldstein, R. A., Cain, M. E., Brodarick, S. M., Geltman, E. M., Jaffe, A. S., Ambos, H. D., and Roberts, R. (1979). *Circulation* **59 & 60** (Suppl. II), II-170.
Brodie, B., Grossman, W., Mann, T., and McLaurine, L. (1977). *J. Clin. Invest.* **59**, 59–68.
Brown, J. J., Davis, D. L., Johnson, V. W., Lever, A. F., and Robertson, J. I. S. (1970). *Am. Heart J.* **80**, 329–342.
Brown, T. M., Matthews, P. O., and Walter, P. F. (1976). *Am. J. Cardiol.* **37**, 123–131.
Burch, G. E. (1956). *Arch. Intern. Med.* **98**, 750–766.
Bussman, W. D., Passek, D., Seidel, W., and Kaltenbach, M. (1979). *Circulation* **59 & 60** (Suppl. II), II-164.
Candell-Riera, J., Figueras, J., Valle, V., Alvarez, A., Gutierrez, L., Cortadellas, J., Cinca, J., Salas, A., and Rios, A. (1981). *Am. Heart J.* **101**, 281–287.

Captopril Multicenter Research Group. (1983). *J. Am. Coll. Cardiol.* **2**, 755–763.
Chatterjee, K. (1982). *In* "Oxford Textbook of Medicine" (J. G. G. Ledingham, D. A. Warrell, and D. J. Weatherall, eds.), Chap. 12.4. Oxford University Press, Oxford, England.
Chatterjee, K., and Parmley, W. W. (1977). *Prog. Cardiovasc. Dis.* **19**, 301–325.
Chatterjee, K., and Parmley, W. W. (1983). *J. Am. Coll. Cardiol.* **1**, 133–153.
Chatterjee, K., and Swan, H. J. C. (1973). *In* "Myocardial Infarction" (E. Corday and H. J. C. Swan, eds.), pp. 51–61. Williams and Wilkins Publishers, Baltimore, Maryland.
Chatterjee, K., Sacoor, M., Sutton, G. C., and Miller, G. A. H. (1971). *British Heart J.* **33**, 565–571.
Chatterjee, K., Parmley, W., Ganz, W., Forrester, J., Walinsky, P., Crexells, C., and Swan, H. J. C. (1973a). *Circulation* **48**, 1183–1193.
Chatterjee, K., Parmley, W. W., Swan, H. J. C., Berman, G., Forrester, J., and Marcus, H. S. (1973b). *Circulation* **48**, 684–690.
Chatterjee, K., Drew, D., Parmley, W. W., Klausner, S. C., Polansky, J., and Zacherle, B. (1976a). *Ann. Intern. Med.* **85**, 467–470.
Chatterjee, K., Swan, H. J. C., Kaushik, V. S., Jobin, G., Magnusson, P., and Forrester, J. S. (1976b). *Circulation* **53**, 797–802.
Chatterjee, K., Parmley, W. W., Massie, B., Greenberg, B., Werner, J., and Klausner, S. (1976c). *Circulation* **54**, 879–883.
Chatterjee, K., Massie, B., Rubin, S., Gelberg, H., Brundage, B. H., and Ports, T. A. (1978). *Am. J. Med.* **65**, 134–144.
Chatterjee, K., Ports, T. A., Parmley, W. W. (1979). *In* "Vasodilator Therapy for Cardiac Disorders" (L. Gould and C. V. R. Reddy, eds.), Chap. 3, pp. 25–62. Futura Publishing Co., Mt. Kisco, New York.
Chatterjee, K., Ports, T. A., and Parmley, W. W. (1981). *In* "Advances and Controversies in Cardiology" (E. Donoso, ed.), Vol. 1, Chap. 8, pp. 136–193. Thieme-Stratton, Inc., New York-Stuttgart.
Chatterjee, K., Rouleau, J.-L., and Parmley, W. W. (1982). *British Heart J.* **47**, 671–678.
Chiariello, M., Gold, H. K., Leinbach, R. C., Davis, M. A., and Maroko, P. R. (1976). *Circulation* **54**, 766–773.
Chiche, P., Baligadao, J. J., and Derrida, J. P. (1979). *Circulation* **59** & **60** (Suppl. II), II-165.
Cody, R. J. (1985). *Am. J. Cardiol.* **55**, 36A–40A.
Cody, R., Covit, A., Schaer, G., and Laragh, J. (1983). *J. Am. Coll. Cardiol.* **1**, 1154–1159.
Cogan, J. J., Humphreys, M. H., Carson, C. J., and Rapaport, E. (1979). *Clin. Res.* **27**, A39.
Cohn, J. N. (1981). *Am. J. Med.* **71**, 135–139.
Cohn, J. N., Franciosa, J. A., and Astargiacomo, A. (1974a). *Circulation* **49** & **50** (Suppl. III), III-103.
Cohn, J., Guiha, N., Broder, M., and Constantinos, J. (1974b). *Am. J. Cardiol.* **33**, 209–214.
Cohn, J. N., Franciosa, J. A., Francis, C. S., Archibald, D., Tristani, F., Fletcher, R., Montero, A., Cintron, G., Clarke, J., Hager, D., Saunders, R., Cobb, F., Smith, R., Loeb, H., and Settle, H. (1982). *New Engl. J. Med.* **306**, 1129–1135.
Colucci, W. S., Wynne, J., Holman, B. L., and Braunwald, E. (1980). *Am. J. Cardiol.* **45**, 337–399.
Creager, M. A., Halperin, J. L., Bernard, D. B., Faxon, D. P., Melidossian, C. D., Gavras, H., and Ryan, T. J. (1981). *Circulation* **64**, 483–489.
Curtiss, C., Cohn, J. N., Vrobel, T., and Franciosa, J. A. (1979). *Circulation* **58**, 763–770.
daLuz, P., Forrester, J., Wyatt, J., Tyberg, J. V., Chagrasulis, R., Parmley, W. W., and Swan, H. J. C. (1975). *Circulation* **52**, 400–407.
Dario, J. O. (1962). *Circulation* **25**, 1002–1014.

Davis, R., Ribner, H. S., Keung, E., Sonnenblick, E., and LeJemtel, T. H. (1979). *New Engl. J. Med.* **301,** 117–121.
DiCarlo, L., Chatterjee, K., Parmley, W., Swedberg, K., Atherton, P., Curran, D., and Cucci, M. (1983). *J. Am. Coll. Cardiol.* **2,** 865–871.
Dunn, R., Botvinick, E., Benge, W., Chatterjee, K., and Parmley, W. W. (1982). *Am. J. Cardiol.* **49,** 1719–1727.
Durrer, J. D., Lie, K. I., vanCapelle, F. J. L., and Durrer, D. (1982). *New Engl. J. Med.* **306,** 1121–1128.
Dzau, V. J., Colucci, W. S., Wilhams, G. H., Curfman, G., Meggs, L., and Hollenberg, N. (1980). *New Engl. J. Med.* **302,** 1373–1379.
Dzau, V. J., Parker, M., Lilly, L., Swartz, S., Hollenberg, N., and Wilhams, G. (1984). *New Engl. J. Med.* **310,** 347–352.
Elkayam, U., Weber, L., Torkan, B., Berman, D., and Rahimtoola, S. (1983). *Am. J. Cardiol.* **52,** 1041–1045.
Elzinga, G., and Westerhof, N. (1973). *Circ. Res.* **32,** 178–186.
Feldman, R. L., and Conti, C. R. (1981). *Circulation* **64,** 1098–1100.
Ferguson, R. K., Brunner, H. R., and Turniga *et al.* (1977). *Lancet* **1,** 775–778.
Ferlinz, J., and Citron, D. (1983). *Am. J. Cardiol.* **51,** 1339–1352.
Fifer, M. A., Collucci, W. S., Lorell, B. H., Jaski, B. E., and Bany, W. H. (1985). *J. Am. Coll. Cardiol.* **5,** 731–737.
Fitchett, D., Neto, J., Oakley, C., and Goodwin, K. (1979). *Am. J. Cardiol.* **44,** 303–309.
Flaherty, J. T., Becker, L. C., Bulkley, B., Weiss, J., Gerstaublish, G., Kallman, G., Silverman, K., Wei, J., Pitt, B., and Weisfeldt, M. (1983). *Circulation* **68,** 576–588.
Forrester, J. S., Ganz, W., Diamond, G., McHugh, T., Chonette, D. W., and Swan, H. J. C. (1972). *Am. Heart J.* **83,** 306–311.
Fouad, F. M., Tarazi, R., Bravo, S. L., Hart, N. J., Castle, L. W., and Salcedo, E. E. (1982). *Am. J. Cardiol.* **49,** 1489–1496.
Franciosa, J. A., and Cohn, J. N. (1979). *Circulation* **50,** 1085–1091.
Franciosa, J. A., Guiha, N. M., Limas, C. J., Rodriguera, E., and Cohn, J. N. (1972). *Lancet* **1,** 650–657.
Franciosa, J. A., Pierpont, G., and Cohn, J. N. (1977). *Ann. Intern. Med.* **86,** 388–393.
Franciosa, J. A., Wilen, M. M., and Jordan, R. A. (1985). *J. Am. Coll. Cardiol.* **5,** 101–107.
Francis, G. S. (1985). *Am. J. Cardiol.* **55,** 15A–21A.
Francis, G. S., Goldsmith, S. R., Ziesche, S., and Cohn, J. N. (1982). *Am. J. Cardiol.* **49,** 1152–1156.
Garthoff, B., Kazda, S., Knorr, A., and Thomas, G. (1983). *Hypertension* **5** (Suppl. II), II-34–II-38.
Gavras, H., Flessas, A., Ryan, T. J., Brunner, H. R., Faxon, D. P., and Gavras, I. (1977). *J.A.M.A.* **238,** 880–882.
Genest, J., Granger, P., deChamplain, J., and Boucher, R. (1968). *Am. J. Cardiol.* **22,** 35–42.
Gold, H. K., Chiariello, M., and Leinbach, R. C. (1976). *Herz* **1,** 161–166.
Goldberg, M. J., Franklin, B. A., Rubenfine, M., Kevin, N. Z., Willens, H. J., and Ruskin, R. (1983). *J. Am. Coll. Cardiol.* **2,** 887–893.
Goldman, S. A., Johnson, L. L., Escala, E., Cannon, P. J., and Weiss, M. B. (1980). *Am. J. Med.* **68,** 36–42.
Goldstein, J. A., Vlahakes, G. J., Verrier, E. D., Schiller, N. B., Tyberg, J. V., Ports, T. A., and Parmley, W. W. (1982). *Circulation* **65,** 513–522.
Goldstone, R., Martin, K., Zypser, R., and Horton, R. (1981). *Prostaglandins* **22,** 587–598.
Gould, L., and Reddy, C. V. R. (1979). *In* "Vasodilator Therapy for Cardiac Disorders" (L. Gould and C. Reddy, eds.), Chap. 4, pp. 63–75. Futura Publishing Co., New York.

Gould, L., Zahir, M., Shariff, M., and Giuliani, M. (1970a). *Japanese Heart J.* **11,** 17–25.
Gould, L., Zahir, M., Shariff, M., and Giuliani, M. (1970b). *Japanese Heart J.* **11,** 141–148.
Gould, L., Reddy, C. V. R., Kalanithi, P., Espinai, L., and Gomprecht, R. F. (1974). *Am. Heart J.* **88,** 144–148.
Gould, L., Reddy, C. V. R., and Blatt, C. J. (1975). *British Heart J.* **37,** 647–654.
Gray, R., Chatterjee, K., Vyden, J. K., Ganz, W., Forrester, J. S., and Swan, H. J. C. (1975). *Am. J. Cardiol.* **36,** 56–61.
Greenberg, B. H., Massie, B. M., Brundage, B. N., Botvinick, E. H., Parmley, W. W., and Chatterjee, K. (1978). *Circulation* **58,** 273–279.
Hacking, B. E. F., Cope, G. D., Clarke, G. M., and Taylor, R. R. (1981). *Am. J. Cardiol.* **48,** 345–352.
Halperin, J. L., Faxon, D. P., Creager, M. A., Bass, T. A., Melidossian, C. D., Gavras, H., and Ryan, T. J. (1982). *Am. J. Cardiol.* **50,** 967–972.
Hanrath, P., Schluter, M., Sonntag, F., Diemert, J., and Bleifeld, W. (1983). *Am. J. Cardiol.* **52,** 544–548.
Haupt, H., Hutchins, G., and Moore, W. (1983). *Circulation* **67,** 1268–1272.
Heel, R. C., Brogden, R. W., Speight, T. M., and Avery, G. S. (1980). *Drugs* **20,** 409–452.
Helfant, R., Pine, R., Meister, S., Feldman, M. S., Trout, R. G., and Banka, V. S. (1974). *Circulation* **50,** 108–112.
Hermiller, J., Magorien, R., Leitke, M., Unverferth, D., and Leier, C. (1983). *Am. J. Cardiol.* **51,** 791–795.
Hockings, B. E. F., Cope, G. D., Clarke, G. M., and Taylor, R. R. (1981). *Am. J. Cardiol.* **48,** 345–352.
Horowitz, J., Antman, E., Lorell, B., Varry, W., and Smith, T. (1983). *Circulation* **68,** 1247–1253.
Ichikawa, L., Pfeffer, J. M., Pfeffer, M. A., Hostetter, T. H., and Brenner, B. M. (1985). *Circ. Res.* **55,** 669–675.
Johnston, C. I., Davis, J. O., Robb, C. A., Mackenzie, J. W. (1968). *Circ. Res.* **22,** 113–125.
Judson, W. E., Hollander, W., and Willeins, R. W. (1956). *Circulation* **13,** 664–694.
Jugdutt, B. (1983). *Circulation* **68,** 673–684.
Kaneho, Y., Ikeda, T., Takeda, T., and Ueda, H. (1967). *J. Clin. Invest.* **46,** 705–716.
Kirk, E. S., LeJemtel, T. H., Nelson, G. R., and Sonnenblick, E. H. (1978). *Am. J. Med.* **65,** 189–196.
Klausner, R., Ratshin, R., Tyberg, J. V., Lappin, H. A., Chatterjee, K., and Parmley, W. W. (1976). *Circulation* **54,** 615–623.
Klein, H., Tordiman, T., Ninio, R., Sarelli, P., Oren, V., Long, R., Geton, J., Pauzner, C., Segni, E., David, D., and Kaplinsky, E. (1983). *Circulation* **67,** 558–565.
Klein, R. C., Amsterdam, E. A., Pratt, C., Laslett, L., Miller, M., Lee, G., DeMaria, A. N., and Mason, D. T. (1978). *Clin. Res.* **26,** 243A.
Koch-Weser, J. (1976). *New Engl. J. Med.* **295,** 320–323.
Kotter, V., VanLeitner, E. R., Wunderlich, J., and Schrader, R. (1977). *British Heart J.* **39,** 1196–1224.
Kramer, B. L., Massie, B., and Topic, N. (1983). *Circulation* **67,** 807–816.
Krebs, R. (1983). *Hypertension* **5** (Suppl. II), II-125–II-129.
Kubo, S., Nishioka, A., Nishimura, H., Sonotani, N., and Takatsu, T. (1980). *Japanese Circ. J.* **44,** 427–437.
Leier, C. V., Huss, P., Magorien, R. D., and Unverferth, D. V. (1983). *Circulation* **67,** 817–822.
Levine, T. B., Franciosa, J. A., and Cohn, J. W. (1980). *Circulation* **62,** 35–41.
Levine, T. B., Francis, G. S., Goldsmith, S. R., and Cohn, J. N. (1983a). *Circulation* **67,** 1070–1075.

Levine, T., Olivari, M., Garberg, V., Sharkey, S., and Cohn, J. N. (1983b). *Circulation* **69**, 548–553.
Lorell, B., Leinbach, R., Pohost, A., Gold, H., Dinsmore, R., Hutter, A., Pastore, J., and DeSanctis, R. (1979). *Am. J. Cardiol.* **43**, 465–471.
McAnulty, J., Hattenhauer, M., Rosch, J., Kloster, F. E., and Rahimtoola, S. H. (1975). *Circulation* **51**, 140–145.
McGregor, M. (1982). *Circulation* **66**, 689–692.
McKay, C. R., Chatterjee, K., Ports, T. A., Holly, A. N., and Parmley, W. W. (1982). *Am. Heart J.* **104**, 575–580.
Magnusson, P., Shell, W. E., Forrester, J. S., Charuzi, Y., Singh, B. N., and Swan, H. J. C. (1976). *Circulation* **53** & **54** (Suppl. II), II-28.
Magorien, R. D., Brown, G. P., Unverferth, D. V., Nelson, S., Boudoulas, H., Bambach, D., and Leier, C. V. (1982). *Circulation* **65**, 528–533.
Mahler, F., Ross, J., O'Rourke, R. A., and Covell, J. (1975). *Am. J. Cardiol.* **35**, 626–634.
Markham, R. V., Gilmore, A., Pettinger, W., Braten, D., Corbett, J. R., and Firth, B. (1983). *Am. J. Cardiol.* **52**, 774–781.
Massie, B., Chatterjee, K., Werner, J., Greenberg, B., Hart, R., and Parmley, W. W. (1977). *Am. J. Cardiol.* **40**, 794–801.
Massie, B., Ports, T., Chatterjee, K., Ostlund, J., O'Young, J., Haughbom, F., and Parmley, W. (1981). *Circulation* **63**, 269–278.
Massie, B. M., Packer, M., Hanlon, J., and Combs, T. (1983). *J. Am. Coll. Cardiol.* **2**, 338–344.
Matsui, S., Murakawi, F., Takekishi, N., Emoto, J., and Matoba, M. (1983). *Am. J. Cardiol.* **51**, 1364–1368.
Mehta, J., Mehta, P., Roberts, A., Faro, R., Ostrowski, N., and Brigman, C. (1983). *J. Am. Coll. Cardiol.* **2**, 625–630.
Meister, S., and Helfant, R. (1972). *New Engl. J. Med.* **287**, 1024–1029.
Merril, A. J., Morrison, J. L., and Brannon, E. S. (1946). *Am. J. Med.* **1**, 468–472.
Milnar, W. (1975). *Circ. Res.* **36**, 565–570.
Minami, M., Yasuda, H., Yamazaki, N., Kajima, S., Nishiyima, H., Matsumura, N., Togashi, H., Koike, Y., and Saito, H. (1983). *Circulation* **67**, 1324–1329.
Moore, T. J., Crantz, F. R., Hollenberg, N. K., Koletsky, R. J., Leboff, M. S., Swartz, S. L., Levine, L., Podolsky, S., Dluhy, R. G., and Williams, G. H. (1981). *Hypertension* **3**, 168–173.
Mueller, H., Religa, A., Evans, R., and Ayres, S. (1974). *Am. J. Cardiol.* **33**, 158.
Mulkherje, D., Feldman, M. S., and Helfant, R. H. (1975). *Circulation* **51** (Suppl. II), 221.
Murgo, J., Westerhof, N., Giolma, J., and Altobelli, S. A. (1980). *Circulation* **62**, 105–116.
Nelson, G., Silke, B., Forsyth, D., Verma, S., Hussain, M., and Taylor, S. (1983). *Am. J. Cardiol.* **52**, 1036–1040.
Nicholls, M. G., Espiner, E. A., Ikram, H., Maslowski, A. H., Lun, S., and Scandrett, M. S. (1981). *J. Clin. Endocrin. Metabol.* **52**, 1253–1256.
Nichols, W., and Pepine, C. (1982). *Prog. Cardiovasc. Dis.* **24**, 293–306.
Nichols, W. W., Conti, C. R., Waller, W. E., and Milnor, W. R. (1977). *Circ. Res.* **40**, 451–458.
Noble, M. I. M., Gabe, I. T., Trenchard, D., and Guz, A. (1967). *Cardiovasc. Res.* **1**, 9–20.
Olivari, M. T., Carlyle, P. F., Levine, B., and Cohn, J. N. (1983a). *J. Am. Coll. Cardiol.* **2**, 872–878.
Olivari, M. T., Levine, T. B., and Cohn, J. N. (1983b). *J. Am. Coll. Cardiol.* **2**, 411–417.
Onoyama, K., Hirakata, H., Iseki, K., Fujimi, S., Omae, T., Kobayashi, M., and Kawahara, Y. (1981). *Hypertension* **3**, 456–459.

Opie, L. H. (1980). *Lancet* **1**, 750-753.
O'Rourke, M., and Taylor, M. (1967). *Circ. Res.* **20**, 365-385.
Packer, M. (1983). *J. Am. Coll. Cardiol.* **2**, 841-852.
Packer, M., Meller, J., Gorlin, R., and Herman, M. V. (1979a). *Circulation* **59**, 531-539.
Packer, M., Meller, J., Medina, N., Gorlin, R., and Herman, M. (1979b). *Circulation* **59 & 60** (Suppl. II), II-182.
Packer, M., Meller, J., Medina, N., Yushak, M., and Gorlin, R. (1982). *New Engl. J. Med.* **306**, 57-62.
Packer, M., Medina, N., and Yushak, M. (1984). *Circulation* **70**, II-305.
Parmley, W. W., and Chatterjee, K. (1978). *In* "Current Problems in Cardiology," Vol. II, No. 12, pp. 8-75. Yearbook Publications, Chicago.
Parmley, W. W., Chuck, L., Chatterjee, K., Swan, H. J. C., Klausner, S. C., Glanz, S. A., and Ratshin, R. A. (1976). *European J. Cardiol.* **4**, 105-120.
Patel, D., Defreitas, F., and Fry, D. (1963). *J. Appl. Physiol.* **18**, 134-140.
Pederson, O. L. (1983). *Hypertension* **5** (Suppl. II), II-74–II-79.
Pepine, C., and Nichols, W. (1982). *Prog. Cardiovasc. Dis.* **24**, 307-318.
Pepine, C., Nichols, W., and Conti, C. (1978). *Circulation* **58**, 460-465.
Pepine, C., Nichols, W., Curry, R., and Conti, C. R. (1979). *J. Clin. Invest.* **64**, 643-654.
Perry, H. (1973). *Am. J. Med.* **54**, 56-72.
Peterson, K. L., Sklavon, D., Ludbrook, P., Uther, J. B., and Ross, J. (1974). *Circulation* **49**, 1088-1101.
Pettinger, W. (1980). *New Engl. J. Med.* **303**, 922-926.
Pierpont, G. L., Francis, G. S., and Cohn, J. N. (1981). *British Heart J.* **46**, 522-527.
Polese, A., Fiorentini, C., Olivari, M., Guazzi, M. (1979). *Am. J. Med.* **66**, 825-830.
Ports, T. A., Chatterjee, K., Wilkinson, P., Avakian, D., and Parmley, W. W. (1983). *Am. Heart J.* **106**, 1036-1042.
Powers, E. R., Reison, D. S., Berke, A., Weiss, M. B., and Cannon, P. J. (1982). *Circulation* **66** (Suppl. II), II-211.
Quyyami, A. A., Wagstaff, D., and Evans, T. R. (1983). *Am. J. Cardiol.* **51**, 1353-1357.
Raemsch, K. D., and Sommer, J. (1983). *Hypertension* **5** (Suppl. II), II-18–II-24.
Raskin, N. H., and Rishman, R. A. (1965). *New Engl. J. Med.* **273**, 1182-1185.
Ratliff, N., and Hackel, D. (1980). *Am. J. Cardiol.* **45**, 217-224.
Rietveld, A., Merrman, L., Essed, C., Trimbos, M., and Hagemeijer, F. (1983). *J. Am. Coll. Cardiol.* **2**, 776-779.
Rigo, P., Murray, M., Taylor, D., Weisfeldt, M., Kelly, D., Strauss, H., and Pitt, B. (1975). *Circulation* **52**, 268-274.
Roberts, W., and Cohen, L. (1972). *Circulation* **46**, 138-147.
Roberts, W., and Perloff, J. (1972). *Ann. Intern. Med.* **77**, 939-944.
Romankiewicz, J. A., Brogden, R. N., Heel, R. C., Speight, T. M., and Avery, G. S. (1983). *Drugs* **25**, 6-40.
Ross, J., Jr. (1976). *Prog. Cardiovasc. Dis.* **18**, 255-264.
Rouleau, J.-L., Warnica, J., and Burgess, J. (1981). *Am. J. Med.* **71**, 147-152.
Rouleau, J.-L., Chatterjee, K., Benge, W., Parmley, W. W., and Hiramatsu, B. (1982). *Circulation* **65**, 671-678.
Sarnoff, S. F., and Farr, H. W. (1944). *Anesthesiology* **5**, 1-69.
Scheidt, S., Wilner, G., Fillmore, S., Shapiro, M., and Killip, T. (1973). *British Heart J.* **35**, 908-916.
Sharpe, D. N., Botvinick, E. H., Shames, D. M., Schiller, N. B., Massie, B. M., Chatterjee, K., and Parmley, W. W. (1978). *Circulation* **57**, 483-490.
Sharpe, D. N., Coxon, R. J., Douglas, J. E., and Long, B. (1980). *Lancet* **2**, 1154-1157.

Shell, W. E., and Sobel, B. E. (1974). *New Engl. J. Med.* **297**, 481–486.
Sonnenblick, E. (1962). *Am. J. Physiol.* **202**, 931–939.
Stinson, E. B., Holloway, E. L., Derby, G., Oyer, P. E., Hollingsworth, J., Griepp, R. B., and Harrison, D. C. (1975). *Circulation* **51**, 1–26.
Swan, H. J. C., Ganz, W., Forrester, J. S., Marcus, H., Diamond, G., and Chonette, D. (1970). *New Engl. J. Med.* **283**, 447–451.
Swartz, S. L., and Williams, G. H. (1982). *Am. J. Cardiol.* **49**, 1405–1407.
Synhorst, D., Lauer, R., Doty, D., and Brady, M. (1976). *Circulation* **54**, 472–477.
Talseth, T. (1976). *J. Clin. Pharmacol.* **10**, 183–187.
Taylor, S. H., Sutherland, G. R., MacKenzie, G. J., Staunton, H. P., and Donald, K. W. (1965). *Circulation* **31**, 741–754.
Taylor, W. R., Forrester, J., Magnusson, P., Forrester, J. S., and Swan, H. J. C. (1976). *Am. J. Cardiol.* **38**, 469–473.
Tecklenberg, P. L., Fitzgerald, J., Allaire, B. I., Alderman, E. L., and Harrison, D. C. (1976). *Am. J. Cardiol.* **38**, 956–958.
Thomas, J. A., and Marks, B. H. (1978). *Am. J. Cardiol.* **41**, 234–243.
Turini, G. A., Brunner, H. R., Ferguson, R. K., Rivier, J. L., and Gavras, H. (1978). *British Heart J.* **40**, 1134–1142.
Turini, G. A., Brunner, H. R., Gribic, M., Waeber, B., and Gavras, H. (1979). *Lancet* **1**, 1213–1215.
van Zwieten, P. A., van Meel, J. C., and Timmermans, P. (1983). *Hypertension* **5** (Suppl. II), II-8–II-17.
Vlodarer, Z., and Edwards, J. (1977). *Circulation* **55**, 815–820.
Wackers, F., Lie, K., Sakole, E., Res, J., VanDerSchoot, J., and Durrer, D. (1978). *Am. J. Cardiol.* **42**, 358–375.
Walinsky, P., Chatterjee, K., Forrester, J., Parmley, W. W., and Swan, H. J. C. (1974). *Am. J. Cardiol.* **33**, 37–41.
Walsh, R. W., Porter, C. B., Starling, M. R., and O'Rourke, R. A. (1984). *J. Am. Coll. Cardiol.* **3**, 1044–1050.
Wartman, W., and Hellerstein, H. (1948). *Ann. Intern. Med.* **28**, 41–73.
Watkins, L., Burton, J. A., Haber, E., Cant, J. R., Smith, F. W., and Barger, A. C. (with technical assistance of McNeil, S. E., and Sherrill, S. M.). (1976). *J. Clin. Invest.* **57**, 1606–1617.
Weber, K. T., Kinasewitz, G. T., West, J. S., Janicki, J. S., Reichek, N., and Fishman, A. P. (1980). *New Engl. J. Med.* **303**, 242–250.
Wei, J., Hutchins, G., and Buckley, B. (1979). *Ann. Intern. Med.* **90**, 149–154.
Wilson, J. R., Sutton, M., Schwartz, J., Ferraro, N., and Reichek, N. (1983). *Am. J. Cardiol.* **52**, 299–303.
Witzgall, H., Hirsch, F., Scherer, B., and Weber, P. C. (1982). *Clin. Sci.* **62**, 611–615.
Zelis, R., and Flaim, S. F. (1982). *Prog. Cardiovasc. Dis.* **25**, 437–459.
Zelis, R., Flaim, S. F., Liedtke, A. J., and Nevis, S. H. (1981). *Ann. Rev. Physiol.* **43**, 455–476.
Zucker, I. H., Earle, A. M., and Gilmore, J. P. (1977). *J. Clin. Invest.* **60**, 323–331.
Zucker, I. H., Shire, L., and Gilmore, J. P. (1979). *Am. J. Physiol.* **236**, H554–H560.

# 3 Pump Failure: Role of Vasopressor Agents

## C. V. Ramana Reddy and Nabil El-Sherif

## I. Introduction

With the advent of modern techniques of coronary care and improved methods of treating ventricular arrhythmias, the in-hospital mortality rate from acute myocardial infarction (AMI) has been dramatically reduced from 30 to 10% (Resnekov, 1973). Currently, derangement of left ventricular (LV) pump function accounts for most of the in-hospital deaths after AMI. This pump failure in the majority is due to loss of a critical mass of left ventricular muscle and in some due to strategically located mechanical abnormalities that interfere with cardiac function. The extreme forms of pump failure—pulmonary edema and shock—carry high mortality despite therapeutic heroics. These syndromes have been found to be associated with larger infarctions than those exhibited by patients who succumbed to AMI but who did not die as a consequence of pump failure (Page et al., 1971). It is a well-known fact that the prognosis for patients with larger infarcts is worse than for those with smaller infarcts. When 40% of the LV is infarcted, LV pumping function falls to a level at which survival is unusual (Page et al., 1971; Alonso et al., 1973).

Recent observation that the pattern of myocardial death in AMI is that of ischemia and necrosis of an enlarging wave front progressing over hours to days (Reimer and Jennings, 1979; Gutovitz et al., 1978) and their prognosis is related to infarct size has led to extensive work in an effort to reduce myocardial ischemia and limit permanent cardiac damage. A number of therapeutic modalities are currently available to treat pump failure in AMI. However, their use is only of temporary benefit since long-term prognosis in the majority of patients was not altered. Hence, it is imperative that all efforts should be directed at early institution of therapies to prevent pump failure in AMI rather than treat after the fact. Early myocardial revascularization appears to be promising in improving survival following AMI (Braunwald, 1985; Kennedy et al., 1985).

In this chapter, we will attempt to discuss the pathophysiologic mechanisms underlying pump failure in AMI. Pharmacotherapy, in particular, vasoactive drugs, will be reviewed.

## II. Pathophysiology

### A. Definition and Incidence of Pump Failure at AMI

Pump failure is an abnormal physiologic state caused by the inability of the heart to deliver sufficient blood to satisfy the metabolic requirements of the tissues. Shock in AMI is, in most cases, a continuance of pump failure and is best defined as a complex pathophysiologic state of marked reduction in tissue blood flow and oxygen delivery below levels required to meet metabolic demands, resulting in progressive impairment of organ function despite compensatory mechanisms (Thal and Kinney, 1967; Jacobson, 1968; Rackley et al., 1975). The diagnosis of shock is based on the demonstration of inadequate tissue perfusion and impaired cellular and organ function. In most cases, shock in AMI represents a vicious cycle of progressive ischemic damage culminating in irreversible myocardial dysfunction ( Page et al., 1971; Gutovitz et al., 1978; Geddes et al., 1980). Although impaired LV function is an important factor in the genesis of pump failure and shock, reduction in venous return (vasomotor and microcirculatory dysfunction), abnormalities in peripheral vascular regulation, disturbances in rhythm, abnormalities in oxygenation, and acid–base metabolism may all play a role.

Clinical and radiologic signs of mild to moderate heart failure have been observed in approximately half of all patients admitted with AMI (Wolk et al., 1972). Severe heart failure or pulmonary edema is less common, occurring in approximately 12% of these patients (Wolk et al., 1972). The incidence of shock following AMI remains at 10 to 15% and carries a mortality of 50 to 100% (Scheidt et al., 1970; Loeb et al., 1976; Rackley et al., 1975; Amsterdam et al., 1976). The high mortality is related chiefly to extensive irreversible myocardial dysfunction.

Mild to moderate pump failure in AMI manifests itself with signs of pulmonary congestion, prominent third and fourth heart sounds, and radiologic evidence of vascular blurring, dilatation of pulmonary arteries, and parenchymal clouding. One may or may not have cardiomegaly. The murmur of papillary muscle dysfunction is not uncommon. The cardinal feature of shock is inadequate tissue blood flow manifested by signs of peripheral vasoconstriction, altered sensorium, oliguria (urine output less than 20 ml/hr), and, usually, hypotension with peak systolic pressure less than 90 mm Hg. It is important to stress that shock can occur without hypotension. The latter occurs relatively late indicating inadequate reflex vasoconstriction. Decrease in systolic pressure by 30 mm Hg or more below the baseline value can decrease the perfusion pressure and flow may drop below critical levels required for cellular viability. It is equally important to stress that one has to rule out other extracardiac factors that may cause hypotension and low cardiac output prior to establishing the diagnosis of shock in AMI.

## B. Determinants of Myocardial Oxygen Demand and Supply

Final infarct size in AMI is the end result of factors determining myocardial oxygen consumption and supply. Several studies have demonstrated the potential for reduction of ischemia and thereby infarct size by favorable alteration of the cardiac oxygen supply–demand balance (Maroko and Braunwald, 1973). Understanding of the regulation of myocardial oxygen consumption and supply is fundamental to this approach (Sonnenblick and Skelton, 1971).

The major physiologic factors that determine the heart's demand for oxygen are the heart size, the LV systolic pressure, the heart rate, and the level of myocardial inotropic state. Myocardial tension, which is directly related to LV volume, pressure, and radius, probably has the most influence on myocardial oxygen demand in AMI. Myocardial oxygen consumption is also affected by afterload and preload on myocardium. The resting cardiac size is conventionally related to preload and LV pressure to afterload. These two factors thus influence the LV wall tension. Thus an increased preload at any given level of LV systolic pressure will augment wall tension and vice versa. Similarly an increase in afterload at any level of end-diastolic dimension or volume will also tend to increase wall stress. Understanding these physiologic interactions is of particular importance, especially when assessing the role of vasodilators in treating pump failure.

The heart rate and contractility also affect the myocardial oxygen consumption. According to these considerations, any therapeutic intervention that diminishes heart size, left ventricular pressure, heart rate, and inotropic state will decrease myocardial oxygen demand. Less important to myocardial oxygen consumption are the roles played by myocardial fiber shortening, basal metabolism, and energy required for activation and relaxation.

Ordinarily, an increase in the myocardial oxygen demand is readily met by an increase in myocardial oxygen supply, and this supply is principally related to coronary blood flow. Since oxygen extraction is nearly maximal in the heart, under states of stress, increasing the blood flow is the principal mechanism for augmenting the tissue oxygenation. The mechanical factors that impair the oxygen delivery include severity of atherosclerotic deposition in the coronary arteries, low aortic diastolic pressure, and shortened LV diastolic filling time. Coronary blood flow is also governed by several autoregulatory mechanisms which modulate the coronary vascular resistance and thereby the flow through the coronary arteries. The diseased coronary artery with atherosclerotic narrowing is unresponsive to the autoregulatory stimuli and is incapable of dilating. Hence the mechanical factors, especially aortic diastolic pressure, assume importance in controlling the flow.

Blood flow through the subendocardial layers mainly occurs during diastole and is dependent upon coronary perfusion pressure, major determinants of which are aortic diastolic pressure and the intramyocardial diastolic pressure. The latter is related to LV diastolic pressure. If this parameter is elevated, the net driving force across the coronary vessels is decreased and subendocardial flow is impeded. Thus, in pump failure of AMI it is important to maintain a normal blood pressure while efforts are made to decrease the preload in order to improve the subendocardial flow, thereby preventing further ischemia. At the same time attempts at decreasing the myocardial oxygen demands will help to preserve the ischemic myocardium and improve myocardial function.

### C. Effects of Myocardial Ischemia

The effects of myocardial ischemia on cardiac performance as a pump have been known for more than 45 years. Tennant and Wiggers (1935) first observed diminished myocardial contractility following coronary occlusion in dogs. The myocardial performance as a pump is affected virtually instantly when the flow in a major coronary artery is interrupted. Cardiac contractions weaken within a few beats and in less than a minute the ischemic segment is visibly cyanotic and no langer participates in ejection of blood. Instead it bulges outward with each systole, unable to exert sufficient tension to overcome the intraventricular pressure being generated by the unaffected, still normally perfused, remainder of the heart muscle. Sudden interruption of myocardial bloody supply has similar consequences in man (Katz, 1978).

### D. Hemodynamic Consequences

The fundamental physiologic abnormality underlying pump failure in AMI is depression of myocardial contractility as a result of loss of a part of functioning myocardium (Swan *et al.*, 1972; Amsterdam, 1973). This depression of ventricular performance generally results in a spectrum of derangement of hemodynamic parameters of cardiac function. The initial hemodynamic abnormality is a reduction in systemic blood pressure, cardiac output, stroke output, cardiac work, stroke work, and LV ejection fraction, with resultant elevation of LV filling pressure (Scheidt et al., 1970, Gunnar et al., 1968; Karliner and Ross, 1971; Amsterdam et al., 1973). Derangement of underlying hemodynamic function may be marked in congestive heart failure without hypotension, but it is quantitatively of lesser degree than cardiogenic shock (Regan et al., 1971)

The diminution of contractile mass leads to regional ventricular dyssynergy, decreased ejection fraction, and a larger diastolic volume (Regan et al., 1971; Ambrose et al., 1985). Consequently, LV filling pressure and left atrial mean pressure rise (Hamosh and Cohn, 1971; Regan et al., 1971). Although these increases are in part related to reduced systolic function, a more important contributing factor is decreased compliance and distensibility of the ischemic myocardium (Sasayama et al., 1985). A major consequence of this is that the normal ventricular function (Starling) curve is depressed, flattened, and shifted to the right. In progressive cardiogenic shock a descending limb may also be described (Bradley et al., 1970; Rackley and Russell, 1972; Ratshin et al., 1972). In severe forms of pump failure, such as shock states, the depressed stroke volume may be relatively fixed (Bradley et al., 1970).

Increase in pulmonary venous pressure results as a consequence of increased left atrial pressure, which in turn produces transudation of fluid, and pulmonary edema results. Systemic arterial hypoxemia may result as a consequence of impaired alveolar-capillary diffusion and venous admixture caused by pulmonary edema. (Loeb et al., 1971). Pulmonary arterial pressure is also elevated in severe forms of pump failure as a result of passive transmission of elevated LV diastolic pressure and increased pulmonary vascular resistance due to hypoxia and acidosis. Right ventricular failure may result from significant pulmonary hypertension or from infarction involving the right ventricle.

### E. Power Failure and Infarct Size

It has been well established that power failure in the absence of mechanical complications such as ventricular septal rupture or mitral regurgitation occurs strictly in proportion to the extent of myocardial ischemia and infarction size. If an area of myocardial ischemia is large, even transient asynergy can lead to clinical evidence of heart failure. Hemodynamic evidence of LV failure is evident when the contraction ceases or is seriously impaired in 20 to 25% of the LV (Buja and Roberts, 1974). Lesions involving more than 40% of LV myocardium are associated with severe degrees of pump failure and shock syndrome. Presumably, it is within this relatively narrow range of LV damage (between 20 and 40%) that the entire spectrum of heart failure from mild to severe becomes clinically apparent. The net loss of critical mass of LV muscle producing pump failure may not necessarily be acute. Small acute infarction superimposed on a previous infarction may result in pump failure of varied severity. Patients with small subendocardial infarctions also suffer and succumb to severe pump failure (Grande et al., 1983). These patients, however, have severe two- or three-vessel disease and or infarction–infarction fibrosis.

Pump failure and shock associated with posterior infarctions is more likely to be due to papillary muscle dysfunction or rupture than to the size of the infarction.

Marginal extension of a recent infarction can occur, resulting in a larger infarction area. Experimental and pathologic studies have confirmed that following AMI a variable area of ischemia (border zone) consisting of depressed but viable myocardial cells exists surrounding an irreversible zone of central necrosis (Maroko et al., 1971; Page et al., 1971; Alonso et al., 1973; Cox et al., 1968; Jennings et al., 1975; Reimer and Jennings, 1979; Braunwald, 1976). This border zone, under adverse conditions of increased oxygen demand, may progress to irreversible necrosis and result in further hemodynamic impairment leading to pump failure and shock. Since the fine balance between the oxygen supply and demand affect the outcome of this border zone, one should direct the initial therapy of AMI towards salvaging this ischemic myocardium.

### F. Power Failure and Infarction Locations

Although it is widely recognized that patients with larger infarcts are at risk of developing pump failure, several studies have shown that the relationship between infarct size and cardiogenic shock was independent of infarct location (Scheidt et al., 1970; Watson et al., 1970; Page et al., 1971; Buja and Roberts, 1974). There exists, however, substantial evidence that derangement of cardiac pump function is greater and occurrence of shock more frequent in anterior than inferior infarctions (Amsterdam, 1973; Ratshin et al., 1973; Miller et al., 1974, 1976; Amsterdam et al., 1975). The left anterior descending artery supplies a greater quantity of left ventricular myocardium than either the right or left circumflex arteries. The majority of the patients with pump failure and shock syndrome exhibit extensive involvement of the left anterior descending artery with or without significant atherosclerotic narrowing of the other two major coronary vessels (Wackers *et al.*, 1970). The extent to which myocardial necrosis is transmural is another important predisposing factor in the development of pump failure in AMI. Transmural infarcts, in particular anterior ones, are more prone to infarct expansion (Disproportionate regional dilatation of the infarct zone leading to acute cardiac dilation), aneurysm formation, and myocardial rupture. Nontransmural infarcts are not usually associated with these complications. Infarct expansion has two negative effects on LV function. First, the disproportionate stretching and dilatation of the infarct segment leads to an increase in the effective size of the infarct in relation to the total LV circumference. Second, infarct expansion increases the net cavity dilatation with resultant increase in volume. This poses additional hemodynamic burden to the LV. The normal myocardium, which is often oxygen-limited by virtue of obstructive coronary artery disease, faces increased oxygen demand. Thus infarct expansion adversely effects the LV function and pump failure may ensure. Factors that predispose to or contribute to infarct expansion are exercise, hypertension, elevated preload and afterload, and use of drugs that interfere with healing processes, such as corticosteroids.

Inferior infarction, however, is usually associated with substantially less myocardial damage. However, posterior-inferior infarctions may be associated with profound pump failure and shock due to papillary muscle rupture or right ventricular infarction. Combined anterior and inferior infarction is associated with the most severely impaired cardiac function and highest frequency of shock, a finding consistent with pathological data previously noted relating the extent of involved myocardium to functional derangement (Hughes *et al.*, 1971a).

About one-third of patients with inferior infarctions have occult infarction of the right ventricle and in some, right ventricular involvement is of such severity that cardiogenic shock may follow (Leinbach, 1980). This form of cardiogenic shock is both serious and important to recognize since its treatment is different from the more usual form of cardiogenic shock that predominately affects the left ventricle. Treating the hypotension inappropriately with vasopressors will increase the myocardial oxygen demand and aggravate ischemia. Right-heart monitoring not only provides the clues to the diagnosis of this entity but aids in guiding the appropriate therapy, which is fluid administration, frequently in large amounts (Leinbach, 1980).

### G. Role of Coronary Collateral Circulation

Collateral coronary circulation probably plays an important role in exerting protective effects on the myocardium in AMI. This potential beneficial role remains controversial in the pathogenesis of pump failure in AMI. In a study of 20 patients with acute transmural infarction who required emergency cardiac catheterization and angiography, Williams *et al.* (1975) found that the presence of collateral circulation to the infarcted area resulted in preservation of ventricular function. The incidence of shock and mortality were significantly less in patients with demonstrable collateral vessels to the area of infarction. This and the observation that the histologic size of an infarct is often smaller than the total area supplied by the occluded vessel lends support to the beneficial role of collateral coronary circulation. Some postmortem studies demonstrating lack of any relationship between collateral vessels and presence and extent of myocardial infarction, however, contradict the above conclusions (Zoll *et al.*, 1951; Snow *et al.*, 1955). The determinants that stimulate collateral channels to one area of ischemic myocardium but not to the others and the capacity for blood flow in these channels remains incompletely understood. However, the documented ability of collaterals to augment regional myocardial function in man suggests a potential for maintenance of local cell viability in myocardial infarction and critical reduction in extent of damage which may be sufficient to avert shock in some patients (Smith *et al.*, 1972; Elayda *et al.*, 1985).

## H. Mechanical Disturbances of Left Ventricular Function

The mechanical complications of AMI may significantly exacerbate the already existing pump failure or precipitate shock. Thus acute mitral regurgitation, ventricular septal rupture, and a large ventricular aneurysm may critically overload an already injured ventricle and further impair pump performance.

Acute mitral regurgitation as a result of ischemia of papillary muscle is more common than rupture (Heinkkila, 1967). Papillary muscle dysfunction produces varying degrees of mitral regurgitation from mild to severe (Burch *et al.*, 1968). In addition ischemia and/or infarction of the underlying myocardium with acute ventricular dilatation may produce mitral incompetence. The resultant volume overload impairs LV performance, further leading to a decrease in forward stroke volume and elevation in left atrial and pulmonary venous pressures. Rupture of papillary muscle is a catastrophic complication commonly involving the posterior papillary muscle (Cederquidt and Soderstrom, 1964; Robinson *et al.*, 1965; Estes *et al.*, 1966; Heinkkila, 1967). This lesion produces severe mitral regurgitation leading to fulminant pulmonary edema and low cardiac output state. It carries a high mortality: 90% succumb within 2 weeks.

3. Pump Failure: Role of Vasopressor Agents 93

Acute rupture of the ventricular septum is a grave complication of AMI and carries a high early mortality, the majority dying within 1 week (Sanders et al., 1956, 1957; Bernard and Kennedy, 1965). The defect most frequently involves the lower portion of the muscular septum (Switinbank, 1959) and is usually associated with extensive myocardial infarction involving the anteroseptal region as well as the LV free wall and, not uncommonly, the posterior region (Selzer et al., 1969). Abrupt clinical deterioration as a result of biventricular failure leading to shock is the rule.

Rupture of the LV free wall close to the interventricular septum occurs more commonly than interventricular septal rupture (London and London, 1965). Acute hemopericardium and tamponade result in death within minutes to hours. Most patients with cardiac rupture have had systemic hypertension, which along with an increase in end-diastolic volume augments intramyocardial wall stress. This additional mechanical stress is a contributing factor disrupting the structural integrity and leading to cardiac rupture (Oblath et al., 1952; Griffith et al., 1961; Van Tassel and Edwards, 1972).

Segmental wall motion abnormalities in the form of hypokinesis, akinesis, and dyskinesis may contribute to impaired LV function. Paradoxic motion of the infarcted segment results in diversion of stroke volume, thus reducing cardiac output. In general pump failure becomes evident where dyssynergy involves more than 20% of LV myocardium (Klein et al., 1967). Hemodynamic consequences as a result include increased end-diastolic volume, elevated LV filling pressure, and decreased stroke volume. The former may increase the myocardial oxygen requirements and augment myocardial ischemia. Dyskinesis may lead to mitral incompetence due to papillary muscle dysfunction. Serious ventricular arrhythmias may occur from this electrically unstable tissue.

## I. Peripheral Circulation and Feedback Mechanisms

The decrease in cardiac output following AMI evokes a number of compensatory mechanisms which help to restore blood flow to vital organs. In addition to local vasoregulatory mechanisms, sympathetic stimulation is a major expected response (Dole and O'Rourke, 1983). A reduction in mean arterial pressure, pulse pressure, and rate of pressure rise will inhibit baroreceptor activity, resulting in enhancement of sympathetic tone and a reduction of vagal tone (Abboud et al., 1976). The sympathoadrenal system is stimulated, releasing catecholamines. A chemoreceptor reflex is also said to be operative in the presence of tissue ischemia which further augments sympathoadrenal activity. The net effect produces increases in heart rate, myocardial contractility, and venous and arterial tones. Systemic pressure is maintained through arterial vasoconstriction (Abboud *et al.,* 1976).

Sympathetic-mediated vasoconstriction is more pronounced in skeletal muscle and cutaneous and splanchnic vascular beds. Coronary and cerebral vasculature possessing autoregulatory capacity are least affected, the overall effect being redistribution of blood flow to the vital organs. The renin–angiotensin system producing angiotensin II also becomes operative thorugh reduction in renal perfusion pressure and stimulation of renal nerves. Angiotensin II, a potent vasoconstrictor, contributes to maintenance of blood pressure (Abboud *et al.,* 1976; Errington and Rocha e Silva, 1974).

In mild to moderate pump failure, these compensatory mechanisms help maintain reasonable stability in the already depressed circulatory state. In severe forms of pump failure, these compensatory mechanisms fail to provide adequate tissue perfusion. Occasionally, a fall in peripheral resistance occurs but is accompanied by no change or rise in cardiac output. Impairment of sympathetic reflex vasoconstriction in AMI has been demonstrated experimentally (Agress *et al.,* 1952; Toubes and Brody, 1970; Hanley *et al.,* 1971) and clinically (Hughes *et al.,* 1971b). it has been attributed to inhibition of vasoconstriction and competitive vasodilation produced by inhibitory reflexes from receptors in the myocardium. These receptors are activated by chemical or mechanical stimuli arising in the infarcted and ischemic cardiac muscle and mediated by vagal and sympathetic efferent pathways (Constantin, 1963; Sleight and Widdicombe, 1966; Kezdi *et al.,* 1970; Mark, 1983). Thus such cardiac depressor reflexes may be of pathophysiologic significance in the development of pump failure.

## J. Extramyocardial Factors in the Pathophysiology of Pump Failure

A number of extramyocardial factors have been identified to play significant roles in the pathogenesis of pump failure in acute myocardial infarction. In some instances these factors perpetuate the already existing pump dysfunction leading to shock syndrome. Recognition of these specific contributing factors is of utmost importance since they are usually correctable and prompt therapy may prevent further deterioration of the circulatory state. These factors are discussed under the physiologic classification of pump failure in AMI (see Table I). (Tolano and Lesch, 1979).

## TABLE I.
Causes of Pump Failure in Acute Myocardial Infarction

I. Pump failure due to inappropriate preload
   A. Inadequate preload
      1. Volume depletion
         a. Excessive diarrhea
         b. Fluid restriction
         c. Vomiting
         d. Phlebotomy
         e. Gastrointestinal hemorrhage
      2. Right ventricular infarction
   B. Excessive preload
      1. Excessive hydration
      2. Salt and water retention
      3. Severe mitral regurgitation
      4. Ventricular septal rupture
      5. Ventricular aneurysm
II. Pump failure due to inappropriate afterload
   A. Inadequate peripheral vascular impedence
      1. Inhibition of reflex sympathetic tone
      2. Activation of left ventricular baroreceptors
      3. Global catecholamine depletion
      4. Sepsis
   B. Excessive peripheral vascular resistance
III. Pump failure due to inappropriate left ventricular contractility
   A. Depressed contractility due to massive infarction
   B. Depressed contractility due to negative inotropic drugs
      1. Narcotics
      2. Hypoxia
      3. Antiarrhythmic agents
      4. Antihypertensive medications
      5. Beta-adrenergic blocking drugs
      6. Calcium channel blockers
      7. Sepsis
IV. Pump failure due to inappropriate heart rate and rhythm
   A. Brady arrhythmias
      1. Sinus bradycardia
      2. A–V junctional rhythm
      3. Second- and third-degree A–V block
   B. Tachyarrhythmias
      1. Atrial fibrillation with rapid ventricular response
      2. Atrial flutter with low grade A–V block
      3. Paroxysmal supraventricular tachycardia
      4. Ventricular tachycardia
      5. Ventricular fibrillation
V. Pump failure due to cardiac compression
   A. Cardiac rupture
   B. Chamber perforation (pacemaker wire, etc.)
   C. Pericardial effusion

## III. Role of Vasopressor Agents in the Treatment of Pump Failure

Ideal medical treatment for various forms of pump failure following AMI requires the use of pharmacologic agents that (1) maintain adequate systemic arterial pressure, (2) increase cardiac output, (3) increase the coronary blood flow without major increase in myocardial oxygen cost, and (4) lower peripheral vascular resistance without major chronotropic effects. The use of vasodilators predominates in the treatment of mild to moderate forms of heart failure in AMI; vasopressors are rarely required. Other inotropic agents such as digitalis, although controversial, may be required. Simultaneous use of a vasopressor and a dilator may at times be required in moderate to severe forms of pump failure. Other measures, such as mechanical cardiac assist devices, are usually reserved for severe forms of pump failure. In this chapter we will deal exclusively with the use of vasopressor agents in AMI pump failure.

### A. General Considerations

The most commonly used cardiovascular drugs in the treatment of AMI shock are sympathomimetic agents. The catecholamines have long been the basis for pharmacologic augmentation of the inotropic state of the myocardium. The different pharmacological actions and clinical uses of these drugs is based upon their action on the various adrenergic receptors. These receptors are components of effector cells rather than part of the sympathetic nervous system and act both in ganglionic and effector cells by receiving the mediators and triggering the response of the cell. Sympathetic adrenergic agonists may act directly at the receptor sites (e.g., isoproterenol), or indirectly, like tyramine, by displacing noradrenaline from granules in the terminal part of a sympathetic neuron, or as a false transmitter, like metaraminol, which replaces noradrenalin the terminals. Alquist (1967) has classified receptors into two main types—alpha and beta—according to the differing orders of potency of a series of sympathomimetic amines. Alpha-receptor stimulation results in vasoconstriction. Beta-receptor stimulation produces cardiac stimulation, vasodilatation, and bronchodilatation. Most metabolic responses to adrenergic stimulation are beta-mediated.

The therapeutic rationale for using sympathomimetic agents in AMI shock is to improve the contractile performance of the remaining viable myocardium. Thus augmenting the cardiac output, and to increase circulation to vital organs and improve tissue perfusion. The latter effects are achieved through an increase in perfusion pressure. These favorable effects, nevertheless, are associated with some adverse cardiovascular consequences. The increase in the inotropy and afterload results in additional myocardial oxygen cost, which may further augment the ischemic process. However, the increase in coronary blood flow due to the rise in arterial pressure and the decrease in LV chamber size associated with augmentation of myocardial contractility tend to partly offset this increase in oxygen demand. Vasoconstriction-related increase in the total peripheral vascular resistance reduces blood flow through some vascular beds. An ideal agent would be expected to increase the inotropic state of the myocardium, lower peripheral vascular resistance, cause a minor increase in the myocardial oxygen demand with concomittant increase in the coronary blood flow, and not have major chronotropic effects. With the introduction of new inotropic agents (i.e., dobutamine and dopamine), some of these effects have been achieved.

All blood vessels have both alpha and beta receptors. In some areas, such as skin and kidney, the alpha receptors predominate. In some vascular beds—for example, the nutrient vessels in the skeletal muscle—beta receptors predominate. In other beds, such as coronary, visceral, and connective tissue, both receptors are active. Currently, there are six commonly used adrenergic receptor stimulants in clinical practice. These are epinephrine, norepinephrine, isoproterenol, dopamine, dobutamine, and salbutamol. All stimulate the myocardium directly but to different degrees. Epinephrine, isoproterenol, and dobutamine have strong inotropic properties; that of dopamine is less. Salbutamol is very weak but its action is prolonged.

All the catecholamines have chronotropic properties. Isoproterenol, epinephrine, and salbutamol exert stronger effects than dobutamine and dopamine. Both the inotropic and chronotropic effects of these drugs are antagonized by beta-adrenergic blocking agents. Larger doses of the agonist may be required to evoke a myocardial response in those patients on prior beta blocker therapy.

The effects of catecholamines on peripheral circulation differ considerably. Norepinephrine is a powerful vasoconstrictor. Epinephrine exerts both vasoconstrictor and vasodilator effects, whereas isoproterenol has only vasodilator properties. Salbutamol, a selective beta-2 agonist, exerts less peripheral effects. Dopamine at large doses acts like norepinephrine but in smaller concentrations selectively dilates the renal and mesenteric vasculature. Dobutamine exerts vasodilatory effects, which in part is a reflex response to the increase in cardiac output secondary to positive inotropic effects.

## B. Norepinephrine

Norepinephrine is the naturally occurring sympathetic neurotransmitter substance and has been in use for treatment of cardiogenic shock for many years. It acts principally on alpha-adrenergic vasoconstrictor receptors and has very little beta-adrenergic action, except on the heart (Beta$_1$ action). Beta-adrenergic effects appear at lower doses than the alpha-adrenergic vasoconstrictor effects (Laks *et al.*, 1971; Lucchesi, 1977). The former result in positive inotropic and chronotropic response.

In man, intravenous infusion of norepinephrine at a rate of 10 $\mu$g/minute produces an increase in both systolic and diastolic arterial pressure; the pulse pressure widens. Cardiac output remains unchanged and may decrease due to strong vagal reflex that slows the heart rate, overriding the direct chronotropic effects. Stroke volume increases. Vasoconstriction in most vascular beds results in an elevated peripheral vascular resistance. Venous tone increases as well. Glomerular filtration rate is unchanged or it may decrease when renal blood flow is markedly decreased due to vasoconstriction. Myocardial blood flow increases, an effect attributable to increased coronary perfusion pressure and possibly to indirectly induced coronary vasodilatation. Subendocardial perfusion, however, is not impaired. Isoproterenol, however, given for an equivalent response impaired subendocardial perfusion (Malcolm *et al.*, 1978).

Clinical studies of patients with AMI shock showed that the drug elicited a pressor response in most patients and increased the cardiac output in many (Binder, 1965; Shubin and Weil, 1965; Kuhn, 1967; Loeb *et al.*, 1974a). With the increase in arterial pressure from shock to more normal levels, the accompanying increases in afterload and cardiac work enhance the myocardial oxygen demand. The latter is partially offset by an increase in coronary blood flow associated with a rise in coronary perfusion pressure. Myocardial metabolism shifts from anaerobic to aerobic mode. Careful hemodynamic and metabolic studies by Mueller and co-workers (1972) on AMI shock showed an increase in peripheral vascular resistance and arterial pressure following norepinephrine infusion. Heart rate varied and the cardiac index was unchanged. Coronary blood flow increased. Myocardial lactate metabolism improved. The effects on myocardial oxygen consumption varied and the oxygen extraction remained high. They have demonstrated that norepinephrine is superior to isoproterenol in treating AMI shock, since the latter increased oxygen demands more than the supply. Measurement of LV end-diastolic pressure in animals (Fearon, 1968) and humans (Cudkowicz, 1968) showed an increase with norepinephrine infusion.

In view of the fact that AMI shock in some may in part be due to inadequate peripheral vasoconstriction (Constantin, 1963; Rotman et al., 1974), theoretically, therapeutic benefit can be achieved with the use of norepinephrine in these patients. However, when intense vasoconstriction is present due to hypotension, use of this drug may be deleterious. The alpha-agonist effect may perpetuate the shock syndrome by increasing further the afterload, thus limiting the extent of rise in cardiac output; tissue ischemia and hypoxia result due to critical underperfusion of vital organs (Cohn and Luria, 1965). Drug-induced increased impedence may exacerbate any prexisting mitral or aortic insufficiency.

The side effects of norepinephrine are minimal and less frequent. The most common ones are anxiety, respiratory difficulty, and an awareness of a slow and forceful heart beat. In previously hypertensive patients, pallor, headache, photophobia, sweating, and vomiting may occur. Aggravation of oliguria may result from renal arterial constriction. Reduction in plasma volume may be a problem when the drug is used for a prolonged period. This may be due to fluid transudation at the capillary level secondary to postcapillary sphincter constriction. The decreased plasma volume may aggravate the shock state by reducing the cardiac output further. Ventricular arrhythmias may occur with rapid infusion. Necrosis may result if extravasation occurs. This can be treated by local infiltration with phentolamine.

In summary the alpha-agonist effect of norepinephrine may be of benefit to treat hypotension in AMI shock. Its use, however, is limited to those with inappropriate peripheral vasoconstriction. In modern practice, it is usually reserved for those patients with cardiogenic shock whose hypotension is no longer responsive to the more balanced effects of dopamine and/or dobutamine. Any deficit in plasma volume should be corrected before its use (Lucchesi, 1977) and arterial pressure should not be raised above 100 mm Hg. At such pressure, norepinephrine has been shown to increase cardiac output (Gunnar et al., 1966). Only when the arterial pressure is increased well above these levels does cardiac output begin to decline. Tachyphylaxis is a major problem. Increasing doses may be needed for a sustained effect. Chronic administration results in desensitization (Ball et al., 1982) and "inotropic dependence," and the persistent intense vasoconstriction that occurs may result in permanent damage to the arteriolar vessel wall (Joris and Majno, 1981). Hence prolonged use is not recommended. One must be able either to substitute less potent agents quite promptly after hemodynamic state has been stabilized or to add mechanical support. To further accentuate cardiac output during norepinephrine infusion, one may choose to add vasodilators such as phentolamine or nitroprusside to negate the alpha-adrenergic vasoconstriction.

## C. Metaraminol

Metaraminol is a synthetic amine, the hemodynamic effect of which differs little from that of norepinephrine except in its longer duration of action (Lucchesi, 1977). It is not as potent in its action as norepinephrine. Its efficiency depends upon tissue norepinephrine concentrations. Hence prolonged use may not evoke a pressor response. In patients with depleted norepinephrine stores, the drug may be ineffective (Loeb et al., 1974b). Although it can be substituted for norepinephrine, its use is limited in the treatment of shock.

## D. Isoproterenol

Isoproterenol, a synthetic sympathomimetic amine, is a balanced $beta_1$ and $beta_2$ adrenergic receptor agonist with essentially no vasoconstrictor effects. Intravenous administration of this drug produces a fall in peripheral vascular resistance (Krasnow et al., 1964), mainly due to vasodilation in skeletal muscle vessels and, to some extent, in the renal and mesenteric vasculature. The drug also possesses powerful positive inotropic and chronotropic effects which result in an elevation in cardiac output. The increase in cardiac output is enough to maintain or raise the systolic arterial pressure. The diastolic and the mean arterial pressures, however, fall. Renal blood flow increases. However, the percentage of total cardiac output directed at the renal vasculature is decreased. Sodium excretion in patients with pump failure did not increase following isoproterenol administration (Sandler et al., 1961).

Initial enthusiasm, based on early encouraging reports on this drug, died out as more of its deleterious side effects became apparent in patients with ischemic heart disease. In patients with cardiogenic shock, this drug has been shown to increase the heart rate, myocardial contractility, and cardiac output and to decrease the systemic vascular resistance with variable effects on the arterial blood pressure (Kuhn, 1967). Kuhn (1978) reviewed the hemodynamic measurements in three series totaling 18 patients. Variable effects on cardiac output have been observed, including an increase, often transitory, or no appreciable rise. Effects on arterial pressure have also been variable and often arterial pressure has not risen even in patients in whom an increase in cardiac output has been noted.

Isoproterenol was said to be superior to metaraminol because it produced a greater increase in cardiac output in patients with AMI shock (Smith et al., 1967). In one study, Gunnar and his co-workers (1967a) concluded that isoproterenol was deleterious to patients with cardiogenic

## 3. Pump Failure: Role of Vasopressor Agents

shock. Despite an increase in cardiac output, improvement in arterial pressure could not be achieved in most of the patients. Clinical deterioration was readily apparent in four patients when the drug therapy was switched from norepinephrine to isoproterenol. When compared to norepinephrine, isoproterenol increased the cardiac output slightly more. The mean arterial pressure, however, was consistently lower during isoproternol infusion.

In a study of systemic and coronary hemodynamics in patients with AMI shock, Mueller *et al.* (1972) demonstrated a marked increase in cardiac output, but this was achieved at the expense of an increase in the heart rate, as the stroke volume remained the same. The mean aortic pressure did not change and aortic diastolic pressure fell. Of considerable interest was this drug's adverse myocardial metabolic effects. Despite a slight increase in the coronary blood flow, intensification of myocardial ischemia was observed as evidenced by an abnormal lactate extraction or production. This indicates that myocardial oxygen demands exceeded an overall improvement in oxygen delivery. A major part of coronary perfusion takes place during diastole and hence is dependent upon diastolic filling time and coronary perfusion pressure. Since isoproterenol abbreviates the diastolic filling time and decreases the aortic diastolic pressure, coronary perfusion may be impaired (Brown *et al.*, 1974; Buckberg *et al.*, 1972). Reduced vascular resistance, however, facilitates an increase in the coronary blood flow, the net effect being only a slight increase in the coronary blood flow. Positive inotropic and chronotropic effects increase the myocardial oxygen demands in excess of the coronary blood flow, resulting in anaerobic myocardial metabolism and worsening ischemia.

There is, in addition, experimental evidence that isoproterenol does in fact increase the area of ischemia and the ultimate infarct size (Maroko *et al.*, 1971) as determined by an increase in the size and extent of topical ST elevation over the infarcted ventricle and by release of creatine phosphokinase from the myocardium (Shell *et al.*, 1973). Myocardial necrosis after long-term use of high doses of isoproterenol has been observed. Although coronary flow is increased, blood may be shunted from ischemic to nonischemic areas producing "coronary steal" (Cohen *et al.*, 1976; Sharma *et al.*, 1971).

In addition to its chronotropic effects, isoproterenol is a potent arrhythmogenic agent. The drug may produce severe sinus tachycardia and/or ventricular arrhythmias. It has been used as a provocative agent in electrophysiological testing for ventricular tachycardia (Reddy and Gettes, 1979; Castellanos *et al.*, 1985). This drug is also said to intensify hypoxemia as a result of increased pulmonary arteriovenous shunting due to increased cardiac output through underventilated lungs.

In conclusion, isoproterenol's tendency to produce major increases in myocardial oxygen demands, tachycardia, ventricular arrhythmias, and only modest hemodynamic improvement make it relatively unattractive drug for patients with AMI shock. Currently its use is limited to those patients with symptomatic bradycardia or A–V block until temporary pacing can be instituted. Two other potential indications for its use were suggested by Loeb et al. (1974b):

1. When shock is associated with severe mitral or aortic regurgitation. Decrease in the peripheral vascular resistance decreases the regurgitant flow and increases the forward flow. However, care should be taken to maintain the perfusion pressure at an adequate level.

2. Isoproterenol given in small doses (0.5–2 $\mu$g/min) may be beneficial in those patients with clinical shock and adequate blood pressure. These smaller doses may produce minimal vasodilator effects without the inotropic and chronotropic actions which predominate at larger doses. Concomitant plasma volume expansion may be needed if left ventricular filling pressure tends to fall. If significant hypotension develops, the drug should be replaced by norepinephrine.

### E. Dopamine

This endogenous catecholamine, present as the natural precursor of norepinephrine (Blaschko, 1959), is found in high concentrations in sympathetic nerves and adrenal gland. Dopamine exerts both alpha- and beta-adrenergic stimulation (Lucchesi, 1977). In addition it possesses an unique property that differentiates it from other endogenous catecholamines and synthetic sympathomimetic amines; it produces unusual vasodilation in the renal, mesenteric, coronary, and intracerebral arterial vascular beds (Goldberg, 1972), an effect said to be mediated through the dopamine vascular receptors. This specific dopaminergic affect is not antagonized by propranolol, atropine, or any other standard antagonist (McNay et al., 1963). However, agents such as haloperidol, phenothiazines (Goldberg and Yeh, 1971), and metochlopamide (Thorner, 1975) have been shown to attenuate the action of dopamine selectively.

Since the original report of McDonald et al. (1964) demonstrating the clinical usefulness of dopamine to increase the systemic arterial pressure without compromising renal blood flow and urine output, this drug has gained wide recognition for treatment of cardioganic shock of all etiologies. Dopamine has a powerful inotropic action and increases myocardial contractility and heart rate by direct beta-adrenergic stimulation. Stroke volume and cardiac output increase. These affects are antagonized by beta blockers. Evidence exists that dopamine also releases norepinephrine from myocardial catecholamine storage sites (Goldberg, 1972) and that the action of dopamine is partly indirect (Lumley *et al.*, 1977). Catecholamine depletion in animal experiments reduced the cardiovascular effects of dopamine. This indirect action also accounts for the selective inotropic rather than chronotropic effect, since the myocardial sympathetic terminals to release catecholamines that exert positive inotropic effect are more abundant. Dopamine has significant chronotropic effects as well, mediated through beta stimulation. It can cause tachycardia and, occasionally, ventricular arrhythmias when larger doses are administered (Rosenblum, 1974). These chronotropic effects, however, are less marked than those of isoproterenol. When doses that elevate the blood pressure are given, baroreceptor-mediated bradycardia may occur. Neurogenic vasodilatation unrelated to the level of blood pressure has also been demonstrated (Goldberg, 1972).

Dopamine is less effective than isoproterenol in increasing cardiac output. However, it does not cause the marked vasodilatation of the skeletal muscle vasculature seen with isoproterenol (Gunnar *et al.*, 1967b). Thus the increased cardiac output during dopamine infusion is directed more to the vital organs. At larger doses the predominant effect is marked vasoconstriction of all vascular beds, mediated by alpha stimulation, and the agent acts much like norepinephrine (Goldberg, 1972; Ahlquist, 1976). Dopamine inhibits renal tubular reabsorption of sodium. Natriuresis may in part be related to an increase in glomerular filtration rate and increased urinary output (Ball *et al.*, 1978). Potassium excretion is also enhanced.

Another potential problem with the use of dopamine as an inotrope is the concomitant increase in pulmonary capillary wedge and LV end-diastolic pressure (Leier *et al.*, 1978; Loeb *et al.*, 1977; Hess *et al.*, 1979; Holloway *et al.*, 1975a,b). In some studies dopamine failed to reduce these pressures in patients in whom they were elevated (Stoner *et al.*, 1977; Stemple *et al.*, 1978; Miller *et al.*, 1977). The reason for these findings is unclear but may be related to increased venous return secondary to venoconstriction (Marino *et al.*, 1975; Mark *et al.*, 1970).

Three dose-dependent cardiovascular effects can be elicited with dopamine. Low doses (2–5 $\mu$g/kg/min) produce nonadrenergic vasodilatation of renal, mesenteric, coronary, and cerebral vascular beds (Goldberg, 1972; Hallenberg *et al.*, 1973). Intermediate doses (6–15 $\mu$g/kg/min) have been shown to increase myocardial contractility and cardiac output through beta stimulation. At such doses one may see initial transient vasoconstriction, followed by a longer vasodilatation. Larger doses ($\geq$20 $\mu$g/kg/min) result in predominant generalized vasoconstriction with little or no vasodilatation (Goldberg, 1972; Allwood and Ginsburg, 1964). Selective alpha blockade with phenoxybenzamine opposed this vasoconstriction, leaving only the vasodilator effect of the drug, providing direct evidence that vasoconstriction was alpha mediated. Similarly, evidence has been shown that beta receptors in the renal bed were not involved with dopamine-induced vasodilatation. Beta blockage did not diminish the dopamine-induced increases in the renal blood flow (McNay and Goldberg, 1965).

The most severe adverse effect observed is ventricular arrhythmia. Other significant undesirable effects observed in clinical use are tachycardia, nausea, vomiting, anginal pain, dyspnea, and, rarely, excessive vasoconstriction. Very infrequently aberrant conduction, piloerection, excessive bradycardia, and azotemia have been reported. Sudden marked increases in blood pressure were seen with inadvertent rapid infusions. Hypotension may occur with dopamine treatment, particularly if there is volume depletion (Lucchesi, 1977). Local tissue necrosis may result when the drug extravasates.

The increase in the inotropic state produced by dopamine may have adverse effects on the myocardial metabolism. Although the myocardial blood supply increases through vasodilatation of normal coronary arteries, myocardial oxygen needs may exceed the supply, resulting in anerobic metabolism in patients with coronary artery disease. Clinical studies revealed that the drug increased cardiac work and did not reduce transmyocardial lactate extraction (Amsterdam et al., 1972; Winslow et al., 1970). Mueller and co-workers (1978) demonstrated that dopamine infused at 8 to 28 $\mu$g/kg/min improved cardiac performance but increased myocardial oxygen consumption and lactate production.

Experience with dopamine has been limited largely to various types of shock and only a few studies are available to date dealing with its use in myocardial infarction shock. Despite some hemodynamic improvement, its effect on mortality has been disappointing in cardiac infarction shock (Talley et al., 1969; Holzer et al., 1973). Better results were seen in patients with low-output shock state following cardiac surgery (Holloway et al., 1975a). Thirteen patients with cardiogenic shock were studied by Loeb et al. (1971): dopamine infusion resulted in a mean increase in cardiac output by 40%, while mean blood pressure increased by 6%. There was no significant change in the urinary flow. LV end-diastolic pressure rose along with an increase in the mean heart rate. When compared to isoproterenol in five patients, the latter appeared to have produced higher cardiac output. Dopamine was considered superior to norepinephrine when compared in eight patients. Dopamine seemed to result in higher cardiac output and low systemic vascular resistance.

There have been no specific studies of this drug in treating mild to moderate forms of pump failure following AMI. Since the use of vasodilators predominates in the treatment of heart failure in AMI, vasopressors are rarely required. The potential for its use exists with the vasodilators. Its natriuretic and positive inotropic effects may be beneficial. However, the possible adverse myocardial metabolic effect of this drug should be considered when used in AMI to treat pump failure. Additive effects of dopamine and diuretics when used in combination in improving urinary output and sodium excretion may be of potential benefit in those patients with pump failure complicated by renal insufficiency. In view of its adverse metabolic effects, dopamine should never be used as the primary drug to treat cardiac infarction heart failure. Its use should probably be limited to circumstances where combination vasopressor and vasodilator therapy is called for. Dopamine, by virtue of its selective renal vasodilator effects, relative lack of chronotropic drive, and lesser arrhythmogenicity, is considered superior to the other vasopressors in the treatment of AMI shock. Because of its dose-related cardiovascular effects, it is suggested that the drug be given at an initial dose of 2 $\mu$g/kg/min, gradually increasing the dose according to the hemodynamic response. Infusion rates of 5 to 20 $\mu$g/kg/min are generally required to achieve the desired hemodynamic and renal responses. As the rate of infusion is increased beyond 1000 $\mu$g/min, the alpha-adrenergic vasoconstrictor effects become increasingly dominant until the agent acts much like norepinephrine. If the latter effect is desired, then switching to norepinephrine is more appropriate unless the chronotropic effects of dopamine is also desired. Under these circumstances, excessive vasoconstriction can be negated with concomitant use of vasodilators such as phentolamine or nitroprusside. However, caution must be exercised so that adequate perfusion pressure is maintained, in order not to compromise the coronary flow.

## F. Dobutamine

Dobutamine, a dopamine analog, possesses a beta$_1$ adrenergic agonist effect and minimal beta$_2$ and alpha-adrenergic actions. It has been shown to have relatively major selective inotropic effects (Tuttle and Millis, 1975; Akthar *et al.*, 1975), with what appears to be an attenuated chronotropic effect. Although structurally related to norepinephrine and isoproterenol, the large substituent, an amino nitrogen, is thought to account for the marked differences in the chronotropic activity of dobutamine. This drug was also shown to lack the norepinephrine-releasing action of dopamine (Goldberg, 1972). Beta-adrenergic stimulation of the myocardium produces a dose-related increase in cardiac output. Since dobutamine exhibits minimal beta$_2$ and alpha-adrenergic effects, augumentation of cardiac contractility occurs without major changes in arterial pressure. Increased contractility coupled with a net effect of adrenergic vasodilatation decreases the total peripheral vascular resistance.

In experimental myocardial ischemia, dobutamine linearly increased contractility and cardiac output with minimal effect on heart rate and total peripheral resistance (Tuttle, 1978; Willerson *et al.*, 1976). LV filling pressure tended to fall (Franciosa *et al.*, 1978). Dobutamine has been shown to increase the coronary blood flow exceeding that of myocardial metabolic requirements in normal dogs as well as in dogs with experimental myocardial infarction (Willerson *et al.*, 1976). At concentrations of 4 to 5 µg/kg/min, this drug has been shown to produce minimal effects resulting in no alterations in myocardial oxygen supply consumption ratio. Lactate extraction fell (Willerson *et al.*, 1976; Franciosa *et al.*, 1978). Such doses increased the myocardial blood flow to the normal and moderately ischemic zones (Vatner *et al.*, 1974; Vatner and Baig, 1979). However, in severely ischemic zones, blood flow and endocardial/epicardial flow ratio did not change. Infusion doses of 8 µg/kg/min in one study increased coronary sinus PaO$_2$, myocardial oxygen supply and consumption ratio, and lactate consumption. Increased flow was observed in both myocardial and endocardial layers of the ischemic area (Tuttle, 1978). At larger doses (20 µg/kg/min) dobutamine in experimental AMI improved regional myocardial blood flow to the ischemic and nonischemic areas. Concomitant parallel increases in myocardial oxygen consumption and coronary sinus blood oxygen saturation were observed. Both endo- and epicardial blood flow increased with no significant change in the flow ratio (Liang *et al.*, 1981). Thus the data suggest that dobutamine does not decrease the regional flow to the ischemic myocardium.

Several clinical studies have shown the beneficial effects of dobutamine in pump failure secondary to AMI. Infusion rates ranging from 8 to 20 µg/kg/min in patients with AMI with low output syndrome but not in cardiogenic shock (Goldstein *et al.*, 1980; Keung *et al.*, 1981) have been shown to increase the cardiac output appreciably, with a modest but significant decrease in systemic vascular resistance. Pulmonary capillary wedge pressures decreased consistently. A minimal but significant increase in heart rate was observed. Mean systemic arterial blood pressure did not change or showed minimal decrease. Bernard and Renard (1978) and Crexells (1978) reported similar results. After 24 hr, dobutamine continued to show beneficial hemodynamic effects (Bernard and Renard, 1978). The cardiac index was slightly lower than at 1 hr after infusion, but higher than the baseline value. The chronotropic and arrhythmogenic effects of dobutamine are considerably less than those of other catecholamines in clinical use. These beneficial hemodynamic effects might be expected to influence the myocardial metabolism favorably. Dobutamine, like other sympathomimetic agents, increases the myocardial oxygen consumption through its positive inotropic effects (Vasu *et al.*, 1978). However, in pump failure of AMI dobutamine-induced reduction in LV filling pressure improves the gradient for diastolic coronary blood flow and, in turn, collateral blood flow to the ischemic myocardium. The decrease in heart size decreases the ventricular wall tension. Overall cardiac performance improves. The net effect is a decrease in myocardial oxygen need. Gillespie *et al.* (1977) have demonstrated that dobutamine in doses sufficient to improve ventricular performance in AMI does not increase enzymatically estimated infarct size or precipitate ventricular arrhythmias. In experimental myocardial ischemia (Vatner and Baig, 1979) dobutamine infused at 10 $\mu$g/kg/min did not produce a decrease in the contractile function or blood flow in the severely ischemic zone as long as the heart rate did not increase. Opposite effects were seen in those dogs exhibiting elevated heart rates with dobutamine. Reduction in infarct size was demonstrated in experimental myocardial infarction following dobutamine administration (Tuttle *et al.*, 1973; Liang *et al.*, 1981).

Prolonged dobutamine infusion (72 hr) producing sustained hemodynamic benefit has been shown to produce improvement in the myocellular processes. These processes included reduction in the numbers of electron-dense particles per 100 mitochondria, an increased cristae-to-matrix ratio within the mitochondria, and a decrease in the mitochondrial size (Unverferth *et al.*, 1980). It is possible that these reparative myocellular processes are the result of inotropic intervention.

The positive inotropic properties, lesser arrhythmogencity, and beneficial effects on cardiac metabolism at doses between 5 and 10 $\mu$g/kg/min make dobutamine a very useful catecholamine for acute stimulation of the failing heart when severe hypotension is not present. Dobutamine has limited value in the treatment of cardiac infarction shock. In those with mild hypotension dobutamine may increase the systemic arterial pressure by augmenting the cardiac output. However, in patients with severe hypotension, an increase in systemic vascular resistance is needed to maintain adequate tissue and coronary perfusion. In such cases norepinephrine or dopamine would be preferred over dobutamine. It should also be pointed out that attenuation of hemodynamic effects of dobutamine may occur as early as after 8 hr of its use, requiring upward dose titration to maintain the desired response. This observation is suggestive of a rapid induction of a down-regulation of myocardial beta$_1$ receptors (Unverferth *et al.*, 1978; Klein *et al.*, 1981).

## IV. Future Directions

Recent efforts to discover new selective vasoactive drugs have resulted in the production of novel compounds that possess $beta_2$ adrenergic activity. A small number of orally active synthetic catecholamines have been developed which act largely as vasodilating agents rather than as inotropic agents. Unfortunately, use of these drugs in parenteral form has been associated with several problems including lack of myocardial $beta_1$ receptor selectivity, tachycardia, arrhythmias and tachyphylaxis. Furthermore, the use of these $beta_2$ agonists may be complicated by noncardiovascular side effects such as marked anxiety and tremulousness (Maskin et al., 1984). Clinical studies with these agents are limited to congestive heart failure. Presently, very little information is available with regard to their use in pump failure of AMI.

### A. Pirbuterol

Pirbuterol is an oral catecholamine with desirable short-term hemodynamic effects in patients with heart failure (Awan et al., 1981a,c; Canepa-Anson et al., 1981; Rude et al., 1981; Sharma et al., 1981). These beneficial hemodynamic effects appear to be mediated predominantly via stimulation of vascular $beta_2$ adrenergic receptors. Taken orally, this drug has rapid onset of action ($\frac{1}{2}$ hr) and the hemodynamic changes persist up to $5\frac{1}{2}$ hr. The optimal daily dose is said to be 60 mg (20 mg three times a day). At this dosage, this agent increased cardiac index, stroke volume, and stroke work index with significant reduction in systemic and pulmonary vascular resistance and left ventricular filling pressures and only slight changes in heart rate and blood pressure. Awan et al. (1981c) reported that these beneficial effects of Pirbuterol compared favorably with those of dobutamine. This agent also appears to have a positive inotropic effect, as reflected by an increase in the rate of rise of pressure in the LV (Rude et al., 1981; Timmis et al., 1981). It is not clear whether this drug possesses a direct inotropic effect or this augmentation in LV dP/dT is merely a reflection of reflex release of catecholamines in response to the peripheral vasodilatation. These hemodynamic effects, however, are not associated with any detrimental effects on myocardial oxygen consumption (Rude et al., 1981; Timmis et al., 1981; Fowler et al., 1982).

Since acute hemodynamic benefits are similar to those of dobutamine, it has been suggested that patients with acute congestive heart failure responding favorably to dobutamine infusion may be conveniently treated for long periods with Pirbuterol orally. Although acute and short-term improvement in cardiac performance is evident, long-term benefits have been variably reported (Awan et al., 1981b; Colucci et al., 1981a,b; Dawson et al., 1981; Pamelia et al., 1981, 1983). Some observed significant improvement in indices of cardiac performance during 6 weeks of continued therapy and others have reported attenuation of clinical benefit after only 1 month. Colucci et al. (1981b) noted that this attenuation of the drug effect has been associated with a reduction in lymphocyte beta receptor density. Down-regulation of beta-adrenergic receptors in myocardial and vascular tissue may be responsible for the attenuated responsiveness to Pirbuterol (Kenakin and Ferris, 1983). In one study, long-term use of Pirbuterol not only did not result in significant improvement in functional status, but many patients could not tolerate the optimal daily dose of 60 mg/day because of adverse effects such as tremulousness and nervousness attributable to $beta_2$ agonist activity (Weber et al., 1982).

Despite its acute hemodynamic benefits, Pirbuterol has not been tested in pump failure of AMI.

## B. Salbutamol

Salbutamol is very similar to Pirbuterol in its action and acts predominantly via stimulation of $beta_2$ receptors (Sharma and Goodwin, 1978; Timmis et al., 1981). It produces a decrease in systemic and pulmonary vascular resistance and LV end-diastolic pressure. The changes in arterial blood pressure and heart rate are small. The cardiac output increases, which has been attributed to an effect on venous capacitance vessels increasing venous return (Gibson and Coltart, 1971). As with Pirbuterol, Salbutamol augments LV dP/dT in patients with heart failure (Sharma and Goodwin, 1978), an effect attributed to reflex sympathetic stimulation in response to decrease in systemic vascular resistance, although direct positive inotropic effect can not be entirely ruled out. The drug probably has some $beta_1$ inotropic effects. Bereud and Martin (1978) have shown that salbutamol in high doses or when given intravenously loses its $beta_2$ specificity and produces direct cardiac stimulant effect. When given intravenously at doses of 1.5 $\mu$g/kg/min the drug increased the cardiac output (Gibson and Coltart, 1971) Lal et al. (1972) have used large bolus doses of the drug (1–2 mg at a time) for treatment of cardiogenic shock following AMI. They reported an increase in blood pressure. An increase in cardiac output has been shown by Yacoub and Buyland (1973) in patients with low output states following open heart procedures. This was achieved by a 1.5-mg bolus dose. A fall in systemic and pulmonary vascular resistance occurred. Heart rate, however, increased. Similar improvement in resting and exercise cardiac index was demonstrated in chronic congestive heart failure by Sharma and Goodwin (1978) with intravenous infusion of Salbutamol. Left ventricular filling pressure fell without change in heart rate and blood pressure. The oral form of this drug has also been shown to improve cardiac index in chronic heart failure (Stephens *et al.*, 1979) without change in LV filling pressure, heart rate, and blood pressure.

## C. Other Newer Agents

### 1. Prenalterol

This new selective $beta_1$ adrenoreceptor agonist with minimal $beta_2$ agonist effect appears to increase the inotropic state of the myocardium without increasing the heart rate (Knaus *et al.*, 1978; Waagstein *et al.*, 1981; Kirklin and Pitt, 1981). The drug is active in both parenteral and oral forms (Mattson *et al.*, 1982). Prenalterol increases the arterial systolic pressure but does not affect the diastolic pressure. Improvement in cardiac performance occurs at the expense of increased myocardial oxygen requirements (Wahr *et al.*, 1982). The oral form of this drug has been shown to produce functional improvement in patients with severe heart failure (Sharfe and Coxon, 1982; Lambertz *et al.*, 1984). Other clinical uses for the drug include treatment of hypotension produced by extradural anaesthesia and gram-negative sepsis and reversal of cardiac depressant effects of beta blockade (Reiz *et al.*, 1980; Kulling, 1982). Beneficial effects of this drug in cardiogenic shock following AMI have been described (Coma-Canella *et al.*, 1984).

### 2. Ibopamine

This new predominantly dopaminergic catecholamine appears to be a promising agent because of its ability to improve renal function in patients with heart failure (Stefoni *et al.*, 1981). Its activity as a renal vasodilator may make this an important adjunct to the therapy with a specific inotropic agent.

Other agents undergoing investigation are a new class of catecholamines that have both intrinsic $beta_1$ agonist and antagonist activity. Their clinical use in AMI pump failure is probably limited.

## References

Abboud, F. M., Heistad, D. D., Mark, A. L., and Shmid, P. (1976). *Progr. Cardiovasc. Dis.* **18,** 371–403.

Agress, C. M., Rosenberg, M. J., and Jacobs, H. I. (1952). *Am. J. Physiol.* **170**, 536–549.
Ahlquist, R. P. (1967). *Am. J. Physiol.* **212**, 823.
Ahlquist, R. P. (1976). *Am. Heart J.* **92**, 661–664.
Akthar, N., Mikulic, E., Cohn, J. C., and Chaudry, M. H. (1975). *Am. J. Cardiol.* **36**, 202–205.
Allwood, M. J., and Ginsburg, J. (1964). *J. Clin. Invest.* **43**, 1116–1118.
Alonso, D. R., Scheidt, S., Post, M., and Killip, T. (1973). *Circulation* **48**, 588–596.
Ambrose, J. A., Winters, S. L., Stern, A., Eng, A., Teicholtz, L. E., Gorlin, R., and Fuster, V. (1985). *J. Am. Coll. Cardiol.* **5**, 609–616.
Amsterdam, E. A. (1973). *Am. J. Cardiol.* **32**, 461–471.
Amsterdam, E. A., Bonanno, J. A., Massumi, R. A., Zelis, R., and Mason, D. T. (1972). *Clin. Res.* **20**, 360–386.
Amsterdam, E. A., Choquet, Y., Bonanno, J. A., Massumi, R. A., Zelis, R., and Mason, D. T. (1973). *Clin. Res.* **21**, 232.
Amsterdam, E. A., Miller, R. R., and Foley, D. H. (1975). *In* "Peripheral Circulation" (Zelis, R., ed.), pp. 363–366. Grune and Stratton, New York.
Amsterdam, E. A., DeMaria, A. N., and Hughes, J. L. (1976). *In* "Congestive Heart Failure: Mechanism Evaluations and Treatment" (Mason, D. T., ed.), Dun-Donnelly, New York.
Awan, N. A., Evenson, M. K., Nedham, K. E., Evans, T. O., Hermanovich, J., Taylor, C. R., and Mason, D. T. (1981a). *Circulation* **63**, 96–101.
Awan, N. A., Nedham, K. E., Evenson, M. K., Hermanovich, J., Joye, J. A., DeMaria, H. N., and Mason, D. T. (1981b). *Am. Heart J.* **102**, 555–563.
Awan, N. A., Nedham, K. E., Evenson, M. K., and Mason, D. T. (1981c). *Am. J. Cardiol.* **47**, 665–669.
Ball, C. G., Gates, N. S., and Lee, M. R. (1978). *Clin. Sci. Mol. Med.* **54**, 29–30.
Ball, N., Danks, J. L., Dorudi, S., and Nasmyth, P. A. (1982). *Br. J. Pharmacol.* **76**, 201–210.
Berend, N., and Marlin, G. E. (1978). *Br. J. Clin. Pharmacol.* **5**, 207–211.
Bernard, P. M., and Kennedy, J. H. (1965). *Circulation* **32**, 76–83.
Bernard, R., and Renard, M. (1978). *In* "Proceedings of the European Dobutamine Symposium" (Glynne, A., and Lucas, R., eds.), pp. 68–75. Guy's Hospital, London.
Binder, M. J. (1965). *Am. J. Cardiol.* **16**, 834–840.
Blaschko, H. (1959). *Pharmacol. Rev.* **11**, 307–312.
Bradley, R. D., Jenkins, B. S., and Branthiasaite, M. A. (1970). *Circulation* **42**, 827–837.
Braunwald, E. (1976). *Circulation* **53** (1), 1–2.
Braunwald, E. (1985). *Circulation* **71**, 1087–1092.
Brown, B. G., Gundel, W. D., Gott, V. L., and Covell, J. W. (1974). *Cardiovasc. Res.* **8**, 621–631.
Buckberg, G. D., Fixler, D. E., Archie, J. P., and Hoffman, J. I. E. (1972). *Circulation Res.* **30**, 67–81.
Buja, L. M., and Roberts, W. C. (1974). *In* "Shock in Myocardial Infarction" (Gunnar, R., Loeb, H. S., and Rahimtoola, S. H., eds.), p. 1. Grune and Stratton, New York.
Burch, G. E., DePasquale, N. P., and Phillips, J. H. (1968). *Am. Heart J.* **75**, 399–415.
Canepa-Anson, R., Dawson, J. R., Kuan, P., Warnes, C., Poole-Wilson, P. A., Reuben, S., and Sutton, G. (1981). *Am. Heart J.* **102**, 578–583.
Castellanos, A., Mendoza, I. J., Luceri, R. M., Castillo, C. A., Zamou, L., Saoudi, N., and Myersburg, R. J. (1985). *Am. J. Cardiol.* **55**, 1344–1349.
Cederquidt, L., and Soderstrom, J. (1964). *Acta Med. Scand.* **176**, 287–292.
Cohen, M. V., Sonnenblick, E. H., and Kirk, E. S. (1976). *Am. J. Cardiol.* **37**, 244–249.

Cohn, J. N., and Luria, M. H. (1965). *J. Clin. Invest.* **44,** 1494–1504.
Colucci, W. S., Alexander, R. W., Mudge, G. H., Rude, R., Holman, B. L., Wynne, J., Grossman, W., and Braunwald, E. (1981a). *Am. Heart J.* **102,** 564–568.
Colucci, W. S., Alexander, R. W., Williams, G. H., Rude, R. E., Holman, L. B., Konstam, M. A., Wynne, J., Mudge, G. H., and Braunwald, E. (1981b). *New Engl. J. Med.* **305,** 185–190.
Coma-Canella, I., Sendon, J. L., and Jadrque, L. M. (1984). *Am. Heart J.* **107,** 1195–1201.
Constantin, L. (1963). *Am. J. Cardiol.* **11,** 205–217.
Cox, J. L., McLaughlin, V. W., Flowers, N. C., and Horan, L. G. (1968). *Am. Heart J.* **76,** 650–659.
Crexells, C. (1978). *In* "Proceedings of the European Dobutamine Symposium" (Glynn, A., and Lucas, R., eds.), pp. 76–82. Guy's Hospital, London.
Cudkowicz, L. (1968). *Thorax* **23,** 63–68.
Dawson, J. R., Reuben, S., Poule-Wilson, P. A., and Sutton, G. C. (1981). *Am. J. Cardiol.* **47,** 492.
Dole, W. P., and O'Rourke, R. A. (1983). *In* "Internal Medicine" (J. H. Stein, ed.), pp. 506–515. Little, Brown and Co., Boston.
Elayda, M. A., Mathur, V. S., Hall, R. J., Massumi, E. A., Garcia, E., and de Castro, C. M. (1985). *Am. J. Cardiol.* **55,** 58–60.
Errington, M. L., and Rocha e Silva, M., Jr. (1974). *J. Physiol.* **233,** 46–47.
Estes, E. H., Jr., Dalton, F. M., Entman, M. L., Dixon, H. B., and Hackel, D. B. (1966). *Am. Heart J.* **71,** 356–362.
Fearon, R. E. (1968). *Am. Heart J.* **75,** 634–638.
Fowler, M. B., Bergman, G., Atkinson, L., Howell, L., and Jewitt, D. E. (1982). *Circulation* **66** (II) 137.
Franciosa, J. A., Notargiaromo, A. V., and Cohn, J. N. (1978). *Cardiovasc. Res.* **12,** 294–302.
Geddes, J. S., Adgey, A. A. J., and Pantridge, J. F. (1980). *Am. Heart J.* **99,** 243–256.
Gibson, D. G., and Coltart, D. J. (1971). *Postgrad. Med. J.* **47,** Suppl., 40–44.
Gillespie, T. A., Ambos, M. D., Sobel, B. E., and Roberts, R. (1977). *Am. J. Cardiol.* **39,** 588–594.
Goldberg, L. I. (1972). *Pharmacol. Rev.* **24,** 1–51.
Goldberg, L. I., and Yeh, B. K. (1971). *Eur. J. Pharmacol.* **15,** 36–40.
Goldstein, R. A., Passamani, E. R., and Roberts, R. (1980). *New Engl. J. Med.* **303,** 846–850.
Grande, P., Christiansen, C., and Padersen, A. (1983). *Eur. Heart J.* **4,** 20–25.
Griffith, G. C., Hedge, B., and Oblth, R. W. (1961). *Am. J. Cardiol.* **8,** 792–798.
Gunnar, R. M., Cruz, A., Boswell, J., Co, B. S., Pietras, R. J., Stavrakos, C., Loeb, H. S., and Tobin, J. R., Jr. (1966). *Circulation* **33,** 753–762.
Gunnar, R. M., Pietras, R. J., Stavrakos, C., Loeb, H. S., and Tobin, J. R., Jr. (1967a). *Med. Clin. N. Am.* **51,** 69–81.
Gunnar, R. M., Loeb, H. S., Petras, R. J., and Tobin, J. R., Jr. (1967b). *JAMA* **202,** 1124–1128.
Gunnar, R. M., Loeb, H. S., Pietras, R. J., and Tobin, J. R. (1968). *Prog. Cardiovas. Dis.* **11,** 29–44.
Gutovitz, A. L., Sobel, B. E., and Roberts, R. (1978). *Am. J. Cardiol.* **41,** 409–475.
Hallenberg, N. K., Adams, D. F., and Mendell, P. (1973). *Clin. Sci. Molec. Med.* **45,** 733–735.
Hamosh, P., and Cohn, J. (1971). *J. Clin. Invest.* **50,** 523–533.
Hanley, H. G., Costin, J. C., and Skinner, N. S. (1971). *Am. J. Cardiol.* **27,** 513–521.

Heinkkila, J. (1967). *Br. Heart J.* **29,** 162–169.
Hess, W., Klein, W., Mueller Busch, C., and Tarnow, J. (1979). *Br. J. Anaesth.* **51,** 1063–1069.
Holloway, E. L., Polumbo, R. A., and Harrison, D. C. (1975a). *Br. Heart J.* **37,** 482–485.
Holloway, E. L., Stinson, E. B., Derby, G. C., and Harrison, D. C. (1975b). *Am. J. Cardiol.* **35,** 656–659.
Holzer, J., Karliner, J. S., O'Rourke, R., Pitt, W., and Ross, J., Jr. (1973). *Am. J. Cardiol.* **32,** 79–84.
Hughes, J. L., Salel, A. F., Massumi, R. A., Zelis, R., Amsterdam, E. A., and Mason, D. T. (1971a). *Circulation* **44** (Suppl. II), 179.
Hughes, J. L., Amsterdam, E. A., Mason, D. T., Mansour, E., and Zelis, R. (1971b). *Clin. Res.* **19,** 321.
Jacobson, E. D. (1968). *New Engl. J. Med.* **278,** 834–838.
Jennings, R. B., Ganate, C. E., and Reimer, A. (1975). *Am. J. Pathol.* **81,** 179–198.
Joris, I., and Majno, G. (1981). *Am. J. Pathol.* **105,** 212–222.
Karliner, J. S., and Ross, J., Jr. (1971). *Progr. Cardiovasc. Dis.* **13,** 374–391.
Katz, A. M. (1978). *Hospital Practice* 83–91.
Kenakin, T. P., and Ferris, R. M. (1983). *J. Cardiovasc. Pharmacol.* **5,** 90–94.
Kennedy, J. W., Gonsini, G. G., Timmis, G. C., and Maynard, C. (1985). *Am. J. Cardiol.* **55,** 871–877.
Keung, E. C., Siskind, B. J., Sonnenblick, E. W., Ribner, H. S., Schwartz, W. J., and Lejemtel, T. H. (1981). *J.A.M.A.* **245,** 144–146.
Kezdi, P., Misnor, S. N., Kordenat, R. K., Spickler, J. W., and Stanley, E. L. (1970). *Am. J. Cardiol.* **26,** 642.
Kirlin, P. C., and Pitt, B. (1981). *Am. J. Cardiol.* **47,** 670–675.
Klein, M. D., Herman, M. V., and Gorlin, R. (1967). *Circulation* **35,** 614–630.
Klein, N. A., Siskind, S. J., Frishman, W. H., Sonnenblick, E. H., and Lejemtel, T. H. (1981). *Am. J. Cardiol.* **48,** 170–175.
Knaus, M., Pfister, B., Dubach, U. C., and Imhof, P. R. (1978). *Am. Heart J.* **95,** 602–610.
Krasnow, N., Rolett, E. L., Yurchak, P. M., Hood, W. B., and Gorlin, R. (1964). *Am. J. Med.* **37,** 514–525.
Kuhn, L. A. (1967). *J.A.M.A.* **20,** 757–764.
Kuhn, L. A. (1978). *Am. Heart J.* **95,** 529–534.
Kulling, P. (1982). *Acta Med. Scand.* **659,** 191–199.
Laks, M., Callis, G., and Swan, H. J. C. (1971). *Am. J. Physiol.* **220,** 171–173.
Lal, S., Saridge, R. S., Davies, D. M., Ali, M. M., and Soni, V. (1972). *Lancet* **1,** 853–854.
Lambertz, H., Meyer, J., and Erber, R. (1984). *Circulation* **69,** 298–305.
Leier, C. V., Heban, P. T., Huss, P., Bush, C., and Lewis, R. P. (1978). *Circulation* **58,** 466–475.
Leinbach, R. C. (1980). *J. Cardiovasc. Med.* **5,** 499–506.
Liang, C. S., Yi, J. M., Sherman, L. G., Black, J., Garras, H., and Wood, W. B. (1981). *Circulation Res.* **49,** 170–180.
Loeb, H. S., Winslow, E. B. J., Rahimtoola, S. H., Rosen, K. M., and Gunnar, R. M. (1971). *Circulation* **44,** 163–173.
Loeb, H. S., Johnson, S. A., and Gunnar, R. M. (1974a). *Triangle* **13,** 121–124.
Loeb, H. S., Gunnar, R. M., and Rahimtoola, S. H. (1974b). *In* "Shock in Myocardial Infarction" (Gunnar, R., Loeb, H. S., and Rahimtoola, S. H., eds.), pp. 131–156. Grune and Stratton, New York.
Loeb, H. S., Bredakis, J., and Gunnar, R. M. (1977). *Circulation* **55,** 375–381.
London, R. E., and London, S. B. (1965). *Circulation* **31,** 202–208.

Lucchesi, B. R. (1977). *In* "Cardiovascular Pharmacology" (M. Antonaccio, ed.), pp. 375–377. Raven Press, New York.
Lumley, P., Bradley, K. J., and Levey, G. D. (1977). *Cardiovasc. Res.* **11,** 17–25.
McDonald, R. H., Goldberg, L. I., McNay, J. L., and Tuttle, E. P. (1964). *J. Clin. Invest.* **43,** 1116–1119.
McNay, J. L., McDonald, R. H., and Goldberg, L. I. (1963). *Pharmacologist* **5,** 269–272.
McNay, J. L. and Goldberg, L. I. (1965). *J. Pharmac. Exp. Ther.* **151,** 23–31.
Malcolm, A. D., Coltart, D. J., Rosenfeldt, F. L., and Williams, B. T. (1978). *Br. J. Clin. Pharmccol.* **5,** 359–362.
Marino, R. J., Romagnoli, A., and Keats, A. S. (1975). *Anesthesiology* **43,** 570–572.
Mark, A. L. (1983). *J. Am. Coll. Cardiol.* **1,** 90–102.
Mark, A. L., Iizuka, T., Wondling, M. G., and Eckstein, J. W. (1970). *J. Clin. Invest.* **49,** 259–266.
Maroko, P. R., and Braunwald, E. (1973). *Ann. Intern. Med.* **79,** 720–733.
Maroko, P. R., Kjekshus, J. K., Sobel, B. E., Watanabe, T., Covell, J. W., Ross, J., Jr., and Braunwald, E. (1971). *Circulation* **43,** 67–82.
Maskin, C. S., Lejemtel, T. H., and Sonnenblick, E. H. (1984). *In* "Cardiac Drug Therapy" (Conti, C. R., ed.), pp. 1–17. F. A. Davis, Philadelphia.
Mattson, H., Hedberg, A., and Carlsson, E. (1982). *Acta Med. Scand.* **659** (Suppl.) 9–37.
Miller, R. R., Amsterdam, E. A., Bogren, H. G., Massumi, R. A., Zelis, R., and Mason, D. T. (1974). *Circulation* **49,** 447–454.
Miller, R. R., Olsen, H. A., Vismara, L. A., Bogren, H. G., Amsterdam, E. A., and Mason, D. T. (1976). *Am. J. Cardiol.* **37,** 340–344.
Miller, R. R., Awan, N. A., Joye, J. A., Maxwell, K. S., DeMaria, A. N., Amsterdam, E. A., and Mason, D. T. (1977). *Circulation* **55,** 881–884.
Mueller, H. S., Ayers, S. M., Gianelli, S., Jr., Conklin, E. F., Mazzara, T. J., and Grace, W. J. (1972). *Circulation* **45,** 335–351.
Mueller, H. S., Evans, R., and Ayers, S. M. (1978). *Circulation* **57,** 361–365.
Oblath, R. W., Levinson, D. C., and Griffith, G. C. (1952). *J.A.M.A.* **149,** 1276–1278.
Page, D. L., Caulfield, J. B., Kastor, J. A., DeSanctis, R. W., and Sanders, C. A. (1971). *New Engl. J. Med.* **285,** 133–137.
Pamelia, F. X., Georghiade, M., Bishop, H. L., Olukotern, A. Y., Taylon, C., Watson, D. D., Beller, G. A., Grunwald, A. M., and Carabello, B. A. (1981). *Circulation* **64** (IV), 295.
Pamelia, F. X., Georghiade, M., Bishop, H. L., Beller, G. A., Olukotun, A. Y., Taylor, C. R., Watson, D. D., Grunwald, A. M., Sirowatka, J., and Carabello, B. A. (1983). *Am. Heart J.* **106,** 1369–1376.
Rackley, C. E., and Russell, R. O., Jr. (1972). *Circulation* **45,** 231–244.
Rackley, C. E., Russell, R. O., Jr., and Mantle, J. A. (1975). *Cardiovasc. Clin.* **7,** 251.
Ratshin, R. A., Rackley, C. E., and Russell, R. O., Jr. (1972). *Circulation* **45,** 127–139.
Ratshin, R. A., Massing, G. K., and James, T. N. (1973). *In* "Myocardial Infarction" (Corday, E., and Swan, J. H. C., eds.), pp. 77–80. Williams and Wilkins, Baltimore.
Reddy, C. P., and Gettes, L. S. (1979). *Am. J. Cardiol.* **44,** 705–713.
Regan, T. J., Passannante, A. J., Khan, M. I., Oldewurtel, H. A., and Jesrani, M. U. (1971). *J. Clin. Invest.* **50,** 534–542.
Reimer, K. A., and Jennings, R. B. (1979). *Lab. Invest.* **40,** 633–644.
Reiz, S., Wangstein, F., and Hjalmarson, A. (1980). *Clin. Cardiol.* **3,** 96–105.
Resnekov, L. (1973). *Br. Heart J.* **35,** 1265–1270.
Robinson, J. S., Stannard, M. M., and Long, M. (1965). *Am. Heart J.* **70,** 233–238.
Rosenblum, R. (1974). *Am. Heart J.* **87,** 527–530.

Rotman, M., Chen, J. T. T., Seningen, R. P., Howley, J., Wagner, G. S., Davidson, R. M., and Gilbert, M. R. (1974). *Am. J. Cardiol.* **33**, 357–362.
Rude, R. E., Turi, Z., Brown, E. J., Lovell, B. H., Colucci, W. S., Mudge, G. H., Taylor, C. R., and Grossman, W. (1981). *Circulation* **64**, 139–145.
Sanders, R. J., Kern, W. H., and Blount, S. G., Jr. (1956). *Am. Heart J.* **51**, 736–748.
Sanders, R. J., Newberger, K. T., and Ravin, A. (1957). *Dis. Chest* **31**, 316–323.
Sandler, H. A., Dodge, H. T., and Murdaugh, H. V., Jr. (1961). *Am. Heart J.* **12**, 643–651.
Sasayama, S., Nonogi, H., Miyazaki, S., Sakurai, T., Kawai, C., Eiho, S., and Kawahara, M. (1985). *J. Am. Coll. Cardiol.* **5**, 599–606.
Scheidt, S., Ascheim, R., and Killip, T. (1970). *Am. J. Cardiol.* **26**, 556–564.
Selzer, A., Gerbode, F., and Kerth, W. J. (1969). *Am. Heart J.* **78**, 548–607.
Sharfe, N., and Coxon, R. (1982). *Circulation* 66 (II), 20.
Sharma, B., and Goodwin, J. F. (1978). *Circulation* **58**, 449–460.
Sharma, B., Hoback, J., Francis, G. S., Hodges, M., Asinger, R. W., Cohn, J. N., and Taylor, C. R. (1981). *Am. Heart J.* **102**, 533–541.
Sharma, G. V. R., Kumar, R., Molokhia, F., and Resser, J. V. (1971). *Clin. Res.* **19**, 339.
Shell, W. E., Lavelle, J. F., Covell, J. W., and Sobel, B. E. (1973). *J. Clin. Invest.* **52**, 2579–2590.
Shubin, H., and Weil, M. H. (1965). *Am. J. Cardiol.* **15**, 147.
Sleight, P., and Widdicombe, J. G. (1966). *J. Physiol.* **181**, 235–258.
Smith, H. J., Oriol, A., March, J., and McGregor, M. (1967). *Circulation* **35**, 1084–1091.
Smith, S. C., Gorlin, R., Herman, M. V., Taylor, W. J., and Collins, J. J., Jr. (1972). *J. Clin. Invest.* **51**, 2556–2565.
Snow, P. J. D., Jones, A. M., and Daber, K. S. (1955). *Br. Heart J.* **17**, 503–510.
Sonnenblick, E. H., and Skelton, C. L. (1971). *Mod. Concepts Cardiovasc. Dis.* **40**, 9–11.
Stefoni, S., Coli, L., Mosconi, G., and Prandini, R. (1981). *Br. J. Clin. Pharmacol.* **1**, 69–72.
Stemple, D. R., Kleiman, J. H., and Harrison, D. C. (1978). *Am. J. Cardiol.* **42**, 267–275.
Stephens, J. D., Banim, S. O., and Spurrell, R. A. J. (1979). *Br. Heart J.* **41**, 381.
Stoner, J. D., Bolen, J. L., and Harrison (1977). *Br. Heart J.* **39**, 536–539.
Swan, H. J. C., Forrester, J. S., Diamond, G., Chatterjee, K., and Parmley, W. W. (1972). *Circulation* **45**, 1097–1110.
Switinbank, J. M. (1959). *Br. Heart J.* **21**, 562–566.
Talley, R. C., Goldberg, L. I., Johnson, L. E., and McNay, J. L. (1969). *Circulation* **39**, 361–378.
Tennant, R., and Wiggers, C. J. (1935). *Am. J. Physiol.* **112**, 351–355.
Thal, A. P., and Kinney, J. M. (1967). *Prog. Cardiovasc. Dis.* **9**, 527–557.
Thorner, N. O. (1975). *Lancet* **1**, 662–665.
Timmis, A. D., Bergman, G., Atkinson, L., Monaghan, M., and Jewitt, D. E. (1981). *Am. J. Cardiol.* **47**, 427.
Tolano, J. V., and Lesch, M. (1979). *In* "Diagnosis and Therapy of Coronary Artery Disease" (T. F. Cohen, ed.) pp. 396. Little Brown and Co., Boston.
Toubes, D. B., and Brody, M. J. (1970). *Circ. Res.* **26**, 211–224.
Tuttle, R. R. (1978). *In* "Proceedings of Europe and Dobutamine Symposium" (Glynne, A., and Lucas, R. A., eds.), pp. 58–67. Guy's Hospital, London.
Tuttle, R. R., and Millis, J. (1975). *Circulation Res.* **36**, 181–191.
Tuttle, R. R., Pollack, G. D., Todd, G., and Tust, R. (1973). *Circulation* **48**, 521.
Unverferth, D. V., Leier, C. V., Magorein, R. D., Croskery, R., Svirbely, J. R., Kolibash, A. J., Dick, M. R., Meacham, J. A., and Baba, N. (1980). *J. Pharmacol. Exp. Ther.* **215**, 527–532.
Van Tassel, R. A., and Edwards, J. E. (1972). *Chest*, **61**, 104–116.

Vasu, M. A., O'Keefe, D. D., Kapellakis, G. Z., Vezeridis, M. P., Jacobs, M. L., Daggett, W. M., and Powell, W. J. (1978). *Circulation Res.* **235,** 237–241.
Vatner, S. F., and Baig, H. (1979). *Circulation Res.* **45,** 793–803.
Vatner, S. F., McRitchie, R. J., and Braunwald, E. (1974). *J. Clin. Invest.* **53,** 1265–1273.
Waagstein, F., Reiz, S., Ariniego, R., and Hjalmarson (1981). *Am. Heart J.* **102,** 548–554.
Wackers, F. J., Lie, K. I., and Becker, A. E. (1970). *Br. Heart J.* **32,** 728–731.
Wahr, D., Swedberg, K., Ports, T., Don Michael, T., and Chatterjee, K. (1982). *Circulation* **66** (II), 137.
Watson, A., Hackel, D. B., and Estes, E. H. (1970). *Am. Heart J.* **79,** 613–619.
Weber, K. T., Andrews, V., Janicki, J. S., Likoff, N., and Reichek, N. (1982). *Circulation* **66,** 1262–1267.
Willerson, J. T., Hutton, J., Watson, J. T., Platt, M. R., ar.d Templeton, G. H. (1976). *Circulation* **53,** 828–833.
Williams, D. O., Amsterdam, E. A., Miller, R. R., and Mason, D. T. (1975). *Am. J. Cardiol.* **37,** 345–351.
Winslow, E. B., Loeb, H., Rahimtoola, S. H., Rosen, K., and Gunnar, R. M. (1970). *Circulation* **41-42** (Suppl. III), 207.
Wolk, M. J., Scheidt, S., and Killip, T. (1972). *Circulation* **66** (II), 137.
Yacoub, M. H., and Buyland, E. (1973). *Lancet* **1,** 1260–1261.
Zoll, P. M., Wessler, S., and Schlesinger, M. J. (1951). *Circulation* **4,** 797–815.

# 4 Coronary Artery Spasm and Pharmacology of Coronary Vasodilators

Charles R. Lambert[1] and Carl J. Pepine

## I. Introduction

Coronary artery spasm is now firmly established as a mechanism responsible for myocardial ischemia. The purpose of this chapter is to summarize the evolution of coronary spasm as a concept, particularly with respect to its role in acute myocardial infarction. The pathophysiological mechanisms responsible for coronary spasm will be addressed. Finally, the pharmacology of agents acting directly upon coronary artery smooth muscle will be examined.

## II. Coronary Artery Spasm: Evolution of Current Concepts

The hypothesis that constriction of a coronary artery may lead to angina pectoris can be traced to the writings of Brunton (1867), Fothergill (1879), and Huchard (1889). Osler (1910) outlined his belief that dynamic coronary artery narrowing was the primary mechanism for angina pectoris at rest. Danielopolus (1924) was probably the first to develop the supply–demand concept of myocardial ischemia. He felt that excessive myocardial metabolic demand and/or diminished coronary blood flow could lead to ischemia and angina pectoris. Clinical-pathologic studies of Gallavardin (1925) supported early theories of coronary artery spasm. He found a general correlation between severe coronary atherosclerosis and exertional angina while patients with predominantly rest angina generally had

---

[1] Dr. Lambert is a research fellow supported by the United States Public Health Service and the American Heart Association, Florida Affiliate, Sun Coast Chapter.

minimal occlusive disease. Later Blumgart et al. (1940) similarly found a high correlation between the degree of coronary atherosclerosis at postmortem and angina. They too noted the occasional patient with clinical ischemia premortem and minimal coronary atherosclerosis at autopsy. Both of these studies suggested dynamic vascular occlusion as a possible pathophysiologic mechanism for myocardial ischemia.

A very influential paper by Keefer and Resnick (1928) proposed that the inability of hardened atherosclerotic coronary arteries to constrict was strong reason to minimize the role of vasomotion. These authors felt that the central mechanism of myocardial ischemia must be increased myocardial oxygen demand, an idea that became firmly established. A large investigative effort ensued to delineate physiological determinants of myocardial energy expenditure. The idea of a primary or supply-side contribution to myocardial ischemia by coronary spasm was largely ignored for many years.

Revival of coronary spasm as a possible clinical entity is credited to Prinzmetal and co-workers (1959, 1960). They summarized findings in 32 cases in which ST segment elevation and rest angina were present. This syndrome they named variant angina and hypothesized that it was due to increased coronary artery tone at the site of atherosclerotic stenosis. However, the next milestone in the appreciation of coronary artery spasm awaited the introduction of selective coronary arteriography. Gensini et al. (1962) first published a case of coronary artery spasm during angina, and other angiographic documentation of spasm was described by Dhurandhar et al. (1972), Oliva et al. (1973), and Froment et al. (1973). Questions remained regarding the contribution of catheter or dye and the clinical relevance of such observations remained in doubt until definitive pathophysiological data in human subjects were gathered by Maseri et al. (1975) Guazzi et al. (1971), Berndt et al. (1977), and Chierchia et al. (1980). Preceding spontaneous episodes of angina, no increase in hemodynamic parameters of myocardial oxygen demand occurred. Arteriography during spontaneous angina revealed transient complete coronary artery occlusion which could be reversed by nitrates. Asymptomatic episodes of ischemia were also documented showing the same angiographic findings. Criticisms related to possible dye- or catheter-induced spasm were settled when thallium-201 scintigraphy showed transmural deficits in uptake in association with episodes of variant angina. Finally, a decrease in coronary venous oxygen saturation, providing direct evidence for myocardial hypoxia, was found during episodes of variant angina. This desaturation clearly preceded the onset of angina, ST segment elevation, decrease in dP/dT, and elevation in left ventricular end-diastolic pressure. These studies offered strong evidence in favor of a primary reduction in coronary flow as the initiator of the sequence of events responsible for variant angina. Subsequently, measurements of regional coronary venous flow were made in our laboratory during episodes of coronary spasm (Feldman et al., 1980, 1981b). An example of such a study is illustrated in Fig. 1. Venous flow from the region supplied by the artery in spasm decreased an average of 32% while flow from the noninvolved region remained un-

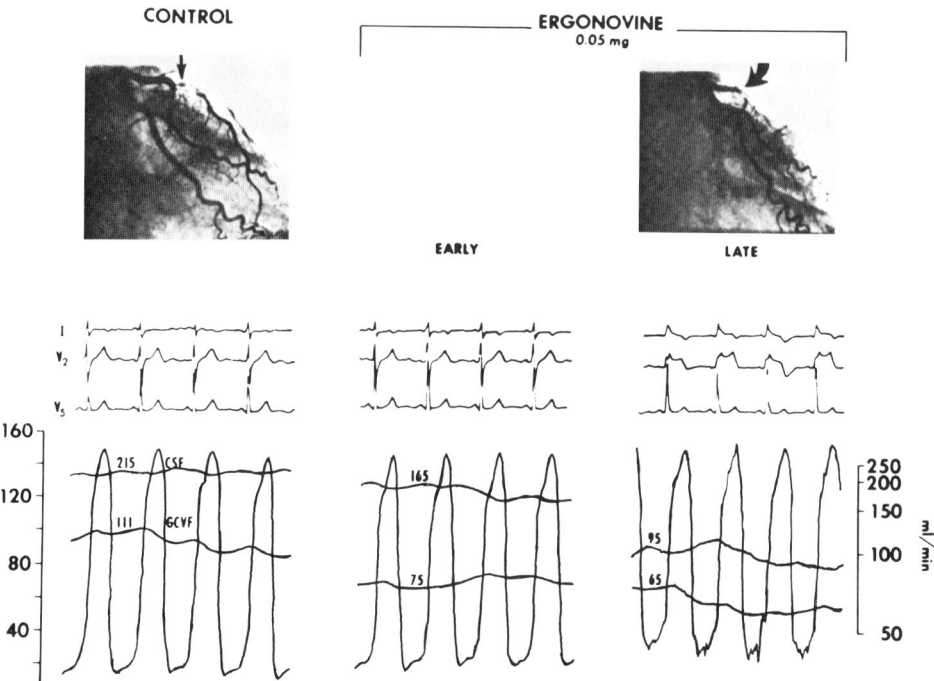

**Fig. 1.** Example of serial coronary flow changes occurring during large vessel (anterior descending) spasm. Above: left coronary arteriograms, right anterior oblique (RAO) projection, before (left control) and after onset of angina evoked with 0.05 mg of ergonovine (right). Before (left) there is severe anterior descending stenosis (small arrow) and after onset of angina (right) both mid- and distal anterior descending segments cannot be visualized beyond the large arrow. Below: representative panels showing ECG, left ventricular pressure and coronary sinus (CSF), and great cardiac vein (GCVF) flow signals recorded continuously after the angiogram shown to the left was filmed until the onset of angina, angiogram shown to the right. Early after ergonovine (middle) administration, both total left ventricular (CSF) and anterior regional (GCVF) blood flows decrease considerably although only minimal ECG T-wave changes and end-diastolic pressure changes occurred as the patient remained asymptomatic. Angina occurred approximately 2 min later as flow declined further and ST segment and further left ventricular end-diastolic pressure elevation became manifest. Although substantial residual anterior regional flow is present, angiography shows no contrast flow in the anterior descending vessel, confirming the presence of spasm. Following nitroglycerin treatment, angina was relieved, and angiographic ECG and hemodynamic changes were restored.

changed. These alterations were similar in magnitude and temporal sequence to those induced by balloon occlusion of a coronary artery during angioplasty (Feldman et al., 1982b).

There is no doubt that transient reversible coronary artery occlusion occurs and results in myocardial ischemia and angina. ST segment elevation is not mandatory. Coronary artery spasm occurs in association with ST depression, T wave changes, or even no electrocardiographic changes in a few patients. Although this syndrome may occur in patients with normal coronary arteries, it is more frequently found superimposed upon coronary atherosclerosis. Appreciation of this association has recently led to a broader concept of dynamic coronary artery stenosis as described later and has laid to rest the view of the "fixed," adynamic atherosclerotic coronary artery.

The natural history of coronary spasm is highly variable and typified by periods of exacerbation and remission (MacAlpin, 1980; Bott-Silverman and Heupler, 1983; Waters et al., 1983). Despite the relative unpredictability of attacks some patients have occurrence in predictable cycles (R. M. Robertson et al., 1979). The frequency of myocardial infarction and rhythm disturbances in patients with coronary spasm is generally agreed to be relatively high. The frequency of infarction has been reported to range from 25 to 40% (Silverman and Flamm, 1971; MacAlpin et al., 1973; Selzer et al., 1976; Conti et al., 1979). The course of patients with spasm first noted in the perioperative period following bypass grafting has shown no recurrence, suggesting a transient mechanical or metabolic cause of the disorder in these cases (Buxton et al., 1982). Although coronary spasm most often occurs at rest or with ordinary activities of life, a few patients have been described who seem to develop spasm with exercise (Specchia et al., 1981; Yasue et al., 1979; DeServi et al., 1981; Chaitman et al., 1981; Boden et al., 1981; Matsuda et al., 1983). Spasm has also been associated with a variable threshold for exertional angina and "walk-through" angina (Brunelli et al., 1981). However, critical review of the role of coronary spasm in exercise-induced angina suggests that these patients almost always have underlying variant angina or other nonexertional angina syndrome. Thus, it appears that exercise-related ischemia found in these cases may be coincident with and simply superimposed upon the syndrome of coronary spasm at rest occurring spontaneously throughout the day (Pepine, 1983).

The exact frequency with which coronary spasm causes myocardial ischemia is unknown due to the highly variable course of the disease with frequent exacerbation and remission periods and lack of a perfect diagnostic test. Although histamine (Ginsburg et al., 1981), adrenalin, and methacholine (Yasue et al., 1974) have been proposed to induce coronary spasm, these agents are not useful in general. The most widely used agent for this purpose is ergonovine. Interpretation of an ergonovine provocation test is easy if a patient with nearly normal coronary arteries has angina, associated ST segment elevation, an ischemic hemodynamic response, and transient coronary artery occlusion with repeat angiography. When such a scenario does not occur difficulty in interpreting the test is not infrequent (Maseri and Chierchia, 1982). In addition, test results may vary in the same patient with time as disease activity and normal coronary reactivity vary or are modified by drugs (Pepine *et al.*, 1982).

Despite these limitations, Bertrand and co-workers (1982b) studied the frequency of methergine-induced coronary artery spasm in 1089 consecutive patients undergoing catheterization for evaluation of chest pain. Excluding patients with spontaneous spasm, left main stenosis, and triple vessel disease, 134 patients developed focal coronary artery spasm. The history of these patients was most frequently rest angina and less often a combined rest and exertional angina syndrome. A high (20%) frequency of coronary artery spasm was found in patients studied after recent myocardial infarction compared to those studied after a remote (6 weeks) infarction. Spasm was superimposed upon atherosclerotic narrowing in 60% of cases. Overall, the frequency of provokable coronary spasm in patients with a history of chest pain was 15%. The percentage of patients presenting with rest angina who had provokable spasm was 38%. Assuming that methergine provocation is synonymous with spontaneous spasm, this figure represents the best approximation of the prevalence of coronary spasm in a patient population with a wide variety of chest pain syndromes.

Coronary spasm has been associated with hyperventilation, the Valsalva maneuver, the cold pressor test, alcohol intake, and administration of various compounds including sympathomimetics, parasympathomimetics, ergot alkaloids, and beta-blocking agents (Yasue *et al.*, 1983). Spasm has been associated with allergic reactions (Druck *et al.*, 1981), eclampsia (Bauer *et al.*, 1982), Raynaud's phenomenon (Robertson and Oates, 1978), and withdrawal from chronic exposure to organic nitrates (Lange *et al.*, 1972). Localized coronary spasm has been noted at the site of transluminal angioplasty (Hollman *et al.*, 1983) and both at the site of and distant from bypass graft anastomoses (Zeff *et al.*, 1982). Symptomatic coronary spasm has also been reported following megavoltage radiotherapy without a cardiac shield (Miller *et al.*, 1983).

Thus, the clinical spectrum of coronary artery spasm is diverse. A modern definition for coronary artery spasm entails transient reduction in the caliber of a coronary artery, sufficient in magnitude to reduce or limit coronary blood flow and result in myocardial ischemia. This ischemic episode may most commonly be asymptomatic, it may give rise to angina pectoris and, as presented below, it may be associated with myocardial infarction and or even sudden death. Coronary spasm has evolved from a hypothetical entity considered insignificant on the basis of the observations of Keefer and Resnick (1928) to a clearly documented pathophysiological mechanism responsible for many episodes of myocardial ischemia.

## III. Coronary Artery Spasm and Myocardial Infarction

The question as to whether coronary artery spasm is primarily responsible for initiation of the sequence of events leading to myocardial infarction has generated a great deal of interest (Lambert and Pepine, 1986). Probably the first firm association between myocardial infarction and coronary spasm was made by Lange and co-workers (1972), who described four patients who developed infarction within 3 days after withdrawal from industrial nitroglycerin exposure. Coronary arteriography later revealed normal vessels in three patients. However, the fourth developed spontaneous spasm of both right and left coronary arteries which was relieved by nitroglycerin. Several episodes of catheter-induced spasm resulting in myocardial infarction were reported subsequently (Cheng *et al.*, 1972; Engel *et al.*, 1976), but here there is always the question of coronary artery dissection or embolus. Weiner and co-workers (1976) described six patients with variant angina who eventually sustained a myocardial infarction. These patients had angiographic studies done later which revealed spasm of the arteries supplying the involved regions of myocardium. Oliva and Breckinridge (1977) reported the results of coronary arteriography in 15 patients within 12 hr of acute myocardial infarction. Coronary artery spasm, defined as total or subtotal occlusion with subsequent opening after nitroglycerin, was found in six (40%) of the patients studied. In each instance, spasm was at the site of an atherosclerotic obstruction. These observations were interpreted as suggesting that coronary artery spasm preceded occlusive thrombus formation and myocardial infarction in some patients.

Maseri and co-workers (1978) reported a systematic study of 187 patients with rest angina. Thirty-seven of these patients evolved a myocardial infarction in areas in which transient ST segment abnormalities were noted earlier. Seventy-six of these patients underwent hemodynamic monitoring together with thallium-201 scintigraphy or coronary angiography during angina episodes. Evidence for vasospasm was seen in all of these patients. Eight patients developed myocardial infarction either during or shortly after hemodynamic studies. Hemodynamic patterns during a typical angina attack were indistinguishable from those seen at the onset of myocardial infarction. After infarction in two patients, occlusion of the coronary artery previously shown to undergo spasm was documented angiographically. One patient who had documented spasm died 6 hr later and had a freshly formed thrombus at autopsy localized to the site of the previously noted spasm. These observations strongly support the role of coronary artery spasm as a primary event in myocardial infarction in some patients with intermittent rest or unstable angina pectoris. Supportive data was reported by Neill and co-workers (1980) who studied 70 patients with unstable angina and reversible ST–T abnormalities in a prospective manner. Coronary arteriography was performed acutely and at 4 months. These studies revealed a high incidence of complete occlusion of arteries at 4 months that had been open but with high-grade atherosclerotic obstructions earlier. These occlusions were associated with myocardial infarction in the region supplied and suggested that the unstable angina period represented intermittent coronary occlusion. Whether this was rapid progression of atherosclerosis, thrombotic occlusion, or secondary to spasm could not be determined. However, the clinical similarity of this patient population to that with spasm studied by Maseri *et al.* (1978) suggests a common mechanism.

Zellinger and co-workers (1982) reported a patient with variant angina and persistent inferior T-wave abnormalities. The patient became symptom-free for a period but later developed recurrent rest angina with marked inferior ST segment elevation. Both symptomatic and asymptomatic periods with ST segment elevation continued despite intravenous nitroglycerin. The patient underwent cardiac catheterization, during which a right coronary artery thombus was fragmented with streptokinase. Subsequent serum creatine phosphokinase (CPK) determinations and electrocardiographic changes indicated myocardial infarction. The authors speculated that during the period of unstable angina, coronary spasm was the operant mechanism for production of intermittent ischemia. Furthermore, they suggested that the timing of arteriographic study in such cases may lead to false conclusions regarding the relative roles of thrombotic versus vasospastic events.

Experience with thrombolytic therapy in acute myocardial infarction has offered some support to the proponents of thrombosis as the primary mediator of myocardial infarction. The primary question remains as to the timing of arteriographic study and the relative lack of data at "time zero" in the course of acute myocardial infarction. Several trials of intracoronary thrombolytic therapy have been published during which intracoronary nitroglycerin was administered to exclude coronary artery spasm. Ganz *et al.* (1981) studied 20 patients within 3 hr of the onset of chest pain. Eighteen of these patients were found to have complete occlusion of a coronary artery and only two opened with intracoronary nitroglycerin. Mathey et al. (1981) studied 39 patients with complete coronary occlusion in a similar time frame and only one nitroglycerin response was seen. Markis et al. (1981) reported nine patients studied within 2 to 4 hr of the onset of pain and none responsed to intracoronary nitroglycerin. Rentrop et al. (1981) studied 29 patients within 1.5 to 16 hr after the onset of chest pain and five responded to intracoronary nitroglycerin. Reduto and co-workers (1981) within a similar time frame found 26 with coronary occlusions, one of which was reversed with nitroglycerin. Mandelkorn et al. (1983) recently reported their experience with intracoronary streptokinase and nitroglycerin in patients with unstable angina, transmural infarction, and nontransmural infarction. Only one patient with unstable angina or nontransmural infarction responded to intracoronary nitroglycerin. After 1.5 to 3 hr, the majority of patients with nontransmural infarction and approximately half of those with unstable angina responded to streptokinase, but not nitroglycerin, with either opening of an occluded vessel, an increase in stenosis diameter, or dissolution of an intracoronary filling defect. These findings are consistent with a thrombotic role for coronary artery diameter reduction in both unstable angina and myocardial infarction after 1.5 to 3 hr. Cipriano and co-workers (1983) reported 11 patients with documented coronary artery spasm either before or after myocardial infarction. Arteriographic study of the vessels supplying infarcted regions showed six which had minimal or no visible atherosclerotic disease. The coincidence of the location of infarction and that of spasm was interpreted as evidence that the latter was probably causally related to the former.

Benacerraf et al. (1983) recently described a 37-year-old man with an evolving inferior myocardial infarction who underwent coronary arteriography approximately 2.5 hr after the onset of chest pain. Angiography initially revealed complete occlusion of the proximal right coronary artery which responded to intracoronary nitroglycerin, revealing a discrete stenosis and some associated intraluminal filling defects suggestive of thrombi. No streptokinase was administered because of previous cardiopulmonary resuscitation. Later catheterization revealed resolution of the intraluminal filling defects and only slight outline irregularity in the area. An ergonovine provocation test was positive and later negative after treatment with diltiazem. These authors postulated that coronary spasm initiated the thrombotic process as suggested by the circumstantial evidence presented.

Another report which lends support to the coronary artery spasm–myocardial infarction connection has been cited earlier, the work by

Bertrand and co-workers (1982b). The high frequency (20%) of provoked coronary artery spasm early after myocardial infarction, which diminishes with time, establishes a temporal if not causal relationship between the two phenomena.

We have had the opportunity to care for several patients who illustrate various ways in which myocardial infarction can be associated with coronary artery spasm. These are illustrated in the following cases. The first patient, a 74-year-old white female, presented with an 8-month history of nonexertional chest pain not responsive to propranolol but improved somewhat with addition of long-acting nitrates and nifedipine. Catheterization at her local hospital revealed 60% narrowing of the proximal left anterior descending coronary artery and she was referred for angioplasty. Examination upon admission was unremarkable and the electrocardiogram was normal. Early on the morning of the scheduled angioplasty, she experienced the sudden onset of crushing substernal pain with associated diaphoresis and nausea. Sublingual nitroglycerin was administered and the ECG shown in Fig. 2 was obtained. She became hypotensive and bradycardic and was taken to the catheterization laboratory where she arrived without pulse or blood pressure despite resuscitative efforts en route. Administration of atropine, phenylephrine, and dopamine led to a systolic pressure of 70 mm Hg and an intra-aortic balloon pump was utilized for support. A left coronary injection revealed a subtotal occlu-

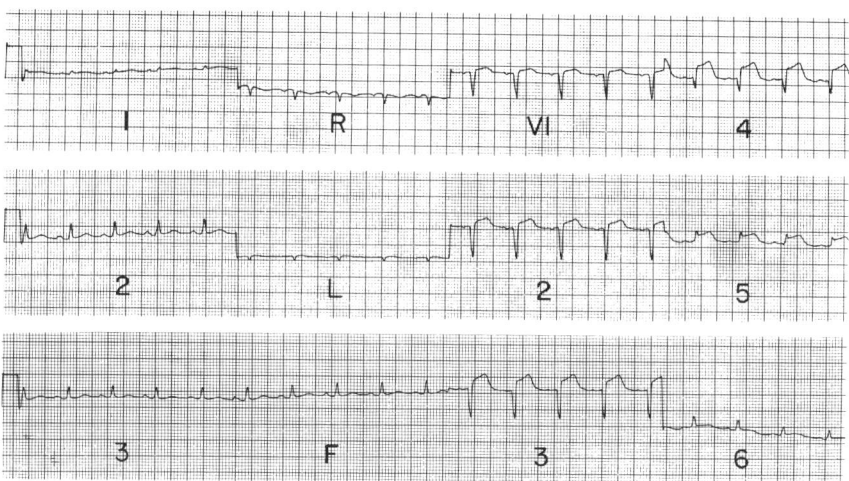

A.S.

**Fig. 2.** Electrocardiogram of patient A.S. with the sudden onset of chest pain prior to hypotension and bradycardia as described in the text. (From Lambert and Pepine, 1986.)

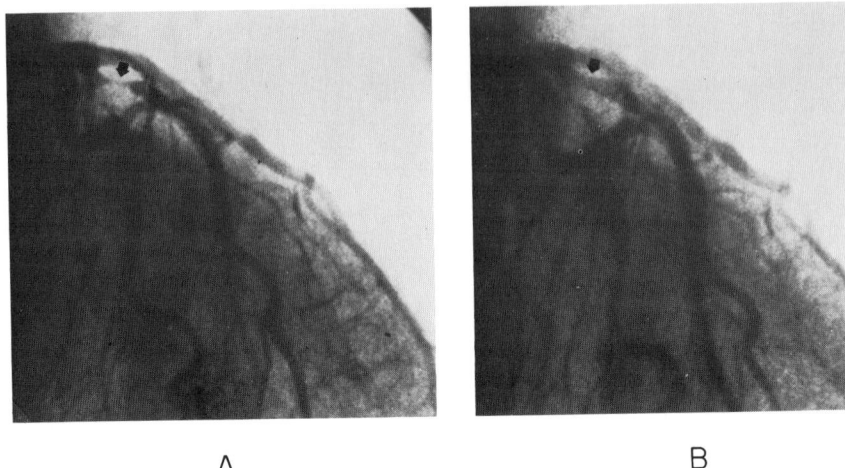

**Fig. 3.** RAO projections of the left coronary system demonstrating focal spasm (A) and relieved by intracoronary nitroglycerin (B). (From Lambert and Pepine, 1986.)

sion of the proximal left anterior descending coronary artery (Fig. 3A). One hundred micrograms of nitroglycerin was then administered into the left coronary system with relief of the obstruction (Fig. 3B). Coincidently, her systolic blood pressure increased to 120 mm Hg without pressors and an intravenous infusion of nitroglycerin was begun. The ST segment elevation noted initially began to resolve, however. Within 10 min it began to worsen again and the systolic blood pressure began to fall. Repeat arteriography revealed reocclusion as in Fig. 3A, and relief again followed intracoronary nitroglycerin. This process repeated itself at 10- to 15-min intervals despite continued intravenous and intracoronary nitroglycerin, intracoronary verapamil, buccal nifedipine, and intracoronary phentolamine. At various times over the next 2–3 hr, spasm involved the left anterior descending artery, a major diagonal branch, and two circumflex branches (Fig. 4A) and required increasing doses of intracoronary nitroglycerin for relief. Figure 4B shows reversal of diffuse spasm with an intracoronary bolus of 1 mg of nitroglycerin. Figure 5A shows subsequent focal spasm of a circumflex branch with later (Fig. 5B) total occlusion suggestive of thrombus. After 1 hr of intracoronary streptokinase, no change was seen; however, after several large (2 mg) bolus injections of intracoronary nitroglycerin relief was produced. Hemodynamic stabilization was eventually achieved with an intravenous infusion of nitroglycerin and verapamil. Final arteriographic study (Fig. 6) revealed a long narrowed area in the anterior descending artery without other focal narrow-

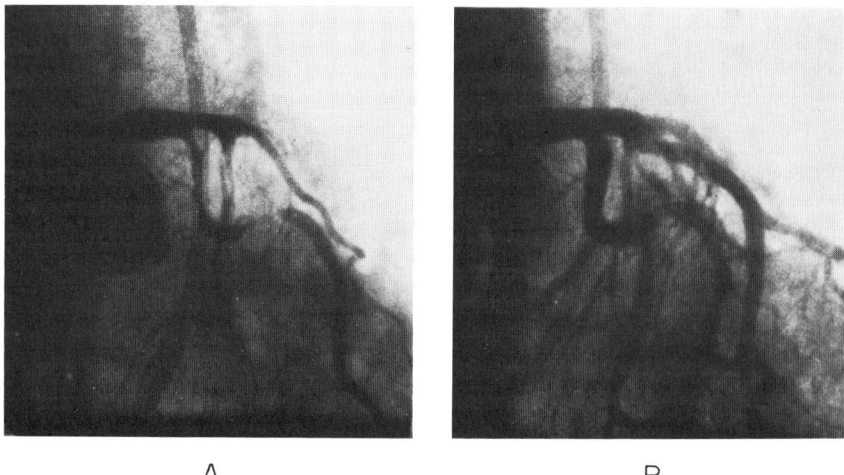

**Fig. 4.** RAO coronary arteriogram demonstrating diffuse spasm involving the left anterior descending, circumflex, and diagonal coronary arteries (A) and relief following large dose of intracoronary nitroglycerin (B). (From Lambert and Pepine, 1986.)

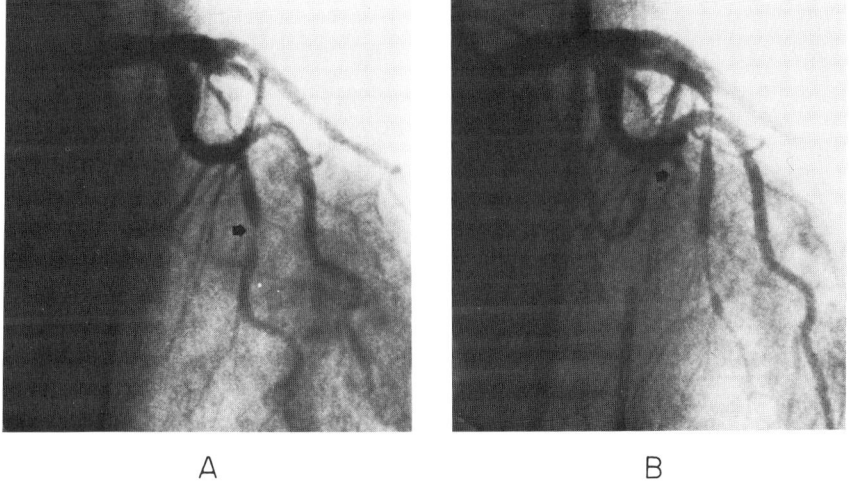

**Fig. 5.** RAO coronary arteriogram demonstrating focal circumflex spasm (A) and proximal circumflex occlusion (B) as described in the text. (From Lambert and Pepine, 1986).

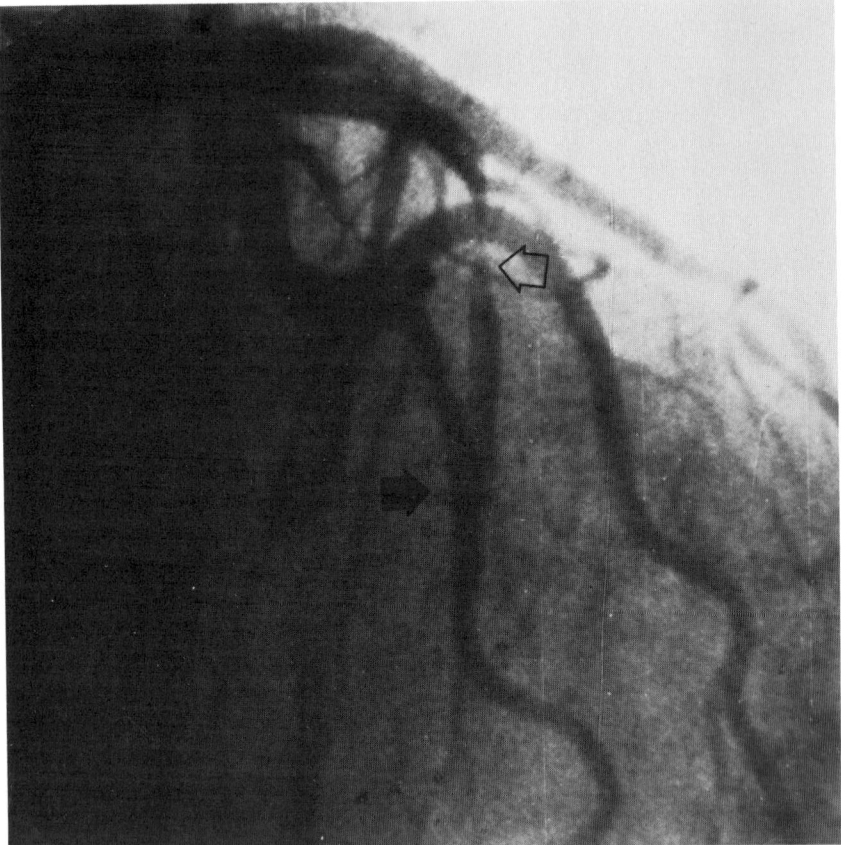

**Fig. 6.** RAO coronary arteriogram illustrating relief of the proximal circumflex occlusion in Fig. 5B and a residual long area of narrowing in the left anterior descending artery (open arrow). (From Lambert and Pepine, 1986.)

ings. The patient evolved enzyme and ECG criteria for a large recently reperfused anterior infarction and, despite her stormy course, is doing well 2 years later.

The second patient, a 68-year-old white male with a history of both rest and exertional angina poorly controlled on beta blockers and nitrates, presented with a prolonged episode of rest pain. The ECG in Fig. 7 (top) was obtained. Cardiac enzymes indicated necrosis. Chest pain recurred several days later and catheterization demonstrated moderately severe obstructions involving the left anterior descending, circumflex, and right coronary arteries. Ergonovine (0.1 mg) intravenously provoked total oc-

## 4. Coronary Artery Spasm and Vasodilators

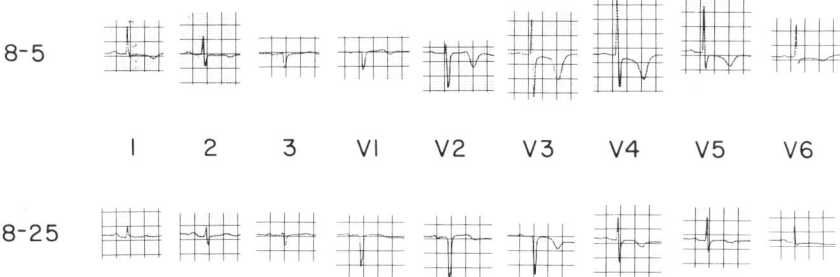

**Fig. 7.** Admission ECGs for patient E.R. as described in the text.

clusion of the proximal left anterior descending coronary artery which was relieved with intracoronary nitroglycerin (Fig. 8). The patient did well taking diltiazem and long-acting nitrates and was discharged with the diagnosis of acute anterolateral subendocardial infarction only to return 1 week later again with an episode of prolonged chest pain at rest. The ECG (Fig. 7, bottom panel) showed evidence for transmural anterior myocardial infarction. Immediate catheterization showed an intraluminal filling defect within the proximal left anterior descending artery in the region of the previously documented spasm (Fig. 9A). Intracoronary streptokinase infusion caused resolution of the filling defect (Fig. 9B). Cardiac enzymes showed evidence for necrosis and the patient did well with combination nifedipine, diltiazem, and nitrate therapy.

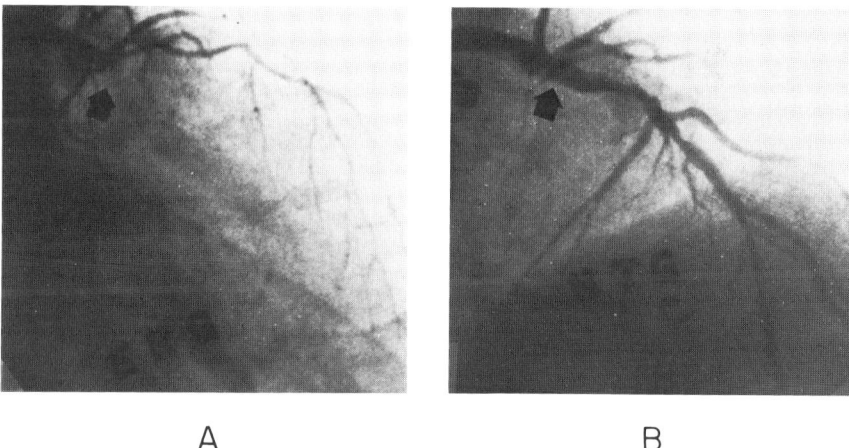

**Fig. 8.** RAO coronary arteriogram revealing total proximal left anterior descending obstruction (A) provoked by ergonovine and relieved by intracoronary nitroglycerin (B).

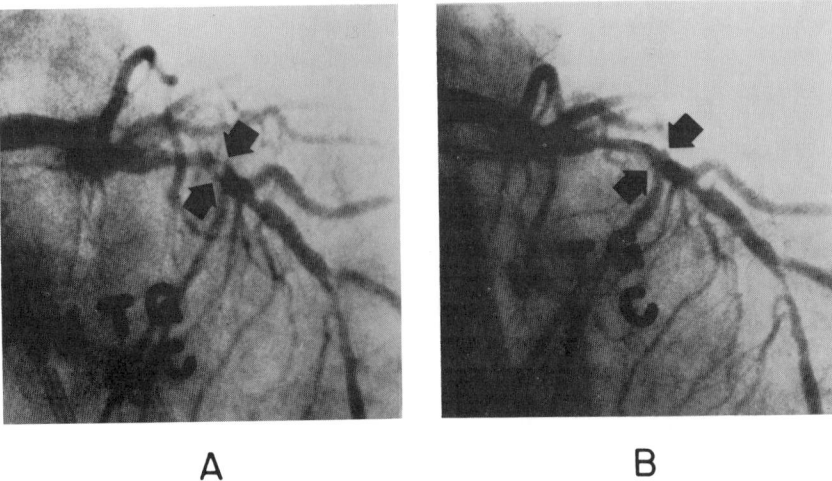

A                B

**Fig. 9.** RAO coronary arteriogram illustrating an intramural filling defect in the left anterior descending artery (A) which disappears following intracoronary streptokinase therapy (B). This defect is located in a portion of the artery previously shown to undergo spasm in Fig. 8.

The third patient is a 62-year-old white male who presented with a 6-year history of both rest and exertional chest pain which was usually nitroglycerin responsive. He underwent cardiac catheterization, with reportedly normal coronary arteries, 5 years previously at a local hospital. He came to our institution with increasing frequency of chest pain and had the admission ECG labeled June in Fig. 10. Serial cardiac enzymes were normal and an exercise stress test (Bruce protocol) to stage IV was without chest pain or ECG changes. He was discharged but continued to have nocturnal chest pain and returned 1 month later with the ECG labeled July in Fig. 10. Serial cardiac enzymes were normal and cardiac catheterization revealed normal coronary arteries with left ventricular anterolateral hypokinesis. Ergonovine stimulation reproduced his chest pain, associated with focal spasm of the left anterior descending artery (Fig. 11) which reversed with intracoronary nitroglycerin. These angiographic findings were accompanied by "pseudonormalization" of electrocardiographic T-wave abnormalities. Right coronary spasm (Fig. 12) was also seen.

These three patients illustrate the array of different manifestations seen with coronary artery spasm in the setting of myocardial infarction. The first case offers data essentially at "time zero" in the course of infarction with "sudden" or near death attributable to severe localized and diffuse

## 4. Coronary Artery Spasm and Vasodilators

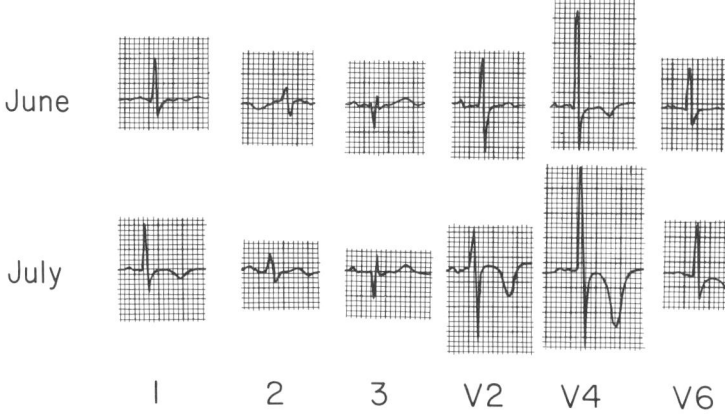

**Fig. 10.** Admission ECGs for patient three as described in the text.

coronary spasm recalcitrant to usual therapy. There was no demonstrable thrombus seen and all coronary occlusions appeared to be due to severe vasotonic influences associated with atherosclerotic disease in some areas but not in others. The second case illustrates the association of myocardial infarction in an area supplied by an artery known to undergo spasm, but with the addition of a focal, nonocclusive thrombus at the time of myocardial damage. Did calcium blockers and nitrates prevent this thrombus from becoming completely occlusive? This case is reminiscent

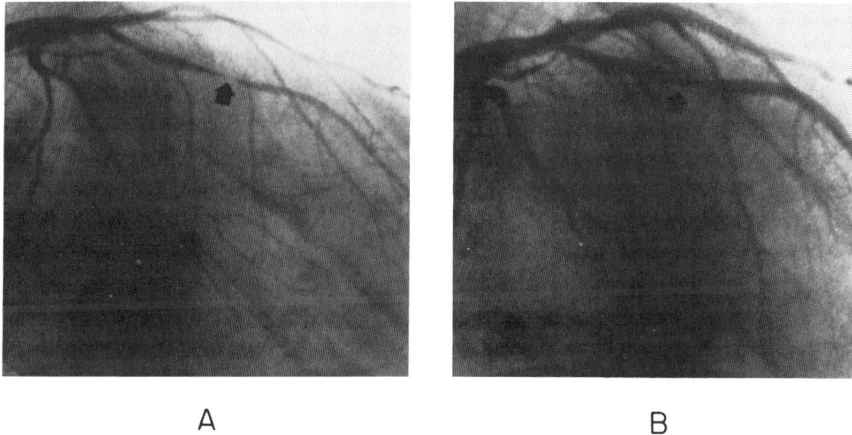

**Fig. 11.** RAO coronary arteriograms illustrating focal left anterior descending spasm (A) provoked by ergonovine and relieved with intracoronary nitroglycerin (B).

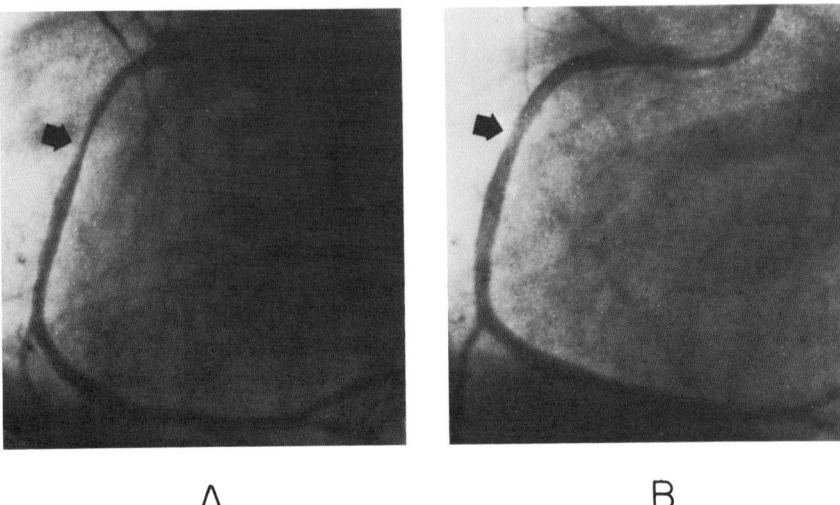

**Fig. 12.** Left anterior oblique (LAO) coronary arteriogram demonstrating focal right coronary artery narrowing after ergonovine (A) relieved by intracoronary nitroglycerin (B).

of the one described by Benacerraf *et al.* (1983). The third case illustrates the relatively uncommon finding of myocardial infarction in a patient with angiographically normal coronary arteries which undergo spasm after provocation at the site of recent infarction.

Thus, there is some direct and considerable circumstantial evidence to implicate coronary artery spasm as a primary phenomenon in the initiation of myocardial infarction. There is also evidence suggesting *in situ* thrombosis as the event present several hours after the onset of the clinical findings of myocardial infarction. A third point of view is more probable, and this is that both thrombosis and coronary artery spasm coexist. The principal problem with clinical studies designed to attempt to delineate the relative roles for spasm versus thrombosis as the primary event in acute myocardial infarction remains the time factor. There will always be a finite time period between the onset of coronary occlusion and clinical presentation and an even longer period of time before angiographic study. An additional consideration is that spasm may become refractory and persist despite intracoronary nitroglycerin, and even paradoxical angiographic responses have been documented following administration of nitroglycerin (Feldman *et al.*, 1978). The answers to these questions await further study using different techniques.

## IV. Pathophysiological Mechanisms

### A. Passive and Active Influences on Vessel Caliber

As noted in the preceding sections, the hypothesis of Keefer and Resnick (1928) that atherosclerotic coronary arteries are incapable of significant vasomotion was directly disproven by clinical observations made with the advent of coronary arteriography. Indeed, in angiographic studies of stenoses of widely varying severity, the capacity for dynamic change in size was a uniform finding (Brown *et al.*, 1981). These observations indicate that the atherosclerotic coronary artery is capable of vasomotion and that both active and passive vasomotion influence stenosis shape and size.

Numerous studies have been performed to define the contribution of passive changes in coronary artery caliber to flow reduction. Important variables which interact to cause such alterations include stenosis geometry, resistance distal to the stenosis, perfusion pressure, and arterial tone (Walinsky *et al.*, 1979; Santamore and Walinsky, 1980; Schwartz *et al.*, 1979; Logan, 1975; Santamore *et al.*, 1982). In the absence of smooth muscle tone, coronary vessels behave like Starling resistors, in which the difference between perfusion pressure and extravascular pressure determines flow. The location of the stenosis as extramural or intramural also plays an important role in determining passive hemodynamic patterns. In arteries without active tone in which a stenosis is created by an external snare, a drop in distal pressure causes a decrease in flow secondary to collapse (i.e., inward protrusion of the vessel wall) (Santamore and Walinsky, 1980; Schwartz *et al.*, 1979). If an intraluminal obstruction of similar magnitude is created, reduction of distal pressure is followed by an increase in flow although calculated resistance increases. These findings are consistent with a waterfall effect, as has been demonstrated in isolated human coronary arteries with eccentric stenoses (Logan, 1975). An extension of this data is that in such eccentric stenoses, if a portion of the arterial wall retains mobility, occlusion will occur primarily as a function of smooth muscle tone. This tone serves as a modulator of critical closing pressure at the point of the stenosis. This principle has been illustrated during ergonovine provocation in an *in situ* canine model of intraluminal obstruction (Sakamoto *et al.*, 1983).

From these observations the concept of a dynamic coronary stenosis has evolved, in which stenosis geometry, smooth muscle tone, distal arteriolar resistance, and perfusion pressure interact to modulate blood flow. This concept is entirely consistent with the clinical findings of reversible coronary occlusion *in vivo*. The degree of vasomotion required for significant limitation of flow is a function of the initial cross-sectional area of the vessel. Thus, in more severe atherosclerotic stenoses, less vasomotion is required for occlusion by the mechanisms cited above than in coronary arteries with less severe atherosclerotic obstructions. This accounts in part for the frequent clinical association of coronary artery spasm with occlusive coronary atherosclerosis (Maseri and Chierchia, 1982).

## B. Endothelium-Dependent Mechanisms

### 1. Mechanical Endothelial Injury

Electron microscopic studies of arteries after spasm was induced by norepinephrine have shown marked endothelial damage (Joris and Majno, 1981). The observed changes included patchy endothelial denudation and adhesions between cells on opposite sides of intimal folds. These changes were felt to be secondary to tight folding of the internal elastic lamina, which in turn compressed endothelial cells directly. Such spasm-induced endothelial disruption might then initiate the sequence of platelet aggregation, plug formation, and the release of vasoactive substances such as thromboxane $A_2$, which might then perpetuate spasm. These studies also offer evidence that spasm-induced endothelial disruption might be an initiating factor leading to localized atherosclerotic disease. An experimental model which supports these contentions is that of Shimokawa and co-workers (1983). Miniature swine were first subjected to balloon-induced endothelial denudation of the circumflex coronary artery and subsequently fed a diet containing 2% cholesterol. This treatment produced local coronary atherosclerosis as documented by angiography. After the development of these lesions, provocative testing with histamine produced localized coronary artery spasm with associated ischemic electrocardiographic changes. Induced spasm was reversed with nitroglycerin and prevented by diphenhydramine or diltiazem. Thus, in this model, mechanical endothelial injury leads to localized atherosclerosis, which increases coronary artery smooth muscle sensitivity to histamine. The possibility that spasm by some other mechanism might initiate the sequence of events by producing the initial endothelial injury rather than using mechanical denudation has not been addressed in such studies.

Kawachi and co-workers (1984) induced localized coronary atherosclerosis in dogs by endothelial denudation and a high-cholesterol diet. Focal coronary spasm was observed in response to ergonovine over a 1- to 6-month period and then *in vitro* studies were performed on the denuded

## 4. Coronary Artery Spasm and Vasodilators

and control sections of arteries. The dose–response curves of denuded and control arteries to phenylephrine were identical while ergonovine or serotonin produced markedly exaggerated responses in the denuded vessels. Thus, in this model, localized endothelial injury led to focal atherosclerosis, *in situ* coronary artery spasm, and marked *in vitro* hypersensitivity to ergonovine and serotonin. Studies of isolated human coronary arteries have demonstrated a potentiated constrictor response to histamine but not ergonovine in atherosclerotic vessels as opposed to controls (Ginsburg *et al.*, 1984).

Other investigators (Arnim *et al.*, 1983) have studied coronary flow responses in isolated rabbit hearts from control and cholesterol-fed groups. Ergonovine and serotonin were without significant differential effect and histamine was not tested.

### 2. Vasoactive Mediators

A great deal of investigation has focused on the area of endothelium-dependent vasoactive compounds in recent years (Furchgott, 1983). The response which was initially shown to be dependent upon the presence of functional endothelial cells is the dose-dependent relaxation produced by acetylcholine. Subsequently bradykinin, ATP, ADP, substance P, and histamine have all been found to exert endothelium-dependent vasodilatory responses. Recently, loss of endothelium-dependent vasodilatory influences has been suggested to play a possible role in coronary vasospasm (Ku, 1982). Supportive studies involved the effects of exogenously administered thrombin on vasomotion in canine coronary arteries. In control vessels, thrombin produced dose-related vasodilation followed by constriction. Vasodilation was dependent on the presence of endothelial cells and was lost after either denudation or exposure to heparin. In arteries taken from an ischemic myocardial region, vasodilation was absent and pronounced vasoconstriction was seen. These observations suggest that ischemia produces endothelial injury which can lead to loss of endogenous vasodilatory influences and thus facilitate vasospasm. The potential implications of this concept with regard to other naturally occurring endothelium-dependent factors, atherosclerosis, and drugs are great.

Prostacyclin, an arachidonic acid metabolite synthesized by endothelial cells, has vasodilatory and antiplatelet effects. Thromboxane $A_2$ is a platelet-dependent factor with powerful aggregatory and vasoconstrictor activity. The balance between thromboxane $A_2$ and prostacyclin has been proposed as a regulatory mechanism which may mediate coronary vasospasm (Mehta, 1983). Presumably, an imbalance in this system and resultant coronary constriction might be caused by mechanical alteration of the endothelium with local platelet aggregation and release of thromboxane $A_2$ coincident with reduction in local synthesis of prostacyclin. There is experimental evidence that the cyclic flow reduction seen in canine models of coronary stenosis is at least in part related to platelet aggregation–disaggregation (Folts *et al.*, 1982). Inhibitors of aggregation or thromboxane $A_2$ generation prevent such flow reductions. Administration of prostacyclin has also been shown to block this response (Aiken *et al.*, 1979). Experimental observations such as these, along with the finding of elevated levels of thromboxane metabolites in the coronary sinus blood of patients with coronary artery spasm (Robertson *et al.*, 1981), led to a trial of intravenous prostacyclin in variant angina patients (Chierchia *et al.*, 1982c). In five patients prostacyclin did not reduce the number, severity, or duration of ischemic attacks. In three patients, the drug had no effect on ergonovine-induced coronary artery spasm. One patient had obvious improvement during infusion periods. These results were felt to be indicative of the variety of mechanisms involved in the production of ischemia in different patients.

These data are supported by determinations of the time course of changes in coronary sinus thromboxane metabolites during rest angina (Robertson *et al.*, 1981). Although, as noted above, levels were elevated, the rise in blood levels of thromboxane metabolites occurred very late in the course of ischemia, suggesting an effect rather than a cause. Administration of thromboxane inhibitors had no effect on the frequency of ischemic events in these patients, and similar results were reported by Chierchia *et al.* (1982b). These observations can be contrasted to those of Lewy *et al.* (1979), who reported that thromboxane inhibition significantly decreased the frequency of variant angina episodes. Cragg and co-workers (1983) studied arachidonic acid metabolites after angioplasty to determine whether alterations in the prostacyclin–thromboxane scheme might mediate postangioplasty vasospasm. Using canine carotid arteries, they showed a 70% decrease in vessel wall prostacyclin production and an 104% increase in vasoconstrictor hydroperoxyacid production postangioplasty. Thus, although the prostacyclin–thromboxane hypothesis for modulation of coronary artery spasm is attractive in its simplicity and may apply in postangioplasty situations, clinical and experimental evidence does not support its role as an important mechanism in coronary spasm.

### C. Nonendothelium-Dependent Mechanisms

#### *1. Sympathetic Nervous System*

The possibility that an increase in sympathetic stimuli to the coronary arteries might precipitate focal or generalized spasm has received a great deal of attention (Maseri and Chierchia, 1982). Electrical stimulation of the central nervous system can cause coronary contriction in animals (Melville *et al.*, 1963, 1969) and the picrotoxin model for coronary artery spasm in cats appears dependent on central mediation of alpha-adrenergic vasoconstriction (Segal *et al.*, 1981). Exacerbation of symptoms in coronary artery spasm patients with administration of beta-adrenergic blockers has been interpreted as possibly being due to unmasking an unopposed alpha-adrenergic constrictor influence in the coronary circulation (Robertson *et al.*, 1982). Studies of general sympathetic nervous system activity in coronary artery spasm patients have shown no elevation over controls (D. Robertson *et al.*, 1979). Robertson and co-workers (1983b) have also studied the time course of arterial and coronary sinus levels of catecholamines during episodes of spasm. Levels rose late in the course of ischemia and these findings were felt to offer support against a sympathetic cause for spasm. Since determination of coronary sinus catecholamines might not detect localized release of norepinephrine, these investigators carried out a double-blind, randomized, placebo-controlled trial of the $alpha_1$ antagonist prazocin in patients with coronary artery spasm (Robertson *et al.*, 1983a). Sympathetic blockade was documented by phenylephrine challenge. Prazocin was without effect on the number or length of ischemic episodes or nitroglycerin consumption. These data suggest a negligible contribution of $alpha_1$ adrenergic influence to clinical coronary artery spasm. Others have implied that the drug may be effective in variant angina patients; however, these data were not collected in a controlled fashion (Tzivoni *et al.*, 1983). Preliminary observations with phentolamine make the contribution of $alpha_2$ mechanisms similarly unlikely (Chierchia *et al.*, 1982a) although conflicting data exist (Levene and Freeman, 1976; Ricci *et al.*, 1979). Plexectomy has been reported to offer some improvement in surgical results in patients with coronary occlusive disease with spasm (Betriu *et al.*, 1983); however, it has been generally ineffective in patients with angiographically normal coronary arteries (Weber *et al.*, 1983).

## 2. Other Vasoactive Substances

Previously, we noted the association of coronary artery spasm with allergic reactions (Druck *et al.*, 1981) and the use of histamine provocation (Ginsburg *et al.*, 1981). The exact role of histamine *in vivo* is uncertain at present. The utility of ergonovine as a provocative agent has led to studies which have defined its mechanism of action as mixed but involving the activation of serotonergic receptors, at least in certain animals (Muller-Schweinitzer, 1980; Holtz *et al.*, 1982). Release of serotonin from aggregating platelets has been proposed as a potential mechanism for coronary artery spasm (VanHoutte, 1983) and there is evidence that serotonin may positively modulate release of cardiac norepinephrine via a prejunctional receptor (Humphrey et al., 1983). Again, the exact role of these mechanisms in clinical vasospasm remains speculative. Hypomagnesemia has been proposed as a mechanism for coronary spasm based on studies of canine arteries (Altura and Trulapaty, 1982); however, this proposal has been refuted by Kalsner (1982). The clinical association of ethanol use and spasm has been suggested to relate to a direct vasoconstrictor action seen *in vitro* (Altura et al., 1983).

### 3. Alterations in Smooth Muscle Activation

A consistent theme in considerations of possible mechanisms for coronary artery spasm has been the probable existence of a hypersensitive vascular wall (Maseri and Chierchia, 1982). The observation of spontaneous phasic activity in rings from human coronary arteries similar to that seen in the portal vein has led to speculation that an alteration in activational mechanisms from tonic to phasic may play a role in intermittent coronary spasm (Ross et al., 1980). In order to investigate this possibility we have used tetraethylammonium chloride to alter activational characteristics of isolated canine and porcine coronary arteries *in vitro*. Exposure of these arteries to ergonovine produces large irregular phasic constrictions which are irregularly synchronized in propagation down the length of the arteries. This activity is dependent upon extracellular calcium and is similar to that observed in isolated human coronaries. A representative recording from such an experiment is shown in Fig. 13. This disorganized phasic activity is currently under investigation as a model for altered activational mechanisms in coronary spasm.

### 4. Small Vessel Spasm

Arteriolar spasm has been suggested as the etiology of the congestive cardiomyopathy seen in Syrian hamsters (Factor and Sonnenblick, 1982). Spasm of resistance vessels secondary to myocardial ischemia produced by large vessel occlusive disease has been proposed as a mechanism for the perpetuation of injury and reflex spasm of large coronary arteries (Hellström, 1982). Mudge et al. (1976) showed an increase in coronary resistance in patients with coronary artery disease during the cold pressor test not seen in normals. In order to determine whether this change was due to large or small coronary artery constriction regional coronary flow measurements and arteriograms were obtained during the cold pressor test in patients without variant angina (Feldman et al., 1982a). Only small changes in epicardial coronary diameter were seen and no coronary artery

### 4. Coronary Artery Spasm and Vasodilators

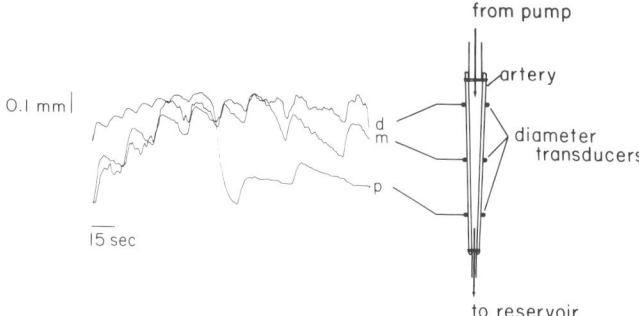

**Fig. 13.** A schematic diagram of an *in vitro* perfused coronary artery used to study constrictions at three points. The three diameter transducers produce records as illustrated on the left when the artery is incubated in 30 mM tetraethylammonium to alter the activational characteristics of the vascular smooth muscle and then exposed to $10^{-6}$ M ergonovine. Phasic irregular constrictions are seen which summate at times and cause portions of the artery to constrict while others relax. Such irregular phasic activity has been proposed as a model for the altered activational state felt to be a mechanism producing spasm *in vivo*.

spasm was demonstrated. Regional coronary resistance decreased 12% in association with normal coronary arteries and increased 22% in association with atherosclerotic coronary arteries. Thus, these patients with ischemic heart disease exhibited an abnormal increase in coronary resistance on an arteriolar level in regions supplied by atherosclerotic arteries. Others have proposed that coronary arteriolar constriction may occur with beta-adrenergic blockade, smoking, static exercise, and mental stress. The connection between these findings and epicardial spasm remains speculative; however, the proposed mechanism noted above by which small vessel spasm in conjunction with ischemia might lead to reflex epicardial spasm is attractive in view of these findings.

## V. Pharmacology of Coronary Vasodilators

### A. Introduction

Recognition that supply-side mechanisms such as coronary artery spasm play an important role in the pathogenesis of myocardial ischemia has fostered increased interest in agents which effect an increase in the caliber of the coronary arteries. Such agents have been shown to affect the tone of both conductance and resistance vessels to varying degrees and are useful in management of all types of ischemic heart disease; however, they have been particularly effective in coronary artery spasm. The main categories of currently available coronary vasodilators include the nitrates, calcium antagonists, and miscellaneous other agents. The general characteristic mechanisms of action and clinical uses for these classes of agents will be outlined below.

### B. Nitrates

*1. Pharmacologic Effects*

Organic nitrates are esters of nitric acid which are available in a wide variety of chemical formulations and dosage forms. Although the pharmacokinetic properties of these various compounds differ, the pharmacologic effects on the cardiovascular system are similar and can be typified by the actions of nitroglycerin (Abrams, 1980). The principal action of nitrates is smooth muscle relaxation, which is nonspecific and may be antagonized in a functional manner by vasoconstrictor substances (Haeusler and Holck, 1982). The principal vascular site at which vasodilation occurs may be tailored by route and rate of administration, an example of which is intracoronary injection for the relief of coronary artery spasm (Pepine *et al.,* 1982). With this route little or no systemic effect is seen and large vessel coronary artery dilation is the predominant effect. With large dose and rapid systemic administration, arterial dilation ensues with hypotension and reflex sympathetic discharge (Mason *et al.,* 1971). With chronic administration either parenterally, sublingually, topically, or orally, there is a predominant systemic venodilator effect with a lesser arterial effect and consequently limited reflex sympathetic changes.

Regional coronary venous flow studies in patients with important coronary occlusive disease of the anterior descending coronary artery reveal an increase or no change in flow with nitroglycerin as oxygen demand decreases (Mehta and Pepine, 1978). Other investigators (Stone *et al.,* 1983) using similar techniques reported a decrease in coronary flow in patients after administration of sublingual nitroglycerin; however, determinants of myocardial oxygen consumption were uniformly decreased. Similar studies of nitroglycerin during pacing-induced angina revealed no increase in coronary flow unless intracoronary administration was used (Fuchs *et al.,* 1983). Relief of angina was associated with systemic administration and a decrease in coronary flow. In animal studies there is no doubt that nitroglycerin dilates large coronary arteries relatively more than it does resistance vessels and that this effect serves to increase blood flow to hypoxic areas where autoregulation has already provided maximum arteriolar dilation (McGregor and Fam, 1972; Epstein *et al.,* 1976). Nitroglycerin may also increase blood flow to ischemic myocardium indirectly by reducing venous return and, consequently, left ventricular filling pressure and wall tension. These latter effects lead to less mechanical hindrance to blood flow, especially in vessels which travel from epicardial to endocardial zones (Gorman and Sparks, 1980; Greenberg et al., 1975). These salutary effects on myocardial blood flow are manifested, in various animal models, as improved contractile function in ischemic areas (Cohen et al., 1973), increased $pO_2$ in the subendocardium (Weiss and Winbury, 1972) and salvage of ischemic myocardium (Epstein et al., 1975; Jugdutt, 1983). Salvage of ischemic myocardium in dogs has been shown to be dependent on maintenance of mean arterial pressure within 10% of normal (Jugdutt, 1983). A large part of the nitroglycerin-induced increase in myocardial blood flow during ischemia in animals had also been related to collateral blood flow (Chiarello et al., 1976; Capurro et al., 1977; Bache, 1978; Becker et al., 1971; Weisse et al., 1972; Bache et al., 1975; Jugdutt, 1983). A similar salutary effect on collateral blood flow in humans has been demonstrated (Cohn et al., 1977; Goldstein et al., 1974). Direct positive inotropic effects of nitrates have been seen *in vitro* with humans and feline ventricular muscle; however, very large concentrations were required and make this unlikely *in vivo* (Strauer, 1971). Mechanisms by which nitrates may limit infarct size are discussed in chapter 2 in this volume.

## 2. Mechanism of Action

The exact mechanism by which nitrates exert their pharmacologic effects remains unknown; however, several possibilities exist. Nitrates are believed to interact with reduced sulfhydryl groups on a receptor which resides on the membrane of the vascular smooth muscle cell (Needleman et al., 1973). A disulfide linkage is formed with the release of inorganic nitrite, which is then thought to act on a common vasodilator intermediate site leading to vascular relaxation. Conversion of the nitrate receptor site by formation of disulfide bonds is thought to be a mechanism responsible for tolerance (Needleman and Johnson, 1973). Another possible mechanism for nitrate action is through elevation of cGMP levels within smooth muscle cells (Axelsson et al., 1979). This seems unlikely in view of the fact that various agents may elevate cGMP levels while inducing smooth muscle contraction (Katsuki and Murad, 1977). There is evidence that nitrates may alter the calcium-dependent characteristics of smooth muscle similar to the calcium antagonists discussed below (Fleckenstein et al., 1975). Nitrates can suppress tetraethylammonium-induced action potentials in coronary artery smooth muscle, and this activity is due primarily to a transmembrane calcium flux (Harder et al., 1979). Nitroglycerin will only suppress this activity in large coronary arteries, unlike the calcium antagonists, which are active in both large and small vessels.

Nitrates have also been implicated in modulation of vasoactive prostanoids in the coronary circulation. Morcillio and co-workers (1980) studied effects of nitroglycerin infusion on myocardial prostaglandin E production and coronary hemodynamics in open-chest dogs. Nitroglycerin provoked a 41% increase in prostaglandin E production, which was prevented by indomethacin. Levin *et al.* (1981) showed a marked increase in synthesis of prostacyclin by cultured human endothelial cells in the presence of nitroglycerin and suggested this as a possible mechanism for *in vivo* vasodilation.

### 3. Clinical Utility

Nitrates remain the cornerstone of therapy in all forms of ischemic heart disease due to their pharmacologic actions noted above. In combination with beta-adrenergic blocking drugs they are the treatment of choice for prevention of effort angina pectoris. Several studies have shown nitrates to be as effective as calcium antagonists in long-term therapy of patients with coronary artery spasm (Freedman *et al.*, 1982; Hill *et al.*, 1982; Ginsburg *et al.*, 1982). Use of intracoronary nitroglycerin in the setting of acute coronary artery spasm has also been established (Pepine *et al.*, 1982). The availability of intravenous nitroglycerin has been associated with growing experience with the management of unstable angina patients and those with evolving myocardial infarction (Flaherty *et al.*, 1975, 1976, 1982; Borer *et al.*, 1975; Come *et al.*, 1975; Epstein *et al.*, 1976; Bussmann *et al.*, 1981). Nitrates are also useful in the management of patients with congestive heart failure (Abrams, 1980) and the hemodynamic principles of such therapy are covered in chapter 2 in this volume.

## C. Calcium Antagonists

### 1. Pharmacologic Effects

The three currently available, "first-generation" calcium antagonists comprise a chemically heterogeneous group of compounds with a number of pharmacologic effects. When they are studied *in vitro*, qualitatively similar effects are observed with the various drugs. These include relaxation of vascular smooth muscle, depression of myocardial contractility, and negative chronotropic and dromotropic effects. The relative potency for these effects *in vitro* for the three first-generation drugs is nifedipine > verapamil > diltiazem (Millard *et al.*, 1983). When pharmacologic studies are done *in vivo*, however, differences between vascular beds, reflex effects and drug sensitivity–potency relationships reveal dissimilar responses between drugs. Thus, although the potency order noted above for *in vitro* studies holds for *in vivo* coronary vasodilation, left ventricular contractility is decreased by verapamil, increased by nifedipine, and unaffected by diltiazem (Millard *et al.*, 1983). Although all three drugs exhibit negative chronotropic effects *in vitro*, reflex changes produce a variable tachycardia *in vivo*, which is worse with nifedipine. Such animal data can be extrapolated in general to the experience with patients, in whom the vasodilator potency remains nifedipine > verapamil > diltiazem. The tendency to delay A–V conduction and depression of contractile function is clearest with verapamil. The action to suppress SA node function is most prominent with diltiazem.

Hemodynamic data regarding depression of contractility with verapamil in humans is conflicting. Compromised left ventricular function in patients with ischemic heart disease given verapamil has been reported in some studies (Chew *et al.*, 1981; Singh and Roche, 1977), but not in others (Ferlinz *et al.*, 1979; Carlens, 1981). Studies of normal men showed no effect of verapamil on left ventricular function either at rest or during exercise (D'Agostino *et al.*, 1983). Overall, when given to patients depressed left ventricular function either due to severe ischemic heart disease, cardiomyopathy, or coadministration of a beta blocker, serious additional functional impairment can result.

Coronary hemodynamic studies in humans have shown a significant increase in coronary sinus blood flow with nifedipine (Stone *et al.*, 1983). Similar studies with diltiazem revealed an increase in coronary sinus flow after an intracoronary bolus but not with prolonged infusion (Bertrand *et al.*, 1982a).

Calcium antagonists have been reported to be effective in preventing ischemic injury in animals. This is presumably due to increased collateral blood flow, redistributed flow to the subendocardium, and reduced myocardial oxygen consumption (Clozel *et al.*, 1983; Henry *et al.*, 1978).

The pharmacokinetics of the calcium antagonists differ with respect to effective dose, onset of action, peak effect, and excretion. A summary of this data for several representative agents is given in Table I.

## 2. Mechanism of Action

As noted above, the calcium antagonists are chemically heterogeneous. However, verapamil and nifedipine show discrete structure–activity relationships with varying potency and selectivity, suggesting specific sites of action (Triggle and Swamy, 1983). This had led to development of a number of verapamil derivatives (i.e., gallopril and tiapamil) which are considerably more potent than verapamil relative to cardiovascular

**TABLE I**
Pharmacokinetics of Calcium Channel Blockers

|  | Nifedipine | Verapamil | Diltiazem |
|---|---|---|---|
| Dose |  |  |  |
| Oral | 10–40 mg q8hr[a] | 80–160 mg q8hr | 30–90 mg q8hr |
| IV ($\mu$g/kg) | 5–15 | 150 | 75–150 |
| Onset of action | 20 min | 30 min | 15 min |
| Peak effect | 1–2 hr | 4–5 hr | 30 min |
| Excretion |  |  |  |
| Renal (%) | ~80 | ~70 | ~35 |
| Fecal (%) | 15 | 15 | 65 |

[a] Also used sublingually.

actions with much less depression of GI motility. Similarly, nifedipine derivatives (i.e., nicardipine and nimoldipine) have been introduced. The basic mechanism of action for this class of compounds, by definition, is the blockade of the voltage-sensitive calcium channel defined in excitable tissues. This leads to a decrease in cellular calcium uptake and subsequent inhibition of excitation–contraction- or stimulus–secretion-coupled responses. Although the voltage-dependent channels influenced by these drugs have been classically held to be separate from receptor-operated calcium channels, recent studies have shown that calcium antagonists may modulate postsynaptic alpha$_2$ receptor responsiveness (Cavero et al., 1983; van Zwieten et al., 1983).

The reduction in transmembrane calcium flux induced by these mechanisms ultimately leads to diminished free activator calcium in the sarcoplasm for transduction of chemical to mechanical energy. Thus, vascular smooth muscle and myocardial muscle activation is decreased, leading to arterial dilation and diminished cardiac contractility. The relatively greater effects of the calcium antagonists on vascular smooth muscle versus myocardium is due to the 10-fold greater sensitivity of the excitation–contraction mechanism of smooth muscle to alterations in transmembrane calcium flux (Fleckenstein, 1977). Similar differences in tissue sensitivities explain the relative effects seen with the calcium antagonists on different portions of the cardiac conduction system.

The characteristics of the binding site for calcium antagonists are unknown. However, Nayler (1980) has associated verapamil with inhibition of ATP-dependent calcium binding and ATPase activation in sarcolemmal

## 4. Coronary Artery Spasm and Vasodilators

membranes. Labeled verapamil bound to carbohydrate residues which were trypsin and phospholipase sensitive. These sites were felt to represent membrane level calcium-dependent modulators of voltage-sensitive calcium channels.

Calcium antagonists have also been shown to have weak platelet antiaggregatory effects (Kiyomoto et al., 1983).

### 3. Clinical Utility and Newer Agents

As alluded to earlier, the calcium antagonists are useful in the therapy of all types of ischemic coronary disease, coronary artery spasm, certain dysrhythmias, and hypertension (Pepine and Conti, 1981). The different relative effects of each drug on arterial tone, ventricular function, and conduction as noted earlier dictates which should be used in a given clinical situation and in combination with what other drugs. The clinical use of these agents for their vasodilator and antiarrhythmic effects as well as potential use in the salvage of ischemic myocardium are discussed in chapters 2 and 8 in this volume.

A number of new calcium antagonists have been developed with differing degrees of specificity with respect to site of action. Felodipine is a dihydropyridine like nifedipine but with less myocardial and more vascular effect; it has been shown to be an effective antianginal agent (Detry et al., 1983). Niludipine is a new agent, also related to nifedipine, which appears to reduce left ventricular work by decreasing systemic blood pressure; however, it has little effect on coronary sinus blood flow in humans (Kurita et al., 1982). Nitrendipine has been shown effective in improving collateral flow to ischemic myocardium in a canine model of chronic coronary occlusion (Warltier et al., 1983). Nicardipine, a similar compound, is currently under investigation for its systemic and coronary vasodilator effects (Taylor et al., 1982; Gelman et al., 1985; Lambert et al., 1985). Bepridil is a calcium antagonist which is chemically unrelated to the three first-generation drugs (Hill et al., 1984). Bepredil is unique in that it has the additional action of blocking the fast sodium channel in cardiac tissues (Kawada et al., 1983) and has ventricular antidysrhythmic properties.

## D. Other Coronary Dilators

A group of coronary vasodilators classed as adenosine potentiators is typified by dipryidamole. These drugs were found to cause arterial dilation, a decrease in heart rate and myocardial contractile force, and increases in coronary flow. The mechanism by which these effects occur involves inhibition of the normal metabolic degradation pathway for adenosine (Olsson et al., 1972; Alfonso, 1970; Scholtholt et al., 1972). These compounds were also found to enhance formation of coronary collaterals in a variety of animals (Haeusler and Holck, 1982). The problem with these compounds in ischemic heart disease is their potential to cause the "coronary steal phenomenon" (McGregor and Fam, 1972). This results from nonspecific dilation of small resistance vessels. In the absence of reduced myocardial oxygen consumption with autoregulatory vasoconstriction and dilation of conductance vessels, competitive flow between ischemic and nonischemic regions can occur. A new steady state is achieved with the potential for flow reduction to ischemic areas unless other measures to produce dilation of conductance vessels or to depress oxygen consumption ensue. Studies of regional coronary venous flow in humans have verified the existence of a coronary steal phenomenon (Feldman et al., 1981a). The results of clinical trials of dipyridamole in ischemic heart disease are conflicting; however, its use to prevent bypass graft closure is accepted after coronary artery bypass surgery (Chesebro et al., 1982).

Molsidomine is a nonnitrate compound with both arterial and venous dilating activity (Hirata et al., 1975; Grund et al., 1978; Holtz et al., 1978; Karsch et al., 1978). It has been used in acute myocardial infarction (Aptecar et al., 1981), angina pectoris (Detry et al., 1981; Majid et al., 1980), and hypertension (Milei et al., 1980). The principal mechanism of action for molsidomine is not known; however, its metabolites have been shown to inhibit platelet aggregation, thromboxane synthesis, and the generation of vasoconstrictor hydroperoxides by human platelets (Darius et al., 1984). The exact place of molsidomine in the therapy of ischemic heart disease remains to be determined.

Amiodarone was originally introduced as a coronary vasodilator and antianginal agent (Charlier et al., 1968; Vastesaeger et al., 1967), although its efficacy in therapy of supraventricular and ventricular dysrhythmias (e.g., Podrid and Lown, 1981; Heger et al., 1981) has drawn more attention. A recent clinical trial has shown chronic amiodarone therapy to be effective in a small number of patients for both the suppression of variant angina and the prevention of ergonovine-induced coronary vasoconstriction (Rutitzky et al., 1982). The mechanism of action was felt to involve both a direct dilator action of the drug and noncompetitive alpha-adrenergic antagonism. In view of frequent, serious toxicity associated with chronic amiodarone administration this agent can not be recommended for management of myocardial ischemia.

## VI. Summary

Coronary artery spasm is an established mechanism in the pathogenesis of transient myocardial ischemia. Through acceptance of spasm, a broader concept of supply-side mechanisms capable of causing transient myocardial ischemia has evolved. These include active and passive disorders acting at both the large epicardial and smaller intramural vessel levels. These disorders are important pathophysiologic mechanisms responsible for rest angina and probably also important in acute myocardial infarction.

Determination of the relative roles of coronary artery spasm, *in situ* thrombosis, and atherosclerotic obstruction is complicated by the lack of data at "time zero" in the course of infarction. Figure 14 is a schematic diagram of three possible mechanisms for the production of infarction which occurs at the arrow on the time axis ("time zero"). The left panel depicts a case of isolated coronary artery spasm with no superimposed atherosclerosis or thrombosis. Although rare, circumstantial clinical evidence for such a mechanism exists and has been reviewed in this chapter. The center panel illustrates a case of isolated thrombosis which occurs in an area of gradually progressive atherosclerosis. The periodic episodes of transient thrombosis preceding "time zero" represent episodic reductions in flow attributed to formation and dissolution of platelet plugs. The right panel represents the case in which atherosclerotic obstruction, vasomotion, and thrombosis all contribute to cause eventual infarction. This is

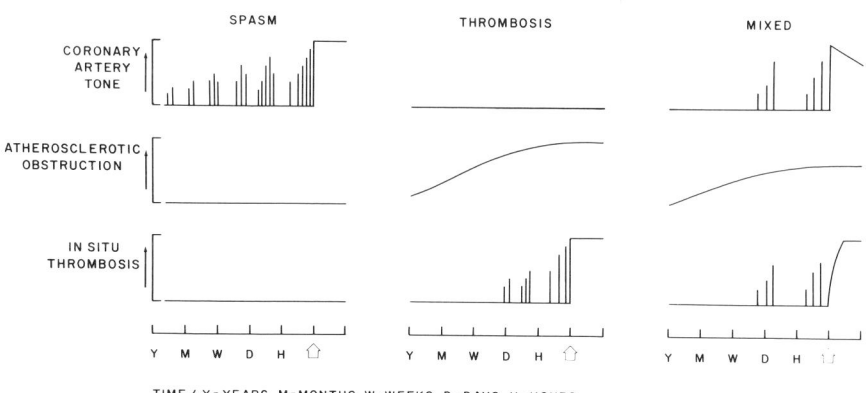

**Fig. 14.** A schematic of possible relative contributions of coronary artery spasm, thrombosis, and atherosclerotic obstruction to myocardial infarction as described in the text.

probably the scenario which best represents the usual case of acute myocardial infarction and accounts for the difficulty in determining a single mechanism causing infarction in clinical studies. In all three cases periods of transient ischemia precede "time zero" and represent the syndrome of unstable or preinfarction angina.

Recognition of the multifactorial etiology for myocardial infarction and the definite contribution of supply-side mechanisms in ischemia has refocused attention upon coronary vasodilators. Nitrates and calcium antagonists form the mainstay of therapy when supply-side mechanisms are suspected. These agents also represent the logical choice for prevention of cardiac events when coronary artery spasm is a contributing factor.

# References

Abrams, J. (1980). *N. Engl. J. Med.* **302,** 1234–1237.
Aiken, J. W., Gorman, R. R., and Shebuski, R. K. (1979). *Prostaglandins* **17,** 483–494.
Alfonso, S. (1970). *Circ. Res.* **26,** 743–752.
Altura, B. M., and Turlapaty, P. D. M. V. (1982). *Br. J. Pharmacol.* **77,** 649–659.
Altura, M. D., Altura, B. T., and Carella, A. (1983). *Br. J. Pharmacol.* **78,** 260–262.
Aptecar, M., Oteroy Garzon, C. A., Vasquez, A., Varini, S., Collia, L., Esteguy, A., and Caruso, S. (1981). *Am. Heart J.* **101,** 369–373.
Arnim, T., Crea, F., Chierchia, S., Thompson, G. R., and Maeri, A. (1983). *Bas. Res. Cardiol.* **78,** 415–422.
Axelsson, K. L., Wikberg, J. E. S., and Andersson, R. G. G. (1979). *Life Sci.* **24,** 1779–1786.
Bache, R. J. (1978). *Circulation* **57,** 557–562.
Bache, R. J., Ball, R. M., Cobb, F. R., Rembert, J. C., and Greenfield, J. C. (1975). *J. Clin. Invest.* **55,** 1219–1228.
Bauer, T. W., Moore, G. W., and Hutchins, G. M. (1982). *Circulation* **65,** 255–259.
Becker, L. C., Fortuin, N. H., and Pitt, B. (1971). *Circ. Res.* **28,** 263–269.
Benacerraf, A., Scholl, J. M., Achard, F., Tonnelier, M., and Lavergne, G. (1983). *Circulation* **67,** 1147–1150.
Berndt, T. B., Fitzgerald, J., Harrison, D. C., and Schroder, J. S. (1977). *Am. J. Cardiol.* **39,** 784–788.
Bertrand, M. E., Dupuis, B. A., Lablanche, J. M., Tilmant, P. Y., and Thieuleux, F. A. (1982a). *J. Cardiovasc. Pharmacol.* **4,** 695–699.
Bertrand, M. E., Lablanche, J. M., Tilmant, P. Y., Thieuleux, F. A., Delforge, M. R., Carre, A. G., Asseman, P., Berzin, B., Libersa, C., and Laurent, J. M. (1982b). *Circulation* **65,** 1299–1306.
Betriu, A., Pomar, J. L., Boruassa, M. G., and Grondin, C. M. (1983). *Am. J. Cardiol.* **51,** 661–667.
Blumgart, H. L., Schlesinger, M. J., and Davis, D. (1940). *Am. Heart J.* **19,** 1–19.
Boden, W. E., Bough, E. W., Korr, K. S., Benham, I., Gheorghiade, M., Caputi, A., and Shulman, R. S. (1981). *Am. J. Cardiol.* **48,** 193–197.
Borer, J. S., Redwood, D. R., Levitt, B., Cagin, N., Bianchi, C., Vallen, H., and Epstein, S. E. (1975). *N. Engl. J. Med.* **293,** 1008–1012.

Bott-Silverman, C., and Heupler, F. A. (1983). *J. Am. Coll. Cardiol.* **2,** 200–205.
Brown, B. G., Bolson, E., Petersen, R. B., Pierce, C. D., and Dodge, H. T. (1981). *Circulation* **64,** 1089–1097.
Brunelli, C., Lazzari, I., Simonetti, A., L'Abbate, A., and Maseri, A. (1981). *Eur. Heart J.* **2,** 155–161.
Brunton, T. L. (1867). *Lancet* **2,** 97–98.
Bussmann, W. D., Passek, D., Seidel, W., and Kaltenbach, M. (1981). *Circulation* **63,** 615–622.
Buxton, A. E., Hirshfield, J. W., Untereker, W. J., Goldberg, S., Harken, A. H., Stephenson, L. W., and Edie, R. W. (1982). *Am. J. Cardiol.* **50,** 444–451.
Capurro, N. L., Kent, K. M., Smith, H. J., Aamodt, R., and Epstein, S. E. (1977). *Am. J. Cardiol.* **39,** 679–683.
Carlens, P. (1981). *J. Cardiovasc. Pharmacol.* **3,** 1–10.
Cavero, I., Shepperson, N., Lefevre-Borg, F., and Langer, S. Z. (1983). *Circ. Res., Suppl. I* **52,** I69–I76.
Chaitman, B. R., Waters, D. D., Theroux, P., and Hanson, J. S. (1981). *Am. J. Cardiol.* **47,** 1350–1358.
Charlier, R., Deltour, G., Baudine, A., and Chaillet, F. (1968). *Arzneimittelforsch* **18,** 1408–1420.
Cheng, T. D., Bashour, T., Singh, B. K., and Belser, G. A. (1972). *Am. J. Cardiol.* **30,** 680–682.
Chesebro, J. H., Clements, J. P., Fuster, V., Elveback, L. R., Smith, H. C., Bardsley, W. T., Frye, R. L., Holmes, D. R., Vlietstra, R. E., Pluth, J. R., Wallace, R. B., Puga, F. J., Orszulak, T. A., Diehler, J. M., Schaff, H. V., and Danielson, G. K. (1982). *N. Engl. J. Med.* **307,** 73–78.
Chew, C. Y. C., Hecht, H. S., Collett, J. T., McAllister, R. G., and Singh, B. N. (1981). *Am. J. Cardiol.* **47,** 917–922.
Chiarello, M., Gold, H. K., Leinbach, R. C., Davis, M. A., and Maroko, P. R. (1976). *Circulation* **54,** 766–773.
Chierchia, S., Brunelli, C., Simonetti, I., Lazzari, M., and Maseri, A. (1980). *Circulation* **61,** 759–768.
Chierchia, S., Crea, F., Davies, G., Berkenboom, G., Crean, P., and Maseri, A. (1982a). *Circulation* **66,** Suppl. II, 247 (abstract).
Chierchia, S., DeCaterina, R., Crea, F., Patrono, C., and Maseri, A. (1982b). *Circulation* **66,** 702–705.
Chierchia, S., Patrono, C., Crea, F., Ciabattoni, G., DeCaterina, R., Cinotti, G. A., Distante, A., and Maseri, A. (1982c). *Circulation* **65,** 470–478.
Cipriano, P. R., Koch, F. H., Rosenthal, S. J., Baim, D. S., Ginsburg, R., and Schroeder, J. S. (1983). *Am. Heart J.* **105,** 542–547.
Clozel, J., Theroux, P., and Bourassa, M. G. (1983). *Circ. Res.* **52,** Suppl. I, I120–I128.
Cohen, M. V., Downey, J. M., Sonnenblick, E. H., and Kirk, E. S. (1973). *J. Clin. Invest.* **52,** 2836–2847.
Cohn, P. F., Maddox, D., Holman, B. L., Markis, J. E., Adams, D. F., and See, J. R. (1977). *Am. J. Cardiol.* **39,** 672–678.
Come, P. C., Flaherty, J. T., Weisfeldt, M., Green, L., Becker, L., and Pitt, B. (1975). *N. Engl. J. Med.* **293,** 1003–1007.
Conti, C. R., Pepine, C. J., and Curry, J. C. (1979). *Curr. Prob. Cardiol.* **4,** 9–70.
Cragg, A., Enzig, S., Castaneda-Zuniga, W., Amplatz, K., White, J. G., and Rao, G. H. R. (1983). *Am. J. Cardiol.* **51,** 1441–1445.
D'Agostino, H. J., Pritchett, E. L. C., Shand, D. G., and Jones, R. H. (1983). *J. Cardiovasc. Pharmacol.* **5,** 812–817.

Danielopolus, D. (1924). *Br. Med. J.* **2**, 553–557.
Darius, H., Ahland, B., Rucker, W., Klaus, W., Peskar, B. A., and Schror, K. (1984). *J. Cardiovasc. Pharmacol.* **6**, 115–121.
DeServi, S., Specchia, G., Curti, M. T., Falcone, C., Gavazzi, A., Bramucci, E., Mussini, A., Angoli, L., Salerno, J., and Bobba, P. (1981). *Am. J. Cardiol.* **48**, 188–192.
Detry, J., Decoster, P. M., and Renkin, J. (1983). *Am. J. Cardiol.* **52**, 453–457.
Detry, J. M., Melin, J., Brasseur, L. A., Cosyns, J., and Rousseau, M. F. (1981). *A. J. Cardiol.* **47**, 109–115.
Dhurandhar, R. W., Watt, D. L., Silver, M. D., Trimble, A. S., and Aldeman, A. G. (1972). *Am. J. Cardiol.* **30**, 902–905.
Druck, M. N., Johnstone, D. E., Standiloff, H., and McLaughlin, P. R. (1981). *Can. Med. Assn. J.* **125**, 1133–1135.
Engel, H. J., Page, H. L., and Campbell, W. B. (1976). *Am. Heart J.* **91**, 501–506.
Epstein, S. E., Kent, K. M., Goldstein, R. E., Borer, J. S., and Redwood, D. R. (1975). *N. Engl. J. Med.* **292**, 29–34.
Epstein, S. E., Borer, J. S., Kent, K. M., Redwood, D. R., Goldstein, R. E., and Levitt, B. (1976). *Circulation* **53**, Suppl. I, I191–I198.
Factor, S. M., and Sonnenblick, E. H. (1982). *Am. J. Cardiol.* **50**, 1149–1152.
Feldman, R. L., Pepine, C. J., and Conti, C. R. (1978). *Am. J. Cardiol.* **42**, 517–519.
Feldman, R. L., Curry, R. C., Pepine, C. J., Mehta, J., and Conti, C. R. (1980). *Circulation* **62**, 149–159.
Feldman, R. L., Nichols, W. W., Pepine, C. J., and Conti, C. R. (1981a). *Circulation* **64**, 333–344.
Feldman, R. L., Pepine, C. J., Whittle, J. L., Curry, R. C., and Conti, C. R. (1981b). *Circulation* **64**, 76–83.
Feldman, R. L., Whittle, J. L., Marx, J. D., Pepine, C. J., and Conti, C. R. (1982a). *Am. J. Cardiol.* **49**, 666–673.
Feldman, R. L., Pepine, C. J., and Conti, C. R. (1982b). *Am. J. Cardiol.* **49**, 948 (abstract).
Ferlinz, J., Easthope, J. L., and Aronow, W. S. (1979). *Circulation* **59**, 313–319.
Flaherty, J. T., Reid, P. R., Kelly, D. T., Taylor, D. R., Weisfeldt, M. L., and Pitt, B. (1975). *Circulation* **51**, 132–139.
Flaherty, J. T., Come, P. C., Baird, M. G., Rouleau, J., Taylor, D. R., Weisfeldt, M. L., Green, H. L., Becker, L. C., and Pitt, B. (1976). *Br. Heart J.* **38**, 612–621.
Flaherty, J. T., Weisfeldt, M. L., Bulkley, B. H., Kallman, C. H., and Becker, L. C. (1982). *Am. J. Cardiol.* **49**, 1024 (abstract).
Fleckenstein, A. (1977). *Ann. Rev. Pharmacol. Toxicol.* **7**, 149–166.
Fleckenstein, A., Nakayama, K., Fleckenstein-Grun, G., and Byon, Y. K. (1975). *In* "Calcium Transport in Contraction and Secretion" (E. Carafoli, F. Clementi, W. Drabikowski, and A. Margreth, eds.), p. 555. North Holland, Amsterdam.
Folts, J. D., Gallagher, K., and Rowe, G. G. (1982). *Circulation* **65**, 248–255.
Fothergill, J. M. (1879). "The Heart and Its Diseases with their Treatment," 2nd Edition. Lindsay and Blakiston, Philadelphia.
Freedman, S. B., Richmond, D. R., and Kelly, D. T. (1982). *Am. J. Cardiol.* **50**, 711–715.
Froment, R., Normand, J., and Amiel, L. (1973). *Arch. Mal. Coeur* **66**, 755–761.
Fuchs, R. M., Brinker, J. A., Guzman, P. A., Kross, D. E., and Yin, F. C. P. (1983). *Am. J. Cardiol.* **51**, 19–23.
Furchgott, R. F. (1983). *Circ. Res.* **53**, 557–573.
Gallavardin, L. (1925). "Les Angines de Poitrine," 1st Edition, pp. 130–132. Paris. Maisson and Cie.
Ganz, W., Buchbinder, N., Marcus, H., Mondkar, A., Maddahi, J., Charuzi, Y., O'Conner,

L., Shell, W., Fishbein, M. C., Kass, R., Miyamoto, A., and Swan, H. J. C. (1981). *Am. Heart J.* **101,** 4–13.

Gelman, J. S., Feldman, R. L., Scott E., Pepine C. J. (1985). *Am. J. Cardiol.* **56,** 232–236.

Gensini, G. G., Digiorgi, S., Murad-Netto, S., and Black, A. (1962). *Angiology* **13,** 550–553.

Ginsburg, R., Bristow, M. R., Knatrowitz, N., Baim, D. S., and Harrison, D. C. (1981). *Am. Heart J.* **102,** 819–822.

Ginsburg, R., Lamb, I. H., Schroder, J. S., Hu, M., and Harrison, D. C. (1982). *Am. Heart J.* **103,** 44–48.

Ginsburg, R., Bristow, M. R., Davis, K., Diabiase, A., and Billingham, M. E. (1984). *Circulation* **69,** 430–440.

Goldstein, R. E., Stinson, E. B., Scherer, J. L., Seningen, R. P., Grehl, R. M., and Epstein, S. E. (1974). *Circulation* **49,** 298–308.

Gorman, M. W., and Sparks, H. V. (1980). *Cardiovasc. Res.* **14,** 515–521.

Greenberg, H., Dwyer, E. M., Jameson, A. G., and Pinkernell, B. H. (1975). *Am. J. Cardiol.* **36,** 426–432.

Grund, E., Muller-Ruchholtz, E. R., Lapp, E. R., Losch, H. M., and Lochner, W. (1978). *Arzneimittelforsch* **28,** 1624–1628.

Guazzi, M., Polese, A., Fiorentini, C., Magrini, F., and Bartorelli, C. (1971). *Br. Heart J.* **33,** 84–94.

Haeusler, G., and Holck, M. (1982). *In* "The Coronary Artery" (S. Kalsner, ed.), p. 644. Oxford Univ. Press, New York.

Harder, D., Belardinelli, L., Sperelakis, N., Rubio, R., and Berne, R. M. (1979). *Circ. Res.* **44,** 176–182.

Heger, J. J., Prystowsky, E. N., Jackman, W. M., Naccarelli, G. V., Warfel, K. A., Rinkenberger, R. L., and Zipes, D. P. (1981). *N. Engl. J. Med.* **305,** 539–545.

Hellström, H. R. (1982). *Am. J. Cardiol.* **49,** 802–810.

Henry, P. D., Schuchleib, R., Borda, L., Roberts, R., Williamson, J. R., and Sobel, B. E. (1978). *Circ. Res.* **43,** 372–380.

Hill, J. A., Feldman, R. L., Pepine, C. J., and Conti, C. R. (1982). *Am. J. Cardiol.* **49,** 431–438.

Hill J. A., O'Brien J. T., Alpert J. S., Gore J. M., Zusman R. M., Christensen D., Boucher C. A., Vetrovec G., Borer J. S., Griedman C., Mack R., Conti C. R., and Pepine C. J. (1985). *Circulation* **71,** 98–103.

Hirata, M., Oku, Y., Tanabe, M., and Kikuchi, K. (1975). *J. Takeda Res. Lab.* **34,** 139–147.

Hollman, J., Austin, G. E., Gruentzig, A. R., Douglas, J. S., and King, S. B. (1983). *J. Am. Coll. Cardiol.* **2,** 1039–1045.

Holtz, J., Bassenge, E., and Kolin, A. (1978). *Bas. Res. Cardiol.* **73,** 469–481.

Holtz, J., Held, W., Sommer, O., Kuhne, G., and Bassenge, E. (1982). *Bas. Res. Cardiol.* **77,** 278–291.

Huchard, H. (1889). "Traite des Maladies du Coeur et des Vaisseaux, Arteriosclerose, Aortities, Cardiopathies Arterielles, Angines de Poitrine." Doin, Paris.

Humphrey, P. P. A., Feniuk, W., and Watts, A. D. (1983). *Fed. Proc.* **42,** 218–222.

Joris, I., and Majno, G. (1981). *Am. J. Pathol.* **102,** 346–358.

Jugdutt, B. I. (1983). *Circulation* **68,** 673–684.

Kalsner, S. (1982). *In* "The Coronary Artery" (S. Kalsner, ed.), p. 586. Oxford Univ. Press, New York.

Karsch, K. R., Rentrop, K. P., Blanke, H., and Kreuzer, H. (1978). *Eur. J. Clin. Pharmacol.* **13,** 241–245.

Katsuki, S., and Murad, F. (1977). *Mol. Pharmacol.* **13,** 330–341.

Kawachi, Y., Tomokie, H., Maruoka, Y., Kikuchi, Y., Araki, H., Ishii, Y., Tanaka, K., and Nakamura, M. (1984). *Circulation* **69**, 441-450.
Kawada, M., Satoh, K., and Taira, N. (1983). *J. Cardiovasc. Pharmacol.* **5**, 604-612.
Keefer, C. S., and Resnick, W. H. (1928). *Arch. Int. Med.* **41**, 769-807.
Kiyomoto, A., Sasaki, Y., Odawara, A., and Morita, T. (1983). *Circ. Res.* **52**, Suppl. I, I115-I119.
Ku, D. (1982). *Science* **218**, 576-578.
Kurita, A., Isojima, K., Mizuno, K., Aozaki, N., Kondo, S., and Hosono, K. (1982). *Cath. Cardiovasc. Diag.* **8**, 373-381.
Lambert C. R., and Pepine C. J. (1986). In: Acute Myocardial Infarction: Emerging Concepts of Pathogenesis and Treatment. (R. H. Cox, ed.), Praeger Publishing, Philadelphia.
Lambert, C. R., Hill, J. A., Nichols, W. W., Feldman, R. L., and Pepine, C. J. (1985). *Am. J. Cardiol.* **55**, 652-656.
Lange, R. L., Reid, M. D., and Tresch, D. D. (1972). *Circulation* **46**, 666-678.
Levene, D. L., and Freeman, M. R. (1976). *J.A.M.A.* **236**, 1018-1022.
Levin, R. I., Jaffe, E. A., Wekster, B. B., and Tack-Goldman, K. (1981). *J. Clin. Invest.* **67**, 762-769.
Lewy, R. I., Smith, J. B., Silver, M. J., Saia, J., Walinsky, P., and Wiener, L. (1979). *Prostaglandins Med.* **2**, 243-248.
Logan, S. E. (1975). *IEEE Trans. Biomed. Eng.* **22**, 327-334.
MacAlpin, R. N. (1980). *J. Hist. Med. All. Sci.* **35**, 288.
MacAlpin, R. N., Kattus, A., and Alvaro, A. (1973). *Circulation* **47**, 946-958.
McGregor, M., and Fam, W. (1972). *In* "The Study of the Systemic, Coronary and Myocardial Effects of Nitrates" (G. G. Gensini, ed.), p. 323. Thomas, Springfield, Illinois.
Majid, P. A., DeFeyter, P. J. F., vanderWall, E. E., Wardeh, R., and Roos, J. P. (1980). *N. Engl. J. Med.* **302**, 1-6.
Mandelkorn, J. B., Wolf, N. M., Singh, S., Shechter, J. A., Kersh, R. I., Rodger, D. M., Workman, M. B., Bentivoglio, L. G., LaPorte, S. M., and Meister, S. G. (1983). *Am. J. Cardiol.* **53**, 1-6.
Markis, J. E., Malagold, M., Parker, J. A., Silverman, K. J., Barry, W. H., Als, A. V., Paulin, S., Grossman, W., and Braunwald, E. (1981). *N. Engl. J. Med.* **305**, 777-782.
Maseri, A., and Chierchia, S. (1982). *Prog. Cardiovasc. Dis.* **25**, 169-192.
Maseri, A., Mimmo, R., Chierchia, S., Marchesi, C., Pesda, A., and L'Abbate, A. (1975). *Chest* **68**, 625-633.
Maseri, A., L'Abbate, A., Biroldi, G., Chierchia, S., Marzilli, M., Ballestra, A. M., Severi, S., Parodi, O., Biagini, A., Bistante, A., and Pesola, A. (1978). *N. Engl. J. Med.* **299**, 1271-1277.
Mason, D. T., Zelis, R., and Amsterdam, E. A. (1971). *Chest* **59**, 296-305.
Mathey, D. G., Kuck, K., Tilsner, V., Krebber, H., and Bleifeld, W. (1981). *Circulation* **63**, 489-497.
Matsuda, Y., Ozaki, M., Ogawa, H., Naito, H., Yoshino, F., Katayama, K., Fujii, T., Matsuzaki, M., and Kusukawa, R. (1983). *Am. Heart J.* **106**, 509-515.
Mehta, J. L. (1983). *Int. J. Cardiol.* **4**, 249-259.
Mehta, J. L., and Pepine, C. J. (1978). *Circulation* **58**, 803-807.
Melville, K., Blum, B., Shister, H., and Silver, M. D. (1963). *Am. J. Cardiol.* **12**, 781-791.
Melville, K., Garrey, H., Shister, E., and Knaack, J. (1969). *Ann. NY Acad. Sci.* **156**, 241-260.
Milei, J., Vasquez, A., and Lemus, J. (1980). *Eur. J. Clin. Pharmacol.* **18**, 231-235.
Millard, R. W., Grupp, G., Grupp, I. L., DiSalvo, J., DePover, A., and Schwartz, A. (1983). *Circ. Res.* **52**, Suppl. I, I29-I39.

Miller, D. D., Waters, D. D., Dangoisse, V., and David, P. R. (1983). *Chest* **83,** 284–285.
Morcillio, E., Reid, P. R., Dubin, N., Chodgaonkar, R., and Pitt, B. (1980). *Am. J. Cardiol.* **45,** 53–57.
Mudge, G. H., Grossman, W., Mills, R. M., Lesch, M., and Braunwald, E. (1976). *N. Eng. J. Med.* **24,** 1333–1337.
Muller-Schweinitzer, E. (1980). *J. Cardiovasc. Pharmacol.* **2,** 645–655.
Nayler, W. G. (1980). *Eur. Heart J.* **1,** 225–237.
Needleman, P., and Johnson, E. M. (1973). *J. Pharmacol. Exp. Ther.* **184,** 709–715.
Needleman, P., Jakschik, B. A., and Johnson, E. M. (1973). *J. Pharmacol. Exp. Ther.* **187,** 324–331.
Neill, W. A., Wharton, T. P., Fluri-Lundeen, J., and Cohen, I. S. (1980). *N. Eng. J. Med.* **302,** 1157–1162.
Oliva, P. B., and Breckenridge, J. C. (1977). *Circulation* **56,** 366–374.
Oliva, P. B., Potts, D. E., and Pluss, R. G. (1973). *N. Engl. J. Med.* **288,** 745–750.
Olsson, R. A., Snow, J. A., Gentry, M. K., and Frick, P. (1972). *Circ. Res.* **31,** 767–778.
Osler, W. (1910). *Lancet* **1,** 839–844.
Pepine, C. J. (1983). *In* "Coronary Artery Spasm and Thrombosis" (S. Goldberg, ed.), pp. 81–86. F. A. Davis, Philadelphia.
Pepine, C. J., and Conti, C. R. (1981). *Mod. Conc. Cardiovasc. Dis. Pts. I and II* **50,** 61–72.
Pepine, C. J., Feldman, R. L., and Conti, C. R. (1982). *Circulation* **65,** 411–414.
Podrid, P. J., and Lown, B. (1981). *Am. Heart J.* **101,** 374–379.
Prinzmetal, M., Kennamer, R., Merliss, R., Wada, T., and Bor, N. (1959). *Am. J. Med.* **27,** 375–388.
Prinzmetal, M., Ekemecki, A., Kennamer, R., Kwoczynski, J. K., Shubin, H., and Toyoshima, H. (1960). *J.A.M.A.* **174,** 1794–1800.
Reduto, L. A., Smalling, R. W., Freund, G. C., and Gould, K. L. (1981). *Am. J. Cardiol.* **48,** 403–409.
Rentrop, P., Blanke, H., Karsch, K. R., Kaiser, H., Kostering, H., and Leitz, K. (1981). *Circulation* **63,** 307–317.
Ricci, D. R., Orlick, A. E., Cipriano, P. R., Guthner, D. F., and Harrison, D. C. (1979). *Am. J. Cardiol.* **43,** 1073–1079.
Robertson, D., and Oates, J. A. (1978). *Lancet* **1,** 452.
Robertson, D., Robertson, R. M., Nies, A. S., Oates, J. A., and Friesinger, G. C. (1979). *Am. J. Cardiol.* **43,** 1080–1085.
Robertson, R. M., Breinig, J. B., and Robertson, D. (1979). *S. Med. J.* **72,** 1297.
Robertson, R. M., Robertson, D., Roberts, J., Maas, R. L., FitzGerald, G. A., Friesinger, C. G., and Oates, J. A. (1981). *New Eng. J. Med.* **304,** 998–1003.
Robertson, R. M., Wood, A. J. J., Vaughn, W. K., and Robertson, D. (1982). *Circulation* **65,** 281–285.
Robertson, R. M., Bernard, Y. D., Carr, K., and Robertson, D. (1983a). *J. Am. Coll. Cardiol.* **2,** 1146–1150.
Robertson, R. M., Bernard, Y., and Robertson, D. (1983b). *Am. Heart J.* **105,** 901–906.
Ross, G., Stinson, E., Schroeder, J., and Ginsburg, R. (1980). *Cardiovasc. Res.* **14,** 613–618.
Rutitzky, B., Girotti, A. L., and Rosenbaum, M. B. (1982). *Am. Heart J.* **103,** 38–43.
Sakamoto, S., Yokoyama, M., Akita, H., Kawashima, S., Okada, T., Mizutani, T., and Fukazaki, H. (1983). *Jpn. Heart J.* **24,** 117–125.
Santamore, W. P., and Walinsky, P. (1980). *Am. J. Cardiol.* **45,** 276–285.
Santamore, W. P., Kent, R. L., Carey, R. A., and Bove, A. A. (1982). *Am. J. Physiol.* **243,** H236–H242.
Scholtholt, J., Nitz, R. E., and Schraven, E. (1972). *Arzneim. Forsch.* **22,** 1255–1259.

Schwartz, J. S., Carlyle, P. F., and Cohn, J. W. (1979). *Am. J. Cardiol.* **43,** 219–224.
Segal, S. A., Pearle, D. L., and Gillis, R. A. (1981). *Eur. J. Pharmacol.* **76,** 447–451.
Selzer, A., Langsto, M., Ruggeroli, C., and Cohn, K. (1976). *N. Eng. J. Med.* **295,** 1343–1347.
Shimokawa, H., Tomoike, H., Nabeyama, S., Yamamoto, H., Araki, H., and Nakamura, M. (1983). *Science* **221,** 560–562.
Silverman, M., and Flamm, M. (1971). *Ann. Int. Med.* **75,** 339–343.
Singh, B. N., and Roche, A. H. G. (1977). *Am. Heart J.* **94,** 593–599.
Specchia, G., DeServi, S., Falcone, C., Angoli, L., Mussini, A., Bramucci, E., Marioni, G. P., Ardissino, D., Salerno, J., and Bobba, P. (1981). *Circulation* **63,** 46–54.
Stone, D. L., Stephens, J. D., and Banim, S. O. (1983). *Br. Heart J.* **49,** 442–446.
Strauer, B. E. (1971). *Pharm. Res. Comm.* **3,** 377–383.
Taylor, S. H., Silke, B., Ahuja, R. C., and Okoli, R. (1982). *J. Cardiovasc. Pharmacol.* **4,** 803–807.
Triggle, D. J., and Swamy, V. C. (1983). *Circ. Res.* **52,** Suppl. I, 117–128.
Tzivoni, D., Keren, A., Benhorin, J., Gottlieb, S., Atlas, D., and Stern, S. (1983). *Am. Heart J.* **105,** 262–266.
VanHoutte, P. M. (1983). *Fed. Proc.* **42,** 233–237.
van Zwieten, P. A., vanMeel, J. C. A., and Timmermans, P. B. M. W. M. (1983). *Circ. Res.* **52,** Suppl. I, I77–I80.
Vastesaeger, M., Gillott, P., and Rasson, G. (1967). *Acta Cardiol.* **22,** 483–490.
Walinsky, P., Santamore, W. P., Wiener, L., and Brest, A. N. (1979). *Cardiovasc. Res.* **13,** 113–118.
Warltier, D. C., Lamping, K. A., Zyvoloski, M. G., Gross, G. J., and Brooks, H. L. (1983). *J. Cardiovasc. Pharmacol.* **5,** 272–277.
Waters, D. D., Bouchard, A., and Theroux, P. (1983). *J. Am. Coll. Cardiol.* **2,** 195–199.
Weber, S., Donzeau-Gouge, G., Chauvand, S., Picard, G., Guerin, F., Carpentier, A., and DeGeorges, M. (1983). *Am. J. Cardiol.* **51,** 1072–1075.
Weiner, L., Kasparian, H., Duca, P. R., Walinsky, P., Gottlieb, R. S., Hanckel, F., and Brest, A. N. (1976). *Am. J. Cardiol.* **38,** 945–955.
Weiss, H. R., and Winbury, M. D. (1972). *Microvasc. Res.* **4,** 273–284.
Weisse, A. B., Senft, A., Khan, M. I., and Regan, T. J. (1972). *Am. J. Cardiol.* **30,** 362–370.
Yasue, H., Touyama, M., Shimamoto, M., Kato, H., Tanaka, T., and Akiyama, F. (1974). *Circulation* **50,** 534–539.
Yasue, H., Omote, S., Takizawa, A., Nagao, M., Miwa, K., and Tanaka, S. (1979). *Am. J. Cardiol.* **43,** 647–652.
Yasue, H., Omote, S., Takizawa, A., and Nagao, M. (1983). *Circ. Res.* **52,** Suppl. I, 147–152.
Zeff, R. H., Iannone, L. A., Kongtahworn, C., Brown, T. M., Gordon, D. F., Benson, M., Phillips, S. J., and Alley, R. E. (1982). *Ann. Thorac. Surg.* **34,** 196–200.
Zellinger, A. B., Abramowitz, B. M., Schick, E. C., and Ryan, T. J. (1982). *Chest* **82,** 188–192.

# 5 Physiologic Basis and Results of Thrombolytic Therapy in Acute Myocardial Infarction

Barry S. Denenberg and James F. Spann

## I. Introduction

The most important predictor of both acute outcome and long-term prognosis following acute myocardial infarction is the amount of myocardium which becomes necrotic during the acute episode (Rude et al., 1981; Roberts, 1980). Attempts to limit infarct size were, until recently, largely unsuccessful. Recent studies with coronary thrombolysis, however, promise to alter dramatically our approach to therapy of myocardial infarction by affording a means to limit infarct size and preserve myocardial function.

Herrick (1912) first proposed that acute coronary obstruction due to thrombi caused myocardial infarction. Whether thrombi were a causative factor or were merely formed secondarily, adjacent to atherosclerotic plaques, however, was not clear. At autopsy patients displayed both infarction in the absence of coronary occlusion and occlusion without myocardial infarction (Friedberg and Horn, 1939; Miller et al., 1951; Branwood and Montgomery, 1956). Hence, the pathophysiology of acute myocardial infarction was still open to considerable question.

It is now clear that myocardial infarction is usually caused by coronary thrombus. Studies in which coronary angiography was performed on patients within the first few hours after the onset of a myocardial infarction have demonstrated an acute thrombus at the border of an atheromatous plaque. DeWood et al. (1981) found total coronary occlusion in 110 of 126 patients evaluated by angiography within 4 hr of the onset of symptoms of an acute myocardial infarction. In 52 of 59 patients who underwent early coronary artery bypass surgery, thrombus was retrieved by Fogarty catheter at the time of surgical reperfusion. Fletcher et al. (1959) first proposed the use of fibrinolytic therapy in acute myocardial infarction to dissolve the causative thrombus. Fibrinolytic therapy is becoming an increasingly widespread method of treating the patient with acute myocardial infarction.

## II. Physiology of Thrombus Formation and Fibrinolytic Enzyme System

Thrombotic occlusion of a coronary artery, usually superimposed on a severe, atherosclerotic narrowing, is present in 80 to 95% of patients during the early hours after the onset of myocardial infarction (DeWood et al., 1981). Arterial thrombi commonly arise at sites of intimal injury, such as trauma, inflammation or, most commonly, atherosclerosis (Schwartz et al., 1978). Arterial thrombi customarily develop in sclerotic arteries in which the luminal or plaque surface has been disrupted. Rupture or ulceration of an atherosclerotic plaque exposes to the lumen the thrombogenic elements in the arterial wall (Chandler, 1974). The cause of rupture of an atheromatous plaque is unclear but may involve a complex interaction of atheromatous plaque, coronary artery spasm, and platelets. Nevertheless, platelets quickly separate from the axial stream of the flowing blood and accumulate at a site of injury to build a thrombotic mass. Platelet adhesion and aggregation is followed by the formation of fibrin around the periphery of platelet aggregate. Fibrin, by enclosing the aggregates, connects and braces the platelet columns as a thrombus develops.

The presence of a thrombus in the intravascular compartment indicates that the rates of formation and deposition of fibrin have exceeded the body's fibrinolytic activity. The proteolytic enzyme plasmin and its proenzyme plasminogen are the components of the major fibrinolytic enzyme system. Small amounts of plasminogen are bound normally in thrombi. In the presence of plasminogen activator, which is released from endothelial cells, plasminogen is enzymatically converted to the active fibrin-dissolving enzyme, plasmin. Plasmin is a relatively nonspecific proteolytic enzyme which hydrolyzes susceptible bonds in a variety of proteins. *In vivo*, however, plasmin is specific for fibrinolysis, due to several factors. First, plasminogen is bound to fibrin. Second, fibrin is required as cofactor for the activation of plasminogen by the endothelial cell activator. Finally, alpha$_2$ antiplasmin, the major antiplasmin in plasma, is unable to inactivate plasmin formed on the fibrin surface, due to the higher affinity of plasmin versus antiplasmin for a similar binding site on fibrin. Thus, using a nonspecific proteolytic enzyme, plasmin, the body can mediate highly selective and localized fibrinolysis without inducing significant proteolytic effects in the circulating plasma (Spann and Sherry, 1984).

The thrombolytic agents currently available for clinical use similarly activate the naturally occurring plasminogen–plasmin enzyme system. Unlike endothelial cell plasminogen activator, however, thrombolytic agents do not require fibrin as a cofactor for the conversion of plasminogen to plasmin. Therefore, infusion of thrombolytic agents into the circulation results in the activation of both the fibrin-bound plasminogen and the circulating plasma plasminogen. Activation of plasminogen to plasmin in the circulating plasma produces a systemic proteolytic state, producing proteolytic degradation of fibrinogen and high concentration of fibrinogen degradation products. Potential for normal fibrin formation is decreased by the hypofibrinogenemias as well as by the fibrinogen degradation products. These biochemical changes rarely cause a generalized hemorrhagic diathesis but may lead to hemorrhagic complications if the patient has a traumatic procedure. In addition, the fibrin that reinforces platelet aggregates of hemostatic plugs is dissolved by plasmin action, resulting in disaggregation of platelets and opening of damaged vessels, leading to possible hemorrhage at sites of prior trauma. Thus, patients who have had critically located hemostatic thrombi, such as those after major surgery or intracranial disease, or who offer the potential for serious hemorrhage from a localized lesion such as an active duodenal ulcer, should not undergo fibrinolytic therapy.

Two thrombolytic agents, both harvested from cell cultures, are approved for clinical use: streptokinase and urokinase. Both agents occasionally produce pyrogenic side effects. Streptokinase can also produce allergic reactions and anaphylaxis. Streptokinase induces thrombolysis indirectly via formation of a streptokinase–plasminogen–activator complex, secondarily converting plasminogen to plasmin. Urokinase directly cleaves plasminogen to plasmin (Fig. 1).

Plasmin circulating in the blood produces a systemic "lytic state," indicated by a decrease in plasma plasminogen, a shortening of the euglobulin lysis time, a decrease in plasma fibrinogen, the appearance of serum fibrin–fibrinogen degradation products, or a prolongation of the prothrombin or thrombin time. Correlation of these assays with clinical results, however, suggests that, while laboratory montoring of therapy is important to assure the presence of a "lytic state," monitoring does not serve as an index of the likelihood of either hemorrhage or clot lysis. The important factors for predicting clot lysis and bleeding complications are the condition of the pathologic thrombus and the hemostatic plugs, not the specific values of biochemical laboratory assays (Marder *et al.*, 1977; Urokinase Pulmonary Embolism Trial: A National Cooperative Study, 1973). The sole reason to perform a laboratory test is to prove that the activator has been effectively delivered to the patient and that it has overcome the inhibitory effect of natural or acquired plasma inhibition.

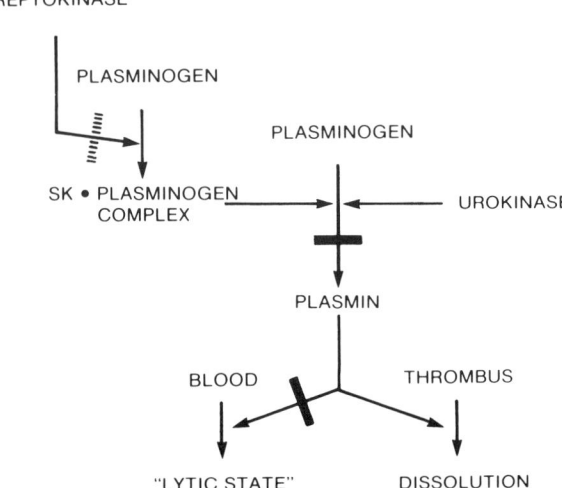

**Fig. 1.** Schematic representation of streptokinase and urokinase activation of plasminogen and the actions of plasmin on the thrombus and in the blood. Streptokinase activates plasminogen indirectly by formation of an activator complex, as opposed to the direct conversion of plasminogen to plasmin by urokinase. Plasmin action on thrombi is indiscriminate, acting on pathologic thrombi and hemostatic plugs. The biochemical changes produced in the blood result in a "lytic state" which is an indicator of effective dose administration of the activator drug. Excessively high levels of antistreptococcal antibodies (interrupted line) may require that a longer than usual dose of activator be infused to achieve a "lytic state." Natural protein inhibitors (solid crossbars) of activation and plasmin play a role in preventing the "lytic state" of infused activators, since standard treatment regimens use enormous quantities of material, and the inhibiting potential of plasma is exceeded. (From Marder, V. J., 1979.)

## III. Early Trials of Long-Duration, Late Intravenous Thrombolytic Therapy in Acute Myocardial Infarction

Twenty-one additional feasibility studies, in series of from 5 to 100 patients, followed the first proposed use of a thrombolytic agent in myocardial infarction by Fletcher *et al.* (1959) and Simon *et al.* (1973). Thereafter, more than a dozen, large multicenter, controlled clinical trials of long-duration, late intravenous therapy in acute myocardial infarction were run (Simon *et al.*, 1973; Stampfer *et al.*, 1982). The majority of trials revealed a trend towards reduced mortality in patients given streptokinase. The European Cooperative Study Group for Streptokinase Treatment in Acute Myocardial Infarction (1979) randomized 315 medium- and high-risk patients to a 24-hr infusion of streptokinase or glucose with 12 hr of the onset of symptoms. The overall mortality rates were significantly lower in the streptokinase group (15.6%) than in the control group (30.6%). While bleeding complications were more frequent in the streptokinase group, only two bleeding complications were clinically important (European Cooperative Study Group For Streptokinase Treatment in Acute Myocardial Infarction, 1979).

Most early studies did not show a statistically significant drop in mortality in streptokinase-treated patients (Stampfer *et al.*, 1982). The dose of streptokinase, however, varied from study to study (Simon *et al.*, 1973). Even more significantly, some studies which did not show a benefit of streptokinase therapy treated patients 12–72 hr after the onset of symptoms (Simon *et al.*, 1973), while the maximum duration of complete ischemia from which the myocardium can recover is thought to be 3 to perhaps 6 hr (Rude *et al.*, 1981). Nonetheless, in a recent reexamination of data pooled from eight randomized trials by Stampfer *et al.* (1982), intravenous streptokinase therapy after acute myocardial infarction reduced mortality over the subsequent few weeks about 20%. Use of the pooled data allowed for a statistically significant finding, whereas when the data were analyzed separately most studies were inconclusive. Stampfer *et al.* (1982) concluded that although pooled data were suggestive of a beneficial effect of intravenous streptokinase, pooled data and data from studies that are too small may be misleading and that a large-scale trial of intravenous streptokinase was needed.

## IV. Intracoronary Streptokinase

### A. Introduction

After animal research showed that the amount of myocardium becoming necrotic after coronary occlusion was not fixed but could be recuced by a number of interventions, particularly the removal of an obstruction with subsequent restoration of flow, and that such reperfusion could lead to salvage of a substantial amount of myocardium (Ginks *et al.*, 1972), it was inevitable that the same procedure should be tried in man. The early intravenous infusion trials of streptokinase to restore flow and limit infarct size were encouraging but, as mentioned above, contained a number of methodological problems. The advance of coronary angiography together with the availability of thrombolytic agents and the belief that coronary thrombosis was the cause of the myocardial infarction, however, led several investigators to instill streptokinase directly into coronary arteries during an acute myocardial infarction in an attempt to limit infarct size (Chazov *et al.*, 1976; Ganz *et al.*, 1981; Rentrop *et al.*, 1979; Mathey *et al.*, 1981; Reduto *et al.*, 1981). It was also hoped that, since intracoronary infusion provided a high concentration of the thrombolytic agent at the site of thrombus with lower systemic concentrations of streptokinase, potential bleeding problems could be avoided. Chazov *et al.* (1976) and Rentrop *et al.* (1979) provided clear evidence that coronary patency could be reestablished by intracoronary streptokinase. Since the initial studies, a number of studies have confirmed reperfusion in coronary arteries in approximately 75% of patients using intracoronary streptokinase (Ganz *et al.*, 1981; Rentrop *et al.*, 1981; Mathey *et al.*, 1981; Reduto *et al.*, 1981).

### B. Technique

Various techniques have been employed for the intracoronary administration of streptokinase. Patients with signs and symptoms of acute myocardial infarction, usually within 12 hr after the onset of symptoms, are brought to the cardiac catheterization laboratory. Clotting parameters are obtained. The patient is premedicated with steroids or, occasionally, Benadryl to decrease the risk of an allergic reaction to streptokinase. The suspected infarct artery is visualized angiographically and determined to be occluded. Intracoronary nitroglycerin is usually given to exclude coronary artery spasm, although the incidence of spasm is reported to be 5% or less. Steptokinase is then infused, usually through the coronary catheter. Subselective infusion by a small catheter that can be passed through the coronary catheter and advanced directly to the site of clot has been used by some groups to infuse streptokinase directly on the thrombus. Subselective infusion is rarely done currently, however, due to the time required for subselective catheter placement, the potential risk for artery dissection, and since nonselective intracoronary infusion has achieved reperfusion rates that are comparable to those achieved by subselective infusion (Smalling *et al.*, 1983). Streptokinase is then infused at a rate of 2000 to 4000 IU/min for a period of 70 to 90 min. Clot lysis usually occurs within 30 min. Some studies have continued intracoronary infusion for 30 min to 1 hr after coronary flow is reestablished in order to continue the lysis of any residual thrombus (Ganz *et al.*, 1983). Some report that puncture of a thrombus with a guide wire can improve the reperfusion rate of occlusions initially resistant to treatment with streptokinase (Mathey *et al.*, 1981). Others believe that use of a guide wire may be associated with a higher incidence of early reocclusion or coronary dissection (Rentrop *et al.*, 1983; Smalling *et al.*, 1983). Nonetheless, once patency of the previously occluded coronary artery is obtained, patients are maintained on a systemic infusion of heparin for 2 to 7 days.

## C. Frequency of Thrombolysis

Intracoronary infusion of streptokinase within the first hours following an acute myocardial infarction results in reestablishment of flow to the area of myocardial infarction in from 60% to greater than 95% of patients (Table I). Rates of clot lysis are highest when patients are infused within 3 to 6 hr after the onset of symptoms.

Spontaneous reperfusion does occur and theoretically could affect the results of reperfusion studies. Spontaneous reperfusion is rare, however, in the first 3 to 4 hr after onset of myocardial infarction. Kennedy et al. (1983) reported a randomized, placebo-controlled study in which 12% of 116 patients had coronary reperfusion without streptokinase infusion

**TABLE I**
Frequency of Reperfusion by Intracoronary Streptokinase

| Study | Number of patients | Number reperfused (%) |
|---|---|---|
| Ganz et al., 1981 | 20 | 19 (95%) |
| Mathey et al., 1981 | 39 | 30 (73%) |
| Merx et al., 1981 | 160 | 129 (81%) |
| Rentrop et al., 1981 | 29 | 22 (76%) |
| Messmer et al., 1983 | 84 | 72 (86%) |
| Schuler et al., 1983 | 21 | 16 (76%) |
| Schwartz et al., 1982a | 27 | 19 (70%) |
| Anderson et al., 1983 | 24 | 19 (79%)[a] |
| Cowley et al., 1983 | 23 | 20 (87%) |
| Cribier et al., 1983 | 80 | 51 (64%) |
| Kennedy et al., 1983 | 118 | 73 (68%)[a] |
| Khaja et al., 1983 | 20 | 12 (60%)[a] |
| Rogers et al., 1983 | 25 | 19 (76%)[a] |
| Serruys et al., 1983 | 89 | 64 (76%) |
| Smalling et al., 1983 | 96 | 69 (72%) |
| Stack et al., 1983 | 24 | 15 (62%) |
| Total | 879 | 649 (74%) |

[a] Randomized trials.

when patients were studied an average of 4.6 hr after symptom onset. With the passage of time, however, spontaneous reperfusion becomes more common. DeWood *et al.* (1981) observed coronary thrombus in 87.3% of patients evaluated within 4 hr of the onset of symptoms, in 85.3% of patients between 4 and 6 hr of onset of symptoms and in only 68.4% ($p$ .005) in patients evaluated 6–12 hr after the onset of symptoms. Nygaard *et al.* (1983) demonstrated patent coronary arteries to the infarct zone in 41% of patients not receiving thrombolytic therapy but having angiograms 2 weeks after myocardial infarction. Thus, recanalization of thrombosed coronary arteries occurring in the first 4 hr after the onset of acute myocardial infarction in streptokinase-treated patients is most probably due to the fibrinolytic therapy, not to spontaneous reperfusion. Since 6 hr is generally considered the outside limit from symptom onset to reperfusion consistent with the salvage of ischemic myocardium, significant salvage of the infarcting myocardium by spontaneous recanalization is unlikely.

## D. Effects of Reperfusion on Clinical Indicators of Infarction

Relief of chest pain, which may be quite dramatic, almost invariably accompanies restoration of blood flow by intracoronary thrombolysis with streptokinase (Ganz *et al.*, 1981, 1983; Rentrop *et al.*, 1981, 1983; Mathey *et al.*, 1981). Along with relief of pain, reduction in ST segment elevation is noted. Most patients, however, either have a loss of R-wave voltage or develop Q waves despite coronary reperfusion, consistent with experimental evidence that irreversible damage and cellular death begin to occur within 20 to 40 min of a coronary occlusion (Rude *et al.*, 1981). Reperfusion would be expected to salvage jeopardized myocardium outside the area of irreversible necrosis. Thus, the presence of Q waves following reperfusion should not be interpreted as a failure to salvage myocardium. In addition, reperfusion does not prevent enzymatic evidence of myocardial infarction. In patients undergoing successful reperfusion with intracoronary streptokinase, the creatine phosphokinase (CPK-MB) rises to a peak in 6 to 8 hr following the onset of pain as opposed to a CPK-MB peak of 12 or more hr after the onset of symptoms in conventionally treated patients (Ganz *et al.*, 1981; 1983; Rentrop *et al.*, 1981, 1983; Mathey *et al.*, 1981). Reperfusion may also result in a higher peak CPK-MB level than would be expected, probably due to an enhanced release and faster washout of the myocardial enzymes (Vatner *et al.*, 1978). Data from our lab (Spann *et al.*, 1984), however, suggested that using CPK-MB may not be a reliable indicator of reperfusion since 10 of 18 patients who did not reperfuse after intravenous steptokinase had a peak value of CPK-MB 13 hr or less after the onset of symptoms.

### E. Salvage of Jeopardized Myocardium by Intracoronary Streptokinase

*1. Effect of Reperfusion on Left Ventricular Function*

In nonrandomized studies of intracoronary streptokinase patients conducted during the period of hospitalization, successfully reperfused patients showed only a small improvement in global left ventricular function while those patients in whom the occluded coronary artery could not be reopened showed no improvement in global left ventricular function (Ganz *et al.*, 1981, 1983; Rentrop *et al.*, 1981, 1983; Mathey *et al.*, 1981). Khaja *et al.* (1983) showed no statistically significant change in global left ventricular function 12 days and 5 months after successful reperfusion. Experimental evidence suggests, however, that an improvement in left ventricular contractile function may not be apparent until a week or longer after reperfusion, since following reperfusion, the previously ischemic myocardium is "stunned" and regains normal biochemical and contractile function only after a delay (Braunwald and Kloner, 1982; Ellis *et al.*, 1983). Coronary reperfusion should not, therefore, be expected to have a marked immediate effect on left ventricular function.

In addition, the global ejection fraction may not be a sufficiently sensitive method for detection of improvement of ventricular function in patients with acute myocardial infarction. Areas of infarction that may potentially benefit from reperfusion are mixed with areas remote from the ischemic zone in measurements of global ventricular function. Compensatory hyperkinesis has been demonstrated in myocardium remote from the ischemic zone, which may artificially increase the global ejection fraction acutely. These hyperkinetic areas may not be present on follow-up studies, thus lowering the global ejection fraction and masking any effect the reperfusion has on regional left ventricular function. Therefore, measurement of changes in regional rather than global left ventricular function is now recognized as a more sensitive method for detecting changes in left ventricular function before and after reperfusion (Sheehan *et al.*, 1982; Stack *et al.*, 1983).

Stack *et al.* (1983) studied 24 patients who underwent intracoronary streptokinase infusion within 6 hr after the onset of symptoms of acute myocardial infarction. Fifteen patients (62%) were successfully recanalized. Sequential studies were done at 24 hr in 19 patients and before discharge (16 days) in 15 patients. At the time of the predischarge study, all patients with reperfusion showed uniform improvement in the jeopardized region while the global ejection fraction showed no improvement or a decrease, due to a decrease in the compensatory wall motion in the uninvolved segments. The regional and global function did not change in the patients who could not be acutely recanalized. The authors concluded that by measuring regional left ventricular function they could document significant salvage of jeopardized myocardium associated with recovery of contractile function in patients reperfused during the first 6 hr of chest pain following acute myocardial infarction.

Sheehan *et al.* (1983) also evaluated regional and global left ventricular function in 52 patients who underwent contrast angiography immediately after intracoronary streptokinase and 6 ± 7 weeks later. Forty-two patients were successfully reperfused. Twenty-two patients who were successfully reperfused underwent coronary artery bypass grafting. Regional wall motion was measured at 100 cords around the left ventricle. Regional hypokinesia improved in 41% of patients with reperfusion by strepto-

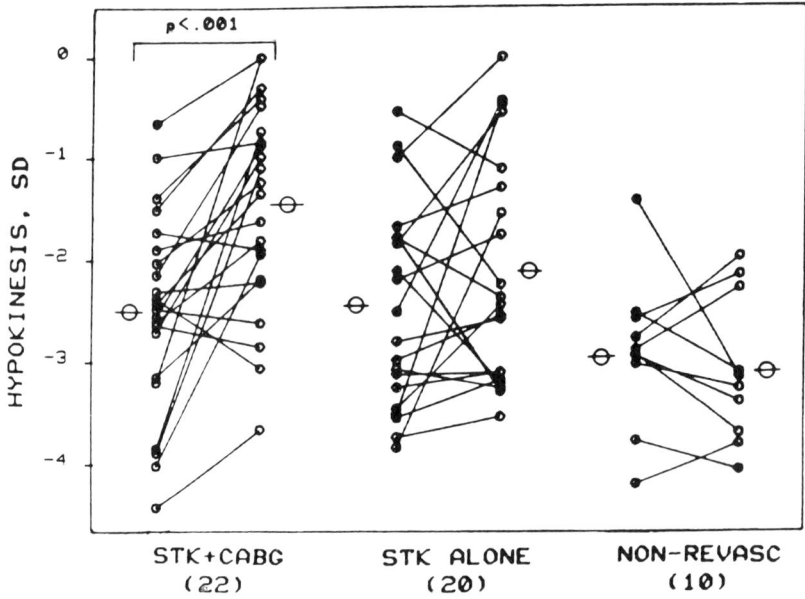

**Fig. 2.** Change in hypokinesia in the region of acute ischemia in acute and follow-up studies in each patient group. STK + CABG, patients who had thrombolysis, optimal reperfusion, and coronary artery bypass surgery; STK, patients with thrombolysis but who developed Q waves or had large residual perfusion defects on thallium scan; Non-Revasc, patients without thrombolysis or with rethrombosis; SD, standard deviation. The number of patients in each treatment group is shown in parentheses. (From Sheehan *et al.*, 1983.)

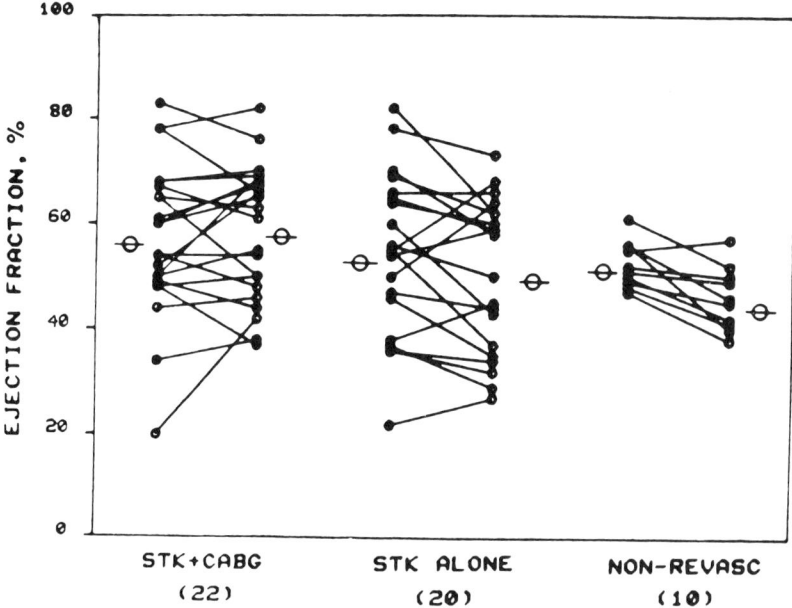

**Fig. 3.** Change in ejection fraction in acute and follow-up studies in each patient group. Abbreviations as in Fig. 2. (From Sheehan et al., 1983.)

kinase alone (Fig. 2). No improvement was seen in patients who were not successfully reperfused. There was no change in the global ejection fraction (Fig. 3), however, because, despite severe hypokinesia in acute myocardial infarction, hyperkinesia, which was present on the opposite wall, decreased at follow-up, masking significant improvement in the infarcted region (Fig. 4). The authors concluded that regional wall motion must be measured to assess adequately the improvement in left ventricular function that occurs with early thrombolysis therapy in acute myocardial infarction.

Cribier et al. (1983) studied patients an average of 3.6 hr after onset of symptoms of acute myocardial infarction by contrast angiography immediately before intracoronary streptokinase therapy, 2 days later, and 3 months later. Again, both regional and global measurements of left ventricular function were made. In those patients with persistent reperfusion, there was a significant improvement in regional wall motion. In those patients in whom no reperfusion was achieved, there was a worsening of regional wall motion. Schwartz et al. (1982a) also demonstrated an improvement in regional ejection fraction but no change in global ejection fraction with successful early reperfusion. While the foregoing were not

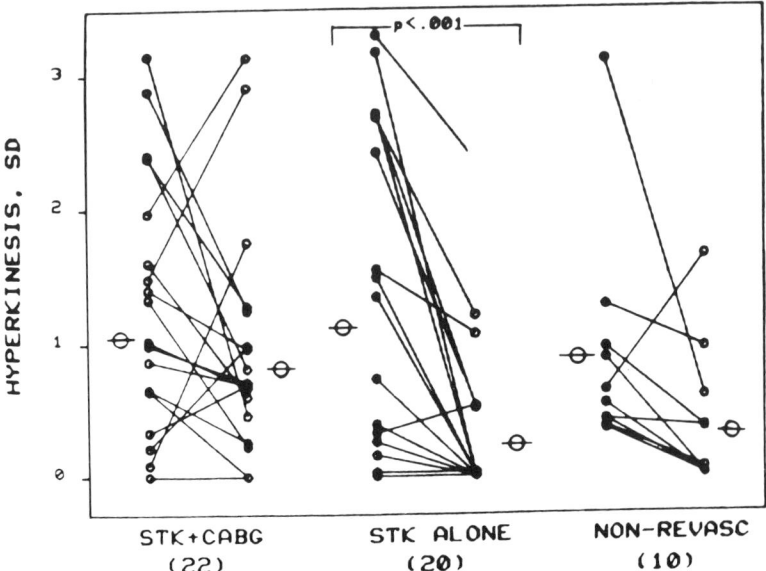

**Fig. 4.** Change in hyperkinesia on the wall opposite the acutely ischemic region in acute and follow-up studies in each patient group. Abbreviations as in Fig. 2. (From Sheehan et al., 1983.)

randomized, controlled trials, the data nevertheless indicate that successful early reperfusion by intracoronary streptokinase in acute myocardial infarction results in partial myocardial salvage, measured by regional left ventricular function. Evaluating global left ventricular function discloses little or no effect of early reperfusion by streptokinase, probably due to the compensatory hyperkinesia in the noninfarcted zone which, on follow-up study, becomes normalized, masking the improvement in motion of the reperfused infarcted area.

The effect of streptokinase on left ventricular function has been studied in several randomized trials. Anderson et al. (1983) randomly assigned 50 patients to receive either intracoronary streptokinase or standard therapy within 3 hr after the onset of symptoms of acute myocardial infarction. Streptokinase infusion was started an average of 4.0 hr after onset of symptoms. Coronary reperfusion was achieved in 19 of 24 patients receiving streptokinase. Radionuclide ejection fraction studied on Day 10 compared to Day 1 had increased an average of 3.9% in patients receiving streptokinase and had decreased an average of 3.0% in patients in the control group ($p < 0.1$). Echocardiographic evaluation of left ventricular wall motion showed significantly greater improvement between Day 1 and Day 10 in the streptokinase group than in the control group.

# 5. Thrombolytic Therapy

Khaja *et al.* (1983) also reported a prospective randomized trial with 20 patients receiving streptokinase and 20 receiving placebo. Twelve patients treated with streptokinase and two patients in the placebo group achieved reperfusion. Streptokinase infusion was started an average of 5.4 hr after onset of symptoms. Global ejection fractions were unchanged in either the placebo or streptokinase treated groups at 12 days or 5 months after admission. Regional ventricular function was measured before and immediately after the streptokinase infusion. No improvement in left ventricular contractile function was observed immediately after streptokinase infusion, apparently due to the "myocardial stun" phenomenon, which may require up to 1 week to abate. Regional ventricular function was not determined later. Improvement in left ventricular function, therefore, could have been missed early due to the stun phenomenon and missed late due to the failure to measure regional function. In an editorial which accompanied these two articles, Swan (1983) suggested several explanations for the difference in the results between the two randomized studies. Differences in the time (4.0 hr versus 5.4 hr) between the onset of symptoms and the initiation of streptokinase therapy may have played a role. Also, in the study by Khaja *et al.* (1983), heparin was not given after lysis of intracoronary clot by streptokinase. In most studies, after lysis of intracoronary clot by streptokinase, heparin was given to reduce the incidence of rethrombosis. Since even with heparin there is a significant incidence of rethrombosis, a higher than average rate of rethrombosis in part could also account for the negative results.

## 2. Salvage of Jeopardized Myocardium Assessed by Thallium-201 Myocardial Scintigraphy

Thallium-201 myocardial scintigraphy has been proposed as a method of indicating salvage of myocardial tissue independent of recovery of left ventricular function. Uptake of thallium-201 requires both bloodflow to deliver the isotope to the myocardium and a myocardial cell with an intact sodium–potassium ATP pump to extract the thallium-201 from the blood, since the isotope acts as a potassium analog.

Markis *et al.* (1981) studied nine patients 3.5 hr after symptoms of acute myocardial infarction. Thallium-201 was injected intracoronary before and after infusion of intracoronary streptokinase. Occluded coronary arteries were opened within 20 min in all patients but reocclusion did occur in one patient. Improved regional perfusion indicating myocardial salvage after recanalization was observed in seven of nine patients. The authors concluded, from the improved regional perfusion, that reperfusion of obstructed coronary arteries after intracoronary thrombolysis salvaged jeopardized myocardium. The authors also studied several patients 2 weeks and 3 months later, and found persistent myocardial thallium uptake, indicating that the salvage of myocardium may persist. The one patient that reoccluded showed worsening of the thallium defect, supporting the view that visualization of myocardium by thallium-201 uptake after recanalization represents cellular uptake of salvaged myocardium consequent to reperfusion.

Schuler *et al.* (1983) studied 21 patients within 4 hr after onset of symptoms of acute myocardial infarction. Recanalization was achieved in 16 patients with intracoronary streptokinase. The size of the thallium-201 perfusion defect was determined from myocardial cross sections from seven-pinhole tomography. The authors found that, following reperfusion, the percent of ventricular circumference displaying a perfusion defect decreased significantly ($p < .001$) from an average of 36% acutely to 19% at 24 hr. In five patients with no reperfusion, the percent of abnormal ventricular circumference from the acute (40%) to 24 hr (41%) was unchanged (Fig. 5). The authors also found that, in patients who had extensive collaterals or subtotal occlusion, the thallium-201 defect at 24 hr was

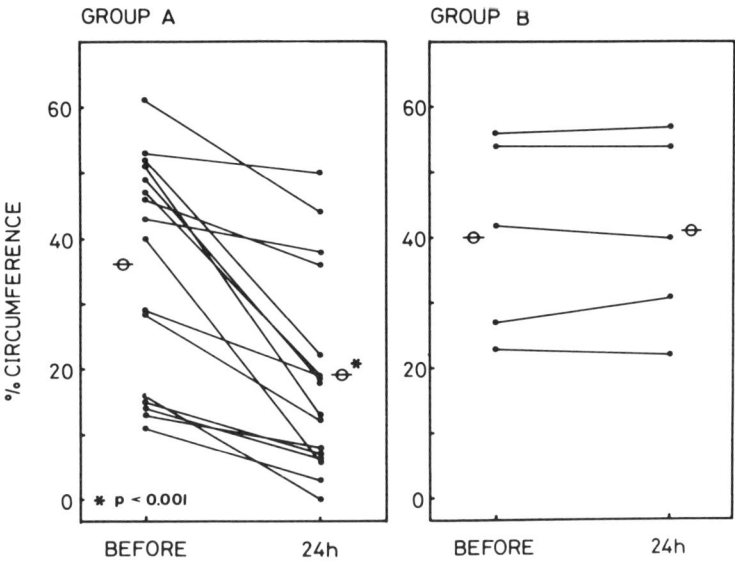

**Fig. 5.** Size of thallium-201 perfusion defects before and 24 hr after thrombolysis expressed as a percentage of left ventricular circumference. In 16 patients in whom the intervention was successful (left), there is significant improvement of thallium-201 uptake; very little change is noted in five unsuccessful cases (right). (From Schuler *et al.*, 1983 by permission of the American Heart Association, Inc.)

most reduced, compared with those patients who had poor or no collaterals and total occlusion. The authors concluded from these data that the patients who benefit most from intracoronary thrombolysis are those with some residual flow, either through a subtotally occluded vessel or by means of extensive collateralization to the ischemic area.

## F. Effect on Myocardial Salvage of Time from Onset of Symptoms to Reperfusion

Animal studies disclose myocardial necrosis beginning after only 20 min of coronary artery occlusion, originating at the subendocardium and progressing in a wave front toward the epicardium (Braunwald and Kloner, 1982). Within 6 hr, the degree of necrosis is influenced by the completeness of the arterial occlusion, the presence of acquired collateral circulation, and hemodynamic and metabolic factors affecting the coronary blood flow and myocardial oxygen demand (Ganz et al., 1983). Thus, in experimental animals, the time of onset of severe ischemia to achievement of reperfusion determines the extent of myocardial necrosis. After 4 to 6 hr of permanent coronary artery occlusion, significant myocardial salvage is unlikely to occur (Sommers and Jennings, 1964). In humans this critical time period will differ from patient to patient and will depend on many factors, including the size of the ischemic involvement, extraneous cardiac demands, and compensatory coronary collateral supply to the jeopardized myocardium (Ganz et al., 1983).

Several studies in humans have explored the effect of the time of onset of symptoms to reperfusion on myocardial salvage. Schwarz et al. (1982b) divided 39 patients, treated with intracoronary infusion of streptokinase, into three groups. Group A consisted of 15 patients with successful reperfusion less than 4 hr (average 3 hr, 10 min) after symptom onset. Group B consisted of 17 patients with successful reperfusion more than 4 hr (average 5 hr, 52 min) after onset of symptoms. Group C consisted of seven patients in whom recanalization was not achieved. Cineangiography was performed before and 4 weeks after streptokinase treatment in each patient. Initial values for global ejection in the three groups were 49% (A), 44% (B), and 49% (C), while regional ejection fractions of the infarction areas were 24% (A), 22% (B), and 27% (C). Four weeks after the streptokinase, patients in Group A had both significantly higher ($p < .05$) average global ejection fraction (59%) and significantly higher ($p < .05$) average regional ejection fractions (39%) of the infarction area than patients in Group B, in which the global ejection fraction averaged 39% and the regional ejection fraction averaged 26% after 4 weeks. Group C had a global ejection fraction of 44% and a regional ejection fraction of 25% 4 weeks after streptokinase. These authors concluded that a greater reduction in infarct size was obtained in patients with early reperfusion compared to patients with late reperfusion.

With the exception of one report, workers consider 4–6 hr as the maximum duration from onset of symptoms to successful reperfusion consistent with myocardial salvage (Swan, 1983). Smalling et al. (1983), however, compared the improvement in global ejection fraction in subsets of patients in whom reperfusion was achieved less than 6 hr, 6–12 hr, and 12–18 hr from onset of symptoms. Each of the groups demonstrated a significant increase in ejection fraction determined by radionuclide techniques within 24 hr of admission to the hospital (Fig. 6). Nevertheless, most clinical data are consistent with the experimental observation that the earlier the reperfusion can be achieved, the more myocardium can be salvaged. The rate of myocardial necrosis, however, is not the same in all patients. Myocardial necrosis may be slowed by collateral flow, intermittent reestablishment of slow, subtotal coronary obstruction, or by local hemodynamic and metabolic factors affecting coronary blood flow and myocardial oxygen demand. If these or other undefined factors are present, late reperfusion may have some benefit.

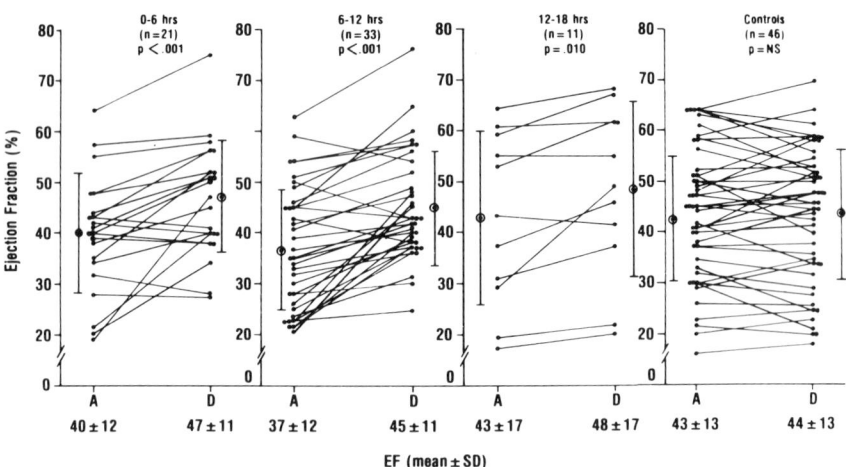

**Fig. 6.** Ejection fraction (EF) on admission to the hospital (A) and at discharge (D) in patients who underwent reperfusion 0–6, 6–12, and 12–18 hr after onset of pain and in control patients ($p$ by paired Students' $t$-test). (From Smalling et al., 1983 by permission of the American Heart Association, Inc.)

## G. Effect of Reperfusion on Mortality

Acute myocardial infarction results in death in approximately 50% of patients before they reach the hospital. During hospitalization, another 10–20% of patients die. Reperfusion with intracoronary streptokinase may improve the survival of these hospitalized patients, either by preserving a critical myocardial mass, by preventing transmural progression of necrosis, thus preventing myocardial rupture, or by terminating myocardial ischemia, preventing lethal arrhythmias. The nonrandomized studies currently available consistently demonstrate that mortality is, indeed, lower among patients who can be successfully reperfused than among those who cannot (Mathey *et al.*, 1981; Ganz *et al.*, 1983; Rentrop *et al.*, 1982, 1983; Smalling *et al.*, 1983). In the two small randomized studies of intracoronary streptokinase (Khaja *et al.*, 1983; Anderson *et al.*, 1983), while there was a trend towards lower early mortality in those patients receiving treatment, this trend did not reach statistical significance, perhaps due to the small number in each group. In a large study by Kennedy *et al.* (1983), however, 134 patients were randomly assigned to intracoronary streptokinase treatment and 116 were controls. The overall 30-day mortality was 18 (7.2%). Five deaths occurred in the streptokinase-treated group (3.7%) while 13 deaths occurred in the control group (11.2%, $p < .02$) (Fig. 7). Intracoronary streptokinase therapy resulted in a nearly threefold reduction in the 30-day mortality after hospitalization for acute myocardial infarction.

## H. Risk of Intracoronary Streptokinase

The major risk associated with intracoronary streptokinase is hemorrhage produced by the systemic lytic state. Even when low-dose intracoronary streptokinase is administered, a systemic lytic state is achieved in most patients (Cowley *et al.*, 1983). Not only is there danger of hemorrhage from traumatic procedures, but previous hemostatic plugs may be dissolved, leading to hemorrhage from sites of previous trauma. If patients with active bleeding or conditions that might predispose to hemorrhage are excluded, however, hemorrhagic complications are rare and the major problem encountered is, then, hematoma formation at the femoral artery puncture site. Intracranial, retroperitoneal, mediastinal, and gastrointestinal bleeding may also occur, although the overall incidence of bleeding complications serious enough to require either transfusion or surgical repair of the site of arterial puncture has varied from 0% (Mathey *et al.*, 1981; Khaja *et al.*, 1983; Anderson *et al.*, 1983) to 7% (Rentrop *et*

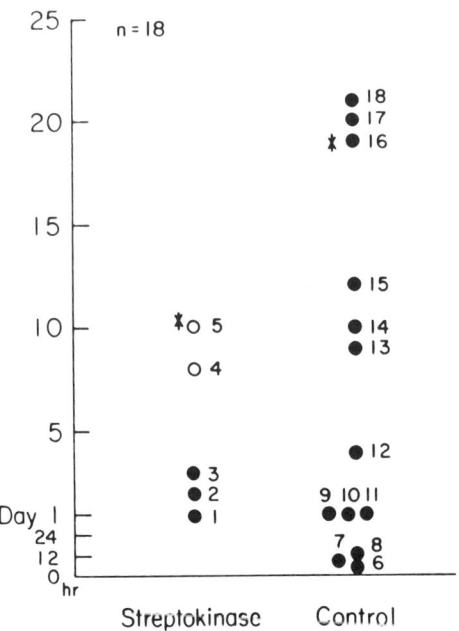

**Fig. 7.** Day of death in five patients treated with streptokinase and in 13 controls. The open dots indicate reperfusion, and the closed dots no reperfusion. Out-of-hospital sudden death is indicated by an asterisk. (From Kennedy *et al.*, 1983.)

*al.*, 1981) and averaged 4.8% in 640 patients from nine series. No patient died from bleeding or suffered major intracranial hemorrhage.

The risk of allergic reaction is posed by streptokinase infusion, since streptokinase is an antigenic protein. To prevent allergic complication, parenteral steroids (Rentrop *et al.*, 1981; Rogers *et al.*, 1983) or Benadryl (Reduto *et al.*, 1981) have been given with no reports of allergic reaction. The risk of allergic reaction, however, may be increased if the patient is reexposed to streptokinase within 6 to 12 months. This, along with antibody inactivation of streptokinase, limits the efficacy of the drug.

Finally, the risk of reperfusion arrhythmia accompanies intracoronary streptokinase. In most studies, lidocaine by bolus and/or infusion is generally begun prior to streptokinase and continued afterwards. Fortunately, ventricular tachycardia and ventricular fibrillation, occurring frequently with reperfusion in experimental animals (Sewell *et al.*, 1955), have not proven a serious problem in man and have not limited therapy. Reperfusion of an occluded right coronary artery has been reported to cause transient bradycardia and hypotension, apparently due to activation of the Bezold–Jurisch reflex, which is initiated by stimulation of

# 5. Thrombolytic Therapy

chemoreceptors of the inferior wall of the left ventricle, resulting in a vagally mediated bradycardia and hypotension (Esente *et al.*, 1983). Reperfusion of patients with an anterior myocardial infarction has been reported to result in a transient acclerated idioventricular rhythm which is usually well tolerated and does not result in hemodynamic impairment (Wei *et al.*, 1983).

## V. Intravenous Streptokinase

### A. Introduction

Although intracoronary administration of streptokinase has been shown to have a high rate of thrombolytic success to reduce mortality and salvage ischemic myocardium, it does require catheterization facilities and trained personnel, not available at many hospitals where acute myocardial infarctions are treated. Moreover, mobilization of support personnel and performqnce of the catheterization may delay administration of streptokinase by several hours, resulting in a greater loss of myocardial tissue. The use of intravenous administration of streptokinase, if safe and effective, would overcome these disadvantages.

High-dose, brief-duration intravenous steptokinase, given early in the course of an acute myocardial infarction, is simple to administer and could prove almost as effective as intracoronary streptokinase. No angiographic facilities or personnel are required, making possible rapid administration of thrombolytic therapy, thereby salvaging more myocardium. Earlier administration also increases the likelihood of successful recanalization. The high dose insures a high concentration of thrombolytic agent in the coronary circulation during the time of infusion, and the shorter thrombolytic state produced would allow for a more rapid recovery from its systemic effects, reducing the risk of bleeding complications.

### B. Frequency of Thrombolysis

Early reports showed that high-dose, brief-duration intravenous administration of streptokinase lysed coronary thrombus in acute myocardial infarction in 46 to 60% of patients (Rogers *et al.*, 1983; Schroder *et al.*, 1983; Taylor *et al.*, 1984; Spann *et al.*, 1982, 1984; Neuhaus *et al.*, 1983). Coronary angiography was performed on 276 patients before and after high-dose, brief-duration intravenous streptokinase (Table II). One hundred and seventy-eight of the 276 patients (65%) achieved coronary reperfusion.

**TABLE II**
Frequency of Reperfusion by Early, High-Dose, Brief Intravenous Streptokinase in Patients with Angiographic Proof

| Study | Number of patients | Number reperfused (%) |
|---|---|---|
| Neuhaus et al., 1983 | 40 | 24 (60%) |
| Rogers et al., 1983 | 16 | 7 (44%) |
| Schroder et al., 1983 | 21 | 11 (52%) |
| Schwarz et al., 1983 | 35 | 16 (46%) |
| Spann et al., 1984 | 43 | 21 (49%) |
| Taylor et al., 1984 | 121 | 99 (82%) |
| Total | 276 | 178 (65%) |

Data from our lab (Spann et al., 1982, 1984) are fairly typical of the results obtained. Coronary angiography was performed before and after intravenous streptokinase infusion as well as 9 to 14 days later. Ventricular function was studied by contrast ventriculography before, 9–14 days later, and at follow-up an average of 8 months later by radionuclide ventriculography. Forty-three patients received streptokinase (850,000 IU in 13 patients or 1,500,000 IU in 30 patients) by systemic intravenous infusion an average of 3.4 hr after the onset of symptoms.

In all patients who were successfully reperfused, a continuous infusion of heparin was maintained when the partial thromboplastin time (PTT) was 50 sec or less to keep the PTT at 1.5 times control values. At follow-up 9–14 days later, all patients who had persistent coronary reperfusion were maintained on oral anticoagulants.

Reperfusion of the occluded coronary artery within 1 hr of streptokinase infusion occurred in 21 of our 43 patients (49%). No serious reperfusion arrhythmias or serious bleeding occurred. Fifteen of those 21 patients, or 35% of the total, had sustained reperfusion 9–14 days later.

Two recent studies of intravenous streptokinase indicate that the rates of reperfusion may be higher than previously thought. Ganz et al. (1984) studied 81 consecutive patients presenting within 3 hr of the onset of acute myocardial infarction. The patients received 750,000 to 1,500,000 IU of streptokinase within 130 ± 41 minutes of symptoms. Reperfusion was recognized by indirect clinical criteria in 78 patients (96%), but, unfortunately, without angiographic proof. Taylor *et al.* (1984) studied a consecutive series of 184 patients. The first 63 patients were treated with intracoronary streptokinase and 44 (70%) had successful thrombolysis. The subsequent 121 patients received intravenous streptokinase immediately after the diagnosis of myocardial infarction and 99 (82%) had successful thrombolysis documented angiographically. Only 58% (14 of 24) of patients requiring transfer from out-of-town hospitals for intracoronary streptokinase treatment had successful thrombolysis while 85% (72 of 85) of patients receiving intravenous streptokinase in local hospitals had successful thrombolysis ($p = .005$). The authors concluded that intravenous streptokinase appeared to be at least as efficacious as intracoronary streptokinase in acute myocardial infarction. The higher rate of thrombolysis seen by Taylor *et al.* (1984) as compared to earlier studies of intravenous streptokinase may be due to the fact that patients were begun on therapy immediately after the diagnosis of acute myocardial infarction was made. In addition, coronary angiography was performed later than in previous studies, indicating that lysis may continue after the infusion of streptokinase is stopped. Further studies are needed to resolve these issues.

In the absence of coronary angiography, it may be difficult to determine with certainty whether reperfusion has occurred after intravenous streptokinase. Patients with early reperfusion have a peak CPK-MB earlier (generally 11–13 hr from onset of symptoms) than do patients without early reperfusion (generally 22–26 hr fron onset of symptoms) (Schroder *et al.*, 1983). There have been reports of early CPK peaks in patients not given streptokinase, however, representing possible spontaneous thrombolysis (Ong *et al.*, 1983). In our series, 18 patients in the reperfusion group had CPK-MB data. Fifteen had an early peak of CPK-MB 26 hr or more after onset. Eighteen patients in the nonreperfusion group had CPK-MB data. Ten had CPK-MB 13 hr or less after onset of symptoms and five had the peak of CPK-MB 26 hr or more after the onset of symptoms. Thus, not only may an early CPK-MB peak be due to spontaneous thrombolysis but may also be seen without thrombolysis. A CPK-MB peak in less than 13 hr may not indicate whether reperfusion was achieved in the individual patient.

Other clinical clues may be used to detect reperfusion. Sudden pain relief occurs in most patients who achieve reperfusion. Ventricular arrhythmias occur in some patients at the time of reperfusion. Rapid return of the ST segment elevation toward the baseline may occur in some patients at the time of reperfusion. When these clinical events occur within several hours after the intravenous infusion of streptokinase and if the CPK-MB values peak with the first 13 hr after the onset of symptoms, reperfusion should be considered probable.

## C. Dose of Intravenous Streptokinase

In early trials of intravenous streptokinase beginning in 1959, a loading dose of 250,000 IU followed by 100,000 IU for 12 to 24 hr was used (Simon et al., 1973; Stampfer et al., 1982). Since it rapidly became clear that, in order to salvage myocardium, early reperfusion was necessary, higher doses given over a short time supplanted a longer continuous infusion. Schroder et al. (1983) infused 500,000 IU of streptokinase to 21 patients within 30 min of the onset of symptoms. All patients had angiographically proven complete occlusion of a coronary artery. Eleven (52%) had reperfused within 1 hr. In the study by Rogers et al. (1983), however, only one of 10 (10%) patients receiving a 15-min infusion of 500,000 IU of streptokinase achieved reperfusion while seven of 16 (44%) patients receiving 1,000,000 IU of streptokinase achieved reperfusion. Neuhaus et al. (1983) reported use of the largest dose to date. Neuhaus et al. infused intravenous streptokinase at a rate of 30,000 to 40,000 IU/min for 30 to 75 min with an average total dose of $1.7 \pm 0.48$ million IU of streptokinase. The reperfusion rate was 60%. Reperfusion rates with larger than 1.7 million units have not been recorded.

In our study (Spann et al., 1982, 1984), 6 of 13 (46%) patients who received 850,000 IU of streptokinase reperfused in 1 hr. Fifteen of 30 patients (50%) who received 1,500,000 IU of streptokinase reperfused in 1 hour. Therefore, although the correct dosage is not yet known, it appears that a dose larger than 500,000 IU should be administered during a 1-hr infusion.

## D. Salvage of Jeopardized Myocardium by Early, High-Dose, Short-Duration Intravenous Streptokinase

Three of the six studies of high-dose, brief-duration, early intravenous streptokinase have reported data on ventricular function before and after streptokinase (Schroder et al., 1983; Spann et al., 1984; Neuhaus et al., 1983). Early and sustained reperfusion was associated with significant improvement of ventricular function in each study.

Schroder et al. (1983) found a significant improvement in regional segmental shortening in the infarct zone as determined by contrast ventriculography 4 weeks after infarction for patients in whom the involved coronary artery reopened. No significant change was observed in patients who were not reperfused. Neuhaus et al. (1983) also studied patients by repeat contrast ventriculography after acute infarction. There was a small increase in global left ventricular function in patients who demonstrated early reperfusion (55 ± 9% ejection fraction acutely to 58 ± 10% 14–24 days later) ($p < .1$), while in those patients who were not reperfused there was a significant drop in global left ventricular function (49 ± 11% ejection fraction acutely to 41 ± 11% 14–24 days later) ($p < .005$). When regional left ventricular function was examined, however, the number of akinetic segments decreased from 17 ± 11 to 13 ± 2 ($p < .02$) in those patients who demonstrated early reperfusion while the number of akinetic segments increased from 26 ± 13 to 33 ± 12 ($p < .05$) in those patients who did not demonstrate early reperfusion.

In our laboratory (Spann et al., 1984), we recently reported on 43 patients who received intravenous streptokinase within 6 hr of acute myocardial infarction. Ventricular function was determined by contrast ventriculography before and 9–14 days later and by radionuclide ventriculography at follow-up 8 months later. Left ventricular regional wall motion was analyzed in contrast ventriculograms by measurement of the percentage of systolic shortening of 66 equidistant hemicords extending perpendicularly from the midline of the ventricular long axis to the contrast border at the endocardium (Wolf et al., 1978). In the reperfused group, the mean shortening fraction of the ventricular hemicords in the initial infarction zone averaged 0.09 ± 0.01 early in infarction and was significantly improved to an average of 0.22 ± 0.03 9–14 days later ($p < .002$). In the nonreperfused group, the mean shortening fraction of the ventricular hemicords in the initial infarction zone did not change from an average of 0.08 ± 0.02 early in infarction and averaged 0.08 ± 0.01 9–14 days later (Fig. 8).

Eight patients in the reperfused group and 12 patients in the nonreperfused group received contrast ventriculography early in infarction and radionuclide ventriculography at follow-up, 10 and 7 months later, respectively. In the reperfused group, the extent of ventricle with depressed contraction averaged 49 ± 4% early in infarction and significantly improved to an average of 24 ± 7% at follow-up ($p < .02$). In the nonreperfused group there was no significant improvement in the extent of the ventricle with depressed contraction, 45 ± 6% early in infarction compared with 47 ± 9% at follow-up.

The above three studies (Schroder et al., 1983; Spann et al., 1984; Neuhaus et al., 1983) were nonrandomized investigations in which all patients received streptokinase. Therefore, it cannot be determined whether streptokinase was responsible in all instances for the rapid reperfusion or for the improvement in left ventricular function seen in all three studies. Randomized and controlled studies are required.

Whether early, brief-duration, high-dose intravenous streptokinase decreases the acute and long-term mortality in acute myocardial infarction

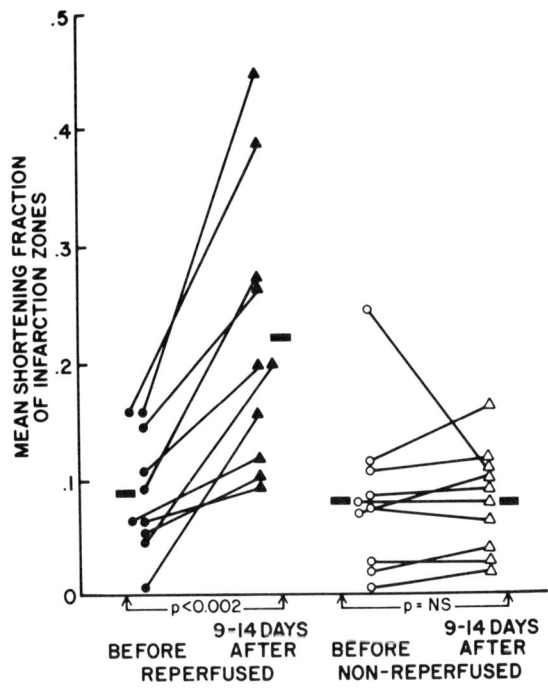

**Fig. 8.** Mean shortening fraction of the ventricular hemicords in the initial infarction zone (circles) and 9–14 days after (triangles) streptokinase infusion in the reperfused patients (closed symbols) and nonreperfused patients (open symbols). Bars indicate the average values. NS, not significant. (From Span et al., 1984.)

has, likewise, not been shown through a randomized and controlled study, although a major trial is currently going forward in 21 German and Swiss hospitals.

The assumption that coronary reperfusion is beneficial rather than harmful could be incorrect if areas of ischemic myocardium salvaged from infarction by reperfusion still remain severely ischemic. Residual ischemia, if present, might predispose the patient who has undergone successful coronary reperfusion to angina, recurrent infarction, arrhythmias, and sudden death. To test for the occurrence of these complications, we followed 41 of our patients for an average of 8 months. We found no increased incidence of death, repeat infarction, angina, or heart failure in the reperfusion group (Spann et al., 1984). We also measured radionuclide left ventricular ejection fractions at rest and during maximum supine bicycle exercise at late follow-up in eight patients in the reperfused group and twelve in the nonreperfused group. During maximum exercise the average left ventricular ejection fraction in the reperfused group increased, while in the nonreperfused group the average ejection fraction did not change during maximum exercise. These results suggest that severe residual ischemia was no more pronounced in patients with persistent reperfusion than in patients without reperfusion. Smalling *et al.* (1983) demonstrated persistent improvement in left ventricular performance and a lower cardiac mortality at 6-month follow-up in patients who achieved reperfusion by intracoronary streptokinase. We conclude that current data indicate no harmful long-term effects from coronary reperfusion and instead suggest long-term benefit.

### E. Risk of Intravenous Streptokinase

The major risk associated with intravenous streptokinase, like intracoronary streptokinase, is hemorrhage produced by the systemic lytic state. The incidence of bleeding complications in studies of intravenous streptokinase has not been different from their incidence in studies of intracoronary streptokinase. In five studies of intravenous streptokinase (Rogers *et al.*, 1983; Schwarz *et al.*, 1983; Neuhaus *et al.*, 1983; Schroder *et al.*, 1983; Spann *et al.*, 1984), the incidence of bleeding complications varied from 0% to 4% and averaged 0.8% of 237 patients. In a recent study by Ganz *et al.* (1984), 12.3% had major bleeding complications. Two elderly patients suffered intracranial hemorrhage. The increased incidence of bleeding complications as compared to the previous studies may have been due to the lack of the usual exclusionary criteria of age greater than 70 and hypertension as well as higher doses of heparin therapy maintaining the partial thromboplastin time (PTT) at greater than 100 seconds.

## VI. Management of Patients after Thrombolytic Therapy

### A. Reocclusion Following Thrombolysis

Lysis of an intracoronary thrombus with streptokinase reverses the immediate cause of coronary obstruction but does not alter the underlying coronary artery disease and does not remove the stimulus that produced the initial thrombus. Accordingly, it is not surprising that, if nothing is done to prevent rethrombosis, there is a very high early reocclusion rate, perhaps as high as 30% (Gold *et al.*, 1983). Several studies using serial coronary arteriography have documented the presence or absence of coronary reocclusion in patients who previously were treated with intracoronary streptokinase (Rentrop et al., 1981; Cribier et al., 1983; Schwarz et al., 1982b; Serruys et al., 1983). In three of these studies, all patients were treated with early heparin. The dose of heparin varied from study to study. The percentage of reocclusion at the time of the follow-up coronary angiogram 2–4 weeks later varied from 5% to 26% and averaged 17% in four studies (Rentrop et al., 1981; Cribier et al., 1983; Schwarz et al., 1982b, Serruys et al., 1983).

Four studies have utilized serial coronary angiography to document the presence of coronary reocclusion in patients who were treated previously with early, high-dose intravenous streptokinase (Rogers et al., 1983; Schroder et al., 1983; Spann et al., 1984; Neuhaus et al., 1983). Again, most patients were treated with early heparin therapy and three of the four series followed up with coumadin as well. The percentage reocclusion at the second coronary angiogram 2–4 weeks later varied from 9% to 29% and averaged 18%, which is very similar to data seen after intracoronary streptokinase. Six of 78 patients reoccluded within 24 hr. Three of these six patients with early reocclusion were successfully treated by repeat administration of intravenous streptokinase.

## B. Management of the Underlying Coronary Artery Disease

Management of the underlying coronary artery disease after successful thrombolysis is an area requiring additional research. The percent of stenosis of the infarction coronary artery remaining after thrombolysis varies widely from patient to patient. Although most patients have residual high-grade lesions, a significant number have less than 60% diameter reduction, judged by visual estimation (Rogers et al., 1983) and less than a 50% diameter reduction, judged by computer-assisted measurement of arterial segment diameter (Serruys et al., 1983). Rogers et al. (1983) noted reocclusion only in vessels with 90% or greater stenosis after thrombolysis. Serruys et al. (1983), by computer-assisted measurement, reported that 31% of patients had a stenosis of less than 50% and only 19% had a stenosis of greater than 70%. Reocclusion was observed in repeat coronary angiography 2 weeks later in 11 patients, while eight other patients displayed clinical evidence of reocclusion in the same myocardial territory. Seventeen of these 19 patients with either angiographically proven or clinically evidenced reperfusion had a stenosis of 58% or more. Computer-assisted measurement of arterial segment diameter technically may give a smaller diameter, thereby explaining the difference between Rogers' finding of reocclusion in patients with 90% or greater stenosis while Serruys found restenosis in patients with a 58% or greater lesion.

In response to the observed frequent reocclusion in lesions of 58% or more, Serruys et al. (1983) performed transluminal coronary angioplasty immediately after successful thrombolysis in 18 patients in whom the stenosis averaged 59%, decreasing stenosis from 59 to 30%. Late follow-up showed reocclusion in only one of these 18 patients. These authors concluded that, although coronary angioplasty is not mandatory in the majority of patients, it is feasible, safe, and seems to prevent reocclusion in patients with high-grade residual stenosis following thrombolysis. Several other studies have found a similar success rate in Percutaneous Transluminal Coronary Angioplasty (PTCA) after successful thrombolytic therapy (Meyer *et al.*, 1982; Papapietro *et al.*, 1983) although further studies are needed before clear-cut clinical guidelines are available.

Coronary artery bypass grafting has also been reported safely employed following streptokinase therapy (Ganz *et al.*, 1983; Messmer *et al.*, 1983; Swan, 1982). In our series (Spann *et al.*, 1984), three patients underwent early coronary bypass surgery 2, 4, and 12 days after streptokinase infusion without operative mortality. Mathey *et al.* (1981) reported on 48 patients with successful thrombolysis and high-grade residual stenosis. Thirty-four patients underwent coronary artery bypass grafting within 10 days of onset of myocardial infarction, while 14 patients underwent successful surgery longer than 10 days after onset of myocardial infarction. Among the 34 patients receiving coronary artery bypass surgery within 10 days of acute myocardial infarction, no patient died. Of the patients with coronary artery bypass grafting later than 10 days after acute myocardial infarction, two died and two had nonfatal reinfarction several months later. Forty-one of the patients were asymptomatic during long-term follow-up.

## VII. Future Directions

Streptokinase is an indirect activator of plasminogen that not only lyses fresh fibrin clots but also produces a systemic lytic state with the ability to prevent formation of additional clots, in addition to having the ability to degrade existing hemostatic plugs. Infusion of a tissue-type plasminogen activator, however, would theoretically only initiate fibrinolysis on the surface of a thrombus and would not digest other plasma proteins essential to normal hemostasis, thus avoiding a systemic lytic state (Collen and Verstraete, 1983). A more specific lysis of the coronary clot could result, with less risk of bleeding complications.

Tissue-type plasminogen activator has been produced from human melanoma tissue cultures (Collen *et al.*, 1982). Using this clot-selective lytic agent, Bergmann *et al.* (1983) demonstrated rapid lysis of an experimentally produced intracoronary thrombus in dogs. In the dog, clot lysis was achieved by either intracoronary or intravenous administration without systemic fibrinolysis. Van de Werf *et al.* (1984) reported successful thrombolysis in six of seven patients with acute myocardial infarction using tissue-type plasminogen activator. Pennicka *et al.* (1983) have synthesized and cloned the human tissue-type plasminogen activator gene, permitting production of large quantities of activator. Gold *et al.* (1983) and Van de Werf *et al.* (1983) have produced coronary thrombolysis using recombinant human tissue-type plasminogen activator without significant systemic fibrinolysis in dogs. The National Heart, Lung, and Blood Institute, on June 1, 1984, will begin a multicenter trial to compare tissue-type plasminogen activator with intravenous streptokinase in acute myocardial infarction. If the results of earlier studies are borne out, a highly effective, specific thrombolytic agent will be available in the future which may make the safe, early, systemic therapy of myocardial infarction a practical reality.

## References

Anderson, J. L., Marshall, H. W., Bray, B. E., Lutz, J. R., Frederick, P. R., Yanowitz, F. G., Datz, F. L., Klausner, S. C., and Hagan, A. D. (1983). *New England Journal of Medicine* **308,** 1312–1318.

Bergmann, S. R., Fox, K. A. A., Collen, D., and Sobel, B. E. (1983). *Journal of the American College of Cardiology* **1,** 615.

Branwood, A. W., and Montgomery, G. L. (1956). *Scot. Med. J.* **1,** 367–375.

Braunwald, E., and Kloner, R. A. (1982). *Circulation* **66,** 1146–1149.

Chandler, A. B. (1974). *Thromb. Res.* **4,** I (Suppl.), 3–23.

Chazov, E. I., Mateeva, L. S., Mazaev, A. V., Sargin, K. E., Sadooskaga, M., and Ruda, Y. (1976). *Ter. Arkh.* **48,** 8–19.

Collen, D., and Verstraete, M. (1983). *Circulation* **68,** 462–265.

Collen, D., Rijken, D. C., VanDamme, J., and Billiau, A. (1982). *Thrombosis and Haemostasis* **48,** 294.

Cowley, M. J., Hastillo, A., and Vetrovec, G. W. (1983). *Circulation* **67,** 1031–1038.

Cribier, A., Berland, J., Champoud, O., Moore, N., Behar, P., and Letac, B. (1983). *British Heart Journal* **50,** 401–410.

DeWood, M. A., Spores, J., Notske, R., Mouser, L. T., Burroughs, R., Golden, M. S., and Lang, H. T. (1981). *New England Journal of Medicine* **303,** 897–902.

Ellis, S. G., Henschke, C. I., and Sandor, T. (1983). *J. Am. Coll. Cardiol.* **1,** 1047–1055.

Esente, P., Giambartolomei, A., and Gensini, G. G. (1983). *Am. J. Cardiol.* **52,** 221–224.

European Cooperative Study Group for Streptokinase Treatment in Acute Myocardial Infarction. (1979). *New England Journal of Medicine* **301,** 797–801.

Fletcher, A. P., Sherry, S., Alkjaersig, N., Smyrniotis, F. E., and Jick, S. (1959). *Journal of Clinical Investigation* **38,** 1111–1119.

Friedberg, C. K., and Horn, H. (1939). *JAMA* **112,** 1675–1679.
Ganz, W., Buchbinder, N., Marcus, H., Mondkar, A., Maddahi, J., Charuzi, Y., O'Connor, L., Shell, W., Fishbein, M. C., Kass, R., Miyamoto, A., and Swan, H. J. C. (1981). *American Heart Journal* **101,** 4–13.
Ganz, W., Geft, I., and Maddahi, J. (1983). *J. Am. Coll. Cardiol.* **1,** 1247–1253.
Ganz, W., Geft, I., Shaw, P. K., Lew, A. S., Rodriguez, L., Weiss, T., Maddahi, J., Bermen, D. S., Cheruzi, Y., and Swann, H. J. C. (1984). *AJC* **53,** 1209–1216.
Ginks, W. R., Syhers, H. D., Maroko, P. R., Covell, J. W., Sobell, B. E., and Ross, J. J. R. (1972). *J. Clin. Invest.* **51,** 2717–2723.
Gold, H. K., Fallon, J. T., Yasuda, T., Khaw, B. A., Guerrero, J. L., Vislosky, J. M., Leinbach, R. C., Harper, R., Hoyng, C., Grossbard, E., and Collen, D. (1983). *Circulation* **68,** (Suppl), 111–38.
Herrick, J. B. (1912). *JAMA* **59,** 2015.
Kennedy, J. W., Ritchie, J. L., Davis, K. B., and Fritz, J. K. (1983). *New England Journal of Medicine* **309,** 1477–1482.
Khaja, F., Walton, J. A., Brymer, J. F., Lo, E., Osterberger, L., O'Neill, W. W., Colfer, H. T., Weiss, R., Lee, T., Kurian, T., Goldberg, A. D., Pitt, B., and Goldstein, S. (1983). *New England Journal of Medicine* **308,** 1305–1311.
Marder, V. J. (1979). *Annals of Internal Medicine* **90,** 802–808.
Marder, V. J., Soulen, R. L., and Atichartakarn, U. (1977). *J. Lab. Clin. Med.* **89,** 1018–1029.
Markis, J. E., Malagold, M., Parker, A., Silverman, K. J., Barry, W. H., Als, A. V., Paulin, S., Grossman, W., and Braunwald, E. (1981). *New England Journal of Medicine* **305,** 777–782.
Mathey, D. G., Kuck, K.-H., Tilsner, V., Krebber, H.-J., and Bleifeld, W. (1981). *Circulation* **63,** 489–498.
Merx, W., Dorr, R., Rentrop, P., Blanke, H., Karsch, K. R., Mathey, D. G., Kremer, P., Rutsch, W., and Schmutzler, H. (1981). *American Heart Journal* **102,** 1181–1187.
Messmer, B. J., Merx, W., Meyer, J., Bardos, P., Minale, C., and Effert, S. (1983). *Annals of Thoracic Surgery* **35,** 70–78.
Meyer, J., Merx, W., and Schmitz, H. (1982). *Circulation* **66,** 905–913.
Miller, R. D., Burchell, H. B., and Edwards, J. E. (1951). *Arch. Int. Medicine* **88,** 597–604.
Neuhaus, K. L., Tebbe, U., Sauer, G., Kreuzer, H., and Kostering, H. (1983). *Clinical Cardiology* **6,** 426–434.
Nygaard, T. W., Gibson, R. S., Craddock, G. B., Sirowatka, J., Crampton, R. S., and Beller, G. A. (1983). *Journal of the American College of Cardiology* (Abst.) **1,** 579.
Ong, L., Reiser, P., Coromilas, J., Scherr, L., and Morrison, J. (1983). *New England Journal of Medicine* **309,** 1–6.
Papapietro, S. E., MacLean, W. A. H., and Stanley, A. W. H., Jr. (1983). *J. Am. Coll. Cardiol.* **1,** 580.
Pennica, D., Holmes, W. E., Kohr, W. J., Harkins, R. N., Vehar, G. A., Ward, C. A., Bennett, W. F., Yelverton, E., Seeburg, P. H., Heyneker, H. L., Goeddel, D. V., and Collen, D. (1983). *Nature* **301,** 214–222.
Reduto, L. A., Freund, G. C., Gaeta, J. M., Smalling, R. W., Lewis, B., and Gould, K. L. (1981). *American Heart Journal* **102,** 1168–1177.
Rentrop, K. P., Blanke, H., Kostering, K., and Karsch, K. R. (1979). *Clinical Cardiology* **2,** 354–363.
Rentrop, K. P., Blanke, H., Karsch, K. R., Kaiser, H., Kostering, H., and Leitz, K. (1981). *Circulation* **63,** 307–317.
Rentrop, K. P., Blanke, H., and Karsch, K. R. (1982). *Am. J. Cardiol.* **49,** 1–8.

Rentrop, K. P., Smith, H., and Painter, L. (1983). *Circulation* **68** (Suppl. I), 55–60.
Roberts, R. (1980). *Circulation* **61**, 458–459.
Rogers, W. J., Mantle, J. A., Hood, W. P., Baxley, W. A., Whitlow, P. L., Reevers, R. C., and Soto, B. (1983). *Circulation* **68**, 1051–1061.
Rude, R. E., Muller, J. E., and Braunwald, E. (1981). *Ann. Intern. Med.* **95**, 736–761.
Schroder, R., Biamino, G., Enz-Rudiger, L., Linderer, T., Bruggemann, T., Heitz, J., Vohringer, H.-F., and Wegscheider, K. (1983). *Circulation* **63**, 536–548.
Schuler, G., Schwarz, F., Hofmann, M., Mehmel, H., Manthey, J., Maurer, W., Rauch, B., Herrmann, H.-J., and Kubler, W. (1983). *Circulation* **66**, 658–664.
Schwartz, C. J., Chandler, A. B., and Gerrity, R. G. (1978). *In* "The Thrombotic Process in Atherogenesis" (A. B. Chandler, K. Eurenius, and G. C. McMillan, eds.), pp. 111–126. Plenum Publishing Corp, New York.
Schwarz, F., Schuler, G., Katus, H., Mehmel, H. C., von Olshausen, K., Hofmann, M., Hermann, H.-J., and Kubler, W. (1982a). *American Journal of Cardiology* **50**, 32–38.
Schwarz, F., Schuler, G., Katus, H., Hofmann, M., Manthey, J., Tillmanns, H., Mehmel, H. C., and Kubler, W. (1982b). *American Journal of Cardiology* **50**, 933–937.
Schwarz, F., Hoffmann, M., Schuler, G., and Kubler, W. (1983). *Journal of the American College of Cardiology* (Abst) 1–615.
Serruys, P. W., Wigns, W., van den Brand, M., Ribeiro, V., Fioretti, P., Simoons, M. L., Kooijman, C. J., Reiber, H. J. C., and Hugenholz, P. G. (1983). *British Heart Journal* **50**, 257–265.
Sewell, W. H., Koth, D. R., and Huggins, C. E. (1955). *Surgery* **38**, 1050–1053.
Sheehan, F. H., Mathey, D. G., Shofer, J., Krebber, H.-J., and Dodge, H. T. (1983). *American Journal of Cardiology* **52**, 431–438.
Simon, T. L., Ware, J. H., and Stengle, J. M. (1973). *Annals of Internal Medicine* **307**, 1178–1179.
Smalling, R. W., Fuentes, R., Matthews, M. W., Freund, G. C., Hicks, C. H., Reduto, L. A., Walker, W. E., Sterling, R. P., and Gould, K. L. (1983). *Circulation* **63**, 131–138.
Sommers, H. M., and Jennings, R. D. (1964). *Lab. Invest.* **13**, 1491–1503.
Spann, J. F., and Sherry, S. (1984). *Drugs* **28**, 462–483.
Spann, J. F., Sherry, S., Carabello, R. A., Mann, R. H., McCann, W. D., Gault, J. H., Gentzler, R. D., Rosenberg, K. C., Maurer, A. H., Denenberg, B. S., Warner, H. F., Rubin, R. N., Malmud, L. S., and Comerota, A. (1982). *American Heart Journal* **104**, 939–945.
Spann, J. F., Sherry, S., Carabello, B. A., Denenberg, B. S., Mann, R. H., McCann, W. D., Gault, J. H., Gentzler, R. D., Belber, A. D., Maurer, A. H., and Cooper, E. M. (1984). *American Journal of Cardiology* **53**, 655–661.
Stack, R. S., Phillips, H. R., Grierson, D. S., Behar, V. S., Kong, Y., Peter, R. H., Swain, J. L., and Greenfield, J. C. (1983). *Journal of Clinical Investigation* **72**, 84–95.
Stampfer, M. J., Goldhaber, S. Z., Yusuf, S., Peto, R., and Hennekens, C. H. (1982). *New England Journal of Medicine* **307**, 1178–1179.
Swan, H. J. C. (1982). *Circulation* **66**, 914–915.
Swan, H. J. C. (1983). *New England Journal of Medicine* **308**, 1354–1355.
Taylor, G. J., Mikell, F. L., Moses, H. W., Dove, J. T., Batchelder, J. E., Thull, A., Hansen, S., Wellons, H. A., Jr., and Schneider, J. A. (1984). *American Journal of Cardiology* **54**, 256–260.
Urokinase Pulmonary Embolism Trial: A National Cooperative Study. (1973). *Circulation* **47** (American Heart Association Monograph No. 30), 1–108.
Van de Werf, R., Bergmann, S. R., Fox, A. A., DeGeest, H., Sobel, B. E., and Collen, D. (1983). *Circulation* (Abst.) **68** (Suppl.), 111–185.

Van de Werf, R., Ludbrook, P. A., Bergmann, S. R., Tiefenbrunn, A. J., Fox, K. A. A., de Geest, H., Verstaete, M., Collen, D., and Sobel, B. E. (1984). *New England Journal of Medicine* **310,** 609–613.
Vatner, S. F., Baig, H., and Manders, W. T. (1978). *J. Clin. Invest.* **61,** 1048–56.
Wei, J. Y., Markis, J. E., and Malagold, M. (1983). *Circulation* **67,** 796–801.
Wolf, N. M., Kreulen, T. H., Bove, A. A., McDonough, M. T., Kessler, K. M., Strong, M., LeMole, G., and Spann, J. F. (1978). *Circulation* **58,** 63–70.

# 6 Electrophysiology of Ventricular Arrhythmias in Myocardial Infarction

## Nabil El-Sherif

## I. Introduction

Ventricular tachycardia and ventricular fibrillation are serious complications of myocardial infarction and ischemic heart disease, the most prevalent form of heart disease in the United States. Different electrophysiological mechanisms may give rise to ischemia-related ventricular arrhythmias. A better understanding of these mechanisms will provide a basis for improved management. More precise information on the mechanisms of ischemia-related ventricular arrhythmias is difficult to obtain from clinical electrophysiological studies because of the limitations on the experimental protocols and techniques that can be utilized. This information could be obtained, however, from successful extrapolations from experimental studies on appropriate animal models to humans. In this chapter the electrophysiological mechanisms of ventricular arrhythmias in general will be outlined, followed by discussion of the mechanisms involved in ischemia-related ventricular arrhythmias.

## II. Electrophysiological Mechanisms of Ventricular Arrhythmias

Ventricular arrhythmias can be caused by either pacemaker activity or reentrant excitation. Each of these two main mechanisms has subclasses (Table I). Pacemaker activity occurs when a cell or a group of closely knit cells result in impulse generation. The mechanism can be normal automatic activity, abnormal automatic activity, or triggered activity (Hoffman and Rosen, 1981). Abnormal automaticity differs from normal automaticity in that it occurs at a level of transmembrane potential considerably less negative than the normal maximum diastolic potential

**TABLE I**
Electrophysiological Mechanisms of Ventricular Arrhythmias

A. Pacemaker activity
   1. Normal automatic activity
   2. Abnormal automatic activity
   3. Triggered activity
      a. Early afterdepolarizations
      b. Delayed afterdepolarizations
   4. Oscillatory depolarizations of membrane potential
B. Reentrant excitation
   1. Circus movement reentry
      a. The ring model
      b. The figure-eight model
      c. The leading circle model
   2. Reflection

or normal resting potential of the fibers involved. Triggered activity differs from both normal and abnormal automaticity in that it requires a prior impulse for initiation. Triggered activity is further subdivided into activity rising from early or delayed afterdepolarizations (Cranefield, 1975). A fourth, less well understood, subclass of pacemaker activity is oscillatory depolarizations of membrane potential. On the other hand, reentrant excitation occurs when the propagating impulse does not die out after complete activation of the heart, as is normally the case, but persists to reexcite the atria or ventricles after the end of the refractory period (Wit and Cranefield, 1979). Reentrant excitation can be subdivided into circus movement excitation and reflection. In circus movement reentry, the activation wave front encounters a site of unidirectional conduction block and propagates in a circuitous pathway before reexciting the tissue proximal to the site of block after expiration of its refractory period. By contrast, in the reflection model of reentrant excitation impulse transmission in both directions is over the same pathway (Antzelevitch *et al.*, 1980).

## A. Pacemaker Activity

### 1. Normal Automatic Activity

Automatic activity is caused by a gradual fall in membrane potential during diastole until it reaches threshold potential and generates an action potential. The diastolic depolarization is believed to result from an outward pacemaker current carried by $K^+$ which gradually declines, thereby allowing the background inward $Na^+$ current to depolarize the cell membrane (Vassalle, 1965; Trautwein, 1973). A recently proposed alternative mechanism suggests that an inward $Na^+$ pacemaker current ($I_f$) increases with time while the outward $K^+$ current remains constant (DiFrancisco, 1981a,b). Automaticity is a normal property of the sinus node, some atrial fibers, the A–V junction, and the His–Purkinje system. The rate of His–Purkinje automaticity is rather slow (Fig. 1A) and characteristically decreases in a hierarchical fashion from the proximal His–Purkinje system to the distal Purkinje network. Normal His–Purkinje automaticity can account for some slow ventricular escape rhythms. However, it is difficult to envision that normal His–Purkinje automatic activity results in ventricular premature beats or ventricular tachycardia. This is especially so if one remembers that normal His–Purkinje automatic activity is constantly being overdrive-suppressed by the much faster supraventricular automatic activity (Vassalle, 1977). It is possible, however, that local release of norepinephrine from sympathetic nerves results in enhancement of the rate of normal His–Purkinje automatic activity (Tsien, 1974), allowing an ectopic pacemaker to reach threshold before being activated by the

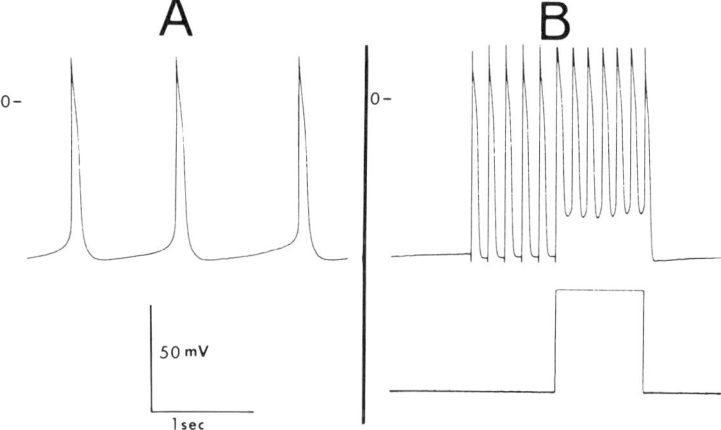

**Fig. 1.** (A) Normal automaticity in a canine Purkinje fiber with a maximum diastolic potential of $-85$ mV. Note the slow diastolic depolarization and the slow rate of automatic firing (9–12 beats per min). (B) Abnormal automaticity induced in a canine Purkinje fiber when the resting potential was reduced from $-78$ to $-56$ mV by the injection of a long-lasting current pulse through a suction electrode. The first six action potentials were stimulated. When the fiber was depolarized, six nonstimulated action potentials occurred. When the membrane potential was brought back to the more negative level, abnormal automatic activity terminated.

supraventricular impulse. It is also possible that entrance block can protect a slow normal His–Purkinje automatic focus from premature discharge by the supraventricular pacemaker, thus creating a parasystolic rhythm (Jalife and Moe, 1976). In this case, the ectopic discharge will capture the ventricles if it falls outside the effective refractory period.

### 2. Abnormal Automatic Activity

Impulses may be generated spontaneously by fibers in which the maximum diastolic potential has been reduced by a variety of interventions. This abnormal automaticity at a low level of diastolic potential has been demonstrated in both Purkinje and myocardial fibers (Hauswirth et al., 1969; Imanishi and Surawicz, 1976; Katzung and Morgenstern, 1977). The example studied most frequently is provided by Purkinje fibers in which the maximum diastolic potential has been decreased by experimental intervention in the range of $-50$ to $-60$ mV (Fig. 1B). A likely cause of automaticity at membrane potentials of around $-50$ mV is deactivation of a $K^+$ current called $ix_i$ (Noble and Tsien, 1968). Because of the low level of membrane potential, action potential upstrokes of abnormal automaticity are dependent on slow inward current (Cranefield, 1975). It is possible that the reduced diastolic potential at which abnormal automaticity occurs might cause entrance block in the focus, thus creating a parasystolic rhythm (Ferrier and Rosenthal, 1980). Unlike normal automaticity, abnormal automaticity may not be overdrive-suppressed (Hoffman and Dangman, 1982). It is therefore easier for an abnormal automatic rhythm to capture the ventricle following a brief transient slowing of the supraventricular rhythm.

### 3. Triggered Activity

Triggered activity is a pacemaker activity caused by afterdepolarizations. An afterdepolarization is a second subthreshold depolarization that occurs either during repolarization (early afterdepolarization) or after repolarization is complete (delayed afterdepolarization) (Cranefield, 1977).

*a. Early Afterdepolarizations.* Early afterdepolarizations occur when the fiber fails to repolarize completely after generating an action potential upstroke. As the membrane potential lingers at intermediate values, oscillatory depolarizations can occur (Fig. 2). Once early afterdepolarizations occur, they can attain threshold and initiate another response. Sometimes the response is followed by complete repolarization and sometimes the first abnormal response is followed by repetitive depolarizations at reduced levels of membrane potential. Early afterdepolar-

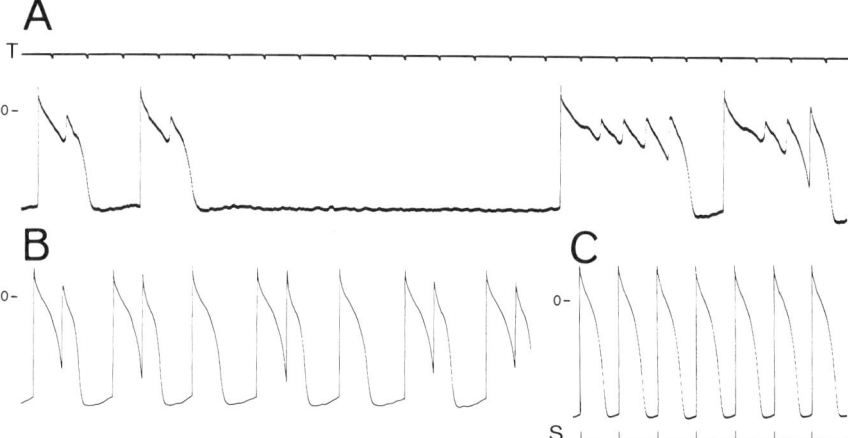

**Fig. 2.** Triggered activity due to early afterdepolarizations in canine Purkinje fibers exposed to anthopleurin-A in a concentration of 100 µg/ml. The drug resulted in prolongation of the action potential duration and the appearance of upstrokes arising from early afterdepolarizations. Following a long diastolic interval (A) the action potential duration became markedly prolonged and a burst of rhythmic activity arising from a low level of membrane potential occurred. Action potentials arising from early afterdepolarization resulted in bigeminal and trigeminal rhythms (B). In (C), the preparation was paced at short cycle lengths, which resulted in shortening of the action potential duration and the disappearance of early afterdepolarizations. This illustrates the bradycardia-dependent nature of the early afterdepolarizations. S denotes the timing of stimulation. The time scale (T) represents 1-sec intervals.

izations can occur if $K^+$ conductance is decreased relative to the conductance of the inward current (Noble and Tsien, 1968). Many types of experimental interventions have been shown to cause early afterdepolarizations (Cranefield, 1975) including marked and abrupt reduction of $[K^+]_o$ (Gadsby and Cranefield, 1977), high concentration of catecholamines (Brooks *et al.*, 1955), and a number of drugs. Experimental drugs such as aconitine (Schmidt, 1950; Matsuda *et al.*, 1981) cause early afterdepolarizations, probably by increasing steady-state $Na^+$ conductance during the plateau phase of the action potential. Figure 2 shows that another experimental drug, anthopleurin-A (AP-A), a polypeptide extracted from a sea anemone, can also prolong action potential duration and induce early afterdepolarizations. Voltage clamp experiments suggest that AP-A causes delayed inactivation of the fast $Na^+$ current (Low *et al.*, 1979). Cesium is another experimental drug that prolongs action potential duration and causes early afterdepolarizations (Brachmann *et al.*, 1983). Cesium has not been shown to enhance an inward current but it is possible that the normal noninactivated $Na^+$ current is sufficient to cause afterdepolarizations if repolarization is sufficiently delayed and outward currents are blocked (Brachmann et al., 1983).

Other clinically used drugs that markedly prolong the time course for repolarization, such as the beta receptor blocking drug sotalol (Strauss et al., 1970) and the antiarrhythmic drugs N-acetyl procainamide (Dangman and Hoffman, 1981) and quinidine (Roden et al., 1985), also cause early afterdepolarizations and triggered activity. This mechanism may explain the multiform ventricular tachycardia (Torsades de Pointes) that is occasionally reported in patients with procainamide or quinidine toxicity associated with prolongation of the QT interval (Krikler and Curry, 1976). As shown in Fig. 2, both the prolongation of action potential duration and the occurrence of early afterdepolarizations caused by AP-A are characteristically bradycardia dependent, that is, they are more pronounced at long cycle lengths (Fig. 2A) and are markedly attenuated or abolished at short cycle lengths (Fig. 2C). The same phenomenon has been shown for the experimental drug cesium (Brachmann et al., 1983) as well as for the clinical drug quinidine (Roden et al., 1985) and may provide a mechanism for bradycardia-dependent ventricular arrhythmias seen in the setting of acute myocardial infarction and in patients with high-grade atrioventricular block (Schwartz, 1936; Langendorf and Pick, 1964). Ventricular premature beats arising from early afterdepolarizations should characteristically exhibit close coupling to the preceding beats and represent one possible mechanism for the R-on-T phenomenon.

*b. Delayed Afterdepolarizations.* Delayed afterdepolarizations occur after phase 3 repolarization has restored maximum diastolic potential to a value that usually is somewhat less than normal. Triggered activity occurs when a delayed afterdepolarization attains threshold potential and terminates following a subthreshold afterdepolarization (Fig. 3). The amplitude and rate of rise of the delayed afterdepolarization are usually a function of both the cycle length and number of preceding action potentials (Rosen et al., 1973; Ferrier et al., 1973; Ferrier, 1976; Wit and Cranefield, 1976, 1977; Aronson, 1981; El-Sherif et al., 1983a) (Fig. 3A). Premature stimulation could also enhance the amplitude of delayed afterdepolarization (Wit and Cranefield, 1977; El-Sherif et al., 1983a). A critically timed premature impulse can be followed by a delayed afterdepolarization that reaches threshold and initiates triggered activity (Fig. 3B). The oscillatory current responsible for delayed afterdepolarizations may be normally present in Purkinje cells and can be enhanced by interventions that increase $[Ca^{2+}]_i$ (Vassalle and Mugelli, 1981). A model that has emerged describing the ionic mechanism responsible for delayed afterdepolarizations suggests one phenomenon common to all preparations exhibiting delayed afterdepolarizations: there is an increase in $[Ca^{2+}]_i$.

6. Electrophysiology of Ventricular Arrhythmias

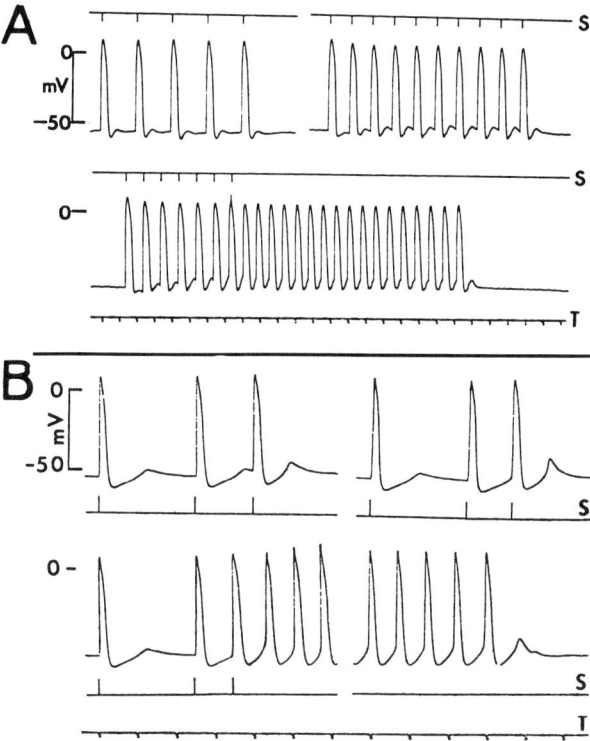

**Fig. 3.** Triggered activity arising from delayed afterdepolarizations in endocardial preparations obtained from 1-day-old canine infarctions. (A and B) Transmembrane recordings from Purkinje cells in the ischemic zone from two different preparations. In (A), the preparation was stimulated at cycle lengths of 2000 msec, 1200 msec, and 1000 msec, respectively. Reduction of the cycle length of stimulation resulted in an increase of the amplitude of the afterdepolarization that reached threshold and initiated triggered activity in the lower recording. The triggered rhythm terminated following a subthreshold delayed afterdepolarization. In (B), the effect of premature stimulation on the amplitude of the delayed afterdepolarization is demonstrated. The preparation was paced at a basic cycle length of 2500 msec. The coupling interval of the premature stimulus was shortened from 1500 msec to 1200 msec to 1000 msec, respectively. This resulted in an increase of the amplitude of the afterdepolarization that reached threshold following the short coupling interval and initiated a triggered rhythm. The rhythm terminated following a subthreshold afterdepolarization. S denotes the timing of stimulation. The time scale (T) represents 1-sec intervals. (Modified from El-Sherif et al., 1983a.)

This could be accomplished directly by increasing $[Ca^{2+}]_o$ and thereby increasing the driving force for calcium or by increasing calcium influx by increasing calcium conductance with catecholamines (Grossman and Furchgott, 1964; Reuter and Scholz, 1977). Indirect increases of $[Ca^{2+}]_i$ occur as a result of inhibiting the $(Na^+,K^+)$-ATPase by digitalis (Lee and

Klaus, 1971) with K-free solutions (Goto *et al.,* 1978) and with Na-free solutions (Reuter and Seitz, 1968; Cranefield and Aronson, 1974). When $[Ca^{2+}]_i$ is sufficiently large, subsequent action potentials initiate oscillatory calcium movements intracellularly, which in turn cause an oscillatory change in membrane conductance that permits a transient inward current (Tsien and Carpenter, 1978; Kass *et al.,* 1978a,b).

In contrast to extrasystoles based on early afterdepolarizations, those resulting from delayed afterdepolarizations should characteristically occur after the end of the T wave, resulting in late coupled ectopic beats.

### 4. *Oscillatory Depolarizations of Membrane Potential*

Spontaneous impulses may arise from oscillatory changes in transmembrane potential that appear to differ from normal phase 4 depolarization (Fig. 4). This mechanism may not be different from delayed afterdepolarizations (Hoffman and Rosen, 1981). However, in contrast to a series of delayed afterdepolarizations that decrease progressively in size like a damped oscillation, oscillatory depolarizations may progressively increase in size, reach threshold, and initiate an action potential. Figure 4 illustrates both types of oscillatory potentials as well as action potentials probably generated by early afterdepolarizations recorded from the same endocardial preparation, obtained from a 1-day-old canine infarction. The figure helps to emphasize the possibility that more than one mechanism for impulse generation may contribute to the arrhythmias that follow myocardial ischemia and infarction.

### B. Reentrant Excitation

#### 1. *Circus Movement Reentry*

*a. The Ring Model of Reentry.* Early experimental observations of Mayer (1908), Garrey (1914), and Mines (1913, 1914) have shown the existence of an entrapped circuit wave (circus contractions or movement) in rings of living cardiac and other tissue cut from a variety of animals including mammals (Fig. 5A). The presence of a fixed anatomical obstacle was considered an important requirement for the occurrence of circus movement. Whether these experiments are related to human cardiac arrhythmias is the hypothesis, first proposed by Mines. Guided by Mines' observations in rings of muscle, Thomas Lewis (1925; Lewis *et al.,* 1920) tried to prove that the atrial flutter wave circulated around a natural opening in the muscles of the auricle (the vena cavae). Schmitt and Erlanger (1928–1929) suggested that a loop composed of a branching pe-

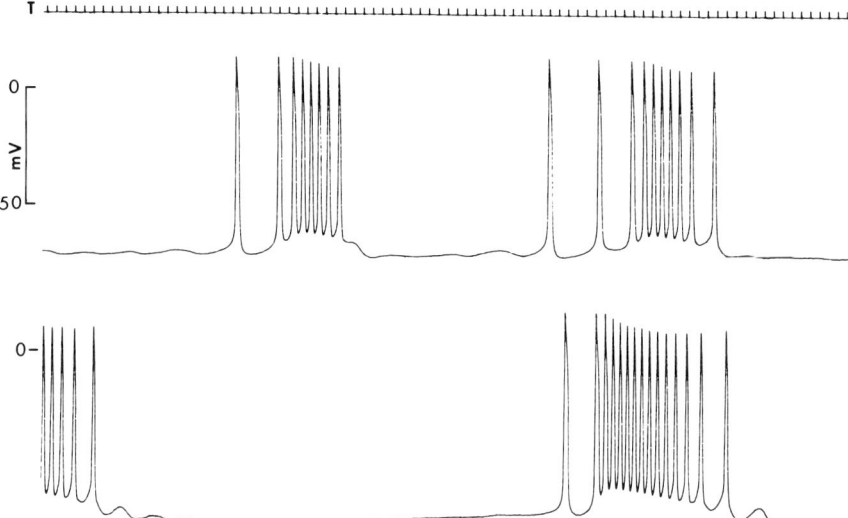

**Fig. 4.** Oscillatory depolarizations of membrane potential. Transmembrane recording from a Purkinje cell in the ischemic zone of an endocardial preparation from a 1-day-old canine infarction. These endocardial preparations commonly show triggered activity arising from delayed afterdepolarizations. The recording was obtained after the preparation was exposed to the calcium-blocking drug verapamil to suppress triggered activity and then to increased extracellular calcium (8.1 m$M$) to reverse the effects of verapamil. Note the presence of two types of oscillatory depolarizations of the membrane potential: those that follow the last action potential in a series of group beats decrease progressively in size like a damped oscillation while those that precede the first action potential progressively increase in size and seem to reach threshold and initiate the action potential. The second action potential in each series of group beats may be generated by a delayed afterdepolarization. However, the action potentials that follow arise before complete repolarization of the preceding action potential and may represent triggered activity from early afterdepolarizations. This activity gradually slows before termination associated with gradual increase of the maximum diastolic potential. The figure illustrates the possibility that more than one mechanism for impulse generation may contribute to the arrhythmias that follow myocardial ischemia and infarction. The time scale (T) represents 1-sec intervals.

ripheral Purkinje fiber bundle and ventricular muscle may sustain a circus movement similar to rings of muscle (Fig. 5B).

Central to the initiation of a circus movement in a ring model is the concept of unidirectional block (Fig. 5C). Here, a stimulus will block in one direction, presumably because of nonhomogeneous refractoriness, but will continue to conduct in the other direction. A circus movement will be established if the returning wave front finds that the site of unidirectional block has recovered excitability, thus permitting conduction to proceed uninterrupted. Although a circus movement in a Purkinje muscle

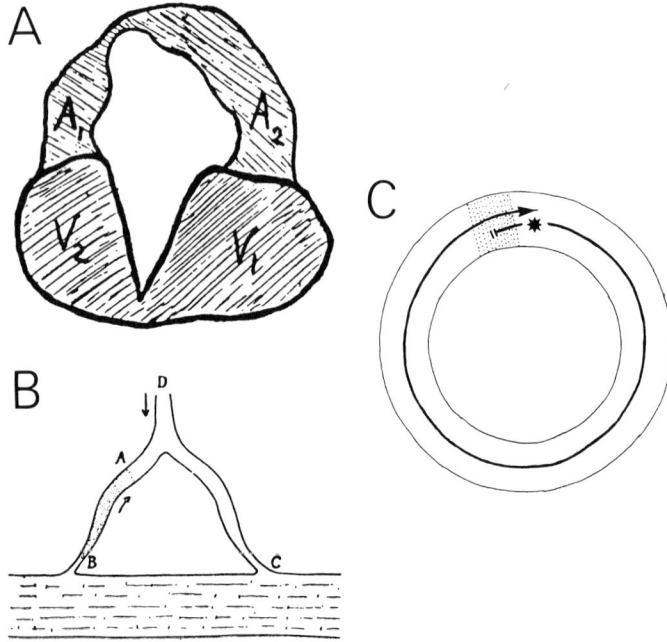

**Fig. 5.** Ring models of reentry. (A) Mines' diagram of a ring preparation comprised of the auricle and ventricle of the tortoise, in which he observed reciprocating rhythm. Both connections between auricle and ventricle could transmit an excitation wave. During reciprocating rhythm, the four portions of the preparation marked V1, V2, A1, and A2 contracted in that order. (From Mines, 1913.) (B) A proposed mechanism for reentry in a Purkinje–muscle loop from the study of Schmitt and Erlanger. The diagram shows a Purkinje fiber bundle, D, that divides into two branches, both connected distally by ventricular muscle. Circus movement will develop if the stippled segment, A–B, is an area of unidirectional conduction. An impulse advancing from D would be blocked at A, but would reach and stimulate the ventricular muscle at C by way of the other terminal branch. The excitation from the ventricular fiber would then reenter the Purkinje system at B and traverse the depressed region at a slow rate so that by the time it arrived at A this site would have recovered from refractoriness and would again be excited. (From Schmitt and Erlanger, 1928–1929.) (C) Diagrammatic illustration of the initiation of circus movement in a ring model emphasizing the importance of unidirectional block. A properly timed stimulus (*) will block in one direction because of nonhomogeneous refractoriness (represented by the stippled zone) but will continue to conduct in the ring in the other direction. A circus movement will be established if the returning wave front finds that the site of unidirectional block has recovered excitability, thus permitting conduction to proceed uninterrupted.

loop is possible, it is difficult to demonstrate in the *in situ* heart. The only two proven examples of a ring model reentry in the intact mammalian heart are (1) the pre-excitation syndrome that was suggested by Mines (1914) shortly after Kent (1914) demonstrated the multiple muscular connections between auricles and ventricles in human hearts, and (2) the circus movement involving both bundle branches (bundle branch reentry) that was first suggested by the experimental observations of Moe and co-workers (1965). What is common to the pre-excitation syndrome and bundle branch reentry is that the anatomical substrate is made in large part of pathways of excitable bundles that are not connected to adjacent atrial and ventricular myocardium. A single simple circulatory wave could thus be established. The circuit could be interrupted with ease by cutting at any point along the insulated excitable bundles but most probably not at the less well-defined atrial or ventricular connections of these pathways.

*b. The Figure-Eight Model of Reentry.* A fixed anatomical obstacle is not required for the development of a circus movement reentry in the atria or ventricles. This was first illustrated by Allessie *et al.* (1973, 1976, 1977), who showed that a properly timed premature stimulus can initiate a circus movement tachycardia in small pieces of atrial myocardium of the rabbit. The initiation of reentry is made possible by the different refractory periods of atrial fibers in close proximity to each other. The premature impulse that initiates reentry blocks in fibers with long refractory periods and conducts in fibers with shorter refractory periods, eventually returning to the initial point of block after excitability recovers there. El-Sherif *et al.* (1981, 1982a, 1983b) and Mehra *et al.* (1983) have demonstrated circus movement reentry in the surviving electrophysiologically abnormal ischemic epicardial layer overlying canine infarction. Ischemia was found to result in lengthening of refractoriness with nonhomogeneous distribution, usually in the form of concentric isochrones of refractoriness with graded increase in refractoriness going from the border zone toward the center of the ischemic zone (El-Sherif, 1985; Gough *et al.*, 1985). A critically timed premature beat that succeeds in inducing reentry results in an arc of unidirectional conduction block around which the reentrant wave front circulates. The arc of conduction block occurs between adjacent sites of short and long refractoriness with the sites of longer refractoriness distal to the arc of block (Fig. 6).

A premature beat that successfully initiates reentry results in a longer arc of conduction block and slower conduction compared to one that fails to induce reentry. When a single premature stimulation ($S_2$) fails to initiate reentry, the introduction of a second premature stimulation ($S_3$) may be necessary. The use of $S_3$ usually results in a longer arc of conduction

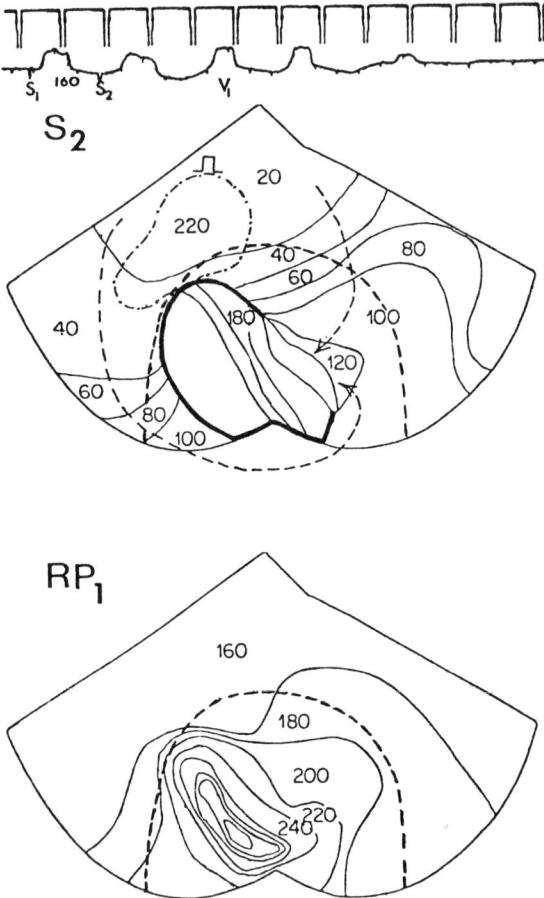

**Fig. 6.** Correlation of isochronal activation and refractory maps of circus movement reentry in the canine postinfarction heart. Recordings were obtained from a dog 4 days after ligation of the left anterior descending artery. The electrocardiogram on top shows that a single premature stimulus, $S_2$, at a coupling interval of 160 msec initiated a short reentrant rhythm. The epicardial activation map of $S_2$ is shown on the top, while the refractory map of $S_1$ as encountered by $S_2$ is shown on the bottom and labeled $RP_1$. Both maps were drawn at 20-msec isochrones. The border of the ischemic zone is outlined on both maps. The epicardial surface is depicted as if the ventricles were folded out after a cut was made from the crux to the apex. The top left and right borders represent the right and left atrioventricular junctions. The two curvilinear surfaces on the right and left are contiguous and extend from the posterior base to the apex of the heart. The ventricles were stimulated from the right ventricular outflow tract. The activation map shows that $S_2$ resulted in a long arc of functional conduction block within the epicardial border of the ischemic zone (represented by the heavy solid line). Epicardial activation circulated around both ends of the arc of block and coalesced into a common reentrant wave front that conducted slowly from lateral to septal border of the ischemic zone before reactivating myocardial zones on the proximal side of the

block and/or slower conduction around the arc. The slower activation travels around a longer, more circuitous route, thus providing time for refractoriness along the proximal side of unidirectional block to expire at one site. Reexcitation of this site will initiate reentry. The beat that initiates the first reentrant cycle, whether it is an $S_2$ or an $S_3$, results in a continuous arc of conduction block. The activation front circulates around both ends of the arc of block and rejoins on the distal side of the arc of block before breaking through the arc to reactivate an area proximal to the block. This results in splitting of the initial single arc of block into two separate arcs. Reentrant activation continues as a figure-eight activation pattern, whereby two circulating wave fronts advance in clockwise and counterclockwise directions, respectively, around two zones (arcs) of conduction block. During a monomorphic reentrant tachycardia, the two arcs of block and the two circulating wave fronts remain fairly stable (Fig. 7). During a pleomorphic reentrant rhythm, however, both arcs of block and the circulating wave fronts can change their geometric configurations while maintaining their synchrony.

*c. The Leading Circle Model of Reentry.* Allessie *et al.* (1973, 1976, 1977) described circus movement tachycardia induced in small pieces of atrial myocardium of the rabbit. The center of the circuit or the vortex is made of excitable tissue. However, the tissue is rendered functionally inexcitable by invasion of the center by multiple centripetal wavelets from the leading circuit outside the vortex (Fig. 8C). A critical analysis of the leading circle model of Allessie and co-workers shows that it may be a special modification of the figure-eight model of reentry that probably can exist only in an isolated preparation but not in the intact heart (see Fig. 8). Thus a figure-eight pattern may be central to the occurrence of "repetitive" reentrant excitation (short of fibrillation) in the interconnected syncytial structure of the atria and ventricles. The dimension of the reentrant circuit in the ventricle could vary from several millimeters to a few centimeters, and depending on the distribution of the pathologic features of the myocardium, these circuits can be located in the epicardial, intramural, or subendocardial regions (El-Sherif, 1985). The long arcs of functional con-

---

arc of block to initiate the first reentrant beat. The refractory map shows that ischemia resulted in a nonuniform refractory distribution with effective refractory periods (ERPs) of 160 and 170 msec located in the normal right and left ventricular epicardium, while the longest ERP (of 320 msec) was located in the center of the ischemic region. The dispersion of refractoriness produced a graded increase in ERP going from the border zone toward the center of the ischemic zone. The arc of functional conduction block encountered by $S_2$ developed between adjacent sites of short and long refractoriness with the sites of longer refractoriness being distal to the arc of block.

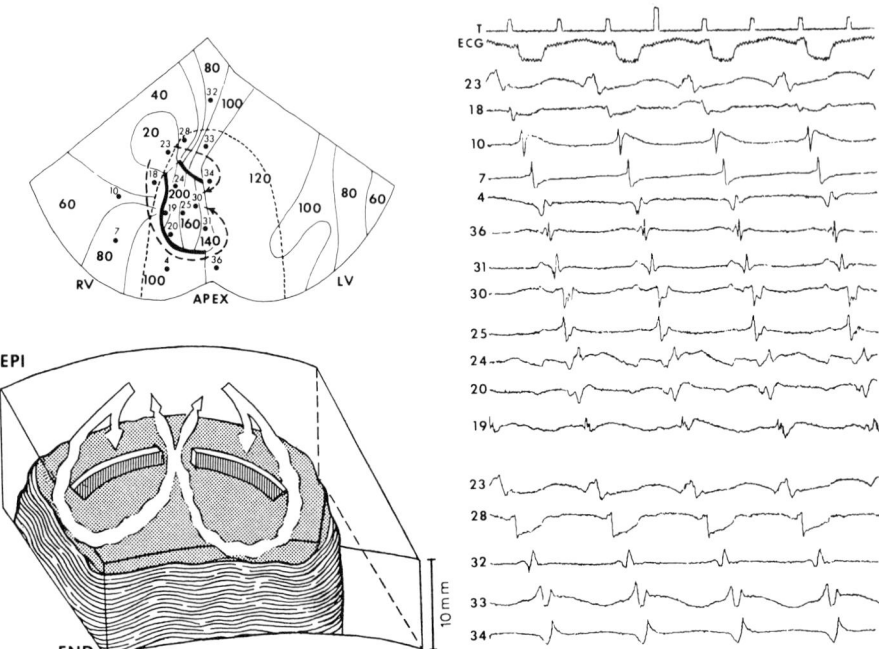

**Fig. 7.** Isochronal activation map during a monomorphic reentrant ventricular tachycardia. Recordings were obtained from a dog 4 days after ligation of the left anterior descending artery. Activation isochrones are drawn at 20-msec intervals. The reentrant circuit has a characteristic figure-eight activation pattern whereby two circulating wave fronts advance in clockwise and counterclockwise directions, respectively, around two zones (arcs) of conduction block (represented by heavy solid lines). The right panel shows selected simultaneous electrograms recorded along the two arcs of functional conduction block and the common reentrant wave front and depicts the presence of diastolic bridging between reentrant beats. A tridimensional diagramatic illustration of the ventricular activation pattern during the reentrant tachycardia is shown at the lower left corner of the figure. In this experimental model, reentrant activation occurs in the surviving thin epicardial layer overlying the infarction. RV, right ventricle; LV, left ventricle; EPI, epicardium; END, endocardium.

duction block that sustain large reentrant circuits in the canine postinfarction ventricle and the small vortices of functional block described by Allessie and co-workers that sustain small reentrant circuits in rabbit atrial myocardium thus may represent two ends of a spectrum of the same electrophysiologic phenomenon.

## 2. Reflection

The term reflection has originally been used to describe reentry in a linear bundle of conducting tissue. Longitudinal dissociation of conduc-

6. Electrophysiology of Ventricular Arrhythmias    201

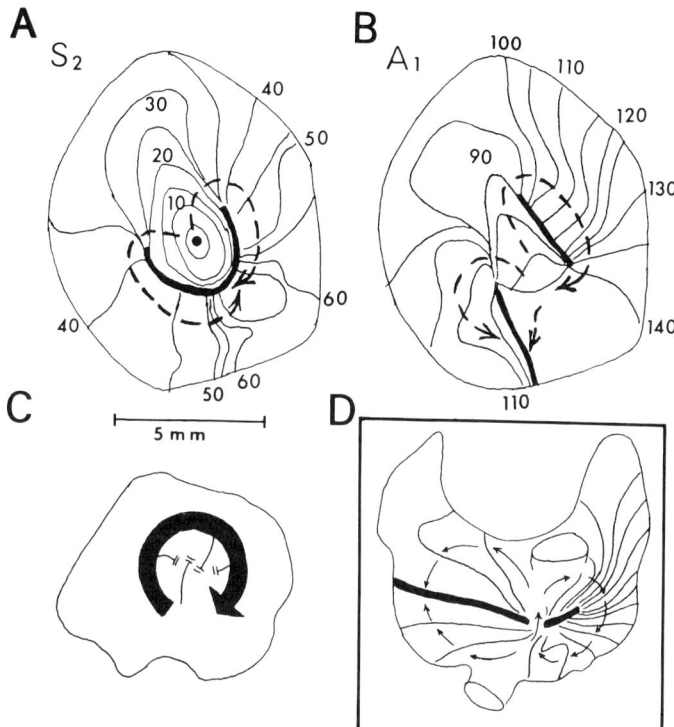

**Fig. 8.** The leading circle model of reentry. (A and B) Isochronal maps of activation of a premature beat ($S_2$) and the first reentrant beat ($A_1$) from an *in vitro* preparation of atrial myocardium of the rabbit. (Slightly modified from Allessie *et al.*, 1976). The arcs of functional conduction block are represented by heavy solid lines instead of the double bars of the original drawing. Isochrones are drawn at 5-msec intervals. Note that the properly timed premature stimulus resulted in a continuous arc of functional conduction block. The activation front circulated around both ends of the arc, coalesced, and then broke through the arc to reexcite myocardial zones on the proximal side of the arc. This resulted in splitting of the original arc into two separate arcs. In (B), a circulating wavefront continued around one of the arcs. However, the second arc of block shifted its site and joined the edge of the preparation so that the second circulating wavefront was aborted. If the preparation in (B) is inserted into the *in situ* heart, the second aborted circulating wavefront would be activated, thus resulting in a figure-eight reentrant pattern. (C) is a diagrammatic illustration of the leading circle model. (From Allessie *et al.*, 1977.) (D) is the *in vivo* isochronal map of atrial activation during atrial flutter in the dog's heart showing an activation pattern similar to that in (B). A single clockwise circulating wave is seen around a zone of functional conduction block. The second potential circulating wavefront in a figure-eight reentry model was prevented when the second arc of block connected to the A–V junction. (Slightly modified from Boineau *et al.*, 1980.)

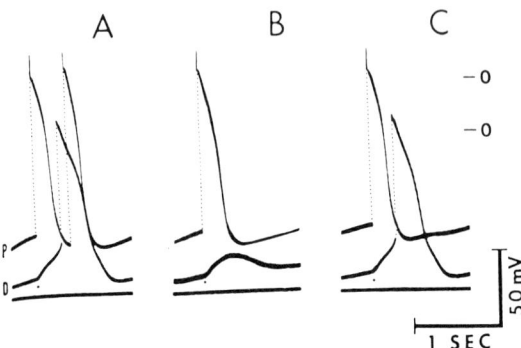

**Fig. 9.** Reflected reentry caused by electrotonic transmission across an excitable gap. Transmembrane potentials recorded from a bundle of Purkinje fibers. The top and middle traces are recordings from proximal (P) and distal (D) segments separated by an inexcitable region. Bottom trace is stimulus marker. In (A), the first action potential in the P trace was stimulated and propagated up to the inexcitable region. Excitation occurred distal to the inexcitable region (D) because of electrotonic current flow. The delay before the distal segment was excited was long enough to allow the proximal segment to recover excitability and permitted a reflected action potential. In (B), the electrotonic current flow was not sufficient to excite the fiber distal to the excitable region. In (C), the distal segment was activated too quickly and reflection did not occur because the proximal segment had not yet recovered excitability. (From Antzelevitch *et al.*, 1980).

tion in the bundle resulting in a microreentrant circuit was thought to be the mechanism (Wit *et al.*, 1972). Later, Antzelevitch *et al.* (1980, 1983), Antzelevitch and Moe (1981), and Jalife and Moe (1981) have described another mechanism which may cause reflection. If a segment of a bundle of Purkinje fibers is inexcitable, impulses conducting along the bundle will block at this segment (Fig. 9B). However, the blocked action potential can generate axial current flow through the inexcitable segment of the bundle, which acts as a passive cable. If the inexcitable segment is sufficiently short relative to the length constant, the current flow across the gap can depolarize the excitable fibers distal to the inexcitable region and can excite an action potential (Fig. 9C). This action potential, if sufficiently delayed, can itself cause retrograde axial current flow across the inexcitable gap. If the total time for to-and-fro transmission across the inexcitable gap exceeds the refractory period of the tissue proximal to the site of block, a "reflected" action potential will be generated (Fig. 9A). The area distal to the inexcitable region may or may not have intrinsic pacemaker characteristics. If there is a cell (or group of cells) with latent automaticity in this area, the retrograde current flow across the inexcitable gap can help bring the membrane potential to threshold. It is possible that reflected reentry could occur in the damaged heart. However, it must be limited to areas where the damage to myocardial fibers is focal, since if the damage is too extensive, electrotonic transmission across the excitable area would fail (Wit and Rosen, 1984).

## III. Electrophysiological Mechanisms of Ventricular Arrhythmias in Myocardial Infarction

### A. Introduction

Following coronary artery occlusion, the area that was originally perfused becomes ischemic. Due to diffusion and collateral circulation, irreversible cell damage spreads from the central zone into the border zone (Reimer et al., 1977; Fenoglio et al., 1979; Schaper et al., 1979). Most infarctions will have one or more areas of necrosis surrounded by ischemic border zones. Purkinje and ventricular muscle fibers in the ischemic zones develop abnormal electrophysiological properties and generate ventricular arrhythmias at various stages following infarction. Since the classic experiments on the dog heart by Harris (1950) it is known that ventricular arrhythmias after coronary occlusion occur in two distinct phases. The first corresponds to the acute phase of ischemia and lasts until 15 to 30 min after coronary occlusion; the second starts 4–8 hr after occlusion and lasts 24–48 hr. The early phase of ventricular arrhythmias is more serious, can degenerate into rapid ventricular tachycardia and ventricular fibrillation, and has been attributed to reentrant excitation in ischemic myocardium (Durrer et al., 1971; Boineau and Cox, 1973; Waldo and Kaiser, 1973; Scherlag et al., 1974; El-Sherif et al., 1975; Janse et al., 1980). The second phase, which is more benign, consists of spontaneous multiform ventricular rhythms having about the same rate as the sinus rhythm and represents ectopic discharge from electrophysiologically abnormal Purkinje fibers (Friedman et al., 1973a,b; Lazzara et al., 1973; Scherlag et al., 1974; Horowitz et al., 1976). It is not known whether such a distinct bimodal distribution of arrhythmia occurs in other animals, including man (Bigger et al., 1977). Furthermore, El-Sherif et al. (1977a,b) have shown that during the second phase of spontaneous ventricular rhythms, as well as following the subsidence of this phase, fast ventricular tachyarrhythmias and ventricular fibrillation could be induced by programmed electrical stimulation of the heart. These tachyarrhythmias, similar to those in the first phase, were attributed to reentrant excitation in ischemic myocardial border zones. Other investigators have shown that ventricular tachyarrhythmias can also be induced by programmed electrical stimulation in the chronic stage of canine myocardial infarction (Garan *et al.*, 1980, 1981; Garan and Ruskin, 1984).

## B. Ventricular Arrhythmias in the Acute Phase of Myocardial Infarction

### 1. Occlusion Arrhythmias

Transmembrane action potentials from intact canine and porcine hearts have been recorded during global and regional ischemia (Kardesh *et al.*, 1958; Downar *et al.*, 1977; Klèber *et al.*, 1978). After coronary artery ligation the cells in the ischemic region show progressive decrease in resting membrane potential, action potential amplitude, duration, and rate of rise of the upstroke (Fig. 10). Eventually, some cells become totally inexcitable. The electrophysiological alterations observed during ischemia can be considered the result of multiple factors including hypoxia, intracellular and extracellular acidosis, and increased extracellular $K^+$, lactate, and many other metabolic byproducts that may accumulate in the extracellular space because of the reduced blood flow. The loss of resting membrane potential has been correlated, to a certain degree, with the accumulation of $K^+$ in the extracellular space (Hill and Gettes, 1980; Hirsche *et al.*, 1980).

In the first 1–3 min of ischemia, the refractory period changes concomitantly with the changes in action potential duration. After this brief initial shortening of the refractory period it begins to lengthen even though action potential duration continues to shorten (Downar *et al.*, 1977). El-Sherif *et al.* (1974) and Lazzara *et al.* (1975) used the term "post-repolarization refractoriness" to indicate that at certain stages of ischemia the membrane may remain inexcitable even when it has been completely repolarized. Such increases in refractory period could exceed the basic cycle length, at which point 2:1 responses occur (Downar *et al.*, 1977) (Fig. 10). The marked dependence of recovery of excitability on the resting potential in partially depolarized ischemic myocardial cells is probably the most important determinant for the occurrence of slow conduction and conduction block in the acute phase of ischemia (Janse and Klèber, 1981). Since the recovery of excitability becomes markedly time dependent, the basic heart rate and the coupling interval of premature beats have a crucial influence on local excitability in cell groups exhibiting a critical range of resting membrane potential. Although in the first several minutes after coronary occlusion conduction is determined mainly by the changes in amplitude and rate of rise of action potentials, in later phases of ischemia the increase in coupling resistance between ischemic cells may play a larger role (Janse and Klèber, 1981).

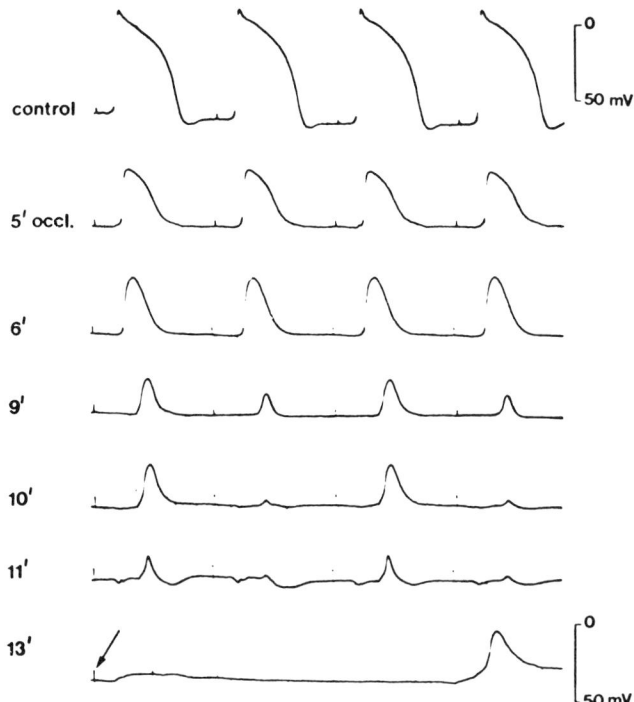

**Fig. 10.** Transmembrane action potentials recorded from the subepicardium of the left ventricle of an *in situ* pig heart before and after occlusion of the proximal left anterior descending artery. The figure shows the typical time course and character of changes which occur in a subepicardial cell in the center of an ischemic region. The heart was paced at a basic cycle length of 390 msec. After 5 min of occlusion, the action potential was reduced in amplitude and duration, and upstroke velocity was decreased. The interval between stimulus artifact and beginning of action potential upstroke is increased. One minute later, the plateau disappeared and the other changes were accentuated. At 9 min, an alternation in amplitude appeared which evolved into 2:1 responses. These responses degenerated further into small spikes which disappeared altogether by 13 min of ischemia. In the bottom trace, the last pacer artifact is indicated by an arrow. It produced no response, but after a pause of 1170 msec, an action potential was produced by a sinus escape. This illustrates the tachycardia-dependent nature of the response of ischemic cells. (From Downar *et al.*, 1977.)

Conduction disorders in the ischemic myocardium have been demonstrated in extracellular recordings and have been correlated with the occurrence of ventricular tachyarrhythmias (Durrer *et al.*, 1971; Boineau and Cox, 1973; Waldo and Kaiser, 1973; Scherlag *et al.*, 1974; El-Sherif *et al.*, 1975). Fractionation of bipolar electrograms into multiple asynchronous spikes has been recorded and was interpreted to suggest marked desynchronization of activation within the area of the recording. The occurrence of continuous electrical activity that bridges the diastolic interval between the sinus beat and the ectopic beat as well as between consecutive ectopic beats was taken as an indication that reentrant excitation is the underlying electrophysiological mechanism for the ventricular arrhythmias (El-Sherif et al., 1977a,b). The fractionation is most commonly seen if a composite electrode that averages the recording from multiple close bipolar electrodes is utilized (El-Sherif et al., 1977a,b). It is also seen in recordings obtained from a bipolar electrode catheter with wide interpolar distance (El-Sherif et al., 1975). The electrode catheter was originally utilized for intracardiac recordings from canine septal myocardium during acute ischemia following ligation of the anterior septal artery. In this study, conduction disorders in the ischemic septal myocardium were tachycardia dependent and the onset of ventricular tachyarrhythmias was characteristically associated with a Wenckebach pattern of conduction delay (El-Sherif et al., 1975) (Fig. 11). The electrode catheter recording technique was later adopted to record fractionated electrical activity in the diastolic interval from the left ventricular cavity in patients with chronic ischemic heart disease and ventricular tachyarrhythmias (Josephson et al., 1978).

Recently, multiple simultaneous close bipolar electrograms and a multiplexer recording system have been utilized to construct isochronal maps of ventricular activation during acute ischemia (Janse et al., 1980). This technique has allowed the demonstration of circus movements around areas of conduction block having a diameter of 1 to 2 cm on the epicardial surface of the ischemic zone during ventricular tachycardia occurring between 2 and 10 min after coronary occlusion. The localization, revolution time, and size of the circus movements changed from beat to beat. Ventricular tachycardia, which could terminate spontaneously or degenerate into ventricular fibrillation, was characterized by the presence of basically one fairly large circus movement. During ventricular fibrillation, reentrant circuits were multiple, seldom completed, and had smaller diameters, on the order of 0.5 cm (Janse et al., 1980) (Fig. 12).

The role of the subendocardial Purkinje network in the initiation of ventricular fibrillation following acute coronary occlusion in isolated perfused canine hearts was studied by Janse et al. (1985). The subendocardium was destroyed by filling the ventricular cavities with phenol. They found that in these hearts ventricular tachycardia, most probably due to reentrant excitation in the epicardial layer, could still be induced by programmed stimulation, although at much slower rates compared to controls. However, the ventricular tachycardia failed to degenerate into ventricular fibrillation. They suggested that a rapidly conducting subendocardial Purkinje system may be a necessary requirement for the development of ventricular fibrillation following acute coronary occlusion.

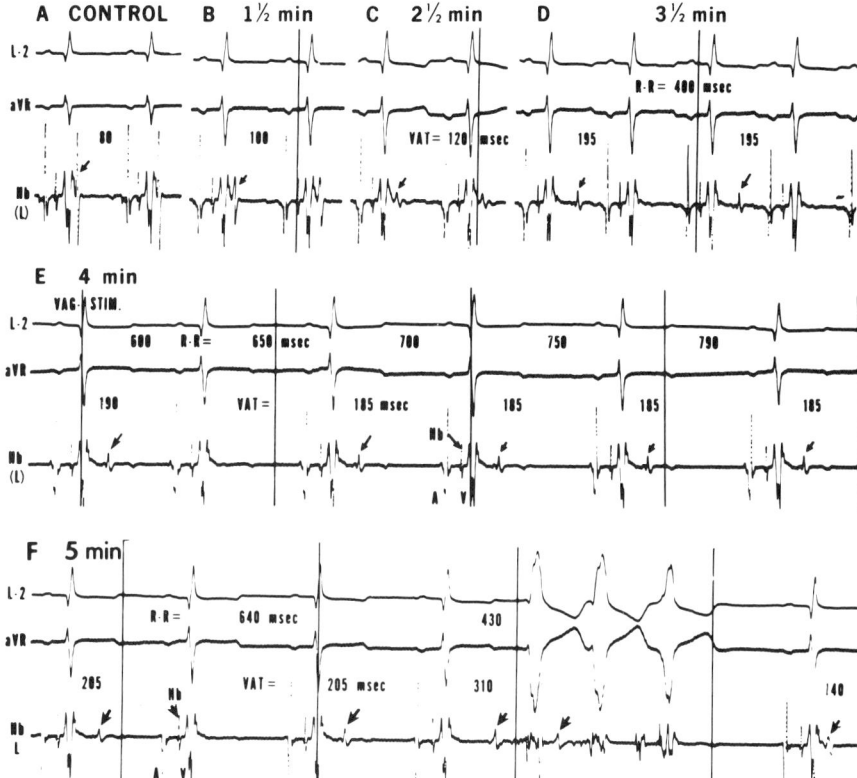

Fig. 11. Electrode catheter recording of the septal myocardium following acute ligation of the anterior septal artery in the dog. Traces from top to bottom are ECG leads II and aVR and an electrode catheter recording of the His bundle from the left side, Hb(L). During control, the Hb(L) recording illustrated a discrete sharp biphasic deflection at the end of the ventricular complex that represented activation of septal myocardium (marked by arrows). Following ligation, there was progressive delay in the inscription of the septal potential with marked decrease in the amplitude of the potential and an increase in its duration. At 3½ min following ligation, the ventricular activation time (VAT) measured from the onset of the ventricular complex to the delayed septal potential increased to 195 msec and the potential was inscribed every other beat, suggesting the occurrence of 2:1 block of this area of septal myocardium. Vagal stimulation applied in (E) slowed the heart rate and resulted in 1:1 conduction of the septal potential. This illustrates the tachycardia-dependent nature of conduction in ischemic myocardium. In (F), 5 min after occlusion, a short ventricular rhythm developed. The onset of the ventricular rhythm was characteristically associated with a Wenckebach pattern of conduction delay of the septal potential. Fractionated electrical activity preceded the onset of the first ectopic beat and bridged at least part of the diastolic interval between consecutive ectopic beats. This suggests that reentrant excitation is the underlying electrophysiological mechanism of the ectopic rhythm. Note that the last ectopic beat was not followed by delayed diastolic activity. (From El-Sherif *et al.*, 1975.)

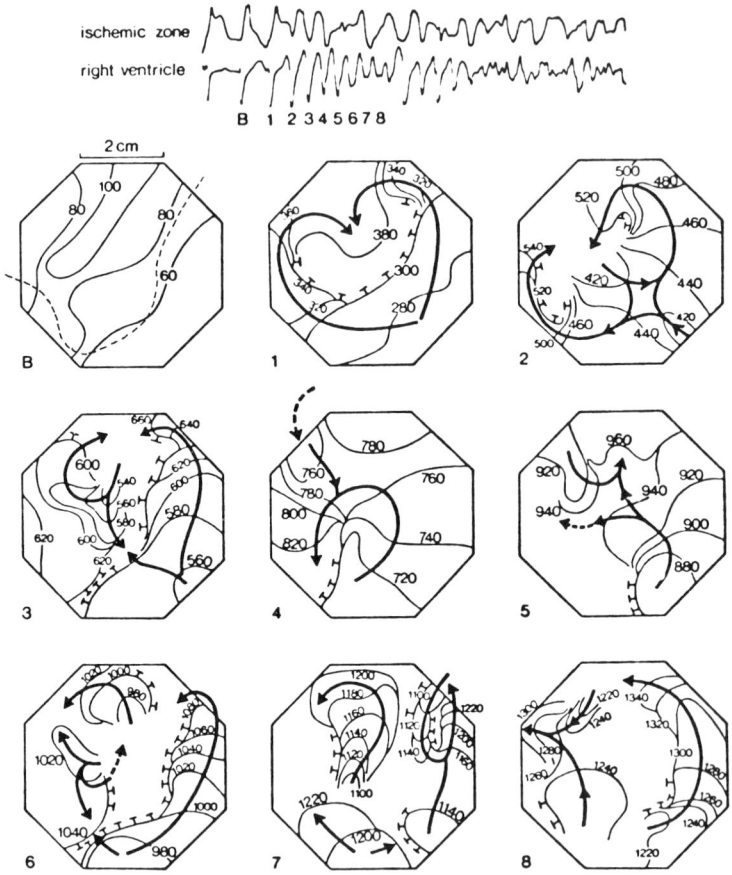

**Fig. 12.** Electrograms recorded from ischemic epicardium and normal right ventricle during a run of ventricular tachycardia that degenerated into ventricular fibrillation $3\frac{1}{2}$ min following left anterior descending artery occlusion in an isolated pig heart. Epicardial isochronal activation maps of the basic beat (B) and first eight ectopic beats are shown. The isochrones separate areas activated within the same 20-msec interval. Numbers are in msec. The interrupted line in the activation map of the basic beat is the ischemic border zone. During the first ectopic beat, earliest activity emerged at 280 msec in the normal zone and was blocked inside the border of the ischemic zone (bars indicate conduction block). The activation wavefront conducted slowly around both ends of the arc of block, coalesced, and then returned to reactivate sites proximal to the arc of block and initiate the first reentrant cycle. A figure-eight reentrant activation pattern continued during the second ectopic beat, and each of the two synchronous wavefronts had a diameter of about 1 cm. Following this, the activation pattern became irregular with fragmentation of wavefronts. Circus movements usually were not completed, and whenever they were their diameter was small (see the circuit in beat 7 with a diameter of 0.5 cm). (From Janse *et al.*, 1980.)

## 2. Reperfusion Arrhythmias

Several studies have investigated the effects of reperfusion following brief coronary artery occlusion (Downar et al., 1977; Murdock et al., 1980; Balke et al., 1981; Penny and Sheridan, 1983). Reperfusion usually results in significant ventricular tachyarrhythmias. The incidence and severity of reperfusion tachyarrhythmias seem to correlate with the duration of prior acute coronary occlusion and the incidence, severity, and time course of ventricular tachyarrhythmias occurring during the preceding period of coronary occlusion (Balke et al., 1981). However, the electrophysiological mechanisms of reperfusion arrhythmias are not very well understood at present. In a study by Downar et al. (1977), ventricular fibrillation frequently occurred on release of coronary occlusion. This was explained by the abruptness and diversity of changes in intracellular responses in both the ischemic and border zone which reperfusion can initiate. The inhomogeneity in responses may be severe enough to preclude organized activation and result in fibrillation. Gradual reperfusion, however, seems to avoid the abrupt precipitation of gross inhomogeneity and significantly reduces the frequency and severity of reperfusion arrhythmias (Sewell et al., 1955). In a study by Ferrier et al., isolated canine Purkinje fibers–papillary muscle preparations, superfused for 40 min with modified "ischemic" Tyrode's solution and then superfused with normal Tyrode's solution showed an orderly sequence of arrhythmias (Ferrier, 1983). Reentry across the Purkinje–muscle junction was seen during simulated ischemia. During 60 min of simulated reperfusion, delayed afterdepolarizations and later protected spontaneous automaticity were seen.

## 3. Role of Injury Current

It has been suggested that the current of injury flowing at the boundary between ischemic and normal tissue could contribute to the genesis of ectopic activity during the acute phase of myocardial ischemia. Janse et al. (1980) have shown that spontaneous ventricular premature depolarizations, which occur frequently 2–10 min following coronary occlusion, consistently arose from the normal subendocardial zone close to the lateral boundary with the ischemic zone (see Fig. 12). In later beats of ventricular tachycardia or ventricular fibrillation, however, circus movement reentry within the ischemic myocardial zone could be demonstrated (Janse et al., 1980). They suggested that if a region of inexcitability is interposed between the normal tissue in the border and the ischemic tissue displaying delayed activity, electrotonic currents generated by the latter could flow across this gap (Janse and Van Capelle, 1982). Properly timed currents, transmitted through a zone of bidirectional block, could trigger automaticity in Purkinje fibers in the normal side of the border zone. This is similar to the mechanism of reflected reentry (Antzelevitch et al., 1980) illustrated in Fig. 9. In a computer simulation study, subthreshold depolarizations caused by injury currents could, when properly timed, induce triggered activity (Janse and Van Capelle, 1982). Thus it is possible that two different electrophysiological mechanisms account for the initial ventricular premature depolarizations and subsequent ventricular tachycardia/fibrillation following acute coronary occlusion.

## C. Triggered Ventricular Rhythms in the Subacute Myocardial Infarction Phase

### 1. In Vitro *Observations*

Following the subsidence of the malignant phase of ventricular tachyarrhythmias that immediately follow acute coronary occlusion, a quiescent arrhythmia-free interval ensues. Approximately 4–8 hr following coronary occlusion, spontaneous multiform ventricular rhythms develop. The ectopic activity, which initially is intermittent in nature, peaks 1–2 days postinfarction and usually subsides by the third day (Harris, 1950). During their peak, the rate of the ectopic rhythms is approximately equal to or only slightly faster than the rate of underlying sinus rhythm and the ectopic rhythms could be easily overdriven by acceleration of the supraventricular rhythm (Scherlag *et al.*, 1974; El-Sherif *et al.*, 1982a). These rhythms were shown to arise from surviving, albeit electrophysiologically abnormal, subendocardial Purkinje networks underlying the infarction (Friedman *et al.*, 1973a,b; Lazzara *et al.*, 1973; Scherlag *et al.*, 1974; Horowitz *et al.*, 1976). The studies of El-Sherif *et al.* (1983a) suggest that triggered activity in ischemic Purkinje fibers may be the underlying mechanism for these rhythms. Triggered activity arising from delayed afterdepolarizations could be demonstrated in depolarized ischemic Purkinje fibers from 1-day-old canine infarction. Similar to other preparations that show triggered activity, the amplitude and rate of rise of the delayed afterdepolarizations in ischemic Purkinje fibers are a function of both the cycle length and number of impulses in a stimulated drive, and premature excitations could enhance the delayed afterdepolarization amplitude (see Fig. 3). However, in contrast to other preparations, in which more than one stimulated action potential is usually required (Rosen and Reder, 1981), triggered activity could commonly be induced by a single action potential in the ischemic preparation (Fig. 13). This may be explained as follows: in almost all other models of triggered activity delayed afterdepolarizations only developed in the presence of a milieu that increased

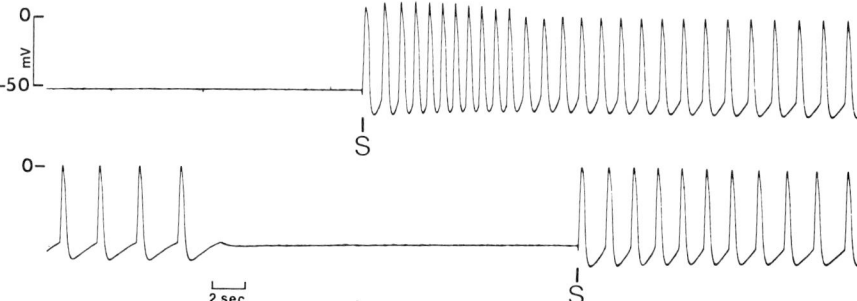

**Fig. 13.** Initiation of triggered activity by a single stimulated action potential. Transmembrane recordings from a Purkinje cell in the ischemic zone of an endocardial preparation from 1-day-old canine infarction. The depolarized cell (resting membrane potential −53 mV) was quiescent. A single stimulated action potential initiated a run of triggered activity. The activity slowed gradually and terminated in the bottom tracing following a subthreshold afterdepolarization. Following another quiescent period triggered activity was again initiated by a single stimulated action potential.

$[Ca^{2+}]_i$ (Vassalle and Mugelli, 1981). The milieu that enhanced $[Ca^{2+}]_i$ caused the cells to be more uniform. Thus a stepwise increase of $[Ca^{2+}]_i$ during a train of stimulated action potentials was usually required to initiate triggered activity (Vassalle and Mugelli, 1981). By contrast, ischemic preparations superfused with normal Tyrode's solution are more heterogeneous, as revealed by the varying degrees of partial depolarizations in contiguous cells. It is possible that the degree of calcium loading among these cells is also different. It is therefore not surprising that a single action potential can initiate triggered activity. The fact that triggered activity in ischemic Purkinje fibers could commonly be induced by a single action potential may explain the persistence of ventricular rhythms in 1-day-old canine infarctions *in vivo* as well as the frequent shift of the pacemaker site (El-Sherif *et al.*, 1983a).

Another characteristic of the ischemic endocardial preparation is that triggered activity can be initiated by normal automatic pacemaker cells when the automatic action potential is followed by a delayed afterdepolarization of sufficient amplitude to reach threshold potential. Triggered action potentials can also give rise to extrasystolic groupings (i.e., bigeminal, trigeminal rhythms, etc.) (El-Sherif *et al.*, 1983a) (Fig. 14). In contrast to abnormal automaticity, triggered activity could be terminated by overdriving pacing and occasionally by a properly timed single premature stimulus (Fig. 15).

Because rhythmic activity in endocardial ischemic preparations is characteristically initiated in partially depolarized Purkinje fibers (maximum

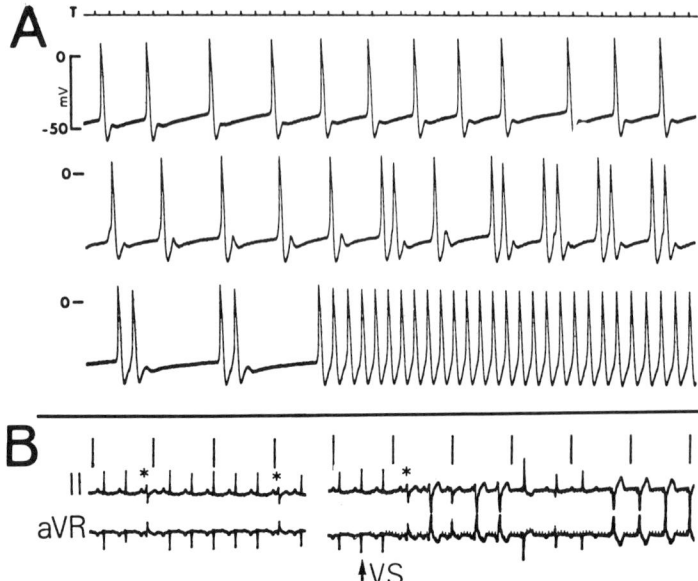

**Fig. 14.** Extrasystolic rhythm due to triggered activity arising from delayed afterdepolarizations. (A) Transmembrane recording from a Purkinje fiber in the ischemic zone of an endocardial preparation from 1-day-old canine infarction. The upper tracing shows a background slow automatic rhythm. Each automatic action potential is followed by a low amplitude delayed afterdepolarization. In the middle tracing, the amplitude of the delayed afterdepolarizations gradually increased, reached threshold, and triggered a single action potential, resulting in a trigeminal rhythm followed by a bigeminal rhythm. In the lower tracing a sustained triggered activity occurred when the subthreshold afterdepolarization that followed the single triggered action potential reached threshold potential. (Modified from El-Sherif *et al.*, 1983a.) (B) Electrocardiographic tracing obtained from a dog 1 day following ligation of the left anterior descending artery. The tracing shows sinus tachycardia and extrasystolic ventricular ectopic beats with late fixed coupling (marked by *). Slight slowing of the sinus rhythm by vagal stimulation (VS) revealed the presence of a multiform ventricular rhythm. The extrasystolic beats and the multiform ventricular rhythm may be the result of triggered activity arising from delayed afterdepolarizations in ischemic Purkinje fibers surviving the infarct.

diastolic potential $-59 \pm 9.9$ mV), it may be difficult to discern from abnormal automaticity. Indeed, in earlier studies of 1-day-old canine ischemic endocardial preparations, rhythmic activity at reduced levels of diastolic potential was considered the result of abnormal automaticity (Friedman *et al.*, 1973a,b; Lazzara *et al.*, 1973). However, when the initiation and termination of these rhythms were carefully analyzed, the majority were found to be due to triggered activity arising from delayed afterdepolarizations (El-Sherif *et al.*, 1983a).

# 6. Electrophysiology of Ventricular Arrhythmias

Entrance and exit block around sites of triggered activity is not uncommon in ischemic subendocardial preparations. The presence of entrance block around a site of triggered activity that is able to exit, at least intermittently, to the rest of the preparation (or the ventricles) can result in a parasystolic rhythm (Fig. 16). It is possible to demonstrate the presence of one or more parasystolic discharges with a varying degree of exit block during the multiform ventricular rhythm seen *in vivo* 1 day following myocardial infarction in the dog (Fig. 17). Ventricular parasystolic rhythms including rapid parasystole with varying exit block have been commonly observed in the setting of acute myocardial infarction and in the postinfarction period in man (Salazar and McKendrick, 1970; Kotler

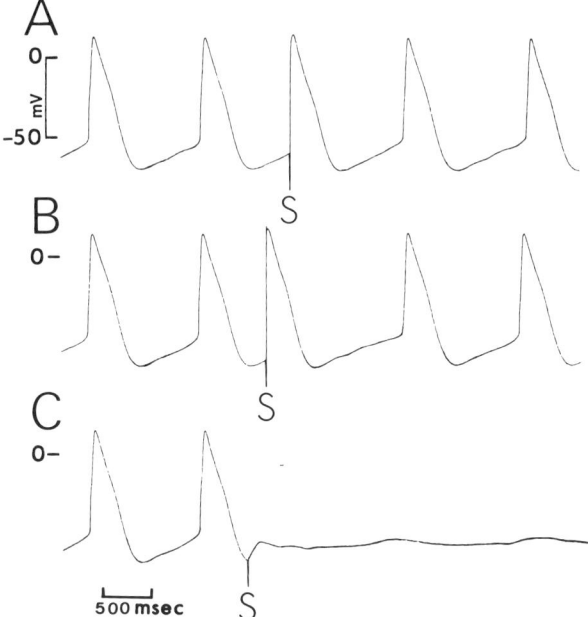

**Fig. 15.** Termination of triggered activity by a single properly timed premature stimulus. Transmembrane recordings from a Purkinje cell in the ischemic zone of an endocardial preparation from a 1-day-old canine infarction. (A) During a regular triggered rhythm, a stimulated action potential introduced late in the diastolic cycle resulted in resetting of the triggered rhythm. (B) A stimulated action potential introduced earlier in the diastolic cycle resulted in lengthening of the first return cycle. This could be attributed to a slight (3 mV) increase of maximum diastolic potential of the premature beat and a slight decrease of the slope of the diastolic potential. (C) A premature stimulus introduced very early in the diastolic cycle resulted in a subthreshold depolarization and was followed by termination of the triggered activity. Note the presence of subthreshold oscillatory depolarizations following termination of triggered activity.

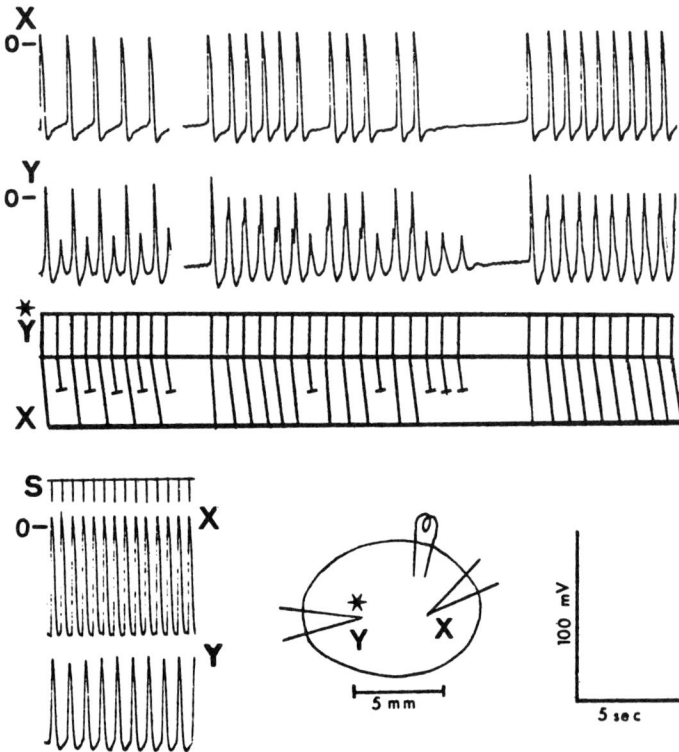

**Fig. 16.** Intermittent parasystolic rhythm due to a triggered automatic pacemaker showing both entrance and exit block. Transmembrane recordings from two Purkinje fibers (X and Y) in the ischemic zone of an endocardial preparation from a 1-day-old canine infarction (see schematic drawing). The recordings show intermittent triggered activity arising from delayed afterdepolarizations. The focus of triggered activity was probably located close to the Y recording (marked by *) and a varying degree of conduction delay and/or block occurred between the two sites. The Y recording showed electrotonic depolarizations that corresponded to the rhythmic discharge of the ectopic focus. Conduction delays between the two sites resulted in an electrotonic depolarization followed by a second larger upstroke in the Y recording. When conduction block occurred, the Y recording only revealed an electrotonic depolarization. In contrast to the Y recording, which could reveal the rhythmic activity of the ectopic focus, the X recording a few mm distant from the ectopic focus showed only delayed conducted action potentials. Each series of triggered activity was initiated by an action potential that was probably generated by background slow Purkinje automaticity arising from a different site in the preparation. The exit block between the focus of triggered activity and the rest of the preparation varied from 2:1 block (top left tracing) to Wenckebach periodicity (top middle tracing) to first-degree block (top right tracing). There was also a period of repetitive conduction block at the end of the middle series of triggered activity. Diagrammatic illustration of the conduction pattern from the ectopic focus is shown at the bottom of the upper tracings. The tracing at the lower left corner shows that when the preparation was stimulated (S) at a rate faster than the ectopic focus entrance block was

## 6. Electrophysiology of Ventricular Arrhythmias

*et al.*, 1973; El-Sherif *et al.*, 1977d). However, the identification of a parasystolic rhythm *in vivo* is sometimes difficult because precisely constant interectopic (parasystolic) intervals are uncommon. Figure 16 illustrates that in addition to intermittence of the discharge of the parasystolic pacemaker, it is possible that changes in the inherent rate of the pacemaker as well as variation of the degree of exit block can occur concomitantly and be responsible for the failure to unravel the exact nature of the ectopic rhythm.

All preparations that show triggered activity, including ischemic Purkinje fibers, may be driven by the same basic mechanism. In almost all other models of triggered activity arising from delayed afterdepolarizations a milieu that increased $[Ca^{2+}]_i$ was present. However, ischemia *per se* results in significant increase in $[Ca^{2+}]_i$. The reduction in pump activity following ischemia (Schwartz *et al.*, 1973; Sobel, 1974) results in an increase in $[Na^+]_i$. This reduces the $Na^+$ gradient, causing a secondary decrease in calcium extrusion by the $Na^+-Ca^{2+}$ exchange (Reuter and Seitz, 1968) and may promote $Ca^{2+}$ release from mitochondria, resulting in an increase in $[Ca^{2+}]_i$ (Carafoli *et al.*, 1974). In preparations showing subthreshold delayed afterdepolarizations, epinephrine or increasing $[Ca^{2+}]_o$ can result in triggered activity (El-Sherif *et al.*, 1983a). Verapamil (El-Sherif *et al.*, 1983a) and other calcium-blocking agents (Gough *et al.*, 1984a,b) inhibit triggered activity either by directly suppressing delayed afterdepolarizations and/or by inducing exit block around sites of triggered activity (Fig. 18). The effects of epinephrine, increased $[Ca^{2+}]_o$, and calcium-blocking agents suggest that, as in other examples of triggered activity, $Ca^{2+}$ is fundamental to the genesis of delayed afterdepolarizations in ischemic Purkinje fibers.

Ouabain at a concentration that has no toxic effect on normal Purkinje fibers may enhance arrhythmias in ischemic Purkinje fibers by increasing the magnitude of delayed afterdepolarizations and enhancing triggered activity (Hariman *et al.*, 1985). It was postulated that the common action of ischemia and digitalis in causing an increase in $[Ca^{2+}]_i$ may work synergistically to cause delayed afterdepolarizations and triggered activity in Purkinje fibers. This may represent the mechanism responsible for increased susceptibility to digitalis toxicity in patients with ischemic heart disease.

---

present. Besides the intermittence of the triggered activity and the varying degree of exit block, the tracings also show that there was a gradual slowing of the frequency of discharge between each new series of triggered activity. All these factors combined can make it very difficult to diagnose parasystolic rhythms in clinical records based on mathematical manipulation of interectopic intervals of manifest ectopic discharge.

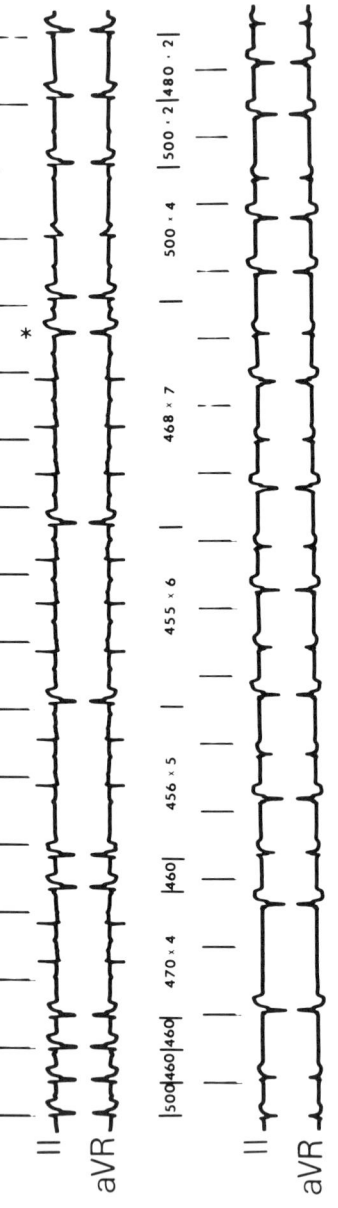

**Fig. 17.** Electrocardiographic recordings from a dog 1 day following ligation of the left anterior descending artery showing ventricular parasystolic rhythms. The recordings were obtained following the administration of propranolol plus verapamil in an attempt to slow or terminate the multiform spontaneous ventricular rhythms. The presence of a parasystolic rhythm was diagnosed when ventricular beats with identical QRS configurations had varying coupling intervals of more than 0.12 sec and interectopic intervals that were multiples of a least common denominator. The upper and lower recordings illustrate two different parasystolic rhythms with varying degrees of exit block and different calculated rates of discharge. In the upper recording, the fast ventricular rhythm at the beginning of the recording is explained by 1:1 conduction from the parasystolic focus while the slower rhythm at the end of the recording represents 2:1 exit block. The asterisk refers to an ectopic beat with a similar QRS morphology to the parasystolic rhythm in the lower recording. The numbers represent milliseconds.

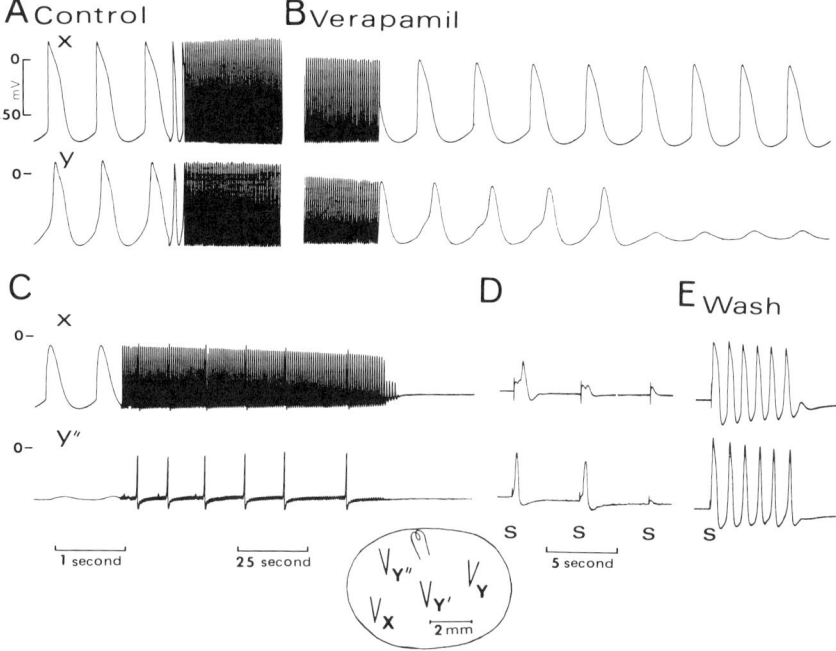

**Fig. 18.** Induction of exit block from site of triggered activity by verapamil. Simultaneous transmembrane recordings from different Purkinje fibers in a small infarcted preparation from a 1-day-old canine infarction. (A) Control triggered activity. Exploring the preparation showed that earliest activity was recorded close to site X, whereas the rest of the preparation was activated 20–60 msec later. (B) Ten min of superfusion with verapamil (2.2 × 10⁻⁶ M) resulted in slowing of the rate of rhythmic activity, depression of action potentials, and increased delay between X and Y before complete conduction block developed. The microelectrode at Y then was moved to two new sites (Y' and Y"). Both sites showed low-amplitude electrotonic potentials simultaneously with action potentials at X. This suggested that the rhythmic activity originated from a site close to X and that exit block developed between this site and the rest of the preparation. (C) Five min later, the action potential at X showed a gradual decrease in amplitude and maximum diastolic potential before the activity spontaneously terminated, at which time the preparation became quiescent. (D) The preparation was stimulated (S) and a Wenckebach type conduction block developed. (E) Ten min of washout of verapamil resulted in improvement of the stimulated action potential and reinitiation of a triggered rhythm. (From El-Sherif et al., 1983a.)

## 2. In Vivo *Observations*

No clinical cardiac arrhythmia has definitely been ascribed to delayed afterdepolarizations. However, some accelerated A–V junctional and idioventricular rhythms as well as some of the atrial and ventricular arrhythmias caused by digitalis toxicity may be explained by delayed after-

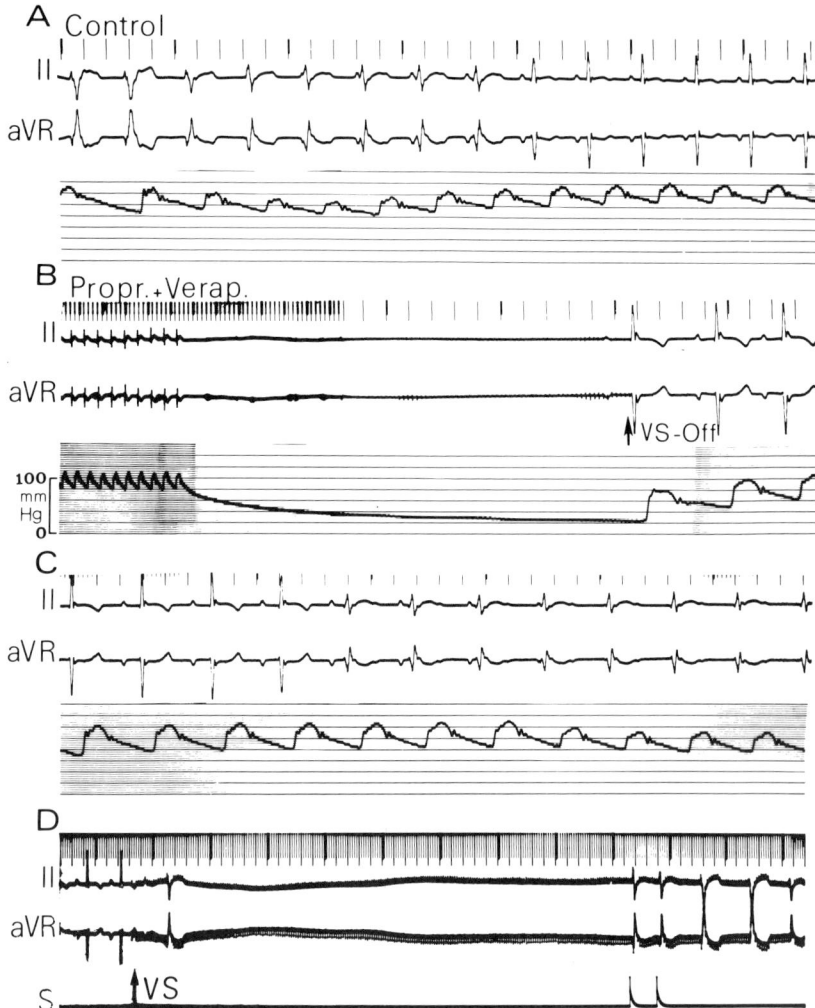

**Fig. 19.** Effect of propranolol and verapamil on spontaneous ventricular rhythms in 1-day-old canine infarction. (A) Control electrocardiographic and arterial pressure recordings. A multiform ventricular rhythm (rate, 120/min) in the first half of the recording was gradually overdriven by a slightly faster sinus rhythm (rate, 125/min). Mean arterial pressure was 100 mm Hg during the control ventricular rhythm and increased to 120 mm Hg during the sinus rhythm. (B) was obtained 4 min following the administration of propranolol, 1 mg/kg and verapamil, 0.4 mg/kg. Mean arterial pressure decreased to 95 mm Hg (5% lower than control). The sinus rhythm was suppressed by vagal stimulation in order to be able to monitor the changes in the ventricular rhythm. The rate of the spontaneous ventricular rhythm gradually decreased to 105/min before it abruptly terminated, resulting in cardiac asystole. The asystolic period was terminated after 10 sec by resumption of the sinus rhythm

depolarizations (Rosen and Reder, 1981). The spontaneous multiform ventricular rhythms in 1-day-old canine infarcts may be due to delayed afterdepolarizations and triggered activity (El-Sherif *et al.*, 1983b). The ventricular rhythms could be suppressed by verapamil following beta-adrenergic blockade resulting in cardiac quiescence. Following quiescence, ventricular rhythms could be initiated only by one or more automatic or stimulated ventricular beats (Fig. 19). Isochronal mapping studies of the induced ventricular rhythms have excluded a circus movement of excitation while elucidating, as in control rhythms, a focal origin from Purkinje fibers surviving the infarct. The failure of verapamil to suppress the spontaneous ventricular rhythms in the absence of beta-adrenergic blockade is consistent with *in vitro* studies that showed that catecholamines or increased $[Ca^{2+}]_o$ can reverse the depressant effect of calcium blocking agents on triggered activity. It also emphasizes the essential role that an intact sympathoadrenal system plays in the maintenance of spontaneous ventricular rhythms. The slower rate of triggered activity *in vitro* compared to the spontaneous ventricular rhythms *in vivo* can also be explained by the intact sympathoadrenal system *in vivo*. The rate of *in vitro* triggered activity can be markedly enhanced by catecholamines. Injection of catecholamines or stimulation of the sympathetic nerves could result in marked acceleration of the rate of spontaneous ventricular rhythms in 1-day-old canine infarctions (up to 240 beats/min) (Bocage *et al.*, 1974).

A recent study by Hariman *et al.* (1984) provided further evidence that the spontaneous ventricular rhythms in 1-day-old canine infarctions are the result of triggered activity arising from delayed afterdepolarizations in ischemic Purkinje fibers. A small apical myocardial infarction was induced in dogs by ligation of multiple distal branches of the left anterior and circumflex coronary arteries. Thirty-two plunge electrodes were placed in the endocardial surface of the area of the infarction. Unipolar electrograms were recorded using a multiplexer recording system at high gains and through low-pass filters. The endocardial area of earliest activity during the ventricular rhythms showed a negative diastolic slope and

---

when vagal stimulation (VS) was turned off. The recording in (C) was obtained a few seconds later and shows that the rate of the sinus rhythm was slower (100/min) compared to control and the PR interval was significantly increased. A ventricular rhythm was reinitiated at a slightly faster rate of 104/min. (D) was obtained 3 min later. The heart was again controlled by the sinus rhythm and when this was suppressed by vagal stimulation (marked by the arrow) a single ventricular ectopic beat occurred. The asystolic interval that followed was terminated after 8 sec by the introduction of two successive ventricular paced beats at a cycle length of 420 msec that reinitiated a ventricular rhythm at a rate of 75/min. S refers to the timing of ventricular stimulation. The heavy time lines represent 1-sec intervals.

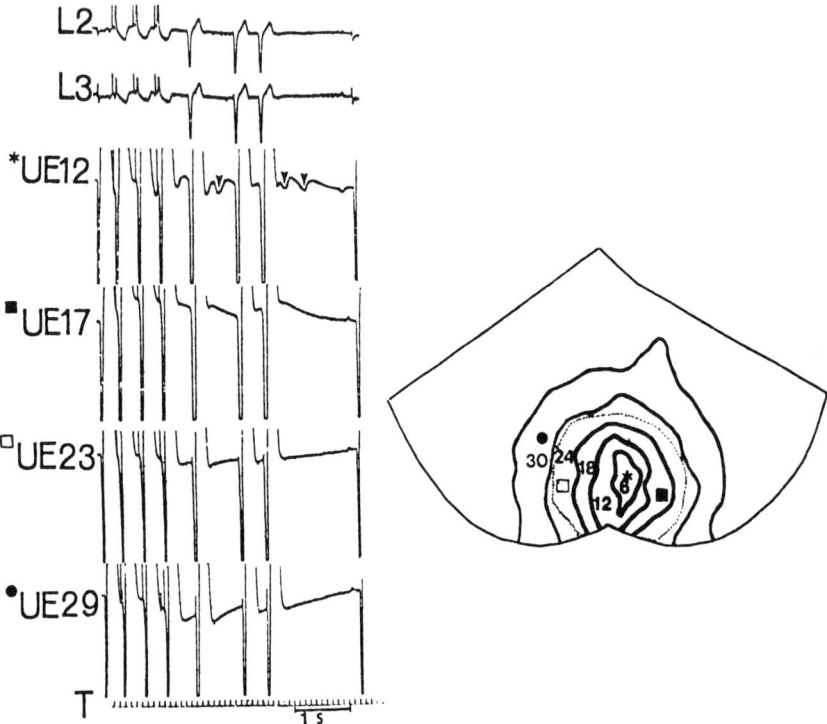

**Fig. 20.** Recordings obtained from a dog 1 day following the creation of a small apical myocardial infarction by ligation of multiple distal branches of the left anterior and circumflex coronary arteries. The surface electrocardiographic leads show three stimulated ventricular beats at a cycle length of 400 msec followed by three spontaneous ventricular beats. Four unipolar electrograms (UE) recorded with high amplifications are displayed. The diagram on the right shows the locations of the electrodes on the endocardial surface of the heart (*, UE 12; ■, UE 17; □, UE 23; ●, UE 29). The infarction is indicated by the dotted line. Numbers in the diagram indicate 6-msec isochrones. Negative-going diastolic slopes preceded the major ventricular deflections in the area of the earliest activation (UE 12 and 17). Positive-going slopes preceded the major ventricular deflection in unipolar electrograms recorded from areas remote to the area of earliest activity (UE 23 and 29). Note that slow negative-going potentials (marked by arrow heads) were recorded from the area of earliest activity during the long diastolic interval between the first and second spontaneous beats and following the third beat. These potentials may represent subthreshold delayed afterdepolarizations that failed to propagate.

upstroke slope preceding each ventricular complex. During spontaneous cessation of ventricular rhythms or cessation induced by propranolol plus verapamil this area showed multiple rhythmic slow negative diastolic potentials before the area became quiescent. These rhythmic slow negative potentials were consistent with subthreshold delayed afterdepolarizations that failed to propagate (Fig. 20).

## D. Reentrant Ventricular Rhythms in the Subacute and Chronic Myocardial Infarction Phase

### 1. Anatomical Substrate of Reentrant Excitation

In the left anterior descending artery (LAD) postligation model blood flow is reduced more in the subendocardium, and resistance to flow in the infarcted tissue causes a redistribution of flow in the epicardial layers. Combined with the enlargement of collateral vessels, this results in sufficient flow to the epicardium that it usually survives (Hirzel *et al.*, 1976). Although the geometry of the infarction varies in different experiments, pathologic studies consistently reveal a layer of surviving epicardial tissue overlying the core of necrotic myocardium (Fig. 21). The epicardial layer varies in thickness from a few cells to a few millimeters (up to 200 cell layers), as verified histologically. Isochronal mapping studies have shown that both the arcs of functional conduction block and the slow activation fronts of reentrant circuits develop in the surviving electrophysiologically abnormal epicardial layer overlying the infarction.

Unlike infarcts caused by permanent LAD occlusion, in which tissue necrosis is usually homogeneous, the infarcts caused by the occlusion–reperfusion technique are mottled with regions of viable myocardium, found throughout the infarct (Karagueuzian *et al.*, 1979; Michelson *et al.*, 1980). It is possible that in the occlusion–reperfusion model reentrant circuits are located intramurally rather than on the epicardial surface. In another canine infarction model described by Garan *et al.* (1980), all

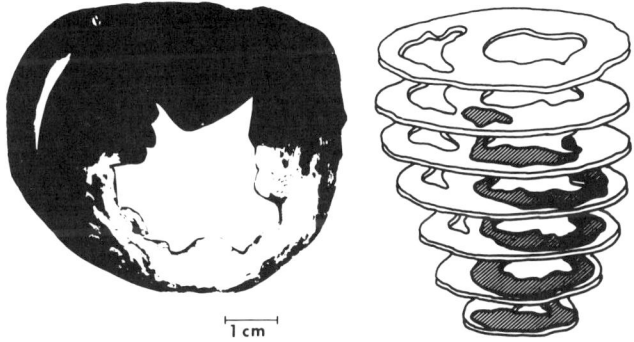

**Fig. 21.** Anatomic characteristics of the infarction 4 days after ligation of the left anterior descending coronary artery in the dog. On the right is a composite drawing of sections stained with nitro blue tetrazolium. The shaded area represents necrotic tissue. The infarction is localized to the anteroseptal region and extends to the endocardial surface. A layer of surviving epicardium of varying thickness is present in all the sections. On the left is a photograph of the fourth section from the top. The dark-stained zone represents normal myocardium; the necrotic areas are unstained.

visible epicardial branches in the left ventricular apical area are ligated. This procedure results in a discrete confluent transmural intrapical infarction, usually with no surviving epicardial layer. Here the reentrant circuits seem to be located subendocardially in the border of the infarction zone, and sustained ventricular tachycardia could be induced several weeks to a few months following infarction. Garan and Ruskin (1984) suggested that reentrant excitation may be confined to a small area, based on the demonstration of continuous electrical activity in endocardial bipolar electrograms. However, there was no detailed mapping of the reentrant pathway similar to what has been demonstrated in the LAD postligation model. In fact, although in the LAD postligation model most reentrant circuits are localized in the surviving epicardial layer, in some dogs subendocardial (El-Sherif *et al.*, 1982a) and intramural reentry (El-Sherif *et al.*, 1985b) could be demonstrated. Thus, depending on the particular anatomical features of the infarction and the geometrical configuration of ischemic surviving myocardium, reentrant circuits could be located in epicardial, subendocardial, or intramyocardial zones.

## 2. Electrophysiological Substrate of Reentrant Excitation

Several investigators have described action potential abnormalities in ventricular tissue removed from subacute or chronic animal or human infarcts (Ten Eick *et al.*, 1976; Myerburg *et al.*, 1977; El-Sherif and Lazzara, 1979; Spear *et al.*, 1979, 1983a; Gilmour *et al.*, 1983). Fewer studies, however, have correlated these abnormalities with conduction (El-Sherif and Lazzara, 1979; Lazzara and Scherlag, 1980; Spear *et al.*, 1983a). El-Sherif and Lazzara (1979) described intracellular recordings from the surviving ischemic epicardial layer overlying 3–5-day-old LAD postligation infarctions in dogs. The cells showed variable degrees of partial depolarization (resting potentials from $-84$ to $-50$ mV), reduced action potential amplitude, and decreased upstroke velocity. Full recovery of responsiveness frequently outlasted the action potential duration, reflecting the presence of postrepolarization refractoriness. In these cells, premature stimuli could elicit graded responses over a wide range of coupling intervals. Slowed conduction, Wenckebach periodicity, 2:1, and high degrees of conduction block could be easily induced by fast pacing or premature stimulation (Fig. 22). Spear *et al.* (1983b) recorded transmembrane potentials and determined conduction characteristics in regions of mottled infarcts of canine epicardium in the occlusion–reperfusion model. At 3 to 5 days, resting potential, action potential amplitude, maximum rate of depolarization, and action potential duration were significantly reduced in

# 6. Electrophysiology of Ventricular Arrhythmias

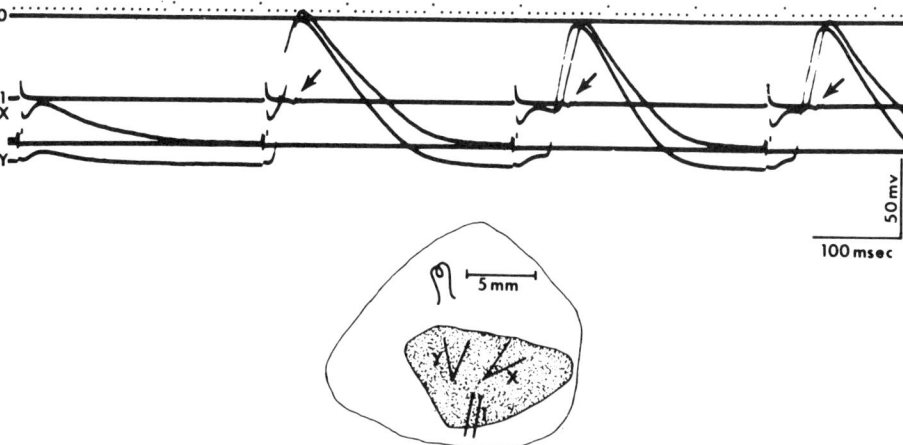

**Fig. 22.** Recordings from a dog with 3-day-old infarction illustrating action potential characteristics in ischemic epicardium. The sketch of the preparation shows two intracellular recordings (X and Y) and a close bipolar recording (1) from the infarction zone (hatched area). Ischemic cells had decreased upstroke velocity, reduced action potential amplitude, and a variable degree of partial depolarization. The two cells were recorded 5 mm apart in the infarction zone but showed significant difference in their resting potentials. The resting potential of the Y cell was only slightly reduced ($-80$ mV), but it still had a poor action potential. The preparation was stimulated at a cycle length of 290 msec, which resulted in a Wenckebach-like conduction pattern. Note that the pacing cycle length exceeded the action potential duration of the two cells, suggesting that refractoriness extended beyond the completion of the action potential (i.e., postrepolarization refractoriness). (From El-Sherif and Lazzara, 1979.)

the infarcted region. Cells on the epicardial surface showed improvement in resting potential, action potential amplitude, and rate of depolarization between 3 to 5 days and 8–15 days after infarction. Action potentials in slowly conducting areas where local conduction block occurred were associated with prepotentials and notches on their depolarization and repolarization phases. It was suggested that the prepotentials and notches are caused by electrotonic interactions resulting from microcircuitous conduction around or across inexcitable areas.

In contrast to the nonhomogeneous slow conduction in the mottled infarct of the occlusion–reperfusion model, a more homogeneous slow conduction was described in epicardium overlying confluent infarcts of the occlusion model (Lazzara and Scherlag, 1980). Spear *et al.* (1983a) have suggested that a depression in action potential depolarization and an increase in effective axial resistance contribute approximately equally to uniform slow conduction in the infarcted myocardium. Similar to the studies of Spear *et al.* (1983b) on mottled infarct, Gardner *et al.* (1984) and Wit and Rosen (1984) have shown that epicardial action potentials in the LAD postligation model that are depressed in the first week postligation return to normal several weeks later. Their studies emphasized the importance of the microanatomy of healed infarcts in the pathogenesis of slow conduction and "fractionated electrograms." They found that as the infarct heals, connective tissue separates the myocardial fibers and distorts their orientation. The interconnections between myocardial fibers appear to be reduced because of the connective tissue formation. Because of this separation on a micro level, individual muscle bundles may be activated asynchronously.

Gardner *et al.* (1984) have suggested that both the arcs of functional conduction block and slow conduction of reentrant excitation could be explained by the characteristic anisotropic properties of the surviving epicardial layer in the canine LAD postligation model. They studied *in vitro* preparations from the epicardial surface of 5-day-old canine infarct. The preparations were stimulated at the relatively long cycle length of 800 msec from two sites parallel and perpendicular to the orientation of the surviving epicardial muscle fibers. Conduction perpendicular to fiber orientation was found to be slower than in the direction parallel to fiber orientation. This study, however, did not take into consideration the fact that unidirectional conduction block and slow conduction, necessary for reentrant excitation, develop in the epicardial layer only in response to premature stimulation with a critically short cycle length. Thus the nature of conduction in the epicardial layer during long cycle lengths may not be related to conduction characteristics in response to a critically short cycle length.

Spear *et al.* (1985) have also studied the influence of fiber orientation on isolated tissues removed from the infarcted regions 8–13 days following coronary artery occlusion and reperfusion. They again studied conduction velocity in directions parallel to and perpendicular to fiber orientation at relatively long cycle lengths, rather than at the critically short cycle length that would result in reentrant excitation. However, they found that the normal dependence of conduction velocity on the orientation of the wave front relative to the myocardial fibers was disrupted. There was poor linear correlation between conduction velocity and the relative angle of the wave front. These findings were attributed to the fact that the infarction may have produced regional discontinuities in the resistance to axial current flow that were heterogeneously distributed in all directions.

In a study by El-Sherif *et al.* (1985a) the role of nonuniform refractory distribution versus anisotropic anatomical properties in the initiation of reentrant excitation in the epicardial layer surviving 3–5 days after LAD ligation was investigated. Reentrant excitation was induced by a single premature stimulus ($S_2$) in the surviving epicardial layer in the form of an arc of functional conduction block in a figure-eight circulating wave. The isochronal activation maps of $S_2$ during epicardial stimulation from at least two sites, one parallel and one perpendicular to fiber orientation of the epicardial ischemic layer, were analyzed. Activation maps were compared with the isochronal refractory maps obtained by determining effective refractory periods (ERPs) at each of 62 epicardial electrode sites. It was found that during stimulation from sites parallel or perpendicular to fiber orientation, the site of arc of conduction block was primarily related to ischemia-induced spatial nonuniformity of ERPs. The arc of block occurred at sites with juxtaposition of long ERPs in ischemic zones and short ERPs in border zones. Although the study could not rule out possible contributions of fiber orientation to spatial nonuniformity, it suggested that ischemia-induced nonuniform refractory distribution is an overriding and paramount factor for the development of arcs of conduction block and reentrant excitation in the canine postinfarction heart.

The ionic changes induced by ischemia that explain altered electrophysiological characteristics of ischemic myocardial cells have not been fully explored. Some studies suggest that depressed ischemic action potentials may be generated by a depressed fast channel rather than representing a slow channel response (El-Sherif and Lazzara, 1979). This was based on experiments that showed that ischemic cells are sensitive to the depressant effect of the fast channel blocker tetrodotoxin but not to the slow channel blockers methoxyverapamil (D-600) or verapamil (Fig. 23A). However, as shown in Fig. 23B, verapamil can depress ischemic myocardial cells with very low resting potential. These observations are similar to those described by Gilmour *et al.* (1983) in diseased human ventricular myocardium and suggest the presence of both depressed fast responses and slow response potentials in ischemic myocardial tissue. The fast channel may be depressed in ischemia for various reasons. This can only be partly explained by cellular depolarization, because the depression is usually out of proportion to the degree of depolarization of the resting potential (see Fig. 23A). The $Na^+$–$K^+$ pump may be depressed in surviving ischemic myocardial cells, leading to intracellular $Na^+$ loading (Schwartz *et al.*, 1973). This can diminish the electrochemical driving force for the inward $Na^+$ current. Ultrastructural changes of the sarcolemmal membrane, as well as the effects of products released by ischemia, including lysophosphoglycerides (Sobel *et al.*, 1978), may be implicated.

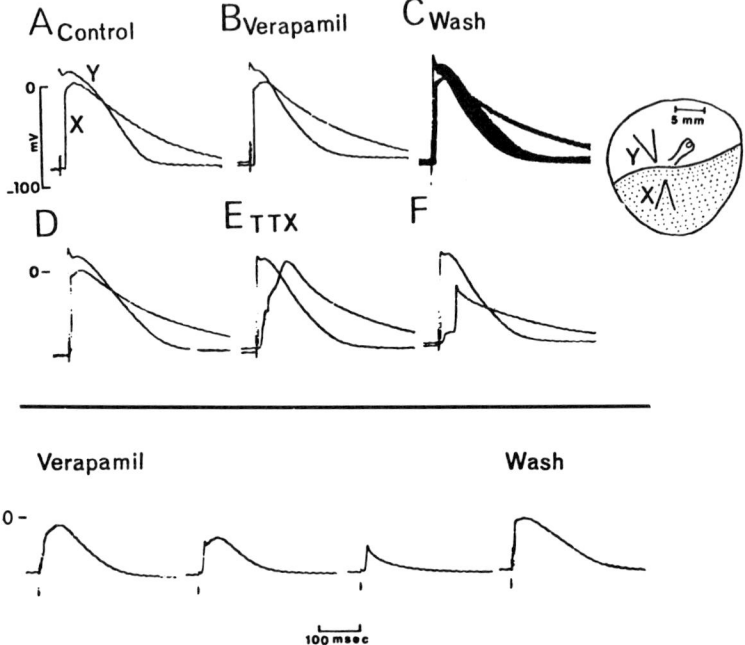

**Fig. 23.** (Upper panel) Action potential recordings of an ischemic (X) and normal (Y) myocardial cells from an epicardial preparation from a 3-day-old canine infarction comparing the effects of tetrodotoxin (TTX) and verapamil. The resting potential of the ischemic cell was similar to that of the normal cell at −82 mV. However, the ischemic cell had a reduced action potential amplitude, decreased upstroke velocity, and a prolonged action potential duration. Verapamil ($1 \times 10^{-6}$ g/ml) had no significant effect on the ischemic cell but resulted in acceleration of the early repolarization phase of the normal cell. On the other hand, TTX ($1 \times 10^{-6}$ g/ml) resulted in marked depression of the ischemic action potential with fractionation of the upstroke and, later, abbreviation of the action potential due to loss of the large amplitude hump on the plateau. This was associated with evidence of conduction delay and block in the ischemic zone. (Lower panel) Action potential recording from an ischemic myocardial cell from another preparation. In contrast to the ischemic cell in the upper panel, the cell in the lower panel had a very low resting potential (−55 mV) and verapamil resulted in marked depression of the cell.

### 3. Interruption of Reentrant Circuits by Cryothermal Techniques

The criteria for proving the presence of circulating excitation as established by Mines (1913, 1914) are (1) an area of unidirectional block must be demonstrated; (2) the movement of the excitatory wave should be observed to progress through the pathway, to return to its point of origin, and then to again follow the same pathway; and (3) "the best test for circulating excitation is to cut through the ring at one point. If impulses continue to arise in the cut ring, circus movement as a cause can be ruled out." Reversible cooling and/or cryoablation of localized areas of the epicardial surface of the reentrant circuit were used to fulfill Mines' criteria for proving the presence of circulating excitation and to identify the critical site along the reentrant circuit at which interruption of reentrant activation could be successfully accomplished (El-Sherif et al., 1983b). These studies have demonstrated that reentrant activation could be successfully interrupted when cooling or cryoablation was applied to the part of the common reentrant wave front immediately proximal to the zone of earliest reactivation (Fig. 24C). At this site, the common reentrant wave front is usually narrow and is surrounded on each side by an arc of functional conduction block. On the other hand, localized cooling to the site of earliest reactivation commonly failed to interrupt reentry (Fig. 24B). The common reentrant wave front usually broke through the arc of functional conduction block to reactivate other sites close to the original reactivation site without necessarily changing the overall reentrant activation pattern. Usually, however, the reentrant cycle length increased by 10 to 30 msec.

The cryothermal experiments underscore the limitations of clinical studies that advanced the notion of an earliest site of ventricular activation during possible reentrant rhythms (Horowitz et al., 1980a). It is obvious that during a continuous reentrant excitation there is no such thing as an earliest site of ventricular activation. On a more practical note, electrograms from the so-called earliest site of ventricular activation were recorded 2–48 msec before the onset of the surface QRS complex. Surgical excisions of these sites were reported to have resulted in termination of the ventricular tachycardia (Horowitz et al., 1980b). In the canine postinfarction heart, electrograms representing the earliest reactivation site preceded the surface QRS by 10 to 40 msec. However, cooling application to this site usually failed to interrupt reentrant activation. Electrograms representing the distal portion of the common reentrant wave front from where the reentrant circuit could be consistently interrupted preceded the surface QRS by 40 to 80 msec, however (El-Sherif et al., 1983b). A plausible explanation for the results of the clinical studies is that the surgical incisions in these studies were in fact extensive and included, in addition to the site of earliest reactivation, parts of the common reentrant wave front.

### 4. Activation Maps during Ventricular Fibrillation

It has been known for some time that ventricular fibrillation requires a critical mass of tissue (Garrey, 1914) and can be sustained only in larger

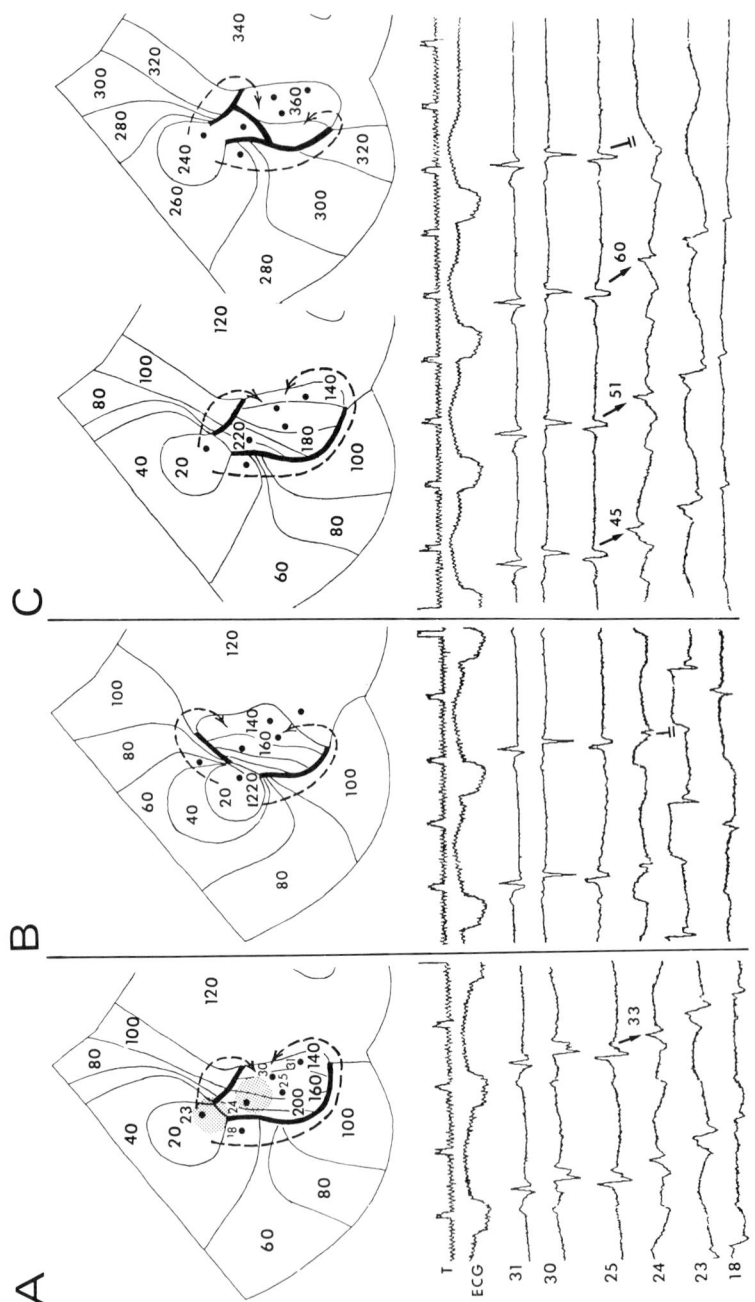

hearts such as those of humans and dogs (Wiggers, 1940). Several studies suggested the presence of activation sequences with some degree of organization during the early phase of ventricular fibrillation (Wiggers, 1940; Moe *et al.*, 1941; deBakker *et al.*, 1979; Janse *et al.*, 1980; Ideker *et al.*, 1981, El-Sherif *et al.*, 1982a). The onset of fibrillation has been mapped by Wiggers (1940) and by Moe *et al.* (1941) using high-speed cinematography and direct electrical recordings from the epicardium. During the onset of electrically induced fibrillation, organized cyclic activation could be followed for two to four cycles. Using a large number of recording sites and multiplexing recording techniques, Janse *et al.* (1980) and El-Sherif *et al.* (1982a) analyzed epicardial activation patterns during the onset of ventricular fibrillation in acute and subacute infarctions, respectively. During acute ischemia, Janse *et al.* (1980) have shown that fragmentation of wave fronts occurred during fibrillation with multiple wavelets following tortuous paths and that circus movements were seldom completed. El-Sherif *et al.* (1982a) have shown the presence of multiple irregular arcs of block as well as complete and incomplete (dead-end) reentrant circuits during ventricular fibrillation in subacute canine infarctions (Fig. 25).

**Fig. 24.** Interruption of reentrant excitation in the surviving epicardial layer overlying 4-day-old canine infarction by cryothermal techniques. The figure illustrates the effects of reversible cooling when the cryoprobe (shaded circles) was applied either to the site of earliest activation (B) or to the distal part of the common reentrant wavefront (C). (A) shows control map. Selected epicardial electrograms are shown on the bottom. At the earliest reactivation site, represented by electrogram 23, the slow reentrant wavefront first reexcited myocardial zones on the other side of the arcs of conduction block. Electrogram 23 preceded the onset of surface QRS by 30 msec. Cooling resulted in a conduction block between sites 24 and 23. The activation potential at 23 was markedly delayed and occurred after the onset of surface QRS. The isochronal map after cooling showed significant changes in the position of the upper arc of conduction block and the clockwise directed wavefront. However, the common reentrant wavefront still reexcited site 18 on the proximal border of the arc of block and adjacent to the original site of early reactivation (site 23). Cooling the original site of early reactivation thus did not interrupt the reentrant circuit but rather resulted in a shift of the early reexcitation site. Conduction of the common reentrant wavefront to the new reexcitation site (sites 24 to 18) was slower compared to control (sites 24 to 23) and resulted in a 20-msec increase in the tachycardia cycle length. (C) shows that when cooling was applied to the distal part of the common reentrant wavefront the reentrant circuit was interrupted. During control, the conduction time between proximal electrode site 25 and the more distal site 24 was 33 msec. Prior to termination of the tachycardia, an incremental beat-to-beat increase of the conduction time between sites 25 and 24 occurred associated with equal increases in the tachycardia cycle length. When conduction block developed between the two sites, the reentrant circuit was terminated and electrogram 24 recorded an electrotonic potential but no local activation potential. This was represented on the isochronal map by an arc of conduction block (heavy solid line) that joined the two separate arcs of conduction block into one. (From El-Sherif *et al.*, 1983b.)

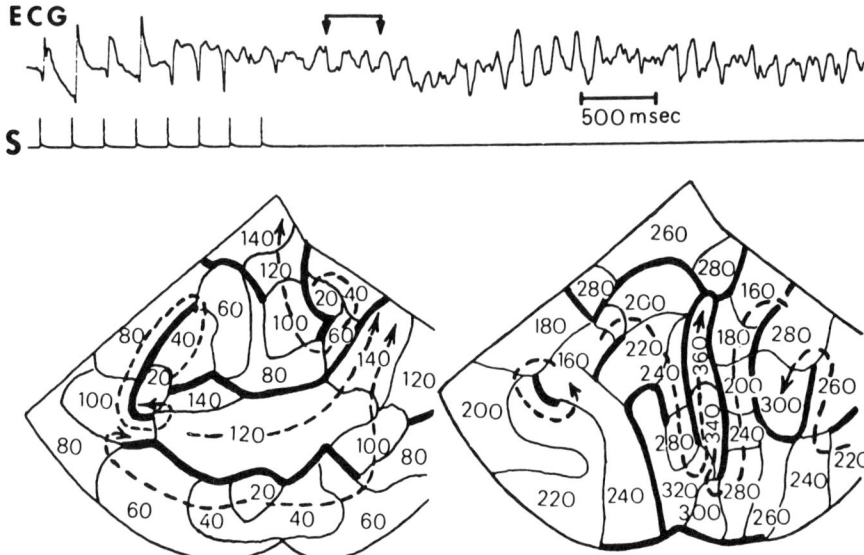

**Fig. 25.** Epicardial activation maps during ventricular fibrillation in canine 1-day-old myocardial infarction. A ventricular tachyarrhythmia that rapidly degenerated into ventricular fibrillation was induced by a burst of rapid ventricular pacing. The arrhythmia started before the termination of pacing and the fifth QRS complex was a nonstimulated beat. The figure illustrates the epicardial isochronal maps during a 360-msec interval (marked by arrows on the ECG) that started only 1 sec after the first nonstimulated beat. Note that epicardial activation is already chaotic with continuously changing multiple asynchronous reentrant circuits, several of which are incomplete (or dead-end) circuits. (From El-Sherif *et al.*, 1982a.)

In another study, El-Sherif *et al.* (1983c) have compared the ventricular activation maps of pleomorphic ventricular rhythms that terminated spontaneously and those that degenerated into ventricular fibrillation in the same dog. It was found that during a self-terminating pleomorphic ventricular rhythm, two synchronous reentrant wave fronts may briefly degenerate into three or four wave fronts but that those soon coalesce into two circulating wave fronts. Reentrant activation finally terminates by fusion of the two separate arcs of functional conduction block. On the other hand, in the same dog, during a pleomorphic ventricular rhythm that degenerates into ventricular fibrillation the initial two synchronous circulating wave fronts progressively degenerated into multiple asynchronous wave fronts that continuously changed their sites and configurations. An important observation in the study was that during self-terminating pleomorphic ventricular tachycardias both the multiple arcs of functional block and circulating wave fronts remained confined within the epicardial layer overlying the infarct. Once functional arcs of block and circulating wave fronts developed in normal myocardial zones, however, ventricular fibrillation did not revert spontaneously. These findings were explained as follows: the development of asynchronous wave fronts in the ischemic epicardial layer resulted in irregular activation of normal epicardium. This accentuated the nonuniform shortening of refractoriness in both ischemic and normal myocardial zones, which in turn resulted in new arcs of functional conduction block and irregular circulating wave fronts. This hypothesis is supported by observations that successive short cycles result in nonuniform shortening of refractoriness in the ischemic zone (El-Sherif, 1985; Gough et al., 1985). Not considered, however, is the activation pattern intramurally and subendocardially. Therefore, another possible explanation is that rapid conduction in the normal Purkinje network invades the epicardial ischemic layer in an irregular fashion, accentuating the degree of nonuniform refractoriness in this layer and thus leading to further degeneration of wave fronts.

## 5. Mechanism of Action of Antiarrhythmic Agents on Ischemia-Related Reentrant Rhythms

Despite extensive studies directed at the cellular mechanisms of antiarrhythmic drugs, direct experimental evidence about their mode of action in ischemia-related reentrant arrhythmias remains scarce and the proposed mechanisms of action remain largely inferential. In the past few years, several electropharmacological studies have been reported on ventricular arrhythmias in the canine subacute myocardial infarction phase. El-Sherif et al. (1977c; El-Sherif, 1978, 1979) have studied the effects of lidocaine, diphenylhydantoin, and procainamide, respectively, on reentrant ventricular arrhythmias in the 3–5 days LAD postligation model. Utilizing composite electrode recordings from the ischemic epicardial layer, the investigators suggested that these drugs prolong refractoriness of potentially reentrant pathways and further depress slow conduction in the ischemic zone. Their antiarrhythmic action was attributed to conduction block of the reentrant pathway. Cobbe et al. (1983, 1984) have studied the effects of sotalol and disopyramide in the same animal model, also using composite electrode recordings, and suggested a similar mechanism of action. Other investigators have studied the effects of disopyramide (Patterson et al., 1980), lidocaine (Patterson et al., 1982), procainamide (Michelson et al., 1981), timolol, and propranolol (Gang et al., 1984) in a canine occlusion–reperfusion model and reported essentially similar results. However, in all of these studies assessment of conduction was based on either recordings from a few sites or on composite electrode

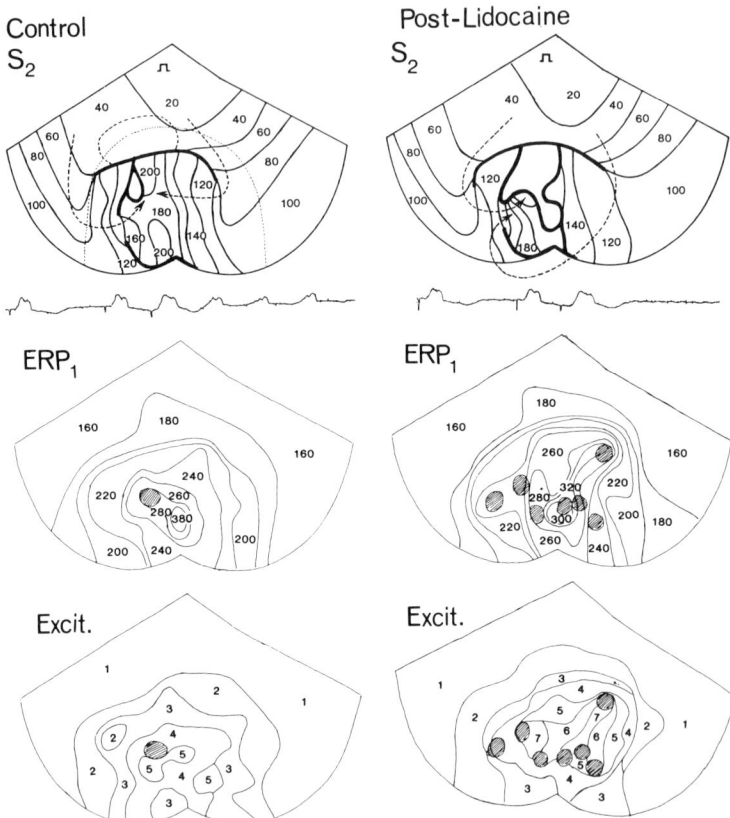

**Fig. 26.** Mechanism of antiarrhythmic action of lidocaine on reentrant ventricular rhythms in 4-day-old canine infarction. Control recordings are shown on the left panel and postlidocaine results on the right. Arranged from top to bottom are the isochronal activation map, the isorefractory map, and the excitability map. The isochrones for the activation and refractory maps are drawn at 20-msec intervals and for the excitability map at 1 mA. During control the reentry zone following $S_2$ stimulation was 80 msec ($S_1$–$S_2$ intervals of 160 to 240 msec). The figure shows that an $S_1$–$S_2$ interval of 175 msec induced a reentrant rhythm. The activation map of $S_2$ shows the development of two arcs of block inside the upper and apical borders of the ischemic zone. The two circulating wave fronts around the upper arc of block coalesced and then reexcited normal myocardial zones on the upper septal border of the ischemic zone initiating a reentrant rhythm. Comparison of the activation and refractory maps shows that the arcs of block developed at areas with nonuniform refractory distribution (crowded refractory isochrones). The excitability map on the bottom shows one inexcitable site (shaded area) and significant increase of the excitability threshold in the central part of the ischemic zone. However, there was no correlation between the excitability threshold and the lengthening of ERP. Following lidocaine, the reentry zone of $S_2$ was markedly reduced but not totally abolished. Only $S_1$–$S_2$ intervals of 160 to 170 msec could induce reentry. The figure shows that an $S_1$–$S_2$ interval of 175 msec failed to initiate a reentrant rhythm. The activation map of $S_2$ shows that both the clockwise and counterclockwise

recordings. Also, assessment of refractoriness was limited. The only study that attempted to investigate the effects of the antiarrhythmic agent lidocaine in acute myocardial ischemia utilizing more detailed analysis of ventricular activation maps was that of Cardinal *et al.* (1981). The authors reported that lidocaine in high concentration reduced the incidence of ventricular fibrillation occurring during occlusion by preventing the fractionation of wave fronts into multiple wavelets and microreentrant circuits. They proposed that lidocaine abolished reentry by converting areas of unidirectional block and slow conduction into areas of total block. This was attributed to the effects of lidocaine in depressing both the active generator properties (fast inward current) and the excitability of membranes in the ischemic zone.

Mehra *et al.* (1984) have investigated the mechanism of lidocaine action on reentrant rhythms in the 3–5 days LAD postligation model by analysis of activation, refractory, and excitability maps before and after lidocaine infusion (4 mg/kg + 50 $\mu$g/kg/min IV). Lidocaine was found to have the following effects:

1. It prolonged the ERPs at most sites in the ischemic zone and increased excitability threshold, with some sites becoming inexcitable.
2. Effective refractory periods and excitability threshold of normal myocardium were not significantly altered.
3. For the premature beat, the conduction time from the normal to ischemic zone was consistently prolonged.
4. In a majority of experiments, lidocaine was able to prevent reentrant rhythms induced by premature beats with long coupling intervals but not at short coupling intervals; in other words, it significantly decreased the zone of reentry.

The common reentrant wave front following premature beats with long coupling intervals was blocked in the ischemic zone, where ERPs were prolonged and excitability threshold had increased (Fig. 26). Premature stimuli at short coupling intervals, however, showed further increase of conduction delay within the ischemic zone, and the delayed reentrant

---

wavefronts blocked at the center of the ischemic zone. Evidence of slowed conduction preceding conduction block was manifested by the counterclockwise wavefront. The postlidocaine refractory map shows no significant change in refractoriness in normal zones and nonuniform lengthening of refractoriness in the ischemic zone. The postlidocaine excitability map shows increase of excitability threshold in the ischemic zone with many sites becoming inexcitable. Correlation of postlidocaine activation, refractory, and excitability maps suggests that the increased conduction delay and conduction block of the premature beat following lidocaine generally occurred at ischemic sites that showed increased nonuniform refractory distribution and decreased excitability.

wave front could still reexcite normal myocardium. Correlation of postlidocaine activation, refractory, and excitability maps suggested that the increased conduction delay and conduction block of the premature beat following lidocaine generally occurred at ischemic sites that showed increased nonuniform refractory distribution and decreased excitability. The study clearly illustrated the potential significance of the correlation of activation, refractory, and excitability maps for understanding the mechanism of action of antiarrhythmic drugs on reentrant rhythms.

## 6. Role of the Autonomic System in Ischemia-Related Reentrant Rhythms

It is widely accepted that sympathetic impulses can facilitate the development of serious ventricular arrhythmias in the setting of acute myocardial ischemia and that sympathectomy and beta-adrenergic blockade can have the opposite effect (for references, see El-Sherif, 1978). The exact mechanisms by which these effects are mediated are not clear. On the other hand, it has been shown that increased vagal tone can promote ventricular electrical stability during acute myocardial infarction and that vagolytic drugs may have the opposite effects. Studies by Martins and Zipes (1980) suggest that the vagus could act on arrhythmias involving ventricular muscle and not only on those involving the specialized conduction system (Kent et al., 1974). Some investigators have questioned the presence of direct vagal effect on ventricular vulnerability and suggested that vagal enhancement of ventricular electrical stability is achieved by counteracting the effects of heightened sympathetic tone. Vagal stimulation has been shown to prolong the left ventricular refractory period; this effect is abolished by beta-adrenergic blockade or sympathectomy (Kolman et al., 1975). A number of mechanisms have been demonstrated that may account for the attenuation of the effects of sympathetic nerve stimulation by simultaneous vagal stimulation. These include both presynaptic and postsynaptic effects of acetylcholine on norepinephrine release and on cAMP generated by adrenergic stimulation (Watanabe et al., 1975; Van Houtte and Levy, 1980).

El-Sherif and Lazzara (1978) have utilized composite electrode recordings to analyze the effects of sympathetic and parasympathetic stimulation on conduction and reentrant rhythms in the ischemic epicardial layer. This study suggested that vagal stimulation has no significant direct electrophysiological effects while sympathetic stimulation resulted in improving conduction in the ischemic zone. However, composite electrode recordings only give an overall estimate of conduction in the ischemic zone and will not be able to detect localized change in activation or refractoriness in response to autonomic stimulation. Barber *et al.* (1983) have used intracoronary injection of vinyl latex solution to eliminate the influence of collateral circulation and create a transmural infarction that includes the superficial epicardial layer. This resulted in disruption of efferent sympathetic neurotransmission in the superficial subepicardium and produced sympathetic denervation in noninfarcted sites apical to the area of necrosis. The study suggests that myocardial infarction can create autonomic imbalance not only in the ischemic area but also in the nonischemic myocardium surrounding the infarction.

## IV. Conclusion

The progress that has been made in less than two decades towards understanding of the electrophysiological alterations and the mechanisms of ischemia-related ventricular arrhythmias reflects the heightened awareness of the revelance and serious nature of this clinical entity. Experimental studies of postinfarction ventricular arrhythmias have usually been conducted in dogs following one- or two-stage occlusion of one or more coronary arteries, although other animal species have also been utilized. A perfect animal model of myocardial infarction that faithfully reproduces the arrhythmias that might occur in man does not exist. Most experimental models create a combination of localized myocardial ischemia and infarction in previously normal hearts. However, in man the majority of ischemias and infarctions occur in hearts with preexisting coronary atherosclerosis. Further, a reliable animal model for spontaneous ventricular tachycardia and ventricular fibrillation is not available even though these arrhythmias are not uncommon in human infarctions. In spite of these and other limitations much progress has been made. There is now convincing evidence that reentrant excitation in ischemic myocardium underlies the spontaneous and often lethal ventricular tachyarrhythmias seen in the acute phase of myocardial infarction as well as ventricular tachyarrhythmias induced by programmed stimulation in the subacute and, possibly, chronic phases. Triggered activity arising from delayed afterdepolarizations in ischemic Purkinje fibers, and possibly abnormal automaticity in ischemic depolarized cardiac cells, may explain some of the spontaneous multiform ventricular rhythms seen in the subacute phase of myocardial infarction and perhaps in the chronic phase as well. The role of the autonomic system and the mechanism of action of the various classes of antiarrhythmic agents on the different types of ischemia-related arrhythmias have been better clarified. With the advent of more sophisticated techniques applicable to both human and animal studies, the future holds promise for better understanding of the electrophysiological alterations associated with ischemia as well as their biophysical and biochemical bases. This undoubtedly will provide a basis for improved clinical management of postinfarction lethal ventricular arrhythmias.

## Acknowledgments

This work was supported in part by the Veterans Administration Medical Research Funds.

## References

Allessie, M. A., Bonke, F. I. M., Schopman, F. J. G. (1973). *Circ Res* **33**:54–62.
Allessie, M. A., Bonke, F. I. M., Schopman, F. J. G. (1976). *Circ Res* **39**:168–177.
Allessie, M. A., Bonke, F. I. M., Schopman, F. J. G. (1977). *Circ Res* **41**:9–18.
Antzelevitch, C., Moe, G. K. (1981). *Circ Res* **49**:1129–1139.
Antzelevitch, C., Jalife, J., Moe, G. K. (1980). *Circulation* **61**:182–191.
Antzelevitch, C., Bernstein, M. J., Feldman, H. N., Moe, G. K. (1983). *Circulation* **68**:1101–1115.
Aronson, R. S. (1981). *Circ Res* **48**:720–727.
Balke, C. W., Kaplinsky, E., Michelson, E. L., Naito, M., Dreifus, L. (1981). *Am Heart J* **101**:449–456.
Barber, M. J., Mueller, T. M., Henry, D. P., Felten, Z. Y., Zipes, D. P. (1983). *Circulation* **67**:787–796.
Bigger, J. T., Dresdale, R. J., Heissenbuttel, R. H., Weld, F. M., Wit, A. L. (1977). *Prog Cardiovasc Dis* **19**:255–300.
Bocage, A. J., Otero, H., Harris, A. S. (1974). *J Electrocardiol* **7**:215–220.
Boineau, J. P., Cox, J. L. (1973). *Circulation* **48**:703–713.
Boineau, J. P., Schussler, R. B., Mooney, C. R., Miller, C. B., Wylds, A. C., Hudson, R. D., Borremans, J. M., Brockus, C. B. (1980). *Am J Cardiol* **45**:1167–1181.
Brachmann, J., Scherlag, B. J., Rosenshtraukh, L. V., Lazzara, R. (1983). *Circulation* **68**:846–856.
Brooks, C., McC., Hoffman, B. F., Suckling, E. E., Orias, O. (1955). "Excitability of the Heart". Grune and Stratton, New York.
Carafoli, E., Tiozzo, R., Lugli, G., Crovetti, F., Kratzing, C. (1974). *J Mol Cell Cardiol* **6**:361–371.
Cardinal, R., Janse, M. J., van Eden, I., Werner, G., Naumann d'Alnoncourt, C., Durrer, D. (1981). *Circ Res* **49**:792–806.
Cobbe, S. M., Hoffman, E., Ritzenhoff, A., Brachmann, J., Kubler, W., Senges, J. (1983). *Circulation* **68**:865–871.
Cobbe, S. M., Hoffman, E., Ritzenhoff, A., Brachmann, J., Kubler, W., Senges, J. (1984). *Am J Cardiol* **53**:1712–1718.
Cranefield, P. F. (1975). "The Slow Response and Cardiac Arrhythmias". Futura Press, Mt. Kisco, New York.
Cranefield, P. F. (1977). *Circ Res* **41**:415–423.

Cranefield, P. F., Aronson, R. S. (1974). *Circ Res* **34**:477–481.
Dangman, K. H., Hoffman, B. F. (1981). *J Pharmac Exp Ther* **217**:851–862.
deBakker, J. M. T., Henning, B., Merx, W. (1979). *Circ Res* **45**:374–378.
DiFrancisco, D. (1981a). *J Physiol* **314**:359–376.
DiFrancisco, D. (1981b). *J Physiol* **314**:377–393.
Downar, E., Janse, M. J., Durrer, D. (1977). *Circulation* **56**:217–224.
Durrer, D., Van Damm, R. T. H., Freud, G. E., Janse, M. J. (1971). *Koninkl Ned Akad Wetenschap Proc, Ser Cx* **74**:321–331.
El-Sherif, N. (1978). *Circulation* **58**:103–110.
El-Sherif, N. (1979). *Am J Cardiol* **43**:429.
El-Sherif, N. (1985). *In* "Cardiac Electrophysiology and Arrhythmias". (D. Zipes and J. Jalife, eds.), Chap 41, pp 363–378. Grune and Stratton, New York.
El-Sherif, N., Lazzara, R. (1978). *Circulation* **57**:465–472.
El-Sherif, N., Lazzara, R. (1979). *Circulation* **60**:605–615.
El-Sherif, N., Scherlag, B. J., Lazzara, R., Samet, P. (1974). *Am J Cardiol* **33**:529–540.
El-Sherif, N., Scherlag, B. J., Lazzara, R. (1975). *Circulation* **51**:1003–1014.
El-Sherif, N., Scherlag, B. J., Lazzara, R. (1977a). *Circulation* **55**:686–701.
El-Sherif, N., Scherlag, B. J., Lazzara, R. (1977b). *Circulation* **55**:702–719.
El-Sherif, N., Scherlag, B. J., Lazzara, R., Hope, R. R. (1977c). *Circulation* **56**:395–402.
El-Sherif, N., Mayorga-Cortes, A., Myerburg, R., Lazzara, R. (1977d). *Circulation* **56** (Suppl III):66.
El-Sherif, N., Smith, R. A., Evans, K. (1981). *Circ Res* **49**:255–265.
El-Sherif, N., Mehra, R., Gough, W. B., Zeiler, R. H. (1982a). *Circ Res* **51**:152–166.
El-Sherif, N., Gough, W. B., Zeiler, R. H., Mehra, R. (1982b). *Circulation* **66** (Suppl II):357.
El-Sherif, N., Gough, W. B., Zeiler, R. H., Mehra, R. (1983a). *Circ Res* **52**:566–579.
El-Sherif, N., Mehra, R., Gough, W. B., Zeiler, R. H. (1983b). *Circulation* **68**:644–656.
El-Sherif, N., Mehra, R., Gough, W. B., Zeiler, R. (1983c). *J Am Coll Cardiol* **1(2)**:621.
El-Sherif, N., Gough, W. B., Zeiler, R. H., Craelius, W., Restivo, M. (1985a). *J Am Coll Cardiol* **5**:390.
El-Sherif, N., Gough, W. B., Zeiler, R. H., Hariman, R. (1985b). *J Am Coll Cardiol* **6**:124–132.
Fenoglio, J. J., Karagueuzian, H. S., Friedman, P. L., Albola, A., Wit, A. L. (1979). *Am J Physiol* **236**:H356–H370.
Ferrier, G. R. (1976). *Circ Res* **38**:156–162.
Ferrier, G. R. (1983). *Circulation* **68** (Suppl III):20.
Ferrier, G. R., Rosenthal, J. E. (1980). *Circ Res* **47**:238–248.
Ferrier, G. R., Saunders, J. H., Mendez, C. (1973). *Circ Res* **32**:600–609.
Friedman, P. L., Stewart, J. R., Fenoglio, J. J., Wit, A. L. (1973a). *Circ Res* **33**:597–611.
Friedman, P. L., Stewart, J. R., Wit, A. L. (1973b). *Circ Res* **33**:612–625.
Gadsby, D., Cranefield, P. F. (1977). *J Gen Physiol* **70**:725–746.
Gang, E. S., Bigger, J. T., Uhl, E. W. (1984). *Am J Cardiol* **53**:275–281.
Garan, H., Ruskin, J. (1984). *J Clin Invest* **74**:377–392.
Garan, H., Fallon, J. T., Ruskin, J. N. (1980). *Circulation* **62**:980–987.
Garan, H., Fallon, J. T., Ruskin, J. N. (1981). *Am J Cardiol* **48**:280–286.
Gardner, P. I., Ursell, P. C., Pham, T. D., Fenoglio, J. J., Wit, A. L. (1984). *In* "Tachycardias, Mechanisms, Diagnosis and Treatment". (M. E. Josephson and H. J. Wellens, eds.), Chap 2, pp 29–60. Lea Febiger, Philadelphia.
Garrey, W. E. (1914). *Am J Physiol* **33**:397–408.
Gilmour, R. F., Jr., Heger, J. J., Prystowsky, E. N., Zipes, D. P. (1983). *Am J Cardiol* **52**:137–144.

Goto, M., Yatani, A., Tsuda, Y. (1978). In "Recent Advances in Studies on Cardiac Structure and Metabolism". Vol II, Heart Function and Metabolism. (T. Kobayashi, T. Sano, M. S. Dhella, eds.), pp 37–44. University Park Press, Baltimore.
Gough, W. B., Zeiler, R. H., El-Sherif, N. (1984a). Am J Cardiol 53:303–306.
Gough, W. B., Zeiler, R. H., El-Sherif, N. (1984b). Cardiovasc Res 18:339–343.
Gough, W. B., Mehra, R., Restivo, M., Zeiler, R. H., El-Sherif, N. (1985). Circ Res 57:432–442.
Grossman, A., Furchgott, R. F. (1964). J Pharmac Exp Ther 145:162–172.
Hariman, R. J., Holtzman, R., Gough, W. B., Mehra, R., Gomes, J. A. C., El-Sherif, N. (1984). J Am Coll Cardiol 3(2):478.
Hariman, R. J., Zeiler, R. H., Gough, W. B., El-Sherif, N. (1985). J Am Coll Cardiol 5:672–679.
Harris, A. S. (1950). Circulation 1:1318–1328.
Hauswirth, O., Noble, P., Tsien, R. W. (1969). J Physiol (Lond) 200:255–265.
Hill, J. L., Gettes, L. S. (1980). Circulation 61:768–778.
Hirsche, H. J., Franz, C., Bös, L., Bissig, R., Lang, R., Schramm, M. (1980). J Mol Cell Cardiol 12:579–793.
Hirzel, H. O., Nelson, G. R., Sonnenblick, E. H., Kirk, E. S. (1976). Circ Res 39:214–222.
Hoffman, B. F., Rosen, M. R. (1981). Circ Res 49:1–15.
Hoffman, B. F., Dangman, K. H. (1982). In "Normal and Abnormal Conduction in the Heart". (A. V. Paes de Carvalho, B. F. Hoffman, M. Lieberman, eds). Futura Press, Mt. Kisco, New York.
Horowitz, L. N., Spear, J. F., Moore, E. N. (1976). Circulation 53:56–63.
Horowitz, L. N., Josephson, M. E., Harken, A. H. (1980a). Circulation 60:1227–1238.
Horowitz, L. N., Josephson, M. E., Harken, A. H. (1980b). N Engl J Med 302:589–597.
Ideker, R. E., Klein, G. J., Harrison, L., Smith, W. M., Kasell, J., Reimer, K. A., Wallace, A., Gallagher, J. J. (1981). Circulation 63:1371–1379.
Imanishi, S., Surawicz, B. (1976). Circ Res 39:751–759.
Jalife, J., Moe, G. K. (1976). Circ Res 39:801–808.
Jalife, J., Moe, G. K. (1981). Circ Res 49:233–247.
Janse, M. J., Klèber, A. G. (1981). Circ Res 49:1069–1081.
Janse, M. J., Van Capelle, F. J. L. (1982). Circ Res 50:527–537.
Janse, M. J., Van Capelle, F. J. L., Morsink, H., Kleber, A. G., Wilms-Schopman, F., Cardinal, R., D'Alnoncourt, C. N., Durrer, D. (1980). Circ Res 47:151–165.
Janse, M. J., Wilms-Schopman, F., Wilensky, R. S., Tranum-Jensen, J. (1985). In "Cardiac, Electrophysiology and Arrhythmias". (D. Zipes and J. Jalife, eds), Chap 40, pp 353–362. Grune and Stratton, New York.
Josephson, M. E., Horowitz, L. N., Farshidi, A. (1978). Circulation 57:659–665.
Karagueuzian, H. S., Fenoglio, J. J., Jr., Weiss, M. B., Wit, A. L. (1979). Circ Res 44:833–846.
Kardesh, M., Hogancamp, C. E., Bing, R. J. (1958). Circ Res 6:715–720.
Kass, R. S., Lederer, W. J., Tsien, R. W., Weingart, R. (1978a). J Physiol (Lond) 281:187–208.
Kass, R. S., Tsien, R. W., Weingart, R. (1978b). J Physiol (Lond) 281:209–226.
Katzung, B. O., Morgenstern, J. A. (1977). Circ Res 40:105–111.
Kent, A. F. S. A. (1914). J Physiol (Lond) 48:22–29.
Kent, K. M., Epstein, S. E., Cooper, T., Jacobowitz, D. M. (1974). Circulation 50:948–955.
Klèber, A. G., Janse, M. J., Van Capelle, F. J. L., Durrer, D. (1978). Circ Res 42:603–613.
Kolman, B. S., Verrier, R. L., Lown, B. (1975). Circulation 52:578–585.
Kotler, N. N., Tabatznik, B., Mower, M. M., Tominaga, S. (1973). Circulation 47:959–966.
Krikler, D. M., Curry, P. V. L. (1976). Brit Heart J 38:117–120.

Langendorf, R., Pick, A. (1964). *In* "Sudden Cardiac Death". (B. Surawicz and E. E. Pellegrino, eds.), pp 97–107. Grune and Stratton, New York.
Lazzara, R., Scherlag, B. J. (1980). *In* "The Slow Inward Current and Cardiac Arrhythmias". (D. C. Zipes, J. C. Bailey, V. El-Harrar, eds.), pp 399–415. Martinus Nijhoff, The Hague.
Lazzara, R., El-Sherif, N., Scherlag, B. J. (1973). *Circ Res* **33**:722–734.
Lazzara, R., El-Sherif, N., Scherlag, B. J. (1975). *Circ Res* **36**:444–454.
Lee, K. S., Klaus, W. (1971). *Pharmacol Rev* **23**:193–261.
Lewis, T. (1925). "The Mechanisms and Graphic Registration of the Heart Beat". Shaw & Sons, London.
Lewis, T., Feil, H. S., Stroud, W. D. (1920). *Heart* **7**:191–233.
Low, P. A., Wm, C. H., Narahashi, T. (1979). *J Pharmac Exp Ther* **210**:417–421.
Martins, J. B., Zipes, D. (1980). *Circ Res* **46**:100–110.
Matsuda, K., Hoshi, T., Nameyamo, S. (1981). *Jpn J Physiol* **9**:419–426.
Mayer, A. G. (1908). *Tortugas Lab* **1**:113–131; Carnegie Institute Publication No. 102, part VII.
Mehra, R., Zeiler, R. H., Gough, W. B., El-Sherif, N. (1983). *Circulation* **67**:11–24.
Mehra, R., Gough, W. B., Zeiler, R. H., El-Sherif, N. (1984). *J Am Coll Cardiol* **2**:542.
Michelson, E. L., Spear, J. F., Moore, E. N. (1980). *Am J Cardiol* **45**:583–590.
Michelson, E. L., Spear, J. F., Moore, E. N. (1981). *Am J Cardiol* **47**:1223–1232.
Mines, G. R. (1913). *J Physiol* **46**:350–383.
Mines, G. R. (1914). *Trans R Soc Can* (Ser 3, Sect IV) **8**:43–52.
Moe, G. K., Harris, A. S., Wiggers, C. J. (1941). *Am J Physiol* **134**:473–492.
Moe, G. K., Mendez, C., Han, J. (1965). *Circ Res* **16**:261–286.
Murdock, D. K., Loeb, J. M., Euler, D. R., Randall, W. C. (1980). *Circulation* **61**:175–182.
Myerburg, R. J., Gelband, H., Nilsson, K. (1977). *Circ Res* **41**:73–84.
Noble, D., Tsien, R. W. (1968). *J Physiol* (*Lond*) **195**:185–214.
Patterson, E., Gibson, J. K., Lucchesi, B. R. (1980). *Am J Cardiol* **46**:792–799.
Patterson, E., Gibson, J. K., Lucchesi, B. R. (1982). *J Cardiovasc Pharmacol* **4**:925–934.
Penny, W. J., Sheridan, D. J. (1983). *Cardiovasc Res* **17**:363–372.
Reimer, K. A., Low, J. E., Rasmussen, M. M., Jennings, R. B. (1977). *Circulation* **56**:786–794.
Reuter, H., Scholz, H. (1977). *J Physiol* (*London*) **264**:49–62.
Reuter, H., Seitz, N. (1968). *J Physiol* (*Lond*) **195**:451–470.
Roden, D. M., Arthur, M., Woosley, R. L. (1985). *J Am Coll Cardiol* **5(2)**:390.
Rosen, M. R., Reder, R. F. (1981). *Ann Int Med* **94**:974–801.
Rosen, M. R., Gelband, H., Hoffman, B. F. (1973). *Circulation* **47**:65–72.
Salazar, J., McKendrick, C. S. (1970). *Brit Heart J* **32**:377–385.
Schaper, W., Frenzel, H., Hort, W., Winkler, B. (1979). *Basic Res Cardiol* **74**:233–239.
Scherlag, B. J., El-Sherif, N., Hope, R., Lazzara, R. (1974). *Circ Res* **35**:372–383.
Schmidt, R. F. (1950). *Pfluegers Arch* **271**:526.
Schmitt, F. O., Erlanger, J. (1928–1929). *Am J Physiol* **87**:326–347.
Schwartz, A., Wood, J. M., Allen, J. C., Bornet, E., Entman, M. L., Goldstein, M. A., Sordahl, L. Z., Suzuki, M., Lewis, R. M. (1973). *Am J Cardiol* **32**:46–61.
Schwartz, S. P. (1936). *Am J Med Sci* **192**:153–163.
Sewell, W. H., Koth, D. R., Huggins, C. E. (1955). *Surgery* **38**:1050–1053.
Sobel, B. E. (1974). *Circ Res* **35** (Suppl III):173–181.
Sobel, B. E., Corr, P. B., Robinson, A. K. (1978). *J Clin Invest* **62**:546–553.
Spear, J. F., Horowitz, L. N., Hodess, A. B., MacVaugh, H., III, Moore, E. N. (1979). *Circulation* **59**:247–256.
Spear, J. F., Michelson, E. L., Moore, E. N. (1983a). *Circ Res* **53**:176–185.

Spear, J. F., Michelson, E. L., Moore, E. N. (1983b). *J Am Coll Cardiol* **1**:1099–1109.
Spear, J. F., Richards, D. A., Blake, G. J., Moore, E. N. (1985). *In* "Cardiac Electrophysiology and Arrhythmias". (D. Zipes and J. Jalife, eds.), Chap 38, pp 337–342. Grune and Stratton, New York.
Strauss, H. C., Bigger, J. T., Jr., Hoffman, B. F. (1970). *Circ Res* **26**:661–678.
Ten Eick, R. E., Singer, D. H., Solberg, L. E. (1976). *Med Clin North Am* **60**:49–67.
Trautwein, W. (1973). *Physiol Rev* **53**:793–835.
Tsien, R. W. (1974). *J Gen Physiol* **64**:293–319.
Tsien, R. W., Carpenter, D. O. (1978). *Fed Proc* **37**:2127–2131.
VanHoutte, P. M., Levy, M. N. (1980). *Am J Physiol* **238**:H275–H281.
Vassalle, M. (1965). *Am J Physiol* **208**:770–775.
Vassalle, M. (1977). *Circ Res* **41**:269–277.
Vassalle, M., Mugelli, A. (1981). *Circ Res* **48**:618–631.
Waldo, A. L., Kaiser, G. A. (1973). *Circulation* **47**:1222–1228.
Watanabe, A. M., Besch, H. R., Jr. (1975). *Circ Res* **37**:309–317.
Wiggers, C. J. (1940). *Am Heart J* **20**:399–412.
Wit, A. L., Cranefield, P. F. (1976). *Circ Res* **38**:85–98.
Wit, A. L., Cranefield, P. F. (1977). *Circ Res* **41**:435–445.
Wit, A. L., Cranefield, P. F. (1979). *Am J Physiol* **235**:H1–H17.
Wit, A. L., Josephson, M. E. (1985). *In* "Cardiac Electrophysiology and Arrhythmias". (D. Zipes and J. Jalife, eds.), Chap 39, pp 343–353. Grune and Stratton, New York.
Wit, A. L., Rosen, M. R. (1984). *In* "Tachycardias, Mechanisms, Diagnosis and Treatment". (M. E. Josephson and H. J. J. Wellen, eds.), Chap 1, pp 1–27. Lea Febiger, Philadelphia.
Wit, A. L., Hoffman, B. F., Cranefield, P. F. (1972). *Circ Res* **30**:1–10.

# 7 The Pharmacology of Antiarrhythmic Drugs

Pasquale F. Nestico and Joel Morganroth

## I. Introduction

Knowledge of pharmacokinetics is extremely important in the application of antiarrhythmic drug therapy. These agents have, normally, a narrow toxic–therapeutic relationship; that is, the toxic concentration only exceeds the effective level by two- or threefold. Also, the plasma concentration after a given dose may vary quite widely from patient to patient. This necessitates enormous skill to adjust the dosage regimen so that effective plasma levels are achieved while avoiding adverse effects. This task is facilitated by understanding drug pharmacokinetics, which consists of a quantitative assessment of drug absorption, distribution, loading and maintenance, metabolism, and excretion. Alterations in pharmacokinetics may account for significant intra- and interpatient variations in serum concentrations as well as alterations of dose requirements in given patients (Shanks and Harrison, 1981; Fenster and Perrier, 1982). Active metabolites may be suspected when the clinical effect of the drug exceeds the therapeutic plasma level of the agent. In some situations and with some drugs, the plasma level after equilibration strongly correlates with the antiarrhythmic effect of the drug (Heger *et al.*, 1982). However, for a specific patient, one must consider the response to the drug of both the patient and the arrhythmia, while the actual plasma level of the agent is of secondary importance.

## II. Pharmacokinetics

### A. Absorption

Most drug absorption occurs in the small intestine, and for most agents the half-time of absorption is in the range of 30 min. Several factors influence the rate of absorption and, ultimately, plasma level. Because tablet preparations have different dissolution rates, different preparations of the same drug may undergo different rates of absorption in the same patient. Therefore, completeness of absorption may vary from 50 to more than 90% and two different preparations of the same drug may not result in the same serum concentration (Fenster and Perrier, 1982). Some agents (i.e., propranolol or verapamil) require that a larger dose be administered orally than intravenously to achieve the same therapeutic effect. This is because a large amount of the drug administered orally is transformed to inactive metabolites in the liver (the so-called obligatory first-pass hepatic effect) before the agent reaches the systemic circulation. Disease states can also alter the rate and completeness of drug absorption. Congestive heart failure can cause decreased intestinal blood flow and mucosal edema and therefore impair the absorption of orally administered drugs. Severe hypotensive states (as occurs with shock or cardiac arrest) decrease reliable absorption of drugs administered intramuscularly by impairing tissue perfusion. In these circumstances, drugs should be given intravenously. Diarrheal states (due to malabsorption syndromes, use of other drugs, or cathartics) may interfere with absorption, as might conditions that delay gastric emptying and therefore the drug's arrival in the small intestine.

## B. Distribution

The volume of distribution of a drug (Vd) is defined as the volume of blood (or plasma) into which the drug mass (M) must be diluted to result in a given plasma concentration (C), so

$$Vd = M/C$$

The volume of distribution and the mass of drug present determine the concentration of drug at any given time (Ct). The volume of distribution is equal to the sum of A and B on the logarithmic plasma concentration axis obtained by extrapolating the alpha and beta phases back to zero time (Fig. 1) (Harrison *et al.*, 1977). For most antiarrhythmic drugs the large volume of distribution indicates that they are present in higher concentrations in some tissues than in the plasma. A large volume of distribution indicates a wide distribution and extensive tissue uptake of the agent. The volume of distribution is dependent on the relative serum and tissue binding characteristics of the drug. In some patients, such as those with renal failure, in whom a change in serum protein or tissue binding may occur, the volume of distribution may be contracted. It is probably a result of a

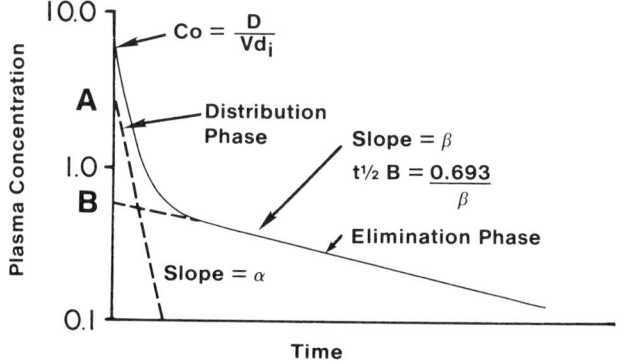

**Fig. 1.** Schematic diagram of the semilogarithmic plot of drug plasma concentration versus time following rapid intravenous injection (From Gibaldi and Perrier, 1975.) $\alpha$, Rate constant for distribution. $\beta$, rate constant for elimination.

decrease in tissue binding of digoxin that quinidine decreases the volume of distribution of digoxin.

The plasma clearance (Cl, defined as the volume of plasma or blood cleared of a drug per unit time) represents a constant fraction (K) of the volume of distribution (Vd) since for most drugs elimination proceeds as a first-order process (that is, the rate of elimination is proportional at all times to drug concentration). Therefore

$$K = Cl/Vd$$

where $K$ represents the first-order rate constant for elimination and has units of time$^{-1}$. This can be expressed in terms of drug half-life ($T_{1/2}$) as

$$K = 0.693/T_{1/2} \text{ and } T_{1/2} = Vd \times 0.693/Cl$$

This last formula illustrates the fact that drug half-life is directly related to volume of distribution and indirectly to drug clearance. This is probably the most important of pharmocokinetic equations.

## C. Administration

### 1. Intravenous Administration

After a given dose of a drug is administered it takes a finite time for the plasma concentration to reach a steady-state level. Steady state is defined as the condition in which the rate of removal is equal to the rate of delivery of drug, so the plasma concentration remains constant. The drug half-life describes both the rate of reduction of drug concentration and the

**TABLE I**
Effects of Half-Life on Drug
Accumulation and Elimination

| Half-lives | % Accumulation | % Remaining |
|---|---|---|
| 1 | 50 | 50 |
| 2 | 75 | 25 |
| 3 | 87.5 | 12.5 |
| 4 | 93.75 | 6.25 |
| 5 | 96.875 | 3.125 |

rate of accumulation to a steady state during a constant infusion. Doubling the infusion will double the drug concentration but has no effect on the time taken to reach the steady-state level. Table I shows the fraction of initial plasma level and of the final steady-state drug concentration achieved after various half-lives of infusion.

*a. Simple Loading Dose.* The use of a loading dose is often necessary in patients requiring urgent medical therapy. This is because it will take too long a time, without the loading dose, to reach a steady-state level. Several methods have been proposed for a rapid therapeutic effect. One of them is the simple loading dose technique. This is not an accepted modality when dealing with antiarrhythmic drugs because side effects occur readily at peak plasma levels.

In general two models, a one-compartment open model and a two-compartment open model, are used to describe and predict serum concentrations for a variety of dose regimens at a given time. In the one-compartment open model drugs enter and are eliminated from a simple homogeneous unit. This unit represents the entire body. However, this model is considered not altogether appropriate because of the time required for the drug to be distributed throughout the volume of the compartment.

For intravenous rapid drug administration the two-compartment open model predicts more precisely drug concentration. In this situation there are two compartments, a central one and a peripheral one (Fig. 2).

The smaller central compartment, into which the drug is administered, reflects plasma concentrations from which elimination occurs. The larger peripheral compartment, acting as a reservoir, represents those tissues that slowly equilibrate with plasma and is connected with the central one

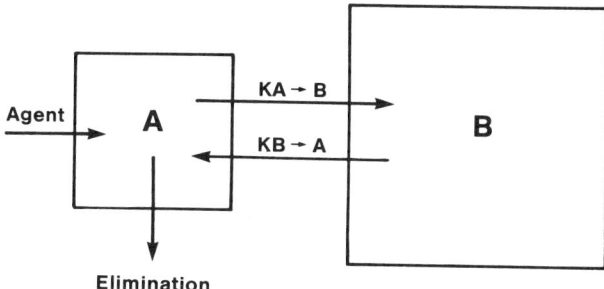

**Fig. 2.** Two-compartment open model: a central compartment (A) and a peripheral compartment (B).

in dynamic equilibrium. The central compartment consists of the blood volume and extracellular fluid of well-perfused organs (i.e., heart, lungs, kidney, and liver). The peripheral compartment, on the other hand, consists of less well perfused tissues (i.e., muscles, skin, and fat tissues).

Immediately after injection of a drug, its concentration is determined by:

$$C0 = D/Vd_i$$

where $D$ represents the dose injected and $Vd_i$ represents the initial volume of distribution (or volume of the central compartment). Two distinct phases are present (Fig.1): the distribution phase, followed by the elimination phase. The first one consists of a rapidly falling plasma drug concentration secondary to the distribution between the central and the peripheral compartment. The elimination phase consists of a slower decrease in plasma drug concentration due to elimination of the agent mainly from the central compartment. It is during the elimination phase, when the drug is in distribution equilibrium, that serum concentration correlates with the pharmacologic effect of the drug.

*b. Loading Dose and Maintenance.* A second method is to give the antiarrhythmic drug as a simple dose followed by a maintenance infusion. This method is not feasible for two reasons (Fig 3). First, to ensure a therapeutic plasma level of the drug, a large single dose is necessary, which will produce toxic levels for an appreciable amount of time (Fig. 3A). This is unsatisfactory. Second, if the simple loading dose is adjusted to avoid toxic peak levels, plasma concentration will fall below the therapeutic range. It will take some time before the plasma levels due to the maintenance infusion will rise into the therapeutic plasma level range

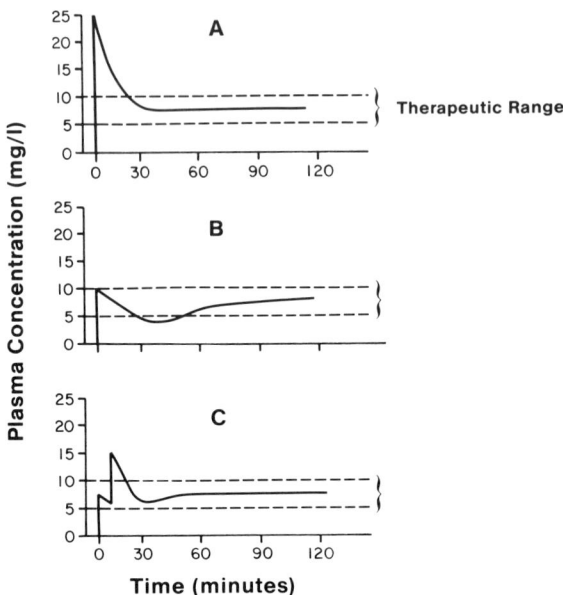

**Fig. 3.** The dashed lines indicate the therapeutic range. (A) the drug is administered as a single large dose with a maintenance infusion begun just after the bolus. (B) the bolus and maintenance infusion is given as in (A) but the bolus is given at a lower dose to avoid side effects. (C) two boluses are given 10 min apart, followed by a maintenance infusion started after the second bolus.

(Fig. 3B), leaving the patient exposed to developing ventricular arrhythmias.

*c. Multiple Loading Dose.* The above problems can be minimized by using the multiple loading dose technique. An initial 1 mg/kg bolus of the drug is given followed by a second bolus of 1 mg/kg 10 min later. After the second bolus the maintenance infusion should begin (Fig. 3C), because if it is started simultaneously with the first bolus, plasma concentration may exceed the therapeutic range for a short time after the second bolus, placing the patient at risk of developing toxic effects.

### 2. Oral Administration

After oral administration, the body behaves as a one-compartment open model. Because of this, only drug clearance and the drug half-life have to be considered in preparing a dosage regimen. The factors that influence volume of distribution and drug eliminations are the same as those previously described. However, in oral administration systemic availability has to be taken into consideration. Systemic availability is the fraction of the dose that reaches the systemic circulation and then the target organ. Two factors reduce the systemic availability: first, incomplete absorption and second, liver and intestinal metabolism. The liver metabolism is called presystemic or "first-pass" elimination. It occurs with several antiarrhythmic agents.

The drug is administered every half-life, and the plasma concentration is monitored by obtaining plasma levels at the end of the dosage interval. The drug dosage is then adjusted such that the trough levels are kept above the minimal therapeutic plasma concentration.

## D. Drug Metabolism and Excretion

Serum elimination half-life is defined as the time taken for drug levels to fall to one-half of their initial value, so that after one half-life, 50% of the drug is left in the body (assuming no further drug is administered). The serum elimination half-life is determined by the function of the organ system that eliminates a given drug from the body. If the drug is metabolized by the liver, then disorders that reduce hepatic blood flow markedly slow the rate of such drug elimination. About 97% of the dose of any drug is removed from the body in a time equal to five half-lives (Harrison *et al.*, 1977).

Several factors (i.e., age, disease states, genetics, concomitant drugs, etc.) may influence the rate and extent of metabolism of a given drug. The acetyltransferase enzyme system, which is genetically controlled, influences drug metabolism depending on whether or not the individual is a "slow" or "rapid" acetylator. Slow acetylators metabolize a drug less rapidly and therefore may require less drug to reach the desired plasma level or pharmacological effect. On the other hand, rapid acetylators may be less predisposed to develop side effects from the parent compound but may be more prone to develop reactions from drug metabolities (Fenster and Perrier, 1982).

Drugs exist in plasma in two forms: free and bound to plasma proteins. The free form is the one capable of distributing into tissues and exerting a pharmacological action. For antiarrhythmic agents the bound form fraction is relatively constant over the clinically relevant range of plasma levels. Therefore, the total serum plasma levels of a given drug correlates well with the pharmacological effects.

## III. Antiarrhythmic Drugs

### A. Class I: Conventional Antiarrhythmic Agents

#### 1. Quinidine

*a. Electrophysiological Actions.* Quinidine suppresses automaticity in normal Purkinje fibers by decreasing the slope of phase 4 diastolic depolarization but exerts little effect on automaticity of the isolated normal sinus node or on the denervated sinus node (Mason et al., 1977) (Table II). In high doses quinidine can cause abnormal automatic discharge in Purkinje fibers (Bigger, 1980). Quinidine has a significant anticholinergic effect (Mason et al., 1977; Mirro et al., 1980), and can cause reflex sympathetic stimulation resulting from alpha-adrenergic blockade. As a result, the drug may increase sinus nodal discharge rate. Furthermore, sinus nodal automaticity can be depressed by quinidine in patients with sick sinus syndrome (Bigger, 1980). Quinidine markedly prolongs the effective refractory period without significantly changing resting membrane potential (Hoffman et al., 1975).

*b. Hemodynamic Effects.* Quinidine is generally considered a myocardial depressant. Overall, depression of contractility appears to be related to the drug concentration. Significant depression of contractility is noted only at considerably high levels while only minor negative inotropic effects are seen at therapeutic plasma concentrations (Hammermeister et

**TABLE II**
Electrophysiology of Conventional Antiarrhythmic Agents[a]

| Agent | Intervals | | | | Electrophysiological intervals | | | | | | |
|---|---|---|---|---|---|---|---|---|---|---|---|
| | Sinus rate | PR | QRS | QT | A–H | H–V | ERP AVN | ERP HPS | ERP A | ERP V | ERP AP |
| Quinidine | -↑ | ↓-↑ | ↑ | ↑ | ↓-↑ | -↑ | ↓ | ↑ | ↑ | ↑ | ↑ |
| Procainamide | – | -↑ | ↑ | ↑ | -↑ | -↑ | -↑ | -↑ | ↑ | ↑ | ↑ |
| Disopyramide | -↑ | – | -↑ | -↑ | – | -↑ | -↓ | ↑ | ↑ | ↑ | ↑ |
| Lidocaine | – | – | – | – | -↓ | -↑ | -↓ | -↑ | – | – | – |
| Tocainide | -↓ | – | – | -↓ | -↑ | – | ↓ | – | -↓ | -↓ | – |
| Propranolol | ↓ | -↑ | – | -↓ | -↑ | – | ↑ | ↓ | – | – | – |
| Bretylium | -↓ | -↑ | – | -↑ | NA | NA | NA | -↑ | NA | -↑ | – |

[a] ↑, Increase; ↓, decrease; –, no change; -↑ or -↓, slight inconsistent increase or decrease; A, atrium; AVN, AV node; HPS, His–Purkinje system; V, ventricle; AP, accessory pathway (WPW); ERP, effective refractory period (longest S1–S2 interval at which S2 fails to produce a response); NA, not available.

al., 1972; Parmley and Braunwald, 1967). Quinidine produces significant peripheral vasodilatation, which is produced by two independent mechanisms (Schmid et al., 1974a; Nelson et al., 1974): a direct action to relax vascular smooth muscle and alpha-adrenergic blockade producing inhibition of adrenergic constrictor tone. Severe hypotension is more likely to occur with parenteral use of the drug. In contrast, oral quinidine in standard doses appears to be well tolerated without significant adverse hemodynamic effects, even in patients with ventricular dysfunction (Cohen et al., 1977). The mild negative inotropic effect of quinidine is of less clinical importance than the effect exerted in the peripheral vascular system.

*c. Pharmacokinetics.* Quinidine is most commonly given by mouth. Plasma quinidine concentrations peak at about 90 minutes after oral administration of quinidine sulfate and at 3 to 4 hr after oral administration of quinidine gluconate. Approximately 80% of plasma quinidine is protein bound (Table III). The intravenous route has not been recommended in therapy, largely because of the circulatory depression likely from a single large dose. About 20% of quinidine is excreted unchanged in the urine. Kessler et al. (1974) recommended that quinidine dosage should not be reduced in patients with renal failure in view of the minor role played by the kidney in elimination. Crouthamel (1975) indicated that congestive heart failure leads to reduction of the rate of absorption and the volume of distribution of the drug with little change in half-life, which is 5–9 hr. Therefore, patients with heart failure tend to have higher peak plasma levels. Data et al. (1976) reported a drug interaction between

**TABLE III**
Pharmacokinetics of Conventional Antiarrhythmic Agents

| Agent | Bioavailability (%) | Volume of distribution (liter/kg) | Plasma protein binding (%) | Effective plasma concentration (mg/liter) | Half-time for elimination (hr) | Total body clearance (ml/min) | Excretion of unchanged drug (%) |
|---|---|---|---|---|---|---|---|
| Quinidine | 60–80 | 2–4 | 80 | 2–6 | 5–9 | 200–300 | 10–40 |
| Procainamide | 70–85 | 1.5–2.5 | 15–25 | 3–8 | 3–7 | 300–700 | 30–60 |
| Disopyramide | 85 | 0.5–1.5 | 50–65 | 2–5 | 6–9 | 100–200 | 40–60 |
| Lidocaine | 35 | 1.0–2.0 | 20–40 | 1–5 | 1–2 | 400–1600 | 10 |
| Tocainide | 9 | 2 | 10–20 | 6–15 | 12–16 | 150–200 | 30–50 |
| Propranolol | 20–50 | 2.5–3.5 | 85–95 | 0.2–0.90 | 3–6 | 400–1000 | 5 |
| Bretylium | 30–50 | 8.2 | <10 | NA[a] | 6–8 | 300–450 | 100 |

[a] NA, not available.

quinidine and the anticonvulsive drugs phenobarbital and phenytoin. Induction of metabolism can change a previously effective dosage to an ineffective one.

The first convincing evidence that the metabolites of quinidine might be pharmacologically active in man came from the studies of Holford *et al.* (1981). Other studies have shown that some quinidine metabolites are active (Conn and Luch, 1964; Drayer *et al.*, 1978) and in the study by Drayer *et al.* (1978) the major active metabolite 3-hydroxyquinidine (Table IV) actually exacerbated test arrhythmias. The rate of formation of this active quinidine metabolite appears to be highly variable (Drayer *et al.*, 1980).

*d. Plasma Level and Dosage.* Plasma concentration guidelines for quinidine were proposed for the first time by Sokolow and Edgar (1950). Plasma level monitoring is highly variable because quinidine is potentially toxic and its kinetics variable. Concentrations of 1.5 to 3 $\mu$g/ml at the end of the dosage interval are generally considered therapeutic and levels of 7 $\mu$g/ml or greater are associated with a high incidence of toxicity.

The dosage required in any given patient can vary quite widely as a result of individual variations, the effects of disease and presence of other drugs, and differences in formulation. The usual oral dose of quinidine sulfate for an adult is 200–400 mg four times daily (Table V). This will result in a steady-state level within about 24 hr; however, the actual dose and dosage interval depends on the preparation used. The dose, if necessary, should be gradually increased in increments of about 50% with careful monitoring of the ECG and QT interval. A loading dose of 600 to 1000 mg produces an earlier effective concentration. Several oral preparations are available. Greenblatt *et al.* (1977) compared the kinetics of the

**TABLE IV**
Metabolites of Conventional Antiarrhythmic Agents

| Agent | Percentage metabolized | Major metabolite | Active metabolites |
|---|---|---|---|
| Quinidine | 60–70 | (3S)-3-Hydroxyquinidine | Yes |
| Procainamide | 40–50 | N-Acetylprocainamide | Yes |
| Disopyramide | 25–35 | Mono-N-dealkylated disopyramide | Yes |
| Lidocaine | 90 | Monoethylglycinexylidide | Yes |
| Tocainide | 60 | N-Carboxytocainide glucuronide | Yes |
| Propranolol | 90 | 4-Hydroxypropranolol | Yes |
| Bretylium | 10 | — | — |

## TABLE V
Dosage and Therapeutic Serum Levels of Conventional Antiarrhythmic Agents

| Agent | Usual dose ranges | | | Effective serum or plasma concentration (µg/ml) | Elimination half-life after oral dose (hr) | Major route of elimination |
|---|---|---|---|---|---|---|
| | Oral maintenance (mg) | Intravenous Loading (mg) | Maintenance (mg) | | | |
| Quinidine | 200–400 q 6 hr | — | — | 3–6 | 5–9 | Liver |
| Procainamide | 250–1000 q 3–6 hr | 6–13 mg/kg at 0.2 to 0.5 mg/kg/min | 2–6 mg/min | 4–8 | 3–5 | Kidneys |
| Disopyramide | 100–200 q 6–8 hr | — | — | 2–5 | 8–9 | Kidneys |
| Lidocaine | — | 1–3 mg/kg at 20 to 50 mg/min | 1 to 4 mg/min | 1–5 | 1–2 | Liver |
| Tocainidine | 400–600 q 8–12 hr | — | — | 4–9 | 10–17 | Liver |
| Propranolol | 10–200 q 6–8 hr | 0.25–0.5 mg, q 5 min for ≤0.15 to 0.20 mg/kg | — | 0.04–0.90 | 3–6 | Liver |
| Bretylium | — | 5–10 mg/kg at 1 to 2 mg/kg/min | 0.5–2 mg/min | 0.5–1.5 | 8–14 | Kidneys |

sulfate and the gluconate salts in normal volunteers. Quinidine gluconate was slowly absorbed with peak levels at 4 hr after dosing and was less available. In contrast, the sulfate was more rapidly absorbed with peak levels of 1.5 hr. Importantly, systemic availability was more varied with the gluconate (40–93%). While the sulfate preparation is given every 6–8 hr, the gluconate is given less frequently, every 8–12 hr. Quinidex extentabs, another preparation, has a relative bioavailability equal to quinidine sulfate tablets, provides up to 12 hr of smooth, sustained release, has the convenience of twice daily (BID) dosage (although some patients may require a three times a day (TID) dosage schedule) and 48 mg more of active quinidine than the gluconate product. The polygalacturonate (Cardioquin) is equivalent to 200 mg of Quinidine sulfate.

## 2. Procainamide

*a. Electrophysiological Actions.* The cardiac actions of procainamide resemble those described for quinidine. It depresses the excitability of both atrial and ventricular tissue, slows conduction, and prolongs the effective refractory period (Table II). Procainamide also depresses myocardial contractility but less so than quinidine. It elevates the threshold to electrically induced fibrillation. The negative inotropic effect of procainamide is dose-related (Harrison *et al.,* 1963; Jawad-Kanbar and Sherrod, 1974). Most studies have shown the occurrence of hypotension after intravenous use (Harrison *et al.,* 1963; Stearns *et al.,* 1952), while others have shown little effect (Burton *et al.,* 1976). The total dose and the rate of administration may explain these differences. In general, however, procainamide is well tolerated even in patients with left ventricular dysfunction, although it should be used with caution under these circumstances.

*b. Hemodynamic Effects.* Most studies have shown a negative inotropic effect after a larger dose of intravenous procainamide, a significant decrease in systemic blood pressure without a significant decrease in systemic vascular resistance (Cote *et al.,* 1973, 1975). The ability of procainamide to produce vasodilatation is well established despite the lack of effect on systemic vascular resistance (Schmid *et al.,* 1974b).

The myocardial depressant effect of intravenous procainamide is dose-related (Harrison *et al.,* 1963; Jawad-Kanber and Sherrod, 1974) and at the doses generally used, the degree of decrease in contractility is of minor importance. Overall, at usual anti-arrhythmic doses, Procainamide has a mild-to-moderate negative inotropic effect and produces a transient decrease in systemic blood pressure.

c. *Pharmacokinetics.* There is a variation in the ratio of daily dose to plasma concentration of procainamide, accounted for by the individual variation in absorption, volume of distribution, and rate of elimination (Koch-Weser and Klein, 1971). The gastrointestinal tract absorption is from 75 to 95%. The biologic half-life is markedly prolonged by renal insufficiency and the plasma concentration from a given dosage may be three times normal in severe renal failure (Koch-Weser and Klein, 1971). Approximately 80% of oral procainamide is bioavailable with 20% bound to serum proteins. The half-life is between 3 and 7 hr (Table III).

Most of the drug is eliminated unchanged in the urine and 10–30% is eliminated by hepatic metabolism (Fenster and Perrier, 1982). One route of metabolism is by acetylation and this is affected by acetylator phenotype. In patients with heart failure, procainamide is cleared less well and if cardiac function is severely compromised, a reduction in dosage by 30 to 50% in initial therapy is recommended. In renal failure the total clearance of the drug is reduced because of a reduction in that fraction eliminated by the kidneys proportionately to the decrease in creatinine clearance. In addition, the clearance of N-acetylprocainamide (NAPA), a metabolite, which is 85% dependent on renal function, would be expected to fall with creatinine clearance, resulting in a more dramatic rise in its level (Drayer *et al.,* 1977). Therefore, the use of procainamide in patients with severe renal insufficiency should be avoided, and if it cannot, both procainamide and NAPA levels should be carefully monitored as well as clinical assessment of efficacy and toxicity.

The major metabolite of procainamide is NAPA (Table IV), which has an elimination half-life of 7 to 8 hr but may exceed 10 hr if high doses are used. Its rate of formation is influenced by a genetically determined pathway, N-acetylation. Slow acetylators develop antinuclear antibodies and the lupus syndrome earlier in therapy than rapid acetylators. Roden *et al.* (1980) compared the clinical pharmacologic properties of procainamide and NAPA in patients with ventricular arrhythmias. NAPA frequently produced adverse effects that limited therapy and was found to be antiarrhythmic in a minority of patients. However, in patients treated on a long-term basis with NAPA, antinuclear antibodies and the lupus syndrome did not develop (Kluger *et al.,* 1981; Stec *et al.,* 1979). Toxic effects of NAPA may explain the occurrence of gastrointestinal side effects in some patients receiving procainamide. Unless NAPA accumulates to plasma levels greater than about 15 $\mu$g/ml in patients who are taking procainamide, its accumulation is of little consequence.

d. *Plasma Level and Dosage.* Procainamide may be given by the oral, intravenous, or intramuscular route (Table V). The drug is quite well absorbed by mouth (75–95%) but plasma levels show very wide variability (up to 10-fold) when the same dose is given to a group of patients. The therapeutic plasma level is 4–8 µg/ml. In many patients the concentration falls above or below the desired therapeutic range, necessitating individual titration of the dose (Koch-Weser and Klein, 1971). Occasionally plasma concentrations exceeding 10 µg/ml have been required (Greenspan et al., 1980).

Koch-Weser (1971) made the first attempt to try to rationalize procainamide therapy. For oral administration it is suggested that a loading dose of twice the maintenance dose should be given followed by the maintenance dose every half-life (i.e., every 3 hr) with 25% dose reduction in patients with heart disease. The minimum maintenance doses used are 250 mg every 3 hr for patients less than 120 lb; 375 mg every 3 hr for patients between 120 and 200 lb; and 500 mg every 3 hr for patients greater than 200 lb. To try to minimize the problem with noncompliance the dosage can be reduced to every 4 hr with the use of a double dose at bedtime. The surface electrocardiogram, looking for QT interval prolongation, and plasma determinations serve as guidelines. For the prolonged-release form of procainamide, dosing is at 6-hr intervals (Giardina et al., 1973). Two sustained oral forms are available. One is Procan-SR, available in 250, 500, and 750 mg tablets; the other is Pronestyl-SR, available in 500 mg tablets. A regimen of intravenous administration of procainamide was devised by Giardina et al. (1973) consisting of giving 100-mg doses at 5 min intervals until either a therapeutic effect was achieved, 1 g had been given, or toxic effects appeared. Another method is to give 6–13 mg/kg at an infusion rate of 0.2 to 0.5 mg/kg/min (Mason and Winkle, 1978). The effect could usually be maintained with a constant-rate intravenous infusion of 2 to 4 mg/min.

### 3. Disopyramide

*a. Electrophysiological Actions.* Disopyramide exerts its action, in a manner similar to quinidine and procainamide, by decreasing membrane responsiveness, hence decreasing excitability, conduction velocity, and contractility (Befeler et al., 1975) (Table II). It has been reported that disopyramide has properties similar to those of lidocaine (decrease in dP/dT) and quinidine (prolongation of action potential) (Kus and Sasyniuk, 1978).

Despite the fact that disopyramide is not a slow channel blocker, at high concentration the drug can slow the sinus nodal discharge rate by a direct action (Katoh et al., 1982) and in patients with sinus node disease can markedly depress sinus nodal activity (LaBarre et al., 1979). Atrioventricular block may occasionally occur (Timins *et al.*, 1981). However, disopyramide may be administered safely to patient who have first degree or Type 1 second-degree A–V block and narrow QRS complexes (Wilkinson 1982.)

*b. Hemodynamic Effects.* Disopyramide has a well-documented negative inotropic effect in both animals (Walsh and Horowitz, 1979) and in man (Jensen *et al.*, 1975; Naqvi *et al.*, 1979; Kotter *et al.*, 1980; Podrid *et al.*, 1980; Bauman, 1981). These studies showed that this drug exerts a negative inotropic effect in association with a direct effect to increase systemic vascular resistance (Naqvi *et al.*, 1979; Kotter *et al.*, 1980). The hemodynamic changes observed included increased intracardiac filling pressures and systemic blood pressure and a decrease in cardiac index and stroke volume. These changes occur in normal subjects (Thadani *et al.*, 1981) but are more remarkable in patients with poor left ventricular function (Leach *et al.*, 1980). In a clinical follow-up study of 100 patients taking disopyramide for the control of arrhythmias, Podrid and co-workers (Podrid *et al.*, 1980) emphasized the importance of careful patient selection before the use of this agent. Of the 100 patients, 16 developed congestive heart failure. In 55% of the patients with history of heart failure, heart failure again developed with disopyramide therapy. Therefore, disopyramide therapy produces a significant negative inotropic effect combined with a peripheral vasoconstrictive effect. These effects have little clinical consequence in patients with normal left ventricular function. However, patients with left ventricular dysfunction and a history of congestive heart failure are at high risk for clinical deterioration. Disopyramide should be avoided in them.

*c. Pharmacokinetics.* Disopyramide is 80–100% absorbed by gastrointestinal tract and is 40–60% excreted unchanged by the kidney (Table III). It has an elimination half-life of 6 to 9 hr in the presence of normal renal function but almost 10 hr in patients with heart failure (Karim, 1975). Investigation of the kinetics of this drug in patients with myocardial infarction revealed that postinfarction patients achieved about twofold lower concentrations of disopyramide after the oral administration of 10 mg than normal subjects (Ward and Kingham, 1976). Disopyramide is 50–65% bound to serum proteins with the percentage bound varying with the total plasma drug concentration. This feature makes interpretation of plasma level difficult and may alter the amount of disopyramide available at a given blood level. Peak blood levels after oral administration are seen in 1 to 2 hr. Bioavailability exceeds 80%.

Approximately 40–60% of Disopyramide is excreted unchanged in the kidneys, requiring that doses and dosing schedules be adjusted in the presence of renal insufficiency (Hinderling *et al.*, 1974). The remainder of the drug presumably undergoes hepatic degradation, with some of the metabolites excreted in the urine. With renal, hepatic, or cardiac insufficiency, loading and maintenance doses need to be reduced. The metabolite *N*-desisopropyl-disopyramide (Table IV) has antiarrhythmic properties but appears to exert less effect than the parent compound. Disopyramide does not appear to be an enzyme inducer (Norpace, 1977).

*d. Plasma Level and Dosage.* The commonest disopyramide dose prescribed is from 100 to 200 mg orally every 6 hr with a range of 400 to 1200 mg/day (Table V). Larger doses of up to 400 mg every 6 hr have been reported effective and safe in some patients with refractory ventricular tachycardia (Gallagher *et al.*, 1977). When using these larger doses, however, caution need to be employed in view of the potential toxicity of disopyramide. Therapeutic plasma levels of disopyramide range from 2 to 5 $\mu$g/ml. Norpace CR (controlled release) capsules are available to give a gradual and consistent release of disopyramide. Thus, for maintenance therapy, Norpace CR provides the benefit of less frequent dosing (every 12 hr) as compared with the 6-hr dosage schedule of immediate-release Norpace capsules. The intravenous (investigational) dose is 1–2 mg/kg as an initial bolus given over 5 to 10 min, followed by an infusion of 1 mg/kg/hr (Kerr *et al.*, 1982).

### 4. Lidocaine

*a. Electrophysiological Actions.* Lidocaine was found, in animal studies, to depress automaticity of Purkinje fibers and this action may be due to an increased potassium conduction (Arnsdorf and Bigger, 1972) (Table II). Lidocaine shortens the action potential duration in both Purkinje and muscle fibers and, to a lesser extent, reduces the effective refractory period of Purkinje fibers. At concentrations of lidocaine up to 3 $\mu$g/ml, membrane responsiveness and conduction velocity of Purkinje fibers are unaffected or increased and depressed only at concentrations above 30 $\mu$g/ml (Bigger and Mandel, 1970). At concentrations of 3 $\mu$g/ml or higher, lidocaine caused a decrease in membrane responsiveness when the abnormally low concentration of potassium present in the standard Tyrode's solution was corrected (Singh and Vaughan Williams, 1971).

*b. Hemodynamic Effects.* In humans, lidocaine depresses arterial pressure and myocardial contractility but less so than procainamide (Harrison *et al.*, 1963). However, clinical significant adverse hemodynamic effects are rarely noted unless left ventricular function is severely impaired.

c. *Pharmacokinetics.* Lidocaine is liver-metabolized. The drug is used only parenterally because oral use results in extensive first-pass hepatic metabolism and unpredictable low plasma levels. The liver removes the drug from circulation so efficiently that the clearance of lidocaine approaches hepatic blood flow. Severe hepatic desease or reduced blood flow (as in heart failure or shock) can greatly decrease the rate of lidocaine metabolism (Stenson *et al.*, 1971). The pharmacokinetic interactions between lidocaine and certain drugs have been studied in animal studies. Propranolol (Branch *et al.*, 1973b) (which decreased cardiac output and hepatic blood flow), and norepinephrine (Benowitz, 1974) (which reduces hepatic blood flow) decrease lidocaine clearance and increase plasma level, while lidocaine clearance is increased by phenobarbital (DiFazio and Brown, 1972) (presumably by microsomal enzyme induction) and by isoproterenol or glucagon (Branch *et al.*, 1973a) (by increasing hepatic blood flow). Cimetidine (Feely *et al.*, 1981) has been shown to reduce hepatic blood flow by 25% in human volunteers. All the above drugs, therefore, may alter both the therapeutic and toxic effects of lidocaine.

Lidocaine undergoes extensive metabolism during its first pass through the liver with less than 10% of the drug excreted unchanged by the kidney (Table III). Its elimination half-life averages about 1 to 2 hr in normal subjects, greater than 4 hr in patients after relatively uncomplicated myocardial infarction, more than 10 hr in patients after myocardial infarction complicated by cardiac failure, and even longer in the presence of cardiogenic shock (Prescott *et al.*, 1976). In patients with low cardiac output the maintenance doses should be reduced by one-third to one-half.

Lidocaine has metabolites (Table IV). The parent drug is de-ethylated in the first pass through the liver to two metabolites: glycinexylidide and monoethylglycinexylidide, both of which have antiarrhythmic activity in humans but are less potent than lidocaine (Narang *et al.*, 1978).

Monethylglycinexylidide, like lidocaine, can produce seizures in animals and glycinexylidide potentiates seizure activity (Blumer *et al.*, 1973). In contrast to lidocaine, both metabolities are excreted in the urine. However, while glycinexylidide may accumulate in renal failure, the other metabolite does not appear, probably because it is further de-ethylated to glycinexylidide. Lidocaine assay systems do not measure these metabolites. Nevertheless, the contribution to the effects of lidocaine by these two metabolites is small and, therefore, the dose of lidocaine does not need adjustment in patients with renal insufficiency.

d. *Plasma Level and Dosage.* The therapeutic range of plasma lidocaine levels is 1.0–5.0 $\mu$g/ml (Table V). In patients with normal hepatic blood flow and function, plasma clearance is about 10 ml/kg/min. Although lidocaine may be given intramuscularly, the intravenous route is most commonly used, Intramuscular lidocaine is given in doses of 4 to 5 mg/kg (250–350 mg) resulting in effective serum levels at about 15 min and lasting for about 90 min.

Several intravenous loading dose regimens have been proposed. A simple loading dose is not appropriate because the volume of distribution at equilibrium of lidocaine exceeds the initial volume of distribution by a factor of three, which is greater than the ratio of toxic to therapeutic plasma concentrations. The main thrust of most dosage schedules is to give a large bolus of lidocaine to provide therapeutic plasma levels. This is immediately followed by a long-term continuous infusion. The most commonly used plan is the multiple bolus continuous infusion technique. The patient receives a 1 mg/kg IV bolus of lidocaine, given at a rate of 50 mg/min. This is followed by a 2 mg/min infusion of the drug. If the initial bolus of lidocaine is ineffective, up to two more boluses of 1 mg/kg may be administered at 5-min intervals. The lidocaine infusion can be increased up to 4 mg/min and is given continuously for 24 hr. At the end of that time, if the patient has no further premature ventricular complexes (PCVs), the infusion is discontinued (Wyman, 1978; Nattel and Zipes, 1980).

### 5. Tocainide

Tocainide, a primary amine analog of lidocaine that is effective orally, exerts electrophysiological effects very similar to those of Lidocaine (Horowitz et al., 1978).

*a. Electrophysiologic Actions.* Tocainide shortens the effective refractory periods of the atria, atrioventricular node, and ventricles (Anderson et al., 1978) and also shortens the action potential duration (Moore et al., 1978) (Table II). The drug has little effect on sinus node automaticity or intracardiac conduction (Horowitz et al., 1978). Tocainide may reduce the QT interval while the PR and QRS intervals are usually unchanged (Young et al., 1980).

*b. Hemodynamic Effects.* The effects of tocainide on cardiac hemodynamics are minor, even in the presence of moderate left ventricular dysfunction (Winkle et al., 1978a). The hemodynamic effects of tocainide in the setting of acute myocardial infarction are determined by the rate of administration and plasma concentration and are quantitatively similar to those of lidocaine (Nyquist et al., 1980). In patients with compensated left ventricular dysfunction, intravenous infusion of this drug moderately decreases mean arterial pressure and slightly increases pulmonary and systemic vascular resistance and left ventricular end-diastolic pressure without altering heart rate and cardiac index (Winkle *et al.*, 1978b).

*c. Pharmacokinetics.* Tocainide differs from lidocaine in that it has pharmacokinetic properties suitable for oral use. The drug is rapidly and completely absorbed, with peak serum levels occurring 60–90 min after oral administration even in patients with acute myocardial infarction (Graffner *et al.*, 1980). Bioavailability is almost 100%, with virtually no hepatic first-pass effect, which is markedly different from lidocaine. The drug is about 50% protein bound (Elvin *et al.*, 1982). Its half-life is 12–16 hr (Table III). There appear to be no important pharmacokinetic interactions between tocainide and digoxin (Ryan *et al.*, 1979), phenobarbital, clofibrate, or salicylamide (Elvin *et al.*, 1980).

Renal excretion of unchanged drug averages 40% while the rest presumably undergoes hepatic degradation (Lalka *et al.*, 1976). In patients with renal dysfunction, tocainide clearance decreases, the mean half-life increases to approximately 30 hr, and the mean total clearance decreases by about 50%. In chronic liver disease, tocainide elimination is only slightly impaired (Oltmanns, 1982).

Tocainide does not at this time appear to have important active metabolites (Table IV) (Ronfeld *et al.*, 1982).

*d. Plasma Level and Dosage.* The suggested optimal range for tocainide concentration is 4–9 µg/ml (Table V). The dosage ranges from 1200 to 1800 mg/day or 400 to 600 mg orally every 8–12 hr. In the presence of renal insufficiency, plasma level monitoring should help to avoid toxicity. In normal renal function, plasma levels of tocainide are stable and can be used to guide therapy in patients with chronic ventricular ectopy (Winkle *et al.*, 1978b). In some patients with resistant arrhythmias, doses of as much as 3200 mg/day have been used but with a high incidence of side effects (Maloney *et al.*, 1980).

## B. Class II: Conventional Antiarrhythmic Agents

Class II antiarrhythmic agents include the beta blockers, of which propranolol is the only one released in the United States for the treatment of arrhythmias.

### 1. Propranolol

*a. Electrophysiological Actions.* In doses that are capable of terminating digitalis-induced arrhythmias, propranolol, like quinidine, causes a reduction in the velocity of the upstroke of the action potential and a reduction in membrane responsiveness. Purkinje fiber repolarization is speeded up and the effective refractory period diminished (Table II). At the same time the action potential duration of the ventricular muscle cells is unchanged (Davis and Temte, 1968). Propranolol in high doses is like quinidine and has a direct negative inotropic action on cardiac muscle; however, it causes less reduction of blood pressure than does quinidine (Parmley and Braunwald, 1967).

Therapeutic doses of propranolol in humans do not exert a direct depressant or "quinidinelike" action but influence cardiac electrophysiology via a beta-blocking action. The dextrorotatory stereoisomer of beta blockers retains the direct membrane action without beta-blocking properties and does not prevent arrhythmias provoked by catecholamine administration (Alexander *et al.*, 1975).

*b. Hemodynamic Effects.* Propranolol may precipitate or worsen heart failure by exerting a negative inotropic effect on cardiac contractility. This agent may cause peripheral vasoconstriction by blocking beta receptors.

*c. Pharmacokinetics.* While all beta blockers exert similar pharmacological effects, they differ markedly in their pharmacokinetics (Koch-Weser and Frishman, 1981).

The kinetics of propranolol are different depending on the route of administration. When given orally, propranolol is almost 100% absorbed from the gastrointestinal tract but undergoes extensive metabolism on its first pass through the liver. Bioavailability is low (20–50%) and the half-life is 3–6 hr (Table III). Bioavailability increases and the drug accumulates during a steady state after chronic oral administration, with a fall in the extraction rate to about 65% (Evans and Shand, 1973).

When given intravenously, propranolol clearance approaches liver blood flow. Like lidocaine, its elimination is flow dependent and hepatic blood flow is responsible for the two- to threefold individual variation in plasma levels (Shand *et al.*, 1970).

Several metabolites of propranolol have been identified (Table IV). One of them, the glucoronide, is not active but can be converted back to propranolol. This may explain persistence of measurable propranolol plasma concentration several days after therapy is stopped (Wallace *et al.*, 1979). Another metabolite, 4-hydroxypropranolol, appears to have beta-blocking properties and is formed mainly after oral administration (Routledge and Shand, 1979).

*d. Plasma Level and Dosage.* There is not clear consensus on the appropriate therapeutic range of propranolol concentrations. In one study, eight of 12 patients with ventricular ectopy were effectively treated with propranolol at plasma levels of 0.04 to 0.09 μg/ml (Coltart *et al.*, 1971). Some patients, though, may require higher levels of up to 0.1 μg/ml to abolish ventricular arrhythmias (Woosley *et al.*, 1977). Plasma levels in the elderly are about twice those in young adults. Smoking also seems to reduce levels but mainly in young people. The appropriate dose of propranolol is best determined by a measure of the patient's physiological response, such as changes in resting heart rate or in the prevention of exercise-induced tachycardia.

When administered orally, an average concentration of about 0.05 μg/ml can be expected with 160 mg of propranolol daily (Nies and Shand, 1975), but the individual variation is great and the dose requires individual titration. Failure of therapy should not be considered until doses of 640 mg daily have been tried or side effects become limiting. In general, 10–200 mg administered every 6 hr is the usual oral dose. If one agent in adequate doses proves to be ineffective, other beta blockers are usually ineffective also.

When given intravenously much smaller doses are required because the extensive first-pass metabolism is avoided. Loading and maintenance regimens have been proposed for the intravenous administration of propranolol. McAllister (1976) proposed a single dose followed by an infusion. Probably it is safer to give an intravenous dose of 0.5 mg/min, every 5 min, until either a total of 0.15 to 0.20 mg/kg has been administered or a desired effect or toxicity is produced. This type of administration must be done very cautiously in patients with significant left ventricular dysfunction, sick sinus syndrome, or conduction blocks.

## C. Class III: Conventional Antiarrhythmic Agents

Class III antiarrhythmic agents include those that have a marked effect causing prolongation of repolarization. Examples include bretylium, amiodarone, and sotalol; the first two will be discussed here.

### 1. Bretylium

*a. Electrophysiological Actions.* The antiarrhythmic mechanism of bretylium can be divided into two types: adrenergic effects and direct myocardial action (Table II). Bretylium alters the cardiac adrenergic stimulation in three ways. First, at high concentration, bretylium initially releases norepinephrine from adrenergic nerve endings. Second, in lower concentrations, the agent inhibits the release of norepinephrine from adrenergic nerves by the action potential (Markis and Koch-Weser, 1971).

Third, bretylium potentiates the action of norepinephrine and epinephrine on adrenergic receptors by blocking reuptake of these agonists into adrenergic nerve endings (Kirpekar and Furchgott, 1964).

Direct myocardial actions of bretylium are known. This drug increases the action potential duration and prolongs the effective refractory period of isolated Purkinje fibers and ventricular muscle fibers (Heissenbuttel and Bigger, 1979; Koch-Weser, 1979). The ratio of effective refractory period to action potential duration is not altered (Bigger and Jaffe, 1971; Wit *et al.*, 1970).

*b. Hemodynamic Effects.* Bretylium has been shown in animals (Gilmore and Siegel, 1962) and in humans (Jorgensen *et al.*, 1971) to exert a positive inotropic effect on cardiac muscle. It has been suggested that bretylium's positive inotropic effect is not a direct effect but rather the result of myocardial release (Chatterjee *et al.*, 1973; Markis and Koch-Weser, 1971). This positive inotropic effect is transient and probably of little clinical importance in most situations.

The most clinically important hemodynamic effect of bretylium in man is orthostatic hypotension, which can often be profound (Taylor *et al.*, 1970). Its mechanism is not fully understood, although it probably results from adrenergic neuronal blockade.

*c. Pharmacokinetics.* Bretylium is effective orally as well as parenterally but it is absorbed poorly and erratically from the gastrointestinal tract.

Kuntzman and co-workers (1970) measured bretylium in the plasma and urine of four volunteers. After 300 mg of bretylium tosylate was administered intramuscularly, plasma concentration peaked after 30 min with subsequent decline following first-order kinetics. Plasma half-life was about 7 hr (Table III) and 70–80% of the administered dose of bretylium was recovered unchanged in the urine within 24 hr. In another study by Romhilt *et al.* (1972) of eight patients, elimination half-lives ranging from 4.2 to 16.9 hr (mean of 9.8 hr) were found. Therefore, since bretylium is excreted unmetabolized in the urine, doses must be adjusted in patients with renal insufficiency (Anderson *et al.*, 1981). Onset of action after intravenous administration occurs within several minutes, but full antiarrhythmic effects may not be seen for 30 min to 2 hr. Bretylium has no known active metabolites (Table IV).

*d. Plasma Level and Dosage.* Bretylium is approved for parenteral administration only. The concentration of bretylium in plasma has not been correlated with the intensity of its antiarrhythmic action and cannot be used to guide individualization of dosage. It is given by intravenous or intramuscular routes at a dosage of 5 to 10 mg/kg body weight with a maximum dose stated to be 30 mg/kg (Table V). It is diluted in 50 to 100 ml of 5% dextrose in water and administered slowly over 10 to 20 min (Holder et al., 1977). Following an initial dose, repeat doses every 6–8 hr or constant intravenous infusion rates of 0.5 to 1 mg/min appear to maintain therapeutic effects. Suppression of ventricular arrhythmias can be maintained for a few days with intravenous or intramuscular infusion. If chronic arrhythmia suppression is needed, another antiarrhythmic agent should be substitued within 3 to 5 days.

2. Amiodarone

*a. Electrophysiological Actions.* The major electrophysiological action of amiodarone is to prolong repolarization and refractoriness in all cardiac tissue studied, including the sinus node, atrium, atrioventricular node, His–Purkinje system, and ventricle (Rosen and Wit, 1983). These effects are seen following chronic oral therapy while little or no prolongation of refractoriness occurs after single intravenous bolus injection except in the atrioventricular node. Along those lines, amiodarone given intravenously to animals and humans produces no significant alterations in the QTc interval while prolonged oral administration results in significant lengthening of the QTc interval (Heger et al., 1982). Some recent data suggests that amiodarone depresses phase 0 in Purkinje fibers and that this use-dependent effect appears to result from selective blockade of inactivated sodium channels (Mason et al., 1983; Yabek et al., 1985).

*b. Hemodynamic Effects.* In patients without depressed left ventricular function, amiodarone (5 mg/kg intravenously) reduced mean arterial pressure, left ventricular end-diastolic pressure, and systemic vascular resistance and slightly increased cardiac index (Cote et al., 1979). In patients with depressed left ventricular function and recurrent ventricular tachycardia, amiodarone (5 mg/kg intravenously over 20 min) resulted in a linear decrease in heart rate and a reduction in stroke work index and cardiac index without any significant changes in systemic vascular resistance or pulmonary capillary wedge pressure. In most patients the deterioration of left ventricular contractility was transient and not severe (Schwartz et al., 1983). Some experimental studies suggest that the hypotensive effects of intravenous amiodarone may be caused by the solvent Tween-80 rather than by the parent compound (Gough et al., 1982). Although well-controlled studies on the hemodynamic effects of chronic administration of oral amiodarone are lacking, present data suggest that the drug does not have severe negative inotropic effects of clinical significance in most patients (Haffajee *et al.*, 1983; Zipes *et al.*, 1984).

   *c. Pharmacokinetics.*   Amiodarone has a reduced clearance rate, large volume of distribution, low bioavailability, and a long half-life. The low bioavailability may relate to incomplete intestinal absorption, while the larger volume of distribution and reduced clearance contribute to the long elimination half-life. Amiodarone may be released slowly from a reservoir or poorly perfused deep compartment, such as fat, into the plasma. After intravenous administration of 400 mg amiodarone to healthy young male volunteers, total plasma clearance was about 8.5 liter/hr, and total blood clearance about 12 liter/hr, with a steady-state distribution volume of approximately 5000 liters. Terminal elimination half-life was 25 days after single dosing and oral bioavailability 35%. Renal elimination of both amiodarone and its metabolite desethylamiodarone was negligible (Holt *et al.*, 1983). Approximately 20–60% of an oral dose of amiodarone enters the systemic circulation with maximal plasma concentration achieved 4–5 hr after drug injection. Amiodarone is then distributed throughout the body to achieve an equilibrium between tissue and plasma. The time course of the equilibrium varies greatly among different tissues (Holt *et al.*, 1983; Kannan *et al.*, 1982). Amiodarone exhibits heterogeneous distribution and equilibrium and is better described by models with three or four compartments.

   *d. Plasma Level and Dosage.*   In 170 patients receiving maintenance amiodarone therapy, a daily dose of 200 mg produced a plasma concentration of approximately 1.0 $\mu$g/ml. A dose of 400 mg daily resulted in plasma concentrations of approximately 2.0 $\mu$g/ml. Terminal elimination half-life after cessation of chronic therapy was about 53 days for the parent compound and 61 days for the metabolite (Holt *et al.*, 1983). Recent data suggest that a large loading dose should be used when beginning amiodarone therapy because the large volume of distribution would be expected to delay the time to achieve minimal effective drug concentration within the body and thus delay the time to onset of clinical efficacy (Mostow *et al.*, 1984).

   The therapeutic level of serum concentrations of amiodarone varies but appears to range between 1.0 and 3.5 $\mu$g/ml (Haffajee *et al.*, 1983). There appears to be a good relation between dosage and steady-state concentration of amiodarone. However, there is considerable overlap of concentrations both for therapeutic efficacy as well as for those concentrations associated with toxicity (Haffajee *et al.*, 1983).

## IV. Summary

These conventional antiarrhythmic agents plus an array of new drugs are important tools for the treatment of ventricular arrhythmias. A markedly variable relation between plasma drug level and effect should raise the possibility that active metabolites may be present. Further knowledge of the pharmacologic properties of these metabolites will help decrease the incidence of adverse effects and increase the frequency of successful therapy. For most antiarrhythmic drugs plasma level guidelines have been proposed. Most drugs do not have a well-characterized relationship between the plasma concentration and the pharmacological effect because of several confounding variables. Despite these limitations, plasma level monitoring of antiarrhythmic drugs can be helpful since they may predict likely adverse effects, especially in patients with severe left ventricular dysfunction.

Clearly a need for more antiarrhythmic agents exists. Newer agents from Class I are being investigated, and these drugs offer combinations of pharmacokinetic properties and electrophysiologic antiarrhythmic effects that are different from those of currently available drugs.

Perhaps insights into the relation between the various pharmacological properties in closely related compounds could allow for the design of more effective and safer drugs.

## References

Alexander, R. W., Williams, L. T., Lefkowitz, R. T. (1975). *Proc. Natl. Acad. Sci. (USA)*, **72**:1564–1568.
Anderson, J. L., Mason, J. W., Winkle, R. A. (1978). *Circulation*, **57**:685–691.
Anderson, J. L., Patterson, E., Wagner, J. G., Johnson, T. A., Lucchesi, B. R., Pitt, B. (1981). *J. Cardiovasc. Pharmacol.*, **3**:485–493.
Arnsdorf, M. F., Bigger, J. T., Jr. (1972). *J. Clin. Invest.*, **51**:2252–2263.
Bauman, D. J. (1981). *Ann. Intern. Med.*, **94**:411–412.
Befeler, B., Castellanos, A., Wells, D. E. (1975). *Am. J. Cardiol.*, **35**:282–287.
Benowitz, N., Forsyth, R. P., Melmon, K. L. (1974). *Clin. Pharmacol. Ther.*, **16**:99–109.
Bigger, J. T., Jr. (1980). *In* "Heart Disease: A Textbook of Cardiovascular Medicine" (E. Braunwald, ed), p. 717. W. B. Saunders Co., Philadelphia.
Bigger, J. T., Jr., Jaffe, C. C. (1971). *Am. J. Cardiol.*, **27**:82–92.
Bigger, J. T., Jr., Mandel, W. J. (1970). *J. Clin. Invest.*, **49**:63–77.
Blumer, J., Strong, J. M., Atkinson, A. J., Jr. (1973). *J. Pharmacol. Exp. Ther.*, **186**:31–36.
Branch, R. A., Shand, D. G., Wilkinson, G. R. (1973a). *J. Pharmacol. Exp. Ther.*, **184**:515–519.

Branch, R. A., Shand, D. G., Nies, A. S. (1973b). *J. Pharmacol. Exp. Ther.*, **187**:581–587.
Burton, J. R., Mathew, M. T., Armstrong, P. W. (1976). *Am. J. Med.*, **61**:215–220.
Chatterjee, K., Mandel, W. J., Vyden, J. K., Parmley, W. W., Forrester, J. S. (1973). *J. Am. Med. Assoc.*, **223**:757–760.
Cohen, I. S., Jick, H., Cohen, S. I. (1977). *Prog. Cardiovasc. Dis.*, **20**:151–163.
Coltart, D. C., Gibson, D. G., Shand, D. G. (1971). *Br. Med. J.*, **1**:490–491.
Conn, H. L., Luch, R. J. (1964). *Am. J. Med.*, **37**:685–699.
Cote, P., Harrison, D. C., Basile, J., Schroeder, J. S. (1973). *Am. J. Cardiol.*, **32**:937–942.
Cote, P., Schook, J., Harrison, D. C., Schroeder, J. S. (1975). *Proc. Soc. Exp. Biol. Med.*, **149**:958–967.
Cote, T., Bourassa, M. G., Delaye, J., Janin, A., Froment, R., David, P. (1979). *Circulation*, **59**:1165–1172.
Crouthamel, W. G. (1975). *Am. Heart J.*, **90**:335–339.
Data, J. L., Wilkinson, G. R., Nies, A. S. (1976). *N. Engl. J. Med.*, **294**:699–702.
Davis, L. D., Temte, J. V. (1968). *Circ. Res.*, **22**:661–677.
DiFazio, C. A., Brown, R. E. (1972). *Anesthesiology*, **36**:238–243.
Drayer, D. E., Lowenthal, D. T., Woosley, R. L. (1977). *Clin. Pharmacol. Ther.*, **22**:63–69.
Drayer, D. E., Lowenthal, D. T., Restivo, K. V. (1978). *Clin. Pharmacol. Ther.*, **24**:31–39.
Drayer, D. E., Highes, M., Lorenzo, B. (1980). *Clin. Pharmacol. Ther.*, **27**:72–75.
Elvin, A. T., Lalka, D., Stoeckel, K. (1980). *Clin. Pharmacol. Ther.*, **28**:652–658.
Elvin, A. T., Axelson, J. E., Lalka, D. (1982). *Br. J. Clin. Pharmacol.*, **13**:872–873.
Evans, G. H., Shand, D. G. (1973). *Clin. Pharmacol. Ther.*, **14**:487–493.
Feely, J., Wilkinson, G. R., Wood, A. J. (1981). *N. Engl. J. Med.*, **304**:692–695.
Fenster, P. E., Perrier, D. (1982). *Mod. Conc. Cardiovasc. Dis.*, **51**:91–96.
Gallagher, J. J., Pritchett, E. L. C., Benditt, D. G. (1977). *Circulation*, **55–56** (Suppl III):225.
Giardina, E. G. V., Heissenbuttel, R. H., Bigger, J. T., Jr. (1973). *Ann. Intern. Med.*, **78**:183–193.
Gibaldi, M., Perrier, D. (1975). "Pharmacokinetics," Vol. 1. Marcel Dekker, New York.
Gilmore, J. P., Siegel, J. H. (1962). *Circ. Res.*, **10**:347–353.
Gough, W. B., Zeiler, R. H., Barreca, P., El-Sherif, N. (1982). *J. Cardiovasc. Pharm.*, **4**:375–380.
Graffner, C., Conradson, T. B., Hofvendahl, S. (1980). *Clin. Pharmacol. Ther.*, **27**:64–71.
Greenblatt, D. J., Pfeifer, H. J., Ochs, H. R. (1977). *J. Pharmacol. Exp. Ther.*, **202**:365–378.
Greenspan, A. M., Horowitz, L. N., Spielman, S. R. (1980). *Am. J. Cardiol.*, **46**:453–462.
Haffajee, C. L., Love, J. C., Alpert, J. S., Sloan, K. C. (1983). *Am. Heart J.*, **106**:935–943.
Hammermeister, K. E., Boerth, R. C., Worbasse, J. R. (1972). *Am. Heart J.*, **84**:643–652.
Harrison, D. C., Sprouse, J. H., Morrow, A. G. (1963). *Circulation*, **28**:486–491.
Harrison, D. C., Meffin, P. J., Winkle, R. A. (1977). *Progr. Cardiovasc. Dis.*, **20**:217–242.
Heger, J. J., Prystowsky, E. N., Zipes, D. P. (1982). *In* "Ventricular Tachycardia—Mechanisms and Management" (M. E. Josephson, ed). Futura Publishing Co., Mount Kisco, New York.
Heissenbuttel, R. H., Bigger, J. T., Jr. (1979). *Ann. Intern. Med.*, **91**:229–238.
Hinderling, P. H., Vres, J., Garrett, E. R. (1974). *J. Pharm. Sci.*, **63**:1684–1690.
Hoffman, B. F., Rosen, M. R., Wit, A. L. (1975). *Am. Heart J.*, **89**:804–808.
Holder, D. A., Sniderman, A. D., Fraser, G., Fallen, E. L. (1977). *Circulation*, **55**:541–544.
Holford, N. H. G., Coates, P. E., Guentert, T. W. (1981). *Br. J. Clin. Pharmacol.*, **11**:187–195.
Holt, D. W., Tucker, G. T., Jackson, P. R., Storey, G. C. A. (1983). *Am. Heart J.*, **106**:840–846.

Horowitz, L. N., Josephson, M. E., Farshidi, A. (1978). *Am. J. Cardiol.*, **42**:276-280.
Jawad-Kanber, C., Sherrod, T. R. (1974). *Chest*, **66**:269-272.
Jensen, G., Sigurd, B., Uhrenholt, A. (1975). *Eur. J. Clin. Pharmacol.*, **8**:167-173.
Jorgensen, C. R., Bache, R. J., Wang, Y., Van Tassel, R. A., Duval, D. L. (1971). *Cicutation* **43** (Suppl II):11-183.
Kannan, R., Nademanee, K., Hendrickson, J. A., Rostini, H. J., Singh, B. N. (1982). *Clin. Pharmacol. Ther.*, **31**:438-444.
Karim, A. (1975). *Angiology*, **26**:85-98.
Katoh, T., Karagueuzian, H., Jordon, J., Mandel, W. (1982). *Circulation*, **66**:1216-1224.
Kerr, C. R., Prystowsky, E. N., Smith, W. M., Cook, L., Gallagher, J. J. (1982). *Circulation*, **65**:869-878.
Kessler, K. M., Lowenthal, D. T., Werner, H. (1974). *N. Engl. J. Med.*, **290**:706-709.
Kirpekar, S. M., Furchgott, R. F. (1964). *J. Pharmacol. Exp. Ther.*, **143**:64-76.
Kluger, J., Drayer, D. E., Reidenberg, M. H. (1981). *Ann. Intern. Med.*, **95**:18-23.
Koch-Weser, J. (1971). *Ann. NY Acad. Sci.*, **179**:370-382.
Koch-Weser, J. (1979). *N. Engl. J. Med.*, **300**:473-477.
Koch-Weser, J., Frishman, W. H. (1981). *N. Engl. J. Med.*, **305**:500-506.
Koch-Weser, J., Klein, S. W. (1971). *J. Am. Med. Assoc.*, **215**:1454-1460.
Kotter, V., Linderer, T., Schroder, R. (1980). *Am. J. Cardiol.*, **46**:469-475.
Kuntzman, R., Tsai, I., Chang, R. M. (1970). *Clin. Pharmacol. Ther.*, **11**:829-837.
Kus, T., Sasyniuk, B. I. (1978). *Can. J. Physiol. Pharmacol.*, **56**:326-331.
LaBarre, A., Strauss, H. C., Scheinman, M. M., Evans, G. T., Bashore, T., Tiedeman, J. S., Wallace, A. G. (1979). *Circulation*, **59**:226-235.
Lalka, D., Meyer, M. B., Duce, B. R. (1976). *Clin. Pharmacol. Ther.*, **19**:757-766.
Leach, A. J., Brown, J. E., Armstrong, P. W. (1980). *Am. J. Med.*, **68**:839-844.
McAllister, R. G. (1976). *Clin. Pharmacol. Ther.*, **20**:517-532.
Maloney, J. D., Nissen, R. C., McColgan, J. N. (1980). *Am. Heart J.*, **100**:1023-1030.
Markis, J. E., Koch-Weser, J. (1971). *J. Pharmacol. Exp. Ther.*, **178**:94-102.
Mason, J. W., Winkle, R. A. (1978). *Circulation*, **58**:971-985.
Mason, J. W., Winkle, R. A., Rider, A. K., Stinson, E. E., Harrison, D. C. (1977). *J. Clin. Invest.*, **59**:481-489.
Mason, J. W., Hondeghem, L. M., Katzung, B. G. (1983). *Pflugers Arch.*, **396**:79-81.
Mirro, M. J., Manalan, A. S., Bailey, J. C., Watanabe, A. M. (1980). *Circ. Res.*, **47**:855-865.
Moore, E. N., Spear, J. F., Horowitz, L. N. (1978). *Am. J. Cardiol.*, **41**:703-709.
Mostow, N. D., Rakita, L., Vrobel, T. R., Noon, D., Blumer, J. (1984). *J. Am. Coll. Cardiol.*, **4**:97-104.
Naqvi, N., Thompson, D. S., Morgan, E. W. (1979). *Br. Heart J.*, **42**:587-594.
Narang, P. K., Crouthamel, W. G., Carliner, N. H. (1978). *Clin. Pharmacol. Ther.*, **24**:654-662.
Nattel, S., Zipes, D. P. (1980). *Cardiovasc. Clin.*, **11**:221-248.
Nelson, L. D., Schmid, P. G., Holmsten, D., Mark, A. L., Heistad, D. D., Abboud, F. M. (1974). *Proc. Soc. Exp. Biol. Med.*, **146**:409-413.
Nies, A. S., Shand, D. G. (1975). *Circulation*, **52**:6-15.
Norpace (1977). "Disopyramide Phosphate, an Antiarrhythmic Drug," Investigational brochure. Searle Laboratories.
Nyquist, O., Forsell, G., Nordlander, R. (1980). *Am. Heart J.* **100**:1000-1095.
Oltmanns, D., (1982). *Kardiol.*, **71**:172.
Parmley, W. W., Braunwald, E. (1967). *J. Pharmacol. Exp. Ther.*, **158**:11-21.
Podrid, P. J., Schoeneberger, A., Lown, B. (1980). *N. Engl. J. Med.*, **302**:614-617.
Prescott, L. F., Adjepon-Yamoah, K. K., Talbot, R. G. (1976). *Br. Med. J.*, **2**:939-941.

Roden, D. M., Reele, S. B., Higgins, S. B. (1980). *Am. J. Cardiol.*, **46**:463–468.
Romhilt, D. W., Bloomfield, S. S., Lipicky, R. J. (1972). *Circulation*, **45**:800–807.
Ronfeld, R. A., Wolshin, E. M., Block, A. J. (1982). *Clin. Pharmacol. Ther.*, **31**:384–392.
Rosen, M. R., Wit, A. L. (1983). *Am. Heart J.*, **106**:829–39.
Routledge, P. A., Shand, D. G. (1979). *Clin. Pharmacokinet.*, **4**:73–90.
Ryan, W., Engler, R., LeWinter, M. (1979). *Am. J. Cardiol.*, **43**:285–291.
Schmid, P. G., Nelson, L. D., Mark, A. L., Heistad, D. D., Abboud, F. M. (1974a). *J. Pharmacol. Exp. Ther.*, **188**:124–134.
Schmid, P. G., Nelson, L. D., Heistad, D. D., Mark, A. L., Abboud, F. M. (1974b). *Circ. Res.*, **35**:948–960.
Schwartz, A., Shen, E., Morady, F., Gillespie, K., Scheinman, K., Chatterjee, K. (1983). *Am. Heart J.*, **106**:848–855.
Shand, D. G., Nuckolls, E. M., Oates, J. A. (1970). *Clin. Pharmacol. Ther.*, **11**:112–120.
Shanks, R. G., Harrison, D. W. (1981). "Pharmacokinetic Principles in Cardiac Arrhythmias: A Decade of Progress." G. K. Hall, Boston.
Singh, B. N., Vaughan Williams, E. M. (1971). *Circ. Res.*, **29**:286–295.
Sokolow, M., Edgar, A. L. (1950). *Circulation*, **1**:576–592.
Stearns, N. S., Callahan, E. J., Ellis, L. B. (1952). *J. Am. Med. Assoc.*, **148**:360–364.
Stec, G. P., Lertora, J. J. L., Atkinson, A. J. J. (1979). *Ann. Intern. Med.*, **90**:799–801.
Stenson, R. E., Constantino, R. T., Harrison, D. C. (1971). *Circulation*, **43**:205–211.
Taylor, S. H., Saxton, C., Davies, P. S., Stoker, J. B. (1970). *Br. Heart J.*, **32**:326–329.
Thadani, U., Manyari, D., Gregor, P. (1981). *Cath. Cardiovasc. Diag.* **7**:27–34.
Timins, B. I., Gutman, J. A., Haft, J. I. (1981). *Chest*, **79**:477–479.
Wallace, T., Conradi, E. C., Walle, U. K. (1979). *Clin. Pharmacol. Ther.*, **26**:686–695.
Walsh, R. A., Horowitz, L. D. (1979). *Circulation*, **60**:1053–1058.
Ward, J. W., Kingham, C. R. (1976). *J. Intern. Med. Res.*, **4** (Suppl 1):49–53.
Wilkinson, P. R., Desai, J., Hollister, J., Gonzales, R., Abbott, J. A., Scheinman, M. M. (1982). *Circulation*, **66**:1211–1216.
Winkle, R. A., Anderson, J. L., Peters, F. (1978a). *Circulation*, **57**:787–792.
Winkle, R. A., Meffin, P. J., Harrison, D. C. (1978b). *Circulation*, **57**:1008–1016.
Wit, A. L., Steiner, C., Damato, A. N. (1970). *J. Pharmacol. Exp. Ther.*, **173**:344–356.
Woosley, R. L., Shand, D. G., Kornhauser, D. M. (1977). *Clin. Res.*, **25**:262A.
Wyman, M. G. (1978). *Am. J. Cardiol.*, **33**:313–317.
Yabek, S. M., Kato, R., Singh, B. N. (1985). *J. Am. Coll. Cardiol.*, **5**:1109–1115.
Young, M. D., Hadidian, Z., Horn, E. R. (1980). *Am. Heart J.*, **100**:1041–1045.
Zipes, D. P., Prystowsky, E. N., Heger, J. J. (1984). *J. Am. Coll. Cardiol.*, **3**:1059–1071.

# 8 Mechanisms and Management of Myocardial Infarction Arrhythmias

Karen J. Friday and Ralph Lazzara

## I. Introduction

Deaths occurring early in the course of myocardial infarction are usually attributable to ventricular arrhythmias. With the advent of rapid access medical care units, and the ability to monitor patients early in the course of myocardial infarction, the incidence of arrhythmias has been well documented. Although the incidence of sudden death during myocardial infarction has been quoted as up to 50% (Gordon and Kannel, 1971), the occurrence of ventricular fibrillation in patients reached soon after the onset of chest pain has been documented as less than 20% (Adgey et al., 1971). Variations among studies may reflect the different time intervals during ischemia at which patient monitoring began (Table I), ranging from the first hour of symptoms to during the coronary care unit (CCU) stay 3–5 days after the acute event. Any of several arrhythmias augured poorly for long-term survival in two studies assessing all arrhythmias monitored in a CCU (Jewitt et al., 1967; Mogenson, 1970) (Table II), but ventricular fibrillation remains the cause of most deaths early in the course of myocardial infarction. Numerous studies have documented ventricular tachyarrhythmias as a significant factor in the mortality early in the infarct period and as predictors of increased risk of sudden death in the posthospital phase of myocardial infarction.

Basic research has been directed at elucidating mechanisms for the arrhythmias occurring during myocardial infarction and at clarifying the electrophysiological effects of antiarrhythmic drugs. Clinical studies have evaluated patients during and after acute myocardial infarction, initially documenting the evolution of arrhythmias and their outcome and subsequently assessing the ability of various interventions to modify the mortality associated with myocardial infarction. Management, and particularly prevention, of the arrhythmias associated with acute ischemia remain foci of controversy and investigation.

## TABLE I
Arrhythmias during Acute Myocardial Infarction[a]

| Study | No. | Time | Arrhythmia | VF | VT | PVCs | AFIB | SVT | BRADY | 2° AVB | 3° AVB |
|---|---|---|---|---|---|---|---|---|---|---|---|
| Adgey et al. (1971) | 284 | 1 Hr | — | 54(19%) | 87(31%) | 163(54%) | 26(9%) | 11(4%) | 125(44%) | — | — |
| Skjaeggestad and Berstad (1974) | 26 | Immed. | 10(38%) | 3(12%) | 5(19%) | 9(35%) | — | — | 5(19%) | — | — |
| Mogenson (1970) | 421 | NS | 404(96%) | 8(2%) | 170(40%) | 133(32%) | 124(29%) | 33(8%) | 88(21%) | 40(10%) | 32(8%) |
| Romhild et al. (1973) | 31 | M, 14 Hr | 31(100%) | 1(3%) | 8(26%) | 31(100%) | 2(7%) | — | — | — | — |
| Jewitt et al. (1967) | 222 | 24 Hr | 163(73%) | 21(9%) | 14(6%) | 75(33%) | 24(11%) | 73(33%) | 65(29%) | 8(4%) | 11(5%) |
| Vismara et al. (1975) | 83 | 3–5 Day | 70(84%) | 4(5%) | 9(11%) | 40(48%) | — | 37(45%) | — | 5(6%) | 2(2%) |
| Denborough et al. (1968)[b] | 412 | NS | 65(16%) | 3(1%) | 3(1%) | — | 9(2%) | — | — | — | — |

[a] Time, delay between symptoms and onset of monitoring; VF, ventricular fibrillation; VT, ventricular tachycardia; PVCs, premature ventricular contractions; AFIB, atrial fibrillation; SVT, supraventricular tachycardia; AVB, A–V block; BRADY, bradycardia; M, mean; NS, not specified.
[b] Not continuous monitoring.

## TABLE II
In-Hospital Mortality Associated with Arrhythmias during Myocardial Infarction[a]

| Arrhythmia | Jewitt et al. (1967) (Number = 222) | | Mogenson (1970) (Number = 421) | |
|---|---|---|---|---|
| | Number | Mortality | Number | Mortality |
| Sinus tachycardia | 73(33%) | 23(32%) | 212(50%) | 59(28%) |
| Sinus bradycardia | 65(29%) | 7(11%) | 90(21%) | 28(31%) |
| Atrial tachycardia | 15(7%) | 4(27%) | 33(8%) | 7(21%) |
| Atrial flutter | 2(1%) | 0(0%) | 40(10%) | 11(28%) |
| Atrial fibrillation | 24(11%) | 7(29%) | 84(20%) | 31(37%) |
| Premature ventricular beats | 75(34%) | 18(24%) | 133(32%) | 35(26%) |
| Ventricular tachycardia | 14(6%) | 6(43%) | 170(40%) | 47(28%) |
| Ventricular fibrillation | 21(9%) | 11(52%) | 8(2%) | 1(13%) |
| Second degree A–V block | 8(4%) | 2(25%) | 40(10%) | 18(45%) |
| Third degree A–V block | 11(5%) | 7(64%) | 32(8%) | 15(47%) |

[a] Patients in the study by Jewitt et al. (1967) were admitted within the first 24 hours after infarction. The time after infarct was not specified in Mogenson's study.

## II. Mechanisms of Cardiac Arrhythmias

Electrical activity in the heart is the expression of ion gradients and flows across the cellular membrane (Fig. 1). The action potential is generated primarily by movements of sodium, potassium, and calcium. The upstroke is mediated by sodium current flowing inward through the "fast" channel. Calcium current flows inward primarily during the plateau via

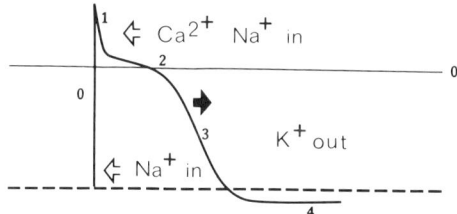

CARDIAC ACTION POTENTIAL

**Fig. 1.** Cardiac action potential: Current flow across the cell membrane sodium ions inward during the rapid upstroke (phase 1). Phase 2 is a plateau during which there is an inward current of calcium and sodium. Phase 3 is rapid repolarization, during which there is an outward flow of potassium.

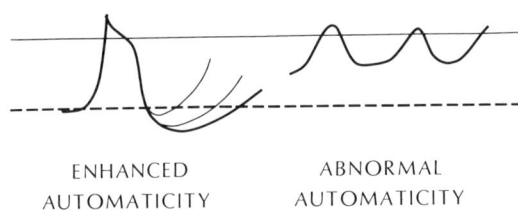

ENHANCED AUTOMATICITY     ABNORMAL AUTOMATICITY

**Fig. 2.** Automaticity occurs in some cells normally (e.g., Purkinje fibers). This spontaneous depolarization may be enhanced (left) by various factors (e.g., catecholamines). Abnormal automaticity (right) occurs when cells are abnormally depolarized and generate an action potential from a less negative threshold.

the "slow" channel. Potassium currents flowing outward are important in the repolarization of the membrane. Arrhythmias are thought to arise from abnormalities of impulse generation or propagation in the various tissues of the heart. Abnormal impulse generation occurs because of enhanced or abnormal automaticity, or because of triggered activity (Hoffman et al., 1975).

### A. Enhanced or Abnormal Automaticity

Specialized cardiac cells demonstrate spontaneous automaticity characterized by slow diastolic (phase 4) depolarization, which generates an action potential when the potential reaches threshold for the activation of the fast sodium current (Fig. 2). In Purkinje fibers, this process occurs at high (more negative) levels of membrane potential. Normal automatic activity may be enhanced by certain factors, such as catecholamines (beta-adrenergic activity). Abnormal automaticity refers to diastolic depolarization of partially depolarized cells which are normally automatic (e.g., Purkinje fibers), or of cells which do not normally display automatic activity (atrial or ventricular muscle cells). Because different ionic currents may be involved in diastolic depolarization occurring at different levels of membrane potential, the sensitivity to pharmacologic interventions may be very different. For example, if inward calcium current is a prominent factor in diastolic depolarization occurring at lower (less negative) levels of membrane potential, calcium channel blocking drugs may be more effective in suppressing abnormal automaticity than in suppressing normal automaticity in Purkinje fibers.

### B. Triggered Activity

Electrical discharge that results from a preceding action potential is considered to be "triggered" (Fig. 3). Triggered activity results from

## 8. Myocardial Infarction Arrhythmias

EARLY AFTERDEPOLARIZATIONS

DELAYED AFTERDEPOLARIZATIONS

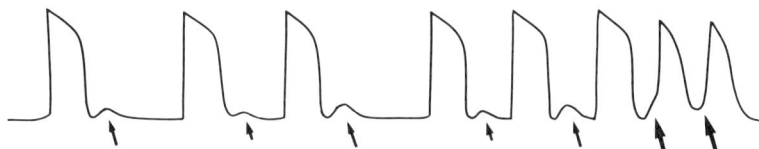

**Fig. 3.** Triggered activity is an electrical discharge arising from the previous action potential. Afterdepolarizations may be "early" (top), arising from the action potential before repolarization is complete, or "delayed" (bottom), arising from shifts in the membrane potential after repolarization is complete.

afterdepolarizations. Early afterdepolarizations represent a plateau or upturn of membrane potential during the terminal phase of repolarization which may produce an upstroke if enough inward current is activated. Delayed afterdepolarizations are transient positive shifts of the membrane potential occurring after repolarization is complete and may produce a triggered discharge if the amplitude is high enough to reach the threshold potential for the fast channel.

The major mechanism for arrhythmia generation through abnormal impulse propagation is reentry.

### C. Reentry

Reentry is the consequence of the formation of a circuit around areas of permanent or functional conduction block (Fig. 4). The circuit is formed when conduction is blocked in one direction but proceeds over another to return to the original site of block, which permits conduction of the returning impulse (unidirectional block). If conduction time around the circuit is long enough, because of slowed conduction, the myocardium adjoining the circuit can be reexcited by the returning reentrant) impulse. Usually, the formation of the reentrant circuit is facilitated by premature

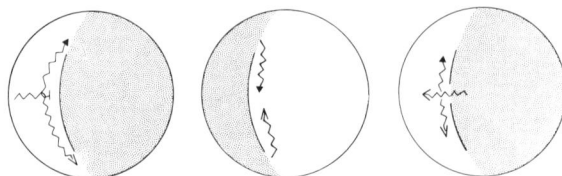

**Fig. 4.** Reentry: Conduction in damaged tissue may be slowed in relatively refractory areas (white) or blocked in absolutely refractory areas (gray). An area of block due to refractoriness is functional and time dependent (left). If conduction is slowed enough, an impulse may be conducted slowly enough around an interface between the refractory and responsive regions that the originally refractory region has recovered the ability to conduct (middle). During conduction in this region, the originally responsive region is refractory (middle). In time, the initial pathway also recovers, usually near the center of the original interface of block, and reentry can occur (right).

excitation, which produces functional block, and slow conduction, the essential elements of the circuit. The circuit may form around a region without propagation (e.g., a scar) or around a region of functional block determined by refractoriness.

These various mechanisms have been identified in animal models and in tissue preparations of myocardial cells, but the metabolic, cellular processes responsible for these mechanisms have not been elucidated. In animals, and in humans *in vivo,* the mechanisms are often more difficult to distinguish from one another. For instance, a premature ventricular beat arising through enhanced automaticity in ventricular tissue may be conducted with adequate delay through an ischemic area of myocardium to set up a reentrant arrhythmia. Determination of the mechanism predominantly responsible for an arrhythmia clinically is frequently inferential.

## III. Mechanisms of Arrhythmias during Infarction

Much of the information which has been obtained on the mechanisms of arrhythmias during myocardial infarction and ischemia has come from studies of the Harris model (Harris and Rojas, 1943) in dogs in which the left anterior descending coronary artery is totally occluded. Although this model has been criticized for its shortcomings, it has provided much insight into how arrhythmias originate and propagate in infarcted tissue.

Arrhythmias occurring in the animal model of acute infarction separate distinctly into two phases. During the acute phase, the first 30 min after occlusion, ventricular fibrillation is common. The initial arrhythmic activity is followed by a period of quiescence. The second phase of arrhythmias begins 4–8 hr after occlusion and lasts up to 2 to 4 days. During this delayed phase, ventricular fibrillation is rare, but there is a marked increase in ventricular ectopy, often complex in morphology (Lazzara *et al.*, 1978b; Fujimoto *et al.*, 1984). Differences in the occurrence and characteristics of arrhythmias have been thought to reflect the role of various mechanisms in the origination of arrhythmias (Fig. 5).

Electrophysiological properties of ventricular myocardial cells change rapidly during ischemia. Fractionation of electrograms in the ischemic area occurs within minutes after the coronary artery is occluded. It reflects irregular conduction, which in turn reflects slowed and irregular upstrokes generated in ischemic cells. Electrograms in the subendocar-

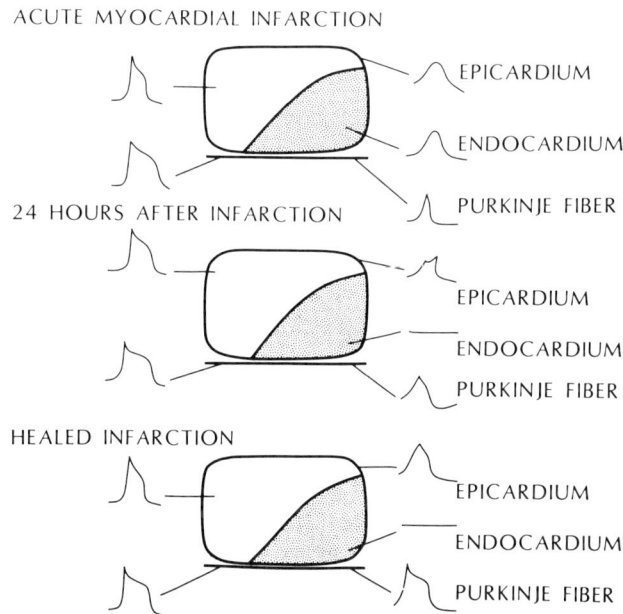

**Fig. 5.** Changes in transmembrane potential during the evolution of myocardial infarction. Action potentials from normal myocardium and Purkinje fibers are at the left, action potentials from damaged tissue are at right. (Top) During acute myocardial infarction, conduction is delayed more in the epicardium than in the endocardium, although the endocardium has the greatest ischemia. Purkinje fibers have a shortened action potential (Middle) Twenty-four hours after the acute event, there is no conduction in the endocardium and conduction in the epicardial cells overlying the infarct is markedly impaired. Purkinje fibers demonstrate prolonged action potentials, enhanced automaticity, and slow upstrokes. (Bottom) In the healed infarct, the epicardial cells which have survived have improved conduction that is not quite normal. No conduction occurs through the infarcted endocardium. Purkinje fibers have been restored to virtually normal. Delays in conduction in different areas of the heart can set up reentrant circuits.

dial, intramural, and subepicardial regions of the infarct show that the conduction delay is greatest in the subepicardium, suggesting that this area is the site for reentry (Lazzara et al., 1978b). Epicardial mapping with multiple electrodes during acute infarction suggests marked conduction delay in this area. This occurs despite evidence that the greatest ischemic damage occurs in the subendocardial areas. Resolution of the acute phase arrhythmias appears to coincide with improvement in the subepicardial electrograms. Most of the evidence to date suggests that the arrhythmias occurring in the acute phase of infarction relate to reentry within ventricular myocardium (El-Sherif et al., 1985).

Purkinje fibers seem to survive the acute phase of ischemia with little initial impairment of conduction. Although reduction in action potential amplitude, duration, and upstroke velocity has been reported, the specialized conduction system does not demonstrate enhanced automaticity or severe conduction delay and is thought to have little role in the acute phase arrhythmias. Some work (Janse et al., 1980) suggests involvement of Purkinje fibers in "re-excitation" created by intensive flow of injury current. However, Purkinje fibers studied in vitro 24 hr after infarction show depression of action potential amplitude, prolongation of action potential duration, and enhanced diastolic depolarization. These changes could lead to both enhanced automaticity and to reentry, and the specialized conduction system is thought to be a major factor in the genesis of arrhythmias in the delayed phase of myocardial infarction (El-Sherif et al., 1977b,c,d; le Marec et al., 1985). Some investigators have shown that ectopic beats occurring this time are preceded by activation of the Purkinje system (Horowitz et al., 1976). At this time, there is little electrical activity demonstrable in the subendocardium, but a cap of subepicardial cells continues to have depressed conduction and could contribute to reentrant arrhythmias. The delayed phase of arrhythmias subsides several days after the infarction, and a study of Purkinje fibers at this time shows a return of the conduction properties to normal, with improvement in the epicardial electrograms (Spear et al., 1983). Limited information is available on the arrhythmias of chronic infarction (Lazzara and Scherlag, 1984). In healing infarctions (El-Sherif et al., 1983b; Gessman et al., 1983), reentry through surviving epicardial cells over the infarction has been documented by cryoablation of the circuit.

Biochemical and metabolic changes which occur in ischemic cells may significantly affect the electrophysiological properties of myocardial cells and of adjacent Purkinje fibers. Such changes include increased extracellular potassium, local tissue acidosis (Gettes et al., 1982), changes in intracellular cyclic AMP and ATP, release of lysophosphoglycerides (Russell et al., 1981), hypoxia (Corr et al., 1981), free radicals, and,

## 8. Myocardial Infarction Arrhythmias

certainly, factors yet to be identified. Elevations of extracellular potassium have been demonstrated in ischemic myocardium (Gettes et al., 1982) and can contribute to some of the conduction delays seen. In vitro studies, however, have shown that correction of potassium levels in ischemic blood alone did not improve conduction properties in myocardial cells. Hypoxia also is not an isolated factor in producing conduction abnormalities in ischemic tissue, as cells perfused with blood in which the oxygen content alone has been reduced do not demonstrate the degree of electrophysiological changes seen with ischemia (Bagdonis et al., 1961). Perfusion of ischemic myocardium with a saline solution of low oxygen content produced improvement in conduction properties in the ischemic areas, suggesting a "washout" of ischemic products (Downar et al., 1977). More recent studies suggest that the combination of high potassium levels, hypoxia, and low pH can reproduce ischemic electrophysiological abnormalities. Lysophosphoglycerides, which may be released in ischemia or in infarction, have been shown to depress conduction in relatively low doses (Corr et al., 1981), but there is controversy as to whether the concentrations at which conduction depression occurs are relevant in vivo. The extent to which these metabolic changes occur in different areas of myocardium during ischemia may produce different degrees of conduction delay. This irregularity of conduction times throughout the ischemic heart may be a factor in the production of reentry.

Calcium current has been implicated in the generation of arrhythmias in several ways. Slow channels conduct inward calcium current primarily during the plateau phase of the cardiac action potential of normal cells. When the fast channel is inactivated, as in cells depolarized by high extracellular potassium, the slow channel may generate an upstroke with a very slow velocity (hence its name, slow channel) and low amplitude (Pappano, 1970). If this slowed conduction were unmasked during ischemia, such as by regional increases in potassium or acidosis, there would be the possibility of block and the substrate for reentrant arrhythmias. Catecholamines may facilitate conduction dependent on slow current when the sodium current has been markedly depressed during ischemia (Pappano, 1970). Local tissue changes would be greatest during the acute process, when reentrant rhythms are thought to be predominant, but the role of the slow channel in conduction delay in ischemic tissue is controversial. Rapid accumulation of intracellular calcium occurs in the areas of infarction and has been postulated (Clusin et al., 1982) to be a contributory factor in the occurrence of ventricular fibrillation during ischemia. This is felt to be a direct effect of the calcium overload in myocardial cells, not confined to the conduction system.

Triggered activity has recently been demonstrated in Purkinje fibers in

1-day-old infarcts (El-Sherif *et al.*, 1983a). Calcium channel blockers have been shown to block this phenomenon (Gough *et al.*, 1984), consistent with the calcium-mediated afterdepolarizations induced by cardiac glycosides (Kass *et al.*, 1978).

Thus, many of the arrhythmogenic mechanisms in acute infarction, such as reentry, triggered activity, and ventricular fibrillation, may be related to calcium imbalance or to calcium-dependent electrical activity.

Both parasympathetic and sympathetic tone have been found to play a role in arrhythmogenesis following infarction. Increased vagal effect in the early phase of infarction has been shown to improve the rate of conduction in the ischemic electrogram (El-Sherif, 1978), increase the ventricular fibrillation threshold, and decrease the incidence of ventricular fibrillation in experimental animals, an effect much more marked with left than right coronary occlusion (Gillis *et al.*, 1976). During the delayed phase of arrhythmias, vagal stimulation enhances the ventricular arrhythmias, presumably by unmasking automatic mechanisms (Scherlag *et al.*, 1974). Atropine given during the different phases counteracts the vagal influences (Goldstein *et al.*, 1973), increasing arrhythmias and ventricular fibrillation when given shortly after occlusion and suppressing the delayed arrhythmias when given 24 hr after occlusion. The increased arrhythmogenicity of atropine was more marked when given to animals with an anterior infarction. Vagal stimulation has been shown to increase the ventricular fibrillation threshold (Kent *et al.*, 1973) with the heart rate controlled, thus the "protective" effect of vagal stimulation may be more than rate-related reduction of ischemia. Cholinergic innervation of the ventricular conduction system has been demonstrated (Kent and Epstein, 1976), suggesting that direct vagal influence on the conduction system may play a role in the increased fibrillation threshold without an effect on ventricular myocardium. Vagal stimulation prolongs repolarization variably throughout normal hearts when sympathetic activity is high, establishing a potential for autonomic imbalance (Martins *et al.*, 1983), although this has not shown to be directly involved in arrhythmogenesis. In some studies, there was a question of enhancement of the vagal effect in the setting of increased sympathetic tone (Rardon and Bailey, 1983), but the role of this balance of autonomic tone in arrhythmias or during ischemia has not been defined.

Although increased sympathetic tone is associated with increases in arrhythmias, the mechanisms involved are not distinct. In normal hearts, sympathetic stimulation has little effect on the conduction properties of myocardium but can increase the rate of automatic firing in Purkinje fibers (Kassenbaum and van Dyke, 1966). During ischemia, sympathetic input may produce a further increase in the rate of firing in automatic Purkinje fibers, which may increase the risk of producing ventricular arrhythmias. During myocardial infarction, there is both an increase in the efferent sympathetic activity and an increase in circulating catecholamines (Corr and Gillis, 1978). Responses to sympathetic stimulation and increased circulating catecholamines are different, perhaps reflecting the irregular distribution of sympathetic receptors in the heart (Kralios et al., 1981). Depletion of myocardial catecholamine stores in ischemic areas has been reported (Barber et al., 1983). Total extrinsic denervation in dogs did not reduce the incidence of ventricular fibrillation after coronary occlusion soon after the denervation but prevented ventricular fibrillation when infarction was produced later after the denervation (Ebert et al., 1969). Myocardial depletion of catecholamines has been shown to reduce arrhythmias with ischemia (Penny, 1984). Since sympathetic fibers generally follow the course of coronary arteries in the subepicardium, transmural infarction may interrupt sympathetic innervation to distal areas of myocardium (Barber et al., 1983). This could lead to an imbalance in autonomic tone in normal myocardium as well as in ischemic areas. Studies have shown an irregular distribution of sympathetic innervation throughout the heart (Kralios et al., 1981), suggesting that sympathetic imbalance may be as much a factor as the total sympathetic outflow, particularly in producing differential areas of conduction in the myocardium. Enhanced alpha-receptor responsiveness has also been shown after sympathetic stimulation (Sheridan et al., 1980), which increases the heterogeneity of conduction. Total extrinsic denervation in dogs eliminated the occurrence of ventricular fibrillation after coronary occlusion (Ebert et al., 1969). Circulating epinephrine has been shown to reduce serum potassium (Brown et al., 1983; Vincent et al., 1984) which could also enhance conduction depression during ischemia.

Experimental evidence shows that just as myocardial ischemia is a very heterogeneous process, so are the biochemical and neural responses to ischemia. The complexity of the ischemic processes, and the responses in different cardiac tissues, presents the milieu for marked disturbances in conduction and the production of lethal arrhythmias. Rapid changes occurring throughout the ischemic myocardium may alter conduction properties as well, allowing different mechanisms of arrhythmias to manifest themselves at different times during infarction.

## IV. Clinical Studies

Clinical studies have suggested different stages in the occurrences of arrhythmias during the evolution of acute myocardial infarction (Adgey et

**TABLE III**
Incidence of Arrhythmias in 284 Patients Seen within 1 Hr of Acute Myocardial Infarction[a]

| Arrhythmia | 1 Hr | 1–2 Hr | 2–4 Hr | >4 Hr | Total |
|---|---|---|---|---|---|
| Bradyarrhythmia | 88(31%) | 10(3.5%) | 6(2%) | 21(7%) | 125(44%) |
| Ventricular fibrillation | 28(10%) | 12(4%) | 2(0.7%) | 12(4%) | 54(19%) |
| Ventricular tachycardia | 10(3.5%) | 16(6%) | 6(2%) | 55(19%) | 87(31%) |
| Premature ventricular beats | 70(25%) | 36(13%) | 16(6%) | 41(14%) | 163(57%) |
| Atrial fibrillation/flutter | 11(4%) | 0 | 0 | 15(5%) | 26(9%) |
| Supraventricular tachycardia | 1(0.4%) | 0 | 0 | 10(3.5%) | 11(4%) |

[a] From Adgey et al. (1971).

*al.*, 1971) (Table III). Differences among studies (Table I) in the types and frequencies of arrhythmias observed reflect the time elapsed between the onset of infarction, the duration of monitoring, and the classification of arrhythmias. Ventricular fibrillation has been categorized as being "primary," occurring in the absence of any hemodynamic compromise, or "secondary," accompanied by such evidence of decreased left ventricular function as rales, hypotension, or pulmonary edema (Campbell, 1983). Such a distinction is more than semantic, as there are marked differences clinically between primary and secondary ventricular fibrillation, including the time course of occurrence during infarction, the response to drugs, and the prognosis for survival (Logan *et al.*, 1981). Ventricular arrhythmias are most often the cause of early hospital mortality (Norris *et al.*, 1968a), and a major objective of therapy during infarction is the prevention and treatment of ventricular fibrillation.

When patients have been monitored from the first minutes of symptoms (Adgey *et al.*, 1971) (Table III), the incidence of primary ventricular fibrillation is maximal within the first hour and rapidly decreases in the ensuing hours. The incidence of primary ventricular fibrillation within the first 4 hrs of infarction was initially shown to be 19% (Adgey *et al.*, 1971), but a later study by the same group (Dunn *et al.*, 1985) showed an incidence of 1.5% in patients treated with placebo early in the infarct period. Placebo treated patients have had a similar low incidence of ventricular fibrillation, 1.2% in a study of lidocaine (Koster and Dunning, 1985) or 1.5% in a study of metoprolol (MIAMI, 1985) early in the infarct period. Another study (Skjaeggestad and Berstad, 1974), which reported arrhythmias in 26 patients who had an infarction while being monitored in the CCU, found nine had significant arrhythmias, three with primary ventricular fibrillation, all within the first 30 min of infarction. These authors postulated that the lower incidence of arrhythmias in this group than in other series may have been due to a high incidence of small infarcts in their group of patients. In one study with continuous monitoring from the time of admission to the CCU (Campbell *et al.*, 1981), ventricular fibrillation was again an arrhythmia seen early in the course of the infarct, but the incidence of other ventricular arrhythmias, particularly ventricular tachycardia and premature ventricular beats, increased with time. Several of the studies which have attempted to assess prevention of ventricular fibrillation in the setting of myocardial infarction have been criticized for the low incidence of ventricular fibrillation in either treated or untreated groups, which may well reflect delays in initiating treatment, or observation of arrhythmias. Most clinical studies show that primary ventricular fibrillation is an arrhythmia of the first 6 hr of infarction, although some cases do occur later. Delays in seeking medical attention and in hospitalization (McNeilly and Pemberton, 1968; Moss *et al.*, 1977; Armstrong *et al.*, 1972) can exceed the high-risk interval for many patients, and patients reaching the CCU may already be in a lower risk group.

A significant contribution of coronary care units to treatment of patients with myocardial infarction was continuous monitoring of heart rhythms and the early detection of serious arrhythmias (Lown *et al.*, 1967; Killip and Kimball, 1967; Stock *et al.*, 1967; Pentecost and Mayne, 1968). Review of the information provided by these units lead to the concept of "warning arrhythmias," which included: R on T beats (premature ventricular contractions occurring with such a short coupling interval that they interrupt the preceding T wave), more than five premature ventricular contractions (PVCs) per minute, multiform PVCs, and repetitive patterns of extrasystoles (e.g., couplets, bigeminy) (Lown *et al.*, 1967). However, subsequent evaluations which compared detection of these arrhythmias using continuous tape recordings to the visual monitoring system in most coronary units demonstrated that these "warning arrhythmias" were not detected well, although ventricular fibrillation was adequately noted (Romhilt *et al.*, 1973; Lindsay and Bruckner, 1975). Other studies (Lie *et al.*, 1975; El-Sherif *et al.*, 1976; Bennett and Pentecost, 1972; Dhurandhar *et al.*, 1971) have addressed the validity of these arrhythmias as precursors of ventricular fibrillation. The incidence of these arrhythmias was found to occur equally among patients who developed ventricular fibrillation and those who did not. In addition, up to half the patients who did develop ventricular fibrillation did so with no preceding rhythm disturbance. When "warning" arrhythmias did occur, they often preceded ventricular fibrillation by too brief a period to initiate any preventive therapy (Adgey, 1983). Thus, ventricular fibrillation occurs early in the course of infarction and frequently without any warnings, even without preceding symptoms of infarction.

Two groups have found a much higher incidence of ventricular fibrillation in patients with hypokalemia than those with normal potassium levels (Hulting, 1981; Nordrehaug, 1983, 1985).

Disturbances of autonomic tone have been observed in the earliest period of infarction (Pantridge et al., 1981; Pantridge and Webb, 1973). Defining parasympathetic activity as sinus bradycardia, A–V node block, or hypotension in the absence of bradycardia, and sympathetic activity as sinus tachycardia or transient hypertension in the absence of tachycardia, 74 of 89 patients (83%) seen within the first 30 min of infarction had some evidence of enhanced autonomic tone. Increased parasympathetic activity was seen in 43 patients (50%), and increased sympathetic tone in 31 patients (33%) seen very early in infarction, with a very rapid decrease in the occurrence of augmented autonomic tone later. Site of infarction was a major factor in the autonomic dysfunction, as the incidence of parasympathetic overactivity was significantly higher in patients with posterior infarction than in those with an anterior wall infarct (George and Greenwood, 1967). Recordings of heart rate preceding ventricular fibrillation (Durrer et al., 1978) showed that seven of 20 patients had heart rates greater than 100/min.

In one study (Vismara et al., 1975), patients with acute myocardial infarction had continuous rhythm recordings during the CCU admission, within the first 5 days of infarction, and just before discharge from the hospital, 2–3 weeks later. They found that arrhythmias in the CCU, particularly ventricular fibrillation, did not necessarily predict occurrence of the same arrhythmia later in the hospitalization.

Prognostic value of primary ventricular fibrillation during acute myocardial infarction remains disputed (Friehling et al., 1984). Some studies suggest that there is no difference in long-term survival in patients post-myocardial infarction with and without primary ventricular fibrillation (Lawrie, 1969), while others (Conley et al., 1977; Robinson et al., 1965) found a higher mortality in patients who had had an episode of ventricular fibrillation. Assessment of this data is difficult, because some study groups are small, control groups for comparison varied, and treatment with antiarrhythmic drugs may have altered the natural history in some studies. One study using matched controls (Schwartz et al., 1985) confirmed that in patients with inferior wall infarctions, early ventricular fibrillation did not differentiate outcome. However, in patients with anterior wall infarction, those who had had ventricular fibrillation were at a significantly higher risk of sudden death than those who did not. In modern CCUs, defibrillation is usually prompt and effective. What effect a brief episode of ventricular fibrillation may have on myocardial perfusion and long-term myocardial function is debated.

Programmed electrical stimulation has recently been done in patients who have recently had a myocardial infarction. Inducibility of ventricular arrhythmias at electrophysiological study was the same in patients who did and did not have clinical ventricular arrhythmias during the first 48 hrs of infarction (Table IV) (Richards *et al.*, 1983; Kowey *et al.*, 1984; Waspe *et al.*, 1985; Roy *et al.*, 1985).

Several studies (Moss, 1979) have evaluated the prognostic factors for long-term survival following myocardial infarction. Early studies (Coronary Drug Project Research Group, 1973, 1974; Moss *et al.*, 1974; Denborough *et al.*, 1968) found that patients having any ventricular ectopy on continuous monitoring have a decreased long-term survival rate compared to those with no ectopy. With the availability of more sophisticated arrhythmia analysis, several groups (Kleiger *et al.*, 1981; Bigger *et al.*, 1982; Kotler *et al.*, 1973; Schulze *et al.*, 1977) found that the survival rate decreased with the occurrence of more frequent or complex forms of ectopy during the subacute stages of infarction. In a study of patients with continuous monitoring both in the CCU 3–5 days after infarction and again late in the hospital course just before discharge (Vismara *et al.*, 1977), sudden death occurred in 12 of 56 patients followed prospectively. Comparing the arrhythmias in the acute and the late hospital phase of infarction, there was no difference in the groups with and without subsequent sudden death in arrhythmias occurring in the acute infarct stage, including ventricular fibrillation. However, the sudden death group had a significantly greater incidence of complex ventricular ectopy on the Holter monitors done just before discharge.

In the studies which have evaluated a number of other clinical variables in the postinfarction patients, additional factors, particularly residual left ventricular function, have been at least as significant a factor, if not more so, than ventricular ectopy in predicting long-term survival. Since some studies have suggested a correlation between impaired left ventricular function and increased ectopy (Schulze *et al.*, 1975; Kleiger *et al.*, 1981), it had been postulated that the ectopy may be but another marker of ventricular dysfunction. Recent data from a multicenter postinfarct study (Bigger *et al.*, 1984) demonstrated that increased frequency of ventricular ectopic beats (>10/min) was a risk factor for sudden death after infarction independent of left ventricular dysfunction.

Electrophysiological testing has had a role in predicting the potential for arrhythmias in patients with chronic ischemic heart disease (Mason and Winkle, 1978; Horowitz *et al.*, 1978). Early studies in patients following myocardial infarction had suggested that the occurrence of a repetitive ventricular response to programmed electrical stimulation was a prognostic factor for the development of ventricular arrhythmias (Green *et al.*,

## TABLE IV
Electrophysiological Studies in Patients Post Myocardial Infarction (MI)

| | | | VT/VF during MI[a] | | | No VT/VF during MI | | |
| | | | | EP Results | | | EP Results | |
| Study | Total Number | Time Post MI | Number | VT/VF | Negative | Number | VT/VF | Negative |
| --- | --- | --- | --- | --- | --- | --- | --- | --- |
| Richards et al. (1983) | 165 | 2–28 days | 26(16%) | 6(23%) | 20(77%) | 139(84%) | 32(23%) | 107(77%) |
| Kowey et al. (1984) | 57 | 3–65 days | 17(30%) | 9(53%) | 8(47%) | 40(70%) | 9(23%) | 31(77%) |
| Waspe et al. (1985) | 50 | 7–36 days | 15(30%) | 7(47%) | 8(53%) | 35(70%) | 8(23%) | 27(77%) |
| Roy et al. (1985) | 150 | 8–20 days | 38(25%) | 10(26%) | 18(74%) | 112(75%) | 25(22%) | 87(78%) |

[a] Occurring within first 72 hours of infarction.

1978). The value of the repetitive ventricular response has been questioned (Gomes et al., 1981; Naccarelli et al., 1981), and this is now rarely used. Some studies (Table V) have evaluated patients early in the infarct recovery period with programmed electrical stimulation. Data from some centers suggest that the inducibility of arrhythmias at electrophysiological study soon after a myocardial infarction may portend a higher risk of sudden death or significant arrhythmias later (Denniss et al., 1984; Waspe et al., 1985; Hamer et al., 1982), although this has not been a consistent finding. (Marchlinski et al., 1983; Roy et al., 1985). Variability in induction protocols and in the endpoints used to define a positive study have also confused the question of the validity of induced ventricular arrhythmias. (Wellens et al., 1985; Brugada and Wellens, 1985). Use of antiarrhythmic drugs had made the predictive value of electrophysiologic testing null in some studies (Santarelli et al., 1985).

Arrhythmias occurring within the first 48 hr of infarction and those which occur during the recovery phase seem to be distinguishable by several factors, including prognosis. In a small series of patients undergoing electrophysiological study 24 hr after infarction during sustained ventricular tachycardia (Wellens et al., 1974), the arrhythmia could not be terminated by extrastimuli, suggesting abnormal automaticity rather than reentry as the mechanism involved. One patient studied 5 weeks later had tachycardia terminated by pacing, suggesting the mechanism was then reentry. This clinical picture of changing arrhythmia patterns suggests some correlation in humans with the variability in the arrhythmia substrate during the evolution of a myocardial infarction seen in animal models.

Clinical studies of patients with acute myocardial infarction have defined the major components of the problem of arrhythmia management. First is the prevention of ventricular fibrillation early in the infarct period, and second is protection from sudden death after resolution of the acute infarct process.

## V. Pharmacology of Antiarrhythmic Drugs

Drugs act through a variety of mechanisms to alter the electrical properties of cardiac cells and to modify the processes that generate cardiac arrhythmias. Delineation of these mechanisms is not a simple matter because drugs may have a number of effects which may or may not be important in the suppression of arrhythmias. Conduction and automaticity of different cardiac tissues (sinus node, A–V node, Purkinje fibers,

## TABLE V
Electrophysiological (EP) Testing in Patients after Myocardial Infarction (MI) Prediction of Subsequent Sudden Death or Tachyarrhythmias[a]

| Study | Number | Study time after MI | VF | Events | VT | Events | Noninducible[b] | Events |
|---|---|---|---|---|---|---|---|---|
| Deniss et al. (1984) | 290 | 1–4 Weeks | 46(16%) | 1(2%) | 50(17%) | 7(14%) | 194(67%) | 7(4%)[c] |
| Hamer et al. (1982) | 37 | 7–20 Days | — | — | 12(32%) | 5(42%) | 25(63%) | 2(8%) |
| Marchlinski et al. (1983) | 46 | 8–60 Days | — | — | 10(22%) | 1(10%) | 36(78%) | 5(14%) |
| Waspe et al. (1985) | 48 | 7–36 Days | — | — | 17(35%) | 5(29%) | 31(65%) | 0(0%) |
| Roy et al. (1985) | 150 | 8–20 Days | — | — | 35(23%) | 2(6%) | 115(77%) | 5(4%) |

[a] VF, ventricular fibrillation; VT, ventricular tachycardia; PVC, premature ventricular contraction; RVR, Repetitive Ventricular Response.
[b] Noninducible included patients with ≤5 RVR (Hamel, Roy) <4 RVR (Marchlinski).
[c] $p < .01$ of sudden death or arrhythmias comparing group with inducible VT and that with no VT.

atrial or ventricular muscle) may be modified in different ways and to different degrees.

Classification of antiarrhythmic drugs has been empirical, based on the observation of common properties of agents known to suppress arrhythmias clinically, and deductive, based on the ability of agents to counteract presumed arrhythmogenic mechanisms.

One of the most widely accepted and clinically useful classifications of antiarrhythmic drugs is that of Vaughan Williams (1984b) (Table VI), with the modification of Class I proposed by Harrison (1983, 1985) (Table VII). Although antiarrhythmic drugs may affect the electrophysiological properties of cardiac cells in different ways, the classification uses the mechanism thought to be the primary mode of action. In this system, the major categories are as follows.

**TABLE VI**

Classification of Antiarrhythmic Drugs[a]

Class I: depress sodium channel conduction
  A. Quinidine
    Procainamide
    Disopyramide
  B. Lidocaine
    Mexiletine
    Tocainide
  C. Flecainide
    Lorcainide
    Encainide
Class II: beta-adrenergic blockers
  Propranolol
  Atenolol
  Timolol
  Nadolol
  Metoprolol
  Pindolol
Class III: prolong action potential duration (antifibrillatory action)
  Bretylium
  Bethanidine
  Amiodarone
  Clofilium
Class IV: calcium channel blockers
  Verapamil
  Nifedipine[b]
  Diltiazem
  Bepridil

[a] From Vaughan Williams (1984b) and Harrison (1983).
[b] No known antiarrhythmic effects.

**TABLE VII**
Clinical Subdivisions of Class I Antiarrhythmic Drugs[a]

| Effect on | A<br>Quinidine<br>Procainamide<br>Disopyramide | B<br>Lidocaine<br>Mexiletine<br>Tocainide | C<br>Lorcainide<br>Encainide<br>Flecainide |
| --- | --- | --- | --- |
| QRS | ↑ At high concentration | 0 | ↑ At low concentration |
| Conduction | ↓ At high concentration | 0 | ↓ At low concentration |
| Effective refractory period | ↑ Absolutely and relative to APD | ↓ Relative to APD | Very little change |
| Action potential duration (APD) | ↑ At high concentration | 0 | Very little change |

[a] From Vaughan Williams (1984b).

## A. Class I: Sodium Current Blockers

It is generally thought that the drugs in this group act by blocking the fast, inward current carried by sodium ions (Vaughan Williams, 1984a), depressing the maximum rate of depolarization and slowing conduction. Given the broad spectrum of electrophysiological properties demonstrated by Class I drugs, use of this mechanism as a basis for classification has been debated. To better organize antiarrhythmic properties of drugs in this group, subgroups have been defined (Harrison, 1983, 1985; Vaughan Williams, 1984b) (Table VII). Drugs in Class IA, quinidine, procainamide, and disopyramide, demonstrate a prolongation of the action potential and the effective refractory period and mildly depress conduction in normal myocardium and Purkinje fibers. Clinically, these drugs demonstrate prolongation of the QT interval. Drugs in Class IB, lidocaine, mexiletine, and tocainide, shorten the action potential duration and, to a lesser extent, the effective refractory period. They do not depress conduction appreciably in normal tissue but depress conduction in abnormal or partially depolarized cells in proportion to the degree of abnormality. No electrocardiographic changes occur with these drugs. Drugs in Class IC, including flecainide, encainide, lorcainide, and propafenone, markedly depress conduction in normal myocardium and Purkinje cells. Electrocardiographic changes with these drugs include a widening of the QRS and prolongation of the PR interval without significant QT prolongation out of proportion to the QRS.

Several factors contribute to the spectrum of electrophysiological changes seen with these drugs. One is the modification of vagal tone, with quinidine being mildly and disopyramide moderately vagolytic. Many of the drugs also have central nervous system (CNS) effects that could influence the heart in ways that have not been clarified. A major factor is that the "fast channel" is not a fixed property of cardiac tissue (Hondeghem and Katzung, 1984) but exists in different states dependent primarily on membrane potential in a time-varying fashion, but also on other factors not fully defined. The different states vary in affinity for drug and in kinetics of interaction with antiarrhythmic drugs. Fast channels associated with drug are thought to be blocked. Thus tissue response to drugs which block the fast channel depends on the state of the channel, the membrane affinity for the drug, and the time course of association and dissociation of the drug.

### B. Class II: Beta-Adrenergic Blocking Drugs

In addition to blocking the cardiovascular effects associated with sympathetic outflow, such as tachycardia, studies in animals treated chronically with beta-blocking drugs indicated a prolongation of the action potential duration in myocardial tissue, even in the absence of plasma levels of drug (Anderson et al., 1983). The basis for this class is the general proposition that sympathetic influence generates tachyarrhythmias, but the exact mechanisms by which ventricular arrhythmias are generated by adrenergic stimulation remains undefined. Possible mechanisms include enhancement of normal diastolic depolarization, promotion of afterdepolarizations, and heterogeneous shortening of refractoriness. The means by which this class might operate to counteract the generation of arrhythmias in the ventricle are also unclear. One postulated mechanism is by reduction in intracellular calcium accumulation (Sugiyama et al., 1985).

### C. Class III: Drugs that Prolong Refractoriness

The basic electrophysiological property of drugs in this class is prolongation of the action potential duration. The mechanisms by which this might occur are not completely defined. This class includes drugs with a wide and differing spectrum of electrophysiological properties. Sotalol has some beta-blocking properties. Amiodarone is usually included in this class, but accumulated evidence indicates that it is a potent depressor of the sodium channel (Class I) as well as having beta adrenergic blocking properties. Bretylium (Bacaner, 1966) and bethanidine (Bacaner et al., 1982) both appear to raise the fibrillation threshold but have no class I activity. The basis for inclusion in this class is the simple concept that prolongation of refractoriness limits the rate at which the heart can respond and the closeness of coupling of premature beats.

### D. Class IV: Calcium Channel Blocking Drugs

This group contains many compounds of widely varying structure which have in common the ability to block inward calcium-mediated current. Tissues in which this process occur vary with the different compounds, and the role of these drugs in antiarrhythmic therapy, apart from conduction delay in the A–V node, remains to be ascertained.

Efficacy of antiarrythmic drugs in control of reentrant arrhythmias is thought to be due to an aggravation of conduction depression such that the reentrant circuit cannot be perpetuated (i.e., there is block in the circuit or a prolongation of refractoriness rendering an essential component of the circuit unresponsive). Drugs most effective in suppression of reentrant arrhythmias are in Class I and Class III. Automaticity due to fast channel tissue may be suppressed by Class I drugs; if due to slow channel tissue, by Class IV drugs. Catecholamine-enhanced automaticity or triggered activity can be suppressed by Class II or Class IV drugs (Wit et al., 1975a,b,c).

## VI. Effects of Antiarrhythmic Drugs in Ischemic Tissue

Antiarrhythmic effects of any of the drugs may be modified during acute myocardial ischemia. Levites et al. (1976) that the differences in refractory periods between acutely ischemic myocardium and normal myocardium were attenuated after administration of procainamide. A study *in vitro* of the effects of lidocaine in endocardial cells made hypoxic in tissue bath, or epicardial cells from a 24-hr-old infarcted heart, found a marked depression of conduction in the already depressed ischemic tissue (Lazzara et al., 1978a). No abnormal automaticity was noted in this preparation. Later studies on encainide (Ro et al., 1981) and disopyramide (Yamada et al., 1982) also demonstrated a greater conduction depression in ischemic tissue than normal myocardium. One study (Naito et al., 1981) found no effect of lidocaine or procainamide in prolonging epicardial delay and no antiarrhythmic effect when drugs were given before ischemia. These studies suggested that antiarrhythmic drugs might prevent or abolish propagation in the more depressed segments of reentrant circuits and lessen the potential for reentrant arrhythmias. In addition to different effects on ischemic tissue, studies of drug distribution in animal hearts (Zito et al., 1981; Wenger et al., 1978; Patterson et al., 1982) demonstrated a differential of drug concentrations in normal and ischemic myocardium, reflecting blood flow gradients between ischemic and normal areas of the heart and perhaps altered cellular uptake. This combination of variable drug distribution throughout the heart and the differential effects of drug on the ischemic myocardium could suppress or augment the occurrence of reentry involving ventricular myocardium and Purkinje fibers. Changing properties in ischemic myocardium and Purkinje fibers could influence the effects of drugs during the time course of the infarction. Drugs such as lidocaine, which exert the most pronounced effect on ischemic or depolarized cells, may be more effective during the acute infarct period, when some regions are very depressed.

## A. Lidocaine

Studies *in vitro* suggest a number of mechanisms by which lidocaine exerts its antiarrhythmic effects. Lidocaine depresses membrane responsiveness (relating $\dot{V}_{max}$ of the upstroke to the level of membrane potential at which the action potential is initiated), inhibiting excitation. The depression of myocardial action potential upstroke (decreased $\dot{V}_{max}$ and amplitude), thereby slowing conduction, was more marked at higher concentrations of potassium in the perfusate (Singh and Vaughan Williams, 1971). These effects appear to be concentration dependent (Bigger and Mandel, 1970b). In addition, lidocaine shortens the action potential duration and, to a lesser extent, the effective refractory periods of Purkinje fibers more than of myocardial tissue (Bigger and Mandel, 1979a). The selectively greater effect of lidocaine on action potentials of initially long durations and the lesser effect on action potentials of shorter duration (Wittig et al., 1973) may lessen dispersion of refractoriness and diminish the substrate for reentry. *In vitro* studies (Lazzara et al., 1978a) of lidocaine in cells from ischemic myocardium show a marked depression of conduction in ischemic cells and much less conduction delay in normal myocardium. This suggests that lidocaine may extinguish conduction through ischemic tissue, limiting reentry. In addition to its effect on suppressing arrhythmias due to reentry, lidocaine acts to suppress normal diastolic depolarization and automatic impulse formation. These data from studies *in vitro* suggest that lidocaine would be effective in treating arrhythmias due to both reentry and to automaticity.

Some studies (Faria et al., 1983; Nasser et al., 1980) suggest that treatment with lidocaine reduces infarct size in animals without arrhythmias and without significant improvement in myocardial blood flow. The mechanism for infarct size reduction in not clear, but a local membrane stabilizing effect on myocardial cells has been postulated by both groups.

### B. Bretylium

Bretylium tosylate has a complex and unique combination of electrophysiological properties. Bretylium has antiarrhythmic effects which relate both to its effects on adrenergic function and to its prolongation of the absolute refractory period. Since the latter appears to be the most prominent, it has been classified as a Class III compound in the Vaughan Williams schema (Table VI). In addition, it has been demonstrated to increase the fibrillation threshold, although the mechanism by which this occurs is not understood. The distinction between antiarrhythmic drugs which suppress ventricular ectopy but have little efficacy in clinical or experimental models of ventricular fibrillation (antiectopic) and those which have little effect on ventricular ectopy but which have marked effectiveness in treating ventricular fibrillation (antifibrillatory) (Anderson, 1984b) has been made. This division may be most dramatic in the setting of acute myocardial ischemia.

Adrenergic mechanisms of bretylium include (1) initial release of norepinephrine from adrenergic nerve endings, (2) inhibition of the release of norepinephrine from adrenergic neurons, and (3) block of norepinephrine and epinephrine reuptake into adrenergic nerve endings, potentiating effects of these agonists on adrenergic receptors (Koch-Weser, 1979). Clinical manifestations of the interaction with the adrenergic nervous system are variable and relate to several factors including the resting level of sympathetic activity, doses of bretylium used, and the rate at which it is given (Torresani, 1984). Increased sympathetic tone is noted early in the administration of bretylium with increases in blood pressure, vascular resistance, and heart rate (Chatterjee et al., 1973; Lucchesi, 1984); this effect dissipates within 20 to 30 min. With the adrenergic blockade produced by catecholamine depletion, hypotension, bradycardia, and a fall in vascular resistance can occur (Chatterjee et al., 1973). Although augmentation of catecholamines may be arrhythmogenic (Patterson et al., 1981), in clinical studies this effect has manifested as increased ventricular ectopy (Castle, 1984), with rare instances of arrhythmia aggravation reported (Anderson and Popat, 1981).

Bretylium produces a prolongation of the action potential duration distinct from its adrenergic properties (Wit et al., 1970; Bigger and Jaffe, 1971). In ischemic hearts bretylium prolongs action potential duration along the conduction system; its effect is greater in normal tissue with shorter action potential durations and less in ischemic regions with prolonged action potential duration (Sasyniuk, 1984; Cardinal and Sasyniuk, 1978). Similar effects have been seen with clofilium (Steinberg et al., 1981). This differential effect would mitigate the dispersion of refractoriness and reduce the potential to initiate and sustain reentrant arrhythmias. Bretylium has demonstrated the ability to increase markedly the threshold for ventricular fibrillation in animal models (Bacaner, 1966, 1968), although not studied in the setting of myocardial infarction. This increase in ventricular fibrillation threshold was much more marked with bretylium in the animal models than with other antiarrhythmic drugs such as quinidine, lidocaine, procainamide, and diphenylhydantoin (Bacaner, 1968). Prior treatment with other antiarrhythmic drugs in this study blunted the change in the fibrillation threshold with bretylium. The increased fibrillation threshold occurs with some lag after drug administration, suggesting that myocardial tissue distribution is a major factor in drug efficacy (Anderson et al., 1980b). Oral bretylium has not found to be useful clinically, as absorption is limited and variable (Anderson et al., 1980a).

## C. Beta-Blocking Drugs

Antiarrhythmic effects of beta-blocking drugs have been attributed to several properties. At low doses, blocking of adrenergic stimulation appears to be the primary effect. Increases in catecholamines or sympathetic stimulation can increase the rate of firing of normally automatic tissue, or cause the induction of slow channel responses in partially depolarized cells without changes in the resting potential, action potential amplitude, or $\dot{V}_{max}$ of normal cardiac tissue. Delayed afterdepolarizations are potentiated by beta-adrenergic stimulation. Effectiveness of beta-blocking drugs in suppression of arrhythmias may well depend on resting sympathetic tone. At substantially higher doses than those which block adrenergic stimulation, depression of the fast channel (i.e., depression of $\dot{V}_{max}$), reduction of the action potential amplitude, and shift of the membrane responsiveness curve are manifested by some beta blockers. The clinical significance of this conduction depression is not clear. In ischemic canine heart (Kupersmith et al., 1976), propranolol produced a greater increase in action potential duration in ischemic than normal zones and slowed conduction in ischemic zones with no effect on normal myocardium. Ventricular tachycardia and ventricular fibrillation in an animal model of chronic infarction (Gang et al., 1984) were abolished by both propranolol and timolol. Both drugs increased the fibrillation threshold and prolonged the effective refractory period. An increased fibrillation threshold in normal canine hearts was more marked with propranolol and oxprenolol than with pindolol, which has intrinsic sympathetic activity (Raeder et al., 1983), suggesting that sympathetic blockade may be an important factor in increasing the fibrillation threshold. Some additional studies have hinted at the possibility of some Class III activity as well, with prolongation of the action potential duration (Anderson et al., 1983).

### D. Calcium Channel Blocking Drugs

Verapamil has been shown to depress slow channel conduction in Purkinje fibers from a 24-hr canine infarct model (Dersham and Han, 1981). Another study (El-Sherif and Lazzara, 1979), however, demonstrated that calcium channel blockers verapamil and D-600 actually improved conduction through ischemic myocardium, suggesting little or no role of the slow channel. *In vivo* effects are also controversial, as one group (Kupersmith and Cohen, 1980) could demonstrate no change in conduction in ischemic canine hearts after verapamil was given by intracoronary injection into the infarct area, while another (Hamamoto et al., 1981), using verapamil intravenously, could demonstrate reduction in ischemic induced conduction delay. To date, experimental evidence for any significant role of inward current via the slow channel in reentrant arrhythmias is equivocal.

Pretreatment with calcium channel blockers in animal models has produced a significant reduction in the incidence of ventricular fibrillation early after coronary artery occlusion, whether the drug was nifedipine, nisoldipine, or niludipine (Fagbemi and Parratt, 1981) or diltiazem (Clusin et al., 1982; Nana et al., 1984). A reduction in ischemic conduction delays was shown when diltiazem was given before infarction (Nakaya et al., 1983). Myocardial blood flow was not affected in this study to account for the improvement in conduction. Thus, animal models suggest an antiarrhythmic effect of calcium channel blockers in acute ischemia, particularly if given before the ischemic event. The mechanism by which this occurs is not clear and may possibly be a direct antifibrillatory property of calcium influx inhibition (Clusin et al., 1982).

## VII. Drug Treatment of Arrhythmias during Acute Myocardial Infarction

Treatment of arrhythmias during the acute infarct period involves (1) suppression of observed arrhythmias, and (2) prophylaxis against ventricular fibrillation. Since the advent of coronary care units, treatment and, hopefully, prevention of lethal arrhythmias have been major goals. "Warning arrhythmias" have not been found to be an accurate or effective predictor of patients at risk for ventricular fibrillation, and uniform arrhythmia prophylaxis has been advocated during acute myocardial infarction. Suppression of PVCs following myocardial infarction has been pursued with enthusiasm and touted as a marker of drug efficacy. However, no studies to date suggest any improvement in survival, immediate or long-term, or reduction in the incidence of ventricular fibrillation or sustained ventricular tachycardia with this approach.

## A. Lidocaine

The efficacy of lidocaine in treating ventricular arrhythmias was first noted in the cardiac catheterization laboratory (Southworth *et al.*, 1953). Since then, its use has been widespread, particularly in critical care units for the treatment of ventricular arrhythmias. Given its effectiveness in treating arrhythmias, its availability in parenteral form, the rapid onset of action when given intravenously, and its safety, lidocaine has been the drug most extensively evaluated for suppression and prophylaxis of arrhythmias during acute myocardial infarction (Table VIII). Some of the reports most enthusiastically advocating use of lidocaine were studies without a control population. One review of lidocaine prophylaxis (Noneman and Rogers, 1978), listed a total of 15 studies with a control population in which lidocaine was given prophylactically. These clinical studies demonstrated a wide variation in the time of initiation of therapy following the onset of symptoms. In some studies, no bolus was given (Kostuk and Beanlands, 1969; Baker *et al.*, 1971) and there was no maintenance infusion in others (Valentine *et al.*, 1974; Singh and Kocot, 1976; Sandler *et al.*, 1976; Lie *et al.*, 1978). Because of the rapid tissue distribution of lidocaine given intravenously, both the bolus dose and maintenance infusion are recommended to maintain adequate lidocaine levels (Starge *et al.*, 1981), although the latter may be given intramuscularly and still have efficacy (Sheridan *et al.*, 1977; Barber *et al.*, 1977). Significant drug effect would be difficult to demonstrate in many studies, since no ventricular fibrillation occurred in treated or control groups, possibly because of delay in beginning the study protocol. Some studies did show a reduction in the occurrence of PVCs with lidocaine (Singh and Kocot, 1976; Chopra *et al.*, 1971), but the significance of this is unclear. Of 10 studies with a control population, bolus dose, and maintenance infusion, only one (Lie *et al.*, 1974) demonstrated a clear-cut benefit of prophylactic lidocaine in reduction of the incidence of primary ventricular fibrillation. As with the

**TABLE VIII**
Lidocaine for Arrhythmia Prophylaxis during Acute Myocardial Infarction (MI)[a]

| Study | Time after MI | IV bolus | Maintenance | VF C | VF L | p | Deaths C | Deaths L |
|---|---|---|---|---|---|---|---|---|
| Bennett and Pentecost (1972) | 72% <12 hr | 60 mg | Low 0.5 mg/min | 7/125 | 11/118 | NS | 3 | 8 |
| | 100% <24 hr | — | High 1.0 mg/min | | 5/113 | NS | | 7 |
| Mogenson (1970) | 72% <12 hr | 75–150 mg | 2 mg/min | 1/37 | 0/42 | NS | 7 | 9 |
| Church and Beirn (1972) | 64% <4 hr | 50–75 mg | 2 mg/min | 3/44 | 4/42 | NS | Not given | |
| Bleifeld et al. (1973) | 63% <24 hr | 100 mg | 14–42 μg/kg/min | 2/48 | 0/41 | NS | 2 | 2 |
| Pitt et al. (1971) | Mean L, 9.3 hr C, 7.7 hr | 75 mg | 2.5 mg/min | 0/59 | 0/54 | NS | 4 | 6 |
| Darby et al. (1972) | 81% <12 h | 200 mg | 2 mg/min | 3/100 | 7/103 | NS | 11 | 12 |
| Chopra et al. (1971) | NA | 50–150 mg | 2 mg/min | 4/43 | 3/39 | NS | 4 | 7 |
| O'Brien et al. (1973) | NA | 75 mg | 2.5 mg/min | 9/105 | 2/218 | NS | 7 | 14 |
| Lie et al. (1974) | 100% <24 hr | 100 mg | 3 mg/min | 9/105 | 0/102 | * | 10 | 8 |
| Dunn et al. (1985) | 87% <4 hr | 100 mg | 300 mg IM | 3/96 | 0/108 | NS | 1 | 3 |

[a] Studies using a loading dose intravenously and having a maintenance dose. All studies had a placebo control, but only the last three were double-blind. C, control; L, lidocaine; VF, ventricular fibrillation; p, significance level; NA, not available; *, $p < .002$; NS, not significant.

other studies, there was no difference in mortality between the treated and the control group (Table VIII). This benefit was thought to be due to the high doses utilized and the early initiation of therapy after onset of symptoms. At these doses, there was a 15% incidence of side effects, although none were serious. This study has been criticized (Pentecost *et al.*, 1981) for randomizing only 261 patients of over 700 patients eligible for the study, suggesting some selective process in the study. An analysis of the results from six different studies utilizing a loading dose and a maintenance infusion (deSilva *et al.*, 1981) showed that there was a statistically significant reduction in the occurrence of primary ventricular fibrillation with the prophylactic use of lidocaine. However, the value of statistical analysis of data accumulated from multiple studies is limited because of the variability among studies in design, doses, patient population, and endpoints. In none of the studies has there been a difference in mortality between the group treated with lidocaine and the placebo group (Furberg, 1983). Retrospective studies (Carruth and Silverman, 1982) have shown no difference in arrhythmias or mortality in groups treated with lidocaine and those without. Pentecost *et al.* (1981) reviewed the trend of antiarrhythmic therapy in a CCU over several years, and documented a decline in CCU mortality during a period when use of prophylactic lidocaine also declined. Other criticisms of the studies using lidocaine for prophylaxis of ventricular fibrillation (Bacaner, 1983), have been that the studies have excluded patients with hemodynamic instability, conduction problems, and over age 70.

Most toxic side effects of lidocaine are related to CNS disturbances, particularly seizures, obtundation, lethargy, and hallucinations. Cardiovascular complications include heart block and hypotension (Pfeifer *et al.*, 1976). During acute myocardial infarction, there is a risk of asystole after lidocaine administration, highest in patients with A–V block (Edvardsson *et al.*, 1983). Decreased lidocaine elimination rates, with the potential of increased risk for side effects, occurs with concomitant treatment with beta blockers (Conrad *et al.*, 1983), although this is debatable (Miners *et al.*, 1984), and cimetidine (Feely *et al.*, 1982). Decreased clearance also occurs with heart failure (Davison *et al.*, 1982; Bax *et al.*, 1980; Thomson *et al.*, 1973) and obesity (Abernethy and Greenblatt, 1984) and may occur during acute myocardial infarction due to increased plasma protein binding (Barchowsky *et al.*, 1982). The incidence of side effects (Lie *et al.*, 1974) increases markedly in patients over age 60. Measurement of lidocaine levels in patients early after the onset of chest pain, (Dunn *et al.*, 1985) demonstrated reduced lidocaine levels in the patients who developed myocardial infarction. Use of beta blockers did not seem to affect the lidocaine levels in this study.

Much of the criticism directed at studies using prophylactic lidocaine have been directed at the delay in the onset of therapy and inadequate dose levels early in the course of treatment, when arrhythmias are most likely to occur. Two studies have been done on the efficacy of lidocaine given by ambulance personnel, either as a 400 mg bolus intramuscularly (Koster and Dunning, 1985) or a 100 mg bolus intravenously followed by a 300 mg dose intramuscularly (Dunn et al., 1985). In neither study was the incidence of ventricular fibrillation significantly reduced by lidocaine, and the incidence of ventricular fibrillation was less than 2% in the placebo groups even though seen early in the course of the infarction. In both studies, the occurrence of asystole in the lidocaine treated group was higher than the incidence of ventricular fibrillation in the placebo group, but this was not thought to contribute significantly to overall mortality. The delay in time from the intramuscular injection of lidocaine to the onset of effective levels (Koster and Dunning, 1985) in injections may further compound the difficulty of diagnosing infarction by the use of enzymes, and its use may be of such marginal benefit, that widespread use may not be practical (Lown, 1985). The Belfast group (Dunn et al., 1985; Pantridge et al., 1981) feel that lidocaine cannot be recommended early in the course of myocardial infarction.

Use of lidocaine prophylactically has been advocated vigorously (Wyman and Gore, 1983), recommended thoughtfully (Harrison, 1978; Ribner and Frishman, 1981; Ribner et al., 1979), and proposed for further review (Anderson, 1984a). However, the majority of the studies have indicated no benefits from lidocaine in prevention of fibrillation, yet excess morbidity from side effects; none of the studies have shown an improvement in survival in patients treated with lidocaine over those in the control groups. These studies suggest that prophylactic lidocaine, if beneficial at all, is most effective given after the first hour of infarction to patients at low risk with no evidence of left ventricular dysfunction and no conduction abnormalities.

## B. Other Class I Drugs

Antiarrhythmic agents were used in the treatment of arrhythmias during myocardial infarction even before monitoring of heart rhythms was available (Reynell, 1961) or lidocaine was used as an antiarrhythmic agent. A few studies have evaluated Class IA and IB drugs for treatment of arrhythmias during acute infarction (Table IX). For most of the drugs studied, the end point was suppression of ventricular ectopy and there was the option of withdrawal for lidocaine therapy. Most of the studies

## TABLE IX
Type I Antiarrhythmic Drugs for Arrhythmia Prophylaxis during Acute Myocardial Infarction (MI)[a]

| Study | Drug | No. | Route | Time after MI | VF | | | VT | | |
| --- | --- | --- | --- | --- | --- | --- | --- | --- | --- | --- |
| | | | | | C | D | p | C | D | p |
| Jones et al. (1974) | Quinidine | 70 | PO | <24 hrs | 0/58 | 0/47 | NS | 12/58 | 1/45 | * |
| Jennings et al. (1976) | Disopyramide | 95 | PO | median 8 hr | 5/49 | 1/46 | NS | 14/49 | 4/46 | NS |
| Nicholls et al. (1980) | Disopyramide | 138 | IV/PO | mean 6.8 hr | 7/70 | 3/68 | NS | 4/70 | 6/68 | NS |
| Wilcox et al. (1980) | Disopyramide | 316 | PO | <24 hr | 4/158 | 7/158 | NS | — | — | NC |
| Kumana et al. (1982a) | Disopyramide | 121 | PO | <12 hr | 0/54 | 0/47 | NS | 5/54 | 4/47 | NS |
| Campbell (1983a) | Tocainide | 791 | IV/PO | <6 hr | 6/281 | 11/278 | NS | 11/281 | 3/278 | NC |
| Campbell et al. (1983) | Mexiletine | 97 | PO | <12 hr | 2/53 | 1/44 | NS | 39/53 | 13/44 | ** |

[a] Placebo-controlled studies of antiarrhythmic drugs during acute myocardial infarction. VT, ventricular tachycardia; VF, ventricular fibrillation; C, control (placebo); D, drug; p, significance level: NS, not significant; *, $p < .01$; **, $p < .001$; NC, Not Calculated.

employed oral medications, a factor which could delay the attainment of adequate drug levels too long to accomplish arrhythmia control, as suggested by one group (Campbell *et al.*, 1979). None of the studies demonstrated a significant difference between drug and placebo in the occurrence of ventricular fibrillation (Table IX) or mortality (Furberg, 1983). A reduction in the incidence of ventricular tachycardia was seen with mexiletine, quinidine, and tocainide. Two studies have compared lidocaine to other drugs in the IB class, mexiletine (Horowitz *et al.*, 1981) and tocainide (Rehnqvist *et al.*, 1983). Both studies used small groups of patients with a low incidence of ventricular fibrillation, so the relative value of the three drugs could not be assessed. Tocainide was felt to have equal efficacy to lidocaine for suppression of all ventricular arrhythmias (77.6 versus 70.7%), with an equivalent number of side effects. Lidocaine therapy had to be terminated in three patients because of CNS toxicity. Tocainide did not produce side effects severe enough to cease treatment. Mexiletine was also as effective as lidocaine in suppressing ventricular arrhythmias, with equivalent numbers of patients developing side effects on both drugs.

Difficulties arise in determining drug dosing in the setting of acute myocardial infarction. Patients having an acute infarction have documented lower serum drug levels of lidocaine (Dunn *et al.*, 1985) and disopyramide (Kumana *et al.*, 1982b; David *et al.*, 1983) for equivalent doses than patients without an infarction. Disopyramide kinetics in the recovery period from infarction were not altered (Bryson *et al.*, 1982). One factor postulated for this difference is an increase in binding protein occurring as part of the acute process (Kumana *et al.*, 1982b). Absorption of oral medications may also be delayed in infarction patients, and there may be alteration of elimination kinetics (Pentikainen *et al.*, 1984; Lalka *et al.*, 1978).

If efficacy of antiarrhythmic medication to prevent arrhythmias is ever to occur, the ability to achieve blood levels consistently and rapidly appears to be crucial, requiring parenteral administration.

## C. Bretylium

Bretylium tosylate has been proposed as an alternative to lidocaine for treatment and prophylaxis of the arrhythmias occurring during acute myocardial infarction (Bacaner, 1983). Advantages proposed for bretylium are its unique set of electrophysiological properties, which include increasing the ventricular fibrillation threshold, spontaneous conversion of ventricular fibrillation to sinus rhythm, and positive inotropic effects.

Most of the clinical studies on bretylium have been in patients with ventricular fibrillation refractory to other methods of therapy (Stand *et al.*, 1984; Dhurandhar *et al.*, 1980), lack controls, and give little information about the populations studied, particularly in the incidence of ischemic heart disease. In patients post-myocardial infarction with ventricular fibrillation refractory to treatment with lidocaine and/or procainamide, bretylium generally has been reported to be effective in preventing further recurrences (Table X). There were delays up to 40 min before arrhythmia control could be achieved (Dhurandhar *et al.*, 1980). No controlled studies of the prophylactic use of bretylium in acute myocardial infarction have been reported, but a large study (Torressani, 1984) comparing the use of bretylium to "conventional therapy" for arrhythmia prophylaxis (lidocaine, ajamaline, and procainamide, alone or in combinations) found a significant reduction in the occurrence of primary ventricular fibrillation with bretylium. Other studies either found no effect (Taylor *et al.*, 1970), or no ventricular fibrillation occurring in a small study group without a control population (Day and Bacaner, 1971). In the latter study, prevention of recurrent ventricular fibrillation was achieved much more readily with bretylium than was control of ventricular ectopy.

Direct comparisons of lidocaine and bretylium for the treatment of ventricular fibrillation have been done by rescue squads treating sudden death patients (Haynes *et al.*, 1981). That study showed no difference between bretylium and lidocaine in the success of defibrillation, the incidence of arrhythmia recurrence, or the number of shocks required to achieve a stable rhythm.

**TABLE X**

Bretylium in Acute Myocardial Infarction (MI)

| | | Arrhythmia prophylaxis | | |
| --- | --- | --- | --- | --- |
| | | VF | | |
| Study | No. | Bretylium | Control | $p$ |
| Torresani (1984) | 1255 | 11/843(1.3%) | 21/412(5.1%) | <0.001 |
| Taylor *et al.* (1970) | 101 | 3/38(8%) | 4/38(11%) | NS |
| Day and Bacaner (1971) | 23 | 1/23(95%) | None | — |

| | | Treatment of recurrent ventricular fibrillation | | |
| --- | --- | --- | --- | --- |
| Study | No. | Lidocaine failure | Response | Survivors |
| Dhurandhar *et al.* (1980) | 18 | 17(94%) | 15(83%) | 10(56%) |
| Day and Bacaner (1971) | 8 | 7(88%) | 8(100%) | 7(88%) |

Strong arguments have been made (*Am. J. Cardiol.*, 1984, **54,** 1A–36A) for the use of bretylium in the treatment of arrhythmias. Certainly, there are advantages to using drugs with specific antifibrillatory effects when the objective of therapy is the prevention of primary ventricular fibrillation in acute myocardial infarction.

### D. Beta Blockers

The role of sympathetic activity in the genesis of clinical arrhythmias is not clear. Lown *et al.* (1978) suggested that emotional stress may be an arrhythmogenic factor. Decreased ventricular ectopy during hours of sleep, as opposed to waking hours, has been observed (Lown *et al.*, 1973; Lichstein *et al.*, 1983). Although sympathetic blockade by total extrinsic denervation such as occurs during heart transplantation does not preclude the occurrence of sustained ventricular arrhythmias or sudden death in these patients (Mason *et al.*, 1976), studies suggest that this might be part of the antiarrhythmic effects of beta-blocking drugs.

Enhanced sympathetic activity has been observed (Pantridge *et al.*, 1981) in almost one-third of patients seen within the first 30 min of infarction. The potential for control of arrhythmias mediated by the increased sympathetic activity by beta adrenergic blocking drugs during acute myocardial infarction has been evaluated in several studies. Other factors postulated as advantages for the use of beta blockers early in myocardial infarction are reduction of myocardial oxygen demand, mitigation of ischemia (Mueller *et al.*, 1974), and, ultimately, reduction of infarct size. At least one study (Roberts *et al.*, 1975) has suggested that the occurrence of ventricular arrhythmias is greater in larger infarcts.

Early studies (Balcon *et al.*, 1966; Clausen *et al.*, 1966) did not support the postulated efficacy of propranolol in suppressing arrhythmias during acute myocardial infarction. These studies were later criticized (Singh, 1978) for using small drug doses, especially since the metabolism of propranolol may be increased during acute ischemia. Intravenous use of beta blockers for prophylaxis of arrhythmias during acute infarction has been studied. A significant decrease in deaths occurring in hospital was found in patients treated acutely with atenolol (Sleight *et al.*, 1981; Yusuf *et al.*, 1983). There was also a reduction of sudden death during hospitalization, although patients were not monitored to confirm arrhythmic causes of death. A reduction in the incidence of ventricular fibrillation and ventricular tachycardia was reported (Ryden *et al.*, 1983) in patients given metoprolol early in the infarct period. Beta blockers have been given intravenously to treat arrhythmias during acute infarction. Propranolol (Lemburg *et al.*, 1970) effectively treated atrial flutter (six of six), atrial fibrillation (18 of 18), and paroxysmal ventricular tachycardia (11 of 11), including efficacy in some patients refractory to lidocaine (eight of 11). Practolol (Jewitt *et al.*, 1969) was effective in treating atrial fibrillation but effectively treated ventricular tachycardia in only five of 11 patients. Alprenolol (Lemburg *et al.*, 1972) suppressed ventricular tachycardia and ventricular ectopy as well as controlling atrial flutter and fibrillation, but the study did not differentiate between slowing of ventricular response and converting to sinus rhythm.

Consideration of the negative inotropic effect of beta blockers given to patients with compromised left ventricular function was balanced with potential benefits in improved oxygen utilization and reduction in infarct size. In none of the studies in which beta-blocking drugs were given acutely was heart failure or hemodynamic compromise significantly greater in the treated group, even when patients with early signs of heart failure were treated. When alprenolol was used for treatment of arrhythmias (Lemburg *et al.*, 1972), 39 of 48 patients has some signs of heart failure before treatment with no worsening on drug.

Reduction of infarct size with beta-blocking drugs remains controversial. A reduction in infarct size as determined by lactic dehydrogenase (LDH) I and II enzyme measurements was reported in patients treated with metoprolol within 12 hours of infarction (Hjalmarson *et al.*, 1981), and as determined by creatine phosphokinase (CPK-MB) fraction by patients treated with atenolol (Yusuf *et al.*, 1983). Propranolol given within the first 4 hr of symptoms also demonstrated a reduction in infarct size as measured by enzymes (Peter *et al.*, 1978b). One multicenter center study of propranolol therapy early in the course of infarction (Roberts *et al.*, 1984) was terminated early because there is no significant difference between the control and treatment groups in infarct size measured by CPK-MB or in ejection fractions. The mean time for initiating treatment was 8.5 hr after the onset of symptoms. This delay may have been a factor in the failure to find a difference with beta-blocking drugs.

Some evidence (Ryden *et al.*, 1983) suggests potential efficacy of beta blockers in preventing arrhythmias if given early enough and in adequate doses. This might be of greater efficacy in patients with increased sympathetic activity, although this has yet to be evaluated. Other proposed benefits of beta-blocking therapy, particularly reduction of infarct size, are still debated.

Even though studies suggest control of early arrhythmia with beta blockers, there has been no difference in acute mortality (0–7 days) in the groups treated with beta blockers and those on placebo. (Yusuf *et al.*, 1985) Reported decreased in mortality after the first week of infarction

(Hjalmarsson *et al.*, 1981; Yusuf *et al.*, 1983) may possibly reflect the lower amount of myocardial damage during the infarction.

### E. Calcium Channel Blocking Drugs

Limited information is available using calcium channel blocking drugs to treat arrhythmias during acute myocardial infarction. Efficacy of calcium channel blockers for treatment of chronic ventricular arrhythmias has been limited (Sung *et al.*, 1983; Surawicz, 1982). One study showed a reduction in ventricular ectopy during acute myocardial infarction with tiapamil, a verapamil analog (Menzel and Kirchner, 1982), while another (Lessem, 1982) studied tiapamil after lidocaine had failed to control the ventricular arrhythmias. In this latter study, tiapamil was successful in reducing the number of PVCs but had limited efficacy in suppressing ventricular tachycardia (four of nine) or ventricular fibrillation (two of six). Israeli groups have found intravenous verapamil slowed or abolished a multiform accelerated idioventricular rhythm (Sclarovsky *et al.*, 1983) and suppressed polymorphous ventricular tachycardia (Grenadier *et al.*, 1984) in patients with acute myocardial infarction. Since both these arrhythmias occur rarely during acute infarction, the clinical relevance of this response is unclear. In a study of verapamil initially given intravenously and then continued orally for 6 months, there were no significant differences between the treated and placebo groups in the incidence of ventricular fibrillation, cardiac arrest, or long term mortality. The verapamil treated group did have a greater occurrence of heart failure and high grade AV block. (Danish Study Group on Verapamil in Myocardial Infarction, 1985.) The role of calcium channel blockers in treatment of arrhythmias acutely during infarction appears negligible at this time.

## VIII. Prophylaxis for Postinfarction Sudden Death

Several studies have shown a high incidence of sudden death in patients following myocardial infarction. A number of interventions have been studied to protect damaged myocardium against further injury and, hopefully, prevent lethal arrhythmias as well (May *et al.*, 1982).

### A. Type I Antiarrhythmic Drugs

Antiarrhythmic drugs would seem a likely option to test for prevention of sudden death. Drugs which have been studied include phenytoin (Collaborative Study Group, 1971, Peter *et al.*, 1978b), tocainide (Campbell *et al.*, 1983), mexiletine (Campbell *et al.*, 1981), and aprindine (Hugenholtz *et al.*, 1974). All the studies (May *et al.*, 1982) failed to show any improvement in mortality. Although not at the level of clinical significance, some of the studies actually showed a better outcome in the control group than in the treated group. However, only aprindine had doses titrated in an attempt to achieve suppression of ectopy, although the dosing was limited by side-effects. The studies to date are limited and have shown no benefit from antiarrhythmic therapy given to all patients following infarction regardless of arrhythmia status. There is also a morbidity from the side effects of these drugs as well.

An NIH sponsored study is being formed to address the question of aggressive arrhythmia suppression by antiarrhythmic drugs in patients at high risk post infarction, and whether this is beneficial.

## B. Beta-Blocking Drugs

Reasons for use of beta blockers in the group of patients surviving a myocardial infarction include both protection from further ischemia, and the potential for protection from sympathetic-mediated arrhythmias. Drugs which have been studied (Fig. 6) include alprenolol (Wilhelmsson *et al.*, 1974; Andersen *et al.*, 1979), atenolol (Wilcox, 1981), oxprenolol (Coronary Prevention Research Group, 1980), propranolol (Baber *et al.*, 1982; Beta-Blocker Trial Heart Attack Research Group, 1982), sotalol (Julian *et al.*, 1982), timolol (Norwegian Multicenter Study Group, 1981), practolol (Multicentre International Study, 1975), and metoprolol (Hjalmarsson *et al.*, 1983; MIAMI, 1985). Although all but two of these studies showed an improvement in survival with treatment, only three trials demonstrated a clearly significant reduction in mortality. These trials used propranolol, which has Class I activity at high concentrations; timolol, a nonselective drug; and metoprolol, a more cardioselective agent. Neither timolol or metoprolol depresses fast channel conduction. Pooling the results of all the beta-blocker trials postinfarction (Staessen *et al.*, 1982) showed a mean improvement in survival of 22% from all the studies using prophylactic beta blockers. Given the spectrum of associated properties of the different drugs, this would seem to implicate efficacy of beta-adrenergic blockade in reducing deaths after myocardial infarction. It is not clear whether this is due to a reduction in ischemic events or an antiarrhythmic effect of sympathetic blockade. Timolol (von der Lippe and Lund-Johansen, 1981) and propranolol (Lichstein *et al.*, 1983) both reduced ventricular ectopy on ambulatory monitoring. A re-

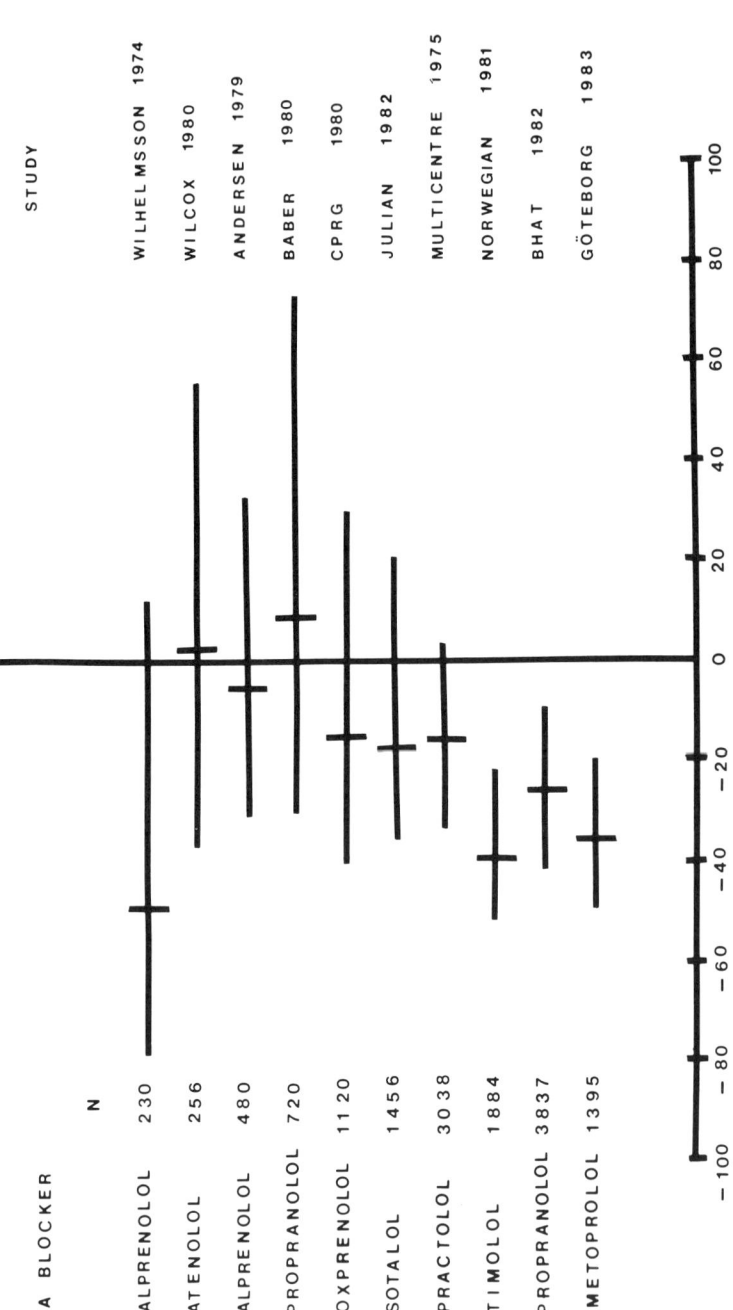

**Fig. 6.** Mean and 95% confidence limits are expressed for the relative mortality rates in patients receiving beta blockers after a myocardial infarction. Confidence limits that do not intersect the null point suggest significant mortality reduction. Timolol, propranolol, and metoprolol have a significant reduction in mortality after myocardial infarction. (Modified from Staessen et al., 1982.)

duction in nonfatal coronary events was seen in the timolol (Norwegian Multicenter Study Group, 1981) and propranolol (Beta-Blocker Heart Attack Trial Research Group, 1983) studies. Whether these factors were synergistic (i.e., a reduction in ischemia reduces the incidence of arrhythmias) is not certain. In the metoprolol study (Hjalmarson et al., 1983) the drug was given intravenously early in the infarct period, and there was evidence of reduced infarct size. This could also play a role in long-term survival after infarction. Recent reviews of the beta-blocker trials in survivors of acute myocardial infarction (Frishman et al., 1983; Singh and Venkatesh, 1984; Staessen et al., 1982; Yusuf et al., 1985) support the use of beta blockers in patients with acute myocardial infarction with no contraindications to beta blockers. Clinically relevant questions that remain are the doses of drug required and the duration of beta blocker therapy.

## IX. Conclusions

Mechanisms of arrhythmias during acute myocardial infarction are complex and not yet well understood. Arrhythmia substrate may be changing throughout the evolution of infarction, potentially making it difficult for a single therapeutic intervention to be effective.

Despite thorough documentation of the increased risk of late mortality in patients with ventricular ectopy after myocardial infarction, there are no data correlating ectopy suppression and decreased mortality in these patients.

Of all clinical studies to date, the most useful antiarrhythmic therapy appears to be that given well before an infarct occurs. In the past decade, clinical studies have demonstrated a marked reduction in the incidence of primary ventricular fibrillation during the first hours of acute myocardial infarction. One might speculate that more aggressive treatment of angina with beta-adrenergic blockers or calcium channel blockers might be a factor in this reduction. For treatment of arrhythmias during the acute ischemic event, bretylium has antiarrhythmic (antifibrillatory) properties which would merit further study in these patients. Beta-adrenergic blockade could also have a role in the prevention of arrhythmias acutely and may help reduce infarct size if given soon enough.

Use of surgery in the early period of infarction is now being studied (DiMarco et al., 1985) and may provide additional options for arrhythmias difficult to control with drugs. Much remains to be learned about the arrhythmias of myocardial infarction and interventions which could control them.

# References

Abernethy, D. R., and Greenblatt, D. J. (1984). *Am. J. Cardiol.*, **53,** 1183–1186.
Adgey, A. A. J. (1983). *Int. J. Cardiol.*, **4,** 224–228.
Adgey, A. A. J., Allen, J. D., Geddes, J. S., James, R. G. G., Webb, S. W., Zaidi, S. A., and Pantridge, J. F. (1971). *Lancet*, **2,** 501–504.
Andersen, M. P., Bechsgaard, P., Fredrickson, J., Hansen, P. A., Jurgenson, H. J., Nielsen, B., Pederson, F., Pederson-Bjergaard, O., and Rasmussen, S. L. (1979). *Lancet*, **2,** 865–867.
Anderson, J. L. (1984a). *Clin. Ther.*, **6,** 125–141.
Anderson, J. L. (1984b). *Am. J. Cardiol.*, **54,** 7A–13A.
Anderson, J. L., and Popat, K. D. (1981). *Arch. Intern. Med.* **141,** 801–802.
Anderson, J. L., Patterson, E., Wagner, J. G., Stewart, J. R., Behm, H. L., and Lucchesi, B. R. (1980a). *Clin. Pharmacol. Ther.*, **28,** 468–478.
Anderson, J. L., Patterson, E., Conlon, M., Pasyk, S., Pitt, B., and Lucchesi, B. R. (1980b). *Am. J. Cardiol.* **46,** 583–592.
Anderson, J. L., Rodier, H. E., and Greer, L. S. (1983). *Am. J. Cardiol.*, **51,** 1196–1202.
Armstrong, A., Duncan, B., Oliver, M. F., Julian, D. G., Donald, K. W., Fulton, M., Lutz, W., and Morrison, S. I. (1972). *Br. Heart J.*, **34,** 67–80.
Baber, N. S., Wainwright, E. D., Horist, G., Thomas, M., Wilson, C., Lewis, J. A., Daves, P. M., Handler, K., and Tuscon, R. (1980). *Br. Heart J.*, **44,** 96–99.
Bacaner, M. B. (1966). *Am. J. Cardiol.*, **17,** 528–534.
Bacaner, M. B. (1968). *Am. J. Cardiol.*, **21,** 504–512.
Bacaner, M. (1983). *Int. J. Cardiol.*, **4,** 133–152.
Bacaner, M. B., Hoey, M. F., and Macres, M. G. (1982). *Am. J. Cardiol.*, **49,** 45–55.
Bagdonis, A. A., Stukey, J. J., Pierce, J., Amer, N. A., and Hoffman, B. F. (1961). *Am. Heart J.*, **61,** 206–218.
Baker, I. A., Collins, J. V., and Evans, T. R. (1971). *Guy's Hosp. Rep.*, **120,** 1–5.
Balcon, R., Jewitt, D. E., Davies, J. P. H., and Oram, S. (1966). *Lancet*, **2,** 917–920.
Barber, J. M., Boyle, D. McC., Hussain, Z., Kelly, J. G., and McDevitt, D. G. (1977). *Br. Heart J.*, **39,** 1361–1364.
Barber, M. J., Mueller, T. M., Henry, D. P., Felten, S. Y., and Zipes, D. P. (1983). *Circulation*, **67,** 787–796.
Barchowsky, A., Shand, D. G., Starger, W. W., Wagner, G. S., and Routledge, P. A. (1982). *Br. J. Clin. Pharmacol.*, **13,** 411–415.
Bastion, B. C., McFarland, P. W., and McLaughlin, J. H. (1980). *Am. Heart J.*, **100,** 1017–1021.
Bax, N. D. S., Tucker, G. T., and Woods, H. F. (1980). *Br. J. Clin. Pharmacol.*, **10,** 353–361.
Bennett, M. A., and Pentecost, B. L. (1972). *Lancet* **1,** 1351–1352.
Bennett, M. A., Wilner, J. M., and Pentecost, B. L. (1970). *Lancet*, **2,** 909–912.
Berke, D. K., Graham, A. F., Schroeder, J. S., and Harrison, D. C. (1973). *Circulation*, **47–48,** Suppl. 3, 112–115.
Beta-Blocker Heart Attack Trial Research Group (1982). *JAMA*, **247,** 1707–1714.
Beta-Blocker Heart Attack Trial Research Group (1983). *JAMA*, **250,** 2814–2819.
Bigger, J. T., Jr., and Jaffe, C. C. (1971). *Am. J. Cardiol.*, **27,** 82–92.
Bigger, J. T., Jr., and Mandel, W. J. (1970a). *J. Pharmacol. Exp. Ther.*, **172,** 239–254.
Bigger, J. T., Jr., and Mandel, W. J. (1970b). *J. Clin. Invest.*, **49,** 63–77.
Bigger, J. T., Jr., Weld, F. M., and Rolnitzky, L. M. (1981). *Am. J. Cardiol.*, **48,** 815–823.

## 8. Myocardial Infarction Arrhythmias 309

Bigger, J. T., Jr., Weld, F. M., and Rolnitzky, L. M. (1982). *Am. Heart J.*, **103**, 660–666.
Bigger, J. T., Jr., Fleiss, J. L., Kleiger, R., Miller, J. P., Rolnitzky, I. M., and the Multicenter Post-Infarction Research Group (1984). *Circulation*, **69**, 250–258.
Bleifeld, W. M., Heinrich, K. W., and Effert, S. (1973). *Eur. J. Clin. Pharmacol.*, **6**, 119–126.
Braunwald, E., Muller, J. E., Kloner, R. A., and Maroka, P. R. (1983). *Am. J. Med.*, **74**, 113–123.
Brown, M. J., Brown, D. C., and Murphy, M. B. (1983). *N. Engl. J. Med.*, **309**, 1414–1419.
Brugada, P., and Wellens, H. J. J. (1985). *Am. J. Cardiol.* **56**, 187–190.
Campbell, R. W. F. (1983). *Am. J. Cardiol.*, **52**, 55C–59C.
Campbell, R. W. F., Achuff, S. C., Pottage, A., Murray, A., Prescott, L. F., and Julian, D. G. (1979). *J. Cardiovasc. Pharmacol.*, **1**, 43–52.
Campbell, R. W. F., Murray, A., and Julian, D. G. (1981). *Br. Heart J.*, **46**, 351–7.
Campbell, R. W. F., Hutton, I., Elton, R. A., Goodfellow, R. M., and Taylor, E. (1983). *Br. Heart J.*, **49**, 557–63.
Cardinal, R., and Sasyniuk, B. I. (1978). *J. Pharmacol. Exp. Ther.*, **204**, 159–174.
Carruth, J. E., and Silverman, M. E. (1982). *Am. Heart J.*, **104**, 545–550.
Castle, L. (1984). *Am. J. Cardiol.*, **54**, 26A–33A.
Chamberlain, D. A., Julian, D. G., Boyle, D. McC., Jewitt, D. E., Campbell, R. W. F., and Shanks, R. G. (1980). *Lancet* **2**, 1324–1327.
Chatterjee, K., Mandel, W. J., Vyden, J. K., Parmley, W. W., and Forrester, J. S. (1973). *JAMA*, **223**, 757–760.
Chopra, M. P., Thadani, U., and Portal, R. W. (1971). *Br. Med. J.*, **3**, 668–670.
Church, G., and Biern, R. (1972). *Circulation*, **45–46** (Suppl 2), 11–139.
Clausen, J., Felsby, M., Jorgenson, R. S., Nielson, B. B., Roin, J., and Strange, B. (1966). *Lancet*, **2**, 920–924.
Clusin, W. T., Bristow, M. R., Karagueuzian, H. S., Katzung, B. G., and Shroeder, J. S. (1982). *Am. J. Cardiol.*, **49**, 606–612.
Collaborative Study Group (1971). *Lancet*, **2**, 1055–1057.
Conley, M. J., McNeer, J. F., Lee, K. L., Wagner, G. S., and Rosati, R. A. (1977). *Am. J. Cardiol.*, **39**, 7–12.
Conrad, K. A., Byers, J. M., III, Finley, P. R., and Burnham, L. (1983). *Clin. Pharmacol. Ther.*, **33**, 133–138.
Coronary Drug Project Research Group (1973). *JAMA*, **223**, 1116–1124.
Coronary Prevention Research Group (1980). In Burley, D. M., Birdwood, G. F., eds., "The Clinical Impact of Beta Adrenergic Blockade," Ciba Laboratories, Basle, p. 173.
Corr, P. B., and Gillis, R. A. (1978). *Circ. Res.*, **43**, 39–47.
Corr, P. B., and Sobel, B. E. (1980). *Adv. Cardiol.*, **27**, 346–360.
Corr, P. B., Lee, B. I., and Sobel, B. E. (1981). *Acta Med Scand.*, Suppl., **651**, 59–69.
Danish Study Group on Verapamil in Myocardial Infarction. (1985). *Eur. Heart J.*, **5**, 516–528.
Darby, S., Bennett, M. A., and Cruickshank, J. C. (1972). *Lancet*, **1**, 817–819.
David, B. M., Ilett, K. F., Whitford, E. G., and Stenhouse, N. S. (1983). *Br. J. Clin. Pharmacol.*, **15**, 435–441.
Davison, R., Parker, M., and Atkinson, A. J. (1982). *Am. Heart J.*, **104**, 203–208.
Day, H. W., and Bacaner, M. (1971). *Am. J. Cardiol.*, **27**, 177–189.
Denborough, M. A., Lovell, R. R. H., Nestel, P. J., and Goble, A. J. (1968). *Lancet*, **1**, 386–388.
Deniss, A. R., Cody, D. V., Ho, B., Russell, P. A., Young, A. A., Ross, D. L., and Uther, J. B. (1984). *J. Am. Coll. Cardiol.*, **3**, 610.
Dersham, G. H., and Han, J. (1981). *J. Pharmacol. Ther.*, **216**, 216–264.

deSilva, R. A., Hennekens, C. H., Lown, B., and Casscells, W. (1981). *Lancet,* **2,** 855–858.
Dhurandhar, R. W., MacMillan, R. L., and Brown, K. W. G. (1971). *Am. J. Cardiol.,* **27,** 347–351.
Dhurandhar, R. W., Pickron, J., and Goldman, A. M. (1980). *Heart and Lung,* **9,** 265–270.
DiMarco, J. P., Lerman, B. B., Kron, I. L., and Sellers, T. D. (1985). *J. Am. Coll. Cardiol.,* **6,** 759–768.
Downar, E., Janse, M. J., and Durrer, D. (1977). *Circulation,* **55,** 455–462.
Dunn, H. M., Kinney, C. C., Campbell, N. P. S., Shanks, R. G., and Adgey, A. A. J. (1984a). *Int. J. Cardiol.,* **5,** 96–98.
Dunn, H. M., McComb, J. M., Campbell, N. P. S., Shanks, R. G., and Adgey, A. A. J. (1984b). *J. Am. Coll. Cardiol.,* **3,** 618.
Dunn, J. M., McComb, J. M., Kinney, C. D., Campbell, N. P. S., Shanks, R. G., MacKenzie, G., and Adgey, A. A. J. (1985). *Am Heart J.,* **110,** 353–362.
Durrer, D., Janse, M. J., and Lie, K. I. (1978). *Adv. Cardiol.,* **25,** 145–154.
Ebert, P. A., Vanderbeck, R. B., Allgood, R. J., and Sabiston, D. C. (1969). *Cardiovasc. Res.,* **4,** 141–147.
Edvardsson, Nils, Holmberg, S., Talwar, K. K., and Olsson, S. B. (1983). *Cardiology,* **70,** 333–340.
El-Sherif, N. (1978). *Circulation,* **58,** 103–110.
El-Sherif, N., and Lazzara, R. (1979). *Circulation,* **60,** 605–615.
El-Sherif, N., Myerburg, R. J., Scherlag, B. J., Befeler, B., Aranda, J. M., Castellanos, A., and Lazzara, R. (1976). *Br. Heart J.,* **38,** 415–422.
El-Sherif, N., Scherlag, B. J., Lazzara, R., and Hope, R. R. (1977a). *Circulation,* **55,** 686–702.
El-Sherif, N., Hope, R. R., Scherlag, B. J., and Lazzara, R. (1977b). *Circulation,* **55,** 702–719.
El-Sherif, N., Lazzara, R., Hope, R. R., and Scherlag, B. J. (1977c). *Circulation,* **56,** 225–234.
El-Sherif, N., Scherlag, B. J., Lazzara, R., and Hope, R. R. (1977d). *Circulation,* **56,** 395–402.
El-Sherif, N., Gough, W. B., Zeiler, R. H., and Mehra, R. (1983a). *Circ. Res.,* **52,** 566–579.
El-Sherif, N., Mehra, R., Gough, W. B., and Zeiler, R. H. (1983b). *Circulation,* **68,** 644–656.
El-Sherif, N., Gough, W. G., Zeiler, R. H., and Hariman, R. (1985). *J. Am. Coll. Cardiol.,* **6,** 124–132.
Fagbemi, O., and Parratt, J. R. (1981). *Br. J. Pharmacol.,* **74,** 12–14.
Faria, D. B., Cheung, W. M., Ruberio, L. G. T., and Maroko, P. (1983). *J. Am. Coll. Cardiol.,* **1,** 1447–1452.
Feely, J., Wilkinson, G. R., McAllister, C. B., and Wood, A. J. (1982). *Ann. Int. Med.,* **96,** 592–594.
Friehling, T., Kowey, P. R., Meister, S. G., and Engel, T. R. (1984). *Cardiovasc. Rev. Rep.,* **5,** 552–561.
Frishman, W. H., Furberg, C. D., and Friedewald, W. T. (1983). *N. Engl. J. Med.,* **310,** 830–837.
Fujimoto, T., Peter, T., Katoh, T., Hamamoto, H., and Mandel, W. (1984). *Am. Heart J.,* **107,** 201–209.
Furberg, C. D. (1983). *Am. J. Cardiol.,* **52,** 32C–36C.
Gang, E. S., Bigger, J. T., Jr., and Uhl, E. W. (1984). *Am. J. Cardiol.,* **53,** 275–281.
George, M., and Greenwood, T. W. (1976). *Lancet* **2,** 739–740.
Gessman, L. J., Agarwal, J. B., Endo, T., and Helfant, R. H. (1983). *Circulation,* **68,** 657–666.

Gettes, L. S., Hill, J. L., Saito, T., and Kagiyama, Y. (1982). *Am. Heart J.* **103**, 667–672.
Gillis, R. A., Corr, P. B., Pace, D. G., Evans, D. E., DiMicco, J., and Pearle, D. L. (1976). *Cardiology*, **61**, 37–49.
Goble, A. J., Sloman, G., and Robinson, J. S. (1966). *Br. Med. J.*, **1**, 1005–1009.
Goldstein, R. E., Karsh, R. B., Smith, E. R., Orlando, M., Norman, D., Farnham, G., Redwood, D. R., and Epstein, S. E. (1973). *Circulation*, **47**, 1180–1190.
Goldstein, S., Moss, A. J., and Greene, W. (1972). *Arch. Int. Med.*, **129**, 720–724.
Gomes, J. A. C., Kang, P. S., Khan, R., Kelen, G., and El-Sherif, N. (1981). *Br. Heart J.*, **46**, 159–167.
Gordon, T., and Kannel, W. B. (1971). *JAMA*, **215**, 1617–1625.
Gough, W. B., Zeiler, R. H., and El-Sherif, N. (1984). *Am. J. Cardiol.* **53**, 303–306.
Greene, H. L., Reid, P. R., and Schaeffer, A. H. (1978). *N. Engl. J. Med.*, **299**, 729–734.
Grenadier, E., Alpan, G., Maor, N., Keidar, S., Bininbom, C., Margulies, T., and Palant, A. (1984). *Am. J. Cardiol.*, **53**, 1280–1283.
Hamamoto, H., Peter, T., Fujimoto, T., and Mandel, W. J. (1981). *Am. Heart J.*, **102**, 350–357.
Hamer, A., Vohra, J., Hunt, D., and Sloman, G. (1982). *Am. J. Cardiol.*, **50**, 223–229.
Han, J., Goel, B. G., Yoon, M. S., and Rogers, R. (1971). *Am. J. Cardiol.*, **34**, 171–178.
Harris, A. S., and Rojas, A. G. (1943). *Exp. Med. Surg.*, **1**, 105–122.
Harrison, D. C. (1978). *Circulation (ED)*, **58**, 581–584.
Harrison, D. C. (1983). *Am. J. Cardiol.*, **52**, 1C–2C.
Harrison, D. C. (1985). *Am. J. Cardiol.*, **56**, 185–187.
Haynes, R. E., Chinn, T. L., Copass, M. K., and Cobb, L. A. (1981). *Am. J. Cardiol.*, **48**, 353–356.
Herlitz, J., Elmfeldt, D., Holmberg, S., Malek, I., Nyberg, G., Pennert, K., Ryden, L., Swedberg, K., Vedin, A., Waagstein, F., Waldenstrom, A., Waldenstrom, J., Wedel, H., Wilhelmsson, L., Wilhelmsson, C., and Hjalmarson, A. (1984a). *Am. J. Cardiol.*, **53**, 9D–14D.
Herlitz, J., Edvardsson, N., Holmberg, S., Ryden, L., Waagstein, F., Waldenstrom, A., Swedberg, K., and Hjalmarson, A. (1984b). *Am. J. Cardiol.*, **53**, 27D–31D.
Hjalmarson, A., Herlitz, J., Malek, I., Ryden, L., Vedin, A., Waldenstrom, A., Wedel, H., Elmfeldt, D., Holmberg, S., Nyberg, G., Swedberg, K., Waagstein, F., Waldenstrom, J., Wilhelmsen, L., and Wilhelmsson, C. (1981). *Lancet*, **2**, 823–827.
Hjalmarson, A., Herlitz, J., Holmberg, S., Ryden, L., Swedberg, K., Vedin, A. Waagstein, F., Waldenstrom, A., Waldenstrom, J., Wedel, H., Wilhelmson, L., and Wilhelmsson, C. (1983). *Circulation*, **67**, I26–I32.
Hoffman, B. F., Rosen, M. R., and Wit, A. L. (1975). *Am. Heart J.*, **89**, 115–122.
Hondeghem, L. M., and Katzung, B. G. (1984). *Ann. Rev. Pharmacol. Toxicol.* **24**, 387–423.
Horowitz, J. D., Anavekar, S. N., Morris, P. M., Goble, A. J., Doyle, A. E., and Louis, W. J. (1981). *J. Cardiovasc. Pharmacol.*, **3**, 409–419.
Horowitz, L. N., Spear, J. F., and Moore, E. N. (1976). *Circulation*, **53**, 56–63.
Horowitz, L. N., Josephson, M. E., Farshidi, A., and Kastor, J. (1978). *Circulation*, **58**, 986–997.
Hugenholtz, P. G., Hagemeijer, F., Lubsen, J., Glazer, B., Van Durme, J. P., and Bogaert, M. G. (1974). *Acta Med Scand., Suppl.* **581**, 572–578.
Hulting, J. (1981). *Acta Med. Scand., Suppl.* **647**, 109–116.
Hurst, V. W., Morris, J. J., Zeft, H. J., Hackel, D. B., and McIntosh, H. D. (1967). *Circulation*, **36**, 294–303.
Janse, M. J., VanCappelle, F. J. L., Morsink, H., Kleber, A. G., Wilms-Schopman, F., Cardinal, R., d'Alnoncourt, C. N., and Durrer, D. (1980). *Circ. Res.*, **47**, 151–165.

Jennings, G., Jones, M. B. S., Besterman, E. M. M., Model, D. G., Turner, P. P., and Kidner, P. H. (1976). *Lancet*, **1**, 51–54.
Jewitt, D. E., Balcon, R., Raftery, E. B., and Oram, S. (1967). *Lancet*, **2**, 734–738.
Jewitt, D. E., Mercer, C. J., and Shillingford, J. P. (1969). *Lancet*, **2**, 227–230.
Jones, D. T., Kostuk, W. J., and Gunton, R. W. (1974). *Am. J. Cardiol.* **33**, 655–660.
Julian, D. G., Prescott, R. J., Jackson, F. S., and Szekely, P. (1982). *Lancet*, **2**, 1142–1147.
Kass, R. S., Lederer, W. J., Tsien, R. W., and Weingart, R. (1978). *J. Physiol.*, **281**, 187–208.
Kassenbaum, D. G., and van Dyke, A. R. (1966). *Circ. Res.*, **19**, 940–946.
Kent, K. M., and Epstein, S. E. (1976). *Cardiology*, **61**, 61–74.
Kent, K. M., Smith, E. R., Redwood, D. R., and Epstein, S. E. (1973). *Circulation*, **47**, 291–298.
Killip, T., and Kimball, J. T. (1967). *Am. J. Cardiol.*, **20**, 457–464.
Kleiger, R. E., Miller, J. P., Thanavaro, S., Province, M. A., Martin, T. F., and Oliver, G. C. (1981). *Circulation*, **63**, 64–70.
Koch-Weser, J. (1979). *N. Engl. J. Med.*, **300**, 473–477.
Koch-Weser, J., Klein, S. W., Foo-Canto, L. L., Kastor, J. A., and deSanctis, R. W. (1969). *N. Engl. J. Med.*, **281**, 1253–1260.
Koster, R. W., and Dunning, A. J. (1985). *N. Engl. J. Med.*, **313**, 1105–1110.
Kostuk, W. J., and Beanlands, D. S. (1969). *Circulation*, **40**, (Suppl. 3), 125.
Kotler, M. N., Tabatznik, B., Mower, M. M., and Tominaga, S. (1973). *Circulation*, **47**, 959–966.
Kowey, P. R., Friehling, T., Meister, S. G., and Engel, T. (1984). *J. Am. Coll. Cardiol.*, **3**, 690–5.
Kralios, A., Bugni, W. J., McDonnell, M. A., Tsagaris, T. J., and Kuida, H. (1981). *Am. Heart J.*, **101**, 440–448.
Kumana, C. R., Rambihar, V. S., Willis, K., Gupta, R. N., Tanser, P. H., Cairns, J. A., Wildeman, R. A., Johnston, M., Johnson, A. L., and Gent, M. (1982a). *Br. J. Clin. Pharmacol.*, **14**, 519–527.
Kumana, C. R., Rambihar, V. S., Tanser, P. H., Cairns, J. A., Gupta, R. N., Wildeman, R. A., Johnston, M., Johnson, A. L., and Gent, M. (1982b). *Br. J. Clin. Pharmacol.*, **14**, 529–537.
Kupersmith, J., and Cohen, R. (1980). *J. Pharmacol. Ther.*, **215**, 394–400.
Kupersmith, J., Shiang, H., Litwak, R. S., and Hormu, M. V. (1976). *Circ. Res.*, **38**, 302–307.
Lalka, D., Wyman, M. G., Goldreyer, B. N., Ludden, T. M., and Cannom, D. S. (1978). *J. Clin. Pharmacol.*, **18**, 397–401.
Lassers, B. W. (1969). *Lancet*, **1**, 1172–1174.
Lawrie, D. M. (1969). *Lancet*, **2**, 1085–1087.
Lawrie, D. M., Higgins, M. R., Godman, J. J., Oliver, M. F., Julian, D. G., and Donald, K. W. (1968). *Lancet* **1**, 523–528.
Lazzara, R., and Scherlag, B. J. (1984). *Am. J. Cardiol.*, **53**, 1B–7B.
Lazzara, R., El-Sherif, N., Hope, R. R., and Scherlag, B. J. (1974). *Circ. Res.*, **35**, 391–399.
Lazzara, R., Hope, R. R., El-Sherif, N., and Scherlag, B. J. (1978a). *Am. J. Cardiol.*, **41**, 872–879.
Lazzara, R., El-Sherif, N., Hope, R. R., and Scherlag, B. J. (1978b). *Circ. Res.*, **42**, 740–749.
leMarec, H., Dangman, K. H., Danilo, P., and Rosen, M. R. (1985). *Circulation*, **71**, 1224–1236.
Lemberg, L., Castellanos, A., and Arcebal, A. (1970). *Am. Heart J.*, **80**, 479–487.

## 8. Myocardial Infarction Arrhythmias

Lemberg, L., Arcebal, A. G., Castellanos, A., and Slavin, D. (1972). *Am. Heart J.*, **30**, 77–81.
Lessem, J. (1982). *Cardiology*, **69** (Suppl. 1), 199–208.
Levites, R., Haft, J. I., Calderon, J., and Venkatachalapathy (1976). *Circulation*, **53**, 982–984.
Lichstein, E., Morganroth, J., Harrist, R., Hubble, E., and the BHAT Study Group (1983). *Circulation*, **67** (Suppl. I), 5–10.
Lie, K. I., Wellens, H. J. J., and VanCapelle, F. J. (1974). *N. Engl. J. Med.*, **291**, 1324–1326.
Lie, K. I., Wellens, H. J. J., Downar, E., and Durrer, D. (1975). *Circulation*, **62**, 755–759.
Lie, K. I., Liem, K. L., Lourditz, W. J., Janse, M. J., Willebrands, A. F., and Durrer, D. (1978). *Am. J. Cardiol.*, **42**, 486–488.
Lindsay, J., and Bruckner, N. V. (1975). *JAMA*, **232**, 51–53.
Logan, J. R., McIlwaine, W. J., Adgey, A. A. J., and Pantridge, J. F. (1981). *Circulation*, **63**, 1163–1167.
Lown, B. (1985). *N. Engl. J. Med.*, **313**, 1154–1155 (ed.).
Lown, B., Fakhro, A., Hood, Wm. B., Jr., and Thorn G. W. (1967). *JAMA*, **199**, 156–166.
Lown, B., Tykocinski, M., Garfein, A., and Brooks, P. (1973). *Circulation*, **61**, 75–87.
Lown, B., DeSilva, R. A., and Lenson, R. (1978). *Am. J. Cardiol.*, **41**, 979–985.
Lucchesi, B. (1984). *Am. J. Cardiol.*, **54**, 14A–19A.
McNeilly, R. H., and Pemberton, J. (1968). *Br. Med. J.*, **3**, 139–142.
Marchlinski, F. E., Buxton, A. E., Waxman, H., and Josephson, M. E. (1983). *Am. J. Cardiol.*, **52**, 1190–1196.
Martins, J. B., Zipes, D. P., and Lund, D. D. (1983). *J. Am. Coll. Cardiol.*, **2**, 1191–1199.
Mason, J. W., and Winkle, R. A. (1978). *Circulation*, **58**, 971–985.
Mason, J. W., Stinson, E. B., and Harrison, D. C. (1976). *Cardiology*, **61**, 75–87.
May, G. S., Eberlein, K. A., Furberg, C. D., Passamani, E. R., and deMets, D. L. (1982). *Prog. Cardiovasc. Dis.*, **24**, 331–352.
May, G. S., Furberg, C. D., Eberlein, K. A., and Geraci, B. J. (1983). *Prog. Cardiovasc. Dis.*, **25**, 335–359.
Menzel, T., and Kirchner, P. (1982). *Cardiology*, **69** (Suppl. 1), 192–198.
MIAMI Trial Research Group (1985). *Eur. Heart J.*, **6**, 199–226.
Miners, J. O., Wing, L. M. H., Lillywhite, K. J., and Smith, K. J. 1984). *Br. J. Clin. Pharmac.*, *18*, 853–860.
Mogenson, L. (1970). *Acta Med Scand., Suppl.*, **513**, 1–80.
Moss, A. J. (1979). *Current Problems in Cardiology*, **4**, 6–53.
Moss, A. J., deCamilla, J., Engström, F., Hoffman, W., Odoroff, C., and Davis, H. (1974). *Circulation*, **49**, 460–466.
Moss, A. J., deCamilla, J. J., Davis, H. P., and Bayer, L. (1977). *Am. J. Cardiol.*, **39**, 635–640.
Mueller, H. S., Ayres, S. M., Religa, A., and Evers, R. G. (1974). *Circulation*, **49**, 1078–1087.
Multicentre International Study (1975). *Br. Med. J.*, **3**, 735–740.
Naccarelli, G. V., Prystowsky, E. N., Jackman, W. M., Heger, J., Renckenberger, R. L., and Zipes, D. P. (1981). *Br. Heart J.*, **46**, 152–158.
Naito, M., Michelson, E. L., Kmetzo, J. J., Kaplinsky, E., and Dreifus, L. S. (1981). *J. Pharm. Exp. Ther.*, **218**, 475–480.
Nakaya, H., Millard, R. W., Lathrop, D. A., Gaum, W. E., Kaplan, S., and Schwartz, A. (1983). *J. Am. Coll. Cardiol.*, **2** 474–480.
Nana, M. A., Nanas, J., Menlove, R. L., and Anderson, J. L. (1984). *J. Cardiovasc. Pharmacol.*, **6**, 780–787.

Nasser, F. N., Walls, J. T., Edwards, W. T., and Harrison, C. E. (1980). *Am. J. Cardiol.*, **46**, 967–975.
Nicholls, D. P., Haybryne, T., and Barnes, P. C. (1980). *Lancet*, **2**, 936–938.
Noneman, J. W., and Rogers, J. F. (1978). *Medicine*, **57**, 501–515.
Nordrehaug, J. E. (1983). *Acta Med Scand., Suppl.*, **647**, 101–107.
Nordrehaug, J. E., Johannessen, K. A., and von der Lippe, G. (1985). *Circulation*, **71**, 645–649.
Norris, R. M., Bensley, K. E., Caughey, D. E., and Scott, P. J. (1968a). *Br. Med. J.*, **3**, 143–146.
Norris, R. M., Caughey, D. E., Scott, P. J. (1968b). *Br. Med. J.*, **2**, 398–400.
Norwegian Multicenter Study Group (1981). *N. Engl. J. Med.*, **304**, 801–807.
O'Brien, K. P., Taylor, P. M., and Croxson, R. S. (1973). *Med. J. Aust.*, **2** (Suppl.), 19–36.
Pantridge, J. F., and Webb, S. W. (1973). *Irish J. Med. Sci., Suppl.*, 26–37.
Pantridge, Webb, S. W., and Adgey, A. A. J. (1981). *Prog. Cardiovasc. Dis.*, **23**, 265–278.
Pappano, A. J. (1970). *Circ. Res.*, **27**, 379–390.
Patterson, E., Gibson, J. K., and Lucchesi, B. (1981). *J. Pharmacol. Exp. Ther.*, **216**, 453–458.
Patterson, R. E., Weintraub, W. S., Halgash, D. A., Maio, J., Rogers, J. R., and Kupersmith, J. (1982). *Am. J. Cardiol.*, **50**, 63–73.
Penny, W. J. (1984). *Eur. Heart J.*, **5**, 960–973.
Pentecost, B. L., and Mayne, N. M. C. (1968). *Br. Med. J.*, **1**, 830–833.
Pentecost, B. L., DeGiovanni, J. V., Lamb, P., Cadigan, P. J., Evemy, K. L., and Flint, E. J. (1981). *Br. Heart J.*, **45**, 42–7.
Pentikainen, P. J., Halinin, M. O., and Helin, J. J. (1984). *J. Cardiovasc. Pharmacol.*, **6**, 1–6.
Peter, T., Ross, D., Duffield, A., Luxton, M., Harper, R., Hunt, D., and Sloman, G. (1978a). *Br. Heart J.*, **40**, 1356–1360.
Peter, T., Norris, R. M., Clarke, E. D., Heng, M. K., Singh, B. N., Williams, B., Howell, D. R., and Ambler, P. K. (1978b). *Circulation*, **57**, 1091–1095.
Pfeifer, H. J., Greenblatt, D. J., and Koch-Weser, J. (1976). *Am. Heart J.*, **92**, 168–173.
Pitt, A., Lipp, H., and Anderson, S. T. (1971). *Lancet*, **1**, 612–616.
Pratt, C., and Lichstein, E. (1982). *J. Clin. Pharmacol.*, **22**, 335–347.
Raeder, E. A., Verrier, R. L., and Lown, B. (1983). *J. Am. Coll. Cardiol.*, **1**, 1442–1446.
Rardon, D. P., and Bailey, J. C. (1983). *J. Am. Coll. Cardiol.*, **2**, 1200–1209.
Rehnqvist, N., Erhardt, L., Ericcson, C. G., Olsson, G., Svensson, G., and Sjögren, A. (1983). *Acta Med. Scand.*, **214**, 21–27.
Reynell, D. C. (1961). *Br. Heart J.*, **23**, 421–424.
Ribner, H. S., and Frishman, W. H. (1981). *Cardiovasc. Rev. Reports*, **2**, 395–412.
Ribner, H. S., Isaacs, E. S., and Frishman, W. H. (1979). *Prog. Cardiovasc. Dis.*, **21**, 287–313.
Richards, D. A., Cody, D. V., Denniss, A. R., Russell, P. A., Young, A. A., and Uther, J. B. (1983). *Am. J. Cardiol.*, **51**, 75–80.
Ro, J. H., Gillon, J., and Kupersmith, J. (1981). *J. Cardiovasc. Pharm.*, **3**, 532–540.
Roberts, R., Husain, A., Ambos, H. D., Oliver, G. C., Cox, J. R., Jr., and Sobel, B. E. (1975). *Br. Heart J.*, **37**, 1169–1175.
Roberts, R., and MILIS Study Group (1984). *N. Engl. J. Med.*, **311**, 218–224.
Robinson, J. S., Sloman, G., Mathew, T. H., and Goble, A. J. (1965). *Am. Heart J.*, **69**, 740–747.
Romhilt, D. W., Bloomfield, Te-Chuan, and Fowler, N. O. (1973). *Am. J. Cardiol.*, **31**, 457–461.

Roy, D., Marchand, E., Theroux, P., Waters, D. D., Pelletier, G. B., and Bourassa, M. G. (1985). *Circulation,* **72,** 487–494.
Ruberman, W., Weinblatt, E., Goldberg, J. D., Frank, C. W., Chaudhary, B. S., and Shapiro, S. (1981). *Circulation,* **64,** 297–305.
Russell, D. C., Lawrie, J. S., Riemersma, R. A., and Oliver, M. F. (1981). *Acta Med Scand, Suppl.,* **651,** 71–79.
Russell, D. C., Lawrie, J. S., Riemersma, R. A., and Oliver, M. F. (1984). *Am. J. Cardiol.,* **53,** 307–312.
Ryden, L., Arnman, K., and Conradson, T. B. (1980). *Am. Heart J.,* **100,** 1006.
Ryden, L., Ariniego, R., Arnman, K., Herlitz, J., Hjalmarson, A., Holmberg, S., Reyes, C., Smedgard, P., Svedberg, K., Vedin, A., Waagstein, F., Waldenstrom, A., Wilhelmsson, C., Wedel, H., and Yamamoto, A. (1983). *N. Engl. J. Med.,* **308,** 614–618.
Saini, R. K., and Antonaccio, M. J. (1982). *J. Pharmacol. Ther.,* **221,** 29–36.
Sandler, G., Dey, N., and Amonkar, J. (1976). *Curr. Ther. Res.,* **20,** 563.
Santarelli, P., Bellocci, F., Loperfido, F., Mazzari, M., Mongiardo, R., Montenero, A. S., Manzoli, U., and Denes, P. (1985). *Am. J. Cardiol.,* **55,** 391–394.
Sasyniuk, B. I. (1984). *Am. J. Cardiol.,* **54,** 1A–6A.
Scherlag, B. J., El-Sherif, N., Hope, R.R., and Lazzara, R. (1974). *Circ. Res.,* **35,** 372–383.
Schulze, R. A., Rouleau, J., Rigo, P., Bowers, S., Strauss, H. W., and Pitt, B. (1975). *Circulation,* **52,** 1006–1011.
Schulze, R. A., Strauss, H. W., and Pitt, B. (1977). *Am. J. Medicine,* **62,** 192–199.
Schwartz, P. J., Zaga, A., Giozia, S., Lombardo, M., Lotto, A., Sbressa, C., and Zappa, P. (1985). *Am. J. Cardiol.,* **56,** 384–389.
Sclarovsky, S., Strasberg, B., Fuchs, J., Lewin, R. F., Arditi, A., Klainman, E., Kracoff, O. H., and Agmon, J. (1983). *Am. J. Cardiol.* **52,** 43–47.
Sheridan, D. J., Rawlins, M. D., Crawford, L., and Julian, D. G. (1977). *Lancet, i,* 824–825.
Sheridan, D., Penksoke, P. A., Sobel, B. E., and Corr, P. B. (1980). *J. Clin. Invest.,* **65,** 161–171.
Singh, B. N. (1978). *Drugs,* **15,** 218–225.
Singh, B. N., and Vaughan Williams, E. M. (1971). *Circ. Res.,* **29,** 286–295.
Singh, B. N., and Venkatesh, N. (1984). *Am. Heart J.,* **107,** 189–200.
Singh, J. B., and Kocot, S. L. (1976). *Am. Heart J.,* **91,** 430–436.
Skjaeggestad, O., and Berstad, A. (1974). *Acta Med Scand.,* **196,** 271–274.
Sleight, P., Yusuf, S., Peto, R., Rossi, P., Ramsdale, D., Bennett, D., Bray, C., and Furse, L. (1981). *Acta Med Scand,* **651,** 185–191.
Sloman, G., Dowling, J., and Vohra, J. (1971). *Br. Heart J.,* **33,** Suppl., 165–170.
Southworth, J. L., McKusick, V. A., Peirce, E. C., and Rawson, R. (1953). *JAMA,* **143,** 717–720.
Spear, J. F., Michelson, E. L., and Moore, E. N. (1983). *J. Am. Coll. Cardiol.,* **1,** 1099–1110.
Staessen, J. C., Bulpitt, J. C., Cattaert, R., Fagard, R., Vanhees, L., and Amery, A. (1982). *Am. Heart J.,* **104,** 1395–1399.
Stand, J. M., Washington, S. E., Barnes, S. A., Dutko, H. J., Chesney, B. D., Easter, C. R., O'Hara, J. T., Kessler, J. H., Schaal, S. F., and Lewis, R. P. (1984). *Ann. Emer. Med.,* **13,** 234–236.
Starge, W., Shand, D. G., Routledge, P. A., Barchowsky, A., and Wagner, G. S. (1981). *Am. Heart J.,* **102,** 872–876.
Steinberg, M. I., Sullivan, M. E., Wiest, S. A., Rockhold, F. W., and Molloy, B. B. (1981). *J. Cardiovasc. Pharmacol.,* **3,** 881–895.
Stock, E., Goble, A., and Sloman, G. (1967). *Br. Med. J.,* **2,** 719–723.

Sugiyama, S., Hattori, M., Miyazaki, Y., Nagai, S., and Ozawa, T. (1985). *J. Electrocardiol.*, **18,** 169–174.
Sung, R. J., Shapiro, W. A., Shen, E. N., Morady, F., and Davis, J. (1983). *J. Clin. Invest.*, **72,** 350–360.
Surawicz, B. (1982). *Am. Heart J.*, **103,** 698–706.
Taylor, S. H., Saxton, C., Davies, P. S., and Stoker, J. B. (1970). *Br. Heart J.*, **32,** 326–329.
Thomson, R. P., Melmon, K. L., Richardson, J. A., Cohn, K., Steinbrunn, W., Cudihee, R., and Rowland, M. (1973). *Ann. Intern. Med.*, **78,** 499–508.
Torresani, J. (1984). *Am. J. Cardiol.*, **54,** 21A–25A.
Valentine, P. A., Frew, J. L., Mashford, M. L., and Slowman, G. (1974). *N. Engl. J. Med.*, **291,** 1327–1330.
Vaughan Williams, E. M. (1984a). *Eur. Heart J.*, **5,** 96–98.
Vaughan Williams, E. M. (1984b). *J. Clin. Pharmacol.*, **24,** 129–147.
Vincent, H. H., Boomsma, F., Veld, A. V. M., Derkx, F. H. M., Wentzing, G. J., and Schalekamp, M. A. D. H. (1984). *J. Cardiovasc. Pharmacol.*, **6,** 107–114.
Vismara, L. A., DeMaria, A. N., Hughes, J. L., Mason, D. T., and Amsterdam, E. A. (1975). *Br. Heart J.*, **37,** 598–603.
Vismara, L., Zakuddin, V., Foerster, J. M., Amsterdam, E. A., and Mason, D. T. (1977). *Am. J. Cardiol.*, **39,** 821–828.
von der Lippe, G., and Lund-Johansen, P. (1981). *Acta Med Scand., Suppl.*, **651,** 253–263.
Waspe, L. E., Seinfeld, D., Ferrick, A., Fink, D., Scavini, G., Wanliss, M., Kim, S. G., Matos, J. A., and Fisher, J. (1985). *J. Am. Coll. Cardiol.*, **5,** 1292–1301.
Wellens, H. J. J., Lie, K. I., and Durrer, D. (1974). *Circulation,* **49,** 647–653.
Wellens, H. J. J., Brugada, P., and Stevenson, W. G. (1985). *Circulation,* **72,** 1–7.
Wenger, T. L., Masterson, C. E., Abou-Dania, M. B., Lee, K. L., Bache, R. J., and Strauss, H. C. (1978). *Circ. Res.*, **42,** 846–851.
Wilcox, R. G. (1981). *Acta Med Scand., Suppl.*, **651,** 193–203.
Wilcox, R. G., Hampton, J. R., Rowley, J. M., Mitchell, J. R. A., Roland, J. M., and Banks, J. C. (1980). *Lancet,* **2,** 765–769.
Wilhelmsson, C., Vedin, J. A., Wilhelmson, L., Tibblin, G., and Werkio, L. (1974). *Lancet,* **2,** 1157–1159.
Wit, A. L., and Bigger, J. T., Jr. (1975). *Circulation,* **51** and **52,** Suppl. III, 96–115.
Wit, A. L., Steiner, C., and Damato, A. N. (1970). *J. Pharmacol. Exp. Ther.*, **173,** 344–356.
Wit, A. L., Hoffman, B. F., and Rosen, M. R. (1975a). *Am. Heart J.*, **90,** 521–533.
Wit, A. L., Hoffman, B. F., and Rosen, M. R. (1975b). *Am. Heart J.*, **90,** 655–675.
Wit, A. L., Hoffman, B. F., and Rosen, M. R. (1975c). *Am. Heart J.*, **90,** 795–803.
Wittig, J., Harrison, L. A., and Wallace, A. G. (1973). *Am. Heart J.*, **86,** 69–78.
Wyman, M. G., and Gore, S. (1983). *Heart and Lung,* **12,** 358–361.
Yamada, S., Nishimura, M., and Watanabe, Y. (1982). *J. Electrocardiol.*, **15,** 31–40.
Yoon, M. S., and Han, J. (1982). *J. Electrocardiol.*, **15,** 109–114.
Yusuf, S., Sleight, P., Rossi, P., Rossi, D., Ramsdale, D., Peto, R., Furze, L., Sterry, H., Pearson, M., Motwani, R., Parish, S., Gray, R., Bennett, D., and Bray, C. (1983). *Circulation,* **67,** Suppl. I, 32–41.
Yusuf, S., Peto, R., Lewis, J., Collins, R., and Sleight, P. (1985). *Prog. Cardiovasc. Dis.*, **27,** 335–371.
Zito, R. A., Caride, V. J., Holford, T., and Zaret, B. L. (1981). *Am. J. Cardiol.*, **47,** 265–270.

# 9 Pharmacologic and Surgical Therapy of Postinfarction Ventricular Arrhythmias

E. Wayne Grogan, Jr. and
Mark E. Josephson

## I. Introduction

Patients who suffer myocardial infarction are at risk of developing ventricular tachyarrhythmias long after the acute infarction. These arrhythmias may, in general, take three forms: (1) frequent or complex ventricular ectopy, including runs of nonsustained ventricular tachycardia (VT) (usually defined as >30 sec of spontaneously terminating VT); (2) ventricular fibrillation (VF); and (3) sustained VT. In this chapter, we will discuss the clinical importance of these arrhythmias, their mechanisms, diagnostic methods used in their evaluation and therapy, and treatment of these arrhythmias using antiarrhythmic drugs, surgery, and newer approaches including arrhythmia termination devices.

## II. Ventricular Ectopy and Nonsustained Ventricular Tachycardia

Survivors of acute myocardial infarction are at increased risk of sudden death in the months and years following infarction (Coronary Drug Project, 1973). Based partly upon early observations that VT in the coronary care unit setting was often preceded by complex ventricular ectopy, including pairs and runs of ventricular premature beats and the "R-on-T" phenomenon (Lown and Wolf, 1971; Lown et al., 1969), many investigators have studied the association of spontaneously occurring ventricular ectopy and the risk of death in the late postinfarction period (Kotler et al., 1973; Schulze et al., 1977; Ruberman et al., 1977, 1981; Anderson et al., 1978; Rehnqvist et al., 1978; Moss et al., 1979; Bigger et al., 1981). These studies have varied widely in techniques used to ascertain the extent of spontaneously occurring ventricular ectopy, with recordings lasting from 1 to 24 hr, and in the care with which other variables were evaluated. However, as a whole these studies have demonstrated that the presence of frequent and/or complex and repetitive ventricular premature depolarizations is associated with a higher risk of death, both sudden and nonsudden. The presence of pairs or runs of three or more ventricular premature depolarizations (VPDs) appears to be particularly highly associated with mortality, and the risk is increased when left ventricular function is impaired (Bigger, 1981; Califf et al., 1978). However, since ventricular arrhythmias are often associated with left ventricular dysfunction, whether ventricular arrhythmias independently contribute to the risk of sudden death or are merely markers of left ventricular dysfunction has been controversial. Bigger and co-workers (1984) have reported that frequent VPDs and runs of VPDs are independently predictive of mortality. A left ventricular ejection fraction of less than 30% was also predictive of high risk, and the two variables were independent of one another. The Myocardial Infarction Limitation Study (MILIS) also found a strong association between repetitive VPDs and mortality independent of the degree of impairment of left ventricular function (Mukharji et al., 1982). Thus, evidence from the most recent of these studies suggests that the presence of complex ventricular ectopy may predict an increased risk of death independent of the degree of left ventricular dysfunction. However, no study has shown that prevalence, frequency, or complexity of VPDs increases the risk of sudden death without increasing total mortality.

In addition, it must be emphasized that demonstration of an association between spontaneous arrhythmias and mortality does not imply that antiarrhythmic therapy can reduce mortality. To date, no study has demonstrated that suppression of ventricular ectopy or nonsustained VT by antiarrhythmic drugs reduces the incidence of death or of sudden death in patients who have had myocardial infarction.

In a series of patients with nonsustained VT evaluated by electrophysiologic study, five of the 33 patients with coronary artery disease, of whom 30 had prior myocardial infarction, died suddenly during follow-up. Three of these five had inducible, sustained VT at the time of electrophysiological study (Buxton et al., 1983, 1984). Although the number of patients was small, there appeared to be a higher risk of sudden death in those patients with severe left ventricular dysfunction as well as in those patients who had inducible sustained VT. As in previous studies, empirically or electrophysiologically guided antiarrhythmic therapy did not appear to influence survival, although this was not performed in a controlled fashion.

Although some have recommended (Lown, 1979) that patients found to have advanced grades of ventricular ectopy following myocardial infarction be treated with antiarrhythmic agents, there is currently no evidence that this is beneficial. If frequent VPDs or nonsustained VT cause disturbing symptoms of palpitations or lightheadedness, treatment directed at reducing the frequency and duration of spontaneously occurring arrhythmias is indicated for symptomatic relief.

The diagnosis and quantitation of complex ventricular ectopy is best performed by 24-hr Holter monitoring. However, if attempts are made to suppress spontaneous arrhythmias, drug efficacy must be assessed very carefully. It has been well shown that there is a great deal of spontaneous variability in VPD frequency (Winkle, 1978; Morganroth *et al.*, 1978; Michelson and Morganroth, 1980) which may simulate drug effects. Drug efficacy must be assessed by monitoring for sufficiently long periods to insure that changes in VPD frequency are due to drug effects rather than to random variability. An 83% reduction in simple VPD frequency must be seen when comparing 24-hr recordings to be sure that the observed change is not due to chance (Morganroth *et al.*, 1978). In the final analysis, sudden death is the endpoint which must be evaluated, not the results of Holter monitoring. The value of Holter monitoring can only be determined by long-term follow-up studies.

Likewise, the role of programmed stimulation with VT induction in the diagnosis and management of patients with spontaneous nonsustained VT has not been established, although preliminary data suggest it can be done safely (Buxton *et al.*, 1983, 1984).

## III. Ventricular Fibrillation

Ventricular fibrillation is seen in two settings in the patient with coronary artery disease: during the acute phase of myocardial infarction, and in the setting of chronic coronary artery disease, weeks or months after acute infarction has occurred. In a series of 234 patients with out-of-hospital VF in Seattle (Baum *et al.*, 1974; Schaffer and Cobb, 1975; Cobb *et al.*, 1975; Weaver *et al.*, 1976), only 16% had ECG evidence of acute myocardial infarction, and 45% had evidence by serum lactic dehydrogenase (LDH) isoenzyme levels of myocardial necrosis. Thus, at least half of the episodes of out-of-hospital VF occur without evidence of myocardial infarction. This distinction is important since patients who are resuscitated from VF occurring during acute infarctions have mortality rates similar to patients with acute infarction who do not suffer VF (Geddes *et al.*, 1967; McNamee *et al.*, 1970). However, patients who experience VF without evidence of acute infarction have a high rate of recurrence, with 36% dead within 1 year and 45% dead within 2 years. In contrast, among those whose VF occurred in the setting of acute infarction, the 2-year mortality rate in the same series was only 14% (Baum et al., 1974).

Those patients who have had VF during the first 48 hr of myocardial infarction may be treated in a similar fashion as patients with infarction who do not suffer VF. Patients who experience VF outside the acute setting of the infarction must be treated differently because of their grave prognosis. A subgroup of these patients may develop VF as a result of myocardial ischemia. These patients have been reported to respond to coronary bypass grafting (Hutchinson et al., 1971; Lambert et al., 1971; Cline et al., 1973; Bryson et al., 1973; Alexander et al., 1974) and might also be expected to respond to aggressive medical treatment for coronary disease. However, this group probably represents only a small fraction of patients with out-of-hospital VF.

Patients who develop recurrent VF during the early convalescent period after infarction often have large anterior infarctions due to left anterior descending coronary artery occlusion, severe left ventricular dysfunction, and conduction abnormalities (Bar et al., 1976; Wald et al., 1979). Medical treatment in this group of patients has been largely unsuccessful and mortality is high. Early studies (Bar et al., 1976; Wald et al., 1979) suggested that surgical intervention with resection of infarction or aneurysm and coronary artery bypass grafting resulted in improved survival. A more recent study of patients who developed VT and/or VF in the early postinfarction period suggests that mortality is high in this group regardless of whether surgical or medical treatment is undertaken (Marchlinski et al., 1983).

When cardiac arrest due to VF occurs outside the periinfarction period, recurrence is common and much effort has been directed toward developing methods to prevent recurrence and prolong survival. This event is usually initiated by VT (Salerno et al., 1981; Pool et al., 1978; Lahiri et al., 1979; Denes et al., 1981). Empirical antiarrhythmic drug treatment to prevent VF has been advocated. However, evidence to support this approach is lacking. In Schaffer and Cobb's series of patients with recurrent VF (1975), 73% of patients who experienced a second episode had been given prophylactic antiarrhythmic drugs after the first episode. However, no data were available to determine whether compliance or dosage was adequate.

Myerburg et al. (1979) noted that patients who maintain stable plasma levels of antiarrhythmic drugs appear to have a lower recurrence rate than patients whose drug levels were found to be erratic. This effect was independent of any effect on VPD frequency measured by Holter monitor. Morady and others (1983) have found low recurrence rates in patients with cardiac arrest treated with amiodarone. This has led some investigators (Nademanee *et al.*, 1981; Peter *et al.*, 1981) to advocate empirical therapy with amiodarone for patients with cardiac arrest without serial electrophysiological testing. However, the side effects of the drug suggest caution in its use.

Several studies have addressed the utility of electrophysiological testing in the management of patients with cardiac arrest. In all studies, the majority of patients have coronary artery disease with prior myocardial infarction. Roy *et al.* (1983) found ventricular tachyarrhythmias inducible in 72 of 119 (61%) survivors of cardiac arrest. These patients were treated with electrophysiologically guided medical therapy, amiodarone, or surgery (endocardial resection with aneurysmectomy in 20 of 22 cases). Sudden death occurred in 15% of the patients treated medically or surgically in whom sustained ventricular arrhythmias were no longer inducible after therapy. Of 12 patients discharged on amiodarone because conventional antiarrhythmic drugs were ineffective, one died suddenly. Of the remaining patients in whom ventricular tachyarrhythmias remained inducible, 27% had recurrent sudden death. Unlike other studies, patients in this group who had no inducible arrhythmias had a 32% death rate regardless of therapy. Thus, absence of inducible VT does not guarantee a benign prognosis.

Ruskin *et al.* (1980) found ventricular tachyarrhythmias inducible in 25 of 31 (81%) of cardiac arrest survivors, although only 49% had sustained arrhythmias induced. After electrophysiologically guided treatment, 19 of the 25 no longer had inducible arrhythmias and none had recurrent sudden death over 15 months of follow-up. In contrast, three of the six patients whose arrhythmias were still inducible died suddenly during follow-up.

Morady *et al.* (1983) were able to induce arrhythmias in 76% of patients with cardiac arrest, and found that conventional agents prevented induction in 26%, but one-third of these patients had recurrences. Most of the remaining patients (23 of 25) were treated empirically with amiodarone and 91% were free of recurrence at 18 months.

Benditt *et al.* (1983) found that ventricular arrhythmias (or rapid atrial fibrillation in two patients with pre-excitation syndrome) could be induced in 88% of the 34 patients with cardiac arrest. In 21, an effective regimen was indentified and this group had the lowest recurrence rate (6%).

Thus, several groups have found that electrophysiological testing is often capable of reproducing a potentially fatal arrhythmia in patients surviving cardiac arrest. In general, electrophysiological study has been helpful in identifying the best therapeutic course of action among conventional antiarrhythmic agents, amiodarone or surgery. It remains to be determined whether empirical therapy with amiodarone or other drugs is superior to this approach. Graboys and co-workers (1982) have reported their experience with a complex technique involving monitoring and exercise testing to identify a drug which suppresses spontaneous ventricular ectopy. Of 123 patients so treated (67 with VF and 57 with VT), survival was markedly better in those patients whose VPDs could be suppressed. However, ventricular function was not carefully evaluated in this study and these findings have yet to be confirmed by others.

## IV. Ventricular Tachycardia

### A. Mechanisms

Recurrent sustained VT is the most extensively studied of the tachyarrhythmias complicating myocardial infarction. Its exact incidence is uncertain, but VT is most commonly seen in patients with sizable infarctions and frequently in patients with ventricular aneurysms. Like all arrhythmias, VT is probably caused by one of three possible mechanisms: enhanced automaticity including "abnormal" or depolarization-induced automaticity, reentry, and triggered activity. The use of electrophysiological testing in patients with VT has helped clarify this question. Automaticity is unlikely to be important except in rare cases of VT. The majority of VTs can be induced and terminated repeatedly by programmed electrical stimulation, a finding which is not seen in automatic rhythms.

Reentry is the most widely accepted hypothesis for the mechanism of VT. According to this hypothesis, a fixed reentrant circuit is present in the diseased ventricle at the border of an infarct or aneurysm. As in the reentrant circuit in patients with the Wolff–Parkinson–White syndrome, two potential pathways must be present with transient block in one and slow conduction in the other. A trigger in the form of a spontaneous VPD or a series of programmed ventricular extrasystoles is able to enter one limb of the reentrant circuit and cause continuous reentry and a sustained tachyarrhythmia. The ability of programmed stimulation to induce and to terminate VT, the reciprocal relationship between the coupling interval of the inducing extrasystole and the first beat of tachycardia, and other features tend to support a reentrant mechanism. Transient entrainment of VT with fixed fusion during ventricular pacing provides further evidence for reentry, as Waldo, *et al.* (1983) have demonstrated in circus movement tachycardias in the Wolff-Parkinson–White syndrome.

The role of triggered activity remains to be demonstrated in VT (Rosen and Reder, 1982). Under certain conditions, isolated Purkinje fibers exhibit afterdepolarizations which reach threshold and cause repetitive firing. Like reentrant arrhythmias, these triggered arrhythmias can be induced and terminated in vitro by programmed stimulation, raising the possibility that some clinical tachycardias may be triggered rather than reentrant. However, few VTs share the characteristics which would be predicted for a triggered rhythm: a direct relation between coupling interval to onset of VT and the tachycardia cycle length, transient overdrive acceleration, and frequent induction with straight pacing. At present, it appears that reentry is the most likely mechanism of VT.

## B. Pharmacological Therapy

Recurrent sustained VT in the patient who has suffered myocardial infarction requires treatment. Depending upon the rate, underlying left ventricular function, and coronary anatomy, patients may have hemodynamic instability, angina, or syncope during VT. If rapid, VT may degenerate to VF and this is an important mechanism in the pathophysiology of out-of-hospital VF (Kempf, 1984). Even if episodes are slow and well tolerated hemodynamically, sustained VT usually requires treatment by the physician or in the hospital emergency room. Thus, most patients should be evaluated to attempt to identify a regimen or course of therapy which will prevent VT recurrence.

Empirical trials of antiarrhythmic drugs are rarely successful unless episodes of VT occur very frequently. More often, episodes of VT are sporadic and unpredictable, and the success of antiarrhythmic drug therapy is impossible to assess by long-term monitoring. Attempts to treat recurrent sustained VT by suppressing frequent or repetitive VPDs may also be unsuccessful, since VPD suppression can be achieved without preventing recurrent VT and, conversely, VT may be prevented without affecting VPD frequency (Myerburg et al., 1979; Herling et al., 1980).

These problems with empirical pharmacological treatment have led to the use of programmed stimulation for induction of ventricular tachyarrhythmias. Using this approach, electrode catheters are inserted percutaneously via femoral or brachial veins and positioned at various locations within the heart. Programmed atrial and ventricular pacing is then carried out. A complete study may consist of incremental atrial pacing and programmed atrial extrastimuli to determine sinus node, atrial, and A–V nodal properties. Rarely, VT may be induced with atrial pacing. Incremental ventricular pacing is performed and one, two, and three extrastimuli are introduced from the right ventricular apex and right ventricular outflow tract during sinus rhythm and ventricular pacing at two paced cycle lengths. This results in induction of sustained VT in 91% of patients who have had spontaneous episodes of this arrhythmia (vandePol et al., 1980). The ability to induce VT in the baseline state enables one to perform serial drug testing of one or more antiarrhythmic agents in an attempt to identify an agent which prevents inducibility. If such an agent is identified, long-term treatment with that agent with maintenance of adequate serum levels is usually successful in preventing recurrence (Fisher et al., 1977; Mason and Winkle, 1978; Horowitz et al., 1978; Josephson and Horowitz, 1979). In contrast, patients who receive drugs which have been found to be ineffective in the electrophysiology laboratory have a high likelihood of recurrent arrhythmia (Mason and Winkle, 1980). Thus, serial electrophysiological testing is useful in rapidly identifying an agent which renders VT noninducible and which will have beneficial long-term results. It is also helpful in identifying a group of patients who do not respond to conventional agents and who would benefit from trials of experimental antiarrhythmic agents or surgery. However, multiple trials of a number of different conventional antiarrhythmic agents may be time-consuming. One approach to limiting the time and expense of serial drug testing involves the use of a discriminant function to identify patients with high or low probability of successful medical treatment for VT. Spielman et al. (1983) used univariate and multivariate analysis to identify eight clinical and electrophysiologic variables which could prospectively predict the response to medical therapy with 92% accuracy in 81% of a group of 31 patients with VT.

The process of serial testing with a large number of conventional antiarrhythmic agents can also be considerably shortened by assessing the response to procainamide. Waxman et al. (1983) have demonstrated that failure to respond to procainamide predicts failure to respond to other conventional agents including disopyramide, quinidine, phenytoin, and lidocaine with 87% certitude. Conversely, patients who respond to procainamide have an 83% likelihood of responding to at least one other conventional agent. Thus, those patients with VT who continue to have inducible tachycardia on procainamide may be spared the time and difficulty of lengthy trials of other conventional agents and may be considered early for other approaches such as the use of experimental agents, surgery, or tachycardia termination devices.

A number of experimental agents are currently available for the treatment of VT. Mexiletine is a Class IB agent which is similar to lidocaine. In one study (Heger et al., 1980), it was associated with frequent side effects and limited efficacy. DiMarco et al. (1981) found that mexiletine prevented VT induction in 13 of 35 patients with inducible VT who were resistant to other agents. Waspe et al. (1983) noted that mexiletine was effective or partially effective in 13 of 44 patients, five of whom responded to mexiletine alone. Side effects were common in this group also, with 61% of patients reporting some adverse effect.

Lorcainide is a Class I agent which can be given intravenously or orally. In 12 patients with inducible sustained VT, lorcainide prevented induction in four. However, sleep disturbances and other neurologic side effects were common (Saksena et al., 1983). In another group of 21 patients, VT remained inducible in all patients after both intravenous and oral lorcainide (Echt et al., 1983).

Propafenone has been effective in suppressing VPDs. However, Doherty et al. (1984) found that 13 of 14 patients treated with intravenous propafenone continued to have inducible VT with no significant changes in mode of induction. Connolly et al. (1983) obtained similar results. Of 16 patients treated with propafenone, VT was rendered noninducible or nonsustained in only two patients. Only two of the five patients treated chronically with propafenone were free of arrhythmia recurrence at 2 and 8 months of follow-up.

Bepridil is a calcium channel blocker which has Class I antiarrhythmic properties as well (Torres et al., 1984). Levy et al. (1984) found bepridil effective in preventing VT inducibility in six of nine drug-refractory patients.

There are a number of other experimental antiarrhythmic agents currently under investigation for the treatment of VT. However, thus far none have emerged as being both widely effective and free of serious side effects.

Amiodarone is a benzfuran derivative which has been widely used as an antiarrhythmic agent in Europe, South America, and, more recently, in the United States. It has been found to be very effective in the treatment of recurrent sustained VT in 50 to 90% of patients treated. Waxman et al. (1982) found amiodarone effective or partly effective in 78% of conventional drug-resistant patients with ventricular tachyarrhythmias. Similarly, Zipes et al. (1984a) report that 139 of 177 (79%) of patients receiving long term amiodarone treatment remained free of recurrent arrhythmias at 16 months. Amiodarone is unique among antiarrhythmic drugs in that in most patients VT continues to be inducible in the electrophysiology laboratory despite lack of clinical recurrence (Heger et al., 1981). Although the mechanism is uncertain, this suggests amiodarone may act not upon the reentrant circuit but by decreasing the frequency of VPDs which trigger VT. Amiodarone is unusual in that a prolonged period of oral loading is required before the drug is effective, suggesting a deep tissue compartment which is slowly saturated with the drug.

VT is usually slowed by amiodarone. When the identical morphology of VT was induced both in the baseline state and after amiodarone loading in

27 patients, a 24% mean increase in cycle length was observed as a result of amiodarone treatment. However, the degree of slowing of VT could not be predicted by the degree of change in any electrocardiographic or electrophysiological parameters (E. W. Grogan, unpublished observations).

The major disadvantage of amiodarone therapy is its side effects. These include the development of corneal microdeposits, hyperthyroidism or hypothyroidism, cutaneous photosensitivity, hyperpigmentation with bluish skin discoloration, and liver function abnormalities. The most serious of amiodarone's side effects is the development of interstitial pneumonitis and pulmonary fibrosis, which can be fatal (Marchlinski *et al.*, 1982). These side effects warrant very careful observation in patients receiving long-term treatment with amiodarone.

### C. Surgical Therapy

Patients who fail to respond to medical therapy for recurrent VT or VF are candidates for surgery. Since the most common anatomic substrate for recurrent ventricular tachyarrhythmias is chronic coronary artery disease with healed myocardial infarction and left ventricular aneurysm, aneurysmectomy was attempted very early in the history of arrhythmia surgery. This first surgical approach to VT was reported by Couch in 1959, who described the excision of left ventricular aneurysmal tissue and the elimination of recurrent VT in a single patient. This was followed by a number of reports of aneurysmectomy with and without coronary bypass grafting for the treatment of ventricular arrhythmias (Ritter, 1969; Hunt *et al.*, 1969; Schlesinger *et al.*, 1971; Thind *et al.*, 1971; Wardekar *et al.*, 1972). However, these reports are sporadic, include few patients, and are selective, so data from these early experiences are difficult to interpret. Coronary bypass grafting alone is usually not effective for recurrent VT unless episodes are associated with acute ischemia (Ricks *et al.*, 1977; Tommaso *et al.*, 1982).

Standard aneurysmectomy has been performed in a number of patients in an attempt to eradicate VT. However, when this procedure is performed without the benefit of ventricular mapping to localize the site of origin of VT, results are not as good (Mason *et al.*, 1982). Although no randomized trials comparing electrophysiologically guided versus unguided surgery have been performed, several authors have retrospectively compared the results of unguided versus electrophysiologically guided aneurysm resection at their respective institutions using historic data for the unguided operations (see Table I). Ostermeyer *et al.* (1982)

## TABLE I
Comparisons (VT) of Electrophysiologically Guided versus Unguided Operations for Ventricular Tachycardia (VT) at the Same Institution[a]

| Author | Years | No. of patients | Operation | Recurrent VT | Death | Months of follow-up |
|---|---|---|---|---|---|---|
| Ostermeyer et al. (1982) | Unguided: 1971–78 | 10 | Aneurysmectomy, CABG[b] | 60% | 50% | 52 |
| | Electrophysiologically guided: 1978–82 | 31 | Primarily encircling endocardial ventriculotomy | 26% | 13% | 12.7 |
| Mason et al. (1982) | Unguided: 1970–79 | 32 | Aneurysmectomy, CABG | 69% | 53% | 42 |
| | Electrophysiologically guided: 1979–81 | 33 | Myocardial resection or incision | 24% | 36% | 14 |
| Harken et al. (1980) | Unguided: 1974–78 | 19 | Aneurysmectomy, CABG | 79% | 68% | 22–66 |
| | Electrophysiologically guided: 1977–79 | 30 | Endocardial resection, CABG | 10% | 17% | 8–30 |

[a] All series are noncurrent, nonrandomized comparisons of patients treated at the same institution.
[b] CABG, coronary artery bypass grafting.

compared 10 patients who had simple aneurysmectomy to 31 patients with electrophysiologically guided encircling endocardial ventriculotomy (EEV). Abolition of VT was significantly more common in the electrophysiologically guided group, and there was a lower early and late mortality. Harken *et al.* (1980) compared 19 patients who underwent nonguided aneurysmectomy to 30 who had map-guided surgery and found a markedly better survival and higher rate of elimination of recurrent VT in the electrophysiologically guided group. Similarly, Mason *et al.* (1982) reported on 32 patients who underwent simple aneurysmectomy and 33 who underwent myocardial incision or resection guided by mapping and found high recurrence rates (56% after 3 months) in the unguided aneurysmectomy group compared to 17% at 3 months in the map-guided group. However, it should be emphasized that these comparisons were not concurrent and, therefore, the groups of patients are not strictly comparable. It has not yet been determined whether modern techniques of VT surgery including endocardial resection can be performed as effectively when unguided by mapping data as when guided by endocardial mapping.

The anatomical explanation for the notable lack of success of unguided aneurysmectomy is the location of the site of earliest endocardial activation during VT. In patients with left ventricular aneurysms, who are the largest group of patients with recurrent VT, the earliest site of endocardial activation during VT has been shown to occur at the border between nonviable aneurysm and the adjacent healthy tissue on the endocardium (Josephson *et al.*, 1979; Horowitz *et al.*, 1980a; Josephson *et al.*, 1981). Frequently, this site of origin is on the interventricular septum. In standard aneurysmectomy, the septum is left intact and the aneurysm border zone is not resected; in fact, a cuff of fibrous tissue from the edge of the aneurysm is often purposely left in place to facilitate suturing. As a result, the site of origin of VT is often left undisturbed by the usual techniques of aneurysmectomy. The unsatisfactory results obtained with coronary bypass grafting and simple aneurysmectomy have led to the development of other techniques for the surgical treatment of VT.

### *1. Ventriculotomy*

Ventriculotomy has been used successfully in patients with VT without coronary disease (Fontaine *et al.*, 1976). Using this approach, epicardial mapping was used to localize the site of earliest breakthrough of VT and a simple ventriculotomy was made at this site. Results were good in this group of patients. However, when this technique was applied to patients with coronary disease, the same investigators (Fontaine *et al.*, 1977) found that the mapping data were difficult to interpret and they were only able to apply the technique to two patients, in one of whom VT recurred. They pointed out several objections to the use of the simple ventriculotomy in coronary artery disease, including the observation that epicardial breakthrough is sometimes located in healthy myocardium, necessitating the incision of normal muscle, which might lead to hemodynamic deterioration. This led them to develop the concept of the encircling endocardial ventriculotomy (EEV).

## 2. Encircling Endocardial Ventriculotomy

Guiraudon and colleagues (1978) reported the use of the EEV for the treatment of recurrent VT. The rationale for this approach is based on observations that surrounding the area of dense scar tissue in the center of the left ventricular aneurysm is an area consisting of an intermixture of normal muscle, ischemic muscle, and fibrosis, from which VT often arises. They reasoned that an incision around the limits of this border zone would interrupt or isolate reentrant circuits which give rise to VT. Since the limits of this area can be delineated by examination from the endocardial side, this can theoretically be done without the benefit of mapping, although in most cases this group's surgery has been guided by the results of intraoperative mapping. The incision extends through endocardium and myocardium, leaving only a thin layer of epicardium and the epicardial coronary vessels along the left ventricular free wall. When the EEV encompasses the septum, the incision is >1 cm deep but not transmural (Guiraudon et al., 1980). The incision is then repaired by a running suture (see Fig. 1). The papillary muscles can be skirted and damage to the mitral valve apparatus avoided. Guiraudon and co-workers (1982) have reported the use of the procedure in 27 patients between 1975 and 1980. Operative mortality was 18%, and VT was prevented for more then 1 year in 16 patients. The mechanism of success of EEV is uncertain. Guiraudon hypothesizes that isolation of the reentrant circuit or interruption by the scar either impairs the ability of the VT to occur or prevents its exit from the encircled zone. However, data of Ungerleider et al. (1982a) suggest that the mechanism may simply be the creation of further ischemic injury to the area from which VT originates by interrupting its blood supply. In animals, the technique causes significant decreases in myocardial blood flow and in regional left ventricular function. Limited data are available regarding ventricular function in humans and it has been suggested that this technique be avoided in patients with severely impaired left ventricular function because of the possibility of further adverse effects on ventricular performance.

Patients who have died following this procedure often died of refractory low cardiac output (Arciniegas et al., 1980). In addition, special tech-

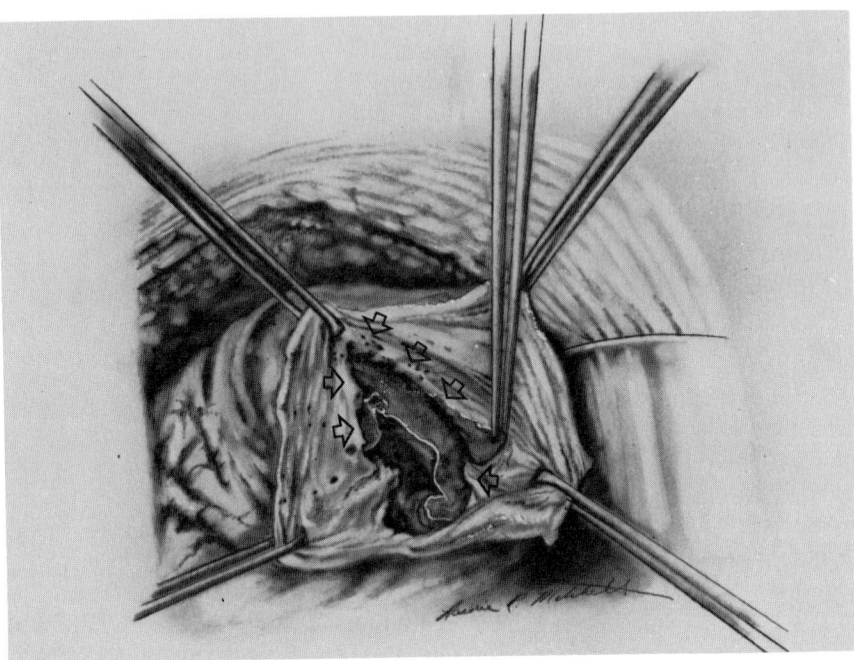

**Fig. 1.** Encircling endocardial ventriculotomy. The arrows indicate the site of the encircling incision at the border of the endocardial scar. (From Josephson and Harken, 1983.)

niques may be necessary to encircle posterior scars (Cox, 1983). Therefore, the EEV may be a useful procedure in selected patients with recurrent VT. It should be used with caution, if at all, in patients with severely impaired left ventricular function. More careful studies are needed to precisely delineate its effects on left ventricular function in patients. However, many investigators have abandoned this procedure in favor of endocardial resection.

### 3. Cryosurgery

Cryosurgery has been used in some patients to treat VT. Cooling of myocardium to −60°C is effective in producing permanent discrete myocardial lesions which have sharply demarcated borders. Gallagher *et al.* in 1978 and Camm *et al.* in 1979 have used this technique to cure patients with VT. Both investigators used the technique of cryomapping, wherein the tissue in question is cooled to 0 to −10°C during VT. This produces electrical inactivity but not irreversible damage in the cooled area. When myocardium necessary for the maintenance of VT is cooled, the tachycardia terminates. This area can then be cooled to −60 to −65°C for 2 min, which effectively destroys it and in some cases cures VT. The ultimate role of this technique requires further exploration. At the University of Pennsylvania, cryothermal techniques have been used primarily as adjunctive therapy in patients undergoing endocardial resection. When the site of origin is near the base of a papillary muscle, precluding extensive endocardial resection in this area, a cryolesion can be placed very close to the base of the papillary muscle in an attempt to destroy the site of origin without interfering with mitral function. Cryothermal techniques are also used to create deeper lesions when mapping with plunge electrodes suggests a deep intramyocardial rather than endocardial site of origin.

## 4. Endocardial Resection

Several observations led to the development of the endocardial resection to treat patients with refractory VT due to coronary disease. Gallagher et al. (1975) noted during epicardial mapping of a patient with VT and a ventricular aneurysm that the earliest epicardial activation occurred after the inscription of the QRS on the surface ECG, suggesting an endocardial or myocardial site of origin. Limited observations by Wittig and Boineau (1975) suggested a subendocardial site of origin. More extensive epicardial and endocardial mapping later by Horowitz et al. (1980) disclosed that VT in the setting of ischemic heart disease invariably arose from the endocardium at the border of the infarction or aneurysm. Since catheter mapping showed the area of origin to be at the margin of the infarct or aneurysm, often on the left ventricular septum, and since standard aneurysmectomy was inadequate both because of failure to remove the site of origin at the border zone and because of inability to resect the septum, the endocardial resection was developed (Josephson et al., 1979).

The technique of endocardial resection is as follows. After opening the chest but before instituting cardiopulmonary bypass, epicardial mapping may be performed. However, as noted, epicardial mapping is not a reliable guide to localizing the site of origin of VT, and this procedure is not often performed. The patient is then placed on normothermic cardiopulmonary bypass and the left ventricle is opened, usually through the aneurysm or scar. Since the ventricle is rapidly decompressed through the ventriculotomy, it is not necessary to cross-clamp the aorta (Harken et al., 1979, 1981). Endocardial mapping is then performed using a bipolar ring electrode on the surgeon's finger (see below). When the areas to be resected have been identified, cold cardioplegia is instituted and a 2-mm thick peel of fibrous endo–myocardium is excised using sharp dissection

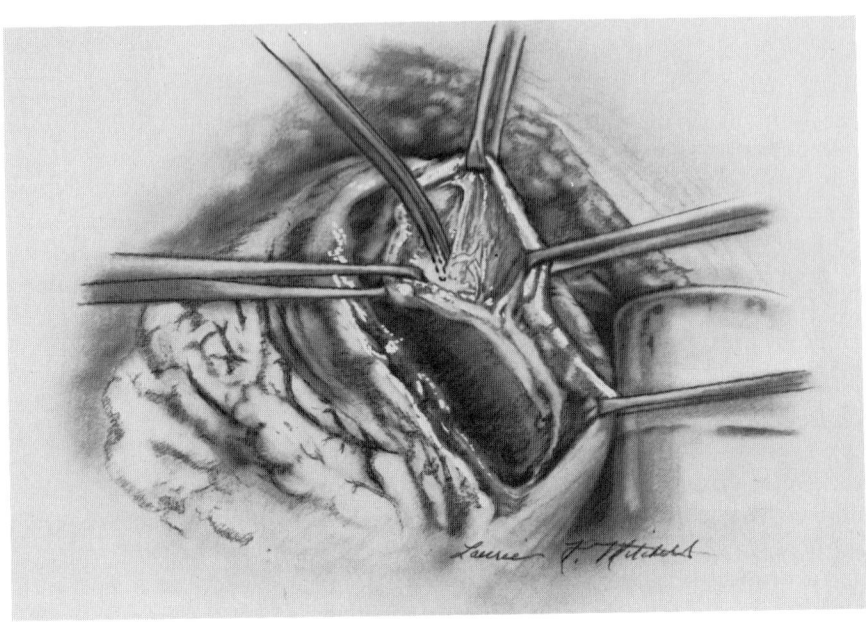

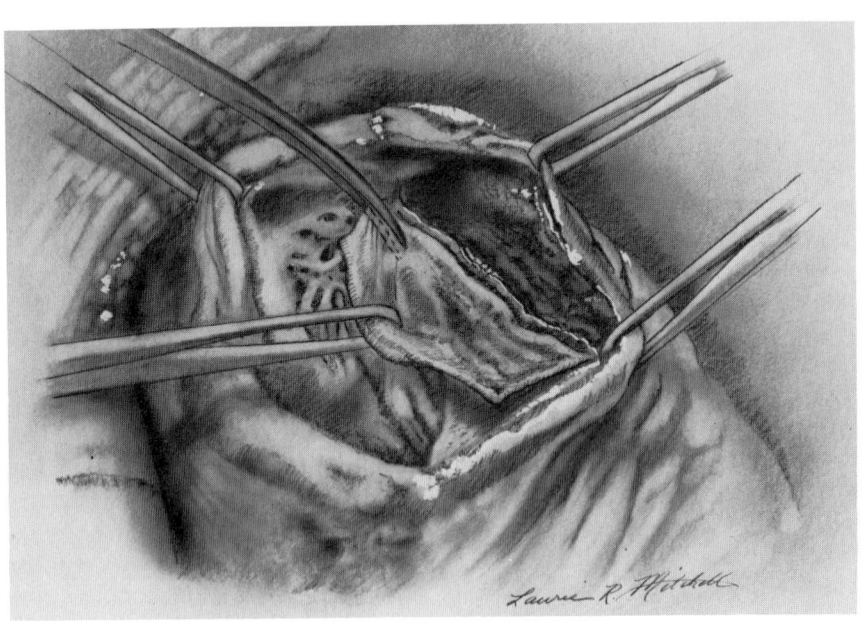

9. Therapy of Ventricular Arrhythmias

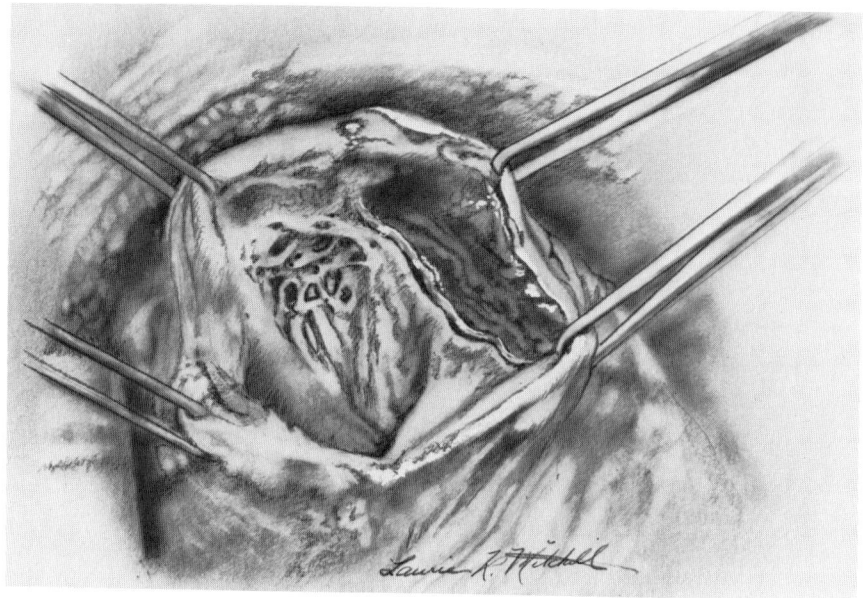

**Fig. 2.** Endocardial resection. In the three photographs, an incision has been made in an apical aneurysm. Sharp dissection is carried out along the endocardial surface of the septum, removing a thin sheet of fibrous scar tissue. (From Josephson and Harken, 1983.)

to develop the natural dissection plane between this fibrous layer and the underlying myocardium (see Fig. 2). The excision includes margins of 3 to 4 cm on all sides of the mapped site of origin of VT. Typically, a sheet of endocardium of 4 to 15 $cm^2$ is removed. Once the endocardium has been excised, aneurysmectomy is carried out in the usual fashion, leaving a cuff of fibrous tissue for suturing. The ventriculotomy is closed using Teflon pledgets to buttress the suture line. Coronary grafts are placed as needed.

The results of endocardial resection in the first 100 patients to undergo this procedure at the Hospital of the University of Pennsylvania have been reviewed (Miller *et al.*, 1984) (see Table II). All patients had prior infarction, 79 of which were anterior and 21 inferior. The mean left ventricular ejection fraction for the group was $28 \pm 9\%$. Preoperatively, 87 patients had catheter mapping of 143 differnt VTs, and 96 patients had intraoperative mapping of 209 different VTs. Surgery was guided by the results of intraoperative or catheter mapping. All patients underwent endocardial resection, 90 had aneurysmectomy, 61 patients had a mean of 1.6 coronary bypass grafts each, and 13 patients had cryolesions placed.

Nine patients died during or after surgery, six due to refractory heart failure, two due to perioperative infarction, and one due to electrome-

**TABLE II**
Results of Ventricular Tachycardia (VT) Surgery in 100 Patients[a]

| Result | No. of patients |
|---|---|
| Operative deaths | 9 |
| Complete clinical success (no VT, on no drugs) | 60 |
| Partial clinical success (no VT, on drugs) | 23 |
| Spontaneous VT despite drugs | 4 |
| Cardiac arrest | 4 |
| Late deaths not due to VT or cardiac arrest | 20 |

[a] Results of endocardial resection in 100 patients treated at the Hospital of the University of Pennsylvania. Mean follow-up, 23 months. (From Miller et al., 1984 by permission of the American Heart Association, Inc.)

chanical dissociation. Of the 91 survivors, 60 had no spontaneous or inducible VT on no medications (complete success) and 23 had no VT on medications (partial success). Thus, the rate of complete or partial success among survivors was 91%. Of the 89 survivors who underwent postoperative electrophysiological study, no VT could be induced in 64 (72%). Of this group of noninducible survivors, three had late VT recurrences controlled with drugs, and three died suddenly. Of the 25 patients (28%) who had inducible VT postoperatively, VT was made noninducible with drugs in 10, of whom one died suddenly 11 months postoperatively, and nine remained free of recurrent VT. Fifteen patients continued to have inducible VT despite drugs, of whom four continue to have periodic recurrent episodes of VT.

At a mean of 28 months of follow-up, 14 patients of the 91 survivors have had spontaneous recurrent VT and four continue to have episodes despite medical therapy.

Late death occurred in 24 due to congestive heart failure in 10, myocardial infarction in five, sudden death in four, and various other causes in five (see Fig. 3).

Multivariate analysis was performed to identify characteristics associated with success or failure of surgery. Surgical failure was strongly associated with multiple morphologies of VT, disparate sites of origin, and inferior wall sites of origin. VT characteristics associated with greater

## 9. Therapy of Ventricular Arrhythmias

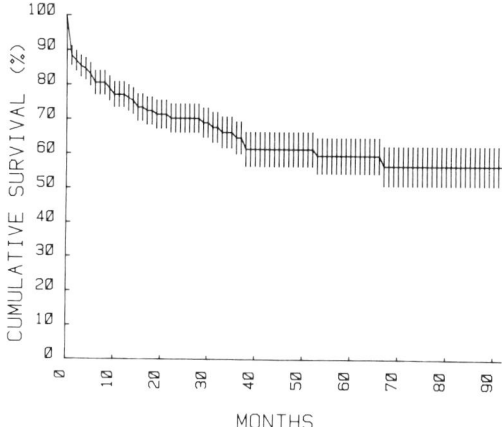

**Fig. 3.** Survival following endocardial resection. Actuarial survival is shown for the first 90 patients to undergo endocardial resection at the Hospital of the University of Pennsylvania. (From Harken and Josephson, 1984.)

failure rate include nonseptal sites of origin and right bundle branch block morphology VT. Left bundle branch block morphology VTs and septal sites of origin (all left bundle branch block morphology VTs arose from the septum) were more likely to be cured by endocardial resection. Tachycardias which recurred postoperatively included both those which occurred clinically preoperatively and those which were only seen as a result of induction in the electrophysiology laboratory. Therefore, preoperative and intraoperative electrophysiological study and endocardial mapping were essential to induce and map all tachycardias, including those which had not been detected clinically, in order to guide endocardial resection.

Hemodynamic effects of endocardial resection have been described for a smaller group of 37 patients undergoing endocardial resection at the University of Pennsylvania (Josephson *et al.*, 1980b, 1982a). Thirty-one of 34 survivors underwent cardiac catheterization. The mean ejection fraction increased from 27 to 40% because of removal of noncontractile left ventricular segments. Left ventricular end-diastolic pressure decreased from 18 to 13 mm Hg, and the cardiac index was unchanged (2.7 to 2.6 liters/min/m$^2$ preoperatively and postoperatively). There was no consistent improvement in the level of ventricular ectopic activity by Holter monitoring. In addition, there was no relation between VPD frequency or Lown Grade of spontaneous ventricular arrhythmias and the presence of persistent inducibility of VT postoperatively (Kienzle *et al.*, 1983).

Moran *et al.* (1982) have reported their experience with a slightly modified procedure, the "extended endocardial resection," in 40 patients, 23 with VT and 17 with VF. Their technique differs from the technique used at the University of Pennsylvania in that (1) no preoperative catheter mapping is performed, and (2) emphasis is placed on the removal of all visible areas of endocardial scar. This resulted in fairly extensive endocardial resections, involving two or more areas of endocardium in 26 of the 40 patients. In addition, mitral valve replacement was performed in five (12.5%) because of excision of scarred papillary muscles. Epicardial and endocardial mapping were performed intraoperatively, and yielded early sites of activation in 25 patients. In 15 patients, mapping was not performed due to noninducibility in the operating room (two), noninducibility after ventriculotomy (five), repeated degeneration to ventricular fibrillation (four), or because it was not attempted (four). In the other 25 patients, data from activation mapping was used in addition to visual observation of the extent of endocardial scarring to guide the extent of endocardial resection. The overall operative mortality was 10%, with a trend toward higher mortality in the patients with VF. There was also a trend toward less frequent postoperative inducibility in the patients who underwent map-guided versus visually-guided operations, but the number of patients is too small to be significant. Three patients (9.1%) continue to have inducible VT postoperatively.

### 5. VT Mapping

As discussed above, simple aneurysmectomy unguided by activation mapping is not an adequate operation for the treatment of VT and recurrences are common. This is because VT usually arises from the aneurysm's border, often on the interventricular septum, and, consequently, the site of origin of VT is usually not resected in simple aneurysmectomy. This led to the development of the endocardial resection guided by activation mapping to remove the site of origin of VT.

In the catheterization laboratory VT mapping can be performed to localize the site of origin of VT within the limits of the technique to an area of about 4 cm$^2$ (Josephson *et al.*, 1982b). Catheters are typically placed in the right ventricular apex, right ventricular outflow tract, and left ventricle via the femoral vessels. VT is induced and if stable and well tolerated, allowed to continue while recordings are made from various sites within the left and right ventricles. Catheter position at each site is confirmed fluoroscopically in at least two projections (see Fig. 4).

If VT is not tolerated hemodynamically because of too rapid a rate, it may be slowed by the administration of intravenous procainamide. The

## 9. Therapy of Ventricular Arrhythmias

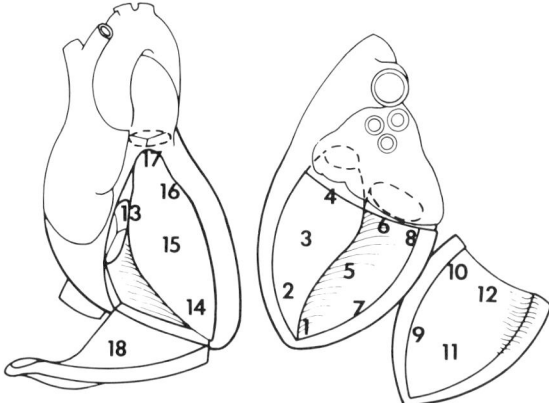

**Fig. 4.** Right and left ventricular catheter mapping sites. (From Josephson *et al.*, 1982b.)

presence of antiarrhythmic drugs does not alter the activation sequence (Josephson *et al.*, 1982b). Alternatively, if VT is tolerated only for brief periods of time it can be repeatedly started, recordings made at one or two sites, and terminated by programmed stimulation. The catheters may then be repositioned and VT once again initiated and terminated until all sites have been mapped. Using these techniques, a site with presystolic electrical activity (prior to the onset of the QRS on the surface ECG) can almost always be identified (see Fig. 5). In patients with coronary artery disease the site of origin is uniformly left ventricular or septal. In addition, the approximate area of VT origin can be inferred by the morphology of VT by a 12-lead surface electrocardiogram (Josephson *et al.*, 1984).

Catheter mapping is important to localize the sites of origin of all VTs so that intraoperative mapping may be concentrated in the proper area. For well-tolerated VTs, catheter mapping can be performed carefully without the time constraints imposed by the operating room. In addition, tachycardias are sometimes not inducible in the operating room and thus surgery must be guided by the results of catheter mapping for any morphology only seen in the electrophysiology laboratory. In the operating room endocardial mapping must be performed through a ventriculotomy while the patient is on normothermic cardiopulmonary bypass. This limits the length of time which can be safely used for mapping, and mapping is usually limited to 1 hr or less. The results of catheter mapping have been found to correlate well with the results of more detailed intraoperative mapping (Josephson *et al.*, 1980a).

In the operating room epicardial mapping has occasionally been used to guide surgery. However, many observers have noted that the earliest site

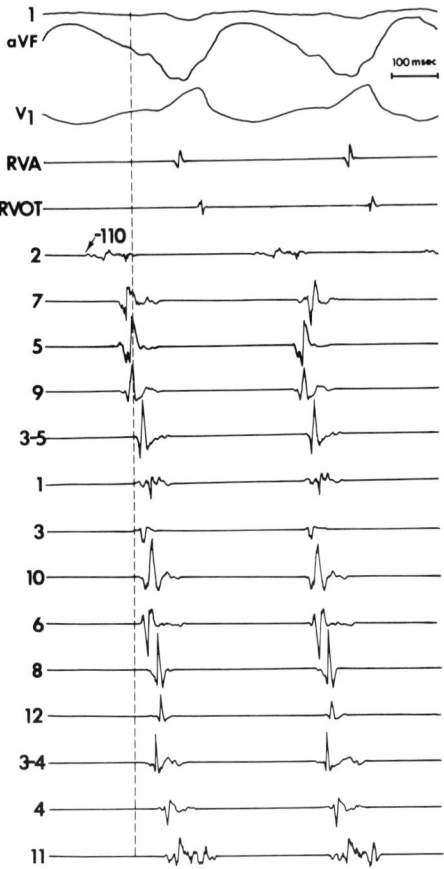

**Fig. 5.** Catheter mapping during sustained ventricular tachycardia. Analog recordings from surface ECG leads 1, aVF, and V₁, electrograms from right ventricular apex (RVA) and right ventricular outflow tract (RVOT), and recordings from 14 sites within the left ventricle are shown. Note that earliest endocardial activation occurs at site 2 (on the apical septum), 110 msec prior to the onset of the QRS on the surface ECG.

of epicardial activation during VT commonly follows the onset of the QRS by surface ECG, suggesting that VT does not arise from the epicardium (see Fig. 6). In contrast, an endocardial site with presystolic electrical activity can almost always be identified, and resection of that site most often leads to cure of clinical and inducible VT. Furthermore, detailed endocardial and epicardial recordings in both animals and humans (Spielman *et al.*, 1978; Horowitz *et al.*, 1980) have revealed that the earliest epicardial activation may be widely separated from the site of earliest endocardial activation during VT and may occur much later in time. Epicardial mapping is thus not a useful guide to VT surgery and endocardial mapping is the technique primarily used to guide resection.

In the operating room, epicardial mapping if performed is done with the pericardium open but before instituting cardiopulmonary bypass. Epicardial mapping may be performed either during normal sinus rhythm or induced VT. The patient is then placed on normothermic cardiopulmonary bypass and the ventricle opened through the scar or aneurysm, most

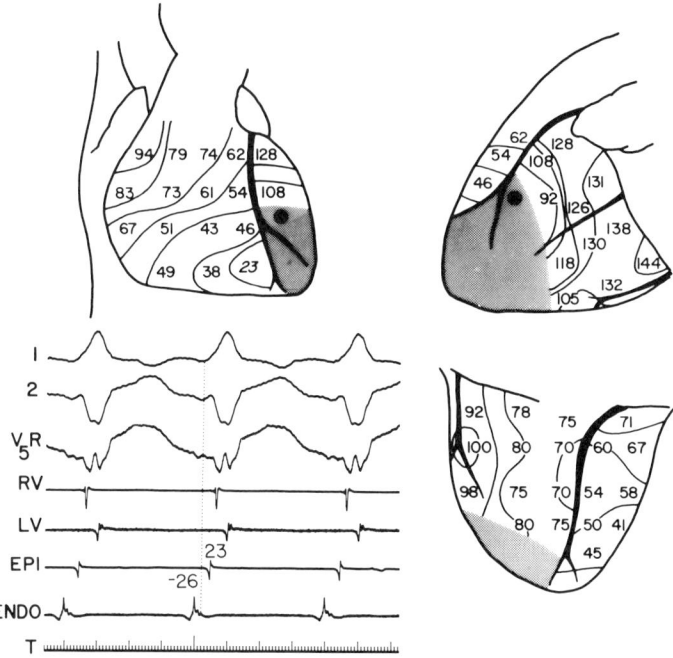

**Fig. 6.** Epicardial and endocardial activation during sustained ventricular tachycardia. Epicardial times and isochronous lines are shown on the anterior, left lateral, and inferior surfaces of the heart (from top left, clockwise). The stippled area represents left ventricular aneurysm, the black dot corresponds to the site of earliest endocardial activation during VT. At lower left are analog recordings from surface ECG leads 1, 2, and $V_5R$, reference electrograms from the right and left ventricles (RV and LV), and electrograms from the sites of earliest epicardial (EPI) and earliest endocardial (ENDO) activation. Note that the site of earliest epicardial activation is several centimeters distant from the site of earliest epicardial activation, and that earliest epicardial activation occurs 23 msec after the onset of the QRS. (From Horowitz et al, 1980b.)

often at the apex. VT is then induced using a previously placed catheter in the right ventricular apex or a plunge electrode inserted at the time of surgery. Endocardial recordings are made during tachycardia at 12 sites around the margin of the ventriculotomy using the hours of the clock to delineate the sites. Serial planes of 12 sites each are recorded beginning at the aneurysm's edge and extending back toward the base in increments of 1 cm. This usually identifies the area of earliest endocardial activation and more detailed higher density recordings may be made in this area, using more closely spaced sites with the bipolar ring electrode or by using arrays of electrodes on fixed plaques. If VT is too rapid or polymorphic, intravenous procainamide can be used to slow VT or to make it more uniform to aid in the mapping process.

Mapping during sinus rhythm has been proposed as a method to guide VT surgery without necessitating VT induction. Areas of endocardial scar frequently show abnormal, low-amplitude, broad or fractionated electrograms. The group at the University of Alabama has used these abnormal electrocardiograms to guide surgery in 16 patients (Arciniegas *et al.*, 1982) and resected all areas with abnormal electrograms during sinus rhythm without attempting to identify the site of earliest activation during VT. EEV was also performed in some patients. Of this group, five patients died, three early and two late, and 11 have survived to between 1 and 54 months without clinical episodes of VT. However, Cassidy *et al.* (1984) have found that sinus rhythm electrogram characteristics may not accurately identify the site of origin of VT. In 52 patients, 14% of sites of origin identified by catheter mapping had normal electrograms during sinus rhythm. Thus, resection of all areas where abnormal sinus rhythm electrograms are recorded may potentially miss a large proportion of the sites from which VTs arise.

Pace-mapping has been advocated as a technique for localizing the origin of VT. This involves pacing at sites on the left ventricular endocardium until a site is found at which pacing closely reproduces the morphology of VT by surface electrocardiogram. Pacing at the site of origin has been found to reproduce the morphology of VT fairly accurately, but markedly different morphologies may be produced by pacing at closely adjacent sites (Josephson *et al.*, 1982c). In addition, accurate pace-mapping is difficult to achieve in the operating room because of inability to record precordial leads with the chest open and the distortion produced by changes in position of the heart within the chest. Thus, activation mapping during VT in the electrophysiology laboratory and in the operating room continue to be the most reliable guides to endocardial resection and other forms of surgery for VT.

### D. Tachycardia Termination Devices

Several classes of automatic devices have been developed for use in the treatment of arrhythmias. Pacemakers can be programmed to deliver predetermined sequences or bursts of extrastimuli either automatically or when activated by the patient or physician during an episode of VT. This may be effective in terminating VT. However, there is a very significant risk of acceleration of VT or conversion to VF by pacing (Roy *et al.*, 1982; Gardner *et al.*, 1982). If this occurs without ready access to defibrillation, the result may be fatal. Therefore, tachycardia-terminating pacemakers must be used with great caution if at all in patients with VT.

New approaches to preventing the initiation of VT with subthreshold stimuli or stimuli programmed to be delivered after spontaneous VPDs which might induce VT are currently under investigation.

A transvenous cardioverter has been used primarily in the hospital setting and in the electrophysiology laboratory to terminate VT. VT can be effectively terminated with low-energy transvenous cardioversion but may accelerate or degenerate to VF. Transvenous cardioversion is not reliably effective in termination of VF. Therefore, without defibrillation capacity, this approach also has very limited applicability. It has been used in a few patients in the automatic mode to date but must be used with great caution (Zipes *et al.*, 1984b).

The automatic implantable defibrillator was originally designed for conversion of VF but may also be used for patients with rapid VT who cannot otherwise be controlled. Twenty-five to 30 joules of energy are delivered between a patch over the left ventricular apex and a spring electrode at the superior vena cava–right atrial junction, or a second epicardial patch. So far the device has proven very effective at detecting VT or VF, discharging, and terminating the arrhythmia (Mirowski *et al.*, 1983). Although still experimental, it may prove to be an important tool in the treatment of recurrent ventricular tachyarrhythmias.

## V. Summary

In conclusion, ventricular tachyarrhythmias are a major cause of death and disability following myocardial infarction. Patients who have ventricular ectopy or nonsustained VT are at increased risk of death and sudden death, but currently there is no available evidence to suggest that empirically or electrophysiologically guided treatment is able to decrease this risk. Patients with cardiac arrest due to VF and patients with recurrent sustained VT are usually found to have inducible ventricular arrhythmias by programmed stimulation in the electrophysiology laboratory. Programmed stimulation may be used to induce VT and to test inducibility on different drugs in an attempt to identify a drug which renders the arrhythmia noninducible. Noninducibility with most drugs is associated with a good long-term clinical outcome. If such a drug cannot be identified, patients should be considered for treatment with amiodarone, arrhythmia surgery, or tachycardia termination devices. Amiodarone is often successful in preventing recurrences despite continued inducibility in the electrophysiology laboratory, but it is associated with significant side effects. VT surgery is associated with a mortality of 8 to 10% but is very effective in preventing recurrent VT. Current tachycardia termination devices consist of experimental pacemakers, the transvenous cardioverter, and the automatic implantable defibrillator. Both the transvenous cardioverter and automatic pacing devices carry significant risks of acceleration of VT or conversion to VF and should only be used with great caution if at all in patients with recurrent VT. The implantable defibrillator appears to be an effective device which can successfully terminate rapid VT or VF and may play an important role in long-term management of these patients.

## Acknowledgments

This work was supported in part by grants from the American Heart Association, Southeastern Pennsylvania Chapter, Philadelphia, PA; and grants #HL06704, #HL07346, #HL28093, and #HL24278 from the National Heart, Lung, and Blood Institute, Bethesda, MD and the Fannie E. Ripple Association, Morristown, NJ.

## References

Alexander, S., Makar, Y., and Ellis, F. H., Jr. (1974). *JAMA* **228**:70–71.
Anderson, R. P., Decanutla, J., and Moss, A. J. (1978). *Circulation* **57**:890–897.
Arciniegas, J. G., Kline, H., Karp, R. B., Kouchoukas, N. T., James, T. N., Kirklin, J. W., and Waldo, A. L. (1980). *Circulation* **62** (III):42.
Arciniegas, J. G., Plumb, R. J., Karp, R. B., Zimmern, S. H., Henthorn, R. W., and Waldo, A. L. (1982). *Am J Cardiol* **49**:935.
Bar, F. W., Lie, K. I., and Wellens, H. J. J. (1976). *Circulation* **54** (Suppl II):37.
Baum, R. S., Alvarez, H. A., and Cobb, C. A. (1974). *Circulation* **50**:1231–1235.
Benditt, G. D., Benson, D. W., Klein, G. J., Pritzkec, M. R., Kriett, J. M., and Anderson, R. W. (1983). *JACC* **2**:418–425.

Bigger, J. T., and Weld, F. M. (1981). *Br Heart J* **45:**717–724.
Bigger, J. T., Weld, F. M., and Rolnitzky, L. M. (1981). *Am J Cardiol* **48:**815–823.
Bigger, J. T., Fleiss, J. L., Kleiger, R., Miller, J. P., Rolnitzky, J. M., and the Multicenter Post-Infarction Research Group (1984). *Circulation* **69:**250–258.
Bryson, A. L., Parisi, A. F., Schechter, E., and Wolfson, S. (1973). *Am J Cardiol* **32:**995–999.
Buxton, A. E., Waxman, H. L., Marchlinski, F. E., and Josephson, M. E. (1983). *Am J Cardiol* **52:**985–991.
Buxton, A. E., Marchlinski, F. E., Waxman, H. L., Flores, B. T., Cassidy, D. M., and Josephson, M. E. (1984). *Am J Cardiol* **43:**1275–1279.
Califf, M., Burks, J. M., Behar, V. S., Margolis, J. R., and Wagner, G. S. (1978). *Circulation* **57:**725–732.
Camm, J., Ward, D. E., Coy-Pearce, R., Rees, J. M., and Spurrell, R. A. J. (1979). *Chest* **75:**621–624.
Cassidy, D. M., Vassallo, J. A., Buxton, A. E., Doherty, J. U., Marchlinski, F. E., and Josephson, M. E. (1984). *Circulation* **69:**1103–1110.
Cline, R. E., Armstrong, R. G., and Stanford, W. (1973). *J Thorac Cardiovasc Surg* **65:**802–805.
Cobb, L. A., Baum, R. S., Alvarez, H., and Schaffer, W. A. (1975). *Circulation* **51 & 52** (Suppl III):223–235.
Connolly, S. J., Kates, R. E., Lebsazk, C. S., Echt, D. S., Mason, J. W., and Winkel, R. A. (1983). *Am J Cardiol* **52:**1208–1213.
Coronary Drug Project Research Group (1973). *JAMA* **223:**1116–1124.
Couch, O. A. (1959). *Circulation* **20:**251–253.
Cox, J. L. (1983). *Ann Surg* **198:**119–129.
Cox, J. L., Gallagher, J. J., and Ungerleider, R. M. (1983). *J Thorac Cardiovas Surg* **83:**865–872.
Denes, R., Gabster, A., and Huang, S. K. (1981). *Am J Cardiol* **48:**9–16.
DiMarco, J. P., Garan, H., and Ruskin, J. N. (1981). *Am J Cardiol* **47:**131–138.
Doherty, J. U., Waxman, H. L., Kienzle, M. G., Cassidy, D. M., Marchlinski, F. E., Buxton, A. E., and Josephson, M. E. (1984). *JACC* **4:**378–381.
Echt, D. S., Mitchell, L. B., Kates, R. E., and Winkle, R. A. (1983). *Circulation* **68:**392–399.
Fisher, J. D., Cohen, H. L., Mehra, R., Altschuler, H., Escher, D. J. W., and Furman, S. (1977). *Am Heart J* **93:**658–668.
Fontaine, G., Guiraudon, G., Frank, R., Coutte, R., and Dragonganne, C. (1976). In "The Conduction System of the Heart" (H. J. J. Wellens, K. I. Lee, and M. J. Janse, eds.), pp 545–563. Kroese BV, Leiden.
Fontaine, G., Guiraudon, G., Frank, R., *et al.* (1977). In "Reentrant Arrhythmias: Mechanisms and Therapy" (H. E. Kulbertus, ed.), pp 334–350. University Park Press, Baltimore.
Gallagher, J. J., Oldham, H. N., Wallace, A. G., Peter, R. H., and Kasell, J. (1975). *Am J Cardiol* **35:**696–700.
Gallagher, J. J., Anderson, R. W., Kassell, J., Rice, J. R., Pritchett, E. L. C., Gault, J. H., Harrison, L., and Wallace, A. G. (1978). *Circulation* **57:**190–197.
Gardner, M. J., Waxman, H. L., Buxton, A. E., Cain, M. E., and Josephson, M. E. (1982). *Am J Cardiol* **50:**1338–1345.
Geddes, J. S., Adgey, A. H. J., and Pantridge, J. F. (1967). *Lancet* **2:**273–275.
Graboys, T. B., Lown, B., Podrid, P. J., and deSilva, R. (1982). *Am J Cardiol* **50:**437–443.

Gradman, A. H., Bell, P. A., and DeBusk, F. (1977). *Circulation* **55**:210–211.
Guiraudon, G., Fontaine, G., Frank, R., Escande, G., Etievent, P., and Cabrol, C. (1978). *Ann Thorac Surg* **26**:438–444.
Guiraudon, G., Fontaine, G., Frank, R., Pavie, A., Grosgogeat, Y., and Cabrol, C. (1980). *In* "Medical and Surgical Management of Tachyarrhythmias" (W. Bircks, F. Loogen, H. D. Schulte, and L. Seipel, eds.), pp 155–172. Springer-Verlag, Berlin.
Guiraudon, J., Fontaine, G., Frank, R., Cabrol, C., and Grosgogeat, Y. (1982). *Arch Mal Coeur* **75**:1013–1021.
Harken, A. H., and Josephson, M. E. (1984). *In* "Tachycardias: Mechanisms, Diagnos, Treatment" (M. E. Josephson and H. J. J. Wellens, eds.), p 483. Lea & Febiger, Philadelphia.
Harken, A. H., Josephson, M. E., and Horowitz, L. N. (1979). *Ann Surg* **190**:456–460.
Harken, A. H., Horowitz, L. N., and Josephson, M. E. (1980). *J Thorac Cardiovasc Surg* **80**:527–534.
Harken, A. H., Josephson, M. E., and Horowitz, L. N. (1981). *Mod Tech Surg* **37**:1–8.
Heger, J. J., Nattel, S., Rinkenberger, R. L., and Zipes, D. P. (1980). *Am J Cardiol* **45**:627.
Heger, J. J., Prystowsky, E. N., Jackman, W. M., Naccarelli, G. V., Warfel, R. A., Rinkenberger, R. L., and Zipes, D. P. (1981). *N Engl J Med* **305**:539–545.
Herling, I. M., Horowitz, L. N., and Josephson, M. E. (1980). *Am J Cardiol* **45**:633–639.
Horowitz, L. N., Josephson, M. E., Farshidi, A., Spielman, S. R., Michelson, E. L., and Greenspan, A. M. (1978). *Circulation* **58**:968–997.
Horowitz, L. N., Josephson, M. E., and Harken, A. H. (1980a). *Circulation* **61**:1227–1238.
Horowitz, L. N. *et al.* (1980b). *N Engl J Med* **302**:591.
Hunt, D., Sloman, G., and Westlake, G. (1969). *Br Heart J* **31**:264.
Hutchinson, J. E., Kemp, H. G., and Schwarz, M. J. (1971). *JAMA* **216**:1645.
Josephson, M. E., and Harken, A. H. (1983). *In* "Cardiac Therapy" (M. R. Rosen and B. F. Hoffman, eds.), p 374. Martinus Nijhoff, The Hague.
Josephson, M. E., and Horowitz, L. N. (1979). *Am J Cardiol* **43**:631–642.
Josephson, M. E., Harken, A. H., and Horowitz, L. N. (1979). *Circulation* **61**:1430–1439.
Josephson, M. E., Horowitz, L. N., Spielman, S. R., Greenspan, A. M., VandePol, C., and Harken, A. H. (1980a). *Circulation* **61**:395–404.
Josephson, M. E., Horowitz, L. N., Harken, A. H., and Kaster, J. A. (1980b). *Circulation* **62** (III):320.
Josephson, M. E., Horowitz, L. N., Waxman, H. L., Cain, M. E., Spielman, A. R., Greenspan, A. M., Marchlinski, F. E., and Ezri, M. D. (1981). *Circulation* **64**:257–272.
Josephson, M. E., Horowitz, L. N., and Harken, A. H. (1982a). *Ann NY Acad Sci* **382**:381–395.
Josephson, M. E., Horowitz, L. N., Spielman, S. R., Waxman, H. L., and Greenspan, A. M. (1982b). *Am J Cardiol* **49**:207–220.
Josephson, M. E., Waxman, H. L., Cain, M. E., Gardner, M. J., and Buxton, A. E. (1982c). *Am J Cardiol* **50**:11–22.
Kempf, F. C., Jr. and Josephson, M. E. (1984). *Am J Cardiol* **53**:1577–1582.
Kienzle, M. G., Doherty, J. U., Roy, D., Waxman, H. L., Harken, A. H., and Josephson, M. E. (1983). *JACC* **2**:853–858.
Kotler, M. N., Tabatznik, B., Mower, M. M., and Tominaga, S. (1973). *Circulation* **47**:959–966.
Lahiri, A., Balasubramanian, V., and Rafferty, E. B. (1979). *Br Med J* **1**:1676–1678.
Lambert, C. J., Adam, M., Geisler, G. F., Verzoga, E., Nazarian, M., and Mitchell, B. F., Jr. (1971). *J Thorac Cardiovasc Surg* **62**:522–528.

Levy, S., Cointe, R., Metge, M., Faugere, G., Valeix, B., and Gerard, R. (1984). *Am J Cardiol* **54**:579–581.
Lown, B. (1979). *Am J Cardiol* **43**:313–328.
Lown, B., and Wolf, M. (1971). *Circulation* **44**:130–142.
Lown, B., et al. (1969). *Am J Med* **46**:705–724.
McNamee, B., Robinson, T., Adgey, G. et al. (1970). *Brit Med J* **4**:204–206.
Marchlinski, F. E., Gansler, T. S., Waxman, H. L., and Josephson, M. E. (1982). *Ann Int Med* **97**:839–845.
Marchlinski, F. E., Waxman, H. L., Buxton, A. E., and Josephson, M. E. (1983). *JACC* **2**:240–250.
Mason, J. W., and Winkle, R. A. (1978). *Circulation* **58**:971–985.
Mason, J. W., and Winkle, R. A. (1980). *N Engl J Med* **303**:1073–1077.
Mason, J. W., Stinson, E. B., Winkle, R. A., Griffin, J. C., Oyer, P. E., Ross, D. L., and Derby, G. (1982). *Circulation* **65**:1148–1155.
Michelson, E. L., and Morganroth, J. (1980). *Circulation* **61**:690–695.
Miller, J. M., Kienzle, M. G., Harken, A. H., and Josephson, M. E. (1984). *Circulation* **70**:624–631.
Mirowski, M., Reid, P. R., Winkle, R. A., Mower, M. M., Watkins, L., Stinson, E. B., Griffith, L. S. C., Kallman, C. H., and Weisfeldt, M. L. (1983). *Ann Int Med* **98**:585–588.
Morady, F., Scheinman, M. M., Hess, D. S., Sung, R. J., Shen, E., and Shapiro, W. (1983). *Am J Cardiol* **51**:85–89.
Moran, J. M., Kehoe, R. F., Loeb, j. M., Lichtenthal, P. R., Sanders, J. H., Jr., and Michaelis, L. L. (1982). Ann Thorac Surg **34**: 538–552.
Morganroth, J., Michelson, E. L., Horowitz, L. N., Josephson, M. E., Pearlman, A. S., and Dunkman, W. B. (1978). *Circulation* **58**:408–414.
Moss, A. J., Davis, H. T., Decamilla, J., and Bayor, L. W. (1979). *Circulation* **60**:998–1003.
Mukharji, J., Rude, R. E., Poole, K., Croft, C., Thomas, L. J., Jr., Strauss, H. W., Roberts, R., Raabe, D. S., Jr., Braunwald, E., Willerson, J. T., and cooperating investigators (1982). *Clin Res* **30**:108A.
Multicenter Post-Infarction Research Group (1983). *New Engl J Med* **309**:331–336.
Myerburg, R. J., Conde, C., Sheps, D. S., Appel, R. A., Kiem, I., Sung, R. J., and Castellanos, A. (1979). *Circulation* **59**:855–863.
Nademanee, K., Cannom, D., Hendrickson, J., Goldreyer, B., and Sorgh, B. (1981). *Circulation* **64** (Suppl II):36.
Nikolis, G. M. B., Bishop, R. L., and Singh, J. B. (1982). *Circulation* **66**:218–223.
Ostermeyer, J., Breithardt, G., Kolvenbach, R., Borggrefe, M., Seipel, L., Schulte, H. D., and Bircks, W. (1982). *J Thorac Cardiovasc Surg* **84**:704–715.
Peter, T., Hamer, A., Weiss, D., and Mandel, W. (1981). *Circulation* **64** (Suppl IV):26.
Pool, I., Kunst, K., and VanDwermeskerken, J. L. (1978). *Br Heart J* **40**:627–629.
Rehnqvist, N., Lundman, T., and Sjögren, A. (1978). *Acta Med Scand* **204**:205–209.
Ricks, W. B., Winkle, R. A., Shumay, N. G., and Harrison, D. C. (1977). *Circulation* **56**:38.
Ritter, E. R. (1969). *Ann Int Med* **71**:1155.
Rosen, M. R., and Reder, R. F. (1982). *Ann Int Med* **94**:794–801.
Roy, D., Waxman, H. L., Buxton, A. E., Marchlinski, F. E., Cain, M. E., Gardner, M. J., and Josephson, M. E. (1982). *Am J Cardiol* **50**:1346–1350.
Roy, D., Waxman, H. L., Kienzle, M. G., Buxton, A. E., Marchlinski, F. E., and Josephson, M. E. (1983). *Am J Cardiol* **52**:969–974.
Ruberman, W., Weinblatt, E., Goldberg, J. D., Frank, C. W., and Shapiro, S. (1977). *N Engl J Med* **297**:750–757.

Ruberman, W., Weinblatt, E., Goldberg, J. D., Frank, C. W., Chaudhary, B. S., and Shapiro, S. (1981). *Circulation* **64**:297–305.
Ruskin, J. N., Dimarco, J. P., and Garan, H. (1980). *New Engl J Med* **303**:607–613.
Saksena, S., Rothbart, S. T., Cappello, G., Bernstein, A., and Somani, P. (1983). *JACC* **2**:538–544.
Salerno, D., Hodges, M., Graham, E., Asinger, R. W., and Mickell, F. L. (1981). *N Engl J Med* **305**:700–709.
Schaffer, W. A., and Cobb, L. A. (1975). *N Engl J Med* **293**:259–262.
Schlesinger, Z., Lieberman, Y., and Neufeld, H. N. (1971). *J Thorac Cardiovasc Surg* **61**:1645.
Schulze, R. A., Jr., Strauss, H. W., and Pitt, B. (1977). *Am J Med* **62**:192.
Spielman, S. R., Michelson, E. L., Horowitz, L. N., Spear, J. F., and Moore, E. N. (1978). *Circulation* **57**:666–670.
Spielman, S. R., Schwartz, J. S., McCarthy, D. M., Horowitz, L. N., Greenspan, A. M., Sadowski, L. M., Josephson, M. E., Waxman, H. L. (1983). *JACC* **1**:401–408.
Thind, G. S., Blakemore, W. S., and Zinsser, H. F. (1971). *Am J Cardiol* **27**:696.
Tommaso, C., Kehoe, R., and Zheutlin, T. (1982). *Circulation* **66** (Suppl II):25.
Torres, V., Flowers, D., Butler, B., Miura, D., and Somberg, J. C. (1984). *JACC* **3**:558.
Ungerleider, R. M., Holman, W. L., Calcagno, D. *et al.* (1982a). *J Thorac Cardiovasc Surg* **83**:850–856.
Ungerleider, R. M., Holman, W. L., Calcagno, D. *et al.* (1982b). *J Thorac Cardiovasc Surg* **83**:857–864.
VandePol, C. J., Farshidi, A., Spielman, S. R., Greenspan, A. M., Horowitz, L. N., and Josephson, M. E. (1980). *Am J Cardiol* **45**:725–731.
Wald, R. W., Waxman, M. D., Corey, P., Gunstensen, J., and Goldman, B. S. (1979). *Am J Cardiol* **44**:329–338.
Waldo, A. L., Plumb, V. J., Arciniegas, J. G., MacLean, W. A. H., Cooper, T., Priest, M. F., and James, T. N. (1983). *Circulation* **67**:73–83.
Wardekar, A., Son, B., Gosaynie, C. B., and Bercu, B. (1972). *Chest* **62**:505.
Waspe, L. E., Waxman, H. L., Buxton, A. E., and Josephson, M. E. (1983). *Am J Cardiol* **51**:1175–1181.
Waxman, H. L., Groh, W. C., Marchlinski, F. E., Buxton, A. E., Sadowski, L. M., Horowitz, L. N., Josephson, M. E., and Kastor, J. A. (1982). *Am J Cardiol* **50**:1066–1074.
Waxman, H. L., Buxton, A. E., Sadowski, L. M., and Josephson, M. E. (1983). *Circulation* **67**:30–37.
Weaver, W. D., Lorch, G. S., Alverez, H. A., and Cobb, L. A. (1976). *Circulation* **54**:895–900.
Winkle, R. A. (1978). *Circulation* **57**:116–121.
Wittig, J. H., and Boineau, J. P. (1975). *Ann Thorac Surg* **20**:117–126.
Zipes, D. P., Prystowsky, E. N., and Heger, J. J. (1984a). *JACC* **3**:1059–1071.
Zipes, D. P., Heger, J. J., Miles, W. M., Mahomed, Y., Brown, J. W., Spielman, S. R., and Prystowsky, E. J. (1984b). *N Engl J Med* **311**:485–490.

# 10 The Role of Beta Blockers in the Prevention of Sudden Cardiac Death in the Postinfarction Patient

Peter L. Frommer and Curt D. Furberg

## I. Introduction

Sudden cardiac death may be the first manifestation of coronary heart disease, but the overwhelming fraction of its victims already carry that diagnosis. For survivors of myocardial infarction, sudden cardiac death is the leading cause of death.

The term "sudden cardiac death" has varied usage. In most recent reports, cardiac deaths occurring within 1 hr of the onset of symptoms and unwitnessed deaths in apparently well persons are referred to as sudden cardiac death, but periods up to 24 hr have also been used. Of the ischemic heart disease deaths within 24 hr, the overwhelming fraction occur within the first hour. Thus the distinction is not of great importance in numbers; but, it is probably significant in regard to the terminal pathophysiological mechanisms causing death.

Ventricular fibrillation is the pathogenetic basis for the major fraction of sudden cardiac deaths. The more quickly rescue teams arrive upon the scene of a cardiovascular collapse, the more frequently this is the rhythm that is encountered; with later arrivals, bradyarrhythmias and cardiac standstill are found with increasing frequency.

With ventricular fibrillation as the primary pathogenetic mechanism for sudden cardiac death, it might be hoped that antiarrhythmic drugs would be effective in its prevention. However, no antiarrhythmic agent has yet been shown effective in reducing the risk of sudden cardiac death either in survivors of acute myocardial infarction as a group or in the patients with the commonly encountered "significant" ventricular arrhythmias. In part, this may be a consequence of the design of reported studies. The sickest patients and those with the most serious arrhythmias have often been excluded for ethical reasons. Generally, antiarrhythmic agents have been studied to demonstrate their success in controlling rhythm disturbances, but their effectiveness in saving life has not been subject to rigorous test due to limitations of sample size. To the extent that antiarrhythmic agents have been studied with survival as the endpoint, after myocardial infarction or in patients with common ventricular arrhythmias, they have not been found persuasively effective (Frommer, 1979; Furberg, 1983).

It has long been recognized that the autonomic nervous system may play a role in sudden cardiac death. Incidents of arousal, anger, and stress—states of high sympathetic outflow—have long been recognized anecdotally as associated with sudden cardiac death. In the animal laboratory, experimental studies have shown that interruption of the sympathetic innervation of the heart will substantially decrease the frequency of ventricular arrhythmias and fibrillation (Yodice, 1941; Harris et al., 1951; Ebert et al., 1968). For example, in dogs with prior cardiac denervation, experimental myocardial infarction did not result in ventricular fibrillation, although this arrhythmia occurred in 60% of controls that had had a sham operation simulating cardiac denervation (Ebert et al., 1968).

Because of these observations, pharmacological blockade of the autonomic nervous system in ischemic heart disease warranted investigation, and it became the topic of research in the animal laboratory and in the clinical setting. The earliest clinical reports dealt with acute and short-term administration of low dosages of beta-adrenergic blockers during myocardial infarction (Snow, 1965). However, the long-term use of beta blockers following myocardial infarction has been the topic of extensive research as well. As detailed below, such therapy is associated with a significant reduction in all-cause mortality and sudden cardiac deaths. A number of reviews and editorials have summarized the clinical trials of chronic beta blockade following myocardial infarction and have commented upon their clinical implications (Baber and Lewis, 1982; Breckenridge, 1982; Hampton, 1982; Rose, 1982; Moss, 1982; Chamberlain, 1983; Furberg et al., 1983; Goldstein, 1983; Griggs et al., 1983; Turi and Braunwald, 1983; Frishman et al., 1984).

Although the beneficial effect of beta blockers in survivors of myocardial infarction has been attributed predominantly to their effects upon the autonomic nervous system, most of these agents have other actions as well, some of which may be beneficial. For example, some have intrinsic antiarrhythmic properties through raising the threshold for ventricular fibrillation and suppressing atrial and ventricular premature depolarizations. Furthermore, beta blockade results in a decreased workload upon the heart, a hemodynamic effect that is compatible with decreased likelihood of myocardial ischemia and infarction and, consequently, with another reason for a lesser likelihood of ventricular fibrillation. Beta blockers have such additional effects as altering platelet aggregation, thromboxane formation, myocardial metabolism, and oxyhemoglobin equilibrium, and elevating certain blood lipids (Frishman, 1983; Shulman *et al.,* 1983); some of these effects are plausibly contributory in preventing episodes of ischemic heart disease, while others may have a deleterious effect.

In this chapter, we summarize the results of the long-term beta blocker usage in patients who are survivors of acute myocardial infarction, focusing upon all-cause and sudden cardiac deaths. However, all survivors of myocardial infarction (MI) are not alike; all do not have similar prognoses; all may not derive similar benefits. Therefore, the question of which patients are more likely to benefit is considered. Several further issues of importance to clinicians are also addressed: when should therapy be started and how long should it be continued? All beta blockers are not identical in their actions; are they equally effective in this setting? Data relevant to these and other questions are examined.

## II. Methods

The effects of long-term beta-blocker therapy in the prevention of sudden cardiac death among survivors of acute myocardial infarction is best assessed by examining the clinical trials that are randomized, controlled, and double-blind; that started therapy after the patients had stabilized a few days from the onset of infarction and continued treatment for at least 12 months; and that randomized over 100 patients. Eight trials, using seven different beta-blocking drugs, fulfilled these criteria (Wilhelmsson *et al.,* 1974; Multicentre International Study, 1975, 1977; Norwegian Multicenter Study Group, 1981; Pedersen, 1983; Beta-Blocker Heart Attack Study Group, 1981, 1982; Hansteen *et al.,* 1982; Julian *et al.,* 1982; Australian and Swedish Pindolol Study Group, 1983; European Infarction Study Group, 1984); their designs are summarized in Table I. The trials involved the participation of 230 to over 3800 patients: 13,290 patients in all. Most patients entered 4 to 28 days from the beginning of their acute illness, and therapy was continued for average periods of 12 to 25 months.

Five other trials are also shown in Table I that have continued beta-blocker therapy for average periods of 3 to 48 months, but they are not included in the main analysis. Three of these began treatment on the day of admission to the hospital (Barber *et al.,* 1975; Andersen *et al.,* 1979;

**TABLE I**
Design of Long-Term Beta-Blocker Trials

| Year | Trial | Patients randomized | Beta blocker | Daily dose (mg) | Entry time after MI in days range (mean) | Length of follow-up months range (mean) |
|---|---|---|---|---|---|---|
| 1974 | Wilhelmsson et al. (1974) | 230 | Alprenolol | 400 | 7–21[a] | 24 (24) |
| 1974/7 | Multicentre International Study (1975, 1977) | 3053 | Practolol | 400 | 7–28 (13.2) | to 36 (14) |
| 1981 | Norwegian Multicenter Study Group (1981), Pedersen (1983) | 1884 | Timolol | 20 | 7–28 (11.5) | 12–33 (17) |
| 1982/3 | Beta-Blocker Heart Attack Study Group (1981, 1982) | 3837 | Propranolol | 180–240 | 5–21 (13.8) | 12–39 (25) |
| 1982 | Hansteen et al. (1982) | 560 | Propranolol | 160 | 4–6 | 12 (12) |
| 1982 | Julian et al. (1982) | 1456 | Sotalol | 320 | 5–14 (8.3) | 12 (12) |
| 1983 | Australian and Swedish Pindolol Study Group (1983) | 529 | Pindolol | 15 | 1–21[b] | 24 (24) |
| 1984 | European Infarction Study Group (1984) | 1741 | Oxprenolol | 160–320 | 14–36 | 12 (12) |
|  | Total | 13290 |  |  |  |  |
| 1979 | Andersen et al. (1979) | 480 | Alprenolol | 400 | 1 (<1.0) | 12 (12) |
| 1980 | Barber et al. (1975) | 298 | Practolol | 600 | 1–3 (<1.0) | 24 (24) |
| 1981 | Hjalmarson et al. (1981) | 1395 | Metoprolol | 200 | 1 (<1.0) | 3 (3) |
| 1980 | Baber et al. (1980) | 720 | Propranolol | 120 | 2–14 (8.5) | 3–9 (6) |
| 1982 | Taylor et al. (1982) | 1103 | Oxprenolol | 80 | 30–2700 (415) | 6–84 (48) |

[a] After discharge.
[b] 75% after 5 days.

Hjalmarson et al., 1981), a potentially confounding feature, as discussed subsequently; one maintained therapy for only 3 to 9 months (Baber et al., 1980); and in the fifth, patients were recruited 1–90 months following myocardial infarction (Taylor et al., 1982), a clinically different group of patients.

## III. Results

### A. All-Cause Mortality

For the eight studies, the populations, the precise admission criteria, the beta-blocker therapy, the period of treatment, concomitant therapy, and the definitions of sudden death varied. Their combined results must be treated with great caution; they can yield general impressions but not precise results. Nevertheless, as summarized in Table II, among the 6510 patients randomized to placebo, there were 659 deaths, a 10.1% all-cause mortality rate for the average 12 to 25 months of therapy. Among the 6780 patients randomized to beta-blocker therapy, there were 530 deaths, a 7.8% all-cause mortality rate. The relative mortality rate expressed as a risk ratio (intervention group mortality devided by control group mortality) is 0.77, indicating an overall reduction in all-cause mortality of 23% ($p < 0.0001$) for these eight trials.

Three of these trials show beneficial effects with individual risk ratios in the range of 0.64 to 0.77 and unequivocal or borderline ($p = 0.05$l) statistical significance (Multicentre International Study, 1975, 1977; Norwegian Multicenter Study Group, 1981; Pedersen, 1983; Beta-Blocker Heart Attack Study Group, 1981, 1982). Four other trials show favorable or neutral risk ratios ranging from 0.51 to 0.97, but individually without statistical significance (Wilhelmsson et al., 1974; Hansteen et al., 1982; Julian et al., 1982; Australian and Swedish Pindolol Study Group, 1983). However, as shown in Fig. 1, the 95% confidence intervals for the risk ratios of these four trials (and for the three other trials) include the risk ratio for the pooled result of the eight studies. Thus, all seven are consistent with the average apparent 23% benefit. In the eighth study (European Infarction Study Group, 1984) recruitment was terminated earlier than scheduled when the intervention group mortality trended toward a less favorable rate than that of the control group; this was not a "statistically significant" unfavorable effect, but the 95% confidence interval does not include the risk ratio based upon the pooled results of the eight studies.

**TABLE II**
All-Cause Mortality in Long-Term Beta-Blocker Trials

| Trial | Drug | Patients randomized Control | Patients randomized Inter-vention | Number of deaths Control | Number of deaths Inter-vention | $p^a$ | Mortality rates Control (%) | Mortality rates Inter-vention (%) | Risk ratio |
|---|---|---|---|---|---|---|---|---|---|
| Wilhelmsson et al. (1974) | Alprenolol | 116 | 114 | 14 | 7 | 0.18 | 12.1 | 6.1 | 0.51 |
| Multicentre International Study (1975, 1977) | Practolol | 1520 | 1533 | 124 | 96 | 0.051 | 8.2 | 6.3 | 0.77 |
| Norwegian Multicenter Study Group (1981), Pedersen (1983) | Timolol | 939 | 945 | 152 | 98 | 0.0003 | 16.2 | 10.4 | 0.64 |
| Beta-Blocker Heart Attack Study Group (1981, 1982) | Propranolol | 1921 | 1916 | 188 | 138 | 0.005 | 9.8 | 7.2 | 0.74 |
| Hansteen et al. (1982) | Propranolol | 282 | 278 | 37 | 25 | 0.16 | 13.1 | 9.0 | 0.69 |
| Julian et al. (1982) | Sotalol | 583 | 873 | 52 | 64 | 0.32 | 8.9 | 7.3 | 0.82 |
| Australian and Swedish Pindolol Study Group (1983) | Pindolol | 266 | 263 | 47 | 45 | 0.96 | 17.7 | 17.1 | 0.97 |
| European Infarction Study Group (1984) | Oxprenolol | 883 | 858 | 45 | 57 | 0.20 | 5.1 | 6.6 | 1.30 |
| Total | | 6510 | 6780 | 659 | 530 | 0.000004 | 10.1 | 7.8 | 0.77 |
| Andersen et al. (1979) | Alprenolol | 242 | 238 | 64 | 61 | 0.92 | 26.4 | 25.6 | 0.97 |
| Barber et al. (1975) | Practolol | 147 | 151 | 46 | 41 | 0.51 | 31.3 | 27.2 | 0.87 |
| Hjalmarson et al. (1981) | Metoprolol | 697 | 698 | 62 | 40 | 0.030 | 8.9 | 5.7 | 0.64 |
| | | $(410)^b$ | $(399)^b$ | $(56)^b$ | $(36)^b$ | $(0.049)$ | $(13.7)^b$ | $(9.0)^b$ | 0.66 |
| Baber et al. (1980) | Propranolol | 365 | 355 | 27 | 28 | 0.91 | 7.4 | 7.9 | 1.07 |
| Taylor et al. (1982) | Oxprenolol | 471 | 632 | 48 | 60 | 0.78 | 10.2 | 9.5 | 0.93 |

[a] $p$ values computed for chi-square test comparing the proportion of deaths in each group.
[b] Randomized patients who actually developed myocardial infarction.

# 10. Beta Blockers in Preventing Sudden Cardiac Death

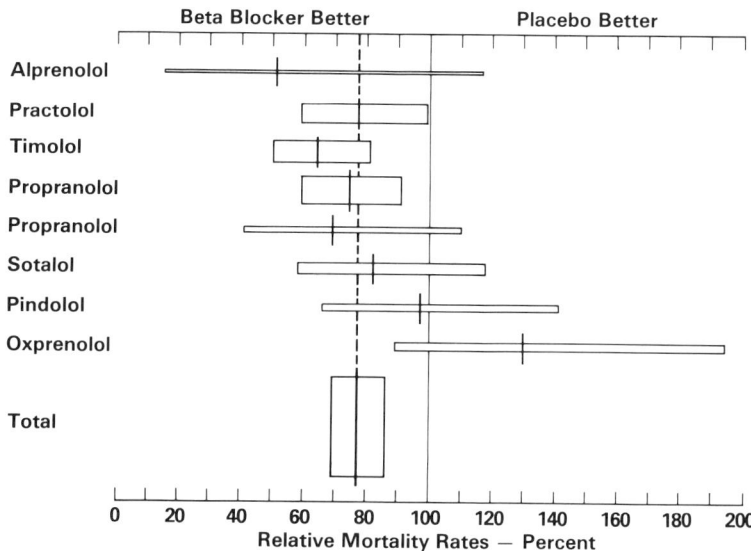

**Fig. 1.** Estimates of approximately 95%-confidence limits of the relative all-cause mortality rates (intervention divided by placebo) in randomized, double-blind trials of beta-blocker therapy beginning after acute myocardial infarction and continuing for at least 12 months. The thickness of each bar is proportional to the number of fatal events in the trial.

Thus, its outcome would not seem to be compatible with the other studies.[1]

The emphasis upon all-cause mortality in a discussion on sudden cardiac death is based upon several factors. All-cause mortality is probably of the greatest importance to patients and physicians. It is most readily ascertainable. It does not involve judgments on the cause or rapidity of death, which may be difficult. In each of these studies, the overwhelming number of deaths were cardiac, and sudden death tends to be the most common form of cardiac death.

The data are here tabulated and analyzed based on the survival of each patient in the group to which he or she was originally assigned—the "intention-to-treat" principle. In several reports, the primary analyses excluded patients "off therapy," accounting for apparent differences

---

[1] It might be argued that the unfavorable trend which resulted in early termination of recruitment might have reversed if the full recruitment had been allowed as planned. It might also be argued that if the one study is "significantly" different from the seven others, its result should not be included in calculating the aggregate results. The all-cause mortality risk ratio would change from 0.77 to 0.73, while the sudden cardiac death risk ratio would change from 0.68 to 0.65. Cautions about the pooled results have already been made; the net effects remain as risk reductions of about one-fourth and one-third, respectively.

from their summarized data. In most studies, from 25 to 30% of the patients were withdrawn from the trial or stopped therapy. Generally the figures for placebo and beta-blocker groups were essentially equal, but in a few trials, the beta-blocker group had a slightly higher withdrawal rate. Analysis on intention-to-treat rather than on the basis of therapy received at the time of death may yield different results. Some argue that only the results of patients who continue on therapy should be compared. However, the bases for the cessation of therapy may be related to the clinical course of the patient. For example, in one of these trials, which reported its results primarily on the basis of deaths while on therapy (Multicentre International Study, 1975), in the month following cessation of therapy, the monthly mortality rate was 14 times that which it was for patients continuing on therapy (Frommer, 1979). In another study, not involving beta-blocker drugs, placebo-treated patients who had stopped taking their placebo had about twice the mortality of those who continued on therapy (Coronary Drug Project Research Group, 1980), further illustrating the hazard of assuming that those who stop therapy are not importantly different from those who continue. Including patients who are nonadherers may dilute the results. Analyzing on the basis of death while on or within 1 month of therapy, the primary mode of analysis in one of these studies (Norwegian Multicenter Study Group, 1981), is perhaps something of a compromise for trials of this type. A favorable result based upon all patients in an intention-to-treat analysis is most persuasive, but it may underestimate the true magnitude of the potential beneficial effect.

Among the five other studies cited but not qualifying for the major analysis, four have risk ratios approximating unity (Barber et al., 1975; Andersen et al., 1979; Baber et al., 1980; Taylor et al., 1982) and would not seem to show benefit; however, the trials were small and the 95% confidence interval for each encompasses the overall 23% beneficial effect observed in the eight studies reviewed. The fifth study (Hjalmarson et al., 1981) shows a substantial and statistically significant beneficial effect with a drug not included among the seven discussed above; its results are consistent with the eight studies summed. An abstract reporting on the use of that drug, metoprolol, starting 1 week after hospital discharge, continuing for a year, and involving 553 patients, also shows a favorable trend, but not with statistical significance (Cats et al., 1983). Unfortunately, the results of the largest study with metoprolol, involving almost 2400 patients treated for 1 year, were anticipated in late 1983 (Cutler, 1983) but remain unreported and unpublished 2 years later; this would be an unusual delay if the results were favorable.

## B. Sudden Cardiac Death

Sudden cardiac death has no standard definition. Each clinical trial used the onset of premonitory or new symptoms as the starting point for the measurement of time. A few report instantaneous death but each reports death within 1 or 24 hr; some also present data for several time intervals. Unwitnessed deaths, typically those occurring within 12 hr of being seen well, are also included. The data in Table III are for deaths within 1 hr or the earliest period reported for each trial. In one of the studies (Multicentre International Study, 1975, 1977), sudden death is reported only for those dying while "on therapy;" because about 40% of patients died "off therapy," the numbers and rates are underestimates.

In seven of the eight trials, the risk ratio for sudden cardiac death is smaller (i.e., more favorable) than for all-cause mortality. For the eight trials combined, the 6510 patients on placebo sustained 357 sudden cardiac deaths, corresponding to a 5.5% rate. For the 6780 patients assigned to beta blockers, the 253 reported sudden cardiac deaths represent a 3.7% rate. This corresponds to a relative risk ratio of 0.68 or a 32% reduction in sudden cardiac deaths ($p < 0.0001$). A statistically significant favorable effect (at $p \leq 0.05$) was observed in each of the three trials for which all-cause mortality was significantly reduced (Multicentre International Study, 1975, 1977; Norwegian Multicenter Study Group, 1981; Pedersen, 1983; Beta-Blocker Heart Attack Study Group, 1981) and for a fourth trial $p < 0.06$. For each of the eight trials, the 95% confidence interval for the risk ratio encompasses the aggregated 32% lower risk in the treated group (Fig. 2). Thus, the result of each study is compatible with this pooled result.

Deaths other than sudden cardiac are also reduced. If sudden cardiac deaths are subtracted from all-cause mortality, the remaining death rates, 4.6% in the control and 4.1% in the treated group, represent an intervention/control ratio of 0.88 ($p < 0.03$). Thus, while the sudden cardiac deaths are reduced by 32%, deaths from all other causes are reduced by 12%.

## C. Nonfatal Myocardial Infarction

A favorable risk ratio has also been reported in the nonfatal myocardial infarction rates. Definition and ascertainment of subsequent myocardial infarction is more difficult and varied. Nevertheless, typical reduction in the beta-blocker treated groups compared to those receiving placebo is on

**TABLE III**
Sudden Cardiac Death in Long-Term Beta-Blocker Trials

| Trial | Drug | Patients randomized | | Definition (hr) | Number of sudden deaths | | $p^a$ | Sudden death rates | | Risk ratio |
|---|---|---|---|---|---|---|---|---|---|---|
| | | Control | Intervention | | Control | Intervention | | Control (%) | Intervention (%) | |
| Wilhelmsson et al. (1974) | Alprenolol | 116 | 114 | ≤24 | 11 | 3 | 0.058 | 9.5 | 2.6 | 0.28 |
| Multicentre International Study (1975, 1977) | Practolol | 1520 | 1533 | ≤1 | 55[b] | 31[b] | 0.011 | 3.6 (5.8)[c] | 2.0 (4.0)[c] | 0.56 (0.69)[c] |
| Norwegian Multicenter Study Group (1981), Pedersen (1983) | Timolol | 939 | 945 | ≤24 | 110 | 66 | 0.0006 | 11.7 | 7.0 | 0.60 |
| Beta-Blocker Heart Attack Study Group (1981, 1982) | Propranolol | 1921 | 1916 | ≤1 | 39 | 64 | 0.050 | 4.6 | 3.3 | 0.72 |
| Hansteen et al. (1982) | Propranolol | 282 | 278 | ≤1 | 23 | 11 | 0.057 | 8.2 | 4.0 | 0.49 |
| Julian et al. (1982) | Sotalol | 583 | 873 | ≤1 | 14 | 25 | 0.71 | 2.4 | 2.9 | 1.19 |
| Australian and Swedish Pindolol Study Group (1983) | Pindolol | 266 | 263 | ≤24 | 31 | 28 | 0.82 | 11.7 | 10.6 | 0.91 |
| European Infarction Study Group (1984) | Oxprenolol | 883 | 858 | ≤1[d] | 24 | 25 | 0.92 | 2.7 | 2.9 | 1.07 |
| Total | | 6510 | 6780 | | 357 | 253 | 0.000002 | 5.5 | 3.7 | 0.68 |
| Andersen et al. (1974) | Alprenolol | 242 | 238 | — | — | — | — | — | — | — |
| Barber et al. (1975) | Practolol | 147 | 151 | — | — | — | — | — | — | — |
| Hjalmarson et al. (1981) | Metoprolol | 697 | 698 | — | — | — | — | — | — | — |
| Baber et al. (1980) | Propranolol | 365 | 355 | — | — | — | — | — | — | — |
| Taylor et al. (1982) | Oxprenolol | 471 | 632 | ≤24 | 25 | 33 | 1.0 | 5.3 | 5.2 | 0.98 |

[a] P values computed for chi-square test comparing the proportion of deaths in each group.
[b] Sudden death data are published only for patients "on therapy;" the 55 and 31 sudden deaths are part of the 78 and 48 all-cause deaths "on therapy."
[c] Sudden death rates calculated when the ratio of sudden to all-cause deaths "on therapy" is extrapolated to patients "off therapy."
[d] Instantaneous witnessed death, found dead, and temporarily resuscitated.

# 10. Beta Blockers in Preventing Sudden Cardiac Death

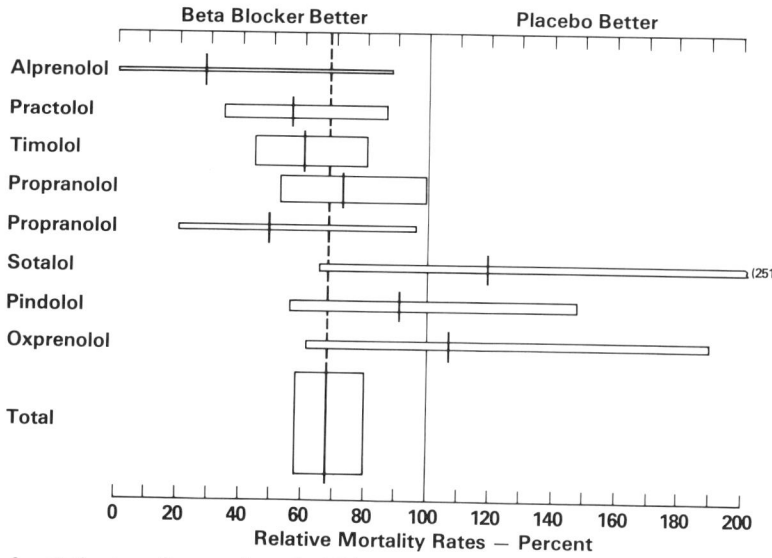

**Fig. 2.** Estimates of approximately 95%-confidence limits of the relative sudden cardiac death rates (intervention divided by placebo) in randomized, double-blind trials of beta-blocker therapy beginning after acute myocardial infarction and continuing for at least 12 months. The thickness of each bar is proportional to the total number of fatal events in the trial.

the order of 25% (Furberg and Bell, 1983). This is a further clear beneficial effect. It also says something about the probable mechanisms of beneficial effects from beta blockers. While their predominant beneficial effect may be in reducing ventricular fibrillation, as evidenced by the reduction in sudden cardiac death, the decreases in nonfatal myocardial infarction and in nonsudden death suggest that other mechanisms play beneficial roles as well.

In summary, when data are pooled from all the randomized, placebo-controlled, double-blind clinical trials that tested the chronic administration of beta blockers to survivors of recent myocardial infarction, enrolled over 100 such patients, and treated them for an average of 12 to 25 months, all-cause mortality decreased by one-fourth (from 10.1% to 7.8%) and sudden cardiac death by one-third (from 5.5% to 3.7%). The saving in life is substantial and real. The major, but not sole, benefit is through the reduction of sudden cardiac death.

## IV. Discussion

### A. Are Beta Blockers Appropriate in All Survivors of Myocardial Infarction?

Each of the trials excluded patients with the standard contraindications to beta-blocker therapy: current congestive heart failure, persistent hypotension, bradycardia (typically below 50 beats/min), conduction disturbances in the form of second or third degree AV block, asthma and bronchoobstructive problems, and diabetes requiring hypoglycemic agents. Patients were also excluded if they were not suitable for a clinical trial for such reasons as the definite need for a beta blocker (e.g., in the management of angina pectoris), anticipated problems in trial adherence or regular contact during the trial period, and coexisting noncardiac disease that might influence survival independently. Most trials recruited from about 25 to over 50% of myocardial infarction survivors at their participating institutions. Most trials also found that approximately 20% of patients had one or more of the cited relative or absolute contraindications to beta-blocker drugs; the balance of nonrecruitment was due to patients in whom the drug was clinically acceptable or even needed but who were not appropriate to the trial or did not accept participation in the trial. Thus, in about one-fifth of myocardial infarction survivors the drugs would seem contraindicated, but about four-fifths would be eligible for such prophylactic therapy or need a beta blocker for other reasons; they constitute the target group for consideration.

### B. Should All Survivors of Myocardial Infarction Who Do Not Have Contraindications to Beta Blockade Receive This Prophylactic Therapy?

There is no easy answer. The prognosis of survivors of myocardial infarction is influenced by previous medical history, the severity of their acute myocardial infarction, and other factors. Those with a less favorable prognosis would potentially have the most to gain, and they do seem to benefit, based upon retrospective sub group analyses in the timolol and Beta-Blocker Heart Attack Trial (BHAT) studies, as well as the Hansteen propranolol study, which was restricted to high-risk patients. In those with a good prognosis, the maximum potential gain is less, and demonstrating benefit with statistical significance is more difficult.

Consider those with a favorable prognosis. In the timolol study (Norwegian Multicenter Study Group, 1981; Pedersen, 1983), patients with a first myocardial infarction and free of complications (cardiogenic shock, persistent hypotension, pulmonary edema, congestive heart failure, incomplete or complete atrioventricular block, atrial fibrillation, or ventricular fibrillation) constituted only 24% of the study group. Of these 422 patients, those on placebo had a 9.5% mortality rate, while those on beta blocker had a 4.5% mortality rate, but these rates are based upon very small numbers of deaths and the apparent difference is without statistical significance. In a post hoc analysis of the BHAT group (Goldstein, 1983), 2289 patients (60%) met these same criteria; mortality rates were 7.3% and 5.3% for the placebo and intervention groups respectively, again a favorable but numerically small trend. The balance of the patients in each study are here considered high-risk groups. For the 1442 such patients in the timolol study, the mortality rates were 18.3% and 12.1%, a substantial and favorable difference. In the 1548 such BHAT patients, the rates were 13.7% and 10.0% respectively. By these analyses, a beneficial effect seems present in both low- and high-risk groups, and it saves more lives among those at high risk.

The BHAT data have also been analyzed using only the clinical status during the acute infarction preceding randomization (Furberg *et al.*, 1984), as shown in Table IV. A prior myocardial infarction was not considered a complication. The criteria for an uncomplicated infarction were as stated above but also required freedom from even brief bouts of ventricular tachycardia and the absence of rales. By these criteria, about 55%

**TABLE IV**

All-Cause and Sudden Cardiac Death Rates by Risk Group and Treatment in BHAT[a]

| Complications prior to randomization | Patients randomized | | All-cause mortality (%) | | Sudden death (<1 hr) (%) | |
|---|---|---|---|---|---|---|
| | Control | Intervention | Control | Intervention | Control | Intervention |
| None | 1079 | 1047 | 6.5 | 6.2 | 3.1 | 2.9 |
| Electrical[b] only | 423 | 443 | 10.9 | 5.2 | 5.9 | 2.9 |
| Mechanical[c] only | 202 | 201 | 16.8 | 10.4 | 5.9 | 3.5 |
| Electrical and mechanical | 217 | 225 | 17.1 | 12.9 | 7.8 | 6.2 |

[a] From Furberg *et al.* (1984).
[b] Ventricular fibrillation or tachycardia (3 or more successive VPBs), heart block of second or third degree, or "new" atrial fibrillation.
[c] Pulmonary edema, cardiogenic shock (oliguria and systolic blood pressure below 90 mm Hg), persistent hypotension (systolic blood pressure below 90 mm Hg for 1 hr or more), basilar rales, or symptoms/signs of congestive heart failure (requiring therapy with digitalis and/or diuretics).

of the patients had no complications. The all-cause mortality in the control and intervention groups was 6.6% and 6.2% respectively, a very small and statistically non-significant difference. In each of the other risk groups: electrical complications only, mechanical complications only, or both, the placebo group mortality rates were 10.9%, 16.8%, and 17.1%, while the intervention group rates were 5.2%, 10.4%, and 12.9%, for favorable differences of 5.7%, 6.4% and 4.2%, or about $5\frac{1}{2}$ lives saved per 100 patients (with complicated MI) treated over 2 years.

These are post hoc categorizations and as such must be looked upon with considerable caution. There is no doubt that those who have the most favorable prognosis following myocardial infarction can have the least to gain from an ideal therapy. However, whether the criteria for "low risk," as defined post hoc in this trial, have general validity would have to be confirmed.

Some studies have identified subgroups of patients in whom beta blockade had unusually favorable effects and others in whom it has seemed to have had relatively neutral or even unfavorable effects. For example, the practolol report (Multicentre International Study, 1975, 1977) suggested that all of the benefit could be attributed to the effects of the drug in patients with anterior wall infarction, with essentially no benefit in those with inferior wall infarction. A similar trend with another cardioselective agent seems to have been observed in the short-term metoprolol study but is not published. However, these analyses are post hoc and the results have not been confirmed in other trials, including BHAT (1982) and the Norwegian Timolol Study (Rodda, 1983).

Another study reported favorable effects in patients under the age of 65 and unfavorable effects in those over this age, with the net effect essentially zero (Andersen *et al.*, 1979). Such an age differential has not been found in other studies (Hawkins *et al.*, 1983; Rodda, 1983).

Until there are more substantial data, it would seem prudent to emphasize long-term beta blockade in those who have had a complicated infarction but to start such therapy in all survivors of myocardial infarction who do not have contraindications to beta blockade; therapy might be discontinued sooner and more readily in those who have a rather favorable prognosis.

### C. Are All Beta Blockers Equally Effective in Improving Prognosis following Myocardial Infarction? Is This a Class Effect of Beta Blockers or Is It Specific for Individual Ones?

Beta blockers are not all alike, as shown in Table V and as discussed by Harrison (1983). Some block both beta-$_1$ and beta-$_2$ adrenoceptors, while

**TABLE V**
Pharmacologic Properties of the
Beta-Adrenergic Blocking Drugs Tested in
Long-Term Trials

| Drug | Cardiac selectivity (beta$_1$-blockade) | Membrane stabilizing activity | Intrinsic sympathomimetic activity |
|---|---|---|---|
| Alprenolol[a] | 0 | + | + |
| Metoprolol | + | 0 | 0 |
| Oxprenolol | 0 | + | + |
| Pindolol | 0 | 0 | ++ |
| Practolol[b] | + | 0 | + |
| Propranolol | 0 | ++ | 0 |
| Sotalol[a] | 0 | 0 | 0 |
| Timolol | 0 | 0 | 0 |

[a] Not available for clinical use in the United States.
[b] No longer in clinical use anywhere.

others are "cardioselective" and block only the former (i.e., they have substantially lesser effect in inhibiting bronchodilation, vasodilation, and glycogenolysis). Some have a membrane stabilizing action (MSA) that causes local anesthesia and decreases the rate of rise in the cardiac action potential; others do not have MSA. Some, in addition to blocking the beta adrenoceptors, have a small intrinsic sympathomimetic action (ISA).

There are persuasive data on the effectiveness of timolol (Pedersen, 1983) and propranolol (Beta-Blocker Heart Attack Trial Research Group, 1982) in the reduction of all-cause and sudden cardiac mortality during long-term therapy following acute myocardial infarction. Both are beta blockers without cardioselectivity and without intrinsic sympathomimetic activity; however they are different in that propranolol has substantial MSA while timolol does not.

The effectiveness of practolol in this circumstance (Multicentre International Study, 1977) is clinically irrelevant because the drug, which was never available in the United States, was taken off the market because of serious side effects. However, from a pharmacological perspective, it is noted that practolol is a beta blocker with cardioselectivity and ISA. Thus ISA does not seem to prevent effectiveness.

Complete data on metoprolol are restricted to a single trial in which the drug was administered acutely and then continued for only 90 days (Hjalmarson *et al.*, 1981). Favorable results from a chronic trial involving 553 patients are available only in abstract form and present a favorable risk ratio but not at a statistically significant level (Cats *et al.*, 1983).

Unfortunately, the results of a trial involving almost 2400 patients was to have been released in late 1983 but remains unreported 2 years later. Metoprolol has cardioselectivity but neither membrane stabilizing action nor ISA.

Oxprenolol, a drug with both MSA and ISA, showed a small unfavorable trend in the European Infarction Study (1984), and recruitment for the study was stopped earlier than planned. In a second study (Taylor *et al.*, 1982), in which the drug was administered in patients beginning 1–90 months (average $13\frac{1}{2}$ months) following myocardial infarction, the results were essentially neutral. Through post hoc analysis, subgroups were developed (those in whom it was started within 5 months, at 6 to 12 months, and later) with reported apparent benefit, no effect, and harm, respectively. It is difficult to rationalize the basis for such a differential response or to reconcile it with continued benefit or no adverse effects in patients receiving beta blockers from the outset and continuing beyond 12 months of therapy. Furthermore, such post hoc hypotheses warrant particular caution.

Alprenolol, another drug with both MSA and ISA, was the first drug studied in a definitive fashion, and it showed a favorable tendency, but in a small study without statistically significant results (Wilhelmsson *et al.*, 1974). A further study, utilizing acute administration followed by chronic therapy, failed to show any substantial beneficial trend (Andersen *et al.*, 1979).

Sotalol, without cardioselectivity, MSA, or ISA, but with specific antiarrhythmic activity, has been shown to have an apparent moderate beneficial effect but without statistical significance (Julian *et al.*, 1982).

The only study with pindolol, a drug with ISA and equivocal MSA, showed no favorable trend (Australian and Swedish Pindolol Study Group, 1983). In this study, 25% of the patients were started on therapy within 5 days, and in this subgroup, those on beta blockers had more deaths than those in the placebo group (12 versus 7 deaths); in those entered beyond 5 days, the intervention group had fewer deaths (33 versue 40). As the authors point out, it is difficult to accept that starting some patients on therapy within the first 5 days can be the sole critical variable for finding no beneficial effect.

Atenolol and nadolol have not been the subject of clinical trials in this clinical setting.

From this summary, it would be hard to argue strongly in favor of or strongly against a class effect by beta blockers or by subgroups of beta blockers. Unequivocally favorable effects have been shown for a drug that lacks cardioselectivity, MSA, and ISA (timolol), for another with only MSA (propranolol), and yet a third that has cardioselectivity and

ISA but no MSA (practolol). For the other beta blockers, there are simply not enough data to assess individual efficacy definitively, though two of those with least or no apparent benefit (pindolol and oxprenolol) have ISA.

In the patient following myocardial infarction in whom the goal is the prevention of all-cause and sudden cardiac death, it would seem prudent to use a drug for which effectiveness has been unequivocally shown: timolol or propranolol. If there are other clinical problems that favor the use of another beta blocker in the postmyocardial infarction patient, a beneficial effect upon all-cause mortality can be hoped for, but not firmly expected.

### D. When Should Chronic Beta-Blocker Therapy Be Started?

There are about 40 reports of the use of beta blockers acutely in the early stages of myocardial infarction with such goals as reduction of mortality, prevention of rhythm disturbances, and reducing the extent of myocardial damage (May, 1983). About as many have shown unfavorable as favorable trends in all-cause mortality. Only a single published study (Hjalmarson *et al.*, 1981) has shown a result that is favorable with statistical significance, and this included continuing the drug for 90 days, with the difference in mortality beginning to appear at about 2 or 3 weeks; whether this is the consequence of acute or chronic therapy remains unclear. In some patients there may be specific reasons for the use of a beta blocker early in the course of acute myocardial infarction for the control of acute problems, but there is no persuasive evidence for its early use in the absence of specific indications.

It would seem prudent to start therapy once the patient is stabilized. In the clinical trials reported, this has generally been from about 4 to 28 days. Some physicians start patients routinely late in the course of hospitalization; others, if they plan to use exercise testing to assess cardiac status early after acute myocardial infarction, may postpone chronic beta-blocker therapy until these tests are complete.

### E. At what Dose Should Beta Blockers Be Given?

In the Norwegian Multicenter Study (1981), timolol was given 10 mg twice daily. In BHAT (1981, 1982), patients received 60 or 80 mg three times daily, with 82% receiving the lower dose. These doses of timolol and propranolol are approximately equivalent in their degree of beta blockade. For other indications these drugs are sometimes effective at lower doses. In the postmyocardial infarction patient, they should be given at these higher levels, even if other symptoms are controlled at a lower dose. In any patient who does not tolerate the full dose of 20 mg timolol or 180 mg propranolol per day, a lesser dose should be tried.

### F. How Long Should Chronic Beta Blockade Be Continued?

This decision must be based upon judgments and interpretations of limited data. No studies have been designed to answer this question. Judgments must be made, based on the clinical and risk status of such patients, their individual response and tolerance to therapy, and familiarity with the survival curves of the clinical trials. In the timolol study (Fig. 3) (Pedersen, 1983), average treatment extended to only 17 months; the mortality curves much beyond that point are based on relatively few patients, and the curves may be substantially influenced by chance. In BHAT (Fig. 4) (Beta-Blocker Heart Attack Trial Research Group, 1982), the major benefit accrued in the first 12–18 months; there does not seem to be substantial divergence in the mortality curves beyond this period. However, the apparent absence of divergence may be due to limited data,

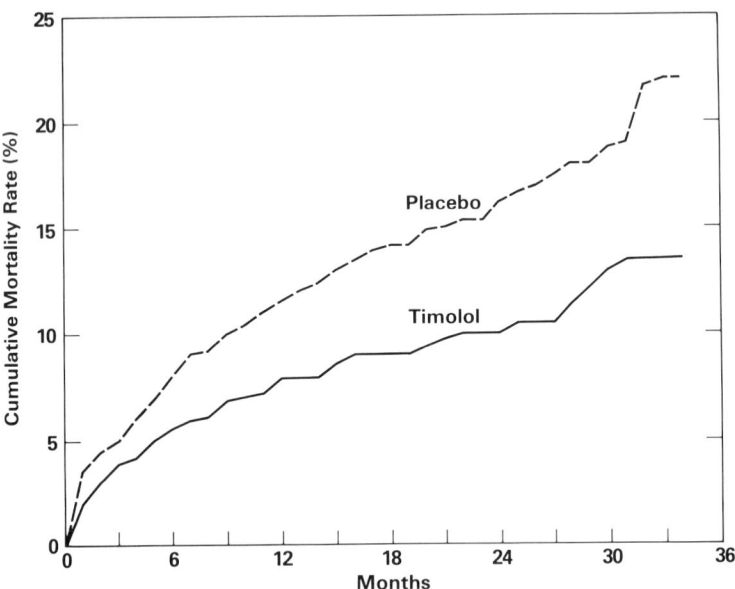

**Fig. 3.** Life table of cumulative mortality curves for timolol and placebo groups (by intention-to-treat). Average follow-up of 17 months. (From Pedersen, 1983.)

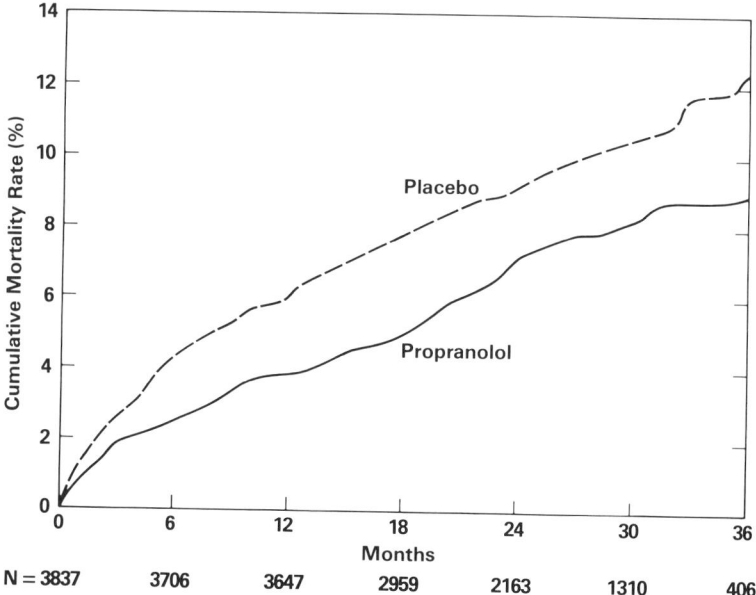

**Fig. 4.** Life table cumulative all-cause mortality curves for propranolol and placebo groups (by intention-to-treat). Average follow up of 25 months. $N$, total number of patients followed through each time point. (From Beta-Blocker Heart Attack Trial Research Group, 1982.)

and even if it were real, survivors might continue to benefit from therapy because continued therapy may be what is keeping some patients alive. Against this argument is the universal observation of survival data following myocardial infarction, which shows substantial mortality in the earliest months, followed by a significantly lower mortality rate.

Twelve to 18 months of therapy would seem a reasonable minimum. Some have advocated 3 years, others advocated continuation indefinitely. In the final analysis, the length of therapy might be based upon clinical judgment of the observed data, recognizing that those whose myocardial infarction was somewhat complicated are at greatest risk and have most to gain, and noting the individual patient's tolerance of the drug.

## G. Should Patients with a Remote Myocardial Infarction Not Already on Beta-Blocker Therapy Be Started on Such a Regimen?

No trial has been conducted to answer this question directly. Inferences can be drawn from what has been said about how long therapy might be continued. A person whose most recent infarct has occurred within the past year might be placed upon beta blockers for purely prophylactic reasons. For those whose most recent infarction is more remote and who have no other indication for beta-blocker therapy, initiation of such a regimen would not seem necessary.

## H. What about the Side Effects of Beta Blockers?

Published trial results yield data that are not uniform but do show reasonably consistent patterns. In most large studies, on the order of 25 to 30% of patients are off protocol before completion of planned therapy; the numbers are generally very similar in the beta-blocker and the placebo control groups, but in some trials, the intervention group has had a stopping rate a few percentage points higher. Such cessation of therapy has been for a variety of reasons including undesired side effects, a specific need for the beta blocker, or simple dropout. The topic has been reviewed by Friedman (1983), and Table VI summarizes the percentages of patients who have stopped therapy for specific reasons. First, it must be remembered that these are all patients in whom beta blockers were not contraindicated at the outset. Then it might be noted that hypotension and bradycardia, though not frequently severe enough to stop therapy, were more frequent causes for cessation of therapy in the intervention than in placebo groups, a finding that is of no surprise. In the aggregate, heart failure was no more common in one group than the other, but in at least one large study (Furberg et al., 1984) it has been encountered more commonly in those who had had mechanical complications during their acute infarction.

**TABLE VI**

Percentage of Patients who Stopped Assigned Therapy, by Reason[a]

|  | Practolol | Timolol | Metoprolol | Propranolol | Sotalol |
|---|---|---|---|---|---|
| Heart failure | 4.1/3.6[b] | 2.9/2.1 | 0.6/1.0 | 4.0/3.5 | 2.6/3.8 |
| Hypotension | 0.6/0.1 | 2.8/1.2 | 4.2/1.9 | 1.2/0.3 | 2.1/0.7 |
| Bradycardia | 0.5/0.1 | 3.9/0.2 | 2.6/0.7 | 0.7/0.3 | 4.4/0 |
| Depression | 0.2/0.3 | NA[c] | 0/0 | 0.4/0.4 | 0/0 |
| Fatigue | 0.3/0.1 | 0.4/0.1 | 0/0 | 1.5/1.0 | 0.9/0.7 |
| Pulmonary problems | NA | 1.1/0.4 | 0/0 | 0.9/0.7 | 0.5/0.2 |

[a] From Friedman (1983).
[b] Treatment group/placebo group.
[c] NA, not available.

**TABLE VII**
Percentage of Patients with Complaints at Any Time during the Beta-Blocker Heart Attack Trial[a]

| Complaint | Propranolol | Placebo | p(Two-sided) |
|---|---|---|---|
| Cardiopulmonary | | | |
|   Shortness of breath | 66.8 | 65.6 | NS[b] |
|   Bronchospasm | 31.3 | 27.0 | <0.005 |
|   Rapid heartbeat | 10.8 | 15.1 | <0.001 |
|   Cold hands, feet | 10.0 | 7.7 | <0.025 |
| Neuropsychiatric | | | |
|   Tiredness | 66.8 | 62.1 | <0.005 |
|   Reduced sexual activity | 43.2 | 42.0 | NS |
|   Depression | 40.7 | 39.8 | NS |
|   Nightmares | 39.7 | 38.9 | NS |
|   Faintness | 28.7 | 26.6 | NS |
|   Insomnia | 21.1 | 18.8 | NS |
|   Blacking out | 9.1 | 10.3 | NS |
|   Hallucinations | 5.9 | 4.5 | NS |
| Gastrointestinal | | | |
|   Diarrhea | 5.5 | 3.6 | <0.01 |

[a] From the Beta-Blocker Heart Attack Trial Research Group (1982).
[b] NS, not significant.

Patients who have had myocardial infarction are not without complaints. Data from BHAT summarizing the percent of patients who complained at any time during the trial of specific cardiopulmonary, neuropsychiatric, or gastrointestinal symptoms are summarized in Table VII. It is not surprising that there are some complaints with a statistically significantly greater frequency in the propranolol-treated group than in the placebo group. However, the small difference or total similarity of the numbers is impressive. A comparison of complaints at any time during the course of the trial may be too coarse a method of quantifying the severity and importance of side effects. Nevertheless, most of the complaints attributed to beta blockade are also voiced in patients receiving placebo, though some plausibly with less frequency or less intensity. Such side effects may be dose- and drug-related.

When patients complain of symptoms that are plausibly attributable to the beta blocker, they may be caused by the beta blocker, but they may also be part of the natural course following myocardial infarction. This is neither a reason for ignoring the complaint nor for automatically stopping the drug; it is another good reason for individual attention to the patient.

## V. Summary

There is firm evidence that certain beta blockers administered to post-myocardial infarction patients who have no contraindication to beta-blocker therapy reduce mortality by about one-fourth (e.g., from about 10% to 7½%) in patients treated 1–2 years. The major effect seems to be a decrease in the sudden cardiac death rate by about one-third, but there is a favorable effect upon other causes of death as well. There is also a decrease of recurrent nonfatal myocardial infarction on the order of 20 to 25%. The drugs are reasonably well tolerated. They are of maximum benefit in terms of lives saved per year of therapy in patients who have had a somewhat complicated myocardial infarction. A beneficial trend is also present in those with uncomplicated infarction, but the effect, in terms lives saved per year of therapy, is substantially smaller. The evidence for such a beneficial effect is persuasive for timolol and propranolol (and probably for practolol, which is no longer on the market). Whether the favorable trends with most other beta blockers are real is presently an unanswerable question. It would seem prudent to start beta-blocker therapy a few days after myocardial infarction, once the patient is stabilized, and to continue therapy for 12 to 18 months, and perhaps longer, keeping in mind the patient's risk of death due to the severity of his myocardial infarction and his tolerance of the drug.

## References

Andersen, M. P., Bechsgaard, P., Frederiksen, J. *et al.* (1979). *Lancet* **2**, 865–868.
Australian and Swedish Pindolol Study Group (1983). *Eur. Heart J.* **4**, 367–375.
Baber, N. S., and Lewis, J. A. (1982). *Br. Med. J.* **284**, 1749–1750.
Baber, N. S., Wainwright, E. D., Howitt, G. *et al.* (1980). *Br. Heart J.* **44**, 96–100.
Barber, J. M., Boyle, D. M. C., Chaturvedi, N. C. *et al.* (1975). *Acta Med. Scand.*, Suppl. **587** 213–219.
Beta-Blocker Heart Attack Study Group (BHAT) (1981). *JAMA* **246**, 2073–2074.
Beta-Blocker Heart Attack Trial Research Group (BHAT) (1982). *JAMA* **247**, 1707–1714.
Breckenridge, A. (1982). *Br. Med. J.* **285**, 37–39.
Cats, V. M., Capelle, F. J. L., Lie, K. I. *et al.* (1983). *Circulation* **68** (Suppl III), III-181.
Chamberlain, D. A. (1983). *Br. Heart J.* **49**, 105–110.
Coronary Drug Project Research Group (1980). *N. Engl. J. Med.* **303**, 1038–1041.
Cutler, J. A. (1983). *Circulation* **67** (Suppl I), I-62–65.
Ebert, P., Allgood, R., and Sabiston, D. (1968). *Ann Surg* **168**, 728–735.
European Infarction Study Group (1984). *Eur. Heart J.* **5**, 189–202.
Friedman, L. M. (1983). *Circulation* **67** (Suppl I), I-89–90.
Frishman, W. H. (1983). *Circulation* **67** (Suppl I), I-11–18.

Frishman, W. H., Furberg, C. D., and Friedewald, W. T. (1984). *N. Engl. J. Med.* **310,** 830–837.
Frommer, P. L. (1979). *In* "Clinical Strategies in Ischemic Heart Disease, New Concepts and Current Controversies." (Corday, E. and Swan, H. J. C., eds.), pp 124–130. Williams & Wilkins Co., Baltimore.
Furberg, C. D. (1983). *Am. J. Cardiol.* **52,** 32C–36C.
Furberg, C. D. and Bell, R. L. (1983). *Circulation* **67** (Suppl I), I-83–85.
Furberg, C. D., Friedewald, W. T., and Eberlein, K. A. (1983). *Circulation* **6,** (Suppl I), I-1–111.
Furberg, C. D., Hawkins, C. M., and Lichstein, E. (1984). *Circulation* **69,** 761–765.
Goldstein, S. (1983). *Circulation* **67** (Suppl I), I-53–57.
Griggs, T. R., Wagner, G. S., and Gettes, L. S. (1983). *J. Am. Coll. Cardiol.* **1,** 1530–1533.
Hampton, J. R. (1982). *Br. Med. J.* **285,** 33–36.
Hansteen, V., Moinichen, E., Lorentsen, E. *et al.* (1982). *Br. Med. J.* **284,** 155–160.
Harris, A., Estandia, A., and Tillotson, R. (1951). *Am. J. Physiol.* **165,** 505–512.
Harrison, D. C. (1983). *Circulation* **67** (Suppl I), I-77–80.
Hawkins, C. M., Richardson, D. W., and Vokonas, P. S. (1983). *Circulation* **67** (Suppl I), I-94–97.
Hjalmarson, A., Herlitz, J., Malek, I. *et al.* (1981). *Lancet* **2,** 823–827.
Julian, D. G., Prescott, R. J., Jackson, F. S., and Szekely, P. (1982). *Lancet* **1,** 1142–1147.
Moss, A. J. (1982). *Int. J. Cardiol.* **1,** 343–349.
Multicentre International Study (1975). *Br. Med. J.* **3,** 735–740.
Multicentre International Study (1977). *Br. Med. J.* **2,** 419–421.
Norwegian Multicenter Study Group (1981). *N. Engl. J. Med.* **304,** 801–807.
Pedersen, T. R. (1983). *Circulation* **67** (Suppl I), I-49–53.
Rodda, B. E. (1983). *Circulation* **67** (Suppl I), I-101–106.
Rose, G. (1982). *Br. Med. J.* **285,** 39–40.
Shulman, R. S., Herbert, P. N., Capone, R. J. *et al.* (1983). *Circulation* **67** (Suppl I), I-19–21.
Snow, P. J. D. (1965). *Lancet* **2,** 551–553.
Taylor, S. H., Silke, B., Ebbutt, A. *et al.* (1982). *N. Engl. J. Med.* **307,** 1293–1300.
Turi, Z. G. and Braunwald, E. (1983). *JAMA* **249,** 2512–2516.
Wilhelmsson, C., Vedin, J. A., and Wilhelmsen, L. (1974). *Lancet* **2,** 1157–1160.
Yodice, A. (1941). *Am. Heart J.* **22,** 545–548.
Yusuf, S., Peto R., Lewis, J. *et al.* (1985). *Prog. in Cardiovas. Dis.* **37,** 335–371.

# Index

## A

Absorption, of antiarrhythmic drugs, 241–242
N-Acetylprocainamide
 activity of, 253
 early afterdepolarizations and, 192
N-Acetyltransferase
 drug metabolism and, 247, 253
 hydralazine metabolism and, 60, 61
Acipimox, hyperlipidemia and, 24
Aconitine, early afterdepolarizations and, 191
Action potential
 abnormalities of, in ventricular infarct tissue, 222–223
 bretylium and, 292–293
 cardiac, ion movements and, 271–272
 lidocaine and, 291
Administration, of antiarrhythmic drugs
 intravenous, 243–244
  loading dose and maintenance, 245–246
  multiple loading dose, 246
  simple loading dose, 244–245
Afterdepolarizations, triggered activity of pacemaker and
 delayed, 192–194
 early, 190–192
Afterload, inappropriate, pump failure and, 95
Afterload reduction, potential benefits of vasodilators in
 aortic input impedance, 48–49
 arterial pressure, 47–48
 systemic vascular resistance, 49
Ajmaline, 301
Aldosterone, 65
 increased systemic vascular resistance and, 41
Allergic reaction, streptokinase infusion and, 172
Alprenolol, 350, 352, 356
 pharmacology of, 361

 prophylaxis for sudden death and, 305, 306, 362
 treatment of arrhythmia during AMI and, 303
Amiodarone, 287
 coronary artery spasm and, 146
 electrophysiological actions, 263
 hemodynamic effects, 263–264
 pharmacokinetics, 264
 pharmacology of, 289
 plasma levels and dosage, 264
 ventricular fibrillation and, 320–321, 325–326
Aneurysm, infarct location and, 91
Aneurysmectomy, ventricular tachycardia and, 326
 electrophysiologically guided, 326–328
Angina pectoris, mechanism of, 117–118
Angioplasty, coronary artery stenosis and, 181
Angiotensin II
 AMI and, 94
 antagonists of, 53, 66–68
 increased systemic vascular resistance and, 41
Animals, experimental, regression of atheroma in, 27–31
Anthopleurin-A, early afterdepolarizations and, 191
Antiarrhythmic drugs
 classification of, 287
 class I
  disopyramide, 254–256
  lidocaine, 256–258
  procainamide, 252–254
  quinidine, 248–252
  tocainide, 258–259
 class II
  propranolol, 259–261
 class III
  amiodarone, 263–264
  bretylium, 261–263
 effects in ischemic tissue, 290–291
  beta-blocking drugs, 293–294

371

bretylium, 292–293
calcium channel blocking drugs, 294
lidocaine, 291–292
mechanism of action on ischemia-related reentrant rhythms, 231–234
pharmacokinetics of
absorption, 241–242
administration, 243–247
distribution, 242–243
metabolism and excretion, 247
pharmacology of, 285–288
beta-adrenergic blocking drugs, 289
calcium channel blocking drugs, 290
drugs prolonging refractoriness, 289–290
sodium current blockers, 288–289
Aortic input impedance, potential benefits of vasodilators and, 48–49
Aprindine, prophylaxis for postinfarction sudden death and, 305
Arrhythmias
in acute phase of myocardial infarction
occlusion arrhythmias, 204–208
reperfusion arrhythmias, 209
role of injury current, 209–210
clinical studies on, 279–285
drug treatment during AMI, 294–295
beta-blockers, 302–304
bretylium, 300–302
calcium channel blockers, 304
lidocaine, 295–298
other sodium current blockers, 298–300
incidence in myocardial infarction, 269–271
intracoronary streptokinase and, 172–173
mechanisms of, 271–272
enhanced or abnormal automaticity, 272
during infarction, 274–279
reentry, 273–274
triggered activity, 272–273
Arterial pressure, as measure of afterload, 47–48
Arterial wall, normal, components of, 13
Arteriolar spasm, congestive cardiomyopathy and, 138–139

Aspirin, atherosis risk and, 24–25
Atenolol, 287, 362
blood lipids and, 25
prophylaxis for sudden death and, 305, 306
treatment of arrhythmias during AMI and, 302
Atheroma
advanced stages of, 4
regression of
in experimental animals, 27–31
in humans, 26–27
Atheromatous plaque, rupture of, thrombus formation and, 156
Atherosclerosis
of coronary arteries, oxygen supply to myocardium and, 88
endothelial injury and, 134–135
Atrial fibrillation, incidence after AMI, 280
Atropine, arrhythmias and, 278
Automatic activity
abnormal, of pacemaker, 190
normal, of pacemaker, 188–190
Automaticity, enhanced or abnormal, arrhythmias and, 272
Autonomic system
role in ischemia-related reentrant rhythms, 234–235
sudden cardiac death and, 348
Autonomic tone, arrhythmias and, 282

**B**

Bepridil, 287
clinical utility of, 145
ventricular tachycardia and, 325
Beta blockers
beneficial effects of, 348–349
appropriateness of beta blockers in all survivors of myocardial infarction, 358
are all beta blockers equally effective?, 360–363
choice of dose, 363–364
how long should therapy be continued?, 364–365
should all survivors of myocardial infarction receive therapy?, 358–360

# Index

should beta blockers be started in patients with remote myocardial infarction?, 365–366
side effects, 366–367
when should therapy be started?, 363
methods, 349–351
results of treatment with beta blockers in patients with myocardial infarction
all-cause mortality, 351–354
nonfatal myocardial infarction, 355–357
sudden cardiac death, 355
effects on ischemic tissue, 293–294
pharmacology of, 289
reasons for stopping therapy, 366
treatment of arrhythmias during AMI and, 302–304
Bethanidine, 287
pharmacology of, 289
Blood glucose, risk of atherosclerosis and, 18, 20
Bradyarrhythmias
incidence after AMI, 280
pump failure and, 95
Bradykinin, captopril and, 66
Bretylium, 287
effects on ischemic tissue, 292–293
electrophysiological actions, 261–262
hemodynamic effects, 262
pharmacokinetics, 262
pharmacology of, 289
plasma levels and dosage, 262–263
treatment of arrhythmias during AMI and, 300–302

## C

Calcium
in arterial walls, 13, 14
nitrates and, 141
Calcium channel blockers
coronary artery spasm and
clinical utility, 145
mechanism of action, 143–145
pharmacologic effects, 142–143
effects on ischemic tissue, 294
pharmacology of, 290
treatment of arrhythmias during AMI and, 304

Calcium current
generation of arrhythmias and, 277–278
Calcium ions
delayed afterdepolarizations and, 192–194
triggered activity and, 210–211, 215
Caliber, of coronary vessels, passive and active influences on, 133–134
Captopril
chronic congestive heart failure and, 75, 76
hemodynamic effects of, 54
mechanism of action, 53
pharmacology, hemodynamics and side effects, 66–68
site of action, 54
Cardiac compression, pump failure and, 95
Cardiac output, low, manifestations of, 40
Cardiac tamponade, 45, 93
Cardiovascular effects, dose-dependent, of dopamine, 103–104
Cardioverter, transvenous, fibrillation and, 341
Catecholamines, see also specific compounds
arrhythmias and, 279
bretylium and, 292
captopril and, 66
early afterdepolarizations and, 191
release, increased systemic vascular resistance and, 40–41
spontaneous ventricular rhythms and, 219
Cesium, early afterdepolarizations and, 191–192
Chlorthalidone, coronary heart disease and, 25
Cholesterol
accumulation in lesions, 14
uptake by smooth muscle cells, control of, 10–11
Cholestipol, hyperlipidemia and, 23
Cholestyramine
hyperlipidemia and, 22–23
regression of atheroma and, 27, 28, 29
Chronic congestive heart failure, therapy of
combination therapy, 76

influence of vasodilator therapy on prognosis, 77
rationale for selection of a specific agent, 75–76
Cigarette smoking, risk of atherosclerosis and, 17–18, 20, 22
Cimetidine, lidocaine and, 257, 297
Ciprofibrate, hyperlipidemia and, 23
Circus movement reentry
  excitation and
    figure-eight model, 197–199
    leading circle model, 199–200
    ring model, 194–197
  of ventricular activation during ischemia, 206
Clinical trials, atherosclerosis and, 19–25
Clofibrate
  hyperlipidemia and, 22, 23, 24
  regression of atheroma and, 27, 30
Clofilium, 287
  effects on ischemic tissue, 293
Clonidine, mechanism of action, 52
Collagen, in atherosclerotic lesions, 4, 5, 10, 11–12, 13, 14, 30
Conduction disorders, ischemia and, 205–206
Congestive heart failure, potential benefits of vasodilators in
  afterload reduction, 47–49
  improvement in diastolic compliance, 51–52
  preload reduction, 49–50
  relief of myocardial ischemia, 50–51
Constrictive pericarditis, 45
Contractility
  disopyramide and, 254
  procainamide and, 252
  quinidine and, 248
Contraindications, to beta blocker therapy, 358
Coronary artery
  bypass grafting, following streptokinase therapy, 181
  pharmacology of vasocilators of, 139–140
    calcium antagonists, 142–145
    nitrates, 140–142
    other, 145–146
Coronary artery disease, management following thrombolysis, 180–181

Coronary artery spasm
  evolution of current concepts, 117–122
  myocardial infarction and, 122–132
  natural history of, 120
  pathophysiological mechanisms of
    endothelium-dependent, 134–136
    nonendothelium-dependent, 136–139
    passive and active influences on vessel caliber, 133–134
Coronary blood flow, variant angina and, 118–120
Coronary circulation, collateral, role in pump failure, 91–92
Cortisol, coronary artery disease and, 20
Creatine phosphokinase, following reperfusion after AMI, 162–163, 175
Cryosurgery, ventricular tachycardia and, 330–331
Cryothermal techniques, interruption of reentrant circuits by, 226–227
Cyanide toxicity, nitroprusside therapy and, 57
Cyclic AMP, vascular relaxation and, 53

## D

Deaths, see also Mortality
  due to acute myocardial infarction, 85
Defibrillator, automatic, implantable, 341
Devices, for termination of tachycardia, 341
Diabetes mellitus, risk of atherosclerosis and, 18, 20–21
Diagnosis, of right ventricular infarction, 44, 45
Diastolic compliance, improvement, vasodilators and, 51–52
Dibutyryl cAMP, mechanism of action, 53
Diet
  coronary heart disease and, 22, 23, 27
  hyperlipidemia and, 16, 17
  regression of atheroma and, 27–30
  serum lipid levels and, 20
Digitalis, delayed afterdepolarizations and, 193, 215, 217, 219
Digoxin, volume of distribution, quinidine and, 243
Diltiazem, 287
  coronary artery disease and, 25
  effects on ischemic tissue, 294

hemodynamic effects of, 54
pharmacology, hemodynamics and side effects of, 70, 142–143
Diphenylhydantoin, arrhythmia and, 231, 293
Dipyridamole
  atherosis risk and, 24–25
  coronary artery spasm and, 145–146
Disadvantages
  of dopamine therapy, 103
  of vasopressors in treatment of pump failure, 97
Disopyramide, 287, 288
  arrhythmia and, 231, 233
  effects on ischemic tissue, 290
  electrophysiological actions, 254–255
  hemodynamic effects, 255
  pharmacokinetics, 255–256
  pharmacology of, 288, 289
  plasma levels and dosage, 256
  treatment of arrhythmias during AMI and, 299, 300
Distribution, of antiarrhythmic drugs, 242–243
Diuretics, acute myocardial infarction and, 71
Dobutamine, pump failure and, 97, 99, 105–107
Dopamine, pump failure and, 97, 99, 102–105
Dosage, of beta blockers, 363–364

**E**

Elastin, lipid binding by, 14
Electrocardiograms, as guides for surgery, 340
Electrophysiological actions, 248
  of amiodarone, 263
  of bretylium, 261–262
  of disopyramide, 254–255
  of lidocaine, 256
  of procainamide, 252
  of propranolol, 259–260
  of quinidine, 248
  of tocainide, 258
Electrophysiological studies, post myocardial infarction patients and, 283–285, 286
Electrophysiological testing, cardiac arrest and, 321

Enalapril
  hemodynamic effects of, 54
  mechanism of action, 53
  pharmacology, hemodynamics and side effects of, 68
Encainide, 287
  effects on ischemic tissue, 290
  pharmacology of, 288
Encircling endocardial ventriculotomy, ventricular tachycardia and, 329–330
Endocardial resection, ventricular tachycardia and, 331–336
Endothelium
  function in atherosclerosis, 11–12
  injury, atherosclerosis and, 8
  pathophysiology of coronary artery spasm and
  mechanical injury, 134–135
  vasoactive mediators, 135–136
Endralazine
  hemodynamic effects of, 54
  pharmacology, hemodynamics and side effects of, 60–61
Enzymes
  of endothelial cells, 12
  of macrophages, 12–13
  of smooth muscle cells, 10, 14–15
Epicardium
  geometry of infarction and, 221–222
  overlying mottled infarcts, conduction in, 223–225
Epinephrine, see also Catecolamines, Norepinephrine
  pump failure and, 97
  triggered activity and, 215
Ergonovine, coronary artery spasm and, 121, 137
Estrogen, regression of atheroma and, 28
Ethanol, coronary artery spasm and, 138
Excretion, of drugs, 247

**F**

Fatty acids, saturated, plasma cholesterol levels and, 16
Fatty streaks, composition of, 4
Felodipine, clinical utility of, 145
Fenofibrate, hyperlipidemia and, 23
Fibrinolysis, plasmin and, 156
Fibrinolytic agents, plasminogen activation by, 157

Fibromuscular intimal thickening
  composition of, 5
  relationship to atherosclerosis, 7
Fibronectin, macrophages and, 13
Fibrous plaque
  description of, 1–4
  relationship to fatty streaks, 4–5
Figure-eight model, of reentrant excitation, 197–199
Flecainide, 287
  pharmacology of, 288
Foam cells, atheroma and, 3–4
Food deprivation, regression of atheroma and, 26

## G

Gallopril, 143
Gemfibrozil, hyperlipidemia and, 23
Glucagon, lidocaine clearance and, 257
Glucose-6-phosphate dehydrogenase, in atherosclerotic lesions, 9
Glutathione reductase, nitroglycerin metabolism and, 58
Glycosaminoglycans, atherosclerotic lesions and, 4, 5, 10, 12, 13–14

## H

Half-life, of drugs, calculation of, 243
Heart failure
  AMI and, 86
  hemodynamic consequences of, 40
    low output in acute myocardial infarction, 42–47
    mechanism of increased systemic vascular resistance, 40–42
    mechanism of increase in preload, 42
Hemodynamic abnormalities
  acute papillary muscle rupture or dysfunction and, 46–47
  in right ventricular infarction, 44–45
  ventricular septal rupture and, 45–46
Hemodynamic consequences, of pump failure, 88–89, 91
Hemodynamic effects
  of amiodarone, 263–264
  of bretylium, 262
  of disopyramide, 255
  of endocardial resection, 335
  of lidocaine, 256
  of procainamide, 252
  of propranolol, 260
  of quinidine, 248–249
  of tocainide, 258–259
Hemodynamic profile, in left myocardial infarction, 43–44
Hemodynamics
  of vasodilators
    calcium entry blockers, 69–70
    converting enzyme inhibitors, 66–68
    endralazine, 54, 60–61
    hydralazine, 54, 60–61
    minoxidil, 54, 62
    nitrates, 54, 57–60
    nitroglycerin, 54, 57–60
    nitroprusside, 54, 55–57
    phentolamine, 54, 62–63
    prazosin, 54, 64–66
    trimazosin, 54, 64
    trimethaphan, 63–64
Hemorrhage, fibrinolytic agents and, 157, 171–172, 179
Heparin
  binding of, 10
  functions in lesions, 14
  in normal arterial wall, 13
Hexamethonium, mechanism of action, 52–53
High density lipoproteins, atherosclerosis and, 17, 20, 21
His-Purkinje system, rate of automaticity of, 189–190
Human, regression of atheroma in, 26–27
Hydralazine
  chronic congestive heart failure and, 75–76
  combined with nitrates or captopril, chronic congestive heart failure and, 76
  hemodynamic effects of, 54
  mechanism of action, 52
  pharmacology, hemodynamics and side effects of, 60–61, 68
  site of action, 54
Hydrochlorothiazide, coronary heart disease and, 25
3-Hydroxyquinidine, activity of, 250
Hypercholesterolemia, risk of atherosclerosis and, 15–17, 20, 21

Hyperlipidemia, hereditary, treatment of, 22–23
  risk of atherosclerosis and, 15–17
Hypertension, risk of atherosclerosis and, 17, 20
Hypertrichosis, minoxidil and, 62
Hypovolemia, acute myocardial infarction and, 47
Hypoxia, conduction properties in ischemia and, 277

## I

Ibopamine, heart failure and, 110
Infarct expansion, pump failure and, 91
Infarct location, power failure and, 90–91
Infarct size
  beta-blocking drugs and, 303
  dobutamine therapy and, 107
  power failure and, 89–90
Injury and repair hypothesis, of atherosclerosis, 8–9
Injury current, role in arrhythmia, 209–210
Inotropic agents, therapy of right ventricular infarction and, 74
Inotropic properties, of dobutamine, 107
Ischemia
  cellular biochemical and metabolic changes in, 276–277
  ionic changes and, 225
  myocardial
    effects in pump failure, 88
    isoproterenol and, 101
Ischemic tissue, effects of antiarrhythmic drugs on, 290–291
  beta-blocking drugs, 293–294
  bretylium, 292–293
  calcium channel blocking drugs, 294
  lidocaine, 291–292
Isoproterenol
  lidocaine clearance and, 257
  pump failure and, 96, 97, 98, 100–102
Isosorbide dinitrate, 59
  dosage of, 58

## L

Leading circle model, of reentrant excitation, 199–200
Lecithin, effect on plasma lipids, 24

Left ventricular contractility, inappropriate, pump failure and, 95
Left ventricular function
  effect of reperfusion on, 163–167
  mechanical disturbances to, pump failure and, 92–93
Left ventricular infarction
  hemodynamic profile in, 43
  low output and, 42–44
Lesions
  atherosclerotic
    early intimal changes and, 1
    function and interaction of components, 9–15
Lidocaine, 287, 288
  arrhythmia and, 231, 233–234, 324
  effects on ischemic tissue, 290, 291–292
  electrophysiological actions, 256
  hemodynamic actions, 256
  pharmacokinetics, 257
  pharmacology of, 288
  plasma level and dosage, 257–258
  side effects of, 297
  treatment of arrhythmias during AMI, 295–298
  ventricular fibrillation and, 280
Lipid
  atherosclerotic lesions and, 4, 5
  effects on arterial cells, 14
Liver, lidocaine metabolism and, 257
Loading dose
  maintenance and, 245–246
  multiple, 246
  simple, 244–245
Lorcainide, 287
  pharmacology of, 288
  ventricular tachycardia and, 325
Low density lipoproteins
  cholesterol and, 16–17
  pathogenesis of atherosclerosis and, 8–9, 10, 12, 14
Low output, in acute myocardial infarction
  acute papillary muscle rupture or dysfunction, 46–47
  causes and compensatory mechanisms, 39
  hypovolemia, 47
  left ventricular infarction, 42–44

right ventricular infarction, 44–45
ventricular septal rupture, 45–46
Lupus syndrome
hydralazine therapy and, 61
procainamide and, 253
Lysophosphoglycerides, ischemia and, 277

## M

Macrophages, pathogenesis of atherosclerosis and, 12–13
Mapping, of ventricular tachycardia, 336–340
Mechanisms, of ventricular tachycardia, 322–323
Membrane potential
abnormal automatic activity of pacemaker and, 190
ischemia and, 204
oscillatory depolarizations of, 194
Metabolism, of drugs, 247
Metabolites, of antiarrhythmic agents, 250
Metaraminol, pump failure and, 96, 100
Methergine, coronary artery spasm and, 121
Methoxyverapamil, ischemic action potentials and, 225
Metoprolol, 287, 356, 360
pharmacology of, 361
prophylaxis for sudden death and, 305, 306, 307, 350, 352, 354, 361–362
side effects of, 366
treatment of arrhythmias during AMI and, 302
ventricular fibrillation and, 280
Mevinolin, hyperlipidemia and, 23
Mexiletine, 287
pharmacology of, 288
prophylaxis for postinfarction sudden death and, 305
treatment of arrhythmias during AMI and, 299, 300
ventricular tachycardia and, 324–325
Minoxidil
hemodynamic effects of, 54
pharmacology, hemodynamics and side effects of, 62
Mitral regurgitation
acute, 46
pump failure and, 92

Molsidomine, coronary artery spasm and, 146
Monoclonal theory, pathogenesis of atherosclerosis and, 9
Mortality, *see also* Death
all-cause, beta blocker therapy and, 351–354
associated with arrhythmia during myocardial infarction, 271
effect of reperfusion on, in myocardial infarction, 171
Myocardial infarction
clinical indicators of, effects of reperfusion on, 162–163
coronary artery spasm and, 122–132
electrophysiological mechanisms of ventricular arrhythmias in, 203–204
acute phase, 204–210
reentrant rhythms in subacute and chronic phases, 221–235
triggered rhythms in subacute phase, 210–220
nonfatal, in study of beta blockers, 355–357
Myocardial ischemia, relief of, potential benefits of vasodilators and, 50–51
Myocardium
determinants of oxygen supply and demand in AMI, 87–88
salvage, effect of time from onset of symptoms to reperfusion, 169–170
salvage by intracoronary streptokinase assessment by thallium-201 myocardial scintigraphy, 167–169
effect on left ventricular function, 163–167

## N

Nadolol, 287, 362
Nicardipine, 144
clinical utility of, 145
Niceritol, hyperlipidemia and, 23
Nicotinic acid, hyperlipidemia and, 22
Nifedipine, 287
chronic congestive heart failure and, 76
coronary artery disease and, 25
effects on ischemic tissue, 294
hemodynamic effects of, 54

Index

mechanism of action, 53, 143–145
pharmacology, hemodynamics and side
    effects of, 69–70, 142–143
Niludipine, 294
    clinical utility of, 145
Nimoldipine, 144
Nisoldipine, 294
Nitrates
    clinical utility of, 142
    mechanism of action, 52, 141–142
    pharmacology, hemodynamics and side
        effects of, 57–60, 140–141
Nitrendipine, clinical utility of, 145
Nitroglycerin
    acute myocardial infarction and, 71–73
    congestive heart failure and, 76
    hemodynamic effects of, 54
    pharmacology, hemodynamics and side
        effects of, 57–60
    reversal of coronary artery spasm and,
        123–127
    site of action, 53–54
Nitroprusside
    acute myocardial infarction and, 71–73
    hemodynamic effects of, 54
    mechanism of action, 52
    pharmacology, hemodynamics and side
        effects of, 55–57
Norepinephrine, *see also* Catecholamines;
    Epinephrine
    bretylium and, 261–262
    His-Purkinje rate and, 189–190
    pump failure and, 97, 98–99
    release, 65
        heart failure and, 40–41

O

Obesity, risk of atherosclerosis and, 18, 20
Occlusion, coronary arrhythmias and, 204–
    208
Ouabain, arrhythmias and, 215
Oxprenolol, 350, 352, 356
    effects on ischemic tissue, 294
    pharmacology of, 361
    prophylaxis for sudden death and, 305,
        306, 362
Oxygen, determinants of myocardial de-
    mand and supply in AMI, 87–88

P

Pacemaker(s), ventricular tachycardia and,
    341
Pacemaker activity, ventricular arrhyth-
        mias and,
    abnormal automatic activity, 190
    normal automatic activity, 188–190
    oscillatory depolarization of membrane
        potential, 194
    triggered activity
        delayed afterpolarization, 192–194
        early afterpolarizations, 190–192
Papillary muscle rupture
    or dysfunction
        low output and, 46–47
        pump failure and, 91, 92
Parasystolic rhythm, entrance block and,
    213–215
Pathogenesis, of atherosclerosis, 7–8
    function and interaction of lesion com-
        ponents, 9–15
    injury and repair hypothesis, 8–9
    monoclonal theory, 9
Pathophysiology
    of pump failure
        definition and incidence at AMI, 86–
            87
        determinants of myocardial oxygen
            demand and supply, 87–88
        effects of myocardial ischemia, 88
        extramyocardial factors, 94–95
        hemodynamic consequences, 88–89
        mechanical disturbances of left ven-
            tricular function, 92–93
        peripheral circulation and feedback
            mechanisms, 93–94
        power failure and infarct location, 90–
            91
        power failure and infarct size, 89–90
        role of coronary collateral circulation,
            91–92
Pentaerythritol tetranitrate, duration of
    action, 58
Peripheral circulation, feedback mecha-
    nisms in pump failure and, 93–94
Personality, risk of atherosclerosis and, 19,
    20
pH, lowered, ischemia and, 277

Phagocytosis, by macrophages in atherosclerotic lesions, 12
Pharmacokinetics, 249
  of amiodarone, 264
  of antiarrhythmic drugs
    absorption, 241–242
    administration, 243–247
    distribution, 242–243
    metabolism and excretion, 247
Pharmacokinetics
  of bretylium, 262
  of disopyramide, 255–256
  of lidocaine, 257
  or procainamide, 253
  of propranolol, 259
  of quinidine, 249–250
  of focainide, 259
Pharmacological therapy, of ventricular tachycardia, 323–326
Pharmacology
  of alprenolol, 361
  of amiodarone, 289
  of antiarrhythmic drugs, 285–288
  of beta blockers, 289
  of bethamide, 289
  of bretylium, 289
  of calcium channel blockers, 290
  of captopril, 66–68
  of diltiazem, 70, 142–143
  of disopyramide, 288, 289
  of enalapril, 68
  of encainide, 288
  of flecainide, 288
  of lidocaine, 288
  of lorcainide, 288
  of metoprolol, 361
  of mexiletine, 288
  of nifedipine, 69–70, 142–143
  of oxyprenolol, 361
  of pindolol, 361
  of practolol, 361
  of procainamide, 252–253, 288
  of propafenone, 288
  of propranolol, 361
  of quinidine, 288, 289
  of sotalol, 289, 361
  of timolol, 361
  of vasodilators, 139–140
    calcium entry blockers, 69–70, 142–143, 290
    converting enzyme inhibitors, 66–68
    endralazine, 60–61
    hydralazine, 60–61, 68
    minoxidil, 62
    nitrates, 57–60, 140–141
    nitroglycerin, 57–60
    nitroprusside, 55–57
    phentolamine, 62–63
    prazosin, 64–66
    trimazosin, 64
    trimethaphan, 63–64
  of verapamil, 70, 142–143
Phenobarbital
  lidocaine clearance and, 257
  quinidine and, 250
Phentolamine
  acute myocardial infarction and, 71
  hemodynamic effects of, 54
  mechanism of action, 52
  norepinephrine therapy and, 99
  pharmacology, hemodynamics and side effects of, 62–63
Phenytoin
  arrhythmias and, 324
  quinidine and, 250
Physical activity, risk of atherosclerosis and, 18–19, 21
Pindolol, 287, 350, 352, 356
  blood lipids and, 25
  effects on ischemic tissue, 294
  pharmacology of, 361
Pinocytosis, by smooth muscle cells, 10–11
Pirbuterol,
  heart failure and, 108–109
  mechanisms of action, 53
Placebo, ventricular fibrillation and, 280
Plasma levels and dosage
  of amiodarone, 264
  of bretylium, 262–263
  of disopyramide, 256
  of lidocaine, 257–258
  of procainamide, 253–254
  of propranolol, 260–261
  of quinidine, 250–252
  of tocainide, 259
Plasmin, fibrinolysis and, 156
Plasminogen activator, production in quantity, 181–182

Platelets, pathogenesis of atherosclerosis and, 8
Platelet-derived growth factor, pathogenesis of atherosclerosis and, 8, 10–11
Postinfarction sudden death, prophylaxis for
 beta-blocking drugs, 305–307
 sodium current blockers, 304–305
Potassium ions, early afterdepolarizations and, 191
Potassium levels
 extracellular, ischemia and, 277
Practolol, 350, 352, 356, 360
 pharmacology of, 361
 prophylaxis for sudden death and, 305, 306, 361
 side effects of, 366
 treatment of arrhythmias during AMI and, 303
Prazosin
 blood lipids and, 25
 chronic congestive heart failure and, 76
 hemodynamic effects of, 54
 mechanism of action, 52
 pharmacology, hemodynamics and side effects of, 64–66, 68
 site of action, 54
Preload
 inappropriate, pump failure and, 95
 mechanism of increase in heart failure, 42
Preload reduction, potential benefit of vasodilators and, 49–50
Premature ventricular beats, incidence after AMI, 280, 281
Prenalterol, heart failure and, 110
Probucol, hyperlipidemia and, 23
Procainamide, 287, 288
 arrhythmia and, 231, 233, 301, 324, 336–337, 340
 effects on ischemic tissue, 290
 electrophysiological actions, 252
 hemodynamic effects, 252
 pharmacokinetics, 253
 pharmacology of, 288
 plasma levels and dosage, 253–254
Prognosis
 as basis for selection of patients for beta blocker therapy, 358–360
 following myocardial infarction, effectiveness of various beta blockers in improvement of, 360–363
Propafenone
 pharmacology of, 288
 ventricular tachycardia and, 325
Propranolol, 287, 350, 352, 356, 358
 absorption of, 242
 arrhythmia and, 231, 233, 302
 blood lipids and, 25
 effects on ischemic tissue, 293–294
 electrophysiological actions, 259–260
 hemodynamic effects, 260
 pharmacokinetics, 260
 pharmacology of, 361
 plasma levels and dosage, 260–261
 prophylaxis for sudden death and, 305, 306, 307, 361, 362, 363
 side effects of, 366, 367
 treatment of arrhythmias during AMI and, 302–303
Prostacyclin(s), 57
 endothelium and, 135–136
 mechanism of action, 53
 nitrates and, 142
Prostaglandin(s), captopril and, 66
Prostaglandin E
 mechanism of action, 53
 nitrates and, 142
Pulmonary edema, AMI and, 86, 89
Pulmonary embolism, acute, 45
Pump failure
 future directions and
  ibopamine, 110
  pirbuterol, 108–109
  prenalterol, 110
  salbutamol, 109–110
 infarct size and, 85
 pathophysiology of
  definition and incidence at AMI, 86–87
  determinants of myocardial oxygen demand and supply, 87–88
  effects of myocardial ischemia, 88
  extramyocardial factors, 94–95
  hemodynamic consequences, 88–89
  mechanical disturbances of left ventricular function, 92–93
  peripheral circulation and feedback mechanisms, 93–94

power failure and infarct location, 90–91
power failure and infarct size, 89–90
role of coronary collateral circulation, 91–92
vasopressor agents in treatment of
  dobutamine, 105–107
  dopamine, 102–105
  general considerations, 96–97
  isoproterenol, 100–102
  metaraminol, 100
  norepinephrine, 98–99
Purkinje fibers
  action potential, infarction and, 276
  lidocaine and, 256
  subendocardial, ventricular rhythms and, 210–211
  ventricular fibrillation following coronary occlusion and, 206

## Q

Quinidine, 287, 288
  arrhythmias and, 324
  early afterdepolarizations and, 192
  electrophysiological actions, 248
  hemodynamic effects, 248–249
  pharmacokinetics, 249–250
  pharmacology of, 288, 289
  plasma levels and dosage, 250–252
  treatment of arrhythmias during AMI and, 299, 300
  volume of distribution of digoxin and, 243
Q waves, following reperfusion after AMI, 162

## R

Receptors, for low density lipoproteins, 10, 12, 13
Reentrant excitation
  circus movement reentry
    figure-eight model, 197–199
    leading circle model, 199–200
    ring model, 194–197
  reflection, 200–203
Reentrant ventricular rhythms
  in subacute and chronic myocardial infarction phases
    activation maps during ventricular fibrillation, 227–231
    anatomical substrate of reentrant rhythms, 221–222
    electrophysiological substrate of, 222–226
    interruption of reentrant circuits by cryothermal techniques, 226–227
    mechanism of action of antiarrhythmic agents on ischemia-related reentrant rhythms, 231–234
    role of autonomic system in ischemia-related reentrant rhythms, 234–235
Reentry, arrhythmia and, 273–274, 322
Reflection, reentrant excitation and, 200–203
Refractoriness, prolongation, drugs and, 289–290
Refractory period, ischemia and, 204
Renal function
  captopril and, 67–68
  nitroprusside therapy and, 57
Renal insufficiency, procainamide and, 253
Reocclusion, of coronary arteries following thrombolysis, 179–180
Reperfusion, arrhythmias and, 209
Rhodanase, nitroprusside metabolism and, 55
Right ventricular infarction
  low output and, 44–45
  therapy of, 74–75
Ring model, of reentrant excitation, 194–197
Risk
  of intracoronary streptokinase, 171–173
  of intravenous streptokinase, 179
  of sudden death
    ventricular ectopy and, 317–319
    ventricular fibrillation and, 319–322
Risk factors, in atherogenesis
  cigarette smoking, 17–18
  diabetes mellitus, 18
  hyperlipidemia, 15–17
  hypertension, 17
  other factors, 18–19

## S

Salbutamol
  mechanism of action, 53
  pump failure and, 97, 109–110
Saralasin, mechanism of action, 53

Serotonin, coronary artery spasm and, 137–138
Shock, pump failure and, 86–87, 90, 91, 98–99, 102, 104, 107, 109
Side effects
　of amiodarone, 326
　of beta blockers, 366–367
　of dopamine, 104
　of isoproterenol, 100–102
　of new vasoactive drugs, 108, 109
　of norepinephrine, 99
　of vasodilators
　　calcium entry blockers, 69–70
　　converting enzyme inhibitors, 66–68
　　endralazine, 60–61
　　hydralazine, 60–61
　　minoxidil, 62
　　nitrates, 57–60
　　nitroglycerin, 57–60
　　nitroprusside, 55–57
　　phentolamine, 62–63
　　prazosin, 64–66
　　trimazosin, 64
　　trimethaphan, 63–64
Sinus node, quinidine and, 248
Smooth muscle, alterations in activation, coronary artery spasm and, 138
Smooth muscle cells, in atherosclerotic lesions, functions of, 9–11
Sodium current blockers
　arrhythmias and, 288–289
　treatment of arrhythmias during AMI and, 298–300
Sotalol, 350, 352, 356
　arrhythmia and, 231, 233
　early afterdepolarizations and, 192
　pharmacology of, 289, 361
　prophylaxis for sudden death and, 305, 306, 362
　side effects of, 366
Spindle cells, atheroma and, 3
Spironolactone, coronary heart disease and, 25
Stenosis
　location, coronary artery caliber and, 133–134
　of reperfused coronary arteries, 180
　　angioplasty and, 181
Streptokinase
　coronary artery occlusion and, 123, 124
　fibrinolysis and, 157
　future directions, 181–182
　intracoronary, 159–160
　　effects of reperfusion on clinical indicators of infarction, 162–163
　　effect of reperfusion on mortality, 171
　　effect on myocardial salvage of time of onset of symptoms to reperfusion, 169–170
　　frequency of thrombolysis, 161–162
　　risk of intracoronary streptokinase, 171–173
　　salvage of jeopardized myocardium by intracoronary streptokinase, 163–169
　　technique, 160–161
　intravenous
　　dosage, 176
　　frequency of thrombolysis, 173–175
　　risk of, 179
　　salvage of jeopardized myocardium by early, high-dose, short-duration therapy, 176–179
Stress, risk of atherosclerosis and, 19
Stroma, of atheromas, 4
Sudden cardiac death
　definition of, 347
　in study of beta blockers following AMI, 355
Sulfhydryl groups, action of nitrates and, 141
Supraventricular tachycardia, incidence after AMI, 280
Surgical therapy, of ventricular tachycardia, 326–328
　cryosurgery, 330–331
　encircling endocardial ventriculotomy, 329–330
　endocardial resection, 331–336
　mapping, 326–340
　ventriculotomy, 328–329
Sympathetic nervous system, coronary artery spasm and, 136–137
Sympathetic tone, arrhythmias and, 278–279, 293
Sympathoadrenal system, AMI and, 93–94
Systemic vascular resistance
　mechanism of increase
　　angiotensin II, 41
　　catecholamine release, 40–41

increased vascular stiffness, 42
vasopressin, 41
potential benefits of vasodilators and, 49

## T

Tachyarrhythmias, pump failure and, 95
Technique, of intracoronary administration of streptokinase, 160–161
Teprotide, mechanism of action, 53
Tetrodotoxin, ischemic action potentials and, 225
Thallium-201, myocardial scintigraphy and assessment of salvage of jeopardized myocardium after intracoronary streptokinase, 167–169
Therapy, for low output in myocardial infarction, 44
Thiocyanate, nitroprusside therapy and, 55, 57
Thrombin, endothelium and, 135
Thrombolysis
  intracoronary streptokinase and, 161–162
  intravenous streptokinase and, 173–175
Thrombolytic therapy
  early trials of long-duration, late intravenous therapy, 158–159
  management of patients after reocclusion following thrombolysis, 179–180
    underlying coronary artery disease, 180–181
Thrombosis, as primary mediator of myocardial infarction, 123–124
Thromboxane $A_2$, coronary artery spasm and, 134, 135–136
Thrombus
  as cause of myocardial infarction, 155
  physiology of formation and physiology of fibrin-olytic system, 156–158
Thyroxin, hyperlipidemia and, 24, 28
Tiapamil, 143
  arrhythmias and, 304
Ticlopidine, risk of atherosclerosis and, 25
Timing, of beta blocker therapy, 363
Timolol, 287, 350, 352, 356, 358, 359
  arrhythmia and, 231, 233
  effects on ischemic tissue, 293–294
  pharmacology of, 361
  prolongation of therapy with, 364
  prophylaxis for sudden death and, 305, 306, 307, 362, 363
  side effects of, 366
  sudden cardiac mortality and, 361
Tocainide, 287, 288
  electrophysiological actions, 258
  hemodynamic actions, 258–259
  pharmacokinetics, 259
  pharmacology of, 288
  plasma levels and dosage, 259
  prophylaxis for postinfarction sudden death and, 305
  treatment of arrhythmias during AMI and, 299, 300
Transmembrane potential, changes during evolution of myocardial infarction, 275–276
Triggered activity
  arrhythmias and, 272–273, 322–323
  of pacemaker
    delayed afterdepolarizations and, 192–194
    early afterdepolarizations and, 190–192
  ventricular rhythms in subacute phase of myocardial infarction
    in vitro observations, 210–217
    in vivo observations, 217–220
Trimazosin
  hemodynamic effects of, 54
  pharmacology, hemodynamics and side effects of, 64
Trimethaphan
  mechanism of action, 52–53
  pharmacology, hemodynamics and side effects of, 63–64

## U

Urokinase, fibrinolysis and, 157

## V

Vagal effect, arrhythmias and, 278
Vascular stiffness, increased systemic vascular resistance and, 42
Vasectomy, coronary artery disease and, 21
Vasoactive mediators, coronary artery spasm and, 135–136

Vasodilation
  classification and mechanisms of, 52–53
  quinidine and, 249
Vasodilators
  clinical applications of
    acute myocardial infarction
      complicated by heart failure, 70–73
      complicated by mechanical defects, 73–74
    chronic congestive heart failure, 75–77
    therapy of right ventricular infarction, 74–75
  pharmacology, hemodynamics and side effects of, 139–140
    calcium entry blockers, 69–70, 142–145
    converting enzyme inhibitors, 66–68
    endralazine, 60–61
    hydralazine, 60–61
    minoxidil, 62
    nitrates, 57–60, 140–142
    nitroglycerin, 57–60
    nitroprusside, 55–57
    other, 145–146
    phentolamine, 62–63
    prazosin, 64–66
    trimazosin, 64
    trimethaphan, 63–64
  potential benefit in congestive heart failure
    afterload reduction, 47–49
    improvement in diastolic compliance, 51–52
    preload reduction, 49–50
    relief of myocardial ischemia, 50–51
  sites of action of, 53–54
Vasopressin, increased systemic vascular resistance and, 41
Vasopressors, in treatment of pump failure
  dobutamine, 105–107
  dopamine, 102–105
  general considerations, 96–97
  isoproterenol, 100–102
  metaraminol, 100
  norepinephrine, 98–99
Ventricular arrhythmias
  electrophysiological mechanisms of, 187–188
    pacemaker activity, 188–194
    reentrant excitation, 194–203

  electrophysiological mechanisms in myocardial infarction, 203–204
    acute phase, 204–210
    reentrant rhythms in subacute and chronic phases, 221–235
    triggered rhythms in subacute phase, 210–220
Ventricular ectopy
  risk of sudden death and, 317–319
  survival and, 283
Ventricular fibrillation
  activation maps during, 227–231
  evidence of myocardial infarction and, 319
  incidence after AMI, 280–281
  primary and secondary, 280
  prognostic value of, 282
  sudden cardiac death and, 347–348
Ventricular septal rupture
  low output and, 45–46
  pump failure and, 93
Ventricular tachycardia
  incidence after AMI, 280, 281
  induction by programmed pacing, 323–324
    drug testing and, 324–326
  mechanisms, 322–323
  pharmacological therapy, 323–326
  surgical therapy, 326–328
    cryosurgery, 330–331
    encircling endocardial ventriculotomy, 329–330
    endocardial resection, 331–336
    mapping of ventricular tachycardia, 336–340
    ventriculotomy, 328–329
  tachycardia termination devices, 341
Ventriculotomy, ventricular tachycardia and, 328–329
Verapamil, 287
  absorption of, 242
  arrhythmias and, 304
  coronary artery disease and, 25
  effects on ischemic tissue, 294
  ischemic action potentials and, 225
  mechanism of action, 53, 143–145
  pharmacology, hemodynamics and side effects of, 70, 142–143
  triggered activity and, 215, 219